# MARINES AND HELICOPTERS 1962 - 1973

By

Lieutenant Colonel William R. Fails, USMC

HISTORY AND MUSEUMS DIVISION
HEADQUARTERS, U.S. MARINE CORPS
WASHINGTON, D.C.
1978

USMC Photo A192655

*Cover Photo:* *UH–1Es at Fire Support Base CUNNINGHAM during Operation DEWEY CANYON in northern I Corps in 1969. Without guns, the UH–1E was an excellent observation aircraft, but it often was diverted to other missions, as here supplying a remote firebase.*

# FOREWORD

This history traces the development of helicopters in the Marine Corps from 1962 to 1973 and is the second in a series of two volumes which between them cover the story of Marines and helicopters from 1946 to the present. In the period covered by this volume, the Marines at last acquired helicopters fully capable of carrying out an amphibious vertical assault, and they further elaborated their helicopter doctrines and tactics. In the Vietnam war, pilots and machines met and surmounted the test of actual combat. The documentary basis for this monograph was primarily the official records of the Marine Corps and Navy Department, but considerable use was made of interviews and correspondence with key individuals involved in all phases of helicopter development.

The author, Lieutenant Colonel William R. (Bob) Fails, USMC (Ret), received his Bachelor of Arts degree in English from Hiram College, Hiram, Ohio, and his Master of Business Administration in Financial Management from The George Washington University, Washington, D.C. His Marine Corps aviation experience includes tours with fixed-wing fighter and attack squadrons, as a flight instructor, and as a helicopter pilot and aircraft maintenance officer. He served in Vietnam in 1965–66 with HMM–263 and again in 1970–71 as S–4 of MAG–16 and facility manager for Marble Mountain Airfield. He came to the History and Museums Division in 1973 from the 34th MAU in the Mediterranean, in which he had been Executive Officer. Now retired, Lieutenant Colonel Fails resides and works in Tempe, Arizona.

Comment copies of the manuscript for this volume were sent to many individuals involved with both the conceptual and operational aspects of Marine helicopter development. In association with Lieutenant Colonel Fails, Dr. Graham A. Cosmas incorporated these comments and edited the manuscript for printing. Dr. Cosmas received his PhD degree in history from the University of Wisconsin and joined the staff of the History and Museums Division in December 1973 after teaching at the University of Texas and the University of Guam.

The History and Museums Division welcomes any comments on the narrative and additional information or illustrations which might enhance a future edition.

E. H. SIMMONS
Brigadier General, U.S. Marine Corps (Ret)
Director of Marine Corps History and Museums

Reviewed and approved:
1 May 1978

# PREFACE

One of the most pervasive characteristics of man is hindsight. It masquerades under many guises: Monday morning quarterbacking, second guessing, and historical writing. When viewed through time, the past becomes distorted. Problems seem simpler, the choices more clear, and the conditions less complex than those of the present. The men who played a part become more heroic or more villainous than they were in life.

This volume is an attempt to portray accurately the difficulties faced and the obstacles conquered by the men who developed helicopters in the Marine Corps, so that the Marines of today and the future may meet the challenges of their own times with the same dedication as their predecessors.

The men who developed helicopters in the Marine Corps had nothing more to rely on than their knowledge of what had preceded them, intelligence liberally used, and both mental and physical courage. The present-day Marine will be well served if he applies nothing more.

This volume is no more the product of one man than is the development of helicopters in the Marine Corps. While the final responsibility must rest squarely on the shoulders of the author, many others were involved. It is impossible to acknowledge all who gave assistance, but special mention has to be made of a few. First there was Henry I. Shaw, Jr, Chief Historian of the Histories and Museums Division at Headquarters Marine Corps. His many hours of counsel, advice, and encouragement in large measure determined the form and thrust of the book. Dr. Graham A. Cosmas, who edited the book for publication and, with me, incorporated the comments of reviewers, was a welcome and expert colleague. Lee M. Pearson, Historian for the Naval Air Systems Command, and his able assistant, M. Frances Mattingly, provided a large amount of material. So did Elsie L. T. Goins of the Aviation History Office, Deputy Chief of Naval Operations (Air Warfare). Major John C. Short and his staff of the division's Historical Reference Section had unlimited patience as I researched through their files.

Many Marines aided me. Major Gary L. Telfer, a ground officer, read many of the technical sections for understandability. Always on the lookout for information were Lieutenant Colonels Alvah J. Kettering, Robert K. Goforth, William C. Ryan III, and Majors Robert M. Rose and William C. Cowperthwait. My special appreciation goes to Colonel David A. Spurlock who always found time in his hyper-busy schedule to explain technical details or provide documents from his own files. His help was invaluable.

Mrs. Keith B. McCutcheon made available to the Marine Corps many of the personal papers of General McCutcheon. They were a great help to me, and will be mandatory for any future research into the history of Marine Corps aviation.

Typing and typesetting were completed by Miss Catherine A. Stoll, layout and charts by Gunnery Sergeant Paul A. Lloyd, and production editorial work by Mr. Paul D. Johnston.

Finally I would like to express my deep and personal appreciation to a Marine who will never read the book: Major Bernard (Bernie) R. Terhorst. On 19 April 1969, while on his second tour in Vietnam, he piloted a helicopter on a night medical evacuation flight. The aircraft was hit by intense fire from the enemy. All on board perished. Major Terhorst was survived by his wife, Barbara, and six children. He and all the other helicopter pilots and crew members who gave their lives for their fellow men, and their families, were the ultimate inspiration for this book.

W. R. FAILS
Lieutenant Colonel, U.S. Marine Corps (Ret.)

# TABLE OF CONTENTS

| | |
|---|---|
| FOREWORD | iii |
| PREFACE | v |
| CHAPTER 1. THE LAST CONCERT | 1 |
|    New Year's Day 1962 | 1 |
|    Marine Helicopters Around the World | 2 |
|    Helicopters ARE Different | 3 |
|    The "Huss" | 5 |
|    The HOK | 10 |
|    The "Deuce" | 12 |
|    The Last of a Breed | 17 |
|    The White Tops | 19 |
|    An Extended Range | 20 |
|    The Conversion | 21 |
|    Soldier Mechanics of the Sea | 22 |
|    Keel-Up LPH | 23 |
|    The Last Concert | 26 |
| CHAPTER 2. MANEUVERS AND DEPLOYMENTS | 27 |
|    Possible Deployment | 27 |
|    SHUFLY | 28 |
|    The 1962 Missile Crisis | 34 |
|    STEEL PIKE I | 36 |
|    Dominican Republic | 37 |
| CHAPTER 3. INTRODUCTION OF THE TURBINES | 42 |
|    More Lift per Aircraft | 42 |
|    The "Huey" | 44 |
|    Replacement for the HUS | 47 |
|    The CH-46 | 52 |
|    The VH-3A | 53 |
|    The VTOLs | 56 |
|    The CH-53 | 58 |
| CHAPTER 4. THE MEN WHO FLEW HELICOPTERS | 63 |
|    Who Wants to Fly Helicopters? | 63 |
|    Sources of Marine Aviators | 64 |
|    Selection of Helicopter Pilots in Training | 67 |
|    Recruiting Expedients | 67 |
|    Transitions | 69 |
|    Training | 70 |
|    Crew Training | 73 |
|    Flight on Instruments | 75 |

| | |
|---|---:|
| **CHAPTER 5. HELICOPTERS SHOOT BACK** | 79 |
| SHUFLY Ends | 79 |
| Land the Landing Force | 80 |
| Armoring | 81 |
| Helicopter Escorts | 82 |
| Early Studies of the LARA | 83 |
| Arming the Transports | 83 |
| Armed Helicopters | 85 |
| Gunships for the Marines? | 86 |
| Armed UH-34s | 87 |
| The Armed UH-1E | 88 |
| **CHAPTER 6. MORE HELICOPTERS FOR AN EXPANDING WAR** | 92 |
| The Buildup | 92 |
| The Viet Cong Worsen the Helicopter Shortage | 95 |
| The "Deuce" Finds a Mission | 97 |
| **CHAPTER 7. THE CH-46 ON ACTIVE SERVICE** | 99 |
| The CH-46 Enters Combat | 99 |
| Problems and Improvements | 99 |
| A New Version | 102 |
| General McCutcheon Takes Charge | 104 |
| **CHAPTER 8. TWO SEPARATE ROLES FOR THE UH-1E** | 109 |
| Expansion and Shortages | 109 |
| Guns or Eyes? | 111 |
| Reorganization | 112 |
| **CHAPTER 9. THE CH-53 ENTERS THE WAR** | 114 |
| A New Role for the Sea Stallion | 114 |
| A Helicopter Retriever | 115 |
| Other Modifications | 116 |
| Retrievers to Vietnam | 117 |
| Requiem for a Heavyweight—the End for the "Deuce" | 119 |
| **CHAPTER 10. MEDIUM TRANSPORT CRISIS** | 121 |
| The CH-46 in Trouble | 121 |
| The CH-46D Arrives in Vietnam | 124 |
| A Premature Funeral for the UH-34 | 125 |
| Last Flights of the "Huss" | 126 |
| **CHAPTER 11. A GENERAL AND HIS PILOTS** | 129 |
| Conscience and Will Power | 129 |
| "There Is No Shortage" | 129 |
| Congress Investigates | 133 |
| **CHAPTER 12. MORE PILOTS FOR THE WAR** | 137 |
| Busy Helicopter Crews | 137 |
| Management Actions | 138 |
| A New Source of Helicopter Pilots | 141 |
| Army Helicopter Training | 142 |
| Post Graduate Flight Training | 144 |
| "We View Our Present Posture with Concern" | 145 |
| The Training Groups | 146 |

| | |
|---|---|
| CHAPTER 13. TWINS AND MIXES | 149 |
|     Continue the March | 149 |
|     Further Improvements of the CH-46 | 150 |
|     The "Huey" Changes Its Skin | 151 |
|     The "Sea Cobra" | 154 |
|     The Twin "Huey" | 157 |
|     Change in the Mix | 158 |
|     Marine Helicopters around the World | 161 |
|     The "Father of Helicopters" Leaves the Ranks | 162 |
| CHAPTER 14. LOOKING TO THE FUTURE | 165 |
|     The LHA | 165 |
|     The CH-53E | 166 |
|     The First Concert | 169 |
| NOTES | 171 |
| CHRONOLOGY | 185 |
| STANDARD AIRCRAFT CHARACTERISTICS | 189 |
| INDEX | 255 |

# CHAPTER ONE

## THE LAST CONCERT

### New Year's Day 1962

New Year's Day 1962 dawned cold and bleak in Washington, D.C. The sky remained overcast and the temperature hovered just above freezing. As most of the residents slept away the revelries of the night before, in a full block of staid but substantial brick buildings located in the southeast section of the city there was a flurry of activity.

For almost 100 years, every New Year's morning the United States Marine Band had staged a well-rehearsed, impromptu concert for the Commandant. Each Commandant had responded, appearing suitably surprised even though he had spent some effort getting dressed in the required formal uniform. At the conclusion of the ritual the band always was invited into the Commandant's House to share with visitors and guests a cup of hot punch. The first of January 1962 was no exception.

At exactly 1045, Lieutenant Colonel Albert F. Schoepper, director and a veteran of 18 years service with the band, two assistant directors, the drum major and 78 members assembled on the north side of the parade ground directly in front of the Commandant's House. Fifteen minutes later as the musicians began their serenade with "Fanfare," General David M. Shoup, Commandant of the Marine Corps (CMC) stepped out the door looking "suitably surprised." [1]

The four interconnected stars of his rank covered the shoulders of his blue uniform, and at the top of the rows of ribbons denoting a total of 22 awards was the unmistakable pale blue background and white stars of the Medal of Honor. He had won it for his leadership in the battle for Betio Island of the Tarawa Atoll in November 1943. On 12 August 1959, as a major general commanding the Recruit Depot at Parris Island, S.C., he had been nominated to the top position in the Marine Corps by President Dwight D. Eisenhower. In so doing, the President had departed from previous tradition and had reached below almost a dozen other candidates who were senior to General Shoup; but the confirmation was given quickly and now he was listening to his third New Year's Day concert as the CMC.

USMC Photo A408673

*General David M. Shoup, 22d Commandant of the Marine Corps. During his term of office, Marine helicopter forces were committed in the Cuban missile crisis and in aid of the South Vietnamese.*

At the conclusion of the program, Lieutenant Colonel Schoepper made a short speech and the CMC responded. Then all adjourned to the punch bowl where they were joined by other members of the band who had not participated in the ceremony.[2]

Of the Marines and their guests gathered that day few could have foreseen that this would be the last New Year's Day for 11 years in which Marines were not engaged in battle. Fewer still could have known that the first major Marine unit to be committed to combat would be a helicopter squadron and that one of the last to be withdrawn also would be a helicopter squadron.

Helicopters in the Marine Corps had come a long way since the first two had been delivered 9 February 1948. At the time, those two fragile Sikorsky-built observation helicopters, designated HO3Ss, represented a total combined capacity of just six passengers—provided conditions for flight were absolutely ideal, which they seldom were.[*]

## Marine Helicopters Around The World

Fourteen years later, the Marine Corps had 341 helicopters of all types.[3] Over half of them, a total of 196, were assigned to Aircraft, Fleet Marine Force, Pacific (AirFMFPac). Unlike the Atlantic Fleet Marine Force (FMFLant), aviation units in the Pacific were a separate command from the rest of the Marine units. Not until 1 July 1965 would the two be consolidated and Major General Avery R. Kier's AirFMFPac merged with FMFPac. General Kier, a pilot with one of the first Marine Reserve Squadrons at Minneapolis in the 1930s, became deputy commander of the consolidated forces under Lieutenant General Victor H. Krulak.[4]

Marine Aircraft Group (MAG) 16, with 64 helicopters, was based at the Marine Corps Air Facility (MCAF), Futema, Okinawa. The newest of all Marine helicopter fields, Futema had been built by Navy construction battalions (CBs) and opened in 1960. In numbers of units, MAG 16 was the smallest of all helicopter groups. Other than the normal Headquarters and Maintenance Squadron (H&MS) 16 and the Marine Air Base Squadron (MABS) 16, it had only three tactical squadrons. Marine Observation Squadron (VMO) 2 had a mixture of helicopters and small fixed-wing aircraft. There were two light transport squadrons: HMRL-261 and -362. On New Year's Day 1962, the latter was temporarily deployed on board the USS *Princeton* (LPH 5), an amphibious assault ship. HMM-362 soon would have a rendezvous with history.

The only helicopter squadron in AirFMFPac not part of a helicopter group was HMRL-161 at Kaneohe, Hawaii. It was attached to what was otherwise an exclusively fixed-wing group, MAG-13, and with 16 helicopters provided the vertical lift capability for the 1st Marine Brigade.

On the west coast of the United States, about 25 miles south of Los Angeles at Marine Corps Air Station (MCAS), Santa Ana was another unit of AirFMFPac. MAG-36 consisted of a H&MS and a MABS, four light transport squadrons )HMRLs-163, -361, -363, and -364), and one medium transport squadron, HMRM- 462, for a total of 105 helicopters; and, 40 miles further south at MCAF, Camp Pendleton, VMO-6 had 11 more plus a complement of fixed-wing observation aircraft.

Fleet Marine Force, Atlantic had concentrated all its helicopter capability at MCAF, New River, North Carolina, at the edge of the sprawling Camp Lejeune complex. There, under MAG-26, were a H&MS and MABS, VMO-1, HMRLs-162, -262, -263, and -264, and HMRM-461 for an aggregate of 108 machines.

One helicopter squadron, not a part of the Fleet Marine Force, was Marine Helicopter Squadron (HMX) 1 at MCAS Quantico, Virginia. It had a dual mission. Its historic role in the Marine Corps, ever since it was commissioned under the command of Colonel Edward C. Dyer on 1 December 1947, had been the "development of helicopter tactics, techniques and equipment for the landing force operation."

Beginning in September 1957, however, it had added another assignment: that of providing special helicopter flights to high-ranking officials in the federal government. This became known as "the Presidential mission." To accomplish both of these tasks, HMX-1 was assigned a total of 26 helicopters representing five different types.

Finally, 11 obsolete helicopters were assigned to fixed-wing air stations to act as search and rescue (SAR) aircraft in the event of an emergency.

At the time, the designation of the squadrons as to "light" or "medium" more accurately reflected earlier hopes of the planners than the actual comparative lift capability of the available helicopters. Before the end

---

[*] For a complete history of the early development of helicopters in the Marine Corps, see: LtCol Eugene W. Rawlins, *Marines and Helicopters, 1946–1962* (Washington: History and Museums Division, Headquarters, U.S. Marine Corps, 1977). Unless otherwise noted, all data for helicopters authorized or on hand is taken from the Marine Corps Aviation Status Board Photograph for the month indicated. In a few instances, aircraft technically possessed are not included in the statistics. The numbers are insignificant and the variety of circumstances is large; such as aircraft loaned to other services and aircraft on bailment (lease) to the manufacturers for special tests or modifications. The status board does include, however, aircraft assigned to a unit but undergoing overhaul and repair (O&R) or progressive aircraft rework (PAR).

of the year, the hard facts would be accepted and what had been a "light" squadron became a "medium." Likewise the "mediums" were redesignated "heavies."[5] Also the individual aircraft were to change designations when in July the Department of Defense directed a system of identifying aircraft which was the same for all military services.[6]*

The Marine Corps helicopters in 1962 represented six different types, only three of which were in use in any significant number by tactical squadrons. All types, however, flew in response to the same laws of aerodynamics.

## Helicopters ARE Different

> The thing is, helicopters are different from planes. An airplane by its nature wants to fly and if not interfered with too strongly by unusual events or by a deliberately incompetent pilot, it will fly.
> 
> A helicopter does not want to fly. It is maintained in the air by a variety of forces and controls, working in opposition to each other; and if there is any disturbance in the delicate balance, the helicopter stops flying immediately and disastrously. There is no such thing as a gliding helicopter.
> 
> This is why being a helicopter pilot is so different from being an airplane pilot; and why, in generality, airplane pilots are open, clear-eyed, buoyant extroverts and helicopter pilots are brooders, introspective anticipators of trouble.
> 
> They know if anything bad has not happened, it is about to.
>
> Harry Reasoner
> ABC Evening News
> 16 February, 1971[7]

Mr. Reasoner, a news commentator, may not have been aware fully of the technical details of why a helicopter did not want to fly, but he described the problem accurately. A lack of appreciation for just what a helicopter could—and could not—do often created misunderstandings. It was the source of numerous myths. The design and employment of helicopters were completely dominated by their aerodynamics. Thus, any understanding of the development of helicopters must start with some knowledge of the basic characteristics. Three are particularly important. The first is the inherent instability of a helicopter.

Given a suitable shape, any aerodynamic body will create lift as the air flows around it. It makes absolutely no difference if the shape is a wing, a propeller, or a rotor blade. The faster the speed of the air, the more lift generated. The forces, however, do not increase uniformly.

An airplane which accelerates from 100 to 300 miles per hour (mph) does not triple the amount of lift from the wings. The increase is nine-fold, for lift is created by the "square" of the velocity of the air. ($100 \times 100$ versus $300 \times 300$). A small change in speed, obviously, creates a disproportionate difference. In a fixed-wing aircraft, with both wings firmly attached to the airplane and moving through the air at the same speed, this is no problem. There is no difficulty with a helicopter either as long as the machine is in a hover in calm air. In such a case, the rotor blades are passing through the air at the same speed at all points around the aircraft. But when a helicopter begins to move forward, the conditions change rapidly. Now as the rotor blade begins to sweep forward to the front of the aircraft, the forward speed of the helicopter is added to the velocity of the air. Conversely, as the blade retreats from the front, the velocity is subtracted. The amount of lift generated on opposite sides of the helicopter is drastically out of balance. This disparity of lift was a major stumbling block to the design of helicopters. Several solutions were proposed. The most common was to install two rotors which turned in opposite directions. In forward flight portions of each were always spinning into the wind, and equal portions turning away from the wind. There was a balance of lift, but two rotors usually turned out to be a complicated and expensive solution.

There were other methods. Igor Sikorsky's rightful claim to be the inventor of the first successful helicopter in the western hemisphere is based on his development of a method for equalizing lift on both sides of the aircraft using a single lifting rotor. As his rotor blades moved around the helicopter, they automatically changed pitch, flexed, twisted, and even adjusted speed so that no matter where they were in relation to the wind, they produced the same amount of lift. The result is termed a "fully articulated" rotor head. Modifications to Sikorsky's basic invention have provided the basis for rotors by most other manufacturers. A fully articulated rotor system, however, has one serious drawback. It results in an aircraft that is completely unstable.

The difference in stability between a helicopter and a fixed-wing aircraft is often compared to a child's swing which is hung by steel rods. If it is pushed from its normal motionless position and then left alone, the swing will sooner or later of its own accord stop exactly where it was originally. The stability of a fixed wing is similar. A helicopter, however, is like the same swing, only this time balanced upside down. If disturbed it will fall away from where it was with ever increasing speed and will never attempt to return to its original position.

To an outside observer a helicopter's instability seems impossible. The whirling rotor blades very much appear to resemble a giant gyroscope—one of the most

---

* See "Standard Aircraft Characteristics," p. 189.

stable devices known. What is seen as a smooth blur, though, is each individual blade moving, twisting, and changing speed to adjust constantly for the differences of lift created by the wind. To demonstrate this phenomenon, cameras have been mounted on a rotor blade and after carefully counterbalancing the others, the helicopter flown. The resulting movie indicates, not the rigid structure of a gyroscope, but what most observers describe as a "writhing wet noodle." [8]

It is somewhat as if an airline pilot were flying a jet liner that had wings made of rubber which constantly changed shape without his knowledge. Sikorsky's solution to the difference in the amount of lift generated on opposite sides of a helicopter is the ultimate source of its instability and vibration.

Designers, engineers, and manufacturers devised a number of systems to compensate for the lack of stability. Most utilized a combination of sensors, electronics, and hydraulic controls. By the late 1960s considerable progress had been made and further refinements were being incorporated into new helicopters.

Brigadier General Jay W. Hubbard, in 1972, had occasion to evaluate the latest developments. General Hubbard, a platoon commander in the 2d Raider Battalion during World War II and one of the more exuberant fighter pilots in the Marine Corps, was at this time commanding general of the 4th Marine Aircraft Wing and Marine Air Reserve Training Command. As some of his units were scheduled to receive new jet-powered helicopters, he completed a familiarization course in the CH-46F. Later he described the results:

> The stability problems that confronted helicopter designers brought out the very best technology as tough engineering problems always seem to do. It was particularly impressive to me . . . to find that the basic trim system in some of our modern helicopters actually amounted to an autopilot. I've also been impressed by both stability and control that first line helicopters demonstrate through a wide airspeed envelope—like flying from zero to 170 knots. It occurs to me that fixed wing flight control technology might welcome some engineers from the rotor community.[9]

In spite of the improvements in handling characteristics brought about by the sophisticated systems, helicopters are still basically no different than the first machines. They remain unstable. Many test pilots consider the electronic systems as "just so much cosmetic window dressing." [10] The fact is constantly brought home to Marines who fly helicopters. Periodically they must demonstrate to an inspector their proficiency in flying with all the stability systems turned off. In most machines the smallest movement will induce an ever increasing swing away from the conditions which prevailed before. If the nose of the aircraft deviates ever so slightly from the intended direction of flight, only the most delicate and precise reaction from the pilot will prevent it from moving even further askew. Even with clear skies and an unencumbered view of the ground, a helicopter without stability systems challenges the very best of pilots. At night or on instruments such flight is seemingly impossible.

Another unique characteristic of a helicopter is termed ground effect. A helicopter rapidly loses efficiency as the air becomes thinner, whether due to an increase in altitude or temperature. The reverse is true also. Under certain circumstances, the rotor can create an artificially dense cushion of air and its lifting ability is dramatically increased. This occurs as the aircraft is close to the ground. The effect is first noticeable when the rotors are at the same altitude as their diameter and continues to intensify until the helicopter lands. The down wash from the rotor literally packs the air under the helicopter and as the aircraft flies in this mass of "thick" air the blades greatly increase their efficiency. A pilot, therefore, finds that it takes less power from the engines to fly at 10 feet than at 100.

Ground effect, however, is present only under specific conditions. The helicopter must be in a hover or moving very slowly. Otherwise it will slide right off the top of the cushion and derive no benefit. The effect is present only when there is a steady wind. If it is gusty from any direction, particularly from the side, it will blow parts of the ground cushion out from under the aircraft.

The surface under the helicopter must be relatively smooth. Otherwise the rotor wash breaks up into a chaos of turbulence. Unless the landing zone is level and the wind steady, the pilot finds ground effect building up momentarily on one side of the aircraft, only to disappear and be created somewhere else for an instant. It makes a smooth landing impossible. The result is much like a sportsman trying to bring his fishing skiff to a perfect docking while bobbing in a fierce storm.

One more phenomenon associated with helicopters is translational lift. As the aircraft is picking up forward speed and passes through approximately 15–20 knots, there is a sudden decrease in the amount of power required to fly. On landing just the reverse occurs and once the helicopter slows below the critical speed, additional power must be added to maintain flight.

The aerodynamic forces which create this paradox are exceedingly complex, but basically involve the relative direction of the wind over the rotor blades. It was an attempt to exploit more fully the advantages of translational lift that resulted in the death of the first Marine ever officially designated as a helicopter pilot,* Major Armond H. DeLalio, who received the certification on 8 August 1946 after completing training with the U.S. Navy. He followed 15 Navy aviators who had qualified earlier.[11] **

In 1952, DeLalio, then a lieutenant colonel, was conducting tests at the Naval Air Test Center (NATC), Patuxent River, Maryland, on jet-assisted takeoffs (JATO) for helicopters. Rockets had been mounted on a HRS-1 model helicopter. When fired, they rapidly accelerated the helicopter to a speed above translational lift. Many problems had been encountered, the most serious of which was "afterburning effect in which a large part of the helicopter is engulfed in a sheet of flame for a short time. The hot gases of the JATO bottle are near to and directed at the runway or ground. Good sized stones are thrown back at the main and tail rotor systems. In the field grass fires would result."[13]

With the tests over 90 percent complete, on 5 January 1952 one of the rockets broke loose, causing an explosion and fire which killed Lieutenant Colonel DeLalio.[14] Seven months after the accident, the Bureau of Aeronautics recommended that the JATO project, which had lain dormant after DeLalio's death, be cancelled. Colonel Edward C. Dyer, head of aviation plans at Headquarters Marine Corps, agreed.[15] Further efforts to provide extra power for a helicopter below the speed of translational lift were shifted to small rocket motors attached to the ends of the main lifting rotor blades.[16]

Helicopter pilots quickly learn to take advantage of both ground effect and translational lift whenever they can. If takeoff is to be made from an open field and the load is heavy, the pilot will raise the helicopter into a very low hover taking full benefit from the dense air in the rotor wash. By starting forward very slowly and keeping the cushion under the aircraft he can accelerate until translational lift is reached and then begin to climb. Likewise on landing, sufficient speed is maintained to keep translational lift until the helicopter is low enough to enter ground effect.

In either case the helicopter can lift extra heavy loads. If neither condition is present, the ability is greatly reduced. This was the cause of some serious misunderstandings. For Marines unaware of these characteristics, it was difficult to believe that a helicopter pilot could lift a large load from an open field where both translational lift and ground effect were present and yet could not hover 100 feet in the air to deliver the cargo to a small, rocky mountain top landing zone.

## The "Huss"

Regardless of their aerodynamic problems, helicopters had become a vital part of the Marine air-ground team, and each machine had a portion of the overall amphibious assault mission to accomplish. By far the most common Marine helicopter in 1962 was the Sikorsky-built HUS (UH-34D) with 225 aircraft assigned[17]. It had arrived at this preeminent position almost by accident. The H-34 series had been purchased by the military initially as an anti-submarine helicopter for the Navy and was originally designated the HSS-1 (SH-34). This particular design was an outgrowth of even earlier models of Sikorsky helicopters, most particularly the HRS-3 (CH-19), which had provided the Marine Corps with much of its helicopter lift capability in the early- and mid-50s. The HSS-1 had made its maiden flight on 8 March 1954 and had been quickly put into service for anti-submarine warfare.[18] *

While the Navy was developing the SH-34, the Marine Corps was concentrating almost exclusively on much larger helicopters and showed limited interest in such a machine. It could be used, however, for minor utility missions and on 1 April 1955 General Lemuel C. Shepherd, Jr., then the Commandant of the Marine Corps, wrote to the Chief of Naval Operations (CNO) requesting that 90 such helicopters be procured to "rapidly shuttle supplies to forward elements, to execute tactical movements of small units and to evacuate battle casualties."[19] Though the Marines did not get 90, they did receive approval and funding for 45.

Production of a utility version of the SH-34 was a relatively simple process which involved removing the equipment for anti-submarine operations, strengthening the cabin floor, and installing cargo tie-down rings. This new model had its first flight in January 1957 and because the modifications from the SH-34 were so slight, formal tests at the NATC Patuxent were not necessary.[20]

The first one was delivered to tactical units on 13 February the same year and by the end of the month, HMRL-261, commanded by Lieutenant Colonel Richard J. Flynn, Jr., had four on hand at New River and

---

* Major General Marion E. Carl is generally credited with being the first Marine to learn how to fly helicopters in July 1945. It was not until some years later, however, that he was officially designated.[12]

** The first naval aviator designated a helicopter pilot was Commander William G. Knapp, USN, who received the certification on 15 April 1944. He retired from the Navy in 1957 and after a long illness died in the Bethesda Naval Hospital in 1965.

---

* Until September 1962, this aircraft was designated the HUS-1; after that date it became the UH-34. The latter designation will be used throughout this volume.

*From 1957 to the mid-1960s, the UH–34 made up the backbone of the vertical lift capability of the Marine Corps. This aircraft is participating in training operations on board the USS* Tripoli *off the California coast in January 1967.*

Lieutenant Colonel William F. Mitchell, who had taken command of HMRL–363 but a week earlier, had three more at Santa Ana. One additional UH–34D was assigned to HMX–1 at Quantico.[21]

From this almost accidental beginning, the UH–34 was to emerge as the mainstay of Marine Corps helicopters until 1968 and was to bear much of the brunt of combat in Southeast Asia for the first six years of the war.

Within a year of General Shepherd's requesting procurement of the limited number of HR–34s, and even before they were first introduced into tactical units, the requirement gained new urgency. The design and production of large assault helicopters continued to encounter technical difficulties, and it appeared that their introduction into the Marine Corps could be long delayed. The problem was recognized in May 1956 when Lieutenant General Vernon E. Megee, Assistant Commandant, gave his approval to a G-3 study which shifted priority to procuring increased numbers of H–34s as an interim helicopter until the true "heavies" could be produced in sufficient quantities.[22] Thus the Marine Corps became increasingly committed to the UH–34.

Like all Sikorsky designs, the UH–34 had a single main lifting rotor, 56 feet in diameter, with a smaller 9 foot, 6 inch anti-torque rotor on the tail pylon. All the blades were constructed entirely of metal, a development still not universally accepted in 1957. The main ones had a leading edge formed of a hollow steel "spar" providing the bulk of the structural strength and lighter "pockets" bonded to the rear of the spar to provide aerodynamic lifting surfaces. These main blades could be folded to permit operations on aircraft carriers and LPHs. The folding operation was a simple manual one in which a mechanic unscrewed a large locking bolt at the point where each main blade attached to the rotor head allowing the blade to pivot to the rear. Other crewmen attached a long crutch to the end of the blade and lowered it into racks that were temporarily installed over the fuselage of the helicopter. To unfold, the mechanics merely reversed the procedure with an additional step of inserting a safety wire through the locking bolt to prevent it from vibrating loose in flight. The rear anti-torque rotor did not fold. Instead the entire tail pylon could be unlocked and rotated 180 degrees until it was parallel to the left side of the fuselage directly in front of its extended position.

With both the main blades and the tail pylon folded, the dimensions of the aircraft were reduced from an extreme length of 65.7 feet to a modest 37 feet and the width from 56 feet to slightly more than 14 feet. It was then easy to move the airplanes on the ship's elevators or pack them tightly on the hanger and flight decks.

The engine was a Wright R–1820–84 which could produce up to 1525 horsepower.* This nine-cylinder workhorse was a slight modification of one that had been in wide use for a number of years in both commercial and military aircraft of all types. Mounted as it was in the very front of the aircraft behind large nose (clam shell) doors, it was comparatively easy for the mechanics to work on. It did require, however, careful coordination on the part of the pilot not to exceed its limitations. The UH–34 had a full set of controls for both the pilot and a co-pilot, who sat above and behind the engine and just forward of the main transmission.**

All helicopters such as the UH–34 that have but a single main lifting rotor possess a similar characteristic. They are very sensitive to the placement of their load as near as possible to the center of gravity of the aircraft. If the load is placed beyond rather narrow limitations, the amount of control the pilot has over adjusting the angle of the rotor to make turns and other maneuvers is restricted and the helicopter cannot fly. Thus the troop compartment of the UH–34 was placed directly under the main transmission and rotor, with the pilots and engine in front being counterbalanced by a long tail structure in the rear. This cabin measured over 13 feet long, almost 5 feet wide and was 6 feet high with a large sliding door on the right side. Canvas bucket seats for 12 passengers could be installed when necessary. In addition a hook underneath the aircraft, stressed to 5,000-pound capacity to allow for any jarring, could be utilized to carry loads externally, and a hoist mounted outside just above the cargo door could be used to lift loads of up to 400 pounds.[23]

One of the most difficult problems faced by Marine Corps planners was to determine accurately how much weight a helicopter could carry when conducting an assault. It was particularly critical for the UH-34s since they were to represent so much of the total lift available. This dilemma stemmed from a variety of causes. There were so many subtle differences between seemingly identical aircraft that the actual weight might vary several hundred pounds. New equipment was often added as aircraft underwent progressive aircraft rework (PAR). A squadron might have but a few of its assigned aircraft with those improvements installed. Slight variations in manufacturing also caused individual aircraft of the same model to vary in basic weight. These two conditions alone created a requirement for each helicopter to be weighed periodically on scales.

A more vexing factor was that the definitions applied by the manufacturers, the operators, and the planners were often confusing. Thus, in 1967 Sikorsky could list an empty weight for the UH-34 of 7,900 pounds [24] and at the same time, the official empty weight published by the Naval Air Systems Command (NavAirSysCom) was 8,090.[25]

Further compounding the problem, the useful load or payload of an individual aircraft had to include all the men and material required for the specific mission. If a crew chief was needed, he was part of the payload as was the fuel necessary to complete the flight. Armament and armor, if installed, further reduced the capability of the helicopter to lift combat Marines. Helicopters were extremely sensitive to the effects of altitude and temperature, both of which, as they increased, rapidly lowered the lifting capability.

While manufacturers were required to verify an "overload" condition under which the aircraft could fly under ideal circumstances, this higher weight put excessive strain on the airframe and rotor components thereby shortening their useful life. An overload also often reduced the maximum airspeed of the helicopter and the amount of shock ("G" loading) it could withstand. Unfortunately, this maximum "overload" condition sometimes gained currency as being the normal or standard load for a helicopter. Different types of takeoff and landing zones also restricted lift capacity. With a short roll on a smooth runway a helicopter could lift a great deal more than if it had to take off straight up and climb several hundred feet before starting forward flight. And finally, particularly in those aircraft with piston engines, the proficiency of the pilot was a critical item in determining absolute payload capability.

Because of these variable factors, Sikorsky could claim that the "useful" load of an H-34 was 5,100 pounds,[26] but NavAirSysCom simultaneously calculated the payload in a standard troop transport mission, as

---

* Engine designations utilize "R" to indicate a radial arrangement of the cylinders. Likewise "T" indicates turbine, "J" pure jet. In piston engines a number such as 1820 indicates maximum displacement or size of the cylinders expressed in cubic inches. The dash number (-84) indicates a particular modification of the basic engine.

** In helicopters the position of the pilot and co-pilot are exactly the reverse of fixed-wing aircraft in which the pilot is on the left side of the cockpit and the copilot on the right. There are many versions of how this practice began but it appears to have been the result of Igor Sikorsky's early experiments with helicopters. Because the engines were mounted backwards from a conventional airplane, the main rotor turned to the left as seen from the cockpit. This required that the anti-torque rotor had to be on the left side of the helicopter to be most efficient. To reduce the danger of an accident from being hit by the tail rotor, all cargo loading and hoist operations were on the right side of the plane. This required that the pilot be on the right side of the cockpit to observe what was being loaded. Once begun, the practice remained and other manufacturers followed Sikorsky's lead.

only 2,700 pounds.[27] Both are correct, but each was using a different set of standards.

By 1962 any competent pilot, co-pilot, or crew chief could calculate exactly the lift capability of the particular aircraft assigned for the flight using a formula termed the HOGE or HIGE. They stood for "hover *out* of ground effect" and "hover *in* ground effect." To do so, however, they needed to know exactly which aircraft they were to fly and the changes incorporated into it, its latest weight on the scale, just what equipment was to be carried, the amount of fuel necessary, exact temperature, humidity, and altitude data for the expected time of takeoff and landing. Such information was seldom available in the heat of a combat assault.

Pilots and crew chiefs attacked the problem from several angles. Most of them adopted as most accurate the solution used by the men who flew helicopters during the first stages of development, and the one that remains today the final criterion for a helicopter pilot. They simply accepted any load put aboard the aircraft and attempted to take off into a hover. If they could, all was well and they proceeded with the mission. If they could not, they unloaded either some cargo or a Marine and attempted to take off again. This process was repeated until a takeoff could be made successfully. While extremely effective in determining the actual load the individual aircraft could lift under the specific set of circumstances existing at that moment, it was hardly conducive to well-organized assault landings. It also gave aviation safety officers nightmares. A second method developed by the Marine Corps Landing Force Development Center (MCLFDC) in 1960 consisted of a series of easily readable charts spelling out the effect of the major variables in lift capability such as altitude, temperature, and fuel required. These in turn were coupled with data from all over the world collected from the National Weather Center so that:

> An S-4 [logistics officer] could be 99% sure that, for example, palletized 2000 lb loads could be externally carried by HUS in area 'X'. He'd also know that there'd be a 30% chance the HUS could carry 200 lbs more. He could palletize some extra 100 or 200 lb loads.[28]

Though well conceived, and based on an accurate knowledge of the problem, the system proved cumbersome and fell into disuse.

A completely different approach to increase the payload, which was later used to great extent in tropical areas, was put forward in 1961 in a perceptive and, at the time, widely read article by Major Herbert A. Nelson, a veteran at the time of over 18 years flying with 1,500 hours in helicopters out of his total of 5,350. He recommended that prior to an assault the UH-34 be stripped of all equipment not needed on that particular mission. Thus "stripping" could include the emergency hatches, winch and hoist, heater and auxiliary power unit. Under certain circumstances even the crew chief was not needed. And there were few times when the large life raft, then required on all flights "out of gliding distance of land" was necessary. This last requirement, like that of carrying parachutes on certain flights, was an irksome holdover from fixed-wing transport operations and bore little relationship to the actual conditions which would exist if a helicopter were to have a major emergency.

Major Nelson calculated that up to 713 pounds could be stripped out of a UH-34 and that a corresponding increase in lift capability, or margin for aircraft and weather variables, would occur. When applied to a 200-sortie assault, the total benefit in combat Marines or cargo was over 142,000 pounds.[29]

Among the items that Major Nelson recommended to leave behind was the 40-pound, catch-all bag carried by the crew chief. He might have understated the potential for weight saving. Crew chiefs in helicopters were (and remain) a vital member of the pilot/co-pilot team. They flew in aircraft, however, that, when necessary in an emergency, could land in any open corn field or rice paddy. With the state of the art at the time, this was not an entirely uncommon occurance. Most crew chiefs had long since forsaken a "catchall" and normally carried a metal cruise box about the same dimensions as a large foot locker. In it would be not only tools for minor repairs, but small parts for all the systems that failed with any imaginable frequency, several cans of hydraulic fluid, an emergency supply of cigarettes, a week's supply of pilfered C-Rations, a clean set of flight clothing and, if the crew chief had had a particularly bad set of luck in his aircraft, some civilian clothes and maybe even a 20-dollar bill.

Crew chiefs on helicopters were prepared for just about any emergency, but their provisions did reduce the capability of the aircraft. Many aircraft maintenance officers combatted this by making frequent inspections and as an ultimate test, ordered the crew chief to pick up his cruise box with one hand. If he could, the weight penalty was reasonable. If he could not, something had to be left behind.

But the crux of the matter was that all these variables combined to make the prediction of the load-carrying capability of the UH-34 a very tenuous occupation. Thus a series of "rule of thumb" guidelines grew up and became widely known among the infantry as well as the helicopter crews. For the UH-34D, as an example, in combat in the humidity of Southeast Asia with both a crew chief and a gunner, armor, and enough fuel for an hour and a half mission, eight combat-equipped Marines (at 250 pounds each) was a normal load. The inability to predict accurately the total amount of lift represented by the UH-34s and other transport helicopters continued to plague the planners. A great deal rested on their estimates, not only for combat assaults but for establishing the number of aircraft required and all the associated personnel, equipment, and ships that were necessary.

This overall lift capability had been reduced seriously a few months before General Shoup was listening to the 1962 New Year's day concert. The reduction had come in a critical area—the Western Pacific.

The Marine Corps had reached a peak of 233 UH-34s on hand in June 1961. Then, in response to an urgent requirement, it had transferred most of its Asian-based helicopter strength to "US Air Force for assignment to Air America as part of the Military Assistance program for Laos." [30]

A total of 31 UH-34s had been involved. Eight of these were diverted from the Marine Corps while they were still being assembled on the production line at Sikorsky. The rest had come from Marine Corps squadrons, mostly the Futema-based HMRL-162 and -163, which were rotated back to the United States in July leaving few helicopters for their replacement squadrons, which would arrive at Futema with only their personnel and records and would take over the aircraft and equipment already on hand. Other than five UH-34s asigned to H&MS-16, the entire vertical lift capability of the Marine Corps in the western Pacific area during July and August of 1961 was entrusted to Lieutenant Colonel Fred A. Steele and his HMRL-261, which was embarked on the helicopter assault ship, the USS *Thetis Bay* (LPH-1) in the South China Sea.[31]

In July, Lieutenant Colonel Archie Clapp, a helicopter pilot since 9 June 1951 and one of the most innovative men in that early age, and his HMM-362 were transferred to Okinawa\*. Unfortunately, when he arrived from Santa Ana and assembled his unit at Futema, the helicopters that should have been awaiting him were gone. It took almost two months before sufficient aircraft could be shipped across the Pacific to make HMM-362 fully operational again.

By the end of July, with the combination of diverted aircraft from the production line, transfers to Laos, and aircraft destroyed in accidents, the Marine Corps was down to 198 UH-34s. The effect continued to be felt and the Marine Corps dropped even more the next month and reached a low of only 187 assigned to units. Then production began to catch up and by September the total was almost back to the level previously obtained: 227. The climb continued until, in February 1964, the Marine Corps would have over 350 UH-34s in service.

In a seemingly endless number of variations, the UH-34 became to helicopter flight operations about what the venerable Douglas DC-3 was to commercial and transport flight. In one modification, it even became a jet-turbine-powered helicopter, as the piston engine was replaced with two 1,000-horsepower General Electric engines. The modification did not necessarily mean an improved payload capability at sea-level conditions, due mostly to the limitations on the amount of power the airframe and rotor systems could be subjected to, but it did increase high altitude performance and provided the safety factor of two engines, in case one should malfunction. Though the Marine Corps never procured this particular model, a version of it was built and widely used by a number of foreign military and civilian operators, most notably the British who built it under the trade name of "Wessex."[32]

To Marines all over the world, the UH-34 became almost a legend in its own time. Ugly, rather crude compared to the new aircraft with which it would soon be faced, but thrifty and economical (in 1959 it had cost but $348,000 in a "fly away" condition at the Sikorsky plant), it demanded the very best technique of the pilot to exploit its potential performance.[33] Before the last one was delivered to the Marine Corps, in 1964, over 540 of these helicopters were sprayed with the paint that indelibly marked them as belonging to the Marine Corps. It was the work horse of a number of international confrontations and of a major war.

By its very reliability, simplicity, and capability, it seems to have given a new slang word to all Marines. When its more sophisticated cousins were grounded periodically for technical problems at the height of the war in Vietnam, the Marine on the ground could always give a radio call for assistance and specify a helicopter that he knew would respond. Using the old designation which never did lose its popularity among Marines and which was much easier to say over a radio, he would broadcast: "Give me a HUS." That word "huss" has been incorporated into the vocabulary of Marines to indicate something good, something beneficial, a favor, or a special set of circumstances that are pleasurable. It takes its place right along with "Gung Ho" and others.

For a helicopter that was to have been nothing more than an interim model standing in the shadow of the big assault machine, and one which had been procured almost as an afterthought by the Marine Corps, to be

---

\* All dates for designation as a Marine helicopter pilot are taken from "Chronological List of Qualified Helicopter Pilots" provided by the Deputy Chief of Naval Operations (Air Warfare) (DCNO-AW), Code OP05D, Washington, D.C.

called a "huss" is not such a bad commendation from the men who actually depended on them: the Marine riflemen in combat.

## The HOK

The most interesting helicopter available in the Marine Corps in 1962—at least from an aerodynamic standpoint—was the standard observation aircraft, the HOK (OH-43D). As other designers were wrestling with the technical problems of producing helicopters with improved performance, and different rotor configurations were still being tested, Charles (Charlie) H. Kaman developed one that was, at the time, ingenious, advanced, and very efficient. Other than the inherent instability of helicopters, the problem that had most bedeviled designers was to devise a way to equalize the amount of lift generated by the rotor blade as it traveled around in a circle. Kaman described his solution to a meeting of the American Helicopter Society in 1953:

> In fact, the single rotor helicopter such as the Sikorsky design violates the principle [of equaled lift] in that it is not symmetrical, whereas the intermeshing rotor helicopter *is* symmetrical. Unlike the single rotor helicopter where, in forward flight, different aerodynamic conditions exist on each side of the rotor disc, the intermeshing helicopter in forward flight has exactly the same condition on the right side of its overall rotor disc as it does on the left side. This is real symmetry, since exactly the same aerodynamic conditions exist for the right wing or rotor as exist for the left wing or rotor.[34]

As could be expected, the OH-43 * had two intermeshing main rotors mounted on pylons which were canted slightly to each side. As these rotors were contra-rotating they provided the desired symmetry and no anti-torque rotor was required, though to aid stability in high-speed forward flight there were fixed vertical and horizontal tail surfaces on booms extending from the rear of the aircraft. Power was supplied by a Pratt and Whitney R-1340-48 engine which could develop up to 600 horsepower.

This machine was unique in many respects. Unlike most helicopters at the time, the OH-43 did not rely on mechanical linkages at the rotor head to change pitch on the blades. Instead, Kaman had invented a system that utilized a small "servo flap" or aileron installed on the outer edges of the blades. When a pilot moved his control stick this small aileron responded and by the very aerodynamic forces generated was able to twist the blade to the desired amount of pitch, allowing the helicopter to maneuver. Initially, Kaman had used wooden blades to achieve the required amount of

---
* Redesignated from HOK in September 1962.

USMC Photo A530120
*A unique feature of the HOK-1, here sitting on the field at Quantico in June 1962, were the small servo-flaps on the rotor blades, which the pilot used to change rotor pitch.*

"twist." The flexing of the wooden blades solved many of the aerodynamic problems but the quality control to insure that all the wood was suitable and could withstand the pressures soon became an insurmountable problem. In the mid-1950s Kaman changed to metal blades that could twist with more predictability. In later models, Kaman would abandon this intermeshing main rotor configuration, but would retain the servo flap system of controlling the pitch of the rotor blades.

This system of rotors in the OH-43 gave it some characteristics superior to other helicopters at the time. It was extremely stable, particularly so in a hover. It could continue to climb at 100 feet per minute at 19,000 feet altitude, performance that was far above even the next generation of helicopters.** [35] For example, the jet-turbine-powered H-46A introduced almost a decade later reached its service ceiling at only 7,300 feet [36]. This ability won the OH-43 acceptance not only as an observation helicopter but, in a turbine-powered version, as a mountain rescue aircraft. The U.S. Air Force used significant numbers of OH-43s for such missions well into the mid-60s.

But the OH-43's high altitude and hover performance were matched by off-setting drawbacks. In forward flight it took a great deal of power to exceed approximately 90 knots. The helicopter was described by one experienced test pilot as performing at that speed as "about like pushing my grandmother's Thanksgiving turkey platter broadside through the air." [37] On

---
** The altitude at which an aircraft can no longer sustain a climb greater than 100 feet per minute is designated as its "service ceiling."

test flights it was discovered also that with rapid and large changes of power, particularly on recovery from a practice autorotation,* the aircraft tended to enter a stage where right rudder was required to go to the left and vice versa, and if not corrected for, the helicopter would unexpectedly enter a violent spin. This control reversal, as it was termed, was compensated for by a system linked to the manifold pressure in the engine which automatically made the correction for the pilot.[38] As long as the mechanism performed correctly, there was no problem; but like all mechanical devices it failed occasionally and when it did a pilot was in for a few thrilling moments.

A total of 81 OH–43's were procured for the Marine Corps. As was the case for many helicopter orders at the time, the delivery schedule underwent a number of revisions. The original contract called for the first delivery in October 1952 with the final deliveries being made in January 1956. After a number of changes, many of which were required to correct the problems discovered during the Fleet Introduction Program (FIP) and which had resulted in several fatal accidents, the first actual delivery was made in April 1953 and the final one in December 1957.[39]

In spite of the difficulties, the obvious advantages of the OH–43 could not be ignored. Rear Admiral Richard F. Stout, then senior member of the board evaluating the aircraft, concluded in his final report that the helicopter had many superior characteristics, one of which was that: "Due to the rotor configuration of the HOK–1 (it has) more stability than other helicopters without automatic stabilization equipment." [40]

Other than its limited top speed and the apprehension of the pilots as to whether the control reversal system would work or not, the OH–43 performed admirably for the Marine Corps. By removing the co-pilot's seat, two litters with wounded Marines could be carried and, if conditions were right, even an attendent could be added. The front of the aircraft was constructed almost entirely of clear plexiglass and the view for an aerial observer was nearly unlimited. The machine could be utilized for many missions that could not be performed economically by any other helicopter—just as long as the occupants were in no great hurry.[41]

By 1962 the OH–43 had become obsolete and the three-year search for a replacement was almost over. Director of Aviation Major General John C. Munn, who was later to become Assistant Commandant, had even suggested at one time that the ubiquitous UH–34 be substituted. He had noted in March, 1959 that:

> The HUS (UH–34) now programmed as the HRS (UH–19) replacement . . . can also perform any mission the HOK is capable of. Admittedly this is using more capability than is needed for the observation mission . . . (but) it has the capability of lifting troops and cargo during the high demand phase of the amphibious assault, prior to the time the HOK (OH–43) . . . type of observation mission becomes an appreciable requirement.[42]

While General Munn admitted that the UH–34 might not make an ideal observation helicopter, he concluded that in light of the budgetary constraints of the time it would have a better chance of being approved than a totally new design.

> Nothing in the foregoing will in any way modify our policy of developing operational requirements and development characteristics for aircraft ideally configured for the particular tasks we want performed. The objective of programming these aircraft will be aggressively pursued. However, our present approach is one of 'all or nothing'. As a result our chances of success in the several areas are remote.[43]

His plan never fully materialized. While the UH–34 was later pressed into service as an expedient for some observation missions, it had several serious drawbacks. The observer had to sit in the cabin, either looking out the open door or craning his neck to see out a window directly behind his seat. This latter procedure, if the mission was of any length, was guaranteed to give one a very stiff neck the next morning. Attempts made in 1965 in Vietnam to put an observer in the co-pilot's seat were generally unsuccessful.

The helicopter that finally did replace the OH–43 would be the first jet-powered one introduced into Marine Corps tactical units. Kaman had done much of the early pioneering of turbine helicopters and had claimed the first "turborotor" system in 1951, the first twin "gas turbine drive" in 1954, and by 1959 no longer produced any helicopters powered by piston engines.[44] It was ironical then that the replacement would not be manufactured by Kaman.

In January 1962, the Marine Corps still had 35 of these unusual aircraft: VMO–6 at MCAF Pendleton and VMO–2 at MCAF Futema each had 11, and VMO–1 at New River, nine. Four additional ones were assigned to HMX–1 at Quantico.[45] In the observation squadrons, these OH–43s were coupled with small fixed-wing aircraft to make up the eyes of the Fleet Marine Force. A total of 32 Cessna built OE–1 and –2s (Bird Dogs) supplemented the capabilities of the helicopters.**

---

* An exercise in controlling and landing the aircraft with the engine turned off.

** Unfortunately, the role of the fixed-wing observation aircraft assigned to helicopter units is beyond the scope of this volume. In most squadrons the pilots interchangably flew either the helicopters or the OEs. Those who fly the OEs were, and still are, the true orphans of Marine Corps aviation. Considered fixed-wing outsiders by the helicopter pilots in their parent aircraft group, they were looked upon with

Not until May 1965 would the OH-43 disappear from the rolls of aircraft assigned to the Marine Corps. Even then, for a few more months, the Futema-based VMO-2 still would be authorized six of them—most probably due to administrative oversight rather than any failure to realize that the HOK had had its day.[46] Though Kaman would build other helicopters for the Marine Corps, none of them would ever be quite as unique as the OH-43. Many commanders appreciated the superb view afforded by that plexiglass cabin, and Marine pilots told more than one sea-story about "the day the control reversal mechanism didn't work" in the HOK.

## The "Deuce"

One model of helicopter had dominated Marine Corps concepts of assault landings for the 14 years from 1948 to 1962 and would continue to overshadow all procurement for another decade. It was the most significant helicopter ever developed for the Marine Corps.

This machine, on which had depended so many hopes of the early planners for a true vertical envelopment capability, was known by many identifications during its service. It had begun with a Sikorsky designation of XHR2S-A. This was a formal way of saying that the aircraft was experimental (X), was a helicopter (H), was designed to be a transport (R), was the second such model in a line of design (2), and was built by Sikorsky (S). The "A" simply identified it as the first version of the type. Later, after testing had been completed, it became the HR2S with the "X" dropped from the designation. Sikorsky, which tried—unsuccessfully—to sell the helicopter to commercial concerns, always referred to it as the S-65. The Department of Defense gave it the name of "Mohave." Under the unified system of designations, it was classified as a CH-37C. Since the most common, and widely known model of helicopter in the Marine Corps at the time was a HRS, the "2" designating a second model took on a special significance and gave rise among Marines, always fond of a good card game, to a long-lasting nickname. To anyone who flew it, tried to maintain it, rode in it, and remembers it, this helicopter is universally referred to as the "Deuce."

Marine Corps interest in a heavy helicopter dated back to 1946, when a special board had been set up at Quantico to study problems of the Corps. Three members of the secretariat of the board—Colonel Merrill B. Twining, Lieutenant Colonel Edward C. Dyer, and Lieutenant Colonel Samuel R. Shaw—began to investigate seriously the use of helicopters in amphibious assaults. This obviously would require helicopters much larger than anything built up to that time. The idea that such a machine could be built gained strength that summer when Colonel Dyer, an air defense expert who had studied the system used by the Royal Air Force in the Battle of Britain and who later would command the first Marine Corps helicopter squadron, visited the Sikorsky plant and discussed the proposal with the inventor himself. As Dyer later recalled, Sikorsky said "We can do that now. This is within our present knowledge. We can build an airplane that will carry 5,000 pounds. We can build airplanes that will carry *much* more than that. We know how to do it. Take my word for it."[47]

Lieutenant Colonel Dyer reported back to Colonel Twining and conveyed Sikorsky's optimism. Both officers then returned to Connecticut for further discussions with Sikorsky of a 5,000-pound-payload helicopter. They also visited Frank Piasecki, the only other major builder of transport helicopters. Piasecki confirmed that there would be no problem in building so large an aircraft.[48]

The idea then languished for a few months but soon was revived. In March 1947, Assistant Commandant of the Marine Corps Lemuel C. Shepherd, Jr. spelled out in detail the helicopter requirements that eventually only the Deuce would begin to meet. In a letter to Admiral Forrest Sherman, then Deputy Chief of Naval Operations (DCNO(OPS)), he stated that "the principal requirement for the helicopter for use in assault landing in amphibious warfare is a minimum payload of 3,500 pounds, or 15 fully equipped infantrymen, but that an extension of the load limit to 5,000 pounds or twenty infantrymen would greatly enhance the value of the aircraft."[49] Shepherd thus called for a helicopter that in one step could take the entire concept of vertical envelopment from an untested idea into actual capability. The attempt was particularly bold since the largest helicopters then flying could, if everything was absolutely favorable, lift the pilot and three passengers; and with that load they seldom could take off without a short run on the ground.

Two years later, Sikorsky reiterated publicly his belief that large helicopters could be built. In an article which appeared in the August 1949 issue of the *Marine Corps Gazette*, he stated:

> I believe that helicopters with a gross weight of 50,000 pounds and a lifting capability of between 30 and 50 per cent of this figure can be designed in the near future. [It will have] a range from 100 up to 1,000 miles and eventually probably up to 2,000 miles

---

scorn as just odd-ball helicopter pilots by their fellow Marines who flew jets. Their contribution to the Marine Corps, however, has been great and their history an interesting one. Possibly in the future they will be suitably recognized.

... utilizing ... inflight refueling or [even] by towing the helicopter.⁵⁰

The idea of building a helicopter so large when those operating were so small and fragile might have intimidated many men, but not the Kiev-born Igor Sikorsky. In 1913, when he was only 24 years old, he had designed and built the world's first four-engine bomber, the "Russkiv Vitiaz" for Czarist Russia. Over the years he continued to produce a long line of extremely large aircraft, both in Russia and in the United States to which he emigrated in 1923. (The Marine Corps was no stranger to Sikorsky aircraft and had utilized his models as transports in the 1930 s.) ⁵¹

Several proposals for the 5,000-pound-lift helicopter were put forward by other manufacturers, most notably Piasecki and McDonnell, but in March 1951 Sikorsky received the contract to begin building what eventually became the "Deuce." *

---
\* See Rawlings, *op.cit.* for an interesting account of the alternatives and the selection process.

Even the most optimistic supporters of heavy helicopters realized that the technology required for such an aircraft would take time to develop and BuAir had calculated cautiously that May 1953 would be the target date for the first flight.⁵² Not until seven months after that on 18 December did the helicopter finally become airborne. A month later the aircraft was officially unveiled by Sikorsky General Manager B. L. Whelan at Bridgeport, Connecticut, before a large group of senior Marine officers led by General Shepherd, who was now Commandant, accompanied by Lieutenant General Oliver P. Smith, Commanding General, FMFLant; Major General Clayton C. Jerome, Commanding General, AirFMFLant; Brigadier General Robert G. Bare, Director of Marine Corps Development Center; Colonel Richard C. Mangrum, Marine Corps Schools, Quantico; Colonel Victor H. Krulak, then Secretary of the Marine Corps General Staff; and Lieutenant Colonel Foster LaHue, aide to the CMC. Similar representatives from the Army, Navy, and Air Force also were present.⁵³

USMC Photo 531855

*A HR2S–1 flies in formation over Quantico with a HRS–3 and a HOK–1, July 1957. Early Marine vertical envelopment doctrine was built around this huge (for its day) helicopter.*

So advanced was the HR2S and so great its lifting potential that a year later a board composed of general officers tasked to study the composition and function of Marine Corps aviation concluded that while small transport helicopters would serve a purpose, only 45 were needed. The rest of the requirements could be met by 9 squadrons of 20 HR2Ss, for a total of 180. Significantly, the senior member of the board, General Smith, and one of the other three generals assigned, General Bare, both had witnessed the first introduction of the HR2S at Bridgeport.[54]

What they and their colleagues had seen was a veritable monster of a machine. Even at this writing (1975) it remains within six inches of being the largest helicopter ever operated by the Marine Corps.[55]

In general layout, the CH–37C was a typical Sikorsky design with one five-bladed main lifting rotor 72 feet in diameter. A 15-foot diameter, four-bladed anti-torque rotor was mounted on a long tail pylon which slanted upward from the rear of the fuselage. Both rotors were powered by two Pratt and Whitney R–2800–54 engines mounted in large nacelles, or pods, attached to the ends of short wings which extended out from the top of the aircraft, an engine arrangement unusual in helicopters. Each engine had 18 cylinders arranged in two rows of nine. Larger aircraft engines had been built, but nothing approaching these ever had been used in a helicopter. Though aircraft piston engines were much more efficient than those installed in automobiles, a rough perspective of their power can be gained by comparing the volume of their cylinders. The cylinders of a typical very large American car engine displace four or five quarts—most are smaller. The two engines in the Deuce displaced almost 20 gallons. Together they could produce up to 4,200 hp.

The engine pods were roughly egg shaped. The front was constructed of a separate round section of metal with the hole for the air intake slightly to the inside and below the center. When this front section was painted white in contrast to the dark green of the rest of the aircraft—as was often the case—the resulting appearance was that of a giant eye-ball. The bolder crew chiefs, when they could get away with it, would add red lines to the white surface to simulate a pair of blood-shot eyes. Viewed from the front, an aircraft so decorated had a distinct appearance which earned it another nick-name: The Cross-Eyed Monster.

The pilot and co-pilot sat in a cockpit mounted high over the front of the airplane and reached by means of a folding ladder. Below them, large clam shell doors opened and a ramp could be lowered to allow vehicles to drive in and out. On the right side

USMC Photo A147156

*Vehicles back into the maw of the mighty "Deuce." In this view, the reasons for its nickname "Cross-Eyed Monster" are readily apparent.*

of the fuselage at the rear of the cargo compartment there was another, slightly smaller door. Extending out this door and running the entire length of the cabin was an overhead trolly (monorail) which was used to load and unload pallets of cargo. While the monorail could be pivoted up and fastened to the ceiling when not needed for cargo on a troop transport mission, occasionally a crew chief would neglect to do so. A generation of heliborne Marines learned always to check the position of that rail prior to jumping in the back door, for when extended it was almost a perfect match of the height of the forehead of a typical man and, if not stowed, could—and often did—inflict a painful wound resulting usually in stitches and a small scar for the victim.

The aircraft was replete with advanced and unusual features. It was the first helicopter known to have retractable landing gear, an innovation which improved its top speed. The main gear extended down from and folded rearward into the engine nacelles.[56] (The original models had but a single large wheel on each strut; later models had two smaller ones.)

Not only did it have fuel tanks for 400 gallons of gasoline located in the fuselage, but two additional 300-gallon fuel tanks could be mounted on the outside of the fuselage. These latter were always a favorite of pilots since, if there was a malfunction in the aircraft, the external tanks could be jettisoned thereby immediately lightening the aircraft to help cope with the emergency.

The Deuce had what was for the time an advanced stabilization system which, unfortunately, had one characteristic that proved troublesome to pilots used to flying the UH-34 who transitioned into the HR2S. In the UH-34, with its stabilization system engaged, to make a small correction in course the pilot had but to place one foot on the rudder in the direction he wished to turn. The same technique in a HR2S caused the stabilization system to react fully and the aircraft would snap almost broadside in the air. Usually after one such experience, a new pilot was careful to remember to put both feet on the rudders to change direction when the stabilization system was engaged.

To control both engines from the cockpit, the Sikorsky engineers had designed an imaginative device. The usual collective levers were on the left side of the pilot and co-pilot and when raised, increased the pitch (lift) of the main rotor blades. Attached to the end of this was what appeared to be a typical piston engine helicopter twist grip to control the amount of power the engines would deliver. To add power the throttle was rotated (or twisted) to the left. It looked much like the throttle twist grip on a motorcycle, though the direction of turn to add power was just the opposite, a condition that made a number of commanding officers of helicopter squadrons with piston engine machines look askance at any pilot that also rode a motorcycle. But this control in the HR2S was not a real throttle at all. Instead it was linked by a simple slip-clutch to the true throttles which were mounted overhead between the pilots. With careful coordination on their part, the one flying the helicopter could use his twist grip to make large changes in power, while the other pilot made precise adjustments in the real ones. This made for very efficient utilization of the engines.

The system, however, that set the HR2S apart from all other helicopters of the time and which insured its rightful position as the most significant machine in the history of vertical amphibious assaults, was its power folding of the main rotor blades. Prior to the introduction of the Deuce, the only way that a helicopter could be sufficiently reduced in size to enable it to be stored on the flight deck of a ship, or easily handled on the elevator and lowered down to the hangar deck, was either to actually remove the rotor blades or gather a crew such as was required for the UH-34 and manually fold them. Both processes were cumbersome but, worst of all, they could be utilized only in relatively small helicopters. If the Marine Corps was to have the size of machine it needed, the blades would be so large that either removal or manual folding by crews of Marines would be such a lengthy process as to limit effectively a flight deck to a very few helicopters.

The engineers at Sikorsky overcame that formidable obstacle and devised a system that enabled the pilot in the cockpit to fold the blades. This first such design was the basis for all other Sikorsky fold mechanisms and was very closely studied by other manufacturers who later devised their own versions of the method. It was an engineering triumph of the first order; for not only did the massive blades have to fold and unfold quickly, they had to do it in sequence to avoid hitting each other, they had to do it precisely to avoid striking the fuselage, and most important they had to fold only when the pilot activated the mechanism so that there was no possibility of them folding while the aircraft was in flight.

To accomplish this feat, the engineers first had to provide sufficient power to move the blades. For this they utilized a 3,000-pound-per-square-inch (psi) hydraulic supply that was generated by a pump on the left (No. 1) engine and served, among other things, to lower and retract the landing gear and operate the nose doors and ramp. They then relied on a complex series of electrical switches, each of which would not operate until the one before it in the sequence was in the proper position, and a number of hydraulically operated pistons that, like the switches, had to be positioned fully before the next one would work.

Even without the fold system, a rotor head in such a large helicopter was extremely complex. The addition of all wires, tubing, and mechanisms from the blade fold interlaced among the other parts created what many observers described as a "pile of lumpy spaghetti."

At times the system did not function perfectly. Frequently a blade would not fold at all or a hydraulic line which had vibrated loose under the spinning encountered in flight would erupt at its proper moment in the sequence with a high pressure geyser of red fluid. But it constituted the first really operable power folding system and assured Marines that the large helicopters they required could be operated from helicopter assault ships.

The planners had the same difficulty in determining the actual payload of the Deuce as they did with other helicopters. Officially it was listed as capable of 6,673 pounds of cargo with 2,400 pounds of fuel plus the normal crew and equipment. Though this was under a maximum overload condition, the first Marine Corps helicopter which could exceed it under the same circumstances would not be introduced until almost 10 years later.

Unfortunately, although impressive in performance, the HR2S proved to be extremely difficult to manufacture. A later age would describe the problem as too much of an advance "in the state of the art." The Sikorsky engineers labored to perfect the design and testing continued, but the Marine Corps became apprehensive about the delays in production. By 1956 it was alarmed.

The same G-3 study that had recommended an increase in the procurement of the UH-34 as an interim helicopter urged reduction of the planned HR2S force from 180 machines to only three squadrons of 15 aircraft each. Previously the Marine Corps had been reduced to only 45 UH-34s but now it was proposing a plan for nine squadrons of them to maintain a limited lift capability pending the arrival of the Deuce —an exact opposite of the ratio that had been adopted only three years previously.[57]

The HR2S however, was not quite ready to be shunted into obscurity. Just as it was about to be dismissed as of questionable value, it would accomplish some feat that set it above and apart from all others. In 1956 when the attention of the Marine Corps had switched to the UH-34, the Deuce, still the largest helicopter in the free world, set a new international speed record of 162.7 mph with Major Roy L. Anderson at the controls.* Major Anderson was one of the original helicopter pilots in the Marine Corps and seven years earlier, when he was assigned as assistant engineering officer of HMX-1, had written the first comprehensive evaluation of the role of helicopters in the Marine Corps to be published in the *Marine Corps Gazette*.[58] He was recognized as the holder of the speed title by the *Federation Aeronautique Internationale*. The aircraft continued to break records. In the same year as Major Anderson's feat, another Deuce flew to 12,000 feet with an 11,500-pound payload, a record-breaking accomplishment then and a respectable one 20 years later.[59]

Performance of individual aircraft, however, did not eliminate the delays in production that continued to plague the HR2S. Not until March 1955 was the first one delivered at New River and accepted by Lieutenant Colonel Griffith B. Doyle, commanding officer of the newly commissioned HMRM-461.[60] It would be one of only 55 "Deuces" ever delivered to the Marine Corps.** [61]

As Lieutenant Colonel Schoepper and General Shoup drank their New Year's Day punch in 1962, Lieutenant Colonel Eugene J. Pope and Major Daniel A. Somerville commanded what remained of the planned fleet of 180 HR2Ss. Now there were only 29 including one still assigned to HMX-1. Lieutenant Colonel Pope's HMRM-461 at New River had 13 machines. On the west coast at Santa Ana, Major Somerville had 15 more.[62] The third squadron, which had been planned even after the reduced requirement, had been activated, but because there were few airplanes available to assign to it, had only a brief existence and was quickly deactivated.[63] No Deuces were assigned to MAG-16 in the western Pacific area. It would

---

* Russia was known to be developing very large helicopters but this was during the period of the Cold War and information on them was scanty. Thus, to insure absolute technical accuracy, the caveat "in the free world" was always applied when describing the size and the capabilities of the Deuce.

** There were other production models, however. The US Army procured almost 100 in a simpler version that did not incorporate the blade folding mechanism necessary for shipboard operations and had a much less sophisticated stabilization system which was all that was necessary if flight on instruments in clouds was not contemplated. These Army HR2Ss were subsequently returned to the factory for, among other modifications, the installation of a stabilization system suitable for instrument flight. The U.S. Navy procured an HR2S-1W, which substituted a large radar dome in place of the clam shell doors in the nose of the airplane, to evaluate as an early warning radar aircraft. It was not adopted. Sikorsky also built a "crane" version in which the entire cabin was eliminated and only the cockpit and enough fuselage to support the engines and rotor systems was retained. This become the prototype of a long series of flying cranes from Sikorsky.

take a war to demonstrate their value and create a need sufficient to justify shipping such large helicopters across an ocean.

In the meantime, Lieutenant Colonel Pope and Major Somerville, and those that succeeded them in command, had to content themselves with the knowledge that, though the vertical assault elements of a regimental landing team (RLT) had been sufficiently streamlined so that the interim UH–34 could carry almost all of the Marines and their equipment, there were at least two vital items that had defied attempts to reduce them to the weight the UH–34 could lift. Both were radio jeeps. The first was the Mark 87, utilized by the air liaison officer which provided the critical link between the infantry commander requesting close air support and the jet attack aircraft that could deliver it. The second was the Mark 83, used by the naval gunfire observer to provide a similar link to the ships off shore and to artillery units firing in support of the assault elements. Both radio jeeps had to go ashore early in an assault, and each was an easy load for a Deuce and an impossible one for any other Marine Corps helicopter. Therefore, in the initial waves of an assault, the Deuces usually would bring in the radio jeeps. When not carrying these two items of equipment, the giants supplemented the lift capability of the UH–34s.

Efforts had begun long before 1962 to procure a replacement for the ailing monster helicopter. The search would be side-tracked several times, but when a new heavy lift helicopter finally was selected and designed, it would be based on the bold engineering efforts made by Sikorsky in designing the HR2S. In the meantime, the Deuce—the dream, the frustration, and the disappointment of Marine Corps planners—continued to furnish what heavy lift capability the Marines had. In 1962, it was not yet ready to be discarded and soon would have its proudest moments.

## The Last of a Breed

The only other helicopter assigned to Marine tactical units in 1962 was the aged HRS–3 (CH–19E). First entering service in 1953, it was the latest model in a long series of HRS designs that had begun in 1946.[64] Earlier versions had provided the Marine Corps with its troop transport capability in the Korean War and the peacetime operations that followed.* The HRS–3's lifting ability was limited. Even with just one pilot as crew, and under ideal circumstances, it accommodated only 1,800 pounds of payload. Were it not for the shortage of UH–34s, the older machines would have been phased out of the squadrons before 1962. The CH–19, however, had been procured by the Marine Corps to fill the initial gap between awarding of the contract for the HR2S and the predicted production date of that large assault helicopter. Thus it had a certain kinship with the UH–34 which had been procured under similar but later circumstances. Both were interim models to maintain a limited lift capability until the HR2S could become fully operational.

The CH–19 had another distinction. It was one of the last helicopters to lack a "stick positioning" system. The absence of such a system was the bane of all pilots who flew such an aircraft. To maneuver any helicopter, the pilot had to be able to make adjustment in the "pitch" (angle) of the rotor blades. Though the actual mechanism for this differed between designers and even to some extent between different aircraft from the same designer, they all had one thing in common: almost without exception, and particularly for the lifting blades, the force required to make the adjustment was so great that no combination of levers and cams even in the smaller helicopters could ever provide enough mechanical advantage for the pilot to control the airplane with any precision, if at all. To overcome this, manufacturers had provided hydraulic pistons, much like power steering in an automobile, to translate the movement of the pilot's stick and collective lever (and in some helicopters, the rudders) into changes in the pitch of the rotor blades. When the pilot moved his controls, he actually was moving valves in the hydraulically-powered control system. This created a situation in which there was no "feedback" from the rotors to keep the control stick and collective in any given position.

In a CH–19, if the pilot took his hands off, the stick simply fell over to the side, the rotors attempted to respond and the aircraft crashed. Early attempts to provide a means to counteract this disturbing characteristic met with little success, though in the HRS–3 Sikorsky engineers had designed a simple locking mechanism which the pilot could engage to keep the collective lever from moving. Even this simple lock was subject to malfunctions and most pilots preferred to keep a firm grip on the collective.[65] Colonel Dyer remembers the problems well:

> Your right hand is on the cyclic pitch (control stick) which determines your direction of flight. Your feet are on the rudders which also determines your direction of flight by controlling the tail rotor and assisting you in turns. The throttle is also on the collective stick. So while your left hand had the throttle and collective, your right hand had the cyclic stick and your feet are on the

---
* For an excellent account of the use of helicopters in Korea, see: Lynn Montross, *Cavalry of the Sky: The Story of U. S. Marine Combat Helicopters* (New York: Harper, 1954).

*Long after it had been retired from assaults, the HRS–3 continued to serve the Marines in a variety of missions. This aircraft of HMX–1 is participating in a test at Quantico in 1955 and is equipped with ROR (Rocket on Rotor), the dome-like device in the center of the rotor blades, which functioned as an auxiliary power unit.*

rudders. And this thing was inherently unstable. That's a big difference between fixed wing and a helicopter. If you turn loose the controls of a fixed wing, and if a fixed wing aircraft is properly trimmed . . . it will tend to restore itself. The helicopter, however, is basically unstable . . . (and) it does *not* tend to restore itself. [Before stick positioning systems were installed] with a helicopter of those days that was basically unstable and with both feet and both hands busy it was quite an operation to turn loose of any of your controls to, let's say, adjust a radio, or something like that. So most of the buttons [for] things like radios were on the sticks. If you had to shift the fuel tank, you would lock your collective stick, make the tank shift and get back to your collective as quickly as you could . . . you couldn't let go of the thing once you had a-hold of it. It was [very] tiring to fly.[66]

High performance Marine aircraft, particularly jets, also used similar hydraulic systems. In most cases, however, this was to improve the response of the aircraft to the pilot's control movement. In helicopters the system was adopted just to get the machine to fly at all. Of all the helicopters the Marine Corps had in 1962, only the HOK did not need stick positioning. It was so stable and aerodynamically unique that the controls would remain in position even if the pilot took his hands and feet off momentarily.[67]

In the others it was not possible. A co-pilot could take over, but he further reduced an already restricted payload. Thus pilots developed a rather elaborate set of contortions to allow them to take their hands and feet off the controls for a few seconds. Modern helicopters have sophisticated mechanisms to compensate for the problem, but the techniques originated by the pioneers still persist. A thigh wedged firmly against the collective lever provided some assurance it would not move; likewise with practice and determination many pilots found that they could still keep both feet on the rudders, yet lock their knees around the control stick to keep it from falling over for at least long enough to switch fuel tanks.

The difference in what it took to fly a jet and what it took to fly a helicopter did not go unnoticed by the young pilot in the Marine Corps. While his fellow aviators soared overhead at supersonic speeds, tracing contrails in the sky in a sleek, stable aircraft that required only a minimum of attention once properly trimmed, the Marine helicopter pilot was struggling along, thousands of feet below with both hands, a thigh, both knees and feet busily engaged in just keeping airborne at 80 knots and desperately wishing for a way to scratch his itchy nose. Attempting to fly classic tight formations under such circumstances produced less than satisfactory results and would have to wait until better stabilization systems were introduced.

On the first day of 1962 the Marine Corps still had four of these HRS-3 aircraft assigned to tactical units: two remaining at HMRL-263 at New River and two at HMRL-161 in Kaneohe, all of which were simply awaiting the arrival of the UH-34. Two more were with Marine Wing Service Group 17 (MWSG-17) at Iwakuni, Japan and were utilized for general utility missions. All of the rest were SAR aircraft.[68]

The HRS-3 had remained in the inventory of Marine helicopters longer than originally anticipated. It was, after all, just a temporary stop-gap until the HR2S began flowing off the production lines. It was to remain a familiar helicopter to Marines for a number of years more, although in a slightly different role. At the height of the war in Vietnam it almost had a brief and spectacular comeback. But in 1962 the HRS-3 was soon to be phased out and with its departure all Marine helicopter pilots would be flying machines with stick positioning in which they finally would be able to scratch their noses—albeit with their knees still locked firmly around the control stick.

## The White Tops

The remaining two types of helicopters assigned to the Marine Corps were unique in that they were both assigned to HMX-1 and it was highly unlikely that either would ever be a part of the assault forces. Both were reserved for the "Presidential mission."

This task was initiated in September 1957 when a UH-34D, piloted by then commanding officer of HMX-1, Major Virgil D. Olson, had lifted President Eisenhower from his vacation home at Newport, Rhode Island to Quonset Point Naval Air Station.[69] Two months later, the Commandant directed HMX-1 to establish a permanent executive flight section with especially prepared helicopters.[70] Because of the distinctive paint scheme of dark glossy green on the lower portion of the fuselage and white on top, these executive mission helicopters were normally called "white-tops" and distinguished by a "Z" designation prior to 1962 and a "V" prefix after adoption of the uniform numbering system.

HMX-1 still had four HUS-1Z (VH-34) aircraft available in January 1962. These had been modified considerably with executive interiors, extra soundproofing, and numerous additional features, and required rigorous maintenance procedures designed to guarantee the safety of the President while flying in them. Regardless of these measures the VH-34 re-

USMC Photo A329349

*A "White-Top" VH-34 of HMX-1 flies over Sugar Loaf Mountain, Rio de Janeiro, Brazil in February 1960. These aircraft were specially outfitted for Presidential missions.*

mained a single-engine aircraft and in case of malfunction the lives of passengers could be jeopardized. Rear Admiral Paul D. Stroop, Chief of the Bureau of Naval Weapons, had requested approval for the purchase of twin-engine helicopters in June 1961. Though he did not specify which of the two suitable aircraft then available should be selected, it was the Sikorsky-built HSS-2 (VH-3) that was chosen. Three of these helicopters were available at HMX-1.[71] They were to become a familiar sight to millions of television viewers as they shuttled back and forth from the front lawn of the White House. A cargo and troop assault version of the HSS-2 was one of the strong competitors for a medium helicopter to replace the UH-34 and the features of this particular model will be discussed more fully later in conjunction with the selection process.

## An Extended Range

> Studies and past experience indicate that the most desirable type of assault shipping for such a [helicopter-borne] force will be ships which can accommodate the necessary embarked troops, the helicopters to land them and the crews to operate and maintain the helicopters. It is becoming increasingly urgent to commence a ship conversion or building program that will parallel the availability of the . . . 36 man helicopter.[72]
> General Clifton B. Cates, USMC
> Commandant of the Marine Corps
> 17 July 1951

With the advent of atomic weapons, it was obvious immediately that the capability of the Marine Corps to conduct amphibious assaults was in jeopardy. It would be impossible to have the masses of ships carrying assault Marines all converge at a single point on a shoreline. Such a concentration of power would present an atomic-equipped enemy with an irresistible target. A method had to be found to disperse the Marines and bring them together only at the moment they assaulted the beaches. Submarines were considered, but technical problems were too great to overcome. Giant seaplanes were a strong contender, but a series of disastrous crashes and a stringent budget caused the Navy to drop the program.

Helicopters seemed to offer the only solution. As unpromising as these machines were, and however many years it might take to develop suitable craft, helicopters had several potential advantages. The most important of these was the fact that they could land Marines far inland from the sea as well as on the beaches. Unlike the seaplanes and submarines, however, helicopters were limited in the distances they could fly.

All the other alternative vehicles had the common advantage that they could transport Marines to the objective area and then carry them in the actual assault. There was no need for any other conveyance between the rifleman embarking from his staging port and his actual attack on the shore. Helicopters lacked the range to combine these functions. Even the HR2S with nothing more for payload than a crew and its maximum fuel load could fly no further than 350 miles. Most helicopters were even more restricted. Efforts to increase the range of helicopters kept running up against the limited payload available in the helicopters of the time. Each pound of fuel carried was a pound less of payload of any kind.

In his famous article in the 1949 *Gazette*, Igor Sikorsky confidently had predicted that: "[a helicopter will have] a range from 100 to 1,000 miles and eventually probably up to 2,000 miles . . . utilizing inflight refueling or [even] by towing the helicopter."[73]

By 1956 HMX-1 had successfully demonstrated inflight refueling from one HRS to another. To avoid the whirling rotor blades they had utilized a probe and drogue system. The former was a long pipe that stuck out in front of the helicopter to receive the fuel, the latter, an aerodynamically stable basket trailing horizontally on the end of the refueling hose from the tanker aircraft. This was the basic technique utilized by fixed wing aircraft and was to form the basis for helicopters when the system was finally adopted for them.[74]

Sikorsky's other prediction was not ignored either. In 1959 the All American Engineering Company of Wilmington, Delaware provided the Marine Corps with the details of a project then being conducted by the U.S. Air Force. This particular method of increasing the range of a helicopter required the pilot to maneuver his machine close to the tail of a C-47 (military version of the DC-3) at which time he could hook on to what amounted to a long tow rope trailing behind the transport. Once attached, the engine of the helicopter could be stopped and the aircraft towed along much like a glider. Under these circumstances, the rotor blades would generate sufficient lift in the wind stream to keep the helicopter airborne. As the objective area was reached, the helicopter pilot would start his engine, engage the rotor, cast loose from the tow rope, and make the assault.[75] The Marine Corps apparently never responded to this proposal, as its lack of feasibility was evident. As one senior Marine aviator later wrote, "The drag of a hel[icopter] of any size was enough to slow the DC-3 down to stall [non-flying] speed."[76]

Interesting as they were, none of these attempts to extend the range of the helicopter promised an early solution to the problem of mobility. The Marine Corps, accordingly, turned to the Navy's proven method of moving aircraft by sea. It began adapting aircraft carriers for helicopter operations.

## The Conversion

In 1962, four ships were available from which a helicopter-borne assault could be launched. All had been converted from other types. The USS *Thetis Bay*, the first of these conversions, had had a checkered career. A product of the Kaiser shipyards in Vancouver, Washington, which had gained fame in World War II as a mass producer of ships, she was not one of those more rapidly rushed to completion. Kaiser received the contract for her on 18 June 1942 but did not lay the keel until three days before Christmas the next year. The ship was launched 16 April 1944 and commissioned five days later. After short service in World War II she went into mothballs along with much of the rest of the fleet. Initially designated simply Maritime Commission Hull No. 1127 (while under construction), she sailed in World War II as CVE 90, an escort carrier; and after conversion to a helicopter assault ship became for a short time CVAH 1 (carrier, assault, helicopter) and finally LPH 6.

The conversion started in the San Francisco Naval Shipyard 1 June 1955 and was finished 1 September 1956. In an unusual event, the vessel was recommissioned prior to the completion of the work. Captain Thomas W. South II* ran up his flag on 20 July 1956 as the commanding officer of the first—and at this time—only ship specifically adapted to conduct helicopter assault operations.

To the Marine Corps, the *Thetis Bay* constituted visible proof that amphibious vertical assaults could be conducted, but compared to other warships of the time, she was not impressive. At maximum load she displaced only 10,866 tons. Modern attack aircraft carriers were being launched at the same time that displaced 56,000, and it would not be long before ship engineers started designing carriers that would displace over 85,000 tons. *Thetis Bay's* overall length of

---

\* Captain South had close association with both aviation and the Marine Corps. The son of Marine Colonel Hamilton D. South, Captain South had flown in the Pacific during World War II and had commanded an experimental unit equipped with remote-controlled assault drones. Captain South, who eventually attained the rank of rear admiral, had a brother, Colonel Hamilton D. South, who was a Marine flier and later Director of Information at HQMC.

USMC Photo A191124

*The USS* Thetis Bay *(LPH 6), the first carrier converted for use as a helicopter assault ship, participates in PHIBEX 1–62 off Puerto Rico in April 1962. UH–34s are operating from her deck.*

501 feet was slightly less than half that of the new attack aircraft carriers, and the conversion's flight deck did not extend the entire length of the ship. Yet this small LPH would have to operate with the HR2S which was 88 feet long as it lifted off with the assault troops. The ship could accommodate 103 Marine officers (including the helicopter pilots) and 901 enlisted men in addition to the 40 officers and 598 men required to operate her. Her two boilers and double propellors could drive this small ship through the water at 19 knots.

Less than a month after the conversion was complete, on 24 September 1956, Colonel Frederick R. Payne had the distinction of being the first Marine helicopter pilot ever to land on an actual LPH when he brought his HRS–3 helicopter down on the flight deck and was eagerly greeted by Captain South.[77]

This ship was always known to pilots and Marines who operated from her as the "Teddy Bear," from her identifying call sign on the radio. The nickname became almost a term of affection among the early pilots operating from her decks rather than any comment on her size. She would serve long after 1962, serve well, and serve courageously. In retrospect, the *Thetis Bay* seems pathetically small. At that time, however, she was the forerunner of all that would come after her.

A second CVE conversion had been approved in the Fiscal Year 1957 program, the USS *Block Island*. Work had begun on 2 January 1958, but budgets were tight. The Navy had other priorities for what funds Congress had approved. The *Forrestal* class of attack aircraft carriers was vital; the atomic submarine and the Polaris missile required huge sums. There was little left over for Marines who still were convinced that a vertical assault in amphibious landings was a valid part of the nation's military strategy. Conversion of the *Block Island* was cancelled.

The newly appointed Commandant, General Randolph McC. Pate, reacted sharply. In one of the more remarkable letters ever sent by a CMC to a CNO, he pointed out the disparity in priorities:

> I view the recent action by the Secretary of the Navy which eliminated the LPH conversion from the Fiscal Year 1957 shipbuilding and conversion program with extreme concern. The Marine Corps has reorganized and introduced new items of equipment to a degree where it is unquestionably ready to exploit the potential of the helicopter. Only one major component of this weapons system is missing—the modern amphibious assault ship.[78]

He continued, to insure that the CNO understood exactly how he felt:

> But without this component of the system our capability in the already developed components is negated. This situation is analogous to one which would exist if the Polaris [missile] were in being, but the submarines to carry it were still years in the future.[79]

The comparison of the Marine Corps vertical assault capability and that of the Polaris submarine was not lost. In essence he had said that the Marine Corps had made great strides to insure that they still maintained the capability of conducting amphibious assaults in an atomic age and flatly challenged the Navy to match these efforts. It was a daring stroke.

The results soon were evident as the lagging conversion program picked up impetus. Six months later, on 30 January 1959, the USS *Boxer* was recommissioned as LPH 4. It was followed in April the same year by the USS *Princeton* (LPH 5) and after some delay, the USS *Valley Forge* (LPH 8.)

These ships were a far cry from the "Teddy Bear." All were of the "*Essex*" class, the first-line attack aircraft carriers of the Pacific campaign in World War II. Weighing in the 38,000-ton class they were nearly four times as large as the *Thetis Bay* and their 888-foot length, with a flight deck almost as long, gave the necessary space for a number of helicopters to load and take off simultaneously. Eight boilers generated 150,000 horsepower, as compared to the 11,200 the two on the *Thetis Bay* could produce, and with this power, gave the carriers a speed well above the rest of the ships in the amphibious fleet.

Each new LPH had accommodations for 171 Marine officers and 1,701 men, including those necessary for the helicopters. Each also officially required over 1,500 sailors to man her, as compared to the 598 on the "Teddy Bear." [80] And in time of tight budgets, where every serviceman was carefully scrutinized to insure that his cost was necessary, this became a point of controversy which had far-reaching implications.

## Soldier Mechanics of the Sea

By definition, Marines are "soldiers of the sea." Marines have been a part of the crew on capital ships, not only since the founding of the U.S. Marine Corps, but far back into the dim reaches of naval history. Since the 1930s, Marine Corps fighter, bomber, and scout squadrons routinely have operated with, and as part of, U.S. Navy carrier air groups (CAGs).

Few Marines have not sailed on a Navy ship, though in most cases they are merely passengers and not members of the regular crew. The large numbers of sailors required to man the *Essex* class LPHs created an entirely different, and to date unique breed of seagoing Marines: the soldier mechanics of the sea. If the Marines were going to have large LPHs, they were going to have to provide part of the crews.

On the 183rd anniversary of the founding of the Marine Corps, 10 November 1958, the first mechanics reported to the yet to be activated USS *Boxer*.[81] They were not Marine detachments, they were not part of the Marine squadrons attached to the CAGs, and they were not passengers: they were full-fledged members of the crew of the ship.

Only in the engineering, navigation, and medical departments were the Marines not used. They filled billets in supply, as cooks and bakers, and disbursing clerks. The Air Department, with the exception of the men who refueled the helicopters and a few Navy officers, was made up completely of Marines. Marines manned

USN Photo 1111758
*The USS* Princeton *(LPH 5), second of the Boxer-class conversions, steams toward Chu Lai, Vietnam, with UH–34s of MAG–36 on her flight deck in August 1965.*

the shops which did the major repairs on the helicopters and, in a more traditional role, even made up the crews for several of the guns.[82]

The initial augmentation on the *Boxer* had been one officer and 92 enlisted men out of a total of 57 officers and 1,077 men. This was to grow until there were 10 officers and 317 Marines serving in the crew.[83] When the USS *Princeton* was converted and reclassified as an LPH on 2 April 1959 the scene was the same.[*]

These aviation officers and men, unfortunately, were not in addition to those required to operate the squadrons. Instead, under the rules then in force within the Department of Defense, they were included in the overall strength of Marine Corps aviation. On 29 July 1960 with the imminent conversion of the third *Essex* class LPH (the *Valley Forge*), Major General Arthur Binney, who at the time was the Director of Aviation, became concerned. He wrote that this practice could not be extended and that the use of Marine aviation officers and men to man Navy ships without any compensating increase in overall strength was extremely difficult due to "an almost impossibly austere manning level" in aviation.[84]

The problem had been recognized. Once again, farsighted officers in the Navy realized that the Marine Corps vertical assault was a vital part of the overall strength of the United States. It had to be preserved, even if some sacrifices had to be made. Negotiations had been going on as to just where these cut-backs could be made. A month previous to General Binney's letter, the Director of the Policy Analysis Division at Headquarters Marine Corps could circulate the results.

The Navy, like the Marine Corps, he pointed out, was under a Department of Defense imposed absolute ceiling of the number of personnel authorized. It was the people to man these large LPHs that was the major stumbling block. The letter declared that the Navy considered the minimum crew for the *Valley Forge* (or the other candidate for the forthcoming fourth—but later abandoned—conversion, the USS *Lake Champlain*) to be at least 1,000 men, though they considered 1,250 more near the actual requirements.[85]

Even though the Commandant had been assigning over 300 Marines to the *Boxer* and the *Princeton*, provision of sufficient sailors to man the next conversion would require the Navy to mothball other ships. In the Navy's first proposed trade-off it calculated that an attack transport ship (APA) required a crew of about 400 men. If three of them were withdrawn from active service, from the Pacific fleet, sufficient men would be released to man the *Valley Forge*. After additional negotiations, the Navy agreed it would be more suitable to decommission just one APA and five landing ships tank (LSTs). It was also concluded that the first of a new type of true LPHs then being built would require a crew "about the same (400) as an APA."[86]

While the *Valley Forge* never would have the same contingent of soldier mechanics of the sea as her two predecessors and the estimates of the number of Navy men required on the true LPHs were to prove conservative, a serious problem once again had been resolved. In the meantime the *Boxer* and the *Princeton* continued to have much of their crews made up of Marines. It was not until 1964 that they would depart. On 15 January the Marines left the *Boxer* and on 31 January, the *Princeton*.[87] Staying behind would be only three permanent crew members: the assistant air operations officer, the combat cargo officer, and his NCO assistant, who are still assigned to all LPHs as the only remaining vestiges of the soldier mechanics of the sea. Those Marines who served on the two ships have a unique and exclusive claim to fame.

Marines supplementing Navy crews, however, really was not the answer to the problem. The disadvantages of converting World War II aircraft carriers to LPHs were becoming increasingly apparent.

## Keel-Up LPH

On the outside, all four of the ships converted into LPHs appeared to meet General Cate's requirements. They all had flight decks and, except for the *Thetis Bay*, were sufficiently large to accommodate all the ground and helicopter elements of the assault team. Inside their gray hulls, however, all the conversions had serious deficiencies.

The original ships had had to provide for just two combat elements: the aircraft and their crews and the sailors to operate the vessels. On a true LPH, a third element had to be accommodated: the assault Marines and their equipment. An LPH had to have large living compartments for the combat troops and storage holds for their gear, and it also had to have elevators for bringing men and material easily and quickly to the flight deck for loading on the helicopters. Efforts to rearrange the interiors of the conversions to accommodate these changes had to contend with the fact that in modern warships most of the bulkheads (walls) are more than partitions; they comprise a vital part of the vessel's structural strength and ability to withstand battle damage. Thus every removal and repositioning of interior bulkheads had to be weighed carefully

---

[*] Commanding officer of the detachment on the *Princeton* was Lieutenant Colonel Homer S. Hill, who also served as air officer. Hill, as a major general, would be Deputy Chief of Staff (Air) at HQMC from 1963–1972.

against the internal integrity of the ship as a whole, and often desirable changes could not be made. As a result, in the USS *Princeton* for example, the assault Marines had to be split up among 27 berthing compartments ranging in size from four to 157 men, totally destroying shipboard unit cohesiveness. The situation was similar on the other three conversions.[88]

The Marine Corps needed a ship designed and built from the keel up to provide for this third element, a ship in which the designers could provide for large troop spaces and cargo elevators right from the initial concept. Such a ship, in essence, would be built around the ship's crew, the helicopters, and the assault Marines. The first such vessel to be built was the USS *Iwo Jima* (LPH 2).* The construction of this unique ship was authorized 27 January 1958 and her keel laid at the Puget Sound Naval Shipyard at Bremerton, Washington on 2 April 1959, just a year after General Pate had compared the lack of such ships to building Polaris missiles without providing submarines to launch them.[89]

What was launched 17 September 1960 still looked from the outside somewhat like a conventional aircraft carrier. Only half as large as the *Essex* class conversions (with a full load displacement of 18,000 tons), *Iwo Jima* was only 592 feet in length, just barely longer than the *Thetis Bay* although with almost twice the "Teddy Bear's" displacement. This combination gave the *Iwo Jima* and the six almost identical ships that were to follow her none of the sleek lines of a fast warship. Instead, she was almost "plump" in her appearance, square sterned, with a short sharp bow that quickly flared out into her 84-foot beam and with a flight deck 52 feet above the water line that covered all but a very small portion of the entire outline of the ship.

Inside her hull was what none of the conversions had, full provisions for all three elements of the amphibious assault team—the helicopters, the combat Marines, and the crew of the ship.

In the simplest terms, an LPH of the *Iwo Jima* class was not a single type ship. She was three completely different vessels stacked on top of each other. At the lowest level was what amounted to an attack cargo ship (AKA) with large holds to store the supplies and equipment of the assault Marines and two large cargo elevators that could bring the material up to either the hangar or flight decks for staging. Both areas were normally used. This storage area was supplemented by an area aft of the hangar deck in which combat vehicles could be carried. To expedite loading at a dock, the designers had included a ramp which could be attached to the aircraft elevators on the outside of the hull, allowing the jeeps and other vehicles to drive directly on to the ship and into the vehicle stowage area.

The second layer of the *Iwo Jima* class extended from the holds up to the hangar deck and was equivalent to an amphibious assault transport (APA). In this section, and a few others scattered throughout the hull, were the large berthing and messing spaces required by 1,900 assault Marines and helicopter mechanics. Though hardly luxurious, these spaces did provide each Marine with a small metal locker to store personal items, separate storage rooms for his pack and rifle, and in the description of one observer who obviously had had experiences with older troop transports: "a comfortable bunk, complete with mattress."[90]

These two layers made the *Iwo Jima* class unique. The provisions for them was what had so seriously handicapped the conversions.

The final layer was more conventional and was what gave the ships their distinctive aircraft carrier-like appearance: the facilities for launching and recovering helicopters from the flight deck, storing them on the hangar deck, and the machine shops and work spaces for the mechanics to maintain the aircraft. To expedite the moving of helicopters from the flight deck to the hangar deck, two elevators, each with a capacity of over 17 tons (a fully loaded HR2S weighed slightly more than 15), were installed, not in the center of the flight deck as had been the case in World War II carriers, but on the outer edge of the flight deck where they operated up and down the outside of the hull. One was on the port side directly abeam the island superstructure; the other one was on the starboard directly aft of the island. To insure that the ships could traverse the Panama and other canals (for when both elevators were extended the ship had an extreme width of 105 feet), the elevators could be folded up along the side of the hull. In actual usage, these aircraft elevators performed an additional function. Cargo could be brought up from the hold to the hangar deck, staged there and moved aboard the lowered elevator. Then to rapidly bring large quantities up to the congested flight deck, the elevator was simply raised. This proved extremely effective, particularly if the cargo was to be carried externally by the helicopter. The same method was used to assemble large units of Marines on the flight deck, ready for boarding their aircraft. The individual teams would form up on the elevator from the hangar deck and with a blare of the klaxon horn, a slight jerk, they would be lifted up to the flight deck beside their waiting helicopters.

---

* The cancelled conversion of the USS *Block Island* was to have been LPH-1. In the redesignation of amphibious ships, the *Thetis Bay* became LPH-6, the *Boxer* LPH-4, *Princeton* LPH-5, and *Valley Forge* LPH-8. The intervening numbers were given to *Iwo Jima* class ships.

*The USS* Guadalcanal *(LPH 7) steams out of Morehead City, N.C. on the way to an exercise in January 1972. This and other* Iwo Jima*-class LPHs were the first ships built from the keel up for helicopter operations.*

Smaller portions of other ships were included also. Above the vehicle stowage area was a hospital that could, in an emergency, accommodate more than 300 casualties (by utilizing the troop berthing space directly aft of it). This particular feature would take on increased importance as the LPHs responded to natural disasters and evacuation of civilians from troubled areas. The deck edge elevators could be utilized in just the reverse of their role in launching assault troops. The sick and wounded were unloaded directly from the helicopters onto one of them, dropped down to the hangar deck and moved to a waiting elevator which lifted them up one deck to a large door leading to the hospital. This fifth elevator, incidentally, was often loudly—and accurately—proclaimed as the only one in the entire ship specifically designed to move people.

In addition, each of the LPHs of this series had a complex communications center for the control of all the helicopters in the assault. Termed the HDC (for Helicopter Direction Center), it and a similar one for the control of supporting fires (FSCC), which were interconnected along with the ships own Combat Information Center (CIC), could act as the coordinating agency for a much larger assault with other ships and aircraft. Though the LPHs to follow were almost identical, the *Iwo Jima* and several of her sister ships had provisions for another function: the offices and communications for both the amphibious force commander and the landing force commander. Ships so modified were tagged "flag configured."

Both as a matter of comfort for the crews and embarked Marines and to assist in maintaining structural strength in a ship that was such a hybrid, the entire vessel was air-conditioned. Popular legend had it that there were no port holes in the LPHs. There were, but what few of them existed were all high in the island structure, an area not normally visited by the assault Marines.

As if the combination of an APA, an AKA, and a helicopter aircraft carrier were not enough, the ship had a space for the crew of 50 officers and 500 Navy men to operate her. The design of such a ship was a remarkable achievement for all the engineers who visions for almost every conceivable situation from played a part. Into her stubby hull were crammed pro-amphibious landing in an atomic age to peacetime disaster rescue missions and most assignments between those two extremes. She was designed to be very versatile. To accomplish all of this, however, the designers had to make a few compromises.

The ships had two separate boilers and associated engines but a single propeller. Such a design saved space for other functions (and was less expensive), though the 22,000 horsepower generated was enough to drive her through the water at a speed slightly in excess of 21 knots. This combination, coupled to the size and shape of the hull, led to some unexpected results.

One characteristic was first noticed shortly after the *Iwo Jima* left the dock on 5 September 1961 for her initial tests at sea. On board were Captain Thomas D. Harris, USN, the first naval officer ever to command a true LPH, his crew learning the intricacies of an entirely new breed of ship, and the officials and engineers from the Puget Sound Naval Shipyard, who had built her.

The next day she returned to dock. Obviously such an innovative design was going to have a number of small discrepancies on her first shakedown. The *Iwo Jima* did. One of the most serious was described in the official reports as: "severe hull vibrations at high power." On 14 September once again she cast off, heading for sea. Most of the original difficulties had been corrected. The vibration persisted. A week later a third trip was made, this time as her official Builder's Sea Trials, a period of testing and exercising the ship to verify if she would perform as predicted.* The hopes of the engineers were vindicated. She performed well. The only disappointment was that "the chief remaining discrepancy was (still) vibration at high power."

This characteristic vibration was never to be cured in any of the class. At about 15 knots the entire ship began to shake every time one of the blades of the screw took a bite of the water. At that speed it was slight throughout all the ship, but more pronounced in the stern and bow Marine berthing areas. As the speed increased, the vibration increased correspondingly in frequency and severity.

Embarked Marines soon learned to recognize it and within a short period of time actually could tell how fast the ship was going by the rattle of the decks. It was as if the builders had given each man aboard the vessel his own private speedometer. As the *Iwo Jima* and her sister ships reached 21 knots the pounding became more pronounced and was inescapable anywhere on board. To the builders this was "severe vibration at high power". To all Marines who experienced it, it was "the twenty-one knot thump."

While on a peacetime deployment, if wakened by the thump in the middle of the night, the Marines knew that another crisis had occurred, that their ship was proceeding at maximum speed, and that the next morning could bring them into action. When the thump began, the ship would come strangely to life, unbidden. Marine officers would begin appearing at the HDC. Assault riflemen would be restless in their bunks and helicopter mechanics would begin worrying about some minor detail on their aircraft that they had postponed repairing. The designers had not intended it this way but they had given each Marine an unavoidable and unmistakable alarm system.

On New Year's Day, 1962, the *Iwo Jima* was in port at San Diego with much of her crew on leave and the rest busy maintaining the ship. She was not quite ready to conduct an assault—but she would be soon.

## The Last Concert

And so a bleak and cold New Year's Day in 1962 was to mark the last time for over a decade that a Commandant could be "surprised" and not have some of his Marines actively engaged in a war. Marine helicopters were stationed around the world. There were several models specifically designed for Marine Corps requirements, and the amphibious ships to give the helicopters and the assault troops the mobility to react in any geographical area bordering on the sea were becoming available rapidly.

The 343 helicopters then in service were far fewer than the Marine Corps thought necessary to carry out the mission it had been assigned, but regardless of their small numbers, the helicopters, combined with the mobility of the new assault ships, gave Marine assault forces a flexibility never before available. Over the next decade, these forces would be called upon a number of times to enforce the decisions of the U.S. Government. These landings, however, were not without cost. By the end of the decade few of the original helicopters would remain. Many of the crews would be gone also.

---

* Designers of ships, much like airplanes, have complex formulas, even computers, to predict how an individual craft will perform. The variables are so great that it is impossible to predict with any absolute certainty. There is only one way to do it: take the ship to sea, or the aircraft into the air, to see if it will perform as expected. Considering the divergent demands that the engineers had to resolve, the *Iwo Jima* class LPH was a resounding success.

# CHAPTER TWO

## MANEUVERS AND DEPLOYMENTS

### Possible Deployment

At the conclusion of the New Year's Day ceremony around the punch bowl, most members of the band and the guests went home to watch the football games. One, at least, did not.

Lieutenant General Wallace M. Greene, Jr., Chief of Staff of the Marine Corps, had serious work to do. He noted in his diary that he had departed promptly at 1230 and returned across the parade ground to his quarters for lunch. At 1330 he started to "review current problems, schedules and pending items of business." He continued until "past midnight."[1]

General Greene was the son of a village shopkeeper in Waterbury, Vermont, a small town of 1,500 near Lake Champlain. A descendent of *Mayflower* immigrants, he included among his forebears the Revolutionary War hero, General Nathanael Greene.[2]

General Greene described his youth as:

> For one thing, everyone knew you, so you had to live up to the community's standards. Another advantage lay in the schooling we received. New Englanders have always been strong supporters of education and in Waterbury we had a good school system. I took Latin for six years and music for 12, and this was a country school.[3]

After graduating from high school in 1925, he entered the University of Vermont with every intention of becoming a doctor. He worked nights to supplement his income and attended classes in the daytime. While still a freshman, he saw an announcement in a newspaper that competitive examinations for the Naval Academy were to be held. As he later explained: "At the time I didn't know much about the Navy, but the tests were free, so I decided to try for the appointment."[4]

He was accepted and the next year began classes at the academy. He still was unsure about the course he had chosen. Only in his senior year did he give any serious thought to the Marine Corps. Then, on a cruise as a midshipman, "I began talking to the captain of the ship's Marine detachment. I decided that if half his stories were true, then I wanted to be a Marine."[5] On graduation in June 1931, he was commissioned a second lieutenant in the Marine Corps.

This flinty Vermonter would preside over the most turbulent and explosive era in the development of helicopters in the Marine Corps. On New Year's Day 1962,

USMC Photo A409014

*Lieutenant General Wallace M. Greene, Jr., Marine Corps Chief of Staff in 1962, became 23d Commandant on 1 January 1964. He participated in many crucial helicopter development decisions.*

he could not foresee what was to come, but one of the problems he pondered was "the possible deployment of the first Marine unit to the Delta area of South Vietnam,"[6] and he also reviewed intelligence reports on the worsening situation in Cuba.[7] In those places and elsewhere, Marine helicopters and the men who flew them soon would be tested.

Between the end of the Korean War and the beginning of 1962 a number of exercises had been held to test the concept of vertical amphibious assaults. All of them had suffered from being relatively small scale, as the necessary LPHs were not available until late in the period. In addition, no matter how realistic the landing, it still remained a peacetime maneuver and there was no sure method to determine if the same procedures would be equally effective in war.

The next three years provided the Marines with four major opportunities to evaluate fully the concept. The first of these, although the smallest operation, was, in retrospect, the most significant.

## SHUFLY

The military situation in South Vietnam had deteriorated seriously in the last half of 1961.* General Maxwell D. Taylor, special military advisor to President Kennedy, had recommended in November an expanded program of U.S. support for the beleaguered government. Many of his suggestions had been approved by the President. They had, however, only a limited immediate effect on the Marine Corps. Its role was still confined to furnishing advisors, members of joint staffs, and specialized communications personnel. The U.S. Army was to supply most of the increased effort—including helicopters.

By December the first two of three helicopter companies planned had been committed. Equipped with the Piasecki-designed tandem-rotor H-21s they represented a small but much-needed increase in mobility for government forces. Each of the aircraft was capable of carrying approximately 10 assault troops in addition to the two gunners who manned machine guns in each door.[8] The H-21, though, suffered a loss of lift capability at high temperature or altitude even more serious than other helicopters of the time and was only marginally suited for night and instrument flight.[9] The JCS became concerned that additional helicopters might be needed. On 17 January 1962, they directed the Commander in Chief, Pacific (CinCPac), Admiral Harry D. Felt, to review the total requirements for Vietnam. The admiral responded on 28 February. Though the third Army helicopter company had arrived, there was a need for one more. He recommended another Army unit be dispatched to the Mekong Delta region of southern Vietnam.[10]

By coincidence, the same day the Commanding General, FMFPac, Lieutenant General Alan Shapley, who had been a member of the Marine Detachment on board the USS *Arizona* when the ship was sunk on 7 December 1941, sent a message to CMC outlining an entirely different plan. The proposal had been developed by Major General Carson A. Roberts, Commanding General, AirFMFPac, who was scheduled to replace General Shapley on 1 July 1962.

The two generals repeated a request from Major General Charles J. Timmes, USA, Chief, U.S. Military Assistance Advisory Group, Vietnam (ChMAAGV) to augment Army squadrons with Marine Corps pilots. Nine officers, he suggested, could be selected at a time and sent to Vietnam for 60 to 90 days of familiarization and indoctrination. Such a program would have been complementary to one General Shapley's command had initiated in May 1961 in which monthly increments of 20 Marines, officers and senior enlisted men, were sent to Vietnam to observe ground operations.

On receiving General Timmes's request, General Roberts pointed out that the Marines would have difficulty working with Army squadrons. Since the Marine pilots would be flying aircraft in which they had no experience, some of the time they spent in the battle zone would have to be used for nothing more than training them to fly the Army H-21. As an alternative he suggested that an entire Marine Corps squadron be sent to the area to replace one of the Army companies. This would increase the total lift available since the 24 UH-34s assigned could carry more and were less susceptible to altitude and heat than the H-21s. In addition, familiarization still could be obtained by rotating pilots from other Marine squadrons. If the helicopters were located in the more mountainous northern portion of RVN they would be operating in an area that was a Marine Corps responsibility under contingency plans then in existence.[11]

While this proposal was being studied, on 6 March the JCS approved the deployment of the fourth Army helicopter unit. The 33d Transportation Light Helicopter Company at Ford Ord, California was alerted to depart 18 April. Apparently unaware of this decision two days earlier in Washington, the Commander, U.S. Military Assistance Command, Vietnam (ComUSMACV), General Paul D. Harkins, informed CinCPac that he agreed with Generals Shapley and Roberts and

---

* For a complete history of this period see: Captain Robert H. Whitlow, *U.S. Marines in Vietnam, 1954-1964: The Advisory and Combat Assistance Era* (Washington: History and Museums Division, Headquarters, U.S. Marine Corps, 1977.)

desired a Marine Corps squadron instead of the fourth Army unit. He requested that it be sent to the Mekong Delta. The Army's 93d Helicopter Company had only recently become fully operational at Da Nang, and to move it south now would result in a decreased level of support just as the monsoon was ending and the weather was becoming more favorable for helicopter operations. "When the tempo of operations permit," he added, "the Marine helicopter squadron will be relocated to the I Corps (northern/Da Nang) area and the 93d helo company to the III Corps [southern] site." [12]

The next day, 9 March, the Commander in Chief, U.S. Army, Pacific, General James F. Collins, added his opinion. He stated that in view of the decision to deploy the company at Fort Ord, no Marine Corps helicopters were necessary in Vietnam. The Army was still anxious, however, to have Marine Corps pilots to augment the units already there.[13]

The issue was not resolved until 19 March. The JCS then approved a Marine Corps squadron instead of the 33d Helicopter Company at Fort Ord. Target date for the squadron to be in place was approximately 15 April.[14] Unlike the Army, which would have to arrange shipping from Hawaii or the West Coast of the United States—a fairly complicated revision of already demanding schedules—the Marine Corps had two squadrons immediately available nearby. Both HMM–261 and HMM–362, the two transport squadrons of MAG–16 in Okinawa, were temporarily in the Philippine Islands. They were scheduled to be the vertical assault portion of a large-scale Southeast Asia Treaty Organization (SEATO) exercise, code named TULUNGAN. The operation was to start 25 March.

The recently promoted commanding general of the 1st Wing, Major General John P. Condon, had already left Iwakuni, Japan and had established his headquarters on Mindoro Island when he received notice on 22 March to deploy a squadron to Vietnam. General Condon, though not designated as a helicopter pilot, was no stranger to them. In later years he described his experience:

> My whirly-bird initiation went back as far as '47 and '48 when the thing was just evolving. General Harris, who was then Director of Aviation, had me evaluate about every helicopter in the country . . . so I covered a lot of helicopter territory kind of early in the game. In fact, some of my bones are still shaking from some of those machines.[15]

Planning began immediately. General Condon selected HMM–362 as the squadron to go. Since the previous October it had been assigned as the helicopter portion of the Special Landing Force (SLF) and had spent most of the intervening months on board the USS *Princeton* (LPH 5) patrolling the South China Sea.

(Lieutenant Colonel Fred A. Steele and the members of HMM–261 were not to be the first in Vietnam but they would have an emergency deployment. Less than two months later, on 17 May, they flew off the ship in the Gulf of Siam and supported contingency operations in northern Thailand. HMM–261 remained at Udorn there until relieved by Lieutenant Colonel Reinhardt Lee and his HMM–162 at the end of June).[16]

By 30 March General Condon had submitted the broad outline of his plan.[17] He proposed a small headquarters group of eight officers and six enlisted men commanded by the chief of staff of the 1st Wing, Colonel John F. Carey, one of the most experienced helicopter pilots in the Marine Corps. On 6 August 1948 he had become the 18th Marine designated and had been the second commanding officer in the history of HMX–1.

To provide the necessary base services, a subunit of MABS–16 with 193 enlisted men and 18 officers also would be sent. This unit was to be led by the current commanding officer of MABS–16, Lieutenant Colonel William W. Eldridge, a helicopter pilot since 5 January 1952. The final element would be Lieutenant Colonel Archie J. Clapp and his HMM–362.

Lieutenant Colonel Clapp had enlisted in the Marine Corps in December of 1940. Two years later he entered flight training and was commissioned in July 1943. He saw combat as a fighter pilot in the campaigns for Iwo Jima and Okinawa. Then, in March 1951 he was assigned to HMX–1 and designated a helicopter pilot on 9 June. In the squadron he expanded his career as a prolific and articulate writer and soon was editing a news sheet distributed throughout the Marine Corps detailing the latest developments in helicopters. After the Korean War he continued to write articles for professional journals. One of them received an honorable mention from the Marine Corps Association contest in 1958. This particular article demonstrated the imaginative approach to a problem that was to make him well suited for his duties in Vietnam. He proposed that helicopters be used as a method to launch and recover fixed-wing aircraft. The helicopter would lift the other airplane to a suitable height and speed and release it. Landing was just the reverse. Such a system would eliminate the need for long runways in a combat area.[18]

As TULUNGAN was concluded and the men of HMM–362 along with the rest of the Marines began reembarking on their ships, planning progressed for what would become known as Operation SHUFLY. Colonel Carey hastily assembled his small staff at Iwakuni. One of their first tasks was to select a site. Of those available in the delta most were surfaced with laterite.[19] Many Marines would learn later that this is

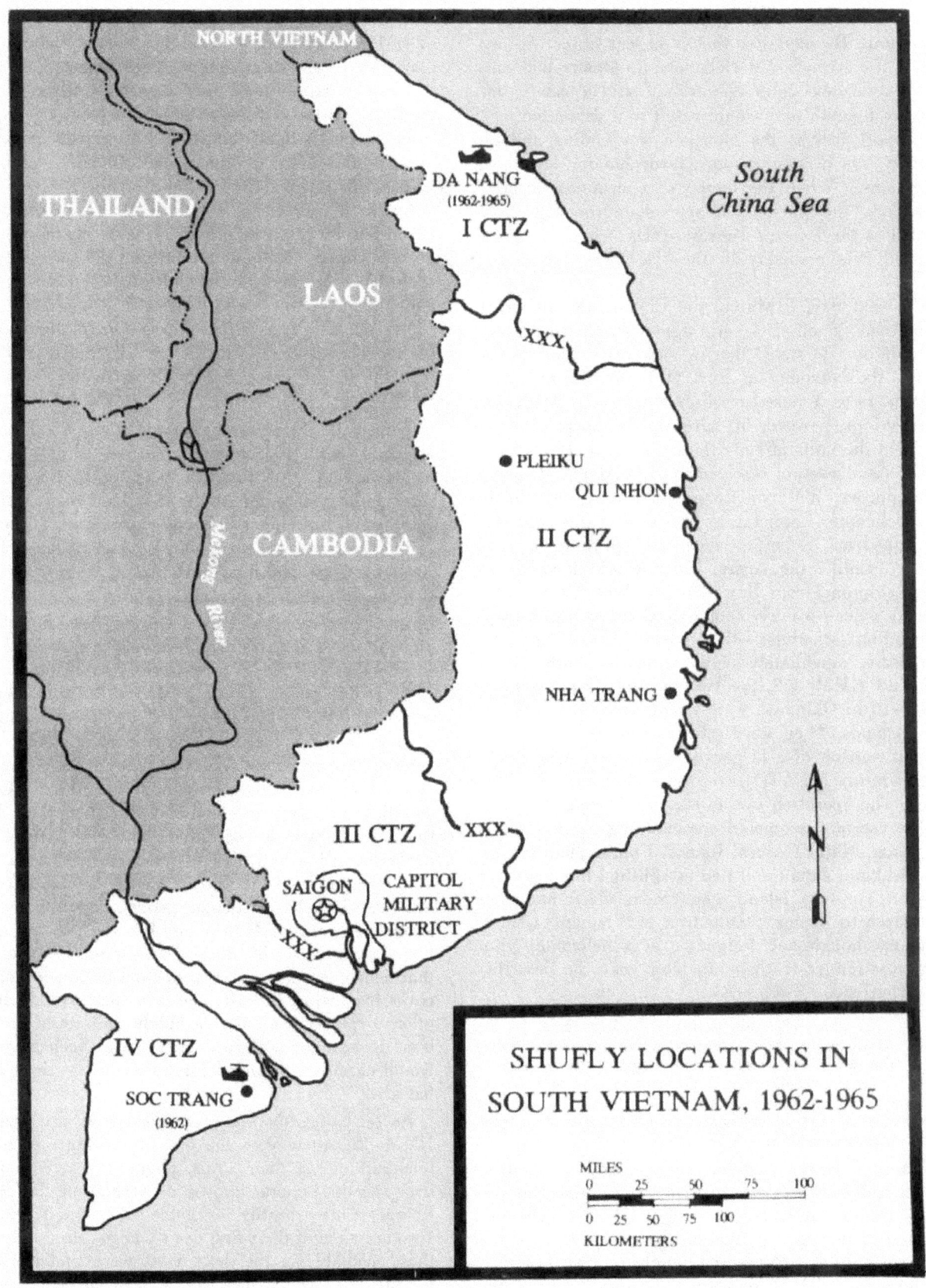

a red clay often used to pave roads and runways in Vietnam. When dry it has the consistency of talcum powder; when wet, bottomless glue. Colonel Carey was concerned that the laterite would damage, not only the helicopters, but the transport aircraft which would be necessary to support his task unit. There was, however, an abandoned airfield that had a suitable concrete runway: Soc Trang. Built by the Japanese during World War II, it was approximately 85 miles south-southwest of Saigon.[20]

To insure flexibility for HMM-362, its normal complement of 24 UH-34s was supplemented by three OE-1 (O1-B) fixed-wing Cessna observation aircraft from Lieutenant Colonel Donald H. Foss's VMO-2 and a C-117 (military version of the improved DC-3 transport) for liaison and supply flights. Approximately 50 additional mechanics were assigned to the squadron for aircraft maintenance.

On the morning of 8 April, Colonel Carey and members of his staff departed Iwakuni in the C-117. After a short stop in Okinawa to pick up others, they proceeded to NAS Cubi Point in the Philippines for final briefings. The next morning they discovered that the aircraft had developed mechanical difficulties and could not proceed to Vietnam. Colonel Carey was remembered as surveying the aircraft and exploding, "We have a war going on and now our horse just died"![21]

There was, fortunately, another C-117 at Cubi on a routine logistics flight for the 1st MAW. Colonel Carey is again remembered as walking over to the pilot, a captain, and saying:

"Too bad your airplane is sick."

The captain responded that his aircraft was in fine shape.

"Oh, no it isn't." Colonel Carey answered. "Yours is over there and it's sick. This one is mine."[22]

A quick switch was made and the party continued on to Soc Trang.

Colonel Carey's determination to arrive on the 9th was prompted by a plan that called for all but fuel and water to be delivered by air. The first KC-130s bringing the MABS subunit to set up the base were due to land that afternoon.*

When the staff finally arrived, they found a runway approximately 3,000 feet long, a dilapidated hangar, and a few long-abandoned buildings. As others began preparations for the arrival of the KC-130s, a pilot of the C-117, Captain James P. Kizer, busied himself by converting the airplane into an improvised control tower. He removed the escape hatch on top of the

---

\* The C-130 is a four-engine turbo-prop aerial refueler which can be converted for cargo and troop transport operations.

Photo courtesy of Lieutenant Colonel James P. Kizer, USMC

*Soc Trang Airfield, SHUFLY's first operating base in the Mekong Delta. Flying from Soc Trang, the Marines quickly learned many vital lessons in helicopter operations and tactics.*

cockpit, turned on the radios, "put my sun glasses on, stuck my head out and said 'Hello there, this is Soc Trang Tower' ";[23] he then was able to give landing information to the KC-130s, the first of which was piloted by General Condon. Lieutenant Colonel Ethridge and his men, on their arrival, immediately set about establishing the necessary facilities to provide for the Marines yet to arrive.

Meanwhile, HMM-362 was busily preparing for the deployment. At the conclusion of TULUNGAN, on 1 April, it reembarked on the USS *Princeton* and proceeded north to Cubi Point in Luzon. There it exchanged some of its aircraft with HMM-261 so that those with the longest time before regularly scheduled overhaul would be assigned to HMM-362. In a "round the clock" operation under the direction of the aircraft maintenance officer, Captain James R. Plummer, and the maintenance chief, First Sergeant Robert A. Schriefer—both of whom were to receive citations later for their skills during SHUFLY—the switch was made.[24] Now with the two squadrons on board, the *Princeton* proceeded back to Okinawa to load the men and equipment that had not been deployed to the Philippines.

On 10 April, still with HMM-261 on board to assist in the unloading, the ship departed. Its destination was 20 miles off the mouth of the Mekong River. Operations were scheduled to start at dawn, 15 April.

In response to a request made on 29 March by the State Department, the landings were to be made as inconspicuously as possible. The Commander, Seventh Fleet, Vice Admiral William A. Schoech, planned to keep the *Princeton* out of sight of land.[25] He also ordered that the escorting jets from the USS *Hancock* (CVA 19) remain well out to sea to be called in only if necessary. This deviation from helicopter assault doctrine which called for the escort "aircraft [to] cover the helicopter waves and provide protection from enemy ground fire" seemed insignificant at the time.[26] It was, however, an ominous indication of further changes to come.

The flights to Soc Trang began on schedule. The only incident recalled by Lieutenant Colonel Clapp occurred shortly after the takeoff of one of the OE-1s.

The engine began to malfunction. The pilot, First Lieutenant Francis M. Walters, Jr., quickly turned back to the *Princeton* and even without a tail hook or arresting wires on the ship made a successful emergency landing. The airplane was repaired and flown to Soc Trang later in the day. By mid-afternoon the transfer was complete. HMM-261 returned to the ship to assume duties as the new SLF squadron.

Within three days in Vietnam, HMM-362 discovered that additional development of tactics and machines was going to be required—a process which was to characterize its entire operation. The first incident was a small, but typical one. Two aircraft had been committed to haul badly needed supplies to an isolated town deep in the delta. Lieutenant Colonel Clapp described it:

> [The pilots] landed and shut down on what appeared to be hard dry ground. In a couple of minutes, though, they noticed that the landing gear was slowly but

USMC Photo

*The commanders responsible for SHUFLY confer after arriving at Soc Trang in April 1962. Major General John Condon, Commanding General, 1st Marine Aircraft Wing (fourth from left) confers with Colonel John Carey (extreme right), the task group commander. Lieutenant Colonel Archie Clapp, HMM-362 squadron commander, is third from left, holding coat and briefcase.*

steadily sinking. Timbers were quickly shoved under the axles, yet [they] were solid on the timbers before the helicopter could be started and rotors engaged for takeoff. After that experience the helicopters always carried a short length of marston matting to be placed under the wheels by the crew chief before the helicopters were shut down in the field."[27]

Lieutenant Colonel Clapp could have added that the problem triggered off a renewed search for an "instant" helicopter landing pad. Several models were later produced in limited quantities.

Another problem the men of HMM–362 could solve immediately, and their experience influenced the design of all helicopters in the future. It had not occurred to the squadron that the small size of the Vietnamese troops "made it difficult for them to embark in the helicopters when they were on solid ground and impossible in mud. The squadron metal-smiths built large jury-rig steps [to the cabin door] from wood and angle iron to solve the problem." [28] Later prefabricated metal steps were added to the UH–34s operating in Vietnam. But the most lasting effect was that the ease of exit and entrance became a factor in the design of future helicopters.

Nine days after their arrival in Soc Trang the Marines had a helicopter shot down. A single bullet pierced an oil line in the engine. The pilot was able to fly the airplane out of the battle to a safe area, but the incident pointed up the vulnerability of the oil system in the UH–34. The vital cooler was located on the bottom of the engine and provided a tempting target for the enemy until later when armor plating was added.*

Lieutenant Colonel Clapp also began refining "short-order" missions, in which the rapid response and mobility provided by the helicopter provided a means to exploit any sighting of the enemy. These operations were subsequently developed into the "Chickenhawk" (or Eagle) fast reaction concept and employed with great success.

To overcome the difficulty of navigating across the featureless swamps and rice paddies of the delta region and yet to provide the surprise resulting from flight at extremely low levels he once again demonstrated his imagination. The leader of a flight would position himself to the rear of the formation high above at 1,500 feet altitude. From there he could identify landmarks and broadcast course corrections to the other helicopters without alerting the enemy to the impending assault.

By the time HMM–362 left Vietnam on 1 August 1962, Lieutenant Colonel Clapp and "Archie's Angels," as the members of his squadron called themselves, had identified almost every area which would eventually require further development in helicopters.

Built-in armor plate was needed. Some integral fire power was necessary though unlike the Army H–21s no machine guns had been mounted in the aircraft. Instead, the crew chief and co-pilot were equipped with "grease gun" submachine guns. "The co-pilot covered the left side of the helicopter while the crew chief covered the right when [they] were close to, or on the ground."[29]

The many studies conducted in the previous 10 years of the possible effect of combat damage had been tested. The helicopter "does not seem to be as fragile as some people think," [30] it was reported.

Landings in the face of heavy fire or "in the vicinity of a machine gun concentration" seemed "foolhardy." Though "some losses will likely occur when operating in an environment" of light enemy fire, "it is not necessary to 'sanitize' an area completely before helicopters con operate in it, if moderate losses are an acceptable factor."[31]

New flight clothing and body armor for helicopter crews were a high priority item.

While the squadron occasionally had fixed-wing aircraft support from the Vietnamese Air Force, the results were uneven. Lieutenant Colonel Clapp accurately predicted what would have to be developed for protection of helicopters in a counterinsurgency war:

> Helicopters need escort aircraft to call on for suppressive fire. The escorting aircraft must have flight characteristics that permit them to stay close to the helicopters and constantly in a position to initiate an attack. A target is not going to be seen until it is firing at the helicopters, and when this happens, even a short delay is too long. The armament of the escort aircraft should be antipersonnel in nature. Their sole mission is to make someone stop shooting at the helicopters. And to make them stop immediately. The results the helicopter leader needs in order for him to get his work done [are to] keep the opposition off his back while he places troops where they are supposed to be.[32]

Unknown to the Marines at Soc Trang, their deployment had created an additional problem. General Shoup had approved the move but he harbored reservations. The Marine Corps was undergoing a major expansion of the helicopter program and planned to add one medium transport squadron to the existing 11 in each of the next four years. The inventory of UH–34s would increase to 294 by fiscal year 1964.[33]

To fill the new units, additional mechanics, technicians, and pilots would have to be recruited and trained, and much of the training would be done by Marines already assigned to helicopters. Any further commitments of active units, therefore would put a severe strain on the planned progress. The Comman-

---

* Armoring of helicopters will be discussed in Chapter 5.

dant feared that the Marine Corps might be asked to provide another squadron to MAG-16 in addition to HMM-362 and HMM-261, resulting in a disruption of the expansion. He indicated that he would oppose the use of the Marine helicopters in Vietnam if this were to be the situation.[34] He made this position clear to Generals Shapley and Roberts on 7 May. The third transport squadron to be sent to the western Pacific was not scheduled to be ready for deployment until March 1964. The plan would be adhered to.[35]

The fears of General Shoup had foundation. Less than a month after his warnings, ComUSMACV stated an urgent need for additional helicopters in Vietnam and requested CinCPac provide another Marine squadron.[36] General Shoup, however, was at least partially successful in his efforts to build up the helicopter program before committing more squadrons to an expanding war in SEA. Not until late fall 1963, would the additional squadron arrive. The three transport units of MAG-16 initially rotated between Vietnam, the ship-borne Special Landing Force, and home station at Futema.

For three years after "Archie's Angels" first touched down at Soc Trang, SHUFLY continued to provide the Marine Corps with information that greatly affected further development of the helicopter. But SHUFLY had become almost a totally land-based operation. The amphibious capability, which gave the Marine Corps such a unique strength, was seldom utilized. The Marine Corps soon was to have an opportunity to evaluate the concept and the machines in an operation which was almost completely sea-based.

## The 1962 Missile Crisis

The first week in October 1962 found Marine Corps helicopters engaged in a wide variety of commitments. HMM-163, led by Lieutenant Colonel Robert L. Rathburn, had replaced HMM-362 in SHUFLY on 1 August. Lieutenant Colonel Rathburn, a fighter pilot in World War II, had made the transition into helicopters and had been designated 23 November 1951.

After turning over all of its equipment and aircraft to HMM-163, "Archie's Angels" had proceeded to new assignments in the United States. HMM-362 was reformed at Santa Ana, but in October found itself once again, as in Futema a year before, awaiting the assignment of aircraft. It was, also, about to have a new mission.

In Thailand, Lieutenant Colonel Steele with HMM-261 had been replaced by the newly arrived HMM-162. The commander, Lieutenant Colonel Reinhardt Leu, was one of the earlier helicopter pilots, having been designated 27 November 1950. Only a small cadre of HMM-261 had been transferred from Thailand to MAG-26 at New River in July, but by mid-September the squadron nearly had regained full strength and was engaged in intensive training.

Lieutenant Colonel Robert L. Cochran had assumed command of MAG-26 on 1 February 1962. Two months later he was promoted. An expert on aviation electronics, he had participated in the battle of Okinawa and had completed flight training after World War II. He had made the transition to helicopters in 1958.

On 1 October he and 74 of his helicopters (out of a total of 122) were deployed to NAS Memphis, Tennessee for what was officially described as "support of Federal operations to control civil disturbances".[37] Rioting had broken out in nearby Oxford, Mississippi when James H. Meredith, a black, had attempted to enroll in the university, and Colonel Cochran and most of his forces had been dispatched on short notice to assist the authorities. They began returning to New River on 8 October.[38]

Eight more of the group's aircraft were embarked in the USS *Shadwell* (LSD 15) in the Mediterranean Sea as the vertical lift component of Battalion Landing Team (BLT) 1/2. These UH-34s were a detachment from HMM-262 commanded by Major Wilbur O. Nelson. Not only did Major Nelson have to start preparing a new subunit for the replacement scheduled for November of the *Shadwell* detachment but on 3 October CMC had announced that his squadron was to undergo a reorganization. The expansion of the helicopter program was progressing on schedule but there remained a serious shortage of pilots to fly the additional aircraft. To alleviate this, one squadron on each coast was to be reformed into a training unit. Experienced fixed-wing pilots were to be ordered to transition training with the first ones due 1 November.[39]

When Colonel Cochran arrived back in New River, he was immediately faced with another challenge. Two of his squadrons, HMM-264 and -261, were scheduled to embark on 16 October for a large-scale exercise (PHIBRIGLEX-62) in the Caribbean. HMM-264, under the command of Lieutenant Colonel Rocco D. Bianchi, would sail in the newest *Iwo Jima*-class LPH, the USS *Okinawa* (LPH-3) which had been commissioned 14 April. In addition to 12 UH-34s, he would be assigned four HR2Ss from Lieutenant Colonel Eugene J. Pope's HMH-461 and two OH-43s from Lieutenant Colonel Earl W. Cassidy, Sr.'s VMO-1. Lieutenant Colonel Frank A. Shook, Jr., was to embark in the USS

*Thetis Bay* with 12 UH–34s. Due to the small size of the "Teddy Bear," no additional aircraft were assigned to HMM–261.[40]

D-day for the landing was scheduled for 23 October with the fleet to arrive back on the east coast a week later. Loading of the 6,000 Marines and their equipment went smoothly, and on 17 October the combined task force sailed with the landing force, under the command of Brigadier General Rathvon McC. Tompkins, Assistant Division Commander, 2d Marine Division, and a winner of the Navy Cross in World War II.

Coincidentally, on the same day in California, the *Iwo Jima* departed for her first deployment in the western Pacific. She would replace the USS *Valley Forge* (LPH 8), an *Essex*-class conversion which had relieved the *Princeton* as the LPH for the Special Landing Force. Plans for all of these units were to change abruptly.

For several years, the situation in Cuba had been growing steadily worse. The day after HMM–264 and –261 and the *Iwo Jima* had left on routine operations, President Kennedy received information indicating that the Russians had introduced missiles into Cuba which were capable of striking the United States. On the 19th, he received further confirmation of the presence of rockets. As the Administration prepared to meet this direct threat to national security, the *Iwo Jima* was ordered to return to the West Coast immediately.[41] PHIBRIGLEX-62 was hastily cancelled and the entire fleet, now numbering over 40 ships, was diverted for new assignments.[42]

On 22 October, President Kennedy went before a nationwide radio and television audience to announce that he was instituting a blockade and quarantine of Cuba to force the removal of the missiles. That same evening, additional Marine helicopter units were alerted for action. The only remaining LPH in the Atlantic, the USS *Boxer*, was ordered to a position off New River, where she was to embark troops and helicopters. The *Boxer* arrived at New River on the 27th and sailed the same day for the Caribbean. On board was HMM–263 under Lieutenant Colonel Clyde H. Slaton, Jr., with 20 UH–34s augmented by four HR2Ss, five OH–43s, and nine O–1s. Also crowded on *Boxer*'s decks were 16 more UH–34s to be delivered to the *Okinawa* and *Thetis Bay* to bring HMM–261 and –264 up to their full complement of 20 aircraft each.[43]

Meanwhile, on the west coast, the *Iwo Jima* had returned to port the same day as the President's announcement and immediately began embarking elements of the 5th Marine Expeditionary Brigade (MEB), commanded by Brigadier General William T. Fairbourn, Assistant Division Commander, 1st Marine Division. The commanding officer of California-based MAG–36, Colonel Earl E. Anderson (later to become Assistant Commandant of the Marine Corps), selected HMM–361 to deploy with the 5th MEB. The squadron had a routine change of command scheduled, and the date was changed to allow Lieutenant Colonel Thomas J. Ross to assume command on 22 October.[44] A detachment of observation aircraft from Lieutenant Colonel Henry K. Bruce's VMO–6 was added to HMM–361. The *Iwo Jima* sailed again on 27 October and this time set course for the Panama Canal.[45] Two weeks later, she was in position in the Caribbean.

The second week in November saw a reduction in tension as the Russians began removing their missiles from Cuba. The amphibious fleets with their LPHs began to plan training maneuvers—within range to permit rapid return to Cuba if necessary.[46]

On 20 November, President Kennedy announced the lifting of the blockade, and the *Okinawa*, *Thetis Bay*, and *Boxer* shortly proceeded back to the New River area to conduct exercises and unload the Marines. All units were home by 2 December.[47] The *Iwo Jima* remained in the Caribbean until 1 December to take part in practice operations at Vieques Island east of Puerto Rico. On 1 December, the ship sailed for the west coast via the Panama Canal.[48] Two weeks later, HMM–361 arrived back at Santa Ana.[49]

Though the Marines had not been engaged in combat during their deployment and had spent almost all of the time at sea, they again had demonstrated the flexibility and mobility available to assault troops in the LPH/helicopter combination. It also had confirmed the necessity of maintaining the LPH construction program and the expansion of Marine helicopter forces as a high priority. As a side effect, the Cuban Crisis had proved invaluable in furthering the indoctrination of many Marines in amphibious vertical assault warfare. Lieutenant General Robert B. Luckey, commander of the landing forces, reviewed the problems at the annual General Officers' Symposium in July 1963. He concluded that "all in all, it was an instructive embarkation drill. As a result, the II Marine Expeditionary Force is better prepared."[50]

More important, the Cuban crisis had demonstrated the need to conduct large-scale exercises incorporating long-range strategic mobility. It would be another two years before sufficient LPHs, helicopters, and crews were available, but when the first such operation was held it would test fully the entire concept of vertical amphibious assault.

## STEEL PIKE I

Lieutenant General James P. Berkeley assumed command of FMFLant on 1 August 1963. Born into a Marine Corps family, he was the son of Major General Randolph Carter Berkeley who had won the Medal of Honor at Veracruz, Mexico in 1914. General Berkeley had followed in his father's footsteps and had enlisted in the Marine Corps in 1927. After almost three years as an enlisted man, including duty in Nicaragua, he was commissioned a second lieutenant on 31 January 1930. He became an expert on communications and served in a variety of billets in that field during World War II. After the war, he was an amphibious warfare advisor to the Argentine Naval War College and to the Argentine Marine Corps.

Three months after assuming command of FMFLant, General Berkeley departed on a trip to those areas in Europe in which his Marines had interest. One of his first stops was on the southwestern coast of Spain. As the general later recounted:

> We'd been interested in the Rota beaches for a long time in the Marine Corps. General Luckey had been over there a number of years before . . . and had surveyed these beaches. We'd been interested in this as an exercise area.[51]

After inspecting the site, General Berkeley "talked to the Commandant of the Spanish Marines . . . about the possibility of having a joint maneuver. The Spaniards were enthused about the idea."[52]

Returning to his headquarters in Norfolk, Virginia, he discussed the area with Vice Admiral John S. McCain, Jr., Commander, Amphibious Force, Atlantic (ComPhibLant). PhibLant was the navy counterpart to FMFLant in landing operations. Coincidentally, Admiral McCain was also the son of a famous military man. His father, Vice Admiral John S. McCain, was the World War II commander of a fast carrier striking force that compiled an enviable battle history in the Pacific as Task Force 38.

Admiral McCain agreed with General Berkeley that a large-scale strategic mobility landing was feasible and desirable. Spain, however, was not the only possibility:

> We [FMFLant staff] physically reconnoitered Jamaica, Panama, Puerto Rico, and Vieques. In addition, Trinidad, Nicaragua, Dominican Republic, Haiti, and areas in South America were investigated. All . . . were inadequate, either from a political, hydrographic or topographic point of view. Therefore we turned our attention to Spain.[53]

> Through Commander-in-Chief, Atlantic Fleet (CinCLantFlt), the matter was brought before the JCS exercise scheduling conference in late January. After [the] presentation . . . a 'Carib Mobex' was recommended by the conference for FY 65 (July 64–June 65), with the understanding that it might be conducted in Spain.[54]

On 31 March, the JCS approved the recommendations of the scheduling conference and shortly thereafter the code name STEEL PIKE was substituted for "Carib Mobex." D-day was set originally for 29 October, but at the request of the Spanish Government, moved up to 26 October.[55]

Three weeks before the landing, ships of the largest amphibious operation in the Atlantic Ocean since World War II began embarking supplies, equipment, and Marines. By the time the fleet arrived off the coast of Spain it consisted of almost 115 U.S. Navy ships, 21,642 men of the II Marine Expeditionary Force, the Mediterranean Ready Amphibious Squadron, and 17 Military Sea Transport Service and commercial charter vessels.[56]

In the objective area the American forces were joined by Spanish units, including 25 additional ships, a Marine battalion landing team, aircraft, and Army forces.[57] The 60 ships of the fleet assigned to carrying the Marines included three LPHs: the *Boxer*, the *Okinawa*, and the newest one, USS *Guadalcanal* (LPH 7).

On board these ships were most of the helicopters in MAG–26. The commanding officer, Colonel Stanley V. Titterud, had been the 24th Marine designated a helicopter pilot. An aviator since he was commissioned in August 1942, he had qualified in helicopters on 11 June 1949.

Six of the seven tactical squadrons in the group with a total of 105 aircraft were committed to STEEL PIKE. There were 80 UH–34s. HMM–261, commanded by Lieutenant Colonel Mervin B. Porter, was in the *Guadalcanal*; HMM–262 with Lieutenant Colonel Edward K. Kirby in the *Okinawa*; and both Lieutenant Colonel Warren L. MacQuarrie's HMM–263 and Lieutenant Colonel Frederick M. Kleppsattel's HMM–264

USMC Photo A450013

*The U.S.S.* Guadalcanal *(LPH 7), with HR2S1s and UH–34s on her deck, participates in Operation STEEL PIKE I in October 1964. In all, seven Marine helicopter squadrons and three LPHs were involved in this major test of the vertical assault concept.*

in the *Boxer*. Each had 20 UH-34s. Major Donald R. Navorska, who had taken command of VMO-1 two months earlier, had 10 of his UH-1Es distributed among all three ships. In addition, Lieutenant Colonel Truman Clark was on board the *Boxer* with eight of the HR2Ss from HMH-461. Finally, the seven UH-34s from HMM-262 which had been on board the USS *Donner* (LSD 20) as part of the Mediterranean ready force rendezvoused with the rest of the group for the operation. The only squadron left at New River, Lieutenant Colonel Eldon C. Stanton's HMM-265, was in the process of converting to a new type of aircraft.

The scheme of maneuver in STEEL PIKE called for one regimental landing team (RLT) to land by boats and another by helicopter in the vicinity of Huelva, on the Atlantic coast of Spain. A second landing to the north would also be made by boat. Both surface thrusts, though, would encounter populated areas in their advance and the final assaults on the inland objectives were planned to be helicopter borne.[58]

The D-day weather was ideal. Clear skies and calm seas prevailed. On hand to observe was a large group of dignitaries, including the CMC, General Greene. The assault was almost classic in its perfection. General Berkeley reported that "all surface and assault elements of landing force executed [operation] on time. Combat efficiency remains excellent."

The only incident to mar the exercise was the collision of two helicopters from HMM-262. The crash resulted in the death of one of the crew chiefs and eight members of BLT 3/8. One pilot, First Lieutenant Donald W. Soper, was critically injured. The rest of the crews and passengers escaped with minor injuries.[59]

As the attack progressed, tests of helicopter operations continued, including the simultaneous lifting of members of the same unit from different ships to a single landing zone. The careful control of so many aircraft within the target area received special attention. To expedite the movement of supplies from the landing zones, lightweight, rough-terrain fork lifts were brought ashore inside the HR2Ss. U.S. fighters practiced escort of the helicopters circling over the transport aircraft, and keeping at bay the Spanish air force which was acting as the "enemy." (Many of the Spanish airplanes were German-designed Messerschmitt ME 109s—the most common fighter of the Nazi Luftwaffe in World War II. Helicopter pilots were often startled when attacked in mock battle by an airplane they had seen only in old newsreels.) General Berkeley utilized the rapid response and versatility of his helicopters and reported that "further helo assaults [are] planned to expedite seizure of force objectives."[60]

By 30 October the assault forces had gained all of the objectives and reembarkation began the next day.

The usefulness of the helicopter had one more demonstration. A Douglas A-4 jet attack aircraft was unable to complete in-flight refueling on the way back to the United States. The pilot spotted an Italian ship, ejected from his airplane beside it, and was picked up promptly. As the freighter passed through the straits of Gibraltar, there was a Marine helicopter hovering above which lifted the pilot on board and returned him to the *Boxer*.

With reembarkation complete, the ships steamed to various European ports to give their crews and the Marines a few days of liberty before returning to the United States. Colonel Titterud and his men arrived back at New River on 28 November.[61]

Major General Louis B. Robertshaw, Deputy Chief of Staff (Air), summed up the operation, saying: "STEEL PIKE has again demonstrated the soundness of Navy-Marine Corps amphibious concepts. The exercise test objectives of the Wing were accomplished proving the validity of the need for such exercises."[62]

The need to conduct another large-scale exercise was satisfied in March 1965 on the west coast. Operation SILVER LANCE was similar to though smaller than STEEL PIKE. Almost 15,000 Marines loaded into 28 ships—only one of which was an LPH—and made an amphibious assault on the beaches of southern California. The initial helicopter landings were limited to 15 UH-34s.[63] Once ashore the Marines conducted extensive counterinsurgency training operations which had been impossible in Spain. Additional large exercises were planned but events intervened. To this date, STEEL PIKE remains the largest amphibious assault ever made utilizing helicopters.

## Dominican Republic

Lieutenant Colonel Kirby's HMM-262 remained at New River for only a short time after returning from STEEL PIKE. Less than two months later, he and his squadron embarked in the *Guadalcanal* as the helicopter squadron of the Caribbean Ready Force. This unit, which consisted of a battalion landing team, specialized support units, and a small headquarters, in addition to the helicopters, was positioned in the Caribbean Sea to deal with any emergency that might develop in that troubled area. If necessary, jet aircraft would be provided to assist them. The units of the ready force normally returned to their home bases after five or six months of deployment. Due to the short time at New River since the STEEL PIKE deployment, HMM-262 was scheduled for an abbreviated tour of three months.

UH–34s loaded with troops leave the deck of the U.S.S. Valley Forge *(LPH 8)* to conduct an assault during Operation SILVER LANCE, 9 March 1965. This exercise similar to STEEL PIKE but smaller in size, involved both a heliborne amphibious assault and counterinsurgency operations.

The squadron's relief, Lieutenant Colonel Kleppsattel's HMM–264, departed Onslow Beach on the USS *Boxer* on 3 April 1965.[64] The *Boxer* met the *Guadalcanal* at Vieques Island east of Puerto Rico for an exercise in conjunction with QUICK KICK VII, after which the pilots and crews of HMM–262 returned to New River and Lieutenant Colonel Kleppsattel's unit assumed the ready force mission. After a short visit for training to Guantanamo Bay, the ships returned to Vieques for another exercise. This one, called PLACE KICK, concluded with a week of extensive training for the Marines on the island. They reembarked on their vessels on 24 April.

That night, CinCLantFlt began to receive reports of riots, demonstrations, and an attempted coup in Santo Domingo from the American embassy there. The next morning the ready force was ordered to move toward the Dominican Republic, but to remain out of sight of land. The fleet, and the Marines, were underway less than an hour later. As the ready force was sailing from Vieques, the situation in Santo Domingo was reported to be disintegrating rapidly, with leftist-led rebels controlling the streets and the local authorities powerless to stop them.

The ships and the Marines arrived off the coast in the predawn hours of 26 April and established contact with the embassy. Late that evening, the ready force was requested to begin the evacuation of Americans starting at first light the next day. Lieutenant Colonel Kleppsattel's helicopters were scheduled to conduct much of the lift.

Kleppsattel had been commissioned a second lieutenant in the Marine Corps in July 1945 and was designated a helicopter pilot on 12 October 1951. He had seen his first combat flying helicopters with VMO–6 in Korea. Subsequently he had served three years as a helicopter flight instructor at Pensacola and before assuming command of HMM–264 had been the operations officer for MAG–26. In the latter position he had instituted an expanded program of night and instrument flying, an effort that was to pay large dividends in Santo Domingo. By 1965 he had amassed almost 4,000 hours of flight time in helicopters and was one of the most experienced pilots in rotary-winged aircraft. To conduct the evacuation, he had 20 UH–34s and two UH–1Es. While there were two HR2Ss attached to the squadron, both were grounded by mechanical troubles.

On 27 April, the squadron lifted a total of 558 civilians from Haina, a small port several miles west of the city. Slightly more were loaded on two American ships in the harbor. The next morning the passengers on the *Boxer* were again moved, this time to the USS *Raleigh* (LPD 1). The ships with the refugees departed for San Juan, Puerto Rico, leaving the *Boxer* to stand by off Santo Domingo. She was needed. During the afternoon of the 28th, Ambassador William Tapley Bennett, Jr., who had been on leave when the rioting began and had just arrived back, relayed requests from the Dominican government to land Marine forces to help restore order. At 1820 they were ordered to go ashore. The *Raleigh* was recalled to the scene and arrived before midnight. The landing zone chosen for the assault was a large polo field on the western outskirts of the city. In the nearby Hotel Embajador—the largest resort hotel in the nation—there were additional refugees and more were arriving hourly.

UH–34s of HMM–264 land U.S. civilians evacuated from the Dominican Republic on the U.S.S. Boxer (LPH 4) in April 1965. In one day, this squadron lifted 558 persons out of the revolt-torn nation.

As night fell clouds formed "right on the deck" and rain began to fall. The training in night and instrument flight became the critical factor. Leaving coordination at the ship to his executive officer "and right arm," Major Thomas L. Spurr, Lieutenant Colonel Kleppsettel led a two-way shuttle of helicopters. On each trip from the ship to the polo field, the UH–34s lifted combat Marines. On the return they carried evacuees. Utilizing a tight diamond formation of four aircraft which Kleppsattel "had always flown in 264" the helicopters took off under radar control.* Unable to see the water or the land, they relied on instructions from the radar operators to bring them to the polo field. There they were guided to a landing by a "black box." This was a series of focused beams of light of different colors which were pre-set on a given angle in the air. A pilot could land by flying the angle indicated by the appropriate color. The return trip to the ship was just the opposite, with radar assistance for the landing.

Shortly before midnight all the Marines were ashore and an additional 684 refugees had been brought to the fleet. Starting before dawn the next day, HMM–264 continued to ferry supplies and equipment to the polo field and evacuate civilians.

At the same time, other units on the east coast had been alerted for movement to the Caribbean. One was HMM–263 at New River. The squadron recently had had a change of command. Lieutenant Colonel Truman Clark had taken over after being relieved in HMH–461 by Major Royce W. Watson. On 29 April, the *Okinawa* was ordered to proceed to a position off Onslow Beach and load BLT 1/2 and the helicopters. In addition to its normal complement of 20 UH–34s, Lieutenant Colonel Clark's unit was augmented with two UH–1Es from VMO–1 and two HR2Ss from his former command HMH–461. The *Okinawa* arrived at dawn 1 May and by late afternoon the embarkation was complete. The ship immediately departed at 21 knots for Santo Domingo and arrived in position the night of 4–5 May. HMM–263 took over helicopter operations, allowing the "Black Knights" of 264 to rest and to repair their aircraft.

The polo field had begun to take on the appearance of a miniature airport. There was a small concrete grandstand on the east side and the Marines had converted the space under it into a combined passenger and cargo terminal. Radios were mounted in the stands and assisted in controlling the constant arrival and departure of helicopters. Both squadrons kept a few

---

* Unlike fixed-wing aircraft formations in which each succeeding aircraft is slightly lower than the one ahead, helicopters fly slightly higher, to escape the down blast from the rotors and to increase the cockpit visibility of the wingmen.

*UH-34s of HMM-264 lift in vehicles for Marine forces establishing positions in Santo Dominigo City, April 1965. The Marine aircraft operated from a polo field hastily converted into a landing field.*

mechanics nearby to make emergency repairs of aircraft. To complete the scene, the Marines had erected a large, handpainted sign announcing the polo field as the home of "The Teenie Weenie Airlines. You call—we haul."[65]

Within the city there were constant clashes between Marine patrols and rebels. Sniper fire was always a hazard.[66] The Marine helicopters were a favorite target but the rebels' aim was poor and none had been hit. Then the snipers got lucky. Captain Thomas ("Tee Squared") P. McBrien was a pilot on one of the UH-1Es attached to HMM-263. The morning of 6 May he was ordered to fly over the city in an attempt to locate four civilian newspapermen who had been caught in an ambush. With him were an aerial observer, First Lieutenant Richard C. Mittelstadt, and the crew chief, Sergeant Thomas Doyle. Sergeant Doyle reported hearing shots go by the aircraft. Almost immediately one penetrated the lower side of the UH-1E striking the pilot. Though painfully wounded, Captain McBrien was able to bring the helicopter to a safe landing at the polo field and was evacuated to the *Okinawa*.[67]

It was the only such incident experienced by the Marine helicopters. McBrien retains the dubious distinction of being one of the very few Marine aviators ever to become a combat casualty in the western hemisphere.*

Intense political negotiations had been going on since the first rioting. By the end of May a compromise solution had been agreed to and the situation became relatively stable. Soon military units from other nations of the Organization of American States were arriving to relieve the U.S. forces. Some Marine units now could be withdrawn.

First priority went to HMM-263 which was scheduled to be transferred to Okinawa in October and needed to return to New River as soon as possible to prepare for the move to the Pacific. Accordingly, on the afternoon of 26 May, the JCS directed the withdrawal of the *Okinawa* with HMM-263 and most of BLT 1/2 on board. The ship headed home as soon as the orders were received and arrived off Onslow Beach the morning of the 29th, after another 21-knot ride. Two weeks later HMM-264 and the *Boxer* left Santo Domingo to take up their normal ready force alert.

The operation in the Dominican Republic was the last test of Marine helicopters before they were fully engaged in combat. It had combined the hostile environment of SHUFLY, the sea-based mobility of Cuba, and the assaults from both land and sea of STEEL PIKE and SILVER LANCE. In retrospect it was much like a final examination before graduation. Most of the grades were good but at least one was marginal. The Dominican Republic confirmed the urgent need for a new generation of helicopters to replace the UH-34 and, particularly, the obsolete HR2S. The requirement, fortunately, had been recognized almost five years previously and by 1965 considerable progress had been made toward meeting it.

---

* Total casualties for Marine units were nine killed and 30 wounded.

# CHAPTER THREE

## INTRODUCTION OF THE TURBINES

### More Lift Per Aircraft

The Marine Corps was faced with one inescapable fact. The total number of aircraft it could possess was strictly limited. The ceiling had been imposed by the Department of Defense and Congress. Since each aircraft required manpower, ships, bases, and operating money, control of the total number of aircraft was in effect control of expenditures in other areas. The limitation had been used as a vital tool of management of the military forces. Any attempt to increase the number resulted in a lengthy and often unsuccessful effort. Conversely, a decrease had been imposed often to reduce funds.

Within the ceiling, however, the Marine Corps had some latitude in deciding what types of aircraft would make up the total. Though it was not easy to do, the mix could be varied. The result was that as additional helicopters were necessary a corresponding number of fixed-wing aircraft often had to be deleted from the inventory—a move that was not universally popular with jet pilots. The same limit was a stumbling block to the introduction of large numbers of very small helicopters into the Marine Corps.

From 1952 to 1963 the total aircraft in the Marine Corps had remained slightly more than 1,050,[1] but in that period the makeup of the force had undergone a significant shift. Even more changes were planned. From a ratio of one helicopter to every five fixed-wing aircraft in 1952, the planned expansion of the helicopter program would result in an almost one-to-one ratio in 1967.

Even this increase in helicopters could not meet the almost insatiable demand for more vertical lift capability. Fortunately, there was another way to meet the requirements: improve the load-carrying capability of each helicopter.

### The Turbine Engines

As installed in helicopters, much of the power of a conventional piston engine was expended just lifting itself. The figure varied somewhat between different models, but most reciprocating engines weighed approximately three pounds for each horsepower they could produce. Typically, the engine in the UH-34 weighed over 3,500 pounds but could develop continuously only 1,275 horsepower. Higher amounts, up to the maximum of 1,525, were restricted to short periods of time. As the size of a piston engine was increased, the weight to horsepower ratio remained about constant, but complexity and reliability became such problems that there was an effective limit to the amount of power. If the Marine Corps was to increase the payload capability of new helicopters, a different source of power would have to be found.

Small turbine engines, fortunately, were becoming available which had much different weight to horsepower ratios. The General Electric-built T-64-G-6 jet turbine could produce 2,270 horsepower continuously, was able to exceed 2,800 for short periods, yet weighed only 728 pounds.[2] Every improvement of the weight-to-power ratio was synonymous with additional lifting capability; hence, conversion from piston to jet engines for helicopters was extremely attractive to the Marines. Like so many other aspects of the development of helicopters, however, the introduction of turbine engines was not as simple a problem as it at first seemed to be.

The basic jet engine contains three main parts. Behind the intake is a large fan used to squeeze the air into a dense mass suitable for efficient operation. The compressed air is fed into burning chambers where it is mixed with fuel and ignited. The result is a massive expansion of hot air which is then directed out the tail pipe. Before leaving the engine the air passes through a turbine which captures some of its force and transmits it back to turn the compressor. The power of the engine is largely determined by the amount of air the compressor can deliver to the burning chambers and the amount of fuel available for combustion. The turbine simply drives the compressor.

# TURBINE INTRODUCTION

In a conventional jet aircraft this is all that is necessary for operation. The hot expanding gasses ejected from the tail pipe provide almost all of the thrust.

The pure jet engine was not suitable for all aircraft. To take advantage of the light weight and large amounts of power which could be generated, in some designs a fourth element was added. An increase in the size and efficiency of the turbine allowed almost all of the power from the compressor and burning chambers to be captured and used to drive not only the compressor but also a gear box mounted on the extreme front of the engine. By converting the high rpm of the jet engine to a slower more powerful force, the gear box now could be used to turn a propeller. The result was a "turbo-prop" engine.

A few designs were given further modification. Instead of a propeller the gear box turned the rotor on a helicopter. When the American Helicopter Society held its 17th annual national forum in Washington, D.C. in May 1961, the members heard the latest developments in helicopter propulsion described:

> At first glance, the . . . turbine appears to be the answer to all helicopter pilots' nightmares, namely, the ability to maintain automatic main rotor rpm; and certainly in most regimes of flight [in small lightly-loaded helicopters] this may be true.[3]

But for most other helicopters all jet engines then available contained a serious flaw. The problem stemmed from two sources. Jet engines operate efficiently only when turning near their maximum allowable speed. The slightest decrease results in a large loss of power. In addition, most of the engines had the turbine and compressor solidly attached to the shaft which connected them. A gear box, if installed, was also fixed to the same shaft. In pure jets, turbo-prop aircraft, and even in small lightly-loaded helicopters this was not a particular disadvantage; but in a large heavily-laden transport helicopter, it could be disastrous.

As previously discussed, the rotor blades of a helicopter achieve lift by the square of the velocity of the air passing around them. To insure that sufficient lift was always available, most helicopters flew with their rotors turning as fast as aerodynamically practicable. Any change in direction of the aircraft was effected by changing the pitch—not the speed—of the blades. Occasionally a pilot inadvertently would allow the rotors to slow up (lose turns) and the aircraft would falter. If not immediately corrected, any further loss of rotor speed would cause the aircraft to enter an uncontrolled descent. The quick response of a piston engine over a wide range of power settings had salvaged many such situations.

In a turbine-driven helicopter with the rotor directly connected to the engine through the gear box, any such loss of turns also slowed the engine. Now the pilot faced a condition in which he needed maximum power to accelerate the rotor, but the engine could produce only a fraction of its full capacity. The more the pilot needed, the less was available. It could become a vicious circle.

The answer was to design a jet engine in which the turbine was not connected to the shaft. This would allow the compressor and burning chambers to operate at maximum efficiency independent of the rotor system. If more power was required rapidly, it would be available. The result was the "free turbine" or "gas-powered turbine" engine.

Two such engines were becoming available at the beginning of the 1960s. The Lycoming-built T–53 developed approximately 900 horsepower while the larger General Electric T–58 was rated up to 1,250 for short periods of time.

Even with free turbines, the problems of installing jets in helicopters were not completely solved. One of the most serious was foreign object damage (FOD) to the engine. As the compressor sucked in large amounts of air for the burning chambers, it did not discriminate about what else it picked up. Fixed-wing jet pilots long had become accustomed to the sight of motorized sweeper trucks scouring the runways and parking aprons to insure that no debris was lying about to be swallowed by engines which could be seriously damaged by a small stone or piece of metal. For helicopters landing in rocky fields, mountain tops, and small clearings in a forest, FOD was going to be a problem. David Richardson, Chief Systems Engineer of the Vertol Division, Boeing Airplane Company, presented his views at the same Helicopter Society forum in 1961:

> Foreign object damage with the helicopter turbine engine is becoming an increasingly significant item. The cost in terms of replacement parts . . . is large. As this paper was being written an engine . . . was removed from a Vertol test helicopter for foreign object damage after less than 60 hours of operation. This was the result of a large foreign object.[4]

He went on to describe a different type of FOD:

> There is another type . . . of foreign particle damage. [These] may be ice, salt water, sand, etc. They do not result in as rapid engine deterioration as caused by large objects, but they may be more costly in that more [of the engine] may be damaged.[5]

He also noted that recently Bureau of Weapons (BuWeps) had begun including specifications for air filters in new helicopter jet engine designs. Richardson concluded that Vertol was working on a filter but needed more information about the effect of sand and grit from the manufacturers of the engines.

Other difficulties challenged the designers. While in a fixed-wing aircraft, the engine was always in a position to receive ample quantities of air, the effect of a helicopter flying sideways or backwards had to be considered.* No matter where the engines were placed on the aircraft, the down wash from the rotor would affect the air surging into the inlet. The results required careful testing. The vibration resulting from the articulated rotor heads was a new factor to any jet. "An engine which has thousands of hours of test time may not withstand the helicopter vibration unless it was designed and tested . . . to the stresses it will be subject to", one report said.[6]

The introduction of turbine engines in helicopters was not just a matter of putting a jet on an existing aircraft. It required a major engineering and design effort and lengthy testing. Enough progress had been made, however, that by 1962 the Marine Corps was about to have jet-powered helicopters.

## The "Huey"

> The proposed replacement for both the HOK and the OE in the VMO squadrons . . . has really been a yo-yo project, alternately being in and out of approved plans, programs and budgets. Again, however, I am happy to state that it is "in."
>
> Colonel Keith B. McCutcheon
> Director of Aviation
> 18 January 1962 [7]

A replacement for the OH–43s had become enmeshed in a difference of opinion as to just what was the mission of the aircraft. One view held that there should be a new aircraft fully configured for observation purposes to replace the O-1s in the VMO squadrons, and a distinctly different type of aircraft for assault support. This position was centered at the Marine Corps Schools at Quantico commanded by Lieutenant General Edward W. Snedeker. A veteran of almost every major campaign in the Pacific from Guadalcanal to Okinawa in World War II and of the Chosin Reservoir in Korea, General Snedeker had been awarded both the Navy Cross and the Silver Star for heroism.

General Shoup, however, insisted that a single type of aircraft, an assault-support helicopter (ASH), could replace both the OH–43s and the O-1s. Attempts to procure either—or both—of the new aircraft were consistently frustrated by performance deficiencies of models proposed by manufacturers or by funding difficulties. By 1960 the continued deterioration of the OH–43s added urgency to finding a suitable new helicopter. General Shoup restated his policy in August that year in a letter to General Snedeker:

> The number one procurement priority in the light observation area is assigned to ASH . . . No new evaluations . . will be commenced until the ASH is programmed and funded.[8]

General Snedeker still held out for two. The ASH could replace the OH–43, but a short takeoff and landing (STOL) attack reconnaissance aircraft to replace and expand the present mission of the O–1s was also needed. General Shoup was not to be swayed and in February 1961 wrote that until "the Assault Support Helicopter is on track, no other light observation type aircraft will be considered".[9]

Difficulties in procuring the replacement aircraft were not confined to the Marine Corps. In September the Deputy Chief of Naval Operations (Air), Vice Admiral Robert B. Pirie, summed up the frustrations of the previous months in a letter to Rear Admiral Paul D. Stroop, Chief of the Bureau of Naval Weapons. Admiral Pirie pointed out that in March he had suggested that "a limited competition be conducted [by BuWeps] to select an aircraft to fulfill the Marine Corps ASH mission."[10] In the same letter he had assured Admiral Stroop that:

> . . . once a satisfactory selection and model evaluation has been made, that every effort would be expended to effect necessary reprogramming of funds within the FY 62 budget to permit the accelerated purchase of the operational vehicles.[11]

BuWeps had indeed conducted an evaluation. "Representatives of the Bureau of Naval Weapons presented the results of the preliminary study of those helicopters under consideration for selection of the assault support helicopter." Admiral Pirie complained that:

> . . . no recommendations were made as to the aircraft best suited to the mission or the most appropriate course of action to be followed in conjunction with an orderly procurement program. Each model reviewed failed to qualify under the recognized guidelines because of one or more deficiencies such as size, cost, capability or lack of qualifications.[12]

"It became apparent," he wrote, "that compromises must be made in regard to funding considerations and aircraft selection." [13]

The crux of the matter was that in August Admiral Stroop had requested CNO to provide 5.1 million dol-

---

* Long a problem almost exclusively in helicopters, the effect of air not entering directly from the front of the engine was the cause of the cancellation of the first trans-Atlantic flight of the giant Boeing jumbo jet—the 747. While waiting for takeoff on 21 January 1970, the wind was blowing from the side. The designers had not taken this into consideration for so large an engine. It overheated and the plane had to return to the terminal—precisely the problem facing helicopters 10 years earlier.

lars for procurement before BuWeps even would request manufacturers to propose the modifications to their helicopters which would make them compatible with the stated requirements of the Marine Corps. Admiral Pirie pointed out that the "CNO cannot receive Congressional Committee approval of funding support for the ASH requirement without selection (first) of a specific model." [14]

To solve the "chicken before the egg" dilemma, he suggested that:

> In the selection of a suitable helicopter, the element of time is of paramount importance. It may well be in the best interests of the service to accept the burden of increased size and cost of an operationally qualified model rather than gamble on a reduced capability or a possible lengthy and costly development program. In such cases, additional potential of such a vehicle in the role of a trainer or light utility vehicle might well be considered.[15]

Admiral Pirie reassured Admiral Stroop that funding could be arranged only if BuWeps would go ahead and select a type of helicopter. The OH-43s rapidly were approaching the end of their usefulness and the "imperativeness of positive action leading to a solution of this increasingly critical subject cannot be overemphasized." [16]

The admiral had made his point. On 16 October, BuWeps solicited bids from 10 different manufacturers for an assault support helicopter for the Marine Corps. Seven responded.[17] *

The original development characteristic (specifications) published on 29 July 1960, had called for an ASH with a total weight of 3,500 pounds, a payload of 800 pounds or three troops, and a cruising airspeed of 85 knots. There was also a long standing requirement "for the provisioning of all helicopters with the necessary attachments for carrying, either internally or externally, of the maximum numbers of canvas litters practicable, such installations not to jeopardize the primary mission of the helicopter." [18]

The aircraft envisioned was similar to a requirement established by the U.S. Army. If both services could procure a single type, costs could be lowered. Even after BuWeps had published the desired specifications, conversations continued with the Army on their need for a light observation helicopter (LOH). Hiller, Bell, and Hughes all had submitted designs but there were too many differences between what the Marine Corps wanted (including carrying litters) and what the Army desired. The Marine Corps indicated "no immediate interest in the proposals to the Army for a LOH." [19]

Evaluation of the seven proposed designs for the ASH continued into the spring of 1962. On 1 March the selection was approved by the Secretary of the Navy and the next day a public announcement was released that the winner was a slight modification of the Bell Helicopter Company's UH-1B. The U.S. Army had procured several hundred of these helicopters and they were already in action in Vietnam. The designation of the Marine Corps version would be UH-1E—soon shortened to "Huey."

Bell had experimented with tandem-rotor helicopters providing additional speed up to the maximum of 120 knots. Due to its small size and rotor design, stabilization of the UH-1E did not require elaborate electronic systems, though several were tested.[20] Sufficient stability could be achieved by mechanical devices. One characteristic of the airplane not universally appreciated at the time was its extremely low silhouette. It was only 12 feet high and the cabin was even lower.

The adoption of the UH-1E did not still all the doubts previously expressed by some Marines. Of particular concern was that the visibility from the aircraft appeared much less than from the OH-43. Colonel Marion E. Carl, who had become the Director of Aviation in February 1962, decided to prove how well a commander could observe from the UH-1E. Colonel Carl, one-time holder of the world's speed record, commander of the first tactical jet squadron in the Marine Corps, World War II ace, and recipient of two Navy Crosses, arrived at the NATC at Patuxent River on a Saturday morning.

One of the aircraft utilized by BuWeps to evaluate the UH-1s had been retained by the center for further

USMC Photo A412088

*The UH-1E was the first turbine-powered helicopter assigned to Marine tactical squadrons.*

---

\* The seven were Bell, Hiller, Kaman, Lockheed, Piasecki, Republic, and Sikorsky. The three not responding were Cessna, Gyrodyne, and Doman.

testing. This helicopter, a UH-1B, was on loan from the U.S. Army. A few days prior to the arrival of Colonel Carl, a truck had backed into the short wing attached to the tail pylon. The stabilizer was damaged beyond repair and there was insufficient time to order a replacement. Across the Potomac River at Fort Belvoir, the Army had a number of UH-1As. A stabilizer was produced and hastily bolted onto the helicopter at Patuxent River.

There was one small problem. The improvements made between the UH-1A and UH-1B included a change in the stabilizers, and the one from Fort Belvoir was only half the size of the one left on the aircraft. Colonel Carl did not seem to be dismayed when he arrived and discovered that the aircraft was decidedly lopsided. He got in the helicopter, along with a test pilot attached to NATC, Marine Captain David A. Spurlock, and took off heading for Washington. The weather was poor with low clouds and intermittent rain. By following highways they soon arrived at the helicopter pad in front of the Pentagon.[21]

There they were met by a delegation of Marine officers, including the Deputy Chief of Staff for Research and Development, Brigadier General Bruno A. Hochmuth. Colonel Carl got out and invited General Hochmuth to get in. He then turned to Captain Spurlock and said, "Show the general how good the visibility is at 3,000 feet."[22] By now the weather had become worse. After a short flight at tree top level to avoid the clouds, a small opening was found and the General and his pilot found themselves evaluating the visibility. The opening, unfortunately, had disappeared. While they were at 3,000 feet, they could see nothing but solid clouds. Later and under better circumstances, the visibility from the UH-1E was found to be excellent and the program was continued.

A total of 72 operational aircraft were required to bring the VMO squadrons up to full strength, replacing both the O-1s and the OH-43s on a one-to-one basis with UH-1Es. The first step was the procurement of four additional aircraft to test fully the modifications from a UH-1B. By October $1.5 million had been provided for the program.[23]

The differences between the Army and Marine Corps versions appeared slight but each was vital if the UH-1E was going to fulfill its role in amphibious warfare. The most important was the installation of rotor brakes. This device was unnecessary when operating from wide open fields and few military or civilian helicopters had them. The major exceptions were the Marine Corps and the Navy. With plenty of room and time, a pilot could shut off the engine of his aircraft after landing and let the rotor slowly wind down to a stop.

On the crowded flight decks of amphibious ships this was impossible. The helicopter had to be landed and the rotor rapidly stopped so that the machine could be moved to a parking area to make way for the next one about to come aboard.[*] Even when flight operations were not being conducted a rotor brake was essential for shipboard operations. As the ship steamed through the water, the wind over the deck often would be sufficient to cause the rotor blades to spin unless locked securely. The Bell solution was a simple brake disk on the main transmission which could be hydraulically activated.

The UH-1E also had to be equipped with radios and communications compatible with both the air and the ground forces. This in turn required that the electrical system of the aircraft be converted from the standard Army direct current to the Navy and Marine Corps alternating current.

The only other significant difference was that much of the UH-1E was constructed of aluminum. Most helicopter designers previously had relied on magnesium to fabricate parts of a helicopter, since the lightness of the metal improved the payload capability of the aircraft and more than compensated for magnesium's inflammability (illumination flares usually are made of magnesium due to the ease of ignition, rapid burning with bright light, and the ability of the metal to burn even under water) and tendency to corrode when exposed to salt air or water. If this corrosion was not halted, the metal soon disintegrated into a pile of white dust. On board ship mechanics constantly had to paint and clean every portion of a helicopter made of magnesium.

By constructing the helicopter of aluminum, much of the problem with corrosion was eliminated. The difference in construction, indistinguishable from previous UH-1s, represented a major improvement in helicopter design. The use of heavier aluminum was possible only as a result of the increased weight/horsepower ratio of the turbine aircraft.

Events moved rapidly once the program was approved and funded. In October even before the four test aircraft had been delivered, funds for the first 30 production models were approved.[24] By the end of January 1963, the aircraft was ready for its first inspection. The configuration engineering inspection (CEI) was a final check to insure that the helicopter was designed as specified. On hand was Colonel George

---

[*] During the May 1965 Dominican Republic crisis, a company of U.S. Army UH-1s was rushed to the scene on board the USS *Guadalcanal*. The lack of rotor brakes required crews to physically catch the blades to bring them to a halt. There were numerous minor injuries from unsuccessful attempts and the loading was considerably delayed.

L. Hollowell, the UH–1E program manager for BuWeps.[25] The aircraft passed the test without difficulty.

The aircraft was then turned back to the manufacturer for avionics and structural testing. Bell completed all the required work on 30 July. The next month the helicopters were delivered to NATC Patuxent River for final trials by the Board of Inspection and Survey (BIS).[26] The evaluation concluded on 10 and 11 December as the UH–1E completed carrier qualifications on board the USS *Guadalcanal* (LPH 2).[27]

Ceremonies at the Bell plant in Fort Worth on 21 February 1964 marked the delivery of the first UH–1E to a Marine tactical squadron. Accepting the helicopter was Colonel Kenneth L. Reusser, commanding officer of MAG–26 and winner of Navy Crosses both in World War II and Korea. Also on hand was the commanding officer of VMO–1, Lieutenant Colonel Joseph A. "Jumpin' Joe" Nelson.[28] The first UH–1E arrived at New River four days later. The schedule called for two additional aircraft to be delivered in March and three each month thereafter.[29] By now the order had grown to over 100 helicopters and almost 15 million dollars.[30] General McCutcheon's yo-yo had finally stopped and a replacement for the aging OH–43s and O–1s was on the way.

## Replacement for the HUS

The search for a replacement for the OH–43 was not the only program to be plagued with delays and disagreements. The process of selecting a successor to the UH–34 encountered similar difficulties.

Though the UH–34 was procured only as an interim helicopter in the late 1950s it remained the backbone of Marine vertical lift capability. In 1957 Sikorsky engineers were working on a new model for the Navy. This helicopter would replace the SH–34s utilized for anti-submarine warfare. Designated the HSS–2 (Helicopter, anti-submarine, Sikorsky) (HS–3 under the unified designation system) it was to be powered by two General Electric T–58 free turbine engines, each of which could develop up to 1,050 horsepower. To provide for emergency landings in the water the lower portion of the fuselage was watertight similar to a boat hull. It had a large door on the starboard side of the cabin, a factor that was to have special significance for the Marine Corps.

General Randolph McCaul Pate, Commandant of the Marine Corps, wrote the CNO on 9 January 1958 requesting procurement of modified HSS–2s to replace the UH–34s. In his letter he pointed out the problems of developing helicopters:

USMC Photo A402599

*General Randolph McC. Pate, 21st Commandant of the Marine Corps, began the process of securing a replacement for the UH–34.*

> The Marine Corps concept for amphibious operations is characterized by the utilization of helicopters to give the amphibious attack increased depth, speed, mobility and flexibility.
>
> Implementation of this concept has progressed somewhat slower than anticipated, particularly in the achievement of a helicopter modernity program.[31]

He went on to point out that the HUS (UH–34) procurement:

> . . . through 1961 falls considerably short of the Marine Corps requirement. In order to satisfactorily alleviate this condition it is requested that a transport version of the HSS–2 which is considered the logical replacement for the present light assault helicopter, be programmed and budgeted for the Marine Corps in

sufficient quantity to operationally support a total of 210 helicopters during the 1962-1966 time frame.[32]

General Pate recommended that the transport version of the HSS-2 be designated the HR3S (Helicopter, Transport—3—Sikorsky). The plan envisioned conversion of all six transport and three composite squadrons then in existence from the HUS-1 to the HR3S. No other aircraft was seriously considered for "at this time there appeared to be no other helicopter available which was competitive with it from either cost or technical viewpoint."[33]

Funds for aircraft procurement were short in 1958 and progress on the design of the HR3S was slow. Then, on 29 March 1959, the HSS-2 made its first public flight.[34] Interest in the assault transport version was rekindled. In July 1959 General Pate requested CNO to provide for a full-sized model of the HR3S as soon as possible.[35] This "mock-up" could be utilized to inspect the proposed changes from the anti-submarine version. It was not until November that the Bureau of Aeronautics responded that until a contract had been awarded for the production of the HR3S no funds could be made available for a mock-up.[36]

In the meantime, a careful review of what modifications were desirable was being conducted within the Marine Corps. Of particular importance was the door on the side which had to be used for troops and cargo. Such a configuration would make it difficult to load small vehicles. If a ramp, similar to that installed in the HR2S, could be included in the HR3S, access to the cabin would be improved. Due to the basic design of the HSS-2, a ramp—if adopted—would have to be in the rear of the cabin and would require a significant redesign of the helicopter.

Not all Marines were convinced that such a method of loading was necessary. In August the Marine Corps Landing Force Development Center reported that:

> [The rear ramp] . . . appears to warrant little consideration since our tactics and techniques are emphasizing the use of external loading with the automatic release cargo hook. This leads to the conclusion that the ramp for internal loading is of small and occasional value. This is particularly true when it is recognized that design investigation for including a ramp, and its design and test will considerably extend the time when new machines could be made available to the FMF.[37]

Not only might it not be necessary to modify the side door but even the watertight boat hull of the standard HSS-2 could prove to be an advantage. MCLFDC proposed loading the helicopters in the well decks of amphibious ships. On reaching the objective area, the deck could be flooded, the aircraft floated out, and the blades unfolded. Sea-based helicopters could be used to augment the capacity of the few LPHs then available. MCLFDC did admit that "launching techniques in an open sea condition would have to be evaluated by extensive testing under operational conditions."[38]

As refinements in the design of the HR3S progressed, General Pate continued to press for a mock-up. In November he again requested CNO to provide the necessary funds. This time he was successful and BuWeps was directed "to proceed with the mock-up as expeditiously as possible."[39] On 1 February 1960, $50,000 was provided to "proceed immediately with all actions necessary to complete the mock-up by 15 June."[40]

Guiding the efforts to procure a replacement for the HUS was the Director of Aviation, Major General John C. Munn, a pilot since 1930 and a veteran of the Guadalcanal campaign in World War II. On 1 December 1959 just two weeks before he was promoted and appointed Assistant Commandant of the Marine Corps, he summed up the progress attained in improving the vertical lift program:

> Tentative programmed procurement (is) 70 HUS per year through 1965. Funding support for the HR3S is scheduled during the FY 62 budget cycle with a buy of ten aircraft. Subsequently, the HR3S is included at a rate of 60 per year. This will likely result in an enforced compensatory reduction in the HUS procurement. A mockup of the assault version of the HSS-2 will be conducted in the near future and detailed specifications are in the final draft form.[41]

The officer who replaced General Munn as director of Aviation was Major General Arthur F. Binney. Among his many decorations gained in almost 30 years in the Marine Corps, General Binney was one of the few Marine aviators still on active duty who had been awarded the Nicaraguan Cross of Valor. He had won it in 1932 for frequent flights over dangerous terrain to rescue a detachment of Marines who had become lost in the jungle.

One of his first acts was to publish further information on the HR3S. The design now called for rear ramp loading and a modified hull to permit safe operations in rough water. General Binney calculated that the new helicopter would be capable of lifting up to 23 fully-equipped combat troops, have a speed over 125 knots, and be fully compatible with the LPHs. By utilizing the basic design of the HSS-2, the new assault helicopter would:

> . . . insure a stable long range production run, minimizing the training problem, simplification of logistic support and a unit cost savings to the government which would not be possible had a new development been undertaken to fulfill this requirement.[42]

He concluded that the HR3S "is a prime program" and asked for "support whenever possible and feasible." [43]

Detailed specifications for the new helicopter were published by CNO on 7 March 1960 as Development Characteristic No. A0 1750–2. The document was a further refinement of one published the previous March. Four items were of special significance. A rear loading ramp was to be included, the fuselage was to be capable of landing in water, the helicopter "must be ready for operational evaluation by 1963," and "It is anticipated that the requirements stated in this Development Characteristic will be met by modification of a helicopter that has already been developed." [44] The development characteristic accurately described only the HR3S among aircraft available at the time.

While the design of the assault transport version was in final review, the HSS–2 was being tested by NATC at Patuxent River. Problems were encountered. The helicopter lacked the desired stability. More disturbing, the main transmission was limited to 2,000 horsepower, even though at peak power the engines could produce more. In the event that more powerful engines could be procured in the future, for them to be installed in the HSS–2 would require extensive—and expensive—alterations to the transmission and drive shafts. [45] Finally, Sikorsky engineers were having difficulty modifying the HSS–2 to provide a rear ramp for vehicles. On 29 June they reported that to give the aircraft the necessary balance, the forward fuselage would have to be extended 30 inches. This would take additional time. [46]

Sikorsky's difficulties did not go unnoticed by other manufacturers. In July 1959, before the selection of the HR3S, Vertol Aircraft Corporation had given presentations at Quantico and at HQMC on one of their new models, the 107A.* [47] This helicopter was designed primarily for civilian use. While it had two free turbine engines it had neither a rear ramp nor a blade-folding mechanism. Thus it could not meet all the desired specifications. The 107 was based on an earlier model, the YHC–1A, three of which were procured by the U.S. Army for evaluation. [48]

The Army model more closely met the specifications and had a rear ramp, though its blades would not fold. However, it was still experimental. The basic design would have to be a proven one before the Marine Corps would indicate much enthusiasm. The scars and disappointments of designing and producing a helicopter from the ground up, such as the "Deuce," were still vivid memories.

In late March 1960, with Sikorsky engineers still wrestling with problems in the HSS–2 and designing a ramp for the HR3S, Vertol dispatched a YHC–1A to the Landing Force Development Center at Quantico. Six experienced helicopter pilots conducted short orientation flights and recorded their observations.

Lieutenant Colonel Victor A. Armstrong, later Major General, flew the aircraft from the plant at Philadelphia to Quantico. He described it as "handling very nicely, with control forces being light and appear adequate for all flight attitudes. The stability augmentation system (SAS) is a fine addition to the control system." [49] Lieutenant Colonel Armstrong added that if the Marine Corps were to consider procurement of the YHC–1A, modifications would have to be made to the ramp area. A jeep could fit inside the fuselage but would not clear the doors over the ramp.

Another pilot who expressed enthusiasm was the Quantico Air Station comptroller, Major Fred M. Kleppsattel (who would command HMM–264 during the Dominican Republic crisis in 1965). He already had amassed 2,360 hours of helicopter flight time. He reported that the center of gravity limitation in a tandem configuration such as this aircraft was 60 inches—far superior to a conventional single main rotor helicopter. [50] (The first helicopter procured by the Marine Corps, the Sikorsky H035, had a center of gravity limit of exactly 3.78 inches.) The four other pilots were equally impressed and all reported that the aircraft had excellent potential as a replacement for the HUS.*

A week after the demonstration, on 8 April 1960, Brigadier General William R. Collins, Director of the Landing Force Development Center, forwarded the comments of the pilots and his own analysis to the Commandant. General Collins had just been promoted and had moved from President of the Tactics and Techniques Board to take command of the center. A survivor of the USS *New Orleans* at Pearl Harbor on 7 December 1941, he later would have command of the Marine ground forces at Guantanamo Bay, Cuba during the first critical eight weeks of the 1962 missile crisis. He said,

> It is understood that present plans are to replace the HUS with the HR3S, beginning sometime during the 1962–1963 period. Before the procurement plans for the HR3S reach fruition, I believe we should run an evaluation of its most serious competitor, the Vertol YHC–1A, a forerunner of the Vertol 107M. The 107M has been

---

* The original Piasecki Aircraft had been reorganized in 1956 into Vertol Aircraft Corporation, The name was derived from *VER*tical *T*ake *O*ff and *L*anding.

* The four were: Majors James W. Ferris, Lloyd J. Engelhardt, and Joseph L. Freitas, Jr., and Captain Guy R. Campo.

proposed by the manufacturers as an HUS replacement.⁵¹

After repeating information he had received about the difficulties being encountered by the HSS–2 and emphasizing the findings of the six pilots who had flown the YHC-1A, General Collins concluded that "It is therefore recommended that CNO be requested to conduct a complete test, evaluation, and comparison of the YHC-1A with the HSS–2 before a final decision is made for a follow on helicopter to replace the HUS."⁵² General Snedeker in his endorsement agreed that an evaluation would be "of valuable assistance in expediting further development and procurement in the event the HSS–2/HR3S fails to measure up to specifications."⁵³

BuWeps did not share the enthusiasm of General Collins. On 4 May it outlined its position to General Binney and proposed to proceed with the development of the HR3S.⁵⁴ This information was followed on 7 June 1960 by a presentation by BuWeps to General Shoup. The Navy concluded that "in all these proceedings, the HR3S–1 was shown to be significantly cheaper in total program cost and to have obvious logistic and training advantages. The Vertol 107M, [however], was presented as being fully as adequate technically as the HR3S–1 to accomplish the assault mission."⁵⁵

General Collins was not to be dissuaded. On 1 July he again submitted his side of the issue and disputed the presentation by BuWeps. He continued to press for obtaining one or more 107s for a comparative evaluation.⁵⁶

On 3 June, Vertol requested BuWeps to allow it to submit proposals for a replacement for the HUS. During conferences that month, Vertol was assured that it would receive full consideration for its 107M. The company then requested an opportunity to present a number of demonstrations and analyses for evaluation purposes within a three-month period.⁵⁷ Much of the rest of the summer was spent by both manufacturers strengthening their arguments as to why their particular model was best for the Marine Corps. On 8 September, BuWeps notified General Shoup that it no longer opposed the position first put forward by General Collins and that it "would secure competitive proposals from Sikorsky and Vertol."⁵⁸ Until the evaluation of the two aircraft had been completed, further work on the mockup of the HR3S was halted.⁵⁹

In view of now having two different models competing for the contract, in October the Commandant directed General Collins to review a revised Development Characteristic. It was subsequently published as AO 17501–3 and called for the new aircraft to be ready for operational evaluation by 1 July 1964, one year later than had been originally scheduled.⁶⁰

Between 9 and 17 February 1961, Admiral Stroop reviewed the different proposals. His task was not easy, for "It was through strong and persistent persuasion by Marine aviation that Vertol was selected over Sikorsky which had been the 'front runner' for a considerable period of time." The admiral recalled:

> . . . Sikorsky, of course, had a head start and . . . was favored by the Bureau Evaluators; however, the Marines persisted in their recommendation for Vertol, the CH–46, and since they were to be the operators and users of the aircraft, their recommendations had to have considerable weight and it . . . resulted in obtaining the CH–46 helicopter to be manufactured by Vertol.⁶¹

On 17 February, Admiral Stroop informed the Assistant Secretary of the Navy for Materiel, Kenneth E. Belieu, that the Marines had prevailed and that the recommendation was to purchase the CH–46. Belieu agreed with the choice.⁶²

Late in the afternoon of 20 February, Admiral Stroop made two long distance telephone calls. The first one was to Lee Johnson, General Manager of Sikorsky Aircraft. Stroop advised Johnson that "Vertol and not Sikorsky had won the HRX competition and that a press release would be issued in a few minutes," at 1730 Washington time. The second call was made to Don Berlin, Vice President and General Manager of Vertol Division, Boeing Airplane Company.* After informing him that Vertol had won the competition, Admiral Stroop extended his congratulations.⁶³

Stroop now had to obtain official acceptance of the contract offer from Secretary of the Navy Fred Korth. Belieu wrote a letter giving the rationale for the decision:

> The choice as to the prime contractor is sound on the basis of operational requirements, technical characteristics (Vertol far excels Sikorsky in this field) and cost wise. As far as cost is concerned our long-range program contemplates 194 aircraft at a total cost of $271 million. By year, the approximate breakdown is as follows:
> 14 helicopters in the '62 buy.
> 60 for each year thereafter.
> On the basis of the estimated cost per lot, Vertol is about $2.5 million lower.⁶⁴

Admiral Stroop personally carried the Assistant Secretary's recommendation to the office of the Secretary of the Navy, "with the thought that I would obtain immediate approval." Stroop felt that quick ap-

---

* The original Vertol Aircraft Company had been purchased by Boeing. In May 1961, Boeing Airplane Company changed its own name to The Boeing Company.

*Colonel Marion E. Carl, Deputy Chief of Staff (Air), receives a painting from representatives of Vertol Division, The Boeing Company, in June 1962, on the occasion of Marine Corps acceptance of the Vertol aircraft as the new medium transport. Colonel Carl was one of the first Marine helicopter pilots, having learned to fly them in July 1945.*

proval was important for two reasons: 'First, we had already experienced considerable delay while Vertol was catching up with Sikorsky; and, in addition, we had a very good price offer from Vertol which would expire in just a few days." The admiral pointed out that the lower price of the Vertol offer was about to expire and advised Secretary Korth that "if he would simply initial the recommendation for Vertol I would carry it back to my office and the procurement would be under way." [65]

For once the Navy was not going to have difficulty in obtaining timely release of the funds required for the initial purchase of helicopters for the Marine Corps, for even as Admiral Stroop and Assistant Secretary Belieu were recommending Vertol as the winner of the competition, they were discussing methods to provide the company with procurement funds ahead of schedule. The first 14 aircraft normally would have been purchased with $21.8 million of FY 62 funds which would not have been available until 1 July. BuWeps, however, had $14.5 million left from FY 61 programs and proposed that it be released to Vertol as soon as possible to take advantage of the low-cost contract.[66]

Apparently unknown to the Marines or Admiral Stroop, two weeks before the recommendation was delivered to Secretary Korth, on 2 February, President Kennedy had ordered all the military services to explore ways to expedite contracts to manufacturers located in areas of high unemployment.[67] The Vertol manufacturing plant was located in Morton, Pennsylvania, a suburb of Philadelphia, and could qualify for the President's program. It was surprising to Admiral Stroop, then, that when he asked Secretary Korth to initial the contract immediately, "the Secretary decided that his staff should study the problem further and to my considerable disappointment, did not give his final approval until after Vertol's offer had expired." The helicopters built at Morton would carry the higher price tag.[68]

## The CH-46

Both the YHC-1A and the Model 107 were based on earlier designs by Frank Piasecki. He had considerable success utilizing two main rotors mounted in a tandem (one on each end of the aircraft) configuration. Since the rotors turned in opposite directions, lift was partially equalized on each side of the aircraft and there was no need for an anti-torque rotor.

The redesign of the 107 into what was originally called the HRB-1 (Helicopter, Transport, Boeing) for the Marine Corps required major modifications. The most pressing one was to install a rotor blade folding mechanism. Without it the helicopter could not operate from amphibious assault ships.

This modification was not an easy task, for the basic 107 design had fully-articulated rotor heads. Thus any addition of weight for a blade fold system would require major revisions of the entire rotor. These modifications in turn would make it necessary to strengthen the transmissions and those parts of the fuselage to which they were attached. Vertol, however, was successful in designing an electrically operated system in which the blades from both the forward and aft rotor heads folded inward and were stored above the center of the aircraft.

The second problem revolved around what Lieutenant Colonel Armstrong noted on the initial orientation flights of the YHC—1A at Quantico. The rear ramp and doors had to be increased in size to permit entry of a jeep. Such change required careful engineering, for the fuselage of an aircraft is much like the shell of an egg. As long as the shell is fully intact, it retains a remarkable amount of strength for its weight. But if a hole is cut into the shell, the strength is quickly lost. Any widening of the rear door would have to be compensated for by greatly increasing the strength of the surrounding fuselage.

The final problem was that new models of the T-58 free turbine were to be installed which could produce more power than the ones in the 107. The greater power was certainly desirable, but it required even more redesign. Most critical were the drive shafts from the two jet engines to the main transmission. These "high speed" shafts had to be balanced precisely. At the speed they were turning, the slightest vibration would create massive strain on the aircraft. All helicopters were subjected to vibration, particularly from a fully articulated rotor head, but the large and relatively slow bumps and thumps from such a source while uncomfortable, did not seriously affect the aircraft. High frequency vibration was another matter for the stress produced was determined by the square of the vibration.*

The engineers at Vertol had their work cut out for them. What finally emerged on 30 April 1962, when the Navy accepted the first aircraft for testing, superficially resembled the YHC-1A and the 107 but was basically an entirely new helicopter.

The CH-46, as the HRB-1 was known under the unified designation system, had two 50-foot, contra-rotating rotors mounted on pylons, directly over the cockpit and the extreme rear of the aircraft.[69] The rotors overlapped each other at the center of the aircraft for a distance of 16 feet. To prevent the blades from striking each other in this overlap area, the two rotors were interconnected by a carefully geared drive shaft.

With the blades folded for movement on the deck of an LPH, the aircraft measured slightly less than 45 feet long and 15 feet wide. With them extended, the aircraft was 83 feet long. The cargo compartment had no obstructions throughout its 24-foot length to hinder the entry of vehicles and troops. It was almost perfectly six feet square. This clean cabin was made possible by the use of small stub wings or sponsons attached to the outside of the fuselage. They doubled as fuel tanks and mounting points for the main landing gear. The sponsons also added stability if the aircraft were landed in the water, for which provisions had been incorporated.

When viewed from the side the CH-46 had two very distinct features. The nose landing gear was much longer than the main ones and gave the aircraft the appearance of squatting down to the rear with the rear tail pylon towering over the rest of the aircraft.

---

* For those engineering minded, the formula is: G (Forces produced) = K (a constant) $\times$ F (frequency)$^2$ $\times$ A (amplitude).

*The CH–46A became the replacement for the UH–34. This aircraft is lifting a 1,780-pound "Mighty-Mite" vehicle on its 10,000-pound-capacity external cargo hook.*

In the aft pylon were both General Electric T–58–8B free-turbine engines and the main transmission. Each engine was connected to the transmission through other gear boxes by individual high-speed drive shafts. Another shaft was placed outside, along the top of the fuselage, and connected the front transmission to the one in the rear. Also in the pylon were the auxiliary power unit (a small jet engine which provided electrical and hydraulic power when the rotors were not turning) and other accessories required by the aircraft. To solve the problem of the bulk of the basic machinery of the aircraft being located directly above the enlarged hole in the egg shell created by expanding the opening for the ramp, the Vertol engineers designed what was essentially a shelf extending rearward from the back of the cabin over the ramp doors. The engines, main transmission, and other equipment were mounted on this platform.

Empty, the CH–46 weighed 11,641 pounds and with 2,400 pounds of fuel and a crew of three was designed to carry either 4,000 pounds of cargo or 17 combat-equipped Marines. Under emergency overload condition, the cargo capacity could be increased to almost 7,000 pounds.[70] Its top speed was 137 knots.

A helicopter which had undergone such an extensive redesign of almost all critical parts as had the 107 to create the CH–46 would require exhaustive testing. Any new aircraft normally encountered areas which would need further refinement and the CH–46 was to be no exception.

The initial flight, which had been scheduled in June 1962, was delayed four months and was not completed until 16 October.[71] The first eight aircraft all were scheduled for the test program. The next six were to be delivered to operating units for initial training of crews.[72]

The first phase of the Navy Preliminary Evaluation (NPE) for the new helicopter was conducted by Patuxent River personnel at the Vertol plant in Morton during the period 14 through 30 January 1963. The changes from the 107 had created new factors in the CH-46. Lieutenant Colonel Perry P. McRoberts reported the results. "The 107 prototype helicopter was very smooth. It was known prior to testing that the additional mass distribution to the rotor heads for the . . . automatic blade folding system would cause vibrations." They were, he noted, "excessively high in all flight regimes."[73] The vibrations from the blade fold system, however, were of low frequency. They made for an uncomfortable ride but imposed little stress on the aircraft. More serious were other vibrations.

There had been "difficulty in assuring proper alignment in the high speed engine shafts. During the testing the aircraft involved was realigned each night to insure proper balance. This problem is related to the [other] vibration problem. Improved methods for realigning are also under study."[74] Any misalignment of the shafts could create extremely high frequency vibrations which could impose serious stress on the aircraft.

The problems were neither unusual nor unexpected. Lieutenant Colonel McRoberts ended his report on a note of optimism: "In spite of the apparent seriousness of some of the items listed above, the inspection team summarized that the evaluation was successful and the momentum generated toward correction of the . . . deficiencies was outstanding."[75]

As the design and testing of the CH-46 continued, the Marine Corps made final plans for the introduction of the new helicopter. In March 1962, Colonel Marion Carl, the Director of Aviation, outlined the program for the next five years. Starting in FY 1963, each year a new CH-46 squadron was to be commissioned until four were formed. (This was the same expansion which had caused General Shoup to be wary of the introduction of Marine helicopters into Vietnam.) In addition during the same period of time, each year one UH-34 squadron would be equipped with the CH-46. According to Colonel Carl's plan the conversion would be complete by FY 1970. At that time, all the UH-34s would have been taken out of service and each of the 15 medium transport squadrons would be operating 24 CH-46s.[76]

The goal for the end of FY 68 was 10 CH-46 squadrons with five other units operating at reduced strength of UH-34s. Procurement of the first 14 CH-46s was now scheduled to be completed in November 1963. Starting the next month, aircraft were to be produced at an initial rate of one per month and increase to five per month in December 1964. By 1967 it was estimated that the manufacturer could produce 96 helicopters per year until conversion was complete.[77]

*Number of Medium Transport Helicopter Squadrons and Type of Aircraft*

|         | HRB (CH-46) | HUS (UH-34) | Total |
|---------|-------------|-------------|-------|
| FY 1962 | 0           | 11          | 11    |
| FY 1963 | 0           | 12          | 12    |
| FY 1964 | 2           | 11          | 13    |
| FY 1965 | 4           | 10          | 14    |
| FY 1966 | 6           | 9           | 15    |
| FY 1967 | 8           | 7           | 15    |
| FY 1968 | 10          | 5           | 15    |

While the build up of the CH-46s was underway, the venerable UH-34 would continue to be purchased until sufficient numbers of the new helicopter could be produced. Not until January 1964 was the Marine Corps to stop receiving the "Huss."

The original schedule required that four CH-46s be delivered in September 1963 for the Fleet Introduction Program (FIP).[78] Additional helicopters were to be available in January 1964. Almost as soon as testing of the aircraft had begun, there was a revision in the time table. In January 1963 BuWeps concluded that the target date a year hence might have to be changed to May, although production was expected to catch up a few months later.[79]

The new design of the CH-46 continued to plague the engineers. The fifth test aircraft was four months late in being delivered and the sixth was provisionally accepted on 24 July, six months behind the original schedule.[80]

The delays centered around the vibration caused by the blade-fold mechanism and the high-speed shafts. At the end of December, NATC reported that the helicopter had successfully passed all portions of phase three of the preliminary evaluation, but it considered "improved vibration levels mandatory for Bureau of Inspection and Survey" trials.[81] Vertol had, however, "on a high priority basis made progress."[82] It was a vexing problem. Several different modifications were attempted. Finally, the last week in August 1964, a solution was found and it was concluded that "NATC flights indicate satisfactory vibration levels for unrestricted Fleet Release."[83]

*CH–46 Helicopters in Operational Squadrons and Total Inventory Assigned.* [79]

| Per End of FY | CH–46 | | UH–34 | |
| --- | --- | --- | --- | --- |
| | Oper* | Inv | Oper | Inv |
| 1962 | 1 | 1 | 278 | 347 |
| 1963 | 10 | 10 | 342 | 402 |
| 1964 | 24 | 31 | 300 | 415 |
| 1965 | 62 | 75 | 283 | 374 |
| 1966 | 109 | 133 | 251 | 311 |
| 1967 | 166 | 203 | 211 | 261 |
| 1968 | 230 | 280 | 155 | 184 |
| 1969 | 249 | 304 | 112 | 118 |
| 1970 | 227 | 277 | 46 | 47 |
| 1971 | 198 | 242 | 9 | 9 |
| 1972 | | | 0 | 0 |

* The difference between operational helicopters and total inventory compensate for aircraft undergoing PAR.

As General McCutcheon was to explain to the Commandant, the engineers had reduced the cockpit vibration to "acceptable limits by the installation of three absorbers. The absorbers constitute a weight reduction in payload of approximately 355 pounds." [84] The loss in lift capability was unfortunate but it represented another example of the difficulties in designing a helicopter.

Even before the absorbers had been agreed on as the solution, on 30 June, the first three CH–46s were delivered to Lieutenant Colonel Eldon C. Stanton's HMM–265 at New River. Stanton, a fighter pilot during the Okinawa campaign in World War II, thus became the first Marine officer to command a squadron of CH–46s.[85] During Operation STEELPIKE in the fall of 1964, his squadron remained at New River converting to the new medium helicopter.

The day after Stanton's unit received its first CH–46s, on 1 July, a second squadron of the aircraft was activated at Santa Ana. This unit, HMM–164, was commissioned under Lieutenant Colonel Herbert J. Blaha. The continued difficulties with vibration and delays in production at Vertol, however, held up delivery of CH–46s to Blaha's squadron until 21 December. In the meantime, his crews operated UH–34s. By mid-1965, HMM–164 had received 23 CH–46s and was engaged in intensive training.

Over six years after General Pate first had recommended a replacement for the interim HUS, the Marine Corps had a medium helicopter that increased the total lift capability without reducing seriously the numbers of other aircraft. The wait was worth it.

## The VH–3A

Ironically the helicopter that had first triggered off the long selection process and which was rejected in favor of the CH–46 still would end up in the Marine Corps. The HSS–2 had first flown on 11 March 1959. As an anti-submarine warfare aircraft, for which it was originally built, it was a very successful design. In the fall of 1961, the HSS–2 set the first of a series of records that culminated on 5 February 1962 when the helicopter became the first officially to exceed 200 miles per hour by logging 210.6 miles per hour over a 19-kilometer course at Windsor Locks, Connecticut. One of the pilots was Marine Captain L. Kenneth Keck, a test pilot at NATC who was later presented the American Helicopter Society's annual Frederick L. Feinberg award for outstanding achievement in helicopters.

In July 1961, Admiral Stroop of BuWeps had received a memorandum from the Secretary of the Navy requesting more modern aircraft than the UH–34s then in use to carry the President and other dignitaries. The Secnav suggested that either the HRB (CH–46) or the HSS–2 would be suitable as both had the additional safety factor of two engines.[86]

Admiral Stroop recommended a version of the HSS–2. In 1962 Sikorsky built eight of these "executive mission" models, with half going to the Army, the others to the Marine Corps. In April 1962 HMX–1 received the first one. Like the predecessor UH–34 White Tops, it contained special electronics and safety features and was fitted with an executive interior. Under the unified designation system, the aircraft became a V (executive) H (helicopter) 3. Over the years it has become a familiar sight to television viewers as the Marines take off and land on the White House lawn.

The ill-fated HR3S, while not suitable for the Marine Corps, was to find new life from an unexpected source. In December 1962, the U. S. Air Force purchased 22 of them for long-range search and rescue missions.[87]

*The VH-3A was the executive mission version of the CH-3. Marines of HMX-1 flew the President in these aircraft, including "Marine One," here taxiing for takeoff at El Toro MCAS in July 1970.*

These helicopters, which had been designed originally for the Marine Corps, were well known to most Marine helicopter pilots in Vietnam, albeit with the U. S. Air Force insignia painted on the side.

## The VTOLS

> There is much potential worth in an aircraft which can hover as efficiently as a helicopter. If we further supplement this hovering ability with the capacity for achieving great speed and carrying heavy loads, we can see that such a hypothetical aircraft would most certainly be a tool of prodigious capability for the military planner.
>
> Lieutenant Commander James R. Williford, USN
> Head, Vertical, and Short Takeoff and
> Landing Branch, Flight Test Division
> Naval Air Test Center
> Patuxent River, Md.[68]

There was never any question that another helicopter would be selected to replace the HOK and the UH-34. In the case of the HR2S the choice was not so obvious.

All helicopters are classified as Vertical Take Off and Landing machines (VTOL, often pronounced "vee-tall"), but not all VTOL aircraft are helicopters. Paralleling the development of early helicopters had been a similar effort in other types of aircraft, which had the same takeoff and landing characteristics. By the late 1950s sufficient progress had been made to indicate that a major breakthrough in non-helicopter VTOL aircraft was within grasp.

Superficially most of these aircraft appeared similar to a normal fixed-wing machine, but in a variety of designs, they were capable of making vertical climbs and descents. Some utilized wings which would swivel 90 degrees from horizontal. The engines then pointed straight up and acted much like the rotor on a helicopter. After the aircraft was safely airborne it could make the transition into normal forward flight by moving the wings and engines back to a conventional position. Other designs had just the engines tilt, leaving the wings stationary. Some designs had the engines inside shrouds to improve the lift capability; some had propellors; some had jet engines from which the blast could be directed downward for take off and landing * Regardless of the particular design, each of the aircraft had one distinctive advantage over helicopters: Once engaged in normal forward flight, they could carry heavier loads at faster speeds because the wings, not a rotor, carried the weight.

In a rotor system, the tip of the blade—which is passing through the air faster than any other portion of the aircraft — encountered serious aerodynamic problems as it approached the speed of sound. Due to this effect, the helicopter was normally limited to speeds of less than 200 knots. A winged VTOL aircraft was not. The biggest problem in such a hybrid design was producing enough lift to permit vertical climbs and descents. No system had been created which equalled

---

* The latter system is utilized in the Marine Corps' AV-8 "Harrier."

the efficiency of a rotor blade of a helicopter for vertical flight.

A compromise solution was the "compound" helicopter. In this design, short wings were attached to what was otherwise a conventional helicopter. At high speeds the wings produced lift and relieved the rotor of some of the load. Under those circumstances, the rotor could turn more slowly than would be necessary in a craft not equipped with wings. This in turn permitted higher speeds for the aircraft. The increase, however, was not as great as that in a winged VTOL, because, as the speed increased even more, the rotor blades once again would have to spin at maximum speed just to keep from producing drag. The compound helicopter, while an improvement, was not enough to warrant the extra complexity.

In 1956 the Marine Corps "could foresee the requirement for a follow on aircraft for the HR2S."[89] In spite of the foresight, 1956 was a time of extremely limited funds and with the much-ballyhooed HR2S finally becoming operational, it was an inauspicious year to discuss a replacement. Two years later the situation suddenly changed. In response to a request in early 1958 by the Joint Coordination Committee on Piloted Aircraft (which was disbanded shortly thereafter) of the Office of the Secretary of Defense, BuWeps conducted a study of the feasibility for a VTOL aircraft which could satisfy requirements of the Air Force, the Army, the Navy, and the Marine Corps for a medium-sized transport aircraft. Major General John C. Munn, Director of Aviation, reported that the study showed "conclusively that it was technically feasible and practical to develop a pressure jet convertiplane [winged VTOL] which would meet all requirements."[90]

The Air Force and Army soon dropped out of the program. The Air Force required a "750 mile radius ... for rescue aircraft"[91] and was unwilling to pursue a development program for an aircraft that did not possess at least this range. The Army withdrew for a different reason. Instead of a winged VTOL transport it decided to develop another helicopter with a three-ton payload capability.* "The Department of Defense reluctantly authorized the Army to proceed with such a program but agreed that the Navy-Marine Corps position of developing a convertiplane was sound."[92] Although the Air Force and the Army were not going to participate, General Munn said, "We should push this program as fast as we can ... welcoming the Army aboard at any point along the route."[93]

---

* This program resulted in the CH-47 "Chinook" built by Vertol.

The development characteristic, entitled VTOL Assault Transport, AO 17501-1 was approved and published by the CNO on 16 March, 1959. It was based on a compound helicopter. In FY 60, $350,000 was provided for initial studies. This money was followed the next year by a request for $2.6 million to complete the initial competition and start procurement of the aircraft to be utilized for testing.

> BuWeps then made a recommendation to CNO that the program would be too expensive for a single service development. Further, that the interim step of obtaining a compound helicopter was unnecessary and efforts should be directed toward a sophisticated VTOL transport. As a result, the funds were reprogrammed and efforts were directed toward a tri-service [Army, Air Force, Navy and Marine Corps] VTOL program.[94]

The specifications developed for this new joint project called for an aircraft which could cruise up to 250 knots. This effectively ruled out a compound helicopter. Like it or not, the Marine Corps would have to look to the tri-service program for a replacement of the aging HR2S.

Three VTOL aircraft eventually were designed and tested. The Vought-Hiller-Ryan XC-142A was initially ordered to make a full evaluation of a four-ton payload transport. The aircraft relied on four General Electric T-64 turbo-prop engines mounted on a tilting wing. They produced sufficient power to allow vertical take offs and landings. Once airborne, the wing moved to a conventional position for forward flight. The first successful transition from VTOL to forward flight was not made until January 1965.[95]

Another system was utilized by the Curtiss X-19A. In this aircraft only the engines tilted while the wing remained in a fixed position. The X-19 was not designed as a transport but was built "to support technology development of other promising concepts."[96]

The final aircraft was the Bell X-22A. It was to be utilized to test missions other than transport. This design had four large propellers installed inside shrouds or ducts. Each fan was mounted on the ends of small wings extending out from the front and rear of the aircraft. Four General Electric T-58 turbine engines were interconnected to the propellers. By tilting the fans, sufficient lift could be produced for VTOL and forward flight.[97]

Even as the competition began, General Greene realized that it would end with nothing more than a prototype for further development and in October 1960 concluded that "the tri-service could not possibly provide a timely follow-on for the HR2S."[98] Simultaneously a new Development Characteristic (AO-17501-3) was prepared calling for a conventional helicopter to replace the "Deuces." Later the winner of the VTOL evaluation was to be the tilt-winged

XC-142A, but it was found "unsuitable for Navy use" and the Navy withdrew from the program in August 1961.[99]

General Greene continued his search for a conventional helicopter. The prescribed characteristics of the new helicopter were very similar to those first proposed for the fixed-wing VTOL. An 8000-pound payload was to be carried over a radius of 100 nautical miles. A helicopter, however, would be unable to meet the original speed requirement so that requirement was revised to a cruise speed of 150 knots. The Development Characteristic was submitted to CNO in October 1960 and approved and published 27 March the next year.

The tri-service VTOL program had delayed the replacement of the HR2S by several years. It was becoming imperative that new aircraft be provided, for by the end of 1961 there were only 29 "Deuces" left in operation. The search for a new helicopter, however, was finally underway.

## The CH-53

Colonel McCutcheon, Director of Aviation, was hopeful.

> The . . . big void in our inventory is the large helicopter. The follow-on to the HR2S is referred to as the HH(X) [Helicopter, heavy, experimental] It is anticipated that BuWeps will go out to industry some time soon in order to complete the evaluation . . . before [July 1962.][100]

On 7 March, BuWeps invited interested manufacturers to submit bids for the replacement for the HR2S. Since time was running short, all proposals had to be based on a helicopter then in existence. Three responded. Kaman Aircraft had initially intended to propose a version of the British-built Fairey Rotodyne. Unable to reach a successful arrangement with Rotodyne, it dropped out of the competition. The two bids received 7 May were from the arch rivals, Vertol and Sikorsky.

Vertol made two separate proposals, both based on the CH-47 "Chinook" it was producing for the U.S. Army. The CH-47 retained the typical tandem rotor configuration of the original Piasecki design. From a distance it resembled the CH-46, though it was half again as large and, in fact, a completely different aircraft. The primary bid from Vertol was to redesign the CH-47 to meet the requirements of the Marine Corps, in a program similar to that which had converted the 107 to the CH-46. New engines, rotors, transmissions, and other components would have to be designed and installed.

Their second proposal was to make the minimum modifications to a CH-47. Blade folding and a rotor brake would be added. Since the aircraft was too tall to fit on the hangar deck of an LPH, the landing gear was to be redesigned so that the helicopter could "kneel down" to insure sufficient clearance. The necessary modifications would weigh enough to reduce the payload capability to 6,000 pounds, a loss which was unacceptable. The minimum proposal was not considered further.[101]

The aircraft proposed by Sikorsky was a direct descendent of the HR2S. The difficulties in designing and manufacturing that giant helicopter had provided the engineers with a wealth of knowledge and at the conclusion of the final refinements of the HR2S, Sikorsky had taken the new-found techniques and applied them to a series of "flying cranes." The crane helicopter was not a new idea. Hughes Aircraft, Piasecki, as well as other manufacturers had all proposed versions. Such a machine had no cabin for passengers or cargo. Instead, only the mechanical components of the helicopter were included along with a small cockpit for the crew. The weight saved by not building a large fuselage could be converted into additional payload which was to be carried externally underneath the aircraft.

The Marine Corps from the start of its development of helicopters had showed interest in such a crane. In 1951 it stated requirements for a "medium and a heavy" cargo lifter with payloads of 25,000 and 50,000 pounds.[102] They were obviously beyond the capability of any designer at the time. Sikorsky, however, continued to pursue the idea. In 1959, at the request of the Navy, it had modified the basic structure of the "Deuce" just enough to manufacture one true "crane" version. Called the S-60, it first flew on 25 March.[103]

In June the Marine Corps expressed interest in the S-60.[104] The S-60, unfortunately, was equipped with the same piston engines as the HR2S. The weight-to-power ratio continued to frustrate designers in their attempts to make a break-through in lift capability. The next version still retained the basic design of the "Deuce" but now was powered by jet engines. Sikorsky designated it the S-64. It was a commercial success. In 1962 Sikorsky proposed as an HHX for the Marine Corps essentially the S-64 with cargo and passenger cabin built back on. The evolution of the "Deuce" had come full circle.

On 26 July Admiral Stroop received approval of BuWeps selection of a new heavy helicopter. This time Sikorsky was the winner. The decision had been based on both technical and production capability factors and—even more important—costs. For research and development for the series, and construction of four aircraft for testing, the winning bid was $15 million.

*The Sikorsky S–60 "Flying Crane," a development from the HR2S, sitting on the field at Quantico in September 1959, became, with later modifications, the ancestor of the CH–53.*

Then in one of the typically frustrating moments in the development of helicopters in the Marine Corps, part of the expected funding was withdrawn.[105] Colonel Hollowell, who was managing the HHX program as well as the UH–1E, reported BuWeps "was now in the position of having sent out requests for proposals, having evaluated and determined that one of the bidders had won, and yet not having enough money" to award the contract.[106]

Because of the funding situation, Colonel Hollowell "was forced to inform Sikorsky that although they had won the competition, we could not do business with them unless they lowered their proposal on the initial research and development program from $15 million to $10 million because we only had $10 million to spend."[107]

The chief of Staff, General Greene, was hardly pleased with the impasse. On 14 August 1962 he wrote the CNO that:

> it is understood that the evaluation of the HHX proposals has been completed by the Bureau of Naval Weapons. The announcement of the results of the evaluation, initially expected in June 1962, continues to slip. It is requested that the announcement of the results of the competition be made as soon as possible in order that steps may be taken . . . to get the program moving again.[108]

Sikorsky had been stung when it had lost the HR3S contract to Vertol. With the HSS–2 and HUS contracts coming to an end, its production lines would be almost vacant if it did not have the HHX contract. Its engineers went to work "with a very sharp pencil" and rebid the research and development contract for $9,995,635.00."[109] Instead of four aircraft for initial tests, only two would be built. On 24 September 1962 the Department of Defense officially announced that Sikorsky had won the competition to design the HHX.[110] The helicopter would be known as the CH–53A.

General Greene and Colonel Hollowell were not alone in their frustration at not getting the CH–53 program off to a speedy start. The new Deputy Chief of Staff (Air), Brigadier General Norman J. Anderson, was about to join them.*

Before being appointed an aviation cadet in 1936, General Anderson had received his degree and had completed graduate work in history. He was designated a naval aviator in 1937 and served at Quantico until April 1940 when his active duty period expired. He continued flying as a pilot for American Airlines. When World War II started, he rejoined the Marine Corps and flew combat operations in the Pacific and Korea, and later in Vietnam.

Five days before the official announcement on the CH–53 contract, he had received a letter which indicated that all FY 64 funds for procurement of production models of the heavy helicopter were to be deleted by the Navy comptroller. The basis was a Navy policy of buying initial test and evaluation aircraft with research and development funds only.[111] The initial aircraft for test and evaluation, Anderson responded, had been properly purchased. The FY 64 funds were for helicopters to be assigned to Marine units. "If follow-on procurement funds are not avail-

---

* In reorganization of HQMC in 1962, the Director of Aviation was retitled Deputy Chief of Staff (Air). The duties remained the same.

able in FY 64 there will be a one-year gap in the production line. The price to the Navy cannot be retained with such a major delay in the program."[112]

General Anderson went on to point out that the program had been approved by Secretary of Defense, Chief of Naval Operations, Secretary of the Navy and all other authorities. In addition, the CH–53 was not a totally new design based on the "crane" version. "The aircraft being procured is a modified, off-the-shelf design. A full R&D effort, as for a new helicopter, was neither planned nor funded." The introduction of the CH–53 into tactical units already had slipped one year because of funding difficulties. Any such action as proposed by the Navy comptroller would further delay it. General Anderson had made his point. Even though funds were difficult to obtain, the planned procurement remained for the moment at 2 aircraft in FY 63, 16 in FY 64, and 18 in FY 65.[113]

There was no mistaking the ancestor of the CH–53. It was obviously the "Deuce." The dimensions were almost identical.[114] The new helicopter was equipped with the familiar 72-foot-diameter main rotor and an anti-torque rotor on the tail similar to that of its predecessor. Close inspection of the transmission and drive trains revealed that they were improved and refined versions of the same systems over which Sikorsky had labored so long 10 years earlier. Two General Electric T–64–GE–6 engines were mounted on either side of the main transmission, although unlike those of the HR2S they were not on stub wings but attached directly to the fuselage.

It was the fuselage which created a distinct appearance. The requirement for a rear loading ramp instead of nose doors had resulted in a cockpit that was in a more normal position. The ramp also required that the tail pylon extend out directly from the top of the cabin area so that vehicles and troops leaving the aircraft could avoid the tail rotor.

Each of the jet engines could produce up to a maximum of 2,850 horsepower for 10 minutes and was rated at 2,270 for continuous operation. In a normal assault mission over a radius of 100 nautical miles, the helicopter could carry 8,000 pounds either in the 30-foot cabin, or externally.

An unusual feature of the design of the CH–53 was capacity for non-stop flights of over 1,500 nautical miles. By filling the cargo compartment with special fuel tanks over 25,275 pounds could be carried. The helicopter could not hover at the resulting gross weight of 25 tons, and needed a runway to take off, but such a range opened new horizons in the employment of the CH–53. The cargo compartment also could carry 38 assault troops, or alternately, 24 litter patients.

Like the HR2S, the new helicopter had landing gear which would retract, a power-operated ramp, and an automatic power blade folding system. The latter was a highly improved version of that which had been first designed for the Deuce. It proved much more reliable, and the geysers of red hydraulic fluid which had so entertained observers of the HR2S became forgotten history. Originally rated as having a top speed of 168 knots, later improvements boosted the CH–53 into the select group of helicopters to exceed 200.

But before the design of the new heavy helicopter had even progressed beyond initial drawings, it appeared for a moment that the entire program was once again in jeopardy. On 12 July 1963, the Secretary of Defense questioned why the Army had ordered the CH–47 Chinook and the Marine Corps the CH–53. Would not a single type be less costly? General Anderson was quick to respond. He and the Army repeated the earlier arguments as to why the need for shipborne

USMC Photo A412901

*The CH–53A was the largest, most powerful helicopter in the Marine Corps when it was introduced in the fall of 1966.*

operations made the CH–47 unsuited unless extensive and expensive modifications were incorporated.[115] Some members of the Office of the Secretary of Defense (OSD) staff were slow to see the difference. In August they deferred all funds for the FY 64 procurement. These were to be the 16 helicopters built after the first two used in testing. If production dates were to be met, the funds would have to be made available prior to 15 September. On 10 September, OSD was still pondering the difference between the Chinook and the CH–53.[116]

Two days before the deadline, OSD agreed that the requirements of the Army and the Marine Corps were different and could not be met by a single type of helicopter. Colonel Robert L. Cochran (commanding officer of MAG–26 during the Cuban crisis), who had replaced Colonel Hollowell, was able to order the 16 aircraft.[117]

The seeming lack of understanding of OSD points out that the road from Marine combat units first establishing a requirement for a new helicopter, to the time when the finished machine is performing in the field, is a long and difficult one. Not only does every factor of funding, selection, development of tactics, and training of personnel have to be carefully coordinated, but even the machine itself has to have each part completely compatible with every other one.

A brief look at some of the problems encountered by Sikorsky in building the CH–53 gives some indication of the difficulties encountered in developing a new aircraft.[118]

The cutbacks in production suffered by Sikorsky in 1960 and 1961 had resulted in many skilled workers and engineers being laid off. With the announcement of the CH–53 contract, Sikorsky tried to reassemble its development team, but many of the former members had found permanent employment elsewhere. It takes years to train such workers and engineers and Sikorsky was hard pressed to find new ones. Two months after the award the company already was reporting severe manpower shortages. Sikorsky had been caught in the boom and bust cycles of defense-related industries. The shortage of engineers, particularly in the airframe design department, was to plague the CH–53. Blueprints were constantly late and Sikorsky was forced to go to other manufacturers to assist it in the design effort.

By March 1963, the company realized that changes in the original concept of the aircraft might increase the weight. In November it was estimated that the helicopter would be 725 pounds heavier than the desired target. The next month a decision was made to replace the steel main rotor head with one just as strong but 500 pounds lighter made of titanium. This and other changes reduced the weight back to acceptable limits but required further design efforts by the already hard-pressed engineers.

Like most major manufacturers, Sikorsky subcontracted the building of many parts of its aircraft to other companies. A late delivery or production difficulties in any one of the subcontractors could cause serious delays throughout the program. As design was progressing, individual components were put through rigorous testing. Occasionally one would be found not compatible with the others and another redesign would have to begin.

The first flight of the CH–53 was originally scheduled for 1 June 1964. Shortages of parts from subcontractors and of government-furnished equipment aggravated the difficulties and the date was repeatedly postponed. The first aircraft to roll off the assembly line was accepted by Sikorsky Flight Test Division on 28 May 1964. It would undergo further testing prior to flight. By October, flight test personnel were working six days a week for a total of 53 hours attempting to improve the schedule. Finally on 14 October a CH–53 took to the air. It was actually the second of the two test aircraft built (Bureau Number 151614) as the other was still undergoing ground tests.*

Sikorsky would continue to struggle to meet deadlines for the next three years. The task was to be complicated by increasing orders from the Marine Corps and U.S. and foreign services for the CH–53 and other helicopters. The company experience was no different, and possibly a little bit better, than other manufacturers of aircraft. The design and production of the CH–53, however, amply illustrates the complexity of developing any new helicopter for the Marine Corps.

In August 1965 the next step in that development was ready. By this time the aircraft was also known as the "Sea Stallion," a name selected personally by the twenty-third commandant, General Greene.[119] The Naval Preliminary Evaluation (NPE) uncovered only a few problems. The most aggravating was a strong shimmy in the nose wheel. The solution was elusive but one was finally devised.

The evaluation included tests on board amphibious ships. No LPHs were available so the USS *Lake Champlain* (CVS–39) was pressed into service in March of 1966. A CH–53 was flown from the plant at Bridgeport, Connecticut, to the ship at nearby Naval Air Station, Quonset Point, Rhode Island. Among the helicopter crew for the tests were Lieutenant Colonel Joseph L. Sadowski, who was later to be commanding officer of the first CH–53 squadron in

---

* BuNo 151614 was subsequently destroyed 2 February 1966 in a freakish accident. Its loss created another delay.

combat, and Master Sergeants C. A. Lamarr and J. A. Reid.[120] No problems were encountered.

The same month NPE was completed. The next step was the Board of Inspection and Survey trials held at Patuxent River. They began 2 June and ended 8 October 1966. Other than a continued shortage of parts and skilled workers at the Sikorsky plant, the BIS trials indicated that the CH–53 was back on track. Rear Admiral Robert L. Townsend, Commander of the Naval Air Systems Command (NavAirSysCom), was briefed by his staff that "reports from the BIS board have shown that the CH–53A completion of BIS was superior to that of any fixed wing or rotary wing aircraft that has been tested at Patuxent River during the past three years."*[121]

The original plan was for a total of 106 CH–53s. Of these 32 would be allowed for aircraft undergoing PAR and normal attrition from accidents. The remaining 74 would be distributed to all five air stations having helicopter units. Ultimately HMM–462 at Santa Ana would have 30 aircraft, HMM–463 at Futema 12, and HMM–461 at New River another 24. A small detachment of six was to be positioned at Kaneohe and two more at Quantico.[122]

The first helicopters delivered to the Marines were intended for the Fleet Introduction Program (FIP). MAG–26 at New River had been the first unit to have the UH–1E and the CH–46. Now it was MAG–36's turn at Santa Ana. On 9 September Major General McCutcheon, who had returned to the position of Deputy Chief of Staff (Air), arrived at the Sikorsky plant to observe the first four FIP aircraft in their final preparations before being turned over to the Marines.[123]

As he accepted the first CH–53 on behalf of the Marine Corps, he told the Sikorsky officials that "this is another milestone for Sikorsky, the Naval Air Systems Command and the Marine Corps". The gen-

---
* BuWeps had been abolished by a reorganization 1 May 1966 which assigned elements to three new commands. Naval Air Systems Command was the aviation portion.

USMC Photo A149242
*Two CH–53Ds of HMH–363 fly in formation over MCAS Santa Ana in June 1968. The CH–53D had still more speed and lifting power than the "A" model.*

eral praised the UH–34 for doing a fine job in Vietnam. He then added: "We have plenty of room out there for the CH–53A."

Major William R. Beeler, commanding officer of HMH–463, received the four aircraft at the plant. On 20 September, after a two-day flight across country, they arrived in Santa Ana.

At long last the "Deuce" had a successor in sight. Now all three main helicopters in the Marine Corps had jet-powered replacements in production and being delivered, the UH–1E, the CH–46, and the CH–53. It was not a moment too soon.

# CHAPTER FOUR

# THE MEN WHO FLEW HELICOPTERS

## Who Wants To Fly Helicopters?

5 September 1960. Lieutenant Colonel Thomas H. Miller, USMC, sets new world's speed record for 500-kilometer course averaging 1216.78 mph in a McDonnell F-4 Phantom II jet fighter. By January 1962, the F-4 has been clocked at 1,606 mph and has flown from Los Angeles to New York in 170 minutes. The Marine Corps is scheduled to receive the Phantom.*

20 February 1962. Lieutenant Colonel John H. Glenn, USMC, becomes first American to orbit the earth reaching speeds up to 17,545 mph in his 81,000-mile trip. Other Marines are being considered for the space program.

5 February 1962. Captain L. Kenneth Keck, USMC, flies in an HSS-2 which sets new world's speed record for helicopters—210.6 mph.**

The difference in speeds of the three records did not go unnoticed. The development of the LPH for mobility and the turbine-powered machines for lift capability had been a long and arduous process for the Marine Corps. The problem which was to prove most thorny, persistent, and demanding was finding the personnel to man and maintain the helicopters. The heart of the issue is contained in the accomplishments of Colonel Miller, Colonel Glenn, and Captain Keck.

Aviation, almost by definition, is a profession of speed and altitude. The aura of dashing pilots executing their daring deeds with cheerful abandon long had permeated the admiring public's view of the flyers and also the flyers' view of themselves. The decades of the 1950s and 1960s had seen an almost continuous succession of new records set, astounding developments, and major breakthroughs. It was a time of jets, supersonics, afterburners, rockets, and space. There was little to attract a pilot to a machine that normally flew at speeds that had been exceeded in 1913 ***; which continually tried to destroy itself; seldom got much above a few thousand feet, even if it was capable of doing so, and many were not; and totally lacked sleekness and aerodynamic beauty.

No pilot in a helicopter was ever going to be declared an "Ace" for shooting down five airplanes, nor could any of them ever hope to take credit for sinking an enemy ship.

A helicopter was slow, low, ugly, uncomfortable, and noisy. It was no consolation to many Marine pilots that it was vital for the prosecution of amphibious warfare. They wanted no part of such a machine. The attitude was spelled out accurately in 1955 by an irate letter to the *Marine Corps Gazette*.

> In the first place, Naval Aviators do not want to fly helicopters. For them being shifted from appealing jets to the whirlybirds is comparable to a hard-charging infantry officer being assigned as Secret and Classified (S&C) files officer when there is a good fire fight going on.**** Naval Aviators want to fly fixed wing aircraft! Secondly, the use of Naval Aviators as helicopter pilots is a waste of trained manpower. [To fly fixed wing aircraft] requires higher physical and mental standards than that of a 'copter pilot.'[1]

Right or wrong the author of the letter correctly identified the problem. Helicopter pilots were considered definitely second-class citizens by their fellow aviators. To order pilots to helicopters was difficult. To get them to volunteer was almost impossible.

Colonel Edward C. Dyer discovered the attitude as he attempted to assemble the pilots for the first Marine Corps helicopter squadron. At the conclusion of his duties in 1947 on the Special Board which had initially recommended helicopters for the Marine Corps,

---

\* Colonel Miller was also one of the first Marines to evaluate the British aircraft that resulted in the AV-8 "Harrier." In 1977, he was a lieutenant general on active duty.

\*\* The pilot of the aircraft was Lieutenant Robert W. Crafton, USN.

\*\*\* Normal cruise speed for the UH-34 and HR2S was approximately 110 knots, roughly equivalent to 128 mph which had been reached on 6 April 1913 by Marcel Prevost in a French Deperdussin aircraft.

\*\*\*\* S&C Files Officer is a very necessary but particularly onerous duty involving a great deal of detailed responsibility and very little authority.

Colonel Dyer had been ordered to form what was to be known as HMX-1. In later years he described the first attempt to recruit pilots:

> I went to the Marine Corps Schools and got permission to interview all the members of the junior course * who were interested in joining the helicopter squadron. The commanding officer of the course [Colonel Peter P.] "Pete" Schrider put out a notice saying that I would be in my office at a certain time. I would give a short briefing on the helicopter and its future and our plans for it in the Marine Corps for anybody who might be interested in later joining the squadron. At the appointed time about 60 guys showed up . . . in the main school building. I brought out some drawings of helicopters of the future that I had gotten from Sikorsky Aircraft—these were big twin engine things, and pretty visionary, although the HR2S turned out to be very much like them.
>
> We had other information on the possible speeds and payload that helicopters would achieve. I described what our squadron hoped to accomplish and how we hoped to go about it. Then I said, 'Now there is a large body of opinion in the Marine Corps that figures helicopters aren't going any place, so if you are interested, stay here and I'll get your names.' [2]

About two-thirds of the group left. Of the less than 20 remaining a few more opted for speedier aircraft and dropped out. "But I ended up with a nucleus of people that later formed HMX-1. I must say that they were all good men . . . and I think they all did a splendid job as we could see later." [3]

The meager results of Colonel Dyer's efforts to recruit volunteers to the first helicopters would recur many times in the future. It made no difference if the claims were unjustified, the second-class syndrome was a fact of life.

Five years later, the situation still was discouraging. The Commandant, General Shepherd, pointed out that as of 22 March 1952, a total of only 344 pilots had been trained in helicopters. Over 40 had left the program and of those remaining, many were reserves and presumably would leave the Marine Corps at the end of the war in Korea. By December there would be a requirement for 487 helicopter pilots.[4]

The problem was compounded by the fact that total manpower in the Marine Corps was held under a tight ceiling. It was a condition identical to that existing with the aircraft. Every pilot assigned to the growing helicopter force had to be offset by the reduction of one in fixed wing, unless another source within the Marine Corps could be found.

Director of Aviation Lieutenant General William O. Brice reported progress at the 1955 General Officers' Conference. General Brice was a veteran of World War I service in the Army. He had been commissioned in the Marine Corps in 1921 and was designated a naval aviator in 1924. He was promoted to brigadier general in 1947. Brice told his fellow generals, ". . . emphasis will be placed on increasing the number of pilots qualified in helicopters." He said, "This action is necessary in order to provide pilots for the increased helicopter lift programmed for the forthcoming years." [5] Recognizing the opinion of helicopter pilots held by many Marines, he added, "There can be no sacrifices made in the aeronautical adaptability and educational background in the selection of applicants for helicopter pilot training." [6]

## Sources of Marine Aviators

The root cause of the chronic shortage of helicopter pilots was the more general shortage in the Marine Corps of recruits for any kind of pilot training. Traditionally, Marine pilots were officers who had been commissioned and who had completed at least Basic School prior to reporting to Pensacola to begin their careers in aviation. The time necessary for this sequence made it attractive only to Marines who already had decided to make a life career of the Marine Corps. For those who were still undecided, there was a reluctance to become obligated for so many years of service. It appeared that a way was needed to recruit directly into aviation.

In early 1955, Lieutenant General Brice called into his office the procurement aids officer at HQMC, Captain Herbert M. Hart. The general asked him what he had to publicize the aviation officer programs. Captain Hart, a ground officer, had to admit that the only material "was an obsolete booklet that was almost out of stock." [7] The general wanted to know why this was so, and the hapless captain could only respond "because we do not have any program to procure aviators directly through Marine Corps channels." Fortunately, there was already in existence a program which seemed ideal to meet the requirement.

The Platoon Leader's Class (PLC) had been a major source of officers entering The Basic School. College students were recruited and spent two summers training with the Marines. On graduation they were commissioned and sent to Basic School. If this source could be tapped, and the officer ordered directly to Pensacola instead of Basic School, the time required could be shortened and a direct method of obtaining pilots would be established. The idea was approved. Some years later, the now Colonel Hart remembered the beginning of the program. "We labored long trying to come up with a cute, gimmicky name for [the program] and finally decided that it would be better to consider it just as part of the routine PLC" recruiting.

---

* Equivalent to the present Amphibious Warfare School.

Thus, the PLC (Aviation) source came into being. The first difficulty was preparing literature and posters to advertise the new way to become a Marine pilot. Photographs were particularly nettlesome to Captain Hart and his crew, since none of them were aviators. This small difficulty did not deter them. He remembered:

> In all our photography, we tried to have at least a "token" pilot. This was not always possible so I bought a set of wings at the post exchange and used these to arbitrarily designate a pilot before a picture was taken. Usually the officer who had most recently flown in a commercial airliner became our pilot for the photograph.
>
> There are still a few ground officers around today as colonels who occasionally are asked about whether they were aviators by officers who remembered seeing them wearing wings in the 1957-era posters.[8]

The ingenuity of Captain Hart in creating "instant" aviators for the photographs assisted the direct recruiting and the PLC (Aviation) program became a success. The basic concept was expanded and by 1963, there was also an Aviation Officer Candidate Course (AOCC) in addition to the PLC (Aviation) and Basic School graduate programs.

There was one other major source: Naval Aviation Cadets (NavCads). The program was initiated in 1935 to augment the supply of officers. All NavCads who completed flight training were eventually commissioned in the Navy or the Marine Corps. Prior to World War II, only college graduates were accepted. But under the demands of the war, the educational requirement was cut to three years of college, then two years, and finally high school graduates were accepted. In the final phases of the war, two years of college were again required.[9]

As far as the Marine Corps was concerned, the cadet program was satisfactory. The Navy held a different view. In December 1957, Rear Admiral Frederick N. Kivette, ACNO(Air), pointed out to General Pate that the Navy had to do all the recruiting for both services and "must procure fairly large numbers . . . to meet Marine Corps requirements."[10] More disturbing to him was that "The Marine Corps has the capability of selecting only those cadets who it considers most desirable, thus in essence leaving the lesser quality to the Navy."[11] There was no question that the capability was being utilized. Since the NavCad did not have to submit his request to become a Marine until near the end of his training, there was time to identify the superior students. Marine officers undergoing training as well as Marine flight instructors conducted an unofficial, informal, but high intensity recruiting campaign to persuade the best cadets to choose the Corps. Their efforts met considerable success.

Admiral Kivette listed other disadvantages of having the Navy recruit all cadets and the Marine Corps select the most promising. He concluded, "It, therefore is requested that the Marine Corps implement a program for procurement of Marine Aviation Cadets and assume the full responsibility for meeting its own input requirements to Flight Training." Finally, he requested that, "this recruiting program be implemented as expeditiously as possible and be fully effective by 1 July 1958."[12]

General Pate agreed that the Navy had a legitimate complaint and directed that studies be made on the possibility of a Marine Corps-managed cadet program. A number of alternatives were proposed. Each study agreed that it would be impossible to meet the target date of 1 July 1958. By the end of the year, however, the issues had been resolved, and on 1 December Major General Carson A. Roberts, at the time Acting Chief of Staff, announced the new Marine Corps Aviation Cadet (MarCad) program. It was very similar to NavCad. Applicants were required to have two years of college (with some permissible exceptions), agree to remain unmarried during their training, and serve three years after they received their wings. Both civilians and enlisted Marines on active duty were eligible.

The first MarCads were to be ordered to Pensacola starting 1 July 1959. In the meantime NavCads who were under training prior to that date would still be offered the opportunity to become Marines. It was not until 21 April 1961 that Second Lieutenant James R. Foster became the last NavCad to be commissioned in the Marine Corps. Lieutenant Foster, a former enlisted man in the Navy, was assigned to jets at Cherry Point, North Carolina.[13]

Two months earlier, the MarCad program began producing pilots, Second Lieutenant Clyde "O" Childress, the first former enlisted man to graduate and be commissioned, arrived at New River in February. He was greeted by the MAG-26 commanding officer, Colonel Paul T. Johnston, and immediately assigned to HMR(L)-262 as a helicopter pilot.[14]

Originally, the Marine Corps planned to obtain 200 pilots a year through the MarCad program. Acknowledging that not all applicants would complete successfully the year and a half of training, it established a quota of 252 to be recruited.[15] A year later Major General Norman J. Anderson did not have encouraging news of the results. From January through December 1960, 242 MarCads had been obtained. Before training started, 12 had been disqualified or dropped out. Of the remaining 230 who began flight instruction, 52 percent did not complete it. Instead of the 200 pilots hoped for, only 110 graduated.[16] The picture was not much brighter for the pilots from officer sources. Only 369 had been recruited to meet a goal of 455. The completion rate was somewhat better with 65 percent graduating, but the net result was still only 210. The Marine Corps had achieved 320 new pilots in 1962. It needed 500.[17] Progress to overcome the chronic shortage was not going to be easy.

To add to the difficulties facing General Anderson, "curtailment of officer training classes in the Marine Corps School system in the coming year will (further) reduce the number of candidates available for training."[18] "As a result," he added, "more candidates will be required from MarCad sources."[19]

Recruiting efforts on college campuses had to be bolstered. He detailed a plan to provide radio and television advertisements and recruiting films. In addition he had obtained CNO approval to "provide indoctrination flights for bona fide MarCad candidates to include combining the flight with transportation to the nearest Naval facility which would provide" for physicals and testing.[20] Not only were civilian sources of MarCads to be combed but General Anderson suggested "that equally intensive recruitment be accomplished in all Marine Corps commands."[21] There could be no repetition of the disastrous attrition rate in 1960. "It is recommended that screening boards of experienced aviators review all applications and interview all candidates carefully to insure that only those qualified candidates who are highly motivated and enthusiastic are recommended."[22]

In the next 10 years, a total of 1,296 MarCads won their wings and a commission in the Marine Corps. In 1968 procurement from officer sources had finally begun to meet total requirements, and the MarCad program was quietly brought to a close. On 22 March that year, Second Lieutenant Larry D. Mullins became the last MarCad to be commissioned. On hand to witness the end of the program was Brigadier General William G. Johnson, Assistant DC/S (Air) and a former NavCad himself.[23]

The MarCad and NavCad programs had served a purpose. They had provided an alternative source of pilots. The lack of a degree, however, proved to be a handicap in later years for the pilots in competition for promotion and assignments. Many of them overcame the difficulty and became successful senior officers in the Marine Corps. Regardless, the fact remained that the Marine Corps felt better served if all its pilots were graduates of college and, when that became possible, discontinued the cadet programs altogether.

## STUDENT AND NAVAL AVIATOR DATA

1. *Student Naval Aviator Inputs*

| End FY | Authorized | | Actual | |
|---|---|---|---|---|
| | MARCAD | OFFICER | MARCAD | OFFICER |
| 60 | 252 | 455 | 242 | 369 |
| 61 | 323 | 430 | 329 | 393 |
| 62 | 407 | 407 | 461 | 324 |
| 63 | 465 | 472 | — | — |
| 64 | 280 | 516 | — | — |

2. *Naval Aviator*

| FY | NATC Output* | | Strengths | T/O Reqm'ts | Shortages |
|---|---|---|---|---|---|
| | Planned | Actual | | | |
| 60 | 500 | 418 | 3932 | 4689 | 557 |
| 61 | 475 | 402 | 3976 | 4720 | 794 |
| 62 | 475 | 320 | 4067 | 4782 | 725 |
| Example: | CY–60 Input | Training Losses | | % Attrition | FY62 Output |
| Mar/Cad | 230 | 120 | | 52.1 | 110 |
| Officer | 326 | 116 | | 35.5 | 210 |
| Total | 556 | 236 | | 42.44 | 320 |

*Calendar Year input (18 months prior) minus flight training attrition results in Fiscal Year output.

## Selection of Helicopter Pilots in Training

Once pilots were recruited, some of them had to be persuaded to specialize in helicopters. Factors at work within the training process made the helicopter option doubly unattractive for the new student aviator. Periodically, a forecast would be made of the needs for each type of pilot in the forthcoming months. This formed the basis for the numbers assigned to the different categories of advanced training, such as jets, propeller aircraft, and helicopters.

As the student neared the end of basic flight training, depending on his academic and flight grades, he received a choice of advanced training until the quota was filled. Those with the highest marks had first opportunity. The next highest group then could select any opening remaining. Though such a system put a premium on speed of learning and ignored depth of learning, it seemed like a convenient way to manage the program. Almost without exception, the highest-graded students chose the glamorous jets. The next group had to be satisfied competing for assignment to propeller aircraft advanced training. What was left got helicopters. The equation was perfect. Helicopter pilots were second-class citizens so second-class pilots got helicopters. The syndrome was self-perpetuating.

The typical attitude prevailing among jet pilots was clearly established in an article in the *Marine Corps Gazette* in 1962.[24] The author invoked the spectre of pilot-caused aircraft crashes to explain why only the most select of pilots could qualify to fly jets. The screening process was rigorous and "this quality input [of students] and careful aptitude analysis" paid off with a new safety record.[25] He went on to say: "It is assumed that all naval aviators are born to fly and that they come equipped with flight aptitude of the highest order. This is nonsense. No two are similar."[26] He then got to the very crux of the syndrome:

> What is flight aptitude? . . . its prime ingredients are headwork, judgement, basic air work and reaction time. Reaction time is of special note because as aircraft performance goes up, reaction time goes down. . . . Aptitude graduates upward in order of increased performance or reaction time.[27]

Even among jet pilots there were those more equal than others. The same article reported "one solution (and a darn good one) mentioned not too long ago was to form an elite cadre of 500 jet pilots, replace them as needed to keep the number constant."[28]

With the benefit of over a decade of hindsight, it is tempting to be harsh with the judgment of the jet pilot. At the time, however, the opinions expressed in the article were widely held and hardly considered radical. It was a simple fact accepted by all fixed-wing pilots—speed of the aircraft equalled superior aptitude. Perpetuation of this myth was helped considerably by the fact that few jet pilots had any contact with, or knowledge of, helicopters. As long as the selection process was based on the reverse assumption that helicopters did not need as proficient pilots as fixed wing, the second-class syndrome would continue to exist, and as long as it did, few pilots would volunteer for helicopters if they had a choice.

## Recruiting Expedients

To secure qualified men to fly helicopters in the face of these obstacles, the Marine Corps considered a number of alternatives. In 1956, Major General Henry R. Paige suggested one of the more original ones. Though not an aviator, General Paige had been deeply involved in the early development of helicopters. In January 1956 he had visited Fort Benning and had received an orientation from the Army on its helicopter program. On his return to Quantico he wrote General Pate suggesting that the Marine Corps "train enlisted pilots on six years enlistments for duty, initially as co-pilots" in helicopters.[29] "Two officer pilots in each helicopter seems uneconomical," he observed.[30] Such a program as he proposed recognized the difficulties in recruiting helicopter pilots and "would also give a group of personnel who make a career in helicopters their principal interest. Now the Marine aviator's interest is divided into many fields of which the helicopter is more or less 'poor relation' and something which few Marine aviators want to make a career of."[31]

He could have added that enlisted co-pilots would avoid transferring fixed-wing aviators into helicopters —a spectre that haunted many jet pilots. In spite of the advantages of the plan, it was directly contrary to the goals spelled out by General Brice and was not adopted at the time.

The idea of only one of the pilots being an officer, however, did not die out entirely. In December 1961 the Director of Aviation, Colonel McCutcheon, held an aviation training conference at El Toro. On his return he reported that: "One point that we tried to sell, but which the field did not buy, concerned the assignment of one vs. two helicopter pilots to passenger carrying aircraft."[32] The attendees at the conference, however, were acutely aware of the "can't let go to scratch your nose" problem, "and were unanimous in expressing a desire to retain two pilots." Colonel McCutcheon went on to say:

> My personal opinion is that there are some occasions when one pilot is sufficient to carry out the particular

mission and that the operational commander involved is the logical person to decide when this situation prevails.[33]

Colonel McCutcheon was reassigned shortly afterwards, but his opinion prevailed. On 18 September 1962 the Navy directive which had established pilot criteria was revised. The new regulation allowed single engine helicopters to be flown under certain conditions by only one pilot. The DC/S (Air) at the time, Brigadier General Norman J. Anderson, commented: "We feel that this is a more realistic approach to the plane commander-co-pilot problem that exists in the helicopter program."[34] The restrictions which remained were such that most combat Marines seldom saw a helicopter with anything but two pilots in it. The basic problem remained unsolved.

Another suggestion of General Paige in the 1956 letter came closer to being adopted.[35] The Marine Corps long had utilized warrant officers. Most were former enlisted men of a number of years of military experience. Many served in highly technical and specialized fields. Some were further designated as limited duty officers (LDOs) and always were assigned the same type of duty. General Paige had wondered if "maybe something in the LDO (helicopter pilot only) line could be worked out."[36]

The Division of Aviation conducted a study in 1960 to investigate the desirability of replacing a portion of the commissioned officer pilots with warrant officers or enlisted pilots. The study concluded "that a commissioned officer structure composed of college graduates was most desirable and recommended . . . restricting warrant officers to technical specialties."[37]

What was desirable was not always possible. During 1960 and 1961 the Marine Corps could not recruit enough college graduates to fill its need for pilots. Warrant officers still might offer a solution. In the summer of 1961 the Warrant Officer, Helicopter Only (WOHELIO) program was initiated. Colonel McCutcheon hoped to reach a goal of 60 the first year and eventually build up to 100.[38] "Our original sources," he noted, "were both active duty and inactive duty reservists [officers] with priority on those who were currently designated" helicopter pilots.[39] At the end of the first six months, 47 reserve lieutenants and captains had been selected and exchanged their insignia for those of a regular warrant officer. Of the total, 11 already were on active duty. The other 36 returned to the Marine Corps from civilian life.[40]

After the initial surge, new applicants were scattered, and Colonel McCutcheon began exploring other methods. "We are now pursuing two other courses of action" he noted in January 1962, "screening Naval aviation pilots* who still meet the criteria for warrant officer programs" and "selecting probably a small number of regular lieutenants and captains that have been twice passed over for promotion."[41] Even the resourceful Colonel McCutcheon had to admit that procuring pilots for helicopters was not an easy task. He concluded, "Where we go from here . . . to get any increase over the 60 is as yet an unsolved problem."[42]

Two years after the WOHELIO program was initiated, only 78 pilots had been produced. "The program began to die on the vine."[43] In September 1963 an attempt was made to revive it in conjunction with the selection of warrant officers for other technical specialities. Once again the goal was set at 100 pilots.

Marine Corps Order 1040.14A announced the new program. "Requirements for the flight training program are the same as those for the Corps' basic Warrant program . . . with the exception" of a higher score in aptitude testing.[44] Unlike the effort in 1960 no previous flight experience was necessary. "Upon successful completion of the screening and basic courses," it was explained, "qualified applicants will be ordered to Naval Air Station, Pensacola for training."[45]

The response to this new program was unimpressive. Only nine enlisted Marines applied and seven of them were found unqualified. An analysis of the failure some years later concluded: "the poor response was due to the fact that the requisites for the warrant officer flight training program were identical to those for the Marine Cadet program except for marital status." Warrant Officers could be married, cadets had to be single but became commissioned officers.[46] "Presumably the nine applicants were married."[47]

A program such as WOHELIO had several inherent defects. First, the idea of anyone other than a commissioned officer flying an aircraft was not universally accepted. In fact, the issue could be explosive. Many years after the event, Brigadier General Samuel R. Shaw could regale his listeners with an anecdote in which the difference of opinion was expressed exactly.

Colonel Shaw had been another of the three members of the secretariat of the special board which in 1947 first had proposed helicopters in the Marine Corps. Though not an aviator, Colonel Shaw had a deep appreciation of the potential—and difficulties—of vertical envelopment. He was also one of those Marines who appear periodically in the Corps in the middle of a controversy over major changes in policy. In 1956, as a colonel serving as Director of Policy

---

* The Marine Corps had previously used a few enlisted men as pilots. Designated naval aviation pilots (NAPs) to distinguish them from the officer naval aviators, a few were still on active duty in 1962.

Analysis at HQMC, he had prepared a paper recommending that enlisted men and warrant officers be used to fly helicopters. He found himself in front of the Commandant, General Pate, accompanied by two senior aviator generals discussing the merits of his proposal. He remembers the conversation as:

> Well, somewhere along the way the generals were both going on at considerable length at a simple fact. To fly an airplane you had to be an officer. That was the central characteristic of people who flew airplanes: they had to be officers. I burst into the conversation. 'Well, how can that be? If they got to be officers, what are all those damned civilians doing flying airplanes?'[48]

General Shaw still chuckles over the results of his remark. "Godalmighty! They tore into me and that was the end of the conversation in front of the Commandant."[49]

A more serious disadvantage of the WOHELIO and other warrant officer programs was that warrant officers were limited in the types of duties they could perform. General Greene pointed out this drawback in a memorandum to the Secretary of the Navy in 1966:

> The Warrant Officer helicopter pilot is restricted in assignment, primarily to operational (flying) billets. Within these billets, he is restricted in assigned responsibility. As his aviation knowledge and pilot proficiency progresses, his responsibilities remain at somewhat the same level.[50]

General Greene continued: "The relatively small size of the Marine Corps demands maximum flexibility in the assignment of the total aviator inventory. The concept of a large Warrant Officer pilot population is in conflict with this requirement."[51]

Periodically there have been attempts to revive the warrant officer program. In each case it seemed to offer a timely solution to an immediate problem. In each case, however, the long-term effects were a handicap which could not be overcome. The Marine Corps simply could not afford to have pilots who could not be assigned to a broad spectrum of duties. To date, no other warrant officer program has been adopted.

## Transitions

By the summer of 1962 the situation was critical. Forty percent of all Marine Corps pilots were needed in helicopters. Only 29 percent were assigned to them.[52] The future looked bleak. Helicopter squadrons were flying in Vietnam, more squadrons were planned, and the growing success of vertical amphibious landings from the new LPHs required a quickened pace of training. The few pilots in helicopters were being stretched thinner and thinner. Some sought a different profession. There was a "marked attrition rate among helicopter pilots, mainly junior officers who feel they aren't going anywhere but up and down."[53] The shortage was so acute that there were restrictions on assigning a helicopter pilot to any duty but in a squadron. The constant deployments and commitments resulted in few of them ever remaining at their home station for any length of time. Helicopter crews could "point to jet and transport pilots, who admittedly have fewer crash projects to meet" in contrast.[54] A number "disliked living out of a sea-bag" to the point where they left the Marine Corps, further compounding the shortage.[55]

General Anderson, DC/S (Air), could see no improvement unless drastic steps were taken. He predicted that by June 1963 the helicopter units would be operating short one-third of the pilots required.[56] The result could only be that even more pilots would leave the Marine Corps when their obligated service was completed. It was a vicious circle. He had, however, another manpower source. At the same time that helicopters were expected to have only 66 percent of their authorized pilots, jet units would have 95 percent, and transports a whopping 114 percent. General Anderson presented a plan to General Shoup, who agreed. It was then forwarded to the CNO who approved it on 30 August 1962. Approximately 500 fixed-wing aviators were to be forced to make a transition into helicopters.* The purpose, General Anderson pointed out, "is to rectify imbalances in the distribution of Marine Aviators . . . caused by abnormally low retention rates of helicopter pilots, increased commitments and requirements for their services."[57]

Those to be selected all had flown at least one tour in fixed-wing aircraft. Most were experienced first lieutenants and captains, though there was a sprinkling of majors and even a few lieutenant colonels. If at all possible, each had been eligible for a routine change of station anyway. Instead of proceeding to the duties they expected, they were to report to helicopters. Help was on the way.

While the overburdened helicopter crews greeted the news with joy, the reaction by most of the 500 fixed-wing pilots chosen was just the opposite. Cries of anguish, incredulous looks of "Why me?", and threats to get out (a few did) resounded throughout the Marine Corps. For those who made a quick trip to HQMC to review their records, hoping to find the reason they had been discarded into helicopters, the experience was even more perplexing. All the information indicated that they were considered among the better officers and pilots in their previous squadrons.

---

* Similar programs on a smaller scale had been utilized in the mid-1950s.

To be transferred to helicopters seemed an odd reward, but General Anderson, well aware of the second-class syndrome, had no intention of having his program turn into a method for culling out weak pilots from fixed-wing units. Not widely known at the time, "to maintain the desired quality level," he had ordered that the final approval of each nomination be made only by his staff at DC/S (Air).[58]

The pilots were to receive a total of 46 hours of classroom instruction, followed by 65 hours of flight in the UH–34.[59] At the completion of the course, they would be designated as co-pilot. The training was to be conducted in two squadrons, one on each coast. HMM–362, which in August had arrived back in the United States after completing its duties on SHUFLY, was designated at Santa Ana. The new commanding officer, Lieutenant Colonel Robert H. Brumley, had to reorganize the unit and set up the program by 5 November when the first transition pilots were due to arrive. In the east coast squadron, HMM–262, Major Wilbur O. Nelson's similar efforts were interrupted by the Cuban missile crisis, but he was able to be ready for the first students on 3 December. Every month for almost the next two years, 10 fixed-wing pilots would be ordered to each of the squadrons for forced transition.

General Anderson planned "that the initial graduates will be used to raise the squadrons to an acceptable strength as expeditiously as possible."[60] As more pilots completed the transition it:

> . . . will permit the assignment of a portion of the existing helicopter population to several hundred other billets and thereby provide a more normal career assignment pattern than has been possible heretofore. Eventually this transition training capability should provide sufficient graduates to [even] permit the reassignment of a . . . number of the existing helicopter population [back to] fixed wing duty.[61]

With the program in full swing he estimated that by June 1964 the relative percentage of pilots available compared to the number required would be 86 percent for helicopters, 85 percent for jets, and 90 percent for transports.

To a former jet pilot, the transition into helicopters was a shock. He immediately recognized that flying a helicopter was not quite as simple as he had been led to believe. The first attempt to perform a simple maneuver, such as keeping the aircraft in a steady hover in gusty winds, generated a certain amount of humility. After landing at night in a confined area surrounded by trees, the jet pilot began to reevaluate his opinion of helicopter pilots. They might fly low and slow, but they definitely were not second class. In many ways the learning process was a two-way street. The fixed-wing aviators brought with them knowledge of other techniques and tactics which could be employed in helicopters. The cross-fertilization of ideas, and the growth of understanding between the two elements within Marine aviation was one of the most significant achievements of the forced transition program.

Even more so was combat training. Many of Archie's Angels and the pilots from the squadrons that followed on SHUFLY were assigned as instructors in HMM–362 and HMM–262. They brought with them the latest developments from Vietnam. The result was that the Marine Corps built up a force of pilots who were experienced in both fixed-wing and helicopters and who had been instructed in the lessons of operations in South Vietnam. It was a fortunate and timely combination which was to prove invaluable in the coming years.

## Training

> Gentlemen. You have studied subsonics, transonics, supersonics, and hypersonics in some detail. We shall now discuss a different regime of flight: Microsonics.
> Presentation on helicopters by Naval Air Test Center, 1962.[62]

Regardless of the source of pilots, they had to be trained to fly aircraft. Colonel Carl simply had learned the fundamentals from a friend at the test center and then taught himself. He was the type of talented and versatile aviator who could do it. Colonel Dyer, prior to the commissioning of HMX–1 in December 1947, was invited by Fred Dawson, then the assistant general manager of Sikorsky "to come up and take pilot training."[63] "So I got Temporary Additional Duty orders from the Marine Corps and came up to Connecticut and took my first helicopter training at the Sikorsky plant at Bridgeport. My instructor was Jimmy Viner . . . the chief test pilot."[64] Major DiLalio had learned to fly them in 1946 at the Navy's Helicopter Development Squadron Three (VX–3) at Floyd Bennet Field, in New York. The same unit later was relocated to Lakehurst, New Jersey and provided a source of training for most of the first Marine pilots. These included First Lieutenant Roy L. Anderson, Captains Robert A. Strieby and Charles D. Garber, and Major Russell R. Riley. The four were among the officers who had responded to Colonel Dyer's first recruiting efforts and became the nucleus of HMX–1 as the squadron was formed. They represent in the lineal list of Marines designated as helicopter pilots numbers two, three, four, and five respectively.[65] All were assigned as instructors to HMX–1 where "initial operations consisted strictly of pilot training."[66]

In June of 1948 the CNO published a new directive requiring formal training of all helicopter pilots "due to the inherent instability . . . and the different nature of control techniques employed." [67] "Only those pilots previously qualified by VX-3 or the U.S. Coast Guard or those qualified after 1 July 1948 under the provisions of the order "will be permitted to solo helicopter type aircraft." [68]

Colonel Dyer did not meet these requirements so "I went back up to Lakehurst and took a check flight, which I passed successfully and I was given my card as a qualified helicopter pilot." [69] Neither did Colonel Carl have the formal certification, but at the time he neglected to receive a check flight. Thus, even though he was the first Marine to learn how to fly a helicopter, it is Major DiLalio who is recognized as the first Marine to be officially designated. The same CNO order established a training syllabus which had to be completed prior to qualification. As all aviators learning to fly helicopters at the time were already experienced in fixed-wing aircraft, the instruction was devoted to only the differences in the types of airplanes.

The course consisted of 39.6 flight hours. The primary stage included practice in a hover "handling stick only" and hovering "handling pitch only." [70] The third stage was operational flying. One flight was devoted to a cross-country navigation over a distance of 100 to 200 miles. Five hours of flight time were allotted, an indication of the speeds of the machines then available. The final check required many maneuvers which were a bit different from those the fixed-wing pilots were accustomed to, such as making "a backward vertical take-off." [71] Or "At five feet altitude, fly a 50-foot-square pattern keeping heading constant at all times. Fly forward on one leg, sideward on second leg, backward on third leg and sideward to starting point." [72] Landings within 12 inches of a predetermined mark were also part of the check.

Surprisingly, many of the basic maneuvers specified 25 years ago still remain today an effective method to teach pilots to fly helicopters. Numerous new ones have been added but the original list remains in use.

By the end of 1949, VX-3 and HMX-1 had qualified a total of 34 Marines including three enlisted pilots. Master Sergeants Arnold G. Fisher and Leonard J. Mounts were designated as of 1 April 1948; and Master Sergeant Samuel R. Wooley on 26 October 1949.[73] They were the 12th, 13th, and 31st Marine helicopter pilots.

As the helicopter program continued to expand, an increasing amount of the available time at HMX-1 was devoted to nothing but training new pilots. The commanding officer, Lieutenant Colonel Edward V. Finn, complained in September 1952 that "80 percent of flight hours are in training and there isn't enough time for the development work." [74] General Shepherd assured him that efforts were being made to have the Navy take over all training, but until such time as it did, the next classes ordered to HMX-1 would be reduced to six students.[75]

VX-3 had its own problems with the expansion. The squadron's helicopters caused increased congestion in the mat area at Lakehurst, and their flights interfered with those of fixed-wing aircraft. The squadron needed a new home. The Navy found one for it at Naval Auxiliary Air Station (NAAS) Ellyson, an unused base near Pensacola, Florida. Built during the construction programs just before World War II, Ellyson had suitable area for practice flights and was located near the Navy's other pilot training facilities at Pensacola. For the next 22 years, it would be a familiar sight for Marine helicopter pilots.

Helicopter Training Unit One (HTU-1) was commissioned on 4 December 1950 and moved to Ellyson 2 January 1951.[76] The commanding officer, Commander Ben Moore, Jr., started out with four officers and four enlisted men. By the time the first class of nine students reported on 15 January, he had three helicopters assigned. The unit was scheduled to grow to 20 officers and 252 men with 20 aircraft. A student class of 24 pilots a month was planned and the first one graduated on 14 March the same year.[77]

Marines arriving later that year for training at Ellyson were confronted with a total of 59 helicopters —of eight different types. Most of them were small. Typical of these trainers, the Hiller-built HTE-2 (OH-23), first introduced into use in January 1951, had a larger engine than the previous model, the HTE-1. (Helicopter Trainer Hiller) [78] The new Franklin 0-335-6 engine could develop 200 horsepower, 22 more than the older aircraft. Even with this increase in power, the performance of the helicopter was slightly less than exhilarating. With 168 pounds of fuel, it could carry an additional 613 pounds of crew or cargo up to its designed limits of 2,400 pounds. Fully loaded, the highest altitude the aircraft could hover out of ground effect was exactly zero. At the same time its maximum rate of climb was also zero. If ground effect or translational lift could not be utilized, someone had to get out or the aircraft could not fly. The designers of the first syllabus had aircraft like the HTE-2 in mind when they established the flight time for the navigational cross country, for it cruised at 67 knots and had a top speed just five knots faster. Fortunately for the heftier Marine pilots, by the end of 1952 the HTE-2s were no longer used.

Most of the other aircraft were members of a long line of Bell Aircraft light helicopters. Bearing the designation of HTL (Helicopter, Light, Bell), H–13, the first of the series, had flown in February 1946. This HTL–1 (Sioux) had been followed by successive models up to the HTL–7. With the HTE–2 gone, 1 January 1953 saw the squadron with eight HTL–4s and 34 HTL–5s. All of them were typical Bell designs with two-bladed main and anti-torque rotors and a clear plastic bubble cockpit.[79]

The first three members of the series had a covering on the tail structure. It was removed in the 4s and 5s to gain an additional 156 pounds of lift capability. Commercial models of the series were widely used and many of the small helicopters seen in motion pictures and television are nothing more than an adaptation of the H–13s. In size and horsepower they were all similar to the HTE–2. The "five" was typical. It was 41 feet long overall with a 35-foot main rotor. The Aircooled Motors 0–335–5 engine could produce 200 horsepower. Fully loaded with 174 pounds of fuel and 606 of payload, it could hover out of ground effect and actually climb at 850 feet per minute.

From 1954, for another 15 years, one variety or another of the H–13 series was to remain the primary aircraft for all helicopter basic training. It was not until February 1969 that the last one would leave Ellyson.[80] In that time, it had built up a legion of anecdotes among Marine pilots. One of the most often told concerned the helicopter's sensitivity to any shifts in weight from side to side. If the student pilot was to conduct a solo flight, sand bags had to be placed in the aircraft to compensate for the absence of the instructor's weight. Periodically a student would manage to get airborne on a solo without the sandbags. The helicopter immediately tipped to the right. The hapless pilot was doomed to nothing but a right hand circle until he could swoop low enough for ground crewmen to throw sandbags into the aircraft and correct the balance.[81]

Some of the TH–13s were equipped with skids, others with conventional landing gear. There was a hearty competition among students to obtain one with wheels. Otherwise the pilot would have to lift the aircraft into a hover and carefully "air-taxi" through the parking apron to the takeoff point. At best, for a fledgling aviator, this is a difficult maneuver. In the close proximity of other helicopters creating their own

USMC Photo 529982

*The HTL series was used extensively for training of helicopter pilots. This HTL–4, at Quantico in 1951, is rigged for medical evacuation missions.*

rotor down wash while taxiing, it was guaranteed to receive critical appraisal from the instructor.[82] It was much easier with wheels.

Advanced training was conducted in a variety of aircraft. Initially there were HRS-1 and —2s (early models of the CH-19) and HUPs. The HUP was a Piasecki-designed, tandem-rotor utility helicopter that was a direct, if distant, ancestor to the CH-46.

The year 1963 marked a turning point in the training of Marine Corps pilots. By that time most of the advanced training was accomplished in the ubiquitous UH-34. The original requirement that only experienced aviators could receive the specialized helicopter training had been dropped in the early 50s. Helicopters were now an advanced phase of normal flight training. The students who reported to Ellyson had received almost 200 hours in fixed-wing propeller trainers. Many were cadets, though the number of officers was increasing. The syllabus which had been set at 60 hours—half in the TH-13, the rest in the UH-34— was to be expanded up to 80 hours "as personnel, and aircraft availability permit."[83]

The year also marked the last time more new Marine pilots would be trained in fixed wing than in helicopters. In July 1964, at the General Officers Symposium, Brigadier General Louis B. ("Ben") Robertshaw, DC/S (Air), explained the program. General Robertshaw, a graduate of the U.S. Naval Academy in 1936, and captain of its football team, had served as an infantry officer for six years prior to entering flight training in August 1942. He had replaced General Anderson in October 1963. He explained that in FY 64 only 40 percent of the pilots needed by the Marine Corps were in helicopters. In three years, however, the total would be 60 percent. "The result is a complete reversal of the distribution ratio of pilots."[84]

The changes in the ratio in training "were necessarily gradual in order to avoid radical changes in the training command."[85] In FY 64, 51 percent of the new pilots were to be helicopter qualified. An additional eight percent would be added in FY 65 and by FY 67 almost two-thirds of all pilots would be trained in helicopters. He went on to explain that even this would not meet all the requirements but that the forced transition program had been successful. It provided an additional source.

Training of helicopter pilots had come a long way since Colonel Dyer and his officers had made the first attempts at HMX-1. But there was other training to do. Once again it was the pioneers at HMX-1 who started it all.

## Crew Training

> Helicopter maintenance requires a high caliber mechanic. No man can bluff his way through this kind of maintenance. The helicopter mechanic must know much more about fundamental mechanical principles and be able to put them into practice. The pilot's safety depends on practically every small part . . . of the helicopter.
> Briefing for CMC
> January 1967[86]

As Colonel Dyer was explaining the helicopter program to prospective pilots in 1947, he also was attempting to obtain the necessary enlisted Marines. He remembered that "I drew up a table of organization and although my ideas were cut down considerably by HQMC, I nevertheless ended up with approximately 81 enlisted men."[87]

"These were all people who were former aviation mechanics, electronics people, parachute men," and other specialists drawn from other aviation units.[88] The helicopter presented new and complex machinery. The new technicians had to be trained. Colonel Dyer arranged for the Marines to attend the Sikorsky Aircraft service school as well as to study at Lakehurst. The first aircraft mechanic assigned to a Marine helicopter squadron was Technical Sergeant Robert V. Yeager, who joined HMX-1 on 21 January 1948.* He arrived from Lakehurst two weeks before the Marine Corps received its first helicopter. From this tiny nucleus was to grow a major educational effort. HMX-1 continued to train mechanics, but it soon became apparent that additional sources were necessary. The Naval Air Technical Training Command at Memphis, Tennessee began to teach helicopter mechanics. By early 1952, the Class "C" School in helicopter fundamentals lasted eight weeks and included 320 hours of instruction.[89] In July 1956 it was further expanded. In addition to the standard eight-week school in reciprocating engines, there was a four-week course emphasizing helicopter fundamentals.[90]

Even this was not enough. Starting on 5 February 1958 the training was reorganized. The new 12-week instruction was designed solely for helicopters and had major new material in "engine principles and flight transmissions and controls."[91] The school was unusual in several respects. It was the only one like it in the Navy and was staffed entirely by Marines. Master Sergeant John P. Maughan, with four years of experience in helicopters, was in charge of the operations. He and his fellow instructors had devised a schedule which required a total of 464 hours of instruction, 314 of which were spent on actual application of the classroom

---

\* Master Sergeant Mounts, one of the NAPs, also carried the occupational specialty rating of aircraft mechanic.

knowledge. As helicopters became increasingly complex, the length of the schools grew correspondingly. In 1965 it was 23 weeks. The same year the Marine Corps had a requirement for 1,465 reciprocating helicopter mechanics just for the HR2S and the UH-34.[92] A program to retrain these Marines into the new helicopters with jet engines had been started.

Regardless of where they were trained, helicopter mechanics were—and are—a unique breed of Marine. The intricacies of the rotor systems demanded a new level of dexterity. As constant attention to proper lubrication was required, most mechanics spent much of their time balanced precariously on top of the aircraft, grease gun in one hand, holding on with another and simultaneously operating the lubricating pump. The power blade folding of the "Deuce" was but one of the ways they could be unexpectedly drenched in red hydraulic fluid. They learned a little bit about electrical systems, hydraulics, avionics, and even metalsmith procedures.

One advantage—in their eyes at least—they did have: they got to fly in the product of their labors. The mechanic normally served double duty as the airborne crew chief of his aircraft. Here they were called upon for still further demonstrations of their versatility. When carrying a load externally underneath the aircraft, the pilot could not see the cargo, and the crew chief, acting as an observer, carefully guided the pilot to the precise location necessary to pick up or drop the load. Likewise, when landing in a confined area, the crew chief kept careful watch to the rear of the helicopter to insure the rotors were clear of the trees.

The close coordination and cooperation necessary between the crew and the pilots occasionally got reinforcement. Master Sergeant Jerome P. Sullivan, a crew chief on both the "Deuces" and the UH-34s in the early 1960s as well as later helicopters, recounted a typical mission: "We had to fly an HR2S from New River up to Norfolk to put on a short demonstration. On takeoff from New River, one of the tires on the left landing gear blew out." This could be a problem, but since there were two wheels on each side, "the pilot decided to go on to Norfolk and ask for a precautionary emergency landing. On touch down, the other left tire blew out. I tried to find another tire but there weren't any to fit." Sergeant Sullivan and the pilots completed the demonstration anyway and without relanding headed back to New River. Shortly after leaving the Norfolk area the pilot called and announced that the temperature of the oil in the main transmission was rising at an alarming rate. "That meant that the strainer (for the lubricating oil) was clogged and we had to make an immediate emergency landing. The only clear spot we could find was in the middle—of all things—a pig pen."

But the pilot "made a safe landing and shut down. Then we drained the oil, cleaned the strainer and put fresh oil back in the transmission." The flight continued, but shortly was interrupted again. The radios failed. Still without tires on the left side, the pilot diverted to the Coast Guard Air Station at Elizabeth City, North Carolina, and made another emergency landing. "We went over to the maintenance people," Sergeant Sullivan remembers:

> ... and we got the radio fixed and took off. We called ahead to let New River know we didn't have any tires on one side and would land in the grass. Somehow the word got scrambled, and when we got to the field all the crash trucks were out for an emergency landing.

"You know," the crew chief mused, "it isn't every airplane crew that can have four emergency landings on the same mission in a single day, and still get the job done."

Sometimes the cooperation among the crews was not the result of mechanical difficulties. A typical, if not routine, mission occurred in 1961. A piece of classified equipment had fallen off a fixed-wing aircraft over the water near the island of Hawaii. Four UH-34s from the Kaneohe-based HMM-161 were dispatched to search for the device. Once again Sergeant Sullivan found himself in austere conditions. "Our base was on an old lava flow near the beach. There was no way you could set up a tent, so we all, pilots and mechanics, just lived and slept in the airplanes together."

For two weeks the pilots and crews "would go out and fly all day, and come back and land on the lava. Then everyone pitched in to conduct the required maintenance on the airplanes before crawling inside to go to sleep."[93]

Crew chiefs became very possessive of the helicopter assigned to them. Most christened their aircraft with nicknames, such as the Road Runner, Champagne Lady, and Coyote—or any other one that struck their fancy. A crew chief always referred to a helicopter in a personal fashion as "my airplane," or "Corporal Smith's airplane." They were usually prepared for the worst and "always carried shaving gear because when you went out on a normal mission you never knew when you might be out for a couple of days."

The feats of helicopter crew chiefs are legendary. They casually performed miracles of repairs in the middle of isolated clearings. They leaped from hovering helicopters to rescue injured persons. They guided the pilots into landing zones that seemed impossibly small. And through it all, they remained consistently cheerful. The tight-knit team of pilots and crew chief

# THE PILOTS

USMC Photo 532039

*A CH–53 crew chief at work. Staff Sergeant James A. Batt of HMH–463 in Vietnam peers through the "Hell Hole" of his aircraft as it prepares to pick up an external load of supplies. A second crew member watches to the rear of the helicopter.*

created a camaraderie that allowed for casual humor. A good example is the lyrics of a song written in 1965 by Sergeants Martin F. Valente and Richard P. Baltos entitled "The Attitude Song."

>  (Sung to the tune of "Sweet Betsy from Pike")
> I'm the greatest co-pilot to ride the left seat.
> My takeoffs are brilliant, my landings are neat.
> I navigate true as we fly through the sky.
> I'm a much better pilot than this other guy.
>
> I am the HAC,* and I sit on the right.
> My co-pilot's lousy, and not very bright.
> If it weren't for me teaching him all that I knew,
> We'd never be able to stay in the blue.
>
> We are the brave, stalwart, underpaid crew.
> The Gunner's the greatest, the Crew Chief is, too.
> Together we bounce along through the blue sky,
> Wondering why those two pilots can't fly.
>
> "ASE" * flies the airplane, the instruments steer.
> We do all the fighting and maintain the gear.
> We give our two pilots the courage it takes,
> To face one more day of the same old mistakes.[94]

Marine helicopter crew chiefs were—and are—ingenious, inventive, universally talented, totally dedicated, and prodigious workers. No pilot has ever served with them and not come away amazed at the caliber of men who maintain the aircraft.

## Flight on Instruments

If there ever was one single point in the development of helicopters where all the difficulties came together, it was flight on instruments. The basic aerodynamics of the machines, the training of the pilots, and the foregone conclusion of a second-class status all combined to produce a problem that challenged even the most perceptive proponents of vertical amphibious assaults.

The pilots of the early helicopters did not fly in clouds or at night except in extreme emergencies. The assumption was that they did not know how. Much to the contrary, as experienced fixed-wing pilots, all of them were well trained in instrument flight techniques and were perfectly capable.

The truth of the matter was that the aircraft themselves were so unstable that no one could control them without seeing outside the cockpit. Flying by utilizing only the instruments in the aircraft by its very nature requires small deliberate corrections of the controls. Any drastic changes became self-compounding and the result is usually what is termed "an unusual attitude." In a fixed-wing aircraft, there are emergency procedures which can be utilized to recover back to normal flight. In an early helicopter there was "virtually no such thing as recovery from an unusual attitude."[95]

HMX–1 and the Navy squadrons all conducted experiments in the early 1950s to establish methods to conduct instrument flight. The progress was discouraging. The problems of instability defeated all but the most modest attempts. One report noted that "future helicopters will be provided with automatic pilots which will equip the helicopter with 'mechanical' stability and relieve the pilot of the stress and strain now existing in controlling instrument flight."[96]

Any significant capability would have to wait until the design and introduction of helicopters with stability systems. The first two to meet those requirements with any degree of success were the mighty "Deuces" and the UH–34, but the problem was not yet solved.

---

\* The term HAC, pronounced "hack," is a Helicopter Aircraft Commander. ASE, pronounced "ace," is the Automatic Stabilization Equipment on an UH–34.

No instruments were available which recognized that helicopters are different. Instead, instruments designed for fixed-wing aircraft were used. Two were particularly important. The artificial horizon appears as a miniature airplane flying against a background simulating the earth. The replica of the airplane moves exactly as does the aircraft itself. The background, however, contains a powerful gyroscope so that it always remains parallel to the ground. The effect is similar to what a pilot would be observing outside on a clear day, his aircraft moving against a fixed horizon. In a conventional airplane such an arrangement accurately portrays the attitude of the fuselage and thus of the wings. In a helicopter, with the rotor constantly moving in different planes, particularly when maneuvering, the fuselage seldom is pointed in the same direction as the rotary wings. The artificial horizon indicated the relationship of the cockpit to the ground, but not the rotor blades, yet the rotor blades controlled the flight. Thus the helicopter pilot found his most valuable instrument usually inaccurate and sometimes grossly so. No one but a helicopter pilot would have accepted an airplane for instrument flight with such a situation existing. Helicopter pilots had to. It was the only thing available.

The second instrument was the air speed indicator. Valuable at any time in flight, this instrument becomes critical on landing and takeoff. In both a fixed-wing aircraft and a helicopter, the pilot requires an exact knowledge of how fast he is going to accomplish a successful maneuver. Once again the helicopters were equipped with an instrument which was designed for fixed-wing aircraft. In this case, the down-wash from the rotor would render the airspeed indicator almost useless below 40 knots—just when the information was most critical. At slow speeds it was impossible to tell if the aircraft was moving forward. sideways, or even backward. Other instruments installed in helicopters were similar. Attempts to provide instruments specifically designed for helicopters were continually frustrated by high costs, weight, or unacceptable complexity.

In spite of the limitations of the stability systems and instruments, by the late 1950s UH-34s and HR2Ss could be found flying in the clouds, particularly up and down the east coast. The situation at Santa Ana was somewhat different. Any aircraft which flies on instruments usually proceeds along a regular route structure. These highways in the sky are controlled by the Federal Aviation Agency (FAA) and are subject to strict rules and regulations. One of them is that an aircraft must be at least 2,500 feet above any mountains which border the airway. Located in the Los Angeles basin, Santa Ana is ringed with mountains. With the additional height required by FAA, the minimum altitude a helicopter could fly on instruments often reached almost 10,000 feet. Even if the helicopter could fly at that altitude—and most could not—the ever-present effect of the thinner air reduced its payload and controllability to a marked degree. The pilots on the West Coast were, for all practical purposes, limited to a small stretch from San Diego to Los Angeles to practice instrument flight on airways. In addition, the presence of the slow moving helicopter created coordination problems with faster fixed-wing aircraft. Most controlling agencies preferred that the helicopters practice somewhere else.

Training on airways was vital, but it ignored a very basic point. Airways flight presupposed that the helicopter would take off and land at an airport. If an airport was available, why utilize a helicopter? Fixed-wing aircraft could do the same task more economically and certainly with more speed and comfort.

If the unique characteristics of a helicopter were to be used, the aircraft had to fly on instruments and land in a small unprepared clearing. Such a mission was an entirely different one than flight on airways. The difficulty was complicated in mountainous terrain. Where a conventional aircraft seldom operated below the tops of the mountains on instrument flight, a helicopter—if it was to perform fully its assigned mission—was seldom going to fly above the tops. It had to be able to navigate at night, in the rain, amid narrow valleys and hills, locate a zone, and make a successful landing. If the pilot committed an error, the result was the same as for his fellow aviator flying jets. All were dead.

By the end of December 1959 enough progress had been made to require all helicopter pilots to be fully rated for instrument flight. The problem of precise navigation off the airways remained.

Several solutions were proposed. In December 1961 the ever-inventive Colonel Archie Clapp described his latest ideas in an article in the *Marine Corps Gazette* entitled "The Missing Link: All Weather Terminal Guidance for Helicopters." [97] "As of now," he wrote, "helicopter operations into rugged, unfamiliar terrain under instrument flight condition (i.e., dark, nighttime or low visibility day-time) is an undertaking bordering on Kamikaze tactics." [98] Colonel Clapp described the procedures that had to be used:

> The only equipment now available in the FMF for guiding helicopters from initial point to landing zone touchdown is the helicopter pilot's eyeballs. One rather primitive visual aid has been provided to augment the eyeball, but that's all. Therefore a night approach into rugged terrain goes something like this: The helicopter pilot studies a contour map of the landing point and determines the best avenue of approach and retirement

based upon surrounding terrain and prevailing wind. He then predicts the altitude he must have at various checkpoints along his route in order to clear the terrain.

> With this planning behind him, the pilot reaches the initial point . . . and commences an approach to the landing site. When (and if) he gains visual contact with the ground, and if the Pathfinders* have accurately set up the best equipment available to them, the pilot sees a light which is either red, amber, or green.
>
> This approach light is a reasonably good aid for establishing a specific glide angle in flat terrain. As a life or death terrain clearance device, however, it is totally inadequate. And, of course, it is completely useless if clouds must be penetrated during the approach.[99]

Colonel Clapp came to the heart of the problem.

> It is difficult to believe that this approach light is the best landing aid our advanced technology can produce. Rather than being technologically infeasible, it is more likely that we don't have an adequate landing aid because of lack of familiarity with the problem.[100]

It was often difficult to explain to a non-helicopter pilot why old fixed-wing instruments were not entirely satisfactory, why it was difficult to obtain sufficient practice even on airways flight, and just what were the hazards of instrument flight in mountains.

He went on to call for an electronic device which would allow the helicopter to home in on it. It should be capable of establishing the direction to the zone, and a gradual rate of descent for:

> The helicopter cannot fly directly over the landing site at cruising altitude, stop and descend like an elevator to the site. As absurd as it might sound, this was proposed by one of the more reputable electronic engineering firms.[101]

Ignorance of ground effect and power settling (another characteristic of helicopters) was not a limited commodity.

Four years later in 1965 this same primitive approach light system was still in use. It was all that Colonel Kleppsattel and the pilots of HMM-264 had in the Dominican Republic. The different colored lights appearing out of the rain and darkness of the polo field provided the only final guidance for landing. Fortunately, the area was relatively flat.

Two months before the publication of Colonel Clapp's article, another proposal was made. The concept was different but could be complementary to his suggestion on terminal guidance. On 6 October 1961, the Landing Force Development Center at Quantico had sent a letter to CMC proposing a development characteristic for a "Self-Contained Navigation System for Helicopter" (SCNS).[102]

Colonel McCutcheon approved the proposal and on 4 December forwarded it to the CNO.[103] The Development Characteristic, No. AO 12501-2, was "designed to provide an advanced navigation system for incorporation in the follow-on aircraft to the HUS and HR2S" either on the production line or in a later modification.[104] The major features called for a capability to provide "sufficient information for enroute navigation of helicopters under all weather conditions, over any type of terrain or water, so that after a flight of one hour's duration during which the helicopter has traveled a distance of at least 100 miles," the airplane would be no more than one-fourth nautical mile from its intended position.[105]

Other features were the ability to operate in flight at a speed of 10 knots backwards to 175 forward. The terrain following was to be such that it must "permit the helicopter to operate with confidence over completely obscured unfamiliar terrain with a flight path" 200 feet above the hills and valleys.[106] Though not required, it was desirable that the system be able to detect wires, cables, or antenna which might obstruct the flight path. The equipment would be required to allow large formations of helicopters to make assaults so a specification was included which could permit up to 32 aircraft "to proceed in company without visual reference to each other." [107]

Finally, the SCNS had to be ready for operational testing prior to 1 July 1964. It was not until 19 March 1964 that the CNO published the Specific Operational Requirements (SOR) No. W-14-09 which set out the details of an all-weather system for Marine helicopters.[108] The concept still included all features of the SCNS, but had been refined and expanded. The new total package was to be called the Integrated Helicopter Avionics System (IHAS). It was to be a computer-controlled system which could present accurate displays to the pilot of his position, the terrain around him, and other aircraft in his formation, all of which could be fed into an automatic flight control system. Three contractors had conducted previous studies on the feasibility of IHAS. They were Texas Instruments, Nortronics, and Teledyne System Company.[109]

In March 1965 Teledyne was awarded a contract to produce four prototype IHAS sets. SCNS was to be a separate component included in the overall system. IHAS represented several firsts in the DOD and Navy development procedures. "The most significant was that this was the first time the Navy had given a single contractor responsibility for the entire avionics package of an aircraft." [110]

---

* Pathfinders are small teams which precede the first helicopters into the landing zone. They provide final guidance to the correct location for the aircraft.

The idea of such a system was so promising that the U.S. Army, in 1962, joined the program. In late 1964 DOD directed that the Navy and the Army would both share the cost on a 60/40 percent basis. Two of the completed experimental sets would be used in the Army development of the attack helicopter AH-56, "Cheyenne." By 1967, however, the difference in requirements had become pronounced and the Army withdrew.

The IHAS was to be developed in three stages. The first would be the SCNS. The second increment would add short range station keeping to allow formation flight on instruments. The third level would be the entire IHAS package. Due to the increase in cost and weight of IHAS, in September 1965 Teledyne recommended only the first two parts be installed in the CH-46. Two sets were ordered for use by Vertol to develop details of the installation. As the equipment was undergoing final design and testing, the Navy ordered sufficient SCNS to equip 91 (later 126) CH-46s and 25 CH-53s. The first flight was to be in June 1968.

It appeared that at long last helicopters would have a full instrument capability in rough terrain. Then, in one of the more frustrating chains of events experienced by the Navy and Marine Corps, the entire concept began to run into difficulty. Testing fell 26 months behind schedule. Cost overruns were encountered which required delicate and lengthy negotiations between the Navy and Teledyne.

It was discovered that when the SCNS was installed in the CH-46, electronic interference blanked out all radio transmissions. In July 1969, after five months of reengineering in a shielded hangar at Vertol, the problem remained unsolved. The last months of 1969 and the spring of 1970 saw one contract after another cancelled due to cost and delays. By the middle of the year, IHAS and all its components were, for all practical purposes, no longer an active program.

The decade of the 60s ended with little progress in instrument equipment for helicopters. A flight into mountainous terrain remained somewhat of a "kamikaze" mission. In view of the difficulties, the fact that so many such flights were successfully completed is a truly memorable chapter in the history of Marine Corps aviation.

# CHAPTER FIVE

## HELICOPTERS SHOOT BACK

### SHUFLY Ends

From 15 April 1962 to 8 March 1965 the brunt of Marine combat in Vietnam was born by Operation SHUFLY. The composition of the unit had remained essentially the same: a squadron of UH-34s augmented by three O-1s and a C-117. The MABS subunit and the small headquarters subsequently were reinforced by a security detachment from the 3d Marine Division on Okinawa.

SHUFLY was scheduled to move from Soc Trang to Da Nang in the summer of 1962. The switch was delayed several times by the strenuous objections of the senior advisor in the delta region, Colonel Daniel B. Porter, Jr., USA, and the Vietnamese commander of the area, Major General Le Van Nghiem. Colonel Porter was aware of the limitations of the Army H-21s which would replace the Marine helicopters. He wrote General Paul D. Harkins, ComUSMACV, that, among other things, "the Marines are better equipped. They have better navigational equipment. They have better maintenance capability. They have better pilots. They have high morale and a will to fly. They can and will fly night operations." [1]

In spite of the objections, on September 16 the first UH-34s arrived at Da Nang after a seven-hour flight from Soc Trang. The aircraft were from HMM-163, commanded by Lieutenant Colonel Robert L. Rathbun, which had relieved "Archie's Angels" of HMM-362 a month earlier.

The climate and terrain which confronted the squadron's "Ridge Runners" when they arrived in Da Nang was very different from the low flat land of the delta. In retrospect the geography of northern Vietnam was to have a major impact on the development of helicopters.

Were it not for the political and military turmoil, the area in which the Marines were to operate could be a paradise for sightseers. Long stretches of white beach border on the South China Sea. The sand is exceptionally fine and in some areas extends several miles behind the surf. Inland, for varying distances but seldom more than a dozen miles, are low-lying farm lands. Much of the area is devoted to the cultivation of rice in small paddies surrounded by clusters of thatched huts and bamboo hedgerows. All of the coastal plain is laced with rivers, streams, and canals which not only serve as irrigation for the rice and a source of fish, but also represent the complete transportation system. Roads are scarce and crude.

Arising abruptly from the low lands are the ramparts of the Annamite Cordillera, a chain of precipitous mountains which runs along the spine of most of Vietnam. Ranging up to 5000 feet high, the mountains have deep gorges cut through by rushing rivers. They are covered with a triple canopy jungle growth of teak and other tropic woods. A few openings exist which allow elephant grass to grow to heights of 10 to 12 feet. Just north of Da Nang, the mountains reach the sea at Hai Van Peninsula, effectively separating the population north and south of it.

Even the weather is different from that which prevails in the delta. From October through March the area is under the influence of the northeast monsoon. Rainfall increases in intensity until the end of January. During the monsoon, a phenomenon occurs which the French called the "crachin" with winds of up to 50 knots and fog and drizzle mixed with the rain. Cloud ceilings lower below 200 feet with visibility restricted to less than a half mile. The crachin may last for a few days early in the season to several weeks during the height of the monsoon. By April the weather begins to clear and the summer is hot, dry, with generally clear skies.

The effect of the weather and terrain was summed up by Lieutenant General McCutcheon:

> The northeast monsoon had a direct impact on all military operations in the area and especially on air operations. Because they can operate with lower ceilings and visibility minimums than fixed-wing aircraft, the helicopters would often perform their mission when the fixed-wing could not, at least along the flat coastal region. Inland, however, the hills and mountains make even helicopter flying hazardous at best. The pilots all developed a healthy respect for the northeast monsoon.[2]

Beginning in the fall of 1962, the pilots and crews would have additional time to gain that respect. The tours in Vietnam were extended to six months at the request of Colonel Julius W. Ireland, who had replaced Colonel Carey as the task unit commander on 1 July.[3]

A year later, in 1963, it appeared that SHUFLY had accomplished its mission. More than 1000 Americans were to be withdrawn by the end of December, and the Marines at Da Nang were to be included.[4]

Within a month after the announcement, their departure had been delayed until sometime in the first half of 1964. The reason was that SHUFLY was about to add another mission to its combat role. It was to train Vietnamese pilots and crews in the UH-34. At the conclusion of the training the Marine helicopters were to be turned over to the Vietnamese Air Force (VNAF).

In September, CinCPacFleet, Admiral Thomas H. Moorer, established a schedule which called for the training to be complete and the aircraft turned over by 31 March 1964. Immediately, the Commander Seventh Fleet, Admiral Roy L. Johnson, registered an objection. When the Marine helicopter units were operating from an LPH they were a part of his force. The admiral long had thought there should be three helicopter transport squadrons available and only recently had won approval of his plan. If the UH-34s were turned over to the Vietnamese, he would have three squadrons, but aircraft enough for only two. He was assured that, if the transfer plan were adopted, replacement aircraft would be provided at the appropriate time by diverting helicopters from the Sikorsky production line to Far East-based MAG-16. In November, the JCS directed Admiral Ulysses S. G. Sharp, CinCPac, to comment on the proposed extention of SHUFLY beyond the originally contemplated December withdrawal date. A series of conferences and consultations resulted in a recommendation that Marines remain until 30 June 1964. This would provide ample time to complete the training and effect the transfer of the aircraft. On 22 January, the JCS approved.[5]

The task would fall first to HMM-362 commanded by Lieutenant Colonel John H. Lavoy. A pilot who had flown helicopters in combat during the Korean War, he had arrived with his squadron in Da Nang on 1 February as the relief for HMM-361. The first training flights with Vietnamese pilots came three weeks later.[6]

Sufficient progress had been made by late April that General Harkins reaffirmed the termination date as 30 June. The 24 UH-34s to replace those turned over to the VNAF had arrived in Okinawa during the first part of the month. It appeared that the Marine Corps commitment to Vietnam once again was going to be reduced to advisors (the numbers of which had expanded considerably since the inception of SHUFLY), staff officers, and specialized communications personnel. As the date of the turnover approached, Lieutenant General Victor H. Krulak, Commanding General, Fleet Marine Force, Pacific, recommended that the squadron be indefinitely retained in Vietnam. It was providing operating units valuable training and experience.[7]

Three weeks before the extended withdrawal date, on 10 June 1964, JCS approved the recommendation to continue Operation SHUFLY. Nine days later, the aircraft were delivered to the VNAF. On 23 June, HMM-162, under the command of Lieutenant Colonel Oliver W. Curtis relieved HMM-364. The training program was not completely terminated. In August, ComUSMACV directed that an additional 97 VNAF pilots and 45 helicopter mechanics receive instruction. The training, however, was not to take precedence over combat operations. By early 1965, combat commitments consumed almost all of the available helicopter flights and only a few more Vietnamese pilots completed the course.[8]

The training program conducted by the SHUFLY squadrons had mixed results. The Vietnamese often lacked the mechanical skills necessary to repair the aircraft. Progress in learning how to keep the helicopters flying was slow.

With one short exception, the SHUFLY squadron represented the only Marine Corps aircraft in Vietnam. In November 1964 Typhoon "Kate" devastated the northern coast of the nation. Lieutenant Colonel (later Major General) Joseph Koler, Jr., in command of HMM-365 in Da Nang, was directed to rescue thousands of inhabitants who were marooned by the flooding rivers and paddies. The SLF squadron was on board the USS *Princeton* at Hong Kong, conducting a routine port visit. On 12 November the ship was ordered to proceed to the coast off Quang Ngai, south of Da Nang, so that HMM-162 could assist in the relief efforts. Lieutenant Colonel Curtis and his squadron arrived on 16 November and did not complete their mission until 23 November. During those few days for the first time, more than one Marine squadron operated within the country.

## Land the Landing Force

The latter part of 1964 witnessed a growing escalation of the United States commitment to combat in Southeast Asia. Laos remained a thorny problem. A frustrating series of political coups in South Vietnam sapped the military energy of the nation. Then, on 4 August, North Vietnamese patrol boats attacked two U.S. destroyers on patrol in the Gulf of Tonkin. Retaliatory air raids were ordered but brought no lessening of North Vietnam's support of the Viet Cong. The security element of SHUFLY was exchanging fire with snipers on an almost regular basis. The airbase at Da Nang became seriously threatened. On 7 March 1965 (6 March, Washington time), the JCS sent the long-waited signal: land the Marines at Da Nang.[9] *

In a quick two-way switch, Lieutenant Colonel Koler's HMM-365, which was back on board the *Princeton*, delivered its equipment and aircraft to Da Nang on the 9th. The officers and men from HMM-162 were flown from Futema to Vietnam the same day and took over the helicopters. The personnel from HMM-365 reembarked on the *Princeton* and sailed to Futema to accept the equipment of HMM-162. On 3 May, VMO-2 arrived from Futema. Its complement of aircraft included three additional O-1s, and most important, six armed UH-1Es.[10]

By April 1965, all elements of the Marine air-ground team were finally reunited. It had been a long, sometimes lonely, existence for the Marines of SHUFLY. The three years of continuous combat since Colonel Clapp and his "Angels" arrived at Soc Trang had provided the Marine Corps with a wealth of experience. The lessons learned were to dominate the development of helicopters for the next decade. One of the first questions to which the Marine Corps tried to apply its SHUFLY experience was that of arming and armoring helicopters.

## Armoring

> On introduction of Marine helicopter squadrons into the Republic of Vietnam, only the UH-34 was involved. At that time no armor plate was installed on the aircraft. As the intensity of enemy resistance increased, it became clear that some type of armor was needed for protection of both aircraft and crew.
>
> CGMFPac message to CMC [11]

In the Marine Corps, helicopter damage from hostile fire was not a new experience. Over 12 years before SHUFLY began, on 20 September 1950, an HO3S-1 observation helicopter was struck while on a reconnaissance mission in the vicinity of Inchon, Korea.[12] The pilot was able to land safely. The incident is the initial one recorded of a Marine helicopter receiving combat damage. Not so fortunate was First Lieutenant Arthur R. Bancroft. Just nine days later, his helicopter was hit and exploded. Lieutenant Bancroft was the first Marine helicopter pilot killed in action.[13]

---

* For more information see: Jack Shulimson and Maj. Charles M. Johnson, *U.S. Marines in Vietnam, 1965: The Landing and the Buildup* (Washington: History and Museums Division, Headquarters, U. S. Marine Corps, 1978.)

In Vietnam, on 23 April 1962, the first SHUFLY helicopter received combat damage. Again, as in Korea, the pilot was able to land safely. It was not until the first week in October that a Marine became a casualty. A crew chief, Lance Corporal James I. Mansfield, was wounded while on a flight to an outpost near Da Nang.[14]

In the time between the incidents involving Lieutenant Bancroft and Corporal Mansfield, the Marine Corps had made a number of studies of protective armor for helicopters. One, in 1960, had concluded that "passive protective measures in the form of armor kits for aircraft and protective vests and helmets for crews must be provided for presently operational helicopters."[15] Subsequently it was suggested that the concept be expanded to include "a means to protect assault airlift pilots and embarked troops from small arms fire and fragments."[16]

Any attempt to add armor plate to helicopters had to resolve two problems immediately. First, it never had been the intention of the Marine Corps to utilize these aircraft to conduct assaults on heavily defended positions. The vulnerability of helicopters had been recognized and appreciated for a long time. The second problem was that, at least until the introduction of the HR2S and the UH-34, most Marine helicopters had difficulty lifting any appreciable payload much less the weight of armor plating. General Binney, Director of Aviation at the time of the suggestion to provide protection for the embarked troops, responded "the weight penalty of armoring the entire troop cabin area will prove to be prohibitive . . . and probably approach a 50 percent reduction in payload."[17]

In the first three and a half months of operation in the Mekong delta, all but six of Colonel Clapp's helicopters had been hit at least once by enemy fire.[18] A study conducted by the Marine Corps Operational Analysis Group pointed out that "four hits, involving three helicopters, were taken in the oil system early in the tour of HMM-362 and directed attention to the vulnerability of this area."[19] The report concluded, "However, whether protection of this area alone is worth an armor penalty of 200-300 lbs or whether rather some lesser degree of protection should be provided to a wider area of the helicopter is an interesting question in view of the hit experience."[20]

Because the helicopter was operating in close proximity to the enemy, the shots did not seem to indicate any particular pattern. They were peppered all over the aircraft. Battle damage did not lend itself to statistical analysis. A solution to the difficulty continued to be elusive for the rest of the war. One effort, much later, was instituted by a team of systems analysts.

They "prescribed the criteria for describing the intensity of enemy fire thusly: 1-15 rounds per minute—light fire. 16-30 rounds per minute—moderate fire. 31 and over rounds per minute—intense fire."[21] Lieutenant Colonel Bertram W. McCauley described the results:

> On after action reports we were required to use these terms to describe enemy fire we encountered on a mission. One of our pilots, after a particularly 'hairy' fight, wrote the word 'withering' under the description of enemy fire. The next day he got a phone call from an indignant systems analyst asking *just* what constituted 'withering fire' to which our stalwart aviator replied: 'One round through the cockpit!'[22]

Regardless of the definition, in 1962 the Marine Corps took immediate steps to provide armor for the SHUFLY helicopters. General Anderson reported in October that "it has been determined that the UH-34 helicopter was extremely vulnerable to small arms fire in the area of the oil cooler system. A program to fabricate easily installed armor kits . . . was initiated in June."[23] Due to the time required to manufacture them, "it was decided to procure a limited number of interim kits made of aluminum and then follow-on kits of armor plate."[24]

The first sets, which consisted of a large protective shield bolted over the bottom of the oil cooler, were shipped to Da Nang in the late summer. They added 160 pounds to the weight of the UH-34s but were effective against .30 caliber gun fire. Eventually further modifications were incorporated and by 1965 the kit weight was approximately 200 pounds.[25]

Protection for the pilots and crew chief was initially provided by standard Navy-issued flak suits. This armor, however, was designed for a person standing erect. When worn sitting down "gaps around the waist and pelvic region" were created and further modifications had to be made.[26]

In 1964, in conjunction with the U.S. Army, the Marine Corps developed a "light-weight plastic . . . dual package outfit consisting of an 'air crew protection' component and a 'vital parts protection' component."[27]

The crew system consisted of a seat plate, a back plate, and side plates for each pilot. It weighed approximately 225 pounds. Similar kits were planned for the UH-1E, the CH-46, and CH-53. Further developments beyond these were stymied by the problem of loss of payload. In late 1965, DC/S (Air), General Robertshaw, concluded that "it appears improbable that complete armor protection for helicopters . . . can presently be provided for routine operations." He continued:

> For the present some helicopter crew protection can be provided, but transparent panels cannot be armored. The prohibitive weight penalty involved in armoring the helicopter cabin compartment will require the embarked troops to rely on body armor for protection.
>
> Until lighter material and body armor . . . can be developed, the Marine Corps will continue to provide armor protection only for aircraft crew members and vital aircraft components.[28]

As limited as the armor protection was, the additional weight combined with the climate and geography of Vietnam significantly reduced the capability of the UH-34. General Krulak sent a message outlining the difficulties:

> Squadrons in RVN [equipped with the UH-34] operate with reduced fuel loads of 1000 vice 1500 lbs leaving a residual lift capability of only 1300 lbs. If the particular mission requires a full fuel load of 1500 pounds, compensation [has to be] made by reducing the payload of either cargo or personnel to about 800 pounds.[29]

He went on to plead for no more armor than absolutely necessary, though he did conclude that the UH-1E possibly could use more than it had.

Even armor was not enough. A method had to be devised which would allow an attack to be made on any enemy shooting at the helicopters. The problem was approached from several different angles.

### Helicopter Escorts

> Attack aircraft, naval gunfire, and artillery prepare the landing zones and approach and retirement lanes by destroying known enemy threats prior to the arrival of the first helicopter wave. Attack aircraft provide protection for helicopters traveling to and from the landing zones. They also provide close air support for the helicopter-borne force.
>
> Helicopter Operations
> FMF Manual 3-3
> 12 June 1963[30]

Classic Marine Corps doctrine was explicit. Protection of the helicopters was the mission of fixed-wing aircraft. Unfortunately, not until April 1965 were Marine Corps attack aircraft permitted in Vietnam. In the meantime, the SHUFLY squadrons had to rely on aircraft from the Vietnamese Air Force, some of which had American co-pilots. The escort consisted of propeller-driven T-28 two-seat trainers and large, single-engine, attack aircraft of the post-Korean War era, the Douglas-built AD series. Occasionally a twin-engine World War II bomber, the B-26, would be added to the protecting air cover. The results were not totally satisfactory. First, there were seldom enough escort aircraft available to neutralize the enemy effectively. Communication between the Marines and the Vietnamese pilots was often difficult. One study conducted in 1962 regretfully concluded: "Preparatory strikes in the Landing Zone or objective area were not made regularly, although supporting air would make an exploratory pass."[31]

Part of the reluctance to provide full support was based on the complications of:

> ... the indistinguishability of the fleeing VC from frightened civilians; the lack of definition of front lines, and the resultant reluctance of ground commanders to call in ... strikes when the location of friendly forces was unknown.[32]

The most serious difficulty was that the training of the Marine air-ground team in close cooperation was not being put to use. Marine attack pilots understood what was required to protect the helicopters, and Marine helicopter pilots knew how best to utilize the protection, but political considerations kept them from working together.

Jets were not the only solution. A requirement for a smaller, less expensive escort long had been recognized. The early reports coming out of the Mekong Delta stirred renewed interest in a Light Armed Reconnaissance Aircraft (LARA).

## Early Studies of the LARA

On 25 July 1962, General Shoup asked the CNO to provide six T-28 aircraft to evaluate "reconnaissance, target-marking, escort and protection of helicopters . . . and for limited close air support in lightly defended areas." He further proposed that the aircraft be considered for a replacement of the fleet of aging O-1 observation planes.[33]

The T-28 was familiar to most Marine pilots. Since the middle 1950s it had been utilized as an intermediate trainer at Pensacola for all pilots. Equipped with a Wright 1820 engine, which was a very slight modification of the one installed in the UH-34, the two-seat trainer had performance roughly equal to the best combat aircraft at the end of World War II. There would be no problem finding pilots capable of flying the North American Aircraft product.

Though General Shoup had requested six of them, the number was subsequently reduced to only four. They were assigned to VMO-6 at Marine Corps Auxiliary Air Field (MCAAF), Camp Pendleton, California. Two of the aircraft were modified with two .50 caliber machine guns housed in pods, and all were to have six bomb racks installed on the wings. The first T-28s arrived at the squadron in February 1963.

Even as the evaluation was beginning, an urgent need developed for the assignment of the aircraft elsewhere. Reports from SHUFLY indicated increasing enemy resistance in the Da Nang area. The VNAF escort was too limited to ensure helicopter assaults without considerable battle damage. On 29 March 1963, General Shoup advised FMFPac that "in order to preclude further hazards of the UH-34D helicopters in fire suppression missions in Vietnam it is desired that a fixed-wing attack capability be provided to HMM-162 (the SHUFLY squadron) at the earliest possible time." The introduction of Marine jets at the moment was still a political impossibility, so the Commandant went on to request that FMFPac "initiate action to provide support by suitably configured T-28 aircraft."[34]

FMFPac answered that the O-1s were badly in need of replacement anyway and assigning T-28s "would place the helicopter squadron in a position to implement a fixed wing support/armed reconnaissance role from within our own resources."[35]

Considerable discussion of the proposal followed throughout the Pacific area commands. Finally, General Harkins cabled from Saigon that he did not concur with replacing the O-1s with the T-28s. He had no objection, however, to testing the four aircraft in helicopter escort roles.[36]

Three days later, on 5 May, Admiral Felt, CincPac, put the entire plan in abeyance. The withdrawal was scheduled the following month and SHUFLY would then be terminated. This revised schedule to withdraw the Marines cancelled the entire project. By the end of the year the evaluation at VMO-6 was complete and the aircraft reassigned. They never were shipped to Vietnam. Marine helicopter pilots still were without Marine escort aircraft and would be for another year and a half.[37]

## Arming the Transports

If the limited fixed-wing support available before 1965 could not suppress enemy fire, the transport helicopters were not completely defenseless. The crew could shoot back. One of the earliest examples of a

USMC Photo 530103

*A Marine North American T-28B "Trojan" trainer stands on the airstrip at Quantico, March 1961. The Marines proposed to arm such aircraft as helicopter escorts.*

helicopter crewman firing at the enemy was recorded in 1953. Staff Sergeant Leo A. Masud in Korea had used a sniper rifle from a CH–19.[38] The accuracy obtained from shooting out the door of that unstable, primitive helicopter, unfortunately, was not recorded. Vietnam was somewhat different.

When he arrived in Soc Trang, Colonel Clapp "decided not to install machine guns on the helicopters as the Army had done." The principal reason was that such an installation would partially obstruct the door on the UH–34, and thus slow up the exit of the assault troops. Colonel Clapp "figured that our best defense was to hold our time on the ground in the landing zone to a bare minimum." To accomplish this, the cabin door had to be clear of any machine guns. The crew chief and the co-pilot were armed with submachine guns. "They, of course, fired only when they could see a VC soldier firing at us."[39] The results were not all that could be desired. A study of operations in the delta concluded that "it can be stated that neither the presence of fixed wing air cover, nor chance of fire from the helicopters appear to deter the Viet Cong from firing."[40] The situation at Da Nang was even more serious. "In many landing zones of the mountainous I Corps area, even those which are 'secure,' helicopters are subject to fire from small arms, machine guns, and even mortars."[41]

By the fall of 1962, the grease guns had been discarded in favor of a M–60 machine gun mounted in the door and fired by the crew chief. The objections of Colonel Clapp had fallen victim to the increasing boldness of the VC in shooting at helicopters. Two lightweight AR–15 automatic rifles also were carried in each aircraft. One was "available in the cabin and one operated by the co-pilot. The forward cabin window on the left side has been removed to permit firing from the left side of the cabin."[42]

In February 1963, the JCS temporarily authorized a change in the rules of defense for helicopter crews. The crews now could "engage clearly defined VC elements considered to be a threat to the safety of the helicopters and their passengers." The authorization to shoot before being shot at, however, lasted less than a week. Another change in the rules again permitted return fire for "defensive purposes only."[43]

The definition of "defensive purposes only" seemed to lose something in the transmission from Washington to Marine helicopter pilots engaged in a deadly struggle in Vietnam. The SHUFLY squadron proudly announced that on 13 March 1963, three UH–34s for the first time had provided close air support from helicopters.[44] Probably as no coincidence, less than two weeks later, General Shoup was striving to have Marine T–28s deployed to Vietnam for helicopter escort.

Even the AR–15 rifles were not enough. In May 1964 they were recalled and another M–60 machine gun—now one on each side of the cabin—substituted.[45] The problems of close-in fire support for the helicopters was pointed out vividly in a widely read report submitted in December 1963 by Lieutenant Colonel (later Major General) William R. Quinn, the Marine Corps representative at the Military Research and Development Center in Thailand. This organization was assigned to assist the Thais in developing specialized capabilities in the field of counterinsurgency. Lieutenant Colonel Quinn, an experienced helicopter and jet pilot, visited SHUFLY the first part of October. He wrote of the frustrations being encountered:

> Most Viet Cong targets are detected from the air by drawing and observing their fire. Under the present rules of engagement this is one of the few ways to identify and be permitted to fire at a VC target. Trying

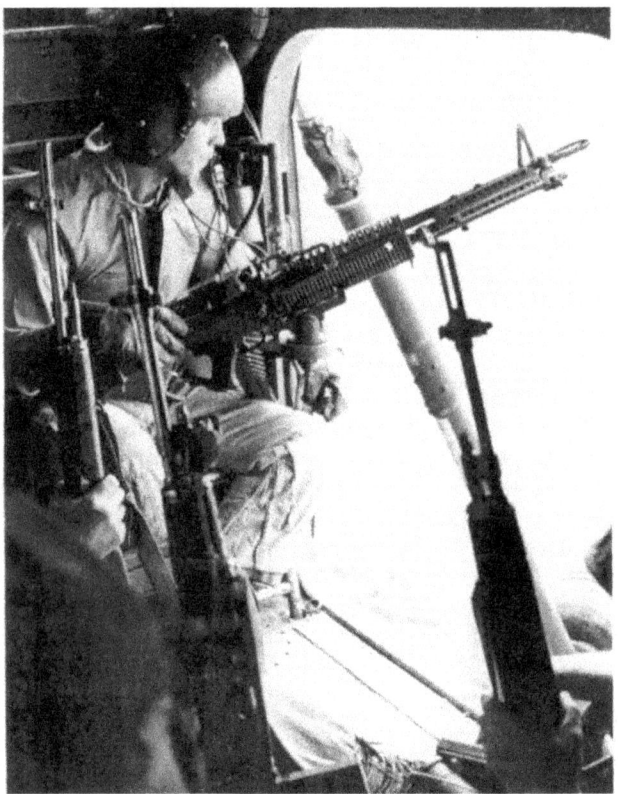

USMC Photo A186600

*A UH–34 door gunner mans his M–60 machine gun during a patrol insert mission in Vietnam, January 1966. The door-mounted machine gun improved the UH–34 firepower protection, but the gun partially blocked troop movement in and out of the helicopter.*

to pinpoint the number and exact location of the individuals doing the firing is quite difficult. Many times you could only tell the general direction from which it was coming . . . the jungle looks so much the same if you look away for a moment, even after seeing a flash, the chances are you cannot return your gaze to the same point with any accuracy."[46]

The battles between helicopter crews and the Viet Cong refused to abate. The results often were disastrous for the Marines. In May 1964, the JCS reminded everyone of just what the relative roles were supposed to be. "Helicopters are for use as transports and their weapons are for the protection of the aircraft and passengers," they cabled. "Armed helicopters will not be used as substitutes for Close Air Support."[47]

Just what was to be substituted for the scarce close air support was not specified, and as 1964 drew to a close, the Marine Corps faced a dilemma in Vietnam. Its fixed-wing aircraft were not permitted to escort its helicopters, and support from the VNAF was limited. The weight penalty from armoring the UH–34 was becoming a serious hindrance to operations, and yet aircraft still were being shot down. Above all, the increasing severity of the opposition was proving more than a match for the two M–60 machine guns installed in the UH–34s. One proposed solution was to design and equip a helicopter specifically to act as an attack aircraft: the gunship.

## Armed Helicopters

The idea of converting a helicopter into an attack aircraft was neither new nor original. Within a year of the Marine Corps receiving its first helicopter, studies began on utilizing it in just such a role. By the spring of 1949 the concept had been expanded to include defense against enemy tanks:

> It is envisioned that the supporting tactics in the use of the helicopter for this purpose might include the use of covering artillery fire . . . to neutralize antiaircraft weapons and the operation of such an anti-tank helicopter from an appropriate level smoke blanket laid by the helicopter itself.[48]

At the time, research was being conducted "in connection with the test firing of rocket type projectiles in an effort to establish the effect . . . on the helicopter." The first tests were disappointing, mainly due to the limited lift capability of the helicopters and their instability as a gun platform.

The idea of an armed helicopter, however, was not abandoned. In 1957 it gained new impetus. Lieutenant Colonel Victor J. Croizat, an authority on French military matters and the first Marine Corps advisor to the Vietnamese armed forces, was dispatched to observe the use of helicopters during the war in Algeria. He was accompanied by Major David Riley. The two Marines returned to Washington on 27 June and submitted a lengthy report a week later.

"[French] armed helicopter proponents," they wrote, "have a twofold thought—protection of helicopter forces and provision for a highly flexible base of fire in support of ground elements until they are debarked and capable of self-support with organic weapons." They had observed or had learned of French Army helicopters armed with machine guns, bazookas, rockets, missiles, and even recoilless cannon. The report concluded that, even though French operations were hampered by the limited number of obsolete helicopters which were utilized, further observations should be made to keep the Marine Corps abreast of the French experiences.[49]

Simultaneously, the Division of Aviation exhibited renewed interest in the development of armed helicopters. Two years after Lieutenant Colonel Croizat returned from Algeria, General Munn wrote of the progress which had been made. Though a number of projects were under way or contemplated, "the basic problem [still remaining] is that of determining whether or not Marine Corps helicopters should be armed." By March 1959 tests had been made on mounting a French-designed, SS–11 wire-guided, air-to-surface missile on an HOK. Also "preliminary information obtained . . . indicate no difficulty in adapting the Zuni air to ground rocket pod to the HUS."[50]

Smaller 2.75-inch rockets and 20 millimeter cannon were under consideration. Probably the most interesting evaluation was the firing of a "Bullpup" from a UH–34. This missile was 11 feet long, weighed approximately 600 pounds, and was mounted on the right hand side of the aircraft. Control was by radio, with the pilot able to steer it through the use of a device on his control stick. In the summer of 1960 the first one was successfully fired by Captain Samuel J. Fulton, a member of HMX–1 which was conducting the evaluation. From an altitude of 1,500 feet the missile traveled over 10,000 yards. Accuracy was rated excellent.

In the next 12 months, 10 more were successfully fired. On the one aircraft that had been especially adapted to the Bullpup, 20mm guns had been added. The total weight, including strengthening of the airplane, missile, and ammunition was 2,378 pounds—almost the maximum possible pay load for the UH–34.[51] During these tests, the Marine Corps was "monitoring the progress being made by the U.S. Army in this field, through close contact with the Marine Corps Liaison Officer at Fort Rucker, Alabama."[52]

The Army had achieved impressive results in developing armed helicopters. In 1958 it successfully had loaded a version of the H-34 with 40 2.75- and 2.5-inch rockets, 9 machine guns, and 2 20mm cannon.[53] In the early 1960s it had conducted experiments with the same aircraft loaded with 20 4.5-inch rockets. In this case, the helicopter was not used for an airborne attack. It was landed and a track-roller dolly inserted under the tail wheel. Soldiers then could swing the entire machine and aim it just as if it were a cannon. As soon as the rockets were launched, everyone got back in, the aircraft took off, returned to home base, and reloaded for another mission.[54]

The enthusiasm of the Army for armed helicopters was based on a very significant difference between its requirements and those of the Marine Corps. The Army was prohibited by law from operating fixed-wing attack aircraft. Thus, if it were to have airborne firepower, it was going to have to rely on armed helicopters.

## Gunships for the Marines?

As General Greene later was to recount, many Marine aviators were "adamantly opposed"[55] to adding helicopter gunships to the inventory of Marine Corps aircraft. This opposition, like a fine-grade golf ball, had many layers, each separate from the others and yet related to them.

Many fixed-wing aviators believed that helicopter pilots were inferior and unsuited to the dramatic and demanding tasks of dropping bombs and shooting rockets and guns. A more substantial reason for opposition was the fact that Marine Corps tactical doctrine, practice, and equipment were all geared to the protection of helicopter transports by fixed-wing aircraft. Incorporation of gunships would require a major change in concept—something not to be taken lightly.

Opponents of gunships continually pointed out that such a helicopter would be relatively slow compared to a fixed-wing aircraft and hence more vulnerable. In addition, even with advanced stability systems, helicopters were far from ideal gun platforms. Even the proponents of armed helicopters had to agree with these arguments, although they insisted that gunships had advantages which outweighed these disadvantages.

Perhaps of most concern to Marine opponents of gunships were the restrictions on the total number of Marine Corps aircraft. If gunships were to be provided, a similar number of fixed-wing aircraft would have to be deleted. Such a course of action was hardly likely to stir enthusiasm among jet pilots. More important, as Major General Norman J. Anderson later wrote:

> ... planners could foresee that at some point in sacrificing fixed-wing capabilities to [helicopters], the Marine Corps would lose its main organizational distinction from the Army: its *combination* of ground and air combat power..* [56]

For example, the procurement of armed helicopters could endanger the LARA program. The requirement for a small, fixed-wing aircraft of modest performance which could fill the gap between jets and helicopters had been validated by VMO-6 with the four T-28s at Camp Pendleton. Preliminary specifications had been published for a twin-engine, two-seat, turbo-prop aircraft which could perform light attack and reconnaissance roles.** An armed helicopter might overlap into the LARA's mission and jeopardize OSD and Congressional support.

Most of the arguments for helicopter gunships came from Marines acquainted with the situation and problems in Vietnam. The war was being fought under peculiar circumstances familiar only to the handful of Marines who had served there. These Marines had difficulty convincing anyone that a helicopter war in Southeast Asia required new approaches to the problem of escort aircraft. Colonel (later Major General) Noah C. New wrote of this frustration:

> The incompatibility of helicopter and jets was a lesson learned early during the Vietnam conflict, but there were so few Marines involved that it was difficult to accept the requirement for helicopter gunships as authentic and authoritative by those who did not have this recent experience. The advocates of helicopter gunships during the period 1962-1964 simply could not present a convincing argument that helicopters had a place in our arsenal of aviation weapons.[57]

Many Marines without experience in SHUFLY could not understand why several fixed-wing jets fully loaded with bombs and napalm could not adequately secure a landing zone for helicopters. The reason, as proponents of gunships tried to explain, was that in the densely populated areas where the helicopterborne assaults were being made, firepower had to be applied with almost surgical precision. The most fundamental tenet in the Marine Corps prosecution of the war was protection of the civilian population from the inroads of the Viet Cong. A village might have but a small element of the enemy in it—often against the will of the citizens. If that small enemy element opened fire on approaching helicopters, a dozen 500-pound bombs in the middle of the village might indeed suppress the fire; but they hardly would "win the hearts and minds" of the frightened or uncommitted residents. It took a long time, however, for supporters of gunships to convince fellow Marines on this point.

---

* Italics in *Anderson Comments*, p. 2.

** The aircraft eventually procured was the North American-built OV-10.

Any attempt to resolve the armed helicopter controversy had to take account of two central and contradictory facts: the war in Vietnam was unique, but Vietnam was not the only area of responsibility of the Marine Corps. During the time SHUFLY was operating with a minimum of support and discussion of the value of armed helicopters was at its peak in the Marine Corps, at least seven major crises occurred in other parts of the world. Each of these could have led to a U.S. military commitment. Fighting continued in Laos, with the U.S. assisting the anti-Communist factions. There were riots and shooting confrontations in Panama over sovereignty of the canal. Haiti simmered; Cyprus exploded. Belgian withdrawal from the Congo left that new African nation in anarchy. Armed conflict with Russia over Berlin and Cuba was a constant possibility.

The Marine Corps had to maintain a readiness to fight in all of these areas and indeed anywhere in the world. Hard experience had taught Marines that they should not put themselves in a position where all of their equipment, doctrine, and tactics were tailored for only one specific theater of war or type of combat. Marines recalled that, 12 years before, they had been more prepared to repeat the beachhead and jungle operations of World War II than to fight in the bitterly cold mountains of North Korea. They had not forgotten the lessons so painfully learned.

General Greene, who had become Commandant on 1 January 1964, fully understood the problem and accurately perceived the dangers. To him fell the burden of maintaining a Marine Corps equipped for and capable of defending the nation in any "clime or place."

On 6 February 1964, this quietly determined Vermonter sat down and personally wrote out his thoughts:

> The highly successful and battle-tested doctrine and techniques of Marine close air support evolved over the years has not changed as a result of our experience in South Vietnam. Marine Corps doctrine calls for tactical fixed wing aircraft to perform offensive and defensive fire missions in support of ground troops and helicopter movement. In South Vietnam, Marine Corps helicopter units have been faced with a special situation in which Marine Corps tactical fixed wing aircraft have not been made available to perform their normal support missions. Consequently, Marine helicopter units have employed that support which has been made available to them. This support has consisted of United States Army armed helicopters used primarily as firing platforms for machine guns and rockets to provide escort for troop-carrying helicopters and to furnish suppressive fires in helicopter landing zones. Certain fixed wing aircraft furnished by the Republic of Vietnam Air Force have also been utilized to provide offensive and defensive close support fires for Marine Corps troop-carrying helicopters. In addition, the crews of Marine Corps helicopters have been armed with rifles and machine guns with which to defend themselves when fired upon. Co-operation by the United States Army and the Republic of Vietnam Air Force has been excellent. As a result of its combat experiences in South Vietnam, the Marine Corps has found that its tactics and techniques of close air support have been reaffirmed. It, nevertheless, does not oppose continued experimentation and possible development of the armed helicopter as a stable firing platform for integrated weapons subsystems designed to provide both offensive and defensive fires against ground targets.[58]

A month later he sent a letter to all Marine Corps general officers "for the guidance of members of your staffs, or for other use as you may consider appropriate." In it he outlined the efforts of the Army to develop an airborne helicopter attack capability and added further details to his position. "This is not to intimate," he stated, "that helicopters so armed cannot be used effectively against limited opposition and in the *environment of the politico-military artificialities* which exist in the Republic of Vietnam."[59] *

## Armed UH-34s

As the termination of SHUFLY kept being postponed, conditions in Vietnam prompted some development of armed helicopters. Since 13 April 1963, Marine helicopters had been escorted by Army UH-1B gunships. Six aircraft from the Utility Tactical Company permanently based in Da Nang and armed with four forward-firing 7.62mm M-60 machine guns and 16 2.75-inch aerial rockets (FEAR), escorted the UH-34s "on all troop carrying missions and on all missions into known V. C. infested areas."[60]

By late summer 1964, even this escort was not sufficient protection. On 17 August, General Greene directed MCLFDC and HMX-1 to begin work on an armament kit for the UH-34.[61] Less than two weeks later the first test firing had been completed.[62] The kit, or TK-1 (Temporary Kit-1) as it was known, consisted of two pods for rockets and two M-60 machine guns. The weapons were mounted on a platform bolted just above the landing gear struts. One pod, containing 18 2.75-inch rockets, was installed on each side of the helicopter. The machine guns were on the right side above the rockets.

The entire installation, including 1,000 rounds of ammunition weighed just over 1,000 pounds. Generals Mangrum and Robertshaw, along with other representatives watched a demonstration of a flight firing on the TK-1 on 8 September. The conclusion was that the kit on a UH-34 "could adequately provide fire support similar to that presently available in Vietnam."[63] The TK-1 was a simple, readily installed modification that could be manufactured easily by

---

* Italics by author.

most aircraft maintenance men. The Station Operations and Engineering Squadron (SOES) at Quantico was to fabricate sufficient numbers for shipment to SHUFLY.

Two of the kits were sent to Okinawa for pilot familiarization. General Krulak, then visiting Futema, decided to test the gun-firing UH-34 himself in order to "satisfy ourselves that they had a reasonable capability." "After the first one was mounted," he later wrote, "I took the opportunity to fire the system from a helicopter in flight." As a result of this experience, Krulak had to agree with the pilots' earlier conclusion that the gun kit, "while better than nothing, was operable only at such short range as to make its overall usefulness doubtful. Nevertheless, we were in favor of its use until something better could be developed." Much later, Krulak ruefully acknowledged that adoption of the gun kits for the UH-34 was "step one in a succession of events which resulted in our sacrificing much of our liaison, observation and forward air controller capability for *ad hoc* gunship roles in the UH-1E era."[64]

In spite of the misgivings of General Krulak and the pilots, the kits were manufactured and the first ones arrived in Vietnam early in November. Testing by HMM-365, however, had to be temporarily suspended due to the squadron's commitment to flood relief during Typhoon Kate. The squadron reported that the limited evaluation accomplished before 17 November indicated that there might be some unforeseen problems. By mid-December, all the kits had been installed, and, although more testing was required, "with proper crew training and utilization, the aircraft [can] perform the mission satisfactorily as armed escort and for fire suppression." Crew training was accelerated by the forced transition program which brought into the squadron pilots with previous experience in aerial gunnery. They were pressed into service as a nucleus of instructors.[65]

The next three months of experience verified that the UH-34 had severe shortcomings as a gunship. Its relatively low speed, the inherent vulnerability of critical rotor systems, and the type of warfare being waged, all made the UH-34 a lucrative target for the Viet Cong. In addition, the helicopter was hardly an ideal gun platform. To achieve the desired accuracy from rockets and fixed machine guns, the aircraft had to be flown in perfectly balanced flight. The instability of a helicopter made this difficult under the best of circumstances, and during violent maneuvers in turbulent air it was impossible.

By the end of April, MAG-16 reported that the TK-1 kits "have not proved effective in combat operations." This evaluation was based on the "bitter experience" that the UH-34 gunships accounted for only 15 percent of the flight time in Vietnam but were taking 85 percent of the hits.[66] A complicating factor was that the TK-1 installations further reduced the already limited payload of assault troops or cargo. The recommendation that no further kits be procured was adopted.

### The Armed UH-1E

Even before the first UH-1E was delivered to the Marine Corps, suggestions had been made to equip it as an armed helicopter. The Army versions were being manufactured with modifications suitable for a full system of armament. "Bell Helicopter, rather than retool, found it cheaper and more advantageous to assemble the Marine UH-1E with identical modifications as those required on the armed version of [the UH-1B/D] Army helicopters."

In November 1963, DC/S (Air) reported that "the Army is very enthused with the [UH-1B/D] as a light weapons fire system," and suggested that 12 aircraft in each VMO should be converted into armed helicopters.[67] The idea, however, became enmeshed in

USMC Photo 532041

*The TK-1 was designed to convert the UH-34 into an armed helicopter. The round rocket pod is mounted below the two machine guns.*

controversy on the role of helicopters as attack aircraft and little progress was made at the time.

A year later, as SHUFLY continued to report difficulties in conducting assaults without conventional fixed-wing escort aircraft, another attempt to arm the UH–1E was made. The CNO sent a letter on 19 September 1964 to BuWeps stating:

> . . . the Marine Corps has an urgent requirement for six Ground Fire Suppression Armament Kits to be installed on the Assault Support Helicopter [UH-1E] within the next 60 to 90 days.

Then, in very precise language which reflected the difference of opinion within the Marine Corps, he spelled out the reason for his request:

> Tactical doctrine requires these helicopters to perform observation, reconnaissance, and rescue missions forward of friendly lines without armed escort. There is no present system of self defense against ground fire for these helicopters.[68]

The armament was to be used only for self-defense. No mention was made of escorting assault troop helicopters. The letter went on to request BuWeps to "select equipment, determine the technical feasibility of the complete system and install the selected equipment in six UH–1E helicopters." [69]

The actual design was to be the responsibility of HMX–1 at Quantico. It had just completed the fabrication of the TK–1 for the UH–34 and had gained experience in modifying guns to fire on helicopters.

On 13 October, CMC directed a high priority project to "develop, evaluate, and service test a readily installable weapons kit for the UH–1E helicopter to provide armed helicopter support for transport helicopters." [70] The official concept now had been expanded to include escort missions.

Three different kits were tested. The first, and that which eventually was adopted, was very much like the TK–1. Among the armament features installed in the UH–1E as a result of Bell's common manufacturing process with the Army versions were attaching points to which the Marines fastened a platform on each side of the aircraft. Two electrically fired M–60C machine guns were mounted on each platform, unlike the TK–1 which had guns only on one side. Two bomb racks were bolted on to the bottom of the platforms. Normally 2.75-inch rocket pods were suspended from the bomb racks, though other items could be carried.

A simple ring and post type of sight was provided which swung up to the top of the cockpit when not needed. To provide the forward point of the sight, a small piece of black tape was placed on the windshield. While the sight seemed crude, it was effective and simple. "Many more elaborate types of sights exist," HMX–1 reported, "but all require major modification of the UH–1E cockpit, introduce added maintenance requirements, or block the pilot's vision." [71]

The kits, dubbed TK–2, were assembled by the Overhaul and Repair Activity, Jacksonville, Florida,

USMC Photo A421904

*An armed UH–1E of VMO–6 escorts UH–34s of HMM–263 supporting a South Korean Marine operation south of Chu Lai in October 1967. This Huey is outfitted with the TK–2 rocket and machine gun kit.*

under the technical direction of HMX-1 and the Marine Corps Landing Force Development Center (MCLFDC). A total of 15 were made.

Test firing at NAS, Patuxent River revealed only minor problems. The most serious was that the expended cartridge links ejected from the left guns could endanger the tail rotor. (The same problem was one of the reasons the UH-34 had no guns on the left side.) The guns were slightly repositioned and later deflector plates were added.

This apparently solved the ejected link problem. However, on the last day of test firing, several additional nicks in the tail rotor were received. It was decided, in view of the time element, to go ahead with the fabrication of the other kits and continue efforts to solve the ejection problem after the kits were completed and delivered to Fleet Marine Force units. The alternative was to hold up delivery to a deploying squadron.[72]

On 15 January 1965 the completed armament sets were shipped to VMO-6 at Camp Pendleton. Once installed on the UH-1Es, they were an immediate success. So much so that on 31 March, CNO requested BuWeps to provide kits for 33 more aircraft. Delivery was promised in July.

Simultaneously with the development of this TK-2, HMX-1 was experimenting with other kits. Two General Electric .50 caliber SM-14 gun pods were evaluated "with excellent results, providing primarily greater effective range."[73] The added weight made the heavier machine guns suitable only for specialized missions. Also tested were two Stoner 63 machine gun pods on temporary loan from the U.S. Air Force. The installation proved unsatisfactory for the UH-1E.

In addition to the rockets and machine guns mounted on the sides of the helicopter, tests were conducted on a rotating turret mounted below the nose of the aircraft. The Emerson Electric TAT-101 turret contained two M-60 machine guns and could be aimed and controlled by the pilot.[74] Beginning in April 1967, UH-1Es were modified to incorporate the turret. A total of 94 kits were purchased. By April 1972, other armament conversions were available which were more suited for the task, and the TAT-101 was removed from those aircraft in which they were installed.

While the TK-1 on the UH-34 was undergoing final testing at HMX-1 and efforts were under way to have approved a similar kit for the UH-1E, General Krulak at FMFPac sent CMC his estimate of the results which could be expected. "The proposed arming of the UH-34 will not provide equivalent protection to replace U.S. Army UH-1Bs." The TK-1s, however, should be provided and "the assignment of Marine UH-1E helos to the 1st Marine Air Wing be expedited for employment in armed escort as required."[75]

USMC Photo A192087

*Marine Huey gunships with TAT-101 chin turrets land to pick up more 2.75-inch rockets at the MAG-39 LZ during Operation NANKING-SCOTLAND II in October 1968. The chin turret further improved the UH-1E's firepower.*

As soon as the pilots at Pendleton finished training, six of the armed UH-1Es were shipped in April to Futema. These six aircraft of Lieutenant Colonel George Bauman's VMO-2 arrived at Da Nang on 3 May 1965. They immediately began to take over the role of escorting the Marine assault troop helicopters.

The introduction into Vietnam of Marine armed helicopters did nothing to still the proponents or opponents of the concept. The situation was not helped by a controversy, which during 1964 was becoming more and more public, between the Air Force and the Army over their respective roles. For airborne firepower, the Army placed almost total reliance on its armed helicopters. The Air Force held that only its fixed-wing aircraft were suitable for close air support and helicopter escort.

The Marine Corps occasionally got dragged into the controversy between the two other services. General Greene made a speech at the National Press Club in Washington, D.C. on 26 March 1964. In it, he once again stated his position on armed helicopters. Press accounts, unfortunately, were written stressing that the "Marines Join Air Force in Opposing Helicopters Ground Support." [76]

He had made no such statement. What General Greene told the reporters was the same thing he had been telling and would continue to tell the Marines:

> This service [armed helicopters] in South Vietnam has been carried out under peculiar circumstances which has led many people to question the Marine Corps' position—and has resulted in some misunderstanding of it. . . . The special situation in South Vietnam has *not* caused us to modify . . . our belief. . . . In South Vietnam, Marine Corps tactical fixed wing aircraft have not been available because of political considerations.

He summed up: "We consider this capability [armed helicopters] must be complementary, rather than competitive with the primary fire support provided by fixed wing aircraft.[77]

Marine attack aircraft, after they were introduced into Vietnam, were used to protect and escort the assault helicopters. So were armed helicopters. Each in its way performed a vital mission. Throughout the conflict in Vietnam, the Marine Corps continued to maintain a balance of weapons which were capable of performing anywhere in the world under almost any conceivable circumstance. The armed helicopter and fixed-wing attack aircraft were just two of them. Much of the credit belongs to General Greene. He, at least, had not forgotten the lessons of previous wars.

# CHAPTER SIX

# MORE HELICOPTERS FOR AN EXPANDING WAR

## The Buildup *

> Helicopters. Here we could characterize our needs as almost a bottomless pit. . . . Our lift capability has doubled . . . but the hunger is still not satisfied.
> And the valor and skill of the pilots has outrun the book. The stars on their air medals are matched only by the stars in their crowns.
>
> Lieutenant General Victor H. Krulak
> Commanding General, FMF Pacific
> 11 July 1967 [1]

At the time of the landing at Da Nang in March 1965, the Marine Corps had a total of 20 helicopter squadrons. Two, HMH-461 and HMH-462, continued to operate the "Deuce." The three observation units had a mixture of old 0-1s and OH-43s and new UH-1Es. Of the 14 medium transport squadrons, 12 were flying the UH-34. One more was to be formed to complete the expansion previously planned by General Shoup. HMM-265 and HMM-164 were in the process of converting to the CH-46. HMX-1 remained at Quantico. A total of 433 helicopters were authorized but only 398 were on hand.[2] The most critical shortage was of CH-46s, resulting from continued delays in production.

On 12 June, the two transport squadrons in Vietnam were joined by Lieutenant Colonel Gene W. Morrison's HMM-161 from Kaneohe. The squadron was initially assigned to the Phu Bai area approximately 40 miles north of Da Nang near the old imperial city of Hue. The squadron in turn was followed by HMM-261, commanded by Lieutenant Colonel Mervin B. Porter, which arrived in Da Nang from New River on 21 June. Meanwhile, Lieutenant Colonel Lloyd F. Childers and his HMM-361 departed Santa Ana and were assigned to Futema on 8 June. There were now five transport squadrons in the western Pacific area: three in Vietnam, one on board the *Iwo Jima* as part of the Special Landing Force and one at Futema. VMO-2 had elements in both Da Nang and Okinawa.

Then, on 28 July, President Lyndon B. Johnson announced to the American people that the U.S. forces in Vietnam would be almost doubled to 125,000 men and that additional reinforcements would be sent if needed. Following the President's speech, the Joint Chiefs of Staff ordered the deployment of MAG-36 from Santa Ana to Vietnam. The commanding officer of the group was Colonel (later Major General) William Gentry Johnson, a veteran of both World War II and Korea, in which he gained extensive experience with night fighter aircraft.

The USS *Princeton* (LPH 5) sailed from Long Beach, California the morning of 11 August. On board were HMMs-362, -363, and -364 commanded by Lieutenant Colonels James Aldworth, George D. Kew, and William R. Lucas. Each squadron was assigned 24 UH-34s. Also, there was VMO-6, commanded by Lieutenant Colonel Robert J. Zitnik. The squadron's 27 UH-1Es would be more than welcome in Vietnam. The group's heavy transport squadron, HMH-462, had been decommissioned two months earlier and the six remaining "Deuces" assigned to the Headquarters and Maintenance Squadron. These aircraft and their crews also were shipped to Da Nang. The *Princeton* arrived at Subic Bay in the Philippine Islands on 27 August. There, the aircraft crews began a three-day period of intensive final training in air-to-ground gunnery in preparation for their entry into combat. The ship departed on 30 August and arrived off Da Nang four days later. Back at Santa Ana, the remnants of the helicopter group were assigned to Marine Wing Service Group (MWSG) 37 with headquarters at the nearby MCAS El Toro.[3]

Five months before the *Princeton* arrived, on 8 March, the headquarters of MAG-16 had moved from Futema to Da Nang. The overall commander of SHUFLY at the time, Colonel John H. King, Jr., assumed command of the helicopter group. A small rear headquarters had remained behind, but even it proceeded to Vietnam on 11 September.[4] Colonel King, a fighter pilot at Guadalcanal in 1942 and commanding officer of VMO-6 in the Korean War, was replaced on 9 August by Colonel Thomas J. O'Connor. Colonel

---

* For more information see: Jack Shulimson and Maj. Charles M. Johnson, *U.S. Marines in Vietnam, 1965: The Landing and the Buildup* (Washington: History and Museums Division, HQMC, 1978.)

O'Connor was an unusual Marine avaitor. Prior to reporting to flight training in May of 1943, he had been a member of the Marine Detachment on board the USS *Savannah* in the November 1942 landings in Africa—a campaign not often associated with a Marine. Before assuming command of MAG–16, he had been Chief of Staff of the 1st Marine Aircraft Wing at Da Nang. Both he and Colonel Johnson were about to have new homes for their men and aircraft, for the rapid buildup of helicopters and other aircraft had completely saturated the airbase. New helicopter airfields were urgently needed.

MAG–16 would be the first to move from the crowded conditions. A few miles east of Da Nang across the Song Han * lay a long peninsula parallel to the ocean. The northern terminus was a mountain which created the south side of the entrance to Da Nang Bay. A few miles further south, the beach was broken by a series of red marble mountains that were almost devoid of vegetation and which rose precipitiously from the coastland. As General McCutcheon was to write later, "For MAG–16, a site had been chosen . . . just north of this Marble Mountain. There was a beautiful stretch of sandy beach along the South China Sea and just inland was a fine expanse of land covered with coniferous trees ten to twenty feet high." [5]

The Marines did not count on the ability of the impoverished Vietnamese to utilize every scrap of material.

> Unfortunately as soon as word got out that Marines were going to construct an air base there, the local Vietnamese came onto the land in droves and removed all the trees including the roots, instead of the few that had to be removed to build the runway and parking areas. Thus, the troops and other inhabitants lost the protection those trees would have afforded against sun, wind, and erosion.[6]

The military construction units in Vietnam were straining to complete other projects so a civilian combine, Raymond, Morrison, Knudson-Brown, Root, and Jones (RMK–BRJ) received the contract to build the airfield. By the end of August the 2,000-foot runway and parking space made of Marston matting was complete. Colonel O'Connor and MAG–16 completed the move from Da Nang on 26 August. A week later MACV officially approved the name recommended for the new installation: Marble Mountain Air Facility (MMAF).[7] When MAG–36 arrived, most of its aircraft and crews waited at Marble Mountain until their own base was ready at Chu Lai farther south.

It was hardly luxurious, but did offer some distinct advantages. Strongbacks, wooden platforms, and framing had been built on which tents were erected. By the end of the year a large wooden mess hall had been completed and in those few moments when not flying or working on the helicopters, the crews could enjoy a hot meal. The cooling breeze from the ocean did not compensate for the heat of the summer, but at least the wind kept away mosquitos—which were the scourge of Da Nang and most of the rest of Vietnam.

The beach was the envy of all the other Marines in the area. Almost pure white sand bordered the clear crystal waters of the ocean. Sunbathing, surfing, and swimming were welcome breaks from the rigors of war, but the fine sand on which the entire base was built created a few problems. It was difficult to construct a road of any permanence, and the vehicles driving through the area often bogged down. Other than sand, the most significant handicap, initially, was that there were no hangars in which the mechanics could work on the aircraft. The heat of the summer and the cold downpours of the monsoon tested even the staunchest of the crew chiefs as they prepared their aircraft for the next combat mission.

Colonel Johnson faced different problems. On 7 May, the Marines had landed 55 miles south of Da Nang at Chu Lai. Construction of a runway for fixed-wing jets had begun two days later, and on 1 June the first aircraft had landed. General McCutcheon remembered that the "peninsula to the northeast of Chu Lai provided a likely site for a helo group." [8]

The construction of the Ky Ha ** helicopter base was begun by U.S. Navy construction battalions (Seabees). They leveled an area 600 by 900 feet which was to serve as parking ramp, landing zone, and take-off runway. Metal matting was urgently needed for other projects, but by using several different types the Seabees were able to pave sufficient space for the helicopters. "But they had no time to do anything else in the way of preparing for MAG–36's arrival." The bulk of the effort fell to Major Jack A. Kennedy and his Marine Air Base Squadron 36. On 2 September it had left the *Princeton* and "began to dig in to stay at Ky Ha." The unit was reinforced with every available Marine who could be spared from the other squadrons. "They unloaded, moved ashore and set about building the camp. At night they also established their own perimeter defense as there was no infantry to do it for them." [9]

In a classic brief understatement, Colonel Johnson reported that on 11 September "we also got our first monsoon rains." The next day a damp Colonel Johnson welcomed the Assistant Commandant, Lieutenant General Richard C. Mangrum, to officially open Ky

---

\* Also variously known as the Tourane River—from the French name of Da Nang—and the Da Nang River.

\*\* Pronounced "key-hah" from the name of a nearby village.

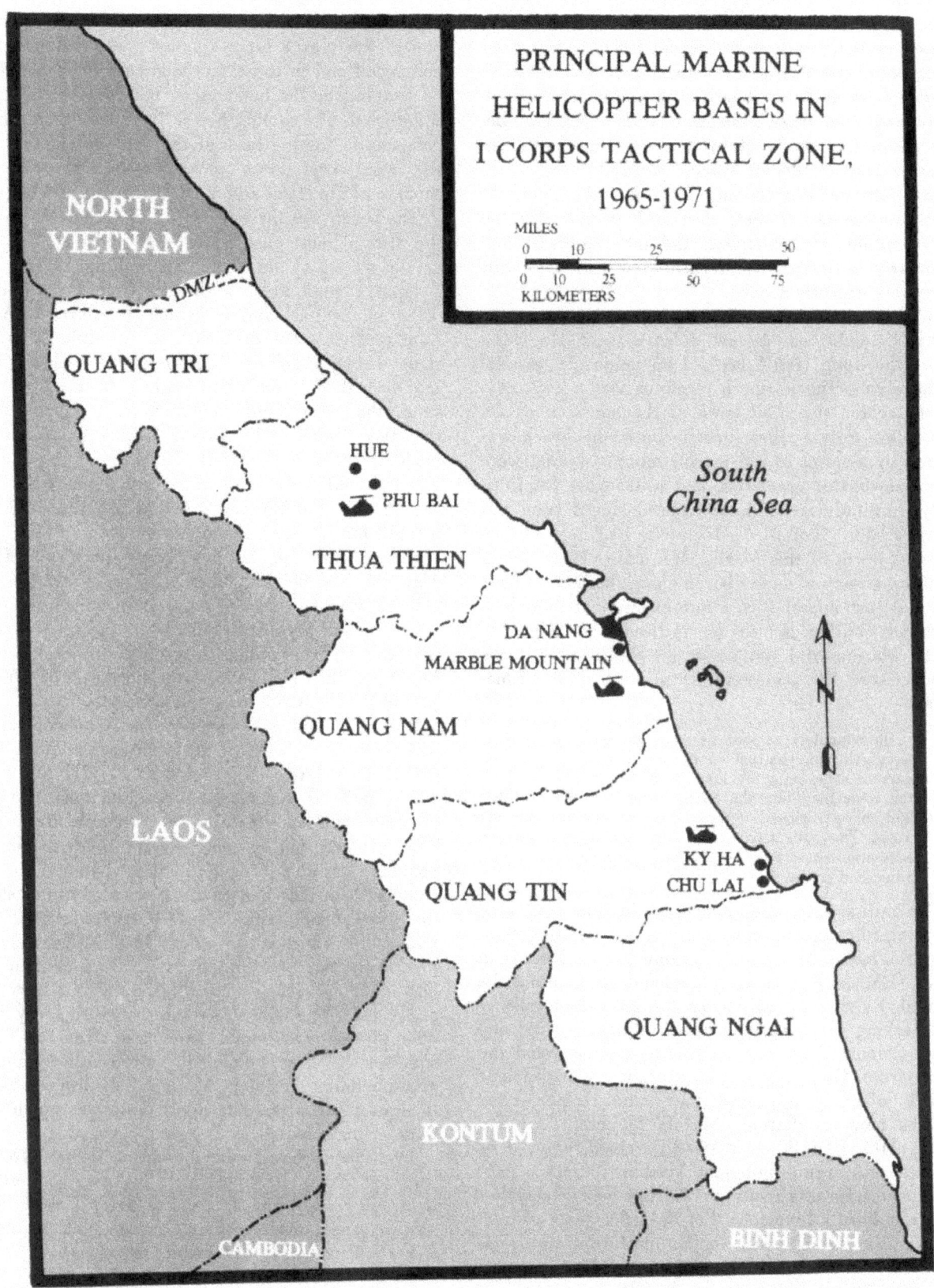

Ha. The torrential rains continued and construction of the camp almost halted. It was not until 17 September that all the Marines could sleep under a tent. Still they were constantly drenched. Colonel Johnson described one solution:

> Our engineering department rigged up a drying tent by erecting a G. P. [General Purpose] tent close to a generator and ducting the hot air blown over the engine into the tent. This allows drying facilities for clothing, boots, etc., in wet weather, a very necessary commodity in this climate.[10]

The Marines of MAG-36 and MAG-16 were learning what had been apparent to the members of the SHUFLY squadron since 1962. The monsoon season in Vietnam is a very wet time of life for everyone. Though the incident occurred some time later and in another area of the country, General Krulak recounted every Marine's opinion of the monsoon. "Not far from the Laos border, I saw this on a piece of a ration box in front of a boy's little hootch. It said, with apologies to G.B. Shaw, 'The rain in Laos falls mainly in the house.'"[11]

There was another thing the Marines were discovering that had been previously noticed by the crews of SHUFLY. When Colonel Carey's staff avoided selecting an airfield in the delta which was paved with laterite, it was due to their knowledge of the characteristics of this red soil. Ky Ha was built in laterite. While the crews at Marble Mountain had to contend with sand in everything, "at Ky Ha it was pure, unadulterated mud."[12]

Dry laterite and sand began to take a toll of helicopters on takeoff and landing. The clouds of dust stirred up by the rotor wash literally sandblasted the rotor blades, causing continued erosion of the metal and requiring frequent changes of the blades. The problem was aggravated by the heavy demands for helicopters. Parts for the machines had been procured on the assumption that each aircraft would fly 40 hours per month. By the end of the summer of 1965, even with the monsoon season starting, the average for the UH-34s was over 70 hours per month.

In August, CinCPacFlt reported a critical shortage of blades for the UH-34s. The problem was so serious that otherwise completely flyable aircraft were grounded because there were no blades for their tail rotors. The end of the month saw the same situation for the UH-1E. For that helicopter, the rotor blades were expected to last for 1,000 hours of flight. In the grit of laterite and sand they were being worn out after only 200 hours. Further aggravating the problem, ejected ammunition links from the guns were still nicking the tail rotor. The modification by HMX-1 had not totally resolved the difficulty. By 22 October, a new

USMC Photo 532040

*The dust and sand of Vietnam eroded rotor blades and clogged turbine engines. This CH-46 raises billowing clouds as it lifts off from a hilltop landing zone in northern I Corps in 1969.*

revision in the gun mounts had been prepared, and was being adapted to the UH-1Es.[13] Efforts to increase the production of rotor blades for both types of helicopter began immediately. By the middle of September, BuWeps could assure the Marine Corps that more rotor blades were on the way to Vietnam. The first ones had been due to arrive 30 August and by January the next year, the supply should be ample.[14] In the meantime some Marine helicopters would have to remain on the ground due to lack of parts.

## The Viet Cong Worsen the Helicopter Shortage

As October drew to a close, MAG-36 continued to improve the base at Ky Ha, in spite of the monsoon rains. Pilots and crews were heavily engaged in combat flights. At Marble Mountain, construction was continuing and though H&MS-16 now had a building for a hangar, most crew chiefs still had to work outside. All but a few of the structures were strongbacked tents. MAG-16 had three of its operating squadrons at Marble Mountain. HMM-263 had arrived on 12 October and replaced HMM-261. The new squadron was under the same commanding officer who had led it during the Dominican Republic crisis earlier in the year, Lieutenant Colonel Truman Clark. Lieutenant Colonel Childers remained with HMM-361 as did Lieutenant Colonel Bauman with VMO-2. The six "Deuces," which had arrived on the *Princeton*, had been assigned to Colonel O'Connor and operated as a subunit under Captain Guss H. Pennel, Jr. The two support squadrons, H&MS-16 and MABS-16 commanded by Lieutenant Colonels Jerome "Jerry" L. Goebel and Thomas E. Vernon were hard at work keeping the base operating and the aircraft flying.

To all of the Marines, 27 October had seemed much like any other day in the helicopter war. A group of VC had been spotted and eight UH-34s from HMM-361 escorted by armed UH-1Es of VMO-2 lifted 75 Vietnamese troops to engage the enemy. "Moderate to heavy small arms fire was received. The escort helicopters laid suppressive fire on these positions."[15] In addition, UH-1Es equipped with loudspeakers had flown over the area just north of MMAF conducting broadcasts to the natives of the area. The aircraft of HMM-263 were busy with routine resupply and administrative flights.

Long after night fell, many Marines were still working. Three of them, Corporal Eugene Mortimer, Lance Corporal Leonard O'Shannon, and Corporal Lawrence Brule were members of H&MS-16. By midnight they had completed their duties in the one hangar and were preparing to get a little sleep before starting again. A few minutes later "we heard three explosions—they sounded like mortars—and we grabbed our weapons and headed for a sandbagged hole."[16] They did not know that "a VC force estimated at 90, and possibly including some personnel from North Vietnam, had launched a well planned and well coordinated attack on the Marble Mountain Air Facility."[17]

Three and possibly four teams conducted the assault. One unit attempted to breach the defenses near the H&MS hangar. There they met Mortimer, O'Shannon, and Brule. "We'd been in the hole only about 20 seconds when we saw about eight people, all armed, running towards us," said O'Shannon. "They were about 30 to 40 feet away. We saw they were Viet Cong. When they got within 15 feet of us, we opened fire with our rifles."[18] Marine Corps training paid off well. All three happened to be "Expert" riflemen and they annihilated the enemy squad, killing seven and wounding and capturing four others.[19]

On the west side of the field, the VC attacked a bunker manned by Marines from MAG-16. Only after all the defending Marines were wounded was the enemy able to penetrate into the area occupied by the maintenance and administrative tents of HMM-361, HMM-263, and VMO-2. "Once in the parking area, they commenced a methodical attack on each helicopter."[20] Seven of the UH-1Es were lined up beside the hangar awaiting the arrival of parts. All were destroyed. Six more on the parking ramp met a similar fate. Two more received major damage and another pair suffered less severe damage.[21] In a matter of moments, MAG-16's UH-1Es had been reduced to four flyable aircraft.

The UH-34s did not escape. Six were destroyed, nine suffered major and 17 minor damage. Few were unscratched. Lieutenant Colonel Clark reported that one of his aircraft, which was considered lightly damaged, had "122 holes in the fuselage from shrapnel."[22] As the remnants of the VC retreated across the parking mat, they were confronted with the six giant "Deuces". Apparently unfamiliar with such a large helicopter they could only push grenades through the machine gun ports in the nose doors. Fortunately all they had left were concussion grenades. The explosions blew off the escape windows from the helicopters, but caused little other damage.

At dawn the next morning, aircraft from the MAG-16 squadron at Phu Bai and from MAG-36 at Ky Ha arrived to bolster the Marble Mountain units. Even with 19 of the helicopters destroyed, 11 more heavily damaged, and most of the rest damaged in some manner, MAG-16, on the day after the attack, flew 333 individual sorties, carrying 312 passengers and 17 tons of supplies.

As initial reports of the attack were received at FMFPac headquarters in Honolulu, it was apparent that additional helicopters would have to be shipped immediately to Vietnam. Almost before the shooting ended, General Krulak requested replacement aircraft "with the highest priority given to the UH-1E."[23] At the time the Marine Corps had only 18 UH-1Es other than those in Vietnam. Two of even this small total were deployed to the Caribbean.[24] Fortunately there were five available at San Diego which already were loaded on board a ship for transfer to the western Pacific area. FMFPac requested CMC to unload them and put them on cargo aircraft for immediate shipment to Vietnam.[25] The next day CMC asked CNO to air-ship five more from HMX-1 at Quantico. By the middle of November, 12 UH-1Es had arrived in Vietnam. Two were from the ship at San Diego, five were from HMX, and five more which had just arrived in October from Santa Ana. Three of these aircraft incorporated a major improvement: The "540" rotor system which increased the speed and performance of the original UH-1E. In Vietnam, however, the Marines and Navy had no parts for the improved helicopter. BuWeps quickly arranged to procure the necessary supplies from the Army, which did have them. More critical was the fact that not only had aircraft been destroyed in the attack but also the precious TK-2 armament kits which had been installed. An urgent program was begun and by 1 December the replacement kits had arrived at Santa Ana where they were assembled and shipped to Vietnam.[26]

The replacements for the destroyed UH-34s also began arriving inside large cargo aircraft.* The combination of the attack on Marble Mountain, aircraft shot down by the enemy, and helicopters destroyed in crashes in the heat and mountains of Vietnam, however, resulted in a shortage of 69 UH-34s throughout the Pacific area by the first of December.[27]

## The "Deuce" Finds a Mission

The insatiable demand for helicopter lift capability in Vietnam gave the powerful but idiosyncratic HR2S a last chance to prove its worth. The "Deuce" never had lived up to the vision of the early Marine helicopter planners of fleets of the huge machines carrying assault troops in massive vertical amphibious landings; but as the Vietnam war expanded, the HR2S found a role, first in filling in back in the United States for other helicopters committed to the war and then by service in combat.

During the late summer of 1965, the continued demands on MAG-26 at New River for aircraft and crews for Vietnam had left the east coast helicopter group short of aircraft to meet its usual required commitments. These included provision of a Caribbean ready force, such as had been on duty when the Cuban and Dominican crises had erupted. Major Richard L. Hawley, commanding officer of HMH-461, proposed a solution. Hawley, a former enlisted Marine who had been commissioned 21 December 1951, had been brought into helicopters by the forced transition program of 1963 and had been assigned to HMH-461 in various capacities since the completion of his training. He recommended that the next Caribbean ready force not use UH-34s, which were in limited supply, but be made up of a full squadron of "Deuces."[28]

The prospect of 12 of these temperamental aircraft deployed together was not greeted with enthusiasm. In the past, a chronic shortage of spare parts had created maintenance problems with the "Deuce," and it was believed that this difficulty would be aggravated if the aircraft were based on board a ship in the Caribbean. Major Hawley, however, was able to point out that the parts situation had improved greatly by mid-1965, as the result of a decision made in 1964 (when it had become apparent that the replacement for the "Deuce," the CH-53, would be delayed in production) to procure a new supply of parts to keep the aging HR2S in operation.

Hawley convinced the Marine Corps that an all-"Deuce" ready force was not only feasible but desirable. On 15 September, HMH-461, with 12 aircraft, deployed on board the USS *Guadalcanal* as the aviation component of the Caribbean Ready Force.[29] It was augmented by two UH-1Es (which were the two deployed when the search started for aircraft to replace the ones destroyed at Marble Mountain.)

By the time the squadron returned to New River on 15 December, it amply had demonstrated that the "Deuce," old and cantankerous as it was, still could outperform any other helicopter then in service in Marine squadrons. On 26 January 1966, nevertheless, HMH-461 went into cadre status to prepare to receive the CH-53, but not until almost a year later on 15 December would the first of the new heavy lifters arrive. In contrast to the original Marine Corps conception of nine squadrons of 20 "Deuces" each, the September 1965 deployment of HMH-461 was the first—and only—time the HR2S deployed in a squadron-size force in the role for which it was designed.

In Vietnam, where the "Deuce" could not be used to conduct vertical amphibious assaults, Marines found many other useful tasks for it. Of increasing importance was the recovery of other helicopters which had been shot down or crashed. Less than two weeks after arriving from Santa Ana, on 12 September 1965, a "Deuce" performed what was claimed as "the first helo lift of a downed aircraft under tactial considerations" when it retrieved a Marine helicopter approximately 15 miles away from Chu Lai and carried it externally back to the airfield."[30]

A typical, though not routine, recovery occurred three days after the attack on Marble Mountain. A UH-34 of HMM-263 flying an assault mission eight miles southwest of Da Nang had been damaged on landing. Recovery was attempted, but daylight ran out before it was accomplished.[31] The Marines guarding the aircraft had to be returned to more secure positions before dark and the helicopter was left unattended during the night. The next morning six UH-34s of HMM-263 escorted by three armed UH-1Es of VMO-2 lifted a platoon of U.S. Marines to the site of the downed aircraft.[32] Experts on the disarming of explosives were included as a Marine reconnaissance team in the area had reported that the Viet Cong had placed booby traps around the aircraft during the night. The recovery force landed in a nearby clearing and set up a defensive perimeter while the experts rendered the booby traps harmless. As the UH-34 would have to be lightened, maintenance personnel from the squadron

---

* Most were shipped in Air Force C-124s. This four-engined propeller aircraft was one of the few large enough to allow the tall UH-34 to fit in.

USMC Photo A186125
*The "Deuce" carries out its mission. A CH-37 of MAG-16 lifts out the stripped hulk of a UH-34 shot down near Da Nang in October 1965.*

were landed and detached the main transmission and rotor, and the rotor blades. This action was necessary since the recovery aircraft would have to hover out of ground effect before reaching translational lift to allow the damaged aircraft to clear surrounding trees.

Two "Deuces" were dispatched. The first lifted the transmission and rotor head and returned to Marble Mountain. The second "Deuce," flown by First Lieutenant Anthony D. Costa, picked up the rest of the UH-34 and started back to Marble Mountain with the load riding steadily beneath the aircraft. Minutes later Costa's "Deuce" was hit by enemy ground fire which cut fuel lines in the left engine. Gasoline from the ruptured hose streamed from the engine and it appeared that there would be an explosion at any moment. Lieutenant Costa, ignoring the danger, kept full power on the engine until he once again could hover, lower the UH-34 to the ground, and then land. The security force, which had boarded other helicopters when the "Deuces" departed, was hastily diverted to the new area. Another "Deuce" was dispatched and once again the UH-34 was airborne under a helicopter and successfully returned to Marble Mountain. Lieutenant Costa's aircraft was repaired and he took off, only to be forced to make another emergency landing before arriving back at home base. The second time, the mechanical difficulty was quickly repaired and he and his crew finally completed the eight-mile trip from the site of the downed aircraft to Marble Mountain. The UH-34 which had caused it all gained the dubious distinction of being shot down twice without even having the engine started between the two incidents.

As Major Hawley's squadron was reduced to a cadre, additional "Deuces" and spare parts were sent to Vietnam. While the big helicopters could perform many missions that neither the UH-34 nor the UH-1E could accomplish, they still had limitations, as Lieutenant Costa's experience had illustrated. Therefore, on 25 January 1966, General Krulak at FMFPac headquarters requested that the "Deuce" be phased out of Vietnam by 1 September 1966. In April, he repeated the request and added that a detachment of three CH-53s should be deployed to Vietnam to replace the "Deuce" as soon as possible.[33]

The rapid buildup of U.S. forces in Vietnam during 1965 had caught the Marine Corps at the beginning of its transition from the older generation of piston-engine helicopters to the new, more powerful generation of turbines. As a result, the reliable UH-34s, supplemented by turbine-powered UH-1Es and by a contingent of powerful but aging HR2Ss, had had to carry the burden of the Marines' first year of large-scale combat against the North Vietnamese and Viet Cong. The new year of 1966 would see jet-powered transport helicopters enter the war, bringing with them a great increase in operational capability but also some new and difficult problems.

# CHAPTER SEVEN

# THE CH-46 ON ACTIVE SERVICE

## The CH-46 Enters Combat

A few months after the attack on Marble Mountain, the first of the new medium helicopters, the CH-46s, entered combat. Efforts to bring the CH-46 into the war had begun in mid-1965. By that time, the tempo of the war had increased, with the Marines no longer confined to defensive action but now actively pursuing the enemy. The demand for more helicopters seemed insatiable, and the UH-34s, reliable as they were, no longer could even begin to meet the requirements. More lift capability was needed immediately.

Only two CH-46 squadrons—HMM-164 and HMM-265—were close to being ready to deploy. On the east coast, HMM-265, now under Major Gregory A. ("Greg") Corliss, had deployed to the Caribbean on board the USS *Okinawa* (LPH 3) in June, the first CH-46 squadron to make a shipboard deployment. On the west coast, HMM-164, which had been left behind and assigned to MWSG-37 when MAG-36 left for Vietnam, was still in training. The original schedule had called for HMM-164 to move to the western Pacific in October 1966, with HMM-265 to follow two months later.[1]

To meet the need for more lift capability, the Marine Corps sped up the departure of these units by about seven months. HMM-164, under Lieutenant Colonel Warren C. Watson, who had taken command on 6 June 1965, sailed for Vietnam on the *Princeton* on 16 February 1966. Watson, who had been a naval aviator since May 1943 and had flown fighters, attack aircraft, and transports in addition to helicopters, had 27 CH-46s under his command, including three which were to be used as spares. On 4 March HMM-164 arrived at Subic Bay. It transferred there to the *Valley Forge* for the rest of the trip to Vietnam.[2]

On the morning of 8 March, the weary UH-34 and "Deuce" crews at Marble Mountain welcomed the sight of 27 CH-46s flying down the white sand of the beach, shuttling the squadron ashore. As one of the pilots watching, Captain Alvah J. ("Jerry") Kettering, later recounted, "Those big airplanes sure were a sight for sore eyes to us '34 crews."[3] The squadron pilots immediately began to familiarize themselves with the tactics and procedures being used by the other units. Initially, the UH-34s continued to fly normal missions, only instead of a second helicopter of the same type in the formation, a CH-46A would be attached. In a few days the indoctrination was over and Lieutenant Colonel Watson with his squadron took on the full burden of combat operations.

Lieutenant Colonel Watson and his crews lost no time in entering combat. In the first 35 days after their arrival in Vietnam, they flew almost 2,700 sorties.* In the same period, eight of the aircraft were hit by enemy fire and though the damage to the helicopters was small, two of the crew members were wounded. General Krulak summed up the first impressions of the new turbine helicopter after a month of operation. "It is emphasized," he wrote, "that the limited period for evaluation of the CH-46 precludes any dogmatic conclusions as to performance and effectiveness of the helo in a combat environment. However, our initial impressions are all favorable." He concluded that "The CH-46 is making a significant contribution to the helo assault capability of the Marine Corps air-ground team in South Vietnam."[4]

Three months later in June 1966 Lieutenant Colonel Herbert E. Mendenhall led his HMM-265 with its 24 CH-46As ashore at Marble Mountain. The squadron had departed New River on 21 April on board the USS *Boxer*.

## Problems and Improvements

The rapid introduction into combat of the CH-46 brought an immediate increase in lift capability, but from the start it also brought difficulties. Some of the problems had become apparent two years before, as the first of the aircraft were delivered to tactical squadrons.

In August 1966, Brigadier General Alan J. Armstrong, Assistant DC/S (Air), reviewed the history. The tests at Patuxent River "in early 1964 revealed

---

* A combat sortie is one requirement completed by one helicopter. Several sorties might be completed on a single flight.

99

that the CH-46A had excellent potential for the Marine Corps assault helicopter mission," he wrote. "However, the mission capability of the CH-46A was seriously compromised by excessive vibration levels and susceptibility of the engines to severe damage in a sand environment." Vertol's engineers "undertook these problems and produced a useable vibration absorber. Engine susceptibility to sand erosion was reduced to [what was then considered] an acceptable level." Like all aircraft in the Marine Corps, he added, the CH-46A "was constantly evaluated for possible improvement."[5]

Among the changes made before the deployment of HMM-265 and HMM-164, were a "four degree rotor trim in the forward transmission to improve the aircraft attitude during landing [the initial aircraft had to land with the nose high in the air, which, among other things, obstructed the view of the pilot at a critical time] and fuselage formation lights for night formation flying." Another change was the direct result of Lieutenant Colonel Clapp's experience in SHUFLY. In 1962 he had decided that the best protection from enemy fire was to spend the minimum amount of time on the ground unloading the assault troops. In a CH-46 the troops exited from the rear, over a lowered ramp. If the aircraft took off with the ramp still down, there was a good possibility of causing damage to the helicopter so "an acceleration in the rear ramp operating time" was included in the modifications.[6]

Other lessons from SHUFLY were incorporated. Armor was added to critical areas of the engines. Armored seats, similar to those which were fitted in the UH-34, were designed and were "installed prior to the introduction of these aircraft into Vietnam."[7] The most important change, however, was that when the CH-46 arrived in combat it would be equipped with machine guns. Vertol designed a kit to be fitted in the aircraft which would allow the crew chief and a gunner to operate either a .50 caliber heavy machine gun or the familiar M-60. The company proposed that it manufacture and install the kits in the first 54 aircraft. The project would be completed in July at a cost of $2,995,000. The schedule was such that some of the modifications would have to be completed on board ship on the way to Vietnam and others would have to be finished after they arrived at Marble Mountain.

The Marine Corps was not satisfied with the offer.

> In view of the contractor [Vertol] time schedule and costs, the O&R Departments [overhaul and repair facilities operated by the Navy and Marine Corps] were requested to undertake a program to expedite installation. Following inspection of the . . . trial installation at Quantico . . . a decision was made to have the kits manufactured and installed by the Navy O&Rs.[8]

At least 16 kits were to be ready in March. Total cost of all 54 was $805,000. "To equip HMM-164 aircraft prior to their WestPac deployment," General Armstrong wrote, teams for the O&R facilities:

> . . . from Cherry Point, North Island, and Jacksonville manufactured and working in two twelve hour shifts at MCAF Santa Ana, installed these kits in record time. This modification was called 'Project Tough.'[9]

Two gun mounts were installed. One was on the left side of the aircraft in an emergency exit door opening immediately behind the cockpit. The other was on the right side, in a window just to the rear of the side passenger door. To complete all of the modifications, including the gun mounts, required approximately 1,400 man hours of labor for each aircraft. The west coast helicopters were finished before HMM-164 departed on the *Princeton*. At New River, HMM-265 had all its aircraft ready by 28 March.[10] Initially, the aircraft were furnished with .50 caliber machine guns. An additional 30 armament kits were built and installed by O&R North Island (San Diego, California) in the CH-46s delivered to HMM-165 in July 1966. From then on "new production helicopters will have the kit mounted by contractor personnel at the plant prior . . . to delivery" to the Marine squadrons.[11]

The addition of the engine and seat armor and the machine guns was not universally applauded. A month after Lieutenant Colonel Watson and his squadron had arrived in Vietnam, General Krulak complained that "the .50 caliber machine gun and the weight of its ammunition constitute a significant reduction in the allowable pay load of the CH-46." Not only was there a reduction of payload but, "the internal mounting of the .50 caliber machine gun restricts its field of fire, and the weapon is limited in elevation due to the dual rotor configuration." "Finally," he wrote, "the .50 caliber does not have the inherent capability of the M-60 to be removed from a downed aircraft and used in defense; it being too heavy for the purpose." General Krulak concluded:

> The weight of the engine armor and the pilot seat armor must also be given consideration in relation to the loss of payload versus the effectiveness of armor. Comments and recommendations with regard to helo armor and arrangement will be addressed separately at a later date after further data are assembled.[12]

Eight months later, in December, he summarized the results of the experience gained in Vietnam. "The addition of armor to this aircraft has reduced its lift capability 967 pounds, from 4850 to 3874 (80 degrees Fahrenheit, at 1500 altitude)." He continued:

The CH-46 which was initially advertised as capable of transporting 25 combat equipped troops, now carries only about 15 in combat. It was also intended to be the ... helicopter capable of lifting the 105mm howitzer which task cannot now be performed without stripping the aircraft of all but essential equipment. With the CH-46, trade of fuel for increased lift is usually not acceptable except for extremely short range missions because of its already limited endurance. Reducing the fuel load to compensate for the current 967 pound armor weight would lower the usable fuel from a total of 2452 pounds to only 1485 pounds, or about 1.3 hours total operation; too little for acceptable combat flexibility.[13]

He agreed that "it is plain that we need protective armor on our helicopters." But, he said:

... up to now ... it appears that our armor installation efforts have been pursued without respect to the missions and tasks assigned, to the capabilities of the aircraft or in the nature of the combat environment in which the particular type is normally expected to operate.

He recommended that:

... an analytical review of present armor requirements be conducted, [and] the objective should be to hold armor weight to the lowest reasonable limit consistent with the mission for each type of helicopter.[14]

For the CH-46, he continued, it should consist of pilot and co-pilot seat armor and limited engine armor in vital areas only, the total weight of which should not exceed 450 pounds.

In spite of General Krulak's advice, the guns and armor remained on the CH-46. On 3 August 1966, Krulak notified the squadrons in Vietnam that the helicopters would continue to be armed, but with the lighter, more portable M-60 machine gun. The .50 caliber guns could be retained and used as desired.[15]

By mid-1966, disturbing reports from the squadrons were citing difficulties with the aircraft. The much admired, beautiful, white sand of the Vietnamese lowlands was proving to be a deadly trap for the turbine engines. When David Richardson of Vertol had spoken to the 1961 meeting of the American Helicopter Society, he obviously did not have operation of the CH-46 in Vietnam in mind. But his fears of sand being sucked into the compressor and causing extensive damage were coming true for HMM-164. The sand was eroding the compressor blades to a point where they could not pump in sufficient air to the burning chambers. The resulting condition, called "compressor stall" caused the engine to lose power and to exceed the maximum temperature allowed. It was a dangerous situation. By the end of April, engines were being ruined and had to be replaced after every 200-300 landings.[16]

All the spare engines the squadron had brought with them had been used earlier in the month.[17] Naval Air Systems Command in Washington, which was in charge of procuring more engines, estimated that, "Based on the programmed flight hours, the current usage rates will generate a need for approximately 32 engine assemblies a month."[18] A series of conferences with the manufacturer, the General Electric Corporation, resulted in the company arranging to have the engines repaired in Japan. This reduced the long time required to ship them from Vietnam to the United States.

In the first week in May, Vertol and General Electric sent a team to Marble Mountain to investigate the problem.[19] The solution the team devised was a large filter, shaped somewhat like an oversized loaf of bread, and similar in function to that utilized in home air conditioners, which was installed on the front of the engines. One of these "100 percent barrier filter" systems was installed on a CH-46 at Marble Mountain. Another was sent to New River. The results of the initial tests were encouraging and by 31 May, MAG-16 could report that "360 landings had been made with no evidence of sand erosion." A week later, MAG-26 confirmed that "753 landings had been completed. Some sand erosion had taken place on the No. 2 engine," but this was the result of an easily corrected fault in the manufacture of the kit.[20] The only difficulty reported was that "a 1% degradation of power is experienced with every 10 landings due to filter clogging," but full power could be restored by cleaning the filter.[21] Even before a contract could be signed, Vertol began constructing other kits. The first shipment of 15 filters was ready by 2 July and 64 more by 25 July.[22]

The sand was not damaging just the engines. The rotor blades were experiencing the same abrasive treatment. The solution was "main rotor blades with nickle plated leading edges" which were air shipped to Vietnam in May. The new blades were estimated "to be good for 1000 landings in sand laden atmosphere," about five to ten times as long as the original stainless steel ones.[23] Finally, the sand and dust were finding their way into the fuel system, causing erratic operation of the engines. The situation became so serious that on 21 July, all CH-46s were grounded and were "to be flown only for heavy lift capability and/or emergency situations." It was a bitter blow for Lieutenant Colonels Watson and Mendenhall and their crews. Some of the pilots were temporarily assigned to the UH-34 squadrons "to supplement pilot strength."[24] Immediately, the Naval Air Systems Command and Vertol began "accelerating fabrication and shipping of ... fuel filters."[25] By the end of August, all the aircraft in HMM-265 and over half of those

*These CH–46s of HMM–161 transporting Marines of the 1st Marine Division in an assault southwest of Da Nang have their .50-caliber machine guns mounted in the doors and air filters fitted over the engine intakes. Both modifications proved necessary under Vietnam conditions.*

in HMM–164 had the barrier filter and fuel filter installed.[26] Soon after, both squadrons were back in full operation. As General Krulak wrote, "These helicopters greatly enhanced the operations [in Vietnam] because of their increased capacity and load carrying characteristics," even though the sand and dirt continued "to cause maintenance difficulties."[27]

### A New Version

Four months before Lieutenant Colonel Watson and his squadron arrived in Vietnam, it had become apparent that the production of CH–46s would have to be accelerated to meet the expected demands of combat. In the 1965 budget, Congress had approved the purchase of 90 of the helicopters the next fiscal year. Late that fall, Roy L. Wilson, Naval Air Systems Command project coordinator for the CH–46, was called to a high-level conference. The question posed to him was, "How many additional CH–46s can be built by 1 July 1967?"[28] Initially, Wilson and his staff thought that Vertol could increase production from the planned seven or eight aircraft per month to a peak of 17. That large an increase, however, would create manufacturing problems costly to the Navy, so the rate was finally established at 14 a month. On 22 September 1965, the Department of Defense notified Vertol to "accelerate the U.S. Marine Corps CH–46 Sea Knight helicopter production schedule by 100 per cent over the previously planned production rate."[29]

At the same time, the company was awarded a contract for $10.7 million to begin procurement of parts for additional helicopters. By January 1966, a total of 184 aircraft had been authorized. Some of these would be CH–46As already on the production line. Most of them would be an improved model: the CH–46D.

In the CH–46, as in most aircraft, the original design underwent a series of improvements. These resulted from development of new manufacturing techniques, experience in actually operating the aircraft, modifications to improve the aircraft's ability to per-

*CH–46s being assembled on the Boeing Vertol production line. The company doubled its Sea Knight production rate in September 1965.*

form its intended mission, and redesign to accept equipment or engines not available when the machine was first built. Under the Department of Defense designation system, if these modifications were significant but did not alter the original purpose of the aircraft, these variations on the initial design were denoted by different letters following the basic model number. So it was for the CH–46. The first model which Boeing-Vertol built for the Marine Corps was designated the CH–46A, and the improved version now to be bought was to be the "D" model.*

The new CH–46D incorporated a number of design changes, many of them the results of rapidly accumulating experience in Vietnam, and it also had a different engine. An important consideration in the original selection of the Vertol entry in the competition with Sikorsky had been the fact that the CH–46A had transmissions and rotor drive components which could be adapted to more powerful engines if they became available. By 1964, such engines were being built, and on 24 January of that year, the CNO had published a new requirement, 14–12 Assault Transport Helicopter Medium, which called for an improved helicopter. Vertol won the contract for what was to be the CH–46D. The new model contained an improvement of the General Electric T58-8 turbine, the T-58-10 (or "Dash Ten" engine as it came to be called), each one of which produced 150 more horsepower than the earlier versions.[30] This 12 percent increase of power resulted in much better performance in a hover and with only one engine operating.

Another significant change was that, unlike the CH–46A, on which only the tail rotor adjusted to give better visibility on landing, in the new machine both the tail and forward rotors automatically corrected for changes in speed. As a result, "The field of view during shipboard operations is significantly improved over the CH–46A helicopter."[31] New rotor blades had been designed which included a cambered—or curved—cross-section instead of the symmetrical design of the earlier ones. The new design "expanded altitude/airspeed capabilities . . . and enhances the service suitability of the CH–46D."[32] Although the new air-

---

* In theory, there could have been a CH–46B and C, but, as was not uncommon, changes could be proposed and a designation assigned and then no aircraft of that designation, or possibly only a test aircraft, ever built. Some military purchasers might accept a modification while others did not. Hence, helicopters in the Marine Corps did not always have their letter designations in strict sequence, and the CH–46 jumped from an "A" version directly to the "D."

If the mission of the aircraft were changed in modification, the first letter of its designation, which indicated purpose, also changed. The Navy SH–34 series, for instance, was the same helicopter as the UH–34, except the former was modified for anti-submarine warfare and the latter as a troop carrier and cargo transport. Except for the special equipment for the different missions, the two aircraft were almost identical.

craft was originally scheduled to be introduced into the Marine squadrons beginning in July 1966, service acceptance trials were not started at Patuxent River until 2 August.[33] The tests, completed on 3 October, consisted of "147 flights for 230.2 hours ... including 15.7 hours of shipboard operations and seven hours of performance evaluation with the engine filters installed [which were] required for operations in sand environment."[34] The report of the test concluded that "the CH-46D offers significant improvements over the CH-46A," and that "Performance characteristics . . . are excellent and all performance guarantees were met."[35] Immediately upon completion of the tests, Patuxent River notified the CNO of the results and recommended that "the model CH-46D be provisionally accepted for service use."[36]

The Marine Corps and Navy did not plan to send "Ds" to Vietnam to replace the "As" already there. Instead, as the CH-46Ds were built they would be assigned to the additional squadrons preparing to leave for the western Pacific and to squadrons in the United States which were converting from the old UH-34. This decision meant that for some time to come, most of the machines in Vietnam would be the original, unimproved "A" version.

The first CH-46Ds arrived at New River in October 1966 but were held temporarily in H&MS-26 until the transfer of HMM-161 from Vietnam on 19 December. Then the helicopters were turned over to this squadron. Simultaneously, CH-46Ds were being delivered to the squadrons at Santa Ana. With the immediate operating problems of the "A" model apparently solved and with the improved "D" version coming into service, it seemed at the end of 1966 that the Marine Corps' difficulties with the CH-46 series were finally over.

## General McCutcheon Takes Charge

In June 1966, as the first CH-46 squadrons were fully committed to the grinding struggle of combat in Southeast Asia, Major General Keith Barr McCutcheon was installed as Deputy Chief of Staff (Air) at Marine Corps headquarters. He would hold this position for the next three and a half critical years.

Among the thousands of Marines who had participated in helicopter development in the Corps since the mid-1940s, McCutcheon consistently had been in the forefront. While he contributed to many areas of the Marine air-ground team, he is best remembered for his work with helicopters. McCutcheon's road to the office of DCS (Air) had been a long, tortuous one.

USMC Photo 532036

*Lift capability was greatly increased with the introduction of the improved CH-46 "D" model. This aircraft is picking up supplies for a remote reconnaissance observation post west of Da Nang in 1969.*

*Lieutenant General McCutcheon dismounts from his UH–1E on a visit to the 7th Marines during his tour as Commanding General, III MAF in 1970. McCutcheon often piloted his own helicopter on such trips. Corporal Thomas F. Norman, the crew chief, holds the general's flack jacket, while Colonel Edmund G. Derning, Jr., the 7th Marines commander, greets McCutcheon.*

McCutcheon was born on 10 August 1915 in East Liverpool, Ohio, a small, economically declining Ohio River industrial town on the edge of Appalachia. He grew up in East Liverpool and graduated from high school there in the grim depression year of 1933. In spite of the depression, McCutcheon's father, a physician, had enough money to pay for a college education for his son, and in the fall of 1933, Keith McCutcheon entered the Carnegie Institute of Technology in nearby Pittsburgh, Pennsylvania.

At Carnegie Tech, where he majored in management engineering, McCutcheon soon demonstrated the keenness of mind and capacity for work that would characterize him thoroughly his life. Besides ranking consistently in the upper one-tenth of his class in scholarship, he worked on the school newspaper, served on the YMCA cabinet, went out for varsity track and intramural athletics, joined a fraternity, and was elected to several journalistic and scholarly honor societies. He also joined his school's Army Reserve Officers' Training Corps (ROTC) unit and completed the four-year course. The course included, besides military tactics and engineering subjects, instruction in "Care of Animals and Stable Management"—an indication of the condition and sense of priorities of the Army at that time.

The continuing depression, with its resulting limited civilian job prospects, combined with a growing interest in aviation, led McCutcheon to seek a military career. Throughout his college years, he tried to get into Army aviation. In 1935, with the help of a Democratic party committeeman from East Liverpool, he obtained one of the few appointments then available to Army flight school, but he failed the entrance physical examination because of high blood pressure—the result, McCutcheon explained, "of finishing a final exam period and a slight sickness." [37]

In January of 1937 (his graduation year), after job applications to several industrial firms, including Lockheed Aircraft, brought no attractive offers, McCutcheon again attempted to enter Army flight school. He obtained and passed a second physical examination, and on 15 May 1937 received orders to report to Randolph Field, Texas, by 1 July to begin the prescribed one-year course of instruction. McCutcheon never reported. The Army informed him that, after his year of training, he would have no guarantee of a commission or of assignment to active duty due to a shortage of funds for aviation officers. McCutcheon therefore requested that his name be removed from the rolls of the July 1937 cadet class. He remained, however, on the eligible list for future classes. He also accepted a second lieutenancy in the Corps of Engineers Reserve.[38]

McCutcheon by this time had a better alternative in sight; he had applied for a commission in the Marine Corps. The Marine Corps McCutcheon hoped to enter consisted of less than 20,000 officers and men in 1937, but it possessed a reputation for valor and an aura of glamor gained in World War I and in Caribbean and Asiatic interventions. Most attractive from McCutcheon's point of view, the Marine Corps had airplanes—in 1937, 102 of them, flown and maintained by an aviation establishment of 140 officers, 15 warrant officers, and 1,117 enlisted men. In these depression years, the few openings for junior officers in the Marines usually were over-subscribed by applicants, many of them young men like McCutcheon of exceptional ability, who turned to the military for lack of other opportunities. This situation permitted the Marine Corps to pick and choose only the best, producing one of the most brilliant generations of officers in the Marines' history. One of those chosen was Keith McCutcheon.

On 7 June 1937, McCutcheon took his Marine Corps physical examination at the Philadelphia Navy Yard. He failed it. Again, high blood pressure—the result of a recent illness and of overwork preparing for examinations—threatened to end his military career before it began. But, as he had with the Army Air Corps, McCutcheon persisted. He appealed for, was granted, and passed a second examination. On 12 August, he was appointed a second lieutenant, USMC, "revocable for two years from the 1st of July 1937." He immediately resigned his Army reserve commission and, on 16 August, reported to the Marine Barracks in Philadelphia for duty and instruction at the officer's Basic School.[39]

After graduation from The Basic School, McCutcheon, assigned as an infantry officer to the Marine detachment on the carrier USS *Yorktown* (CV 5), continued his effort to get into aviation. In September 1938, he applied for Marine Corps flight training and was turned down. He tried again in January 1939 and was informed that no vacancies in the training program existed but that his "preference for this assignment has been recorded for future consideration."[40] In June of that same year, an unexpected vacancy occurred in the flight class scheduled to begin at Pensacola on 1 July, and McCutcheon at last obtained his desire. He was ordered to Pensacola to begin pilot training. On 3 July 1940, he was designated a naval aviator and assigned to Marine Observation Squadron 1 at Quantico.[41]\*

McCutcheon spent a year with the squadron, serving on board carriers and at Guantanamo and San Juan, Puerto Rico. Then he entered further aviation technical training. In September 1941, the Marine Corps sent him to the postgraduate aeronautical engineering school at the U.S. Naval Academy. McCutcheon graduated from this school—typically, number one in his class—in May 1943. He spent the summer touring military and civilian aircraft plants to learn production and design techniques, and in October he began graduate work at the Massachusetts Institute of Technology. Nine months later, he received his Master of Science degree.

In September 1944, McCutcheon, now a lieutenant colonel, became operations officer of Marine Aircraft Group 24, located on Bougainville in the Southwest Pacific. MAG–24 the following month was assigned to provide most of the close air support for the Army in the planned invasion of the Philippines. Lieutenant Colonel McCutcheon received the job of developing the procedures for coordinating Marine air and Army ground forces. This promised to be a difficult task. Marines long had experimented with close air support of ground troops, but no complete doctrine had yet been worked out. What systems the Marines had developed were oriented toward support of beachhead assaults involving large Marine forces in restricted areas rather than toward supporting units of a different service in mobile, wide-ranging land operations.

McCutcheon later recalled that he and his staff were "completely unprepared" for their mission. "Efforts were made immediately to assemble all the available literature on the subject," he continued, "but it became clearly apparent that the existing instructions were published piecemeal in many forms and much of the data was contradictory."[42]

Using as much as they could of the existing doctrine and information and drawing on their own experience and ingenuity, McCutcheon and his group drew up a new, detailed doctrine. McCutcheon's system was based on the principle that "close air support is an additional weapon to be employed at the discretion of the ground commander."[43] Once the concept and instructions had been approved, McCutcheon

---

\* Later redesignated Marine Observation Squadron 151.

supervised the training of both Marines and Army personnel in how to put them to use, and during the offensive in the Philippines he helped direct their implementation. The system proved successful in the campaigns for Luzon and Mindanao. For his part in developing it, McCutcheon was awarded the Legion of Merit by Admiral Thomas C. Kinkaid, Commander of the Seventh Fleet.[44] McCutcheon's plan for controlling close air support constituted a significant contribution to the development and refinement of air-ground cooperation.* Had he accomplished nothing else in the Marine Corps, this achievement alone would have made him a major figure.

To the keen analytical mind which could produce an air support doctrine, McCutcheon added personal courage. In April 1945 he participated in an exploit that won him a Silver Star medal from the commander of the U.S. Army X Corps. Due to its nature, the feat remained classified and was not widely known at the time. The citation gives the details:

> For gallantry in action against the enemy in the vicinity of Malabang Field, Mindanao, Philippine Islands during the period 12 April 1945 to 17 April 1945. Prior to the landings on Mindanao information was received which indicated a possible change in the tactical plans. Lieutenant Colonel McCutcheon volunteered to fly to the Malabang Airfield that had just been reported seized by a small guerrilla force. He arrived at the Airfield five days prior to the landings of American forces. During the ensuing five days, from positions within close range of enemy machine gun and mortar fire and with utter disregard for his own safety, he reported the situation to the landing force afloat, briefed pilots and supervised the direction of air strikes. His accurate information transmitted to the task force commander afloat enabled the formulation of amended plans and resulted in an unopposed landing on Malabang Area. Lieutenant Colonel McCutcheon's unselfish devotion to duty, disregard for his personal safety, and outstanding performance of hazardous duty in the face of the enemy contributed greatly to the successes attained....[45]

By the end of the war, McCutcheon also had won a Distinguished Flying Cross and six Air Medals for his exploits. On his return to the United States in November 1945, he was assigned as an instructor in the Aviation Section of the Marine Corps Schools at Quantico and then, less than a year later, to the Bureau of Aeronautics at the Navy Department in Washington. At the Bureau of Aeronautics, where he remained until December 1949, McCutcheon became deeply involved with the guided missile and pilotless aircraft programs. During this assignment, from April to October 1947, he had the additional duty of Marine Corps aide to the White House. He also took on another title—that of husband. On 1 November 1947, the 32-year-old, highly decorated aviator was married to Marion P. Thompson from East Liverpool.

McCutcheon had been associated with the earliest development of helicopters as an aviation instructor in the Quantico schools, but not until July 1950 did he begin officially flying them. Ordered back to Quantico to take command of HMX-1, McCutcheon took transitional helicopter training with the Navy's Helicopter Squadron 2 at Lakehurst, New Jersey. Always a superior student, he completed the course "in the shortest length of time the Navy had recorded up until then." He assumed command of HMX-1 on 17 August 1950. With his new command, McCutcheon "inherited an experiment which had significant effect on . . . helicopter operations in Vietnam—firing a cockpit controlled 2.36-inch rocket from the side of the helicopter." ** In addition, "bombing from the helo was also evaluated as the HRP-1 (early Piasecki transport helicopter) dropped externally carried bombs from 8,000 feet."[46] ***

In December 1951, the now Colonel McCutcheon was ordered to Korea to take command of the recently deployed HMR-161. He continued to develop new tactics and techniques and to lead his squadron in combat assaults until 5 August 1952. For his service in Korea, he was awarded his second Legion of Merit and four more Air Medals. On his return to the United States he was almost immediately ordered to Frankfurt, Germany, where he served successively as Operations Officer; Assistant Chief; and later Chief, Operations Branch, J-3 Division at the headquarters of the United States European Command. May 1954 saw him back in the United States where he was assigned as Chief, Air Section, Marine Corps Equipment Board, at Quantico.

---

* For additional information, see Robert L. Sherrod, *History of Marine Corps Aviation in World War II* (Washington: Combat Forces Press, 1952) and George W. Garand and Truman R. Strobridge, *Western Pacific Operations: History of U.S. Marine Corps Operations in World War II*, Vol. IV (Washington: Historical Division, HQMC, 1971).

General Vernon E. Megee, USMC (Ret), who commanded all Marine air support control units with the Pacific Fleet in 1945, notes that McCutcheon's system had little direct application to amphibious operations and that, "Development of air support control for the latter type of operations began with Peleliu and continued through Iwo Jima and Okinawa. Thus the latter development was more or less contemporaneous with what occurred in the Philippines." (*Megee Comments*)

** Not to be confused with later experiments with "Bullpup" missile firings from a UH-34.

*** For additional information on developments of the period, see Rawlins, *Marines and Helicopters 1946-1962*, *passim*.

Three years later, he reported to New River as the commanding officer of MAG-26, where he remained until June 1959. This was a particularly productive time for him in the development of helicopters, as he was constantly devising new techniques, developing tactics for the UH-34 and "Deuce," and reorganizing the units and equipment of the helicopter group. A tour as a student at the National War College in Washington followed, and after graduation, in July 1960 he reported to HQMC first as Assistant Director of Aviation, and then—as a colonel—as the Director, in September of that year.

The next spring he was promoted to brigadier general and assumed command of the Hawaii-based 1st Marine Brigade. He and his family remained in Hawaii after this tour and he joined the staff of the Commander-in-Chief, Pacific, as Assistant Chief of Staff for Operations. During this assignment, he participated in the escalation of the war in Vietnam, and helped define clear-cut responsibilities for the conduct of combat air operations involving the Air Force, Navy, and Marine Corps. For exceptionally meritorious service from 1963 to 1965 he was awarded his third Legion of Merit.

Ordered to Vietnam in June 1965, McCutcheon commanded the 1st Marine Aircraft Wing and served as Deputy Commander, III Marine Amphibious Force, earning his first Distinguished Service Medal. He received his major general's stars in January 1966 while still in Vietnam and six months later went to Washington, D.C., to begin work as Deputy Chief of Staff (Air). This, the longest assignment of his career, would tax to the full McCutcheon's resources of character and aviation knowledge and experience.

# CHAPTER EIGHT

# TWO SEPARATE ROLES FOR THE UH-1E

## Expansion and Shortages

When Colonel Reusser accepted the first UH-1E at the Bell plant on 21 February 1964, the Marine Corps planned to equip each of the three VMO squadrons in the active forces with 24 aircraft for observation and assault support roles. It had been hoped that the VMO squadron in the Organized Reserves could be similarly equipped, but approval had not been gained. Even as the first helicopters were arriving at New River and Santa Ana, a controversy was smoldering as to their proper employment. The roots went back to the disagreement between General Shoup and General Snedeker as to whether the combined observation and assault support roles required both a fixed-wing aircraft and a helicopter, or if the UH-1E could perform both missions. At the time of the disagreement, General Shoup had prevailed, and only the UH-1E was procured, but in 1965 he no longer was Commandant.

In July of that year, Major General Louis E. Robertshaw, DC/S(Air), presented a briefing to the annual general officers' symposium in which he outlined a different program. A new fixed-wing aircraft, much like that recommended by General Snedeker, was under study. The OV-10A, a "two-seat, twin engine, light armed reconnaissance aircraft," he reported, "has been proposed for introduction into each of our observation squadrons, including the organized Marine Corps Reserves." Though the Secretary of Defense so far had withheld approval of the OV-10A—which was a joint project of the Army, Air Force, and Navy/Marine Corps—the general remained optimistic. "We plan for the OV-10A to be operational commencing in FY-68. Each VMO squadron will be equipped with 18 OV-10As, and the number of UH-1Es cut in half to only 12." The result would be that the three active duty and one reserve VMOs would be equipped with a total of 72 OV-10A fixed-wing aircraft and 48 UH-1E helicopters.[1]

Another factor influenced the enthusiasm for the OV-10A. SHUFLY had been operating over three years, and the buildup of Marines in Vietnam had occurred only four months before the general spoke. There was a rising clamor for armed helicopters and the opponents and proponents of the concept were busily defending their relative positions. General Robertshaw told the assembled generals, "We *need* this aircraft [the OV-10] to provide close-in escort capability to transport helicopters, especially during operations in rough terrain and conditions of reduced visibility." Assuming that the Secretary of Defense approved the purchase, "we could expect to see the OV-10A in the Fleet Marine Force by the end of FY-68." In the meantime, he concluded, "we will continue to rely on the A-4s and UH-1Es to do the job."[2]

In early October of the same year, General Krulak urgently requested that another VMO squadron be activated for deployment to Vietnam no later than April 1966. General Greene answered reluctantly that the only way to meet the requirement in time was to mobilize the VMO from the reserves. The squadron was equipped with OH-43s which were hardly considered ideal. The only other possibility was to obtain the approval of the Secretary of Defense to commission a fourth squadron in the active forces, but such an effort would entail "a lead time which would be much greater."[3] Under normal circumstances, such an increase in the number of squadrons within the Marine Corps, without an offsetting decrease in fixed-wing units, would be a long and arduous process spanning several years. The war in Vietnam, however, was rapidly demonstrating that the fall of 1965 and the spring of 1966 were not normal times.

Major General William R. Collins had been overall commander of the Marines during the initial landings in 1965 at Da Nang and subsequently was assigned as Assistant Chief of Staff, G-3 at HQMC. In July 1966 he was able to announce that the Secretary of Defense indeed had approved the request of the Marine Corps to activate, not one, but two additional observation squadrons. He added a note of caution, for the units were only "Vietnam temporary add-ons" and not a part of the permanent peacetime Marine Corps.[4] At the conclusion of the war, they probably would have to be disbanded. General McCutcheon, at the same

UH-1Es at Fire Support Base CUNNINGHAM during Operation DEWEY CANYON in northern I Corps in 1969. Without guns, the UH-1E was an excellent observation aircraft, but it often was diverted to other missions, as here supplying a remote firebase.

time, went on to say that under current plans "one of the squadrons will form next month [August] and deploy to WestPac in two 12-plane increments in December and March. The other will form in January and remain on the west coast" at MCALF Camp Pendleton to train additional pilots.[5]

Approval of the new units did not instantaneously create more capability. Additional aircraft had to be supplied and the Marine Corps already was short of UH-1Es as the result of the attack on Marble Mountain. In March 1966, although authorized a total of 76 UH-1Es in the operating units, it had only 58. To alleviate the situation, the Marine Corps that month attempted to borrow UH-1Bs from the Army.[6] The Army had none to spare, for it had found its UH-1 series to be well suited to combat as a light troop transport and for its increasing numbers of gunships. Though Bell was straining to meet the demands for more helicopters, the shortage in the Marine Corps continued. The addition of the two temporary squadrons compounded the problem. Colonel Alan J. Armstrong, who filled the two-month gap between the departure of General Robertshaw as DC/S(Air) on 15 April and the arrival of General McCutcheon on 15 June, continued to press for the loan of Army UH-1Bs. A week after General McCutcheon took over his new duties, he was able to write that the Secretary of the Army finally had agreed to transfer 20 helicopters.[7] The Secretary of Defense approved the decision on 12 July.[8]

Since the Army version had no rotor brake, it was only marginally suitable for shipboard operations. The helicopter forces in Vietnam had first priority for amphibious vertical assaults, so it was necessary that they be equipped with the Marine Corps design. All of the Army aircraft were delivered to New River, releasing UH-1Es for transfer to the Pacific area. While they reduced the amphibious assault capability of the FMFLant forces, the UH-1Bs without rotor brakes were better than nothing. Ten of them arrived in August and 10 more in January 1967.[9]

As the impact of the war became more apparent, it was obvious that the Marine Corps would require additional UH-1Es to meet its needs. A supplemental budget request for FY-66 included a total of 108 aircraft. To compensate for the combat losses, 28 were desired. An additional 45 were destined for the two new squadrons, and hopefully, 35 more could be procured to begin outfitting the organized reserve units. Only 59 were approved, with none for the reserves and only 31 for the add-on squadrons.[10] These were not enough. By May, the Secretary of the Navy had approved switching funds from other programs so that the parts requiring long manufacturing processes for 27 more UH-1Es could be ordered.[11] In July, Congress approved the actions and full procurement of the 27 helicopters was authorized. Simultaneously, VMO-3 was commissioned on schedule at MCALF Camp Pendleton on 1 August under the command of Major Francis R. ("Frank") Murray. The first detachment of 12 UH-1Es departed California for Vietnam on 9 December. A week later, Major Kyle W. Townsend assumed command and on 17 December, he left with the rest of the squadron.

On the same day that Major Townsend took over VMO-3, 15 December, VMO-5, under the command of Lieutenant Colonel Donald K. Tooker, was formed out of the nucleus of a small training subunit which had been operating at Pendleton, nominally as a part of HMM-462. The new squadron continued to serve as a training unit for UH-1E pilots and crews until March 1968.

## Guns or Eyes?

By the end of June 1967, the equivalent of the Marines' entire peacetime helicopter observation forces were committed to combat in Vietnam. Three squadrons, VMOs-2, -3, and -6 had a total of 68 aircraft assigned.[12] Even this many could not meet the requirements, for the versatile UH-1E was being subjected to two different, and often conflicting, demands for specific missions.

In July, General Krulak returned to Washington to report on the progress of the war. He brought with him some startling statistics. He displayed a chart which gave the type of missions being flown in Vietnam by the UH-1E from July 1966 through June 1967.

*UH-1E Task Performance*[13]
*July '66–June '67*

| | |
|---|---|
| Admin/liaison | 5,579 |
| Tactical Air Controller (Airborne) | 1,086 |
| Casualty Evacuation | 1,109 |
| Command and Control | 1,099 |
| Search and Rescue | 116 |
| Reconnaissance | 1,756 |
| Total | 10,745 |

He then announced some shocking information. In addition to the flights he had listed, another 19,597 missions—almost two-thirds of the grand total—had been flown as armed helicopters, a role for which the UH-1E had never been designed for the Marine Corps.[14]

His analysis of the problem of the armed helicopter was a classic—and typical—example of his perception:

> I believe our VMO has not been optimally used. Its function has been altered, in part from predominantly observation, command, control and liaison to the role of the attack aircraft; that is to say, 2.75-inch rocket and machine gun close air support.
>
> You can see from the data [on his chart] that the commanders were largely denied the eyes which are so urgently needed over the jungle environment of much of Vietnam; denied the eyes that were provided them for the purpose, while the bulk of the sorties were in the armed role.

He then continued:

> How did it come about? We all share some of the responsibility. We probably put too many rocket pods on the little aircraft and thus unconsciously encouraged their misuse. The close physical association of the VMO personnel and the personnel of the ground unit often generated *ad hoc* arrangements, which went around the existing tactical air request doctrine. There were some [commanders] reluctant to invest deeply in on-station [fixed wing] close air support because of the obvious cost. This, of course, diminished responsiveness.
>
> The heavy demand for the [fixed wing] air support and the distances sometimes involved, often generated further delays, further reduction in responsiveness and further encouragement [of the ground commanders] to turn to the armed helo as a more responsive weapon.
>
> And then there is the undeniable fact that the armed helicopter has a useful capability in conditions of poor visibility, plus a favorable morale effect on our own people. And finally, the absence of heavy resistance has often allowed us to get away with the use of the helicopter in this role. (But this is not always true. During Operation PRAIRIE, for example, we had a brief brush with a .50 caliber environment and had 4 helicopters shot down in two days.)[15]

He went on to state his opinion that a helicopter—even large, heavily armed, and armored ones capable of speeds over 200 knots such as the experimental aircraft the Army was developing—"would not survive in a high resistance environment." In case any of the assembled general officers had missed the point, General Krulak brought up another example of what he considered was the misuse of the UH-1E:

> Akin to the observation problem is the forward air controller problem. Of our close and direct support attacks, which are delivered under a forward air controller (FAC), well over half are run by a U.S. Air Force forward air controller, airborne in a U.S. Air Force airplane. Why? Not because we do not have the FACs. We do have them and they are good ones. But

*Another role for the UH-1E. Marines rappel from a Huey at Camp Pendleton in April 1970.*

USMC Photo A149377

mostly they are sitting at a battalion command post, in the image of Korea or World War II, where . . . they cannot see to do their job any more than half the time. They are not elevated in an aircraft where they can see, because the aircraft have not been available. We have a small number of 0–1s . . . and we are getting the OV–10A. Here again the UH–1E can do the job—if it is made available and we are thus brought back to the less than optimal use of our VMO capability.[16]

General McCutcheon echoed General Krulak's thoughts, but had some encouraging news. "The observation aircraft situation has improved somewhat in the past year," he reported at the same conference to which General Krulak had spoken. "We are almost in a position to return the 20 Army UH–1Bs we borrowed." Over 70 percent of all the Marine Corps UH–1s of either type were deployed to Vietnam where they "proved so useful in the utility, liaison, administrative and gunship escort roles that they were often pulled away from their observation mission." Assistance was on the way, however, as "we are counting on North American's OV–10A, recently named the 'Bronco,' to help us in the observation and helicopter escort missions." Unfortunately, "The airplane's schedule slipped in service test because of engine and control troubles." In spite of the difficulties in the twin-engine turbo-prop aircraft, he planned that "the first Marine OV–10s will go to Pendleton in November and will deploy in May 1968." [17]

Until the OV–10s could be sent to Vietnam, other expedients would have to be found to support the observation requirements. Attempts were made to convert the ubiquitous UH–34 into an observation helicopter, but the attempts failed because the machine simply was not designed for the mission.* A more promising alternative was to reactivate some old, small, fixed-wing, Cessna-built O–1s—the same type of aircraft which had been assigned to the original SHUFLY. Ten machines, the entire inventory left in the Navy, were hurriedly pulled from storage in the fall of 1966 and shipped to Vietnam. Even though parts were scarce and the Commandant remained concerned over the supply problems, the aircraft made a valuable addition to the aviation forces in Vietnam.[18] The O–1s were so useful that General McCutcheon began negotiations with OSD "to borrow enough 0–1s to keep 1st MAW up to an operating level of 12 until the OV–10s deploy." [19] He eventually was able to obtain the aircraft, which remained in service until the fall of 1969.

## Reorganization

General Krulak and General McCutcheon had identified the problems created by the UH–1Es spending the majority of their flight time in the role of an armed escort. Finding a solution, however, proved a complex and lengthy task. General McCutcheon observed in July 1967 that as:

> . . . a direct result of our experience in Vietnam . . . we know that the VMOs, with 24 UH–1Es each, do not have enough helicopters to meet the demands for both observation and administrative-liaison-utility missions.[20]

A year later, he was still lamenting that "Vietnam has proven that we do not have enough small helicopters for all of the tasks that Marine ingenuity can devise." [21] Any major change in the makeup of the Marine Corps required a lengthy process of review in the Department of Defense and Congress, so in 1967 McCutcheon could only repeat that "If there is anything that we have learned in Vietnam, it is that we need light helicopters and many of them. One squadron per [division—wing team] is completely inadequate." [22] With the introduction of the OV–10 into the VMO squadrons, which was scheduled for the summer of 1968, "The VMOs will drop to 12 UH–1E each and the shortage will be compounded," he wrote.[23]

---
* See Chapter 1.

*An OV–10A flies over the countryside near Da Nang in 1970. This long-awaited aircraft took over some of the reconnaissance and tactical air control missions previously performed by the UH–1E.*

The ever-resourceful General McCutcheon had evolved two plans to strengthen the UH–1E program. First he proposed that the 12 aircraft deleted from each of the squadrons when the OV–10A became operational, and the aircraft approved for the two temporary "add-on" squadrons, be combined "to form a light helicopter squadron for each wing." Second, he wanted to procure helicopters which were specifically designed as armed escorts and assign 12 of them to each of the VMOs, replacing the rest of the UH–1Es.

> The VMO would then have gunships . . . and OV–10A and the pure observation, Tactical Air Controller (Airborne) (TACA), and helicopter escort mission. The HMLs (Helicopter Marine, Light) would have 24 straight UH–1Es each and would pick up the utility, administrative tasks.[24]

The general was optimistic about the program "Because it uses the UH–1E already on hand and requires such modest procurement we think this proposal stands a good chance of approval."[25] The Secretary of Defense agreed with the arguments "but only on a temporary basis." When the Marine Corps requested that he reconsider the decision and include the three squadrons as part of the permanent peacetime force the Secretary of Defense refused. The units were to remain only as temporary ones, General McCutcheon reported in July 1968, and the Office of the Secretary of Defense had stated that "we do not need HMLs" at all when the war in Vietnam was over.[26]

Though the issue was not resolved at the time, General McCutcheon lost no time organizing the three temporary squadrons. On 15 March 1968, HML–267 was formed at Pendleton under the command of Lieutenant Colonel Phillip P. Upschulte, followed a week later by HML–367 at Phu Bai in Vietnam under Lieutenant Colonel Glenn R. Hunter. The final commissioning was that of HML–167 at Marble Mountain with Major Robert C. Finn taking command on 1 April.

As part of the reorganization, the two wartime "add-on" observation squadrons, VMOs -3 and -5, disappeared from the rolls of Marine Corps units. Their personnel were absorbed by the new HMLs. The Marine Corps continued to press for inclusion of the new units in the permanent forces, and subsequently succeeded in this effort.

# CHAPTER NINE

# THE CH-53 ENTERS THE WAR

## A New Role for the Sea Stallion

The CH-53 had been designed as an amphibious vertical assault helicopter, but by early 1966, as it entered final testing, a new and urgent role was being considered for it: that of a flying crane. Helicopter designers long had dreamed of constructing a "flying crane," a machine which could lift more than its own weight. Igor Sikorsky had envisioned such an aircraft in 1948 when he had predicted that helicopters with a gross weight of 50,000 pounds and a lifting capacity of half that figure could be designed in the near future.[1] Until the advent of the turbine-powered helicopter, however, the building of a true flying crane had been impossible.

While a single large aircraft seemed beyond the range of possibility during the 1950s, many experiments had been made with hooking together two, three, or even more helicopters to lift single heavy loads. The Marine Corps pioneered the "multiple lift" concept in 1954 by using two HRS helicopters attached to the load by long cables. To counteract the weight being carried between them, both aircraft had to fly in a steep bank to avoid being pulled together. Although heavy loads could be lifted, the flying proved extremely hazardous and the project was dropped.[2]

Vertol had made early studies of the same type of multiple helicopter lifts, and by the mid-1950s had concluded that a satisfactory procedure could be worked out using light-weight but rigid beams between the aircraft. In 1957, the company received a contract from the Army Transportation Research and Engineering Command to study further possible designs and techniques. In the final recommendation of this study, Vertol proposed a "multilift system composed of equal sized beams . . . with a single beam for two helicopters, three for three helicopters, four for four, and so on."[3] This study led to another contract in 1958 to construct the beams and flight test two-, three-, and four-plane hitches. Tests of this system with two aircraft revealed that as the aircraft entered ground effect on takeoff or landing, their rotor wash intermingled, creating an unstable condition similar to hovering in a gusty wind. More serious, if the load began to sway for any reason, it set up a similar motion in the helicopter. This difficulty could not be overcome, and the contract was cancelled on 12 February 1959. Vertol continued its experiments and tried without success to interest the Marine Corps in using the system with the YHC-1A (which became the CH-46).

The war in Vietnam revived interest in a multiple-lift system, and indeed in flying cranes in general, for use in retrieving aircraft shot down in enemy territory. During the Korean War, in 1951, Marines on several occasions used helicopters to retrieve other helicopters downed close to Communist lines. These lifts involved almost total dismantling of the damaged aircraft and the carrying of different portions by different helicopters.[4] During the years after Korea, the use of helicopters as cranes to retrieve other helicopters continued to be limited by the small lift capability of the available machines. With the "Deuce," more retrievals were possible, but for most aircraft, unless conditions were absolutely perfect, extensive stripping had to be accomplished before they could be lifted. For the UH-34, for instance, either a combination, or all, of the main rotors, the main transmission and rotor head, the engine, or the tail pylon had to be removed before the aircraft could be retrieved with any degree of certainty by the "Deuce."

The war in Vietnam offered no time for this lengthy process. In Korea, where there had been a fixed front line, most damaged helicopters managed to land in American-held territory; but in Vietnam most came down in areas easily reachable by the Viet Cong, who found downed aircraft lucrative targets. Even if security forces—made up of troops urgently needed elsewhere—could guard the aircraft as it was being stripped, the VC would make every effort to stop the recovery, as Lieutenant Costa had found out in his attempts to retrieve a UH-34 with a "Deuce." It was natural, therefore, for the Marines to explore the possibility of using their new heavy helicopter, the CH-53, as a flying crane.

## A Helicopter Retriever

On 7 January 1966, Colonel Alan J. Armstrong, then assigned as Assistant DC/S(Air), wrote a letter to the CNO recounting the conditions existing and those that could be anticipated in the future. "A need exists," he said, "in the Republic of Vietnam for a helicopter capable of retrieving helicopters or light aircraft downed as the result of enemy action or aircraft malfunctions." He pointed out that in combat "Retrieving downed aircraft in a minimum elapsed time is an operational necessity; failure to do so may result in loss of downed aircraft." Even though the planned deployment of the CH-46A would provide "an enhanced retrieval capability as well as an improved heavy external lift" to assist the over-worked "Deuces," "specific information as to procedures, performance data and preparation of the downed aircraft has not been generated to date."

Armstrong requested that testing be completed in three phases. The first, to be completed by 1 April, was to determine the methods for the CH-46A to lift the UH-34 and UH-1E. The second step was to evaluate the CH-53 to lift the CH-46 plus the two smaller aircraft. He asked that this project be completed within the next five months. Finally, tests were to be run on retrieving a CH-53 with another CH-53. The dates were "based on firm CH-46A deployment dates and," in one of the first inklings of future plans for the CH-53, "possible early deployment of the [heavy helicopter] to provide a retriever capability for the CH-46A." [5]

As Colonel Armstrong was writing, the CH-53 was still undergoing testing at Patuxent River prior to introduction of the helicopter into the Marine Corps squadrons. The evaluation as a retriever was incorporated into the normal testing routine. On 16 May, a CH-53 was assigned to begin the project.[6] The next week a UH-1E was successfully lifted into a hover. The day after, on 24 May, a "dud CH-46A . . . weighing 11,217 pounds" was lifted with the retriever carrying a full fuel load.[7] Two more tests were completed in the next two days. One carried the UH-1E in forward flight at a speed of 100 knots, by utilizing two drogue parachutes to stabilize the load. The same demonstration, only with a CH-46, was completed on 26 May. At the conclusion of the initial tests, the "Preliminary performance data . . . indicates the CH-53A with its present engine, the T-64-GE-6, to be an acceptable retriever of the UH-34D and UH-1E aircraft, but only marginally acceptable as a CH-46A retriever." [8]

Additional lifting capability was needed. While an improved engine, the T-64-GE-12 (Dash-12), was scheduled to be installed in the CH-53, it would not be available until Fiscal Year 1968, too late for the first planned deployment. In March, as preparations were underway to begin the retrieval demonstrations at Patuxent River, Major General Robertshaw, DC/S (Air), had decided that an "emergency helicopter recovery capability was to be deployed as early as air crews and maintenance training can be accomplished subsequent to the August 1966 CH-53 deliveries." [9] A detachment of three or four aircraft from HMH-463 at Santa Ana was to be sent to Vietnam. Target date was 1 November. There was no possibility of having the Dash-12 engines ready by then.

There was, however, another alternative. The rated 2,850 horsepower of each of the engines installed was a guarantee that all engines would produce that much as a minimum. Slight variances in the manufacturing process created a situation in which some engines could produce more. The exact power of each individual engine being delivered from the production line could be established only by operating the engine in a test stand. On 3 June, as soon as the preliminary results of the retriever evaluation were known, General Greene approved a letter to the Naval Air Systems Command "requesting utilization of increased shaft horsepower (3080 maximum . . . vice current 2850)" for the CH-53A's engines.[10]

Initially it appeared that speedy approval would be obtained. General McCutcheon, who had returned to the position of DC/S(Air) on 16 June, reported the first week in August:

> To improve lift capability of four CH-53As deploying to Southeast Asia . . . selected T-64 GE-6 engines will be installed. These selected production engines average 200 horsepower each greater than the minimum specification engines.[11]

In addition, NavAirSysCom was to provide these selected engines on a continuing basis to bridge the gap between the T-64-GE-6 and the improved engine, the T-64-GE-12. His optimism was short lived, for Rear Admiral Allen M. Shinn, Commander of NavAirSysCom, refused approval of the request. His basis was that minor modifications were to be incorporated in the Dash-6 the summer of next year and that the Dash-12 engines should be ready in early 1968. Neither date came close to meeting the requirements of the Marine Corps.

General Greene and General McCutcheon were not to be thwarted. "On 27 October 1966, a letter was sent to CNO strongly repeating the increased power requirement for the CH-53A and advocating that an emergency, time-limited, higher horsepower rating be provided by 1 December 1966." [12] Rear Admiral Robert L. Townsend, who had replaced Admiral Shinner in September, was overruled. "The Naval Air Systems Command authorized the Marine Corps to designate and operate eight CH-53As for helicopter retrieval missions," General McCutcheon could report on 12 December. He continued that the General Electric engines "have been hand picked to provide in excess of 3000 shaft horsepower," and, "moreover, these selected engines have been granted an emergency time-limited, higher horsepower envelope in which they may be operated." [13] * He went on to write that the CH-53As:

> Will initially complement and eventually replace the obsolescent CH-37 'Deuce.'
>
> These CH-53As, which will be used primarily as aircraft retriever vehicles, have been provided additional engine horsepower so that the ambient conditions of RVN will not hinder retriever missions. This 3800 pounds of increased lift performance will enable recovery of the CH-46 and lighter helicopters intact on a 100 degree day at sea level or an 86 day at 2000 feet.[14]

The improvements allowed the CH-53A to "recover all USMC helicopters in RVN except itself, without the requirement of prior stripping." [15] ** By December the retrieval testing at Patuxent River had been completed and "the results, techniques, and necessary hardware to accomplish retriever missions have been issued to the fleet for both rotary and fixed-wing recovery." General McCutcheon could conclude, on 22 December, that "The current helicopter retriever requirement has been solved by the introduction of the CH-53A with increased power into RVN." [16] It was a welcome Christmas present for all Marines involved.

## Other Modifications

The specifically selected engines were not the only changes in the CH-53 which were being made during the busy summer and fall of 1966. Three additional ones were the direct result of the experience in Vietnam. Armor was to be added to critical areas of the engines and controls. The installation had been programmed in 1965 and would "be installed prior to introduction of these aircraft into Vietnam." [17] As General Krulak had pointed out in the case of the UH-34 and CH-46 armoring, there was a significant loss of lift. He wrote in December 1966 that the CH-53s would be "tasked primarily for transport of supplies and equipment and they are not regarded as primarily an assault, reconnaissance, evacuation, or observation aircraft. It is noted, however, that the lift capability . . . will be reduced at least 610 pounds with the addition of protective armor." The general went on to recommend that the helicopter be equipped with only "pilot and co-pilot seat armor; limited engine armor in vital areas only" and "the total armor weight not to exceed 450 pounds." [18]

Guns also were to be added. Similar to the installation in the CH-46 and UH-34, one M-60 machine gun was mounted on a swivel base on each side of the cabin. By 1 August, testing, which had been held at Patuxent River along with the regular evaluation, and the evaluation of retriever capabilities (and other specialized tests) had been "satisfactorily completed." [19] The ideas of an armed helicopter with the lifting capability of the CH-53 continued to prove intriguing to some military men, and in 1968 Sikorsky proposed that the aircraft be utilized as an armed heavy bomber. The machine could carry, the company suggested, "2 gun pods with 20mm cannon and 4000 rounds . . . plus 6 rocket launchers with 114 2.75 inch rockets," or bombs, napalm, land mines and a variety of other ordnance.[20] The Marine Corps showed no interest in the project.

The difficulties of operating the CH-53 in the sand and laterite of Vietnam became a matter of concern. Design of fuel filters and air filters for the engines was well underway by the end of July. The plan was "for all [the modifications] to be on early deployment aircraft." [21] On 19 September, the Commandant sent a message to CNO and NavAirSysCom which "requested that deploying aircraft be equipped with a

USMC Photo A422527
*Before being sent to Vietnam, the CH-53s had large filters installed on the air intake of the engines.*

---

* At higher horsepower the turbines create higher temperatures in the burning chambers and on the turbine. To prevent damage, the amount of time the engine could be operated at the increased temperature was limited.

** The "Deuce" was so large it was never considered as being retrievable intact by helicopter.

swirl sand separator system similar to that used on the Army's CH-54A crane" helicopter.[22] The first design was less than satisfactory and Sikorsky reported that after 300 landings in a sand pit, the engines had lost from three to five percent of their rated power due to erosion.[23] Further modifications were made and the resulting engine air particle separator (EAPS) was first installed and flown on a CH-53 by the middle of November at the Sikorsky plant.[24] The new kits "proved very satisfactory and flight tests show it to be airworthy and that performance difference is negligible."[25] Installation on the four aircraft to be deployed to Vietnam was made by Sikorsky personnel and completed 8 December before the aircraft departed.[26]

## Retrievers to Vietnam

The object of all this attention and intense activity was Major William R. ("Bill") Beeler, the commanding officer of HMH-463 at Santa Ana. Beeler's squadron, which had been commissioned 1 March 1966, had been expecting to receive the first CH-53s in late summer. The difficulties in the production line had prevented the original schedule from being met and it was not until 20 September that Beeler landed in California with the first new helicopter. While he and his crews were at the Sikorsky plant in Connecticut, accepting the aircraft, General Krulak sent a warning order to Vietnam, alerting 1st MAW to expect the arrival of a detachment of CH-53s with a retriever capability. The general set a date of 25 October for the unit to be ready to leave Santa Ana.[27] A week before the expected deployment day, General Krulak "postponed HMH-463's readiness date for embarkment of a four aircraft detachment for 25 October 1966 to 1 December 1966. This delay will allow adequate testing of the engine air inlet sand filter," and the incorporation of all other modifications into the aircraft.[28]

On 16 December newly promoted Lieutenant Colonel Beeler assumed the duties of officer in charge of Detachment "A" of the squadron (which had been commanded by Lieutenant Colonel Samuel G. Beal since 21 September). Two days before Christmas, he and the maintenance officer for the detachment, Major James L. Shelton, arrived at Marble Mountain. Most of the remainder of the other 11 officers and 36 Marines joined them in time to mark New Year's Eve in Vietnam. The four precious aircraft had been preserved for the long ocean voyage at O&R North Island and arrived on 8 January on board the USS *Croatan* (TAKV 43). The next few days were spent getting the aircraft ready for combat operations, including

USMC Photo 3d-6-3471-67
*A CH-53 lifts a disabled UH-34 out of Con Thien in northern I Corps in 1967. The CH-53A had enough power to lift a "Huss" with the rotor blades on.*

final installation of the armor and armament kits. On 13 January the detachment completed its first cargo hop. Only four days later, the Viet Cong introduced the crews to small arms fire. Two aircraft were hit but not seriously damaged. Lieutenant Colonel Beeler's crews and aircraft had their first chance to demonstrate the mission for which they had been sent to Vietnam on 25 January, when a UH-34 had mechanical difficulties on the landing platform of a hospital ship. The CH-53 pilot retrieved the stricken aircraft and closed the official report with a terse "No problems encountered."[29] *

During their first weeks of activity, the CH-53s were grounded temporarily after an accident at Santa Ana,

---

* Initial reports from the detachment counted this as an administrative lift. Contemporary official records at HQMC credit the first lift under tactical conditions to 5 February. On that day a UH-1E and a UH-34 were recovered. In the interim, two additional UH-34s had been retrieved. One of these efforts, however, had been unsuccessful.

where one helicopter was seriously damaged when the tail pylon broke in a practice landing in the hills east of the airfield. Initial fears were allayed when an investigation revealed that the failure had most probably occurred when the helicopter had made a landing which imposed stresses beyond the designed limit. Nevertheless, NavAirSysCom "recognized that during combat and in operations from unprepared areas it may be difficult to assure that pilots will stay with specified landing limits." To prevent any recurrence of the accident, NavAirSysCom "developed a structural change to provide an overall improvement in aircraft strength of approximately 30 percent."[30] The changes were quickly incorporated. Even before the kits had arrived in Vietnam, Lieutenant Colonel Beeler and his crews went back to unrestricted flight on 29 January.

From its arrival in January to 22 May, this small detachment of four CH-53s retrieved 103 aircraft, many of which would have been lost if it had not been for Lieutenant Colonel Beeler and his crews. The total included 72 UH-34s, which, General McCutcheon was quick to point out, were enough aircraft to equip three medium transport squadrons. In addition, the unit had recovered 13 CH-46s, 16 UH-1Es, and two Air Force aircraft.

Meanwhile at Santa Ana, the rest of HMH-463 was undergoing intensive pre-deployment training. On 1 May it sailed on board the USS *Tripoli* with 22 CH-53s and arrived at Marble Mountain three weeks later. As Lieutenant Colonel Beal and his crews began flying to their new home, they were greeted by Major General Robertshaw, McCutcheon's predecessor as DC/S (Air), who had overseen much of the development of the CH-53 and now was finishing a tour as Commanding General, 1st Marine Aircraft Wing. The same day, Detachment "A" was reunited with its parent squadron and Lieutenant Colonel Beeler became the executive officer. By the middle of the summer of 1967, Lieutenant Colonel Beal could report that "the squadron is moving over 100 tons of cargo daily, and

USMC Photo A422224

*A CH-53 of HMH-463 prepares to lift a CH-46 damaged by enemy fire near Quang Tri in September 1968. More powerful and reliable than the CH-37, the CH-53 could retrieve any downed helicopter except another CH-53.*

USMC Photo A192651

*A CH–53 places a 12th Marines 150mm howitzer in a mountain top firebase southwest of Da Nang in 1968. The powerful Sea Stallion could lift very heavy loads into high-altitude landing zones.*

on peak days, 250 tons have been carried. Aircraft retrievals are commonplace and occur daily." [31]

General Robertshaw went further:

> We are all impressed with the job being done by the CH–53. We are delighted to note that since the arrival of the full squadron, the CH–53s have carried about 75% of MAG–16's total tonnage and passengers, while flying only about 16% of the flight hours.[32]

The prodigious capacity of the helicopter was demonstrated at the end of August, when one aircraft lifted a load consisting of 75 combat-equipped United States Marines. This type of mission could be accomplished only through increasing the allowable horsepower of the engines. The initial experiments had proved so successful that by the first of August, NavAirSysCom had agreed to allow all the CH–53s in Vietnam to operate the engines at higher temperatures, resulting in each generating approximately 230 extra horsepower.

As rapidly as aircraft could be delivered, crews trained, and parts stocked, additional CH–53s were delivered to Vietnam. By the end of December, 36 of them were in combat.[33] At the same time, HMH–463 had accounted for a total of 370 aircraft retrievals though not all of them were from enemy areas. Brigadier General Armstrong, Assistant DC/S (Air), on 22 January 1968—only a few days past the anniversary of the first CH–53 operational commitment in Vietnam —could state confidently:

> The immediate requirement for a helicopter retriever has been satisfied by the CH–53. Retriever techniques and equipment have proven themselves in Southeast Asia. All CH–53s have been provided uprated engines from 2850 shaft horsepower to 3080 shaft horsepower. Further engine improvement is programmed for CY 69 CH–53 deliveries when the new T–64-12 engine (3400 SHP) is to be incorporated.[34]

The exploits of these large helicopters became widely appreciated by not only the combat Marines and their commanders, but the pilots and crews as well. Gradually, in recognition of its capabilities, it acquired a new nick-name which remains to this time. The CH–53 is known as "The Super-Bird" among those Marines who have seen it perform at its maximum lift and speed capability.

## Requiem for a Heavyweight— the End for the "Deuce"

As the CH–53 proved its worth as a heavy lifter, the machine upon which the entire Marine Corps helicopter doctrine had been based finally was leaving active service. On 1 January 1967, Major Richard L. Hawley, who had commanded the only HR2S squadron ever operationally deployed as a unit, took over as officer in charge of the detachment of "Deuces" at Marble Mountain. He was replaced on 12 April by Captain Steven E. Field. A little over a month later, on 14 May, a "Deuce" made the last operational flight of a HR2S in Vietnam, carrying 20 troops and 3,000 pounds.[35] An era had ended. Since the aircraft had arrived on the *Princeton* in September 1965, this small subunit had flown over 5,300 hours, carried almost 32,000 passengers, and transported 12.5 million pounds of cargo. Though hardly designed for the mission, the "Deuces" also had executed over 600 medical evacuation flights.

When the HR2Ss left Vietnam, the commanding officer of MAG–16, Colonel Samuel F. Martin, summed up the feelings of most Marines:

> The Deuces carried a big share of the logistics cargo lifted by MAG–16. Though their lift capability is replaced many times over by the CH–53s, the belching roar of the "Deuces" will be missed as they pass from the scene.[36]

The crews who had flown them and maintained them would miss them even more. One reporter wrote of their feelings:

> The sentiments—and that's just what it was, sentiment—from tough-talking Marines, were echoed by

Gunnery Sergeant Donald D. Stoltz. "It's a damn shame to see them go. That's all—a damn shame."[37]

In June 1967, for the first time since HMH-461 accepted the initial "Deuce" to be delivered to a Marine Corps tactical squadron in March 1957, the official reports did not list any of these giant helicopters in the active inventory. NavAirSysCom, on 30 July 1968, directed that all the stored "Deuces" be stricken from the records and disposed of at the least expense to the government. Even then the "Deuce" continued to serve the Marine Corps. Three years later, MAG-56 requested use of one last hulk which had been rotting in San Diego, to train a new generation of helicopter pilots in the techniques of aircraft recovery. The Naval Air Systems Command approved the transfer on 25 February 1971.[38] It was the last known reference to the "Deuce" in official records.

To new generations of Marines, it is difficult to remember that this helicopter was the first—and for almost 10 years, the only—aircraft which could conduct a vertical amphibious assault in the manner conceived in 1948 by the early planners. The "Deuce" dominated development of the helicopter for two decades. All machines prior to it were but interim designs awaiting the introduction of it into the Marine squadrons. The lessons learned from this aircraft proved to be the basis for most subsequent development. The "Deuce" established that a power blade fold mechanism could be designed which would permit large helicopters to operate from the confined flight decks of the LPHs.

The lifting capability of the "Deuce" was the limiting factor in what equipment was carried by all assault Marines, and it was the "Deuce" which demonstrated that the Marine Corps had a unique capability in the nation's military forces.

While the idiosyncrasies of the "Deuce" were legendary, it was, and remains, the most significant helicopter ever introduced into the Marine Corps. A search of available records indicates that all of the Marine versions have been broken up and sold for scrap. The mighty "Deuce" deserved a better fate.

# CHAPTER TEN

# MEDIUM TRANSPORT CRISIS

## The CH-46 in Trouble

In the summer of 1967, the Marine Corps had 10 squadrons of CH-46 helicopters.[1] Half were equipped, or being equipped, with the improved "D" model. The rest still had the earlier "A" version. Three of the squadrons were in Vietnam and one was on board the assault ships of a Special Landing Force operating in the South China Sea. The deployed aircraft represented 107 of the 211 CH-46s possessed by the Marine Corps.[2] The remainder of the Marine Corps medium vertical assault capability consisted of five squadrons flying UH-34s, three of which were in Vietnam and one as another SLF squadron. In addition to these 15 transport squadrons which were now available as the result of General Shoup's expansion program, two additional ones had been authorized as part of a temporary wartime fourth helicopter group, MAG-56, based at Santa Ana. "The shortage of helicopter pilots," General McCutcheon lamented in July 1967, "has prevented our manning MAG-56 as an active group."[3] At the time he spoke, only one of the extra transport squadrons, HMM-561, had been formed but it remained in a cadre status with no aircraft assigned. Later it received UH-34s as they became available. The second approved squadron was never activated.

Even with the loss of lift capability in the CH-46As due to the installation of the guns and armor, and in spite of the difficulties with sand the previous May, the CH-46 units had compiled an enviable record. From the time Lieutenant Colonel Watson flew into Marble Mountain until 1 May the next year, they had flown a combined 32,774 hours.[4] "Prior to 1 May 1967," General McCutcheon later was to write:

> ... there had been only isolated incidents/accidents involving the H-46. Statistics gathered by the Naval Aviation Safety Center revealed that the H-46 had an accident trend comparable to other fleet helicopters at a similar time in their development cycle.[5]

Then on 3 May, a CH-46D at Santa Ana crashed, killing all four members of the crew. Within three days the investigators of the accident had determined that the mounting brackets of the main transmission had failed, allowing the front and rear overlapping rotors to intermesh.[6] The result was catastrophic. The solution required a detailed inspection and the addition of steel reinforcements to those transmission mounts which were found faulty. All CH-46 helicopters were temporarily grounded. In Vietnam, "immediate corrective action of a temporary nature enabled the aircraft to fly combat missions while at the same time a detailed inspection program . . . was instituted." Of the 115 transmissions available, including spares, in the Western Pacific, inspection revealed that 46 would have to be repaired.[7] All the aircraft in the United States remained grounded until 13 May, when the Naval Air Systems Command released for flight any CH-46s which had successfully passed inspection.[8]

Unknown to the Navy at the time, a few hours before the message ungrounding the aircraft was sent, another CH-46—this time an "A" model—crashed off the coast of Vietnam when the tail pylon containing the engines, main transmission and aft rotors broke off in flight. All four crew members were killed. General McCutcheon ordered "a comprehensive study of CH-46 material problems," and Vertol "initiated extensive investigation with instrumented flight tests" to determine the exact cause.[9] In June, General Krulak reported "another problem area was highlighted when a CH-46 crashed . . . due to a still undetermined cause. However," he added, "the malfunction under strong suspicion is failure" in the main transmission.[10]

Later the same month, on 20 June, another CH-46A crashed, though two of the four-man crew survived. Once again, even though the aircraft was not recovered from the water, failure of some sort in the rear pylon was suspected.[11]

Ten days later, a CH-46D at Santa Ana crashed when a rotor blade separated from the aircraft. Miraculously, all three of the crew survived. As a result of this latest accident, all CH-46Ds were immediately grounded.[12] Other models of the CH-46 were not affected, which meant that all the "A" model aircraft in Vietnam and on the SLFs could continue flying. Sophisticated X-ray inspection equipment was ordered and double checking of all blades directed. Three days later, on 3 July, still another CH-46 crashed in Viet-

*A CH–46A of HMM–262 prepares to land on the U.S.S.* Guadalcanal *(LPH 7) in July 1966. By 1967, the CH–46 had become the backbone of the Marines' medium helicopter transport capability.*

nam, killing all four Marines of its crew. The aircraft was one of the ungrounded "A" models, and the cause of the crash again was traced to failure of the main transmission. General McCutcheon had had enough. He demanded, and got, a "CH–46 Reliability Review Conference," scheduled to convene the first week in August.[13]

At the end of July, General Krulak became sufficiently concerned about the CH–46 to send a message to Vice Admiral Allen M. Shinn, Commander, Naval Air Forces, Pacific, stating that he "wholeheartedly support the effort to obtain an expedited review of the basic reliability of the aircraft." He continued that:

> The problems with the aft transmission and the rotor blades appear likely to be solved with the programs now in effect. Although hard to equate with the Vietnam record, there remains the possibility that there may be some basic design weakness in the aircraft with respect to transmission mounting and distribution of transmission stresses in the airframe. I hope that the review which [has been] requested clarifies this.[14]

Krulak called attention to two additional effects of the protracted groundings of the CH–46 on the West Coast. HMM–364, equipped with CH–46Ds, was scheduled to deploy to Vietnam in October. The continued difficulties with its helicopters, according to Krulak, "is affecting adversely the replacement pilot and crew training program" for the squadron. In addition, "while I am sure there has been some loss of confidence in the CH–46 . . . I have no evidence that it has yet reached significant proportions." Krulak concluded that, until the results of the reliability conference were known, "we are obligated to keep the CH–46 at work as best we can, since, as you know, it is the backbone of our vertical assault capability in Vietnam."[15]

The conference began on 1 August at the Vertol plant in Morton, Pennsylvania. Members of the DC/S (Air) staff, Naval Air Systems Command, the fleet operators, Vertol, and technical personnel all attended. Among other conclusions, the conferees decided that in the CH–46, "There were no safety or flight discrepancies remaining uncorrected on the aircraft provided recommended inspection procedures were accomplished." These inspection requirements "created an unacceptable maintenance workload [but] the aircraft fixes being installed and test equipment under procurement would reduce the required maintenance workload to an acceptable level." The Vertol representatives suggested that the massive buildup in Vietnam had helped produce the difficulties by reducing the quality of Marine maintenance crews. "The rapid turnover rate of maintenance personnel, their level of technical training and their CH-46 maintenance experience are critical contributing factors in this area." The Marines denied that this was a significant cause of the trouble.[16] *

Other members of the conference blamed the crashes on "rotor blades, drive shaft bearings, and excessive vibration of the aft pylon."[17] The conference ended with a report that since "The vibration level and flight stress loads in the CH-46 were an area of concern," the Naval Air Safety Center should task the Naval Air Test Center at Patuxent River, Maryland, to conduct an expedited CH-46 flight test program to evaluate structural changes to the aft pylon considered necessary as a result of an instrumented flight test program conducted by Boeing Vertol."[18]

It appeared that the difficulties of the CH-46 could be brought under control. Then, on 31 August, a CH-46A from HMM-262 on the SLF "Yawed at 3000 feet and lost the tail pylon." All five crew members died in the flaming crash. The next day in Vietnam, an aircraft was landing, when the "tail pylon separated from aircraft."[19] The crew escaped with minor injuries. This latest incident "precipitated an exhaustive investigation by the accident board and various technical advisors including Vertol engineers." The team of experts "failed to determine the exact cause of the accident." Reluctantly, Major General Norman J. Anderson, who had left DC/S (Air) in November of 1963 and who now commanded the 1st Marine Aircraft Wing in Vietnam, ordered that all CH-46s be "restricted to emergency combat requirements which could not be met by other aircraft."[20]

The first of September saw technicians from Vertol, Naval Air Systems Command, and other agencies converging on Vietnam in an attempt to pinpoint the cause of the failures. The President of Boeing/Vertol, Robert W. Tharrington, accompanied by a Marine helicopter maintenance expert, Major Wyman U. Blakeman, arrived the 17th of the month.[21] They were met by a growing team of experts. Their investigations indicated that "although the specific causes of the CH-46 accidents were varied, the ultimate structural failures occurred in the area of the after pylon."[22]

Back in Washington, General McCutcheon, DC/S (Air), agreed with the recommendation "that interim structural and system modifications be incorporated in the CH-46." The modifications included:

> A strengthening of structural members in the aft pylon and along the ramp closure area. These modifications will improve areas of known weakness . . . and will provide additional strength and durability. . . . several hydraulic and electrical systems modifications will be effected which will minimize the possibility of damage . . . will prevent malfunction of the yaw stability augmentation system with resultant structural damage and will reduce overall maintenance effort . . . power transmission modification will provide a reduction in engine mount . . . wear and structural cracks in the aft transmission . . . area.[23]

Improvements, already underway, to reduce the high frequency vibration in the shafts connecting the engines to the transmissions—an area of concern since the first tests of the helicopter at Patuxent River—were to be expedited. The entire modification program "which will require about 1,000 man-hours per helicopter will be performed by personnel of the Boeing/Vertol Company. Marines will disassemble and reassemble the aircraft."[24]

In the western Pacific area, rather than complete the required work at the airfields in Vietnam which were receiving sporadic attack from the enemy, General McCutcheon approved a plan which would "establish maximum CH-46A repair positions at MCAF Futema, Okinawa."[25] Repairs began on 11 October when 40 helicopters were unloaded from the LPH *Tripoli*. Initially only eight aircraft could be handled at a time, but by early November 16 more work stations were added.[26]

The Marines of Lieutenant Colonel Gregory A. "Greg" Corliss's HMM-262 were selected to move from the SLF to Futema to prepare all of the aircraft. On the squadron's arrival Lieutenant Colonel Corliss turned over command to Major David L. Althoff, who in turn was relieved on 23 November by Major John W. Alber. The modification program on Okinawa "was officially completed at Futema on 20 December. 80 CH-46s had been completed and returned operationally ready to the forces in Vietnam as scheduled."[27] An additional 25 aircraft which had been undergoing normal overhaul in Japan would be completed in February 1968. An additional 111 CH-46Ds were modified at New River, 32 at Santa Ana, and 34 more at overhaul and repair facilities. A total of 325 CH-46As and "Ds" underwent the extensive overhaul.

A year earlier, DC/S (Air), Brigadier General Alan J. Armstrong, had written "The Marine Corps has

---

* Major General Norman J. Anderson, who had succeeded Robertshaw in command of the 1st MAW in June 1967, later recalled that: "The pinnacle was Vertol's proposal that they provide maintenance crews to the Marine Corps in S[outh] V[ietnam] because our Marines were too thin in talent to do justice to the machine. . . . General Krulak upheld my view that the basic contention of ineptitude was nonsense and that we had no desire to introduce more civilians into the combat domain." (*Anderson Comments*)

always been proud of its 'crisis control' capability."[28] The major modification of so many helicopters in such a short time was a tribute to that capability. Every Marine mechanic who worked on the aircraft, the personnel from Vertol, and the officers and men of the units involved, as well as the leaders and staff in all the major commands contributed to the rapid restoration of the CH-46 as a full-fledged member of the amphibious vertical assault team of the Marine Corps.

The temporary loss of the CH-46 had been especially critical in Vietnam, where the CH-46s assigned to MAG-16, MAG-36, and the SLF represented 48 percent of the cargo lift and 47 percent of the personnel lift capability of III MAF.[29] Until the CH-46s could be returned to duty, additional helicopters had to be found. As soon as the seriousness of the problems in the tail pylon became evident, 23 UH-34s were sent in cargo aircraft from Norfolk, Virginia and MCAS Cherry Point, North Carolina. These old reliable work horses arrived on 15 October and immediately were thrown into battle, often flown by CH-46 pilots from the squadrons which were having their aircraft modified. It was during this time, in the fall of 1967, that the "interim" UH-34 (or HUS under the old system) had the unique distinction of having its official designation adopted into the slang of all Marines. "Give me a 'Huss,'" had become indelibly identified as asking for something good.

An additional 10 CH-53s were sent from California to further augment the lift capability in Vietnam. Finally, on 28 September, 31 U.S. Army UH-1s were assigned to General Anderson's forces until the CH-46s could be returned to flight status.

The exact causes of the problems with the CH-46 never were pinpointed with accuracy and complete assurance. There is no doubt that at least a partial reason for the crashes was the extensive modifications made on the aircraft Vertol had sold in 1961—the YHC-1A—to produce the aircraft being flown by the Marine Corps in 1967. The provision of a blade folding mechanism introduced new loads on the transmission and fuselage. The widening of the ramp door and the resulting smaller support on the sides of the fuselage for the "shelf" on which the main components were attached would have weakened the structure of the aircraft, and more powerful engines would add still more strain. The persistent high-frequency vibrations, if uncontrolled, could impose stresses far beyond what the airplanes could withstand. Even the modifications, such as the installation of gun mounts and armor, made on the CH-46As before their deployment to Vietnam and not considered significant enough to warrant full-scale testing, might have been contributing causes. Regardless of what the exact cause was, the modifications installed in the final month of 1967 corrected the problem.

## The CH-46D Arrives in Vietnam

The need for drastic structural modification of the CH-46 delayed the introduction of the improved "D" model to Vietnam. Lieutenant Colonel Louis A. Gulling's "Purple Foxes" of HMM-364 at Santa Ana had been scheduled to be the first squadron to deploy to Vietnam with CH-46Ds, but their movement was held back so that each of their 32 helicopters could have the new modifications installed. Work on the CH-46Ds began on 5 October 1967. On the 28th, most of the unit's pilots and crews flew to Vietnam where they began operating UH-34s to help relieve the medium lift shortage while waiting for their own aircraft to be completed back in California.[30]

On 10 November, the aircraft were ready. They left the United States on board the *Valley Forge* that same day, and 19 days later arrived at Phu Bai, north of Da Nang. The 1st MAW now had 115 CH-46s in the combat area, 83 of them the older, less powerful "A" model. In all, the Marine Corps possessed 222 CH-46s, with 132 of them the improved version.[31]

The difference between the two models was immediately appreciated in Vietnam. Lieutenant General Robert E. Cushman, Jr., then commanding III MAF and a future Commandant, reported in the summer of 1968 that "the advantage of the CH-46 'D's over the 'A's becomes more apparent each day as the temperature rises."[32]

USMC Photo A422347

*A CH-46D arrives in Vietnam. This aircraft of newly-arrived HMM-263 is being stripped of its "Spray-Lat" protective coating at Marble Mountain in January 1969.*

With the arrival in Vietnam of the first "D"s and with the correction of its structural problems, the CH-46 at last was ready to take its place as the heart of the Marines' vertical lift capability, not only in Vietnam but throughout the world. Uncounted Marines since 1967 have conducted assaults from them, depended for food, water, and ammunition upon them, and have returned to their home bases in them. Countless Marines owe their lives to the CH-46, which picked up the wounded—often in the face of enemy fire—and sped them to waiting hospitals. The CH-46 became, and remains, a valuable and respected member of the Marine amphibious assault air/ground team.

## A Premature Funeral for the UH-34

With the return of the CH-46 to full operational status, the replacement of the "Deuce" with the CH-53, and the expansion of the UH-1E program, it appeared by 1967 that the Marine Corps would soon be equipped with nothing but turbine-powered helicopters. Such was not the case. The ever-versatile UH-34 simply refused to leave the scene. No one, in 1955 when General Shepherd had first requested that 90 HUS helicopters be procured, could have foreseen how this aircraft would become such a seemingly permanent fixture of Marine Corps aviation. It was, after all, only an expedient interim model to augment the capability for vertical assault until the "Deuce" could be produced in large numbers. The peak number of UH-34s in the Marine Corps was reached in January 1964 with more than 350 assigned. At that time, Lieutenant Colonel Walter Sienko, commanding officer of HMX-1, accepted the last Marine Corps UH-34 from Mr. Leete P. Doy, vice president of Sikorsky.[33] With Captain Bruce A. Colbert as co-pilot and Staff Sergeant Donald Sabattus as crew chief, the aircraft represented the last of over 500 delivered to the Marine Corps since January 1957. In the intervening years since the first and last delivery, these sturdy aircraft had already amassed a total of 580,000 hours in the air. One single helicopter had already flown 3,745 hours, a phenomenal amount.[34]

Originally, the Marine Corps had planned to introduce the UH-34s into the organized reserve as soon as the CH-46s could replace them in the active forces. This plan had been frustrated by the delays in delivering the CH-46s and by the initial attempts to slow down their purchase to save money. In April 1964, General Robertshaw pointed to "the critical shortage of reserve helicopters available," and complained that "there are currently only 10 UH-34s available to meet a . . . mobilization requirement of 120 helicopters."[35]

Three years later, in the summer of 1967, it appeared that there soon would be enough UH-34s available to provide the reserve squadrons with the total of 73 aircraft which had been approved.[36] Continued losses in Vietnam, the urgent need to augment the combat lift capability during the fall of that year when the CH-46s were having the tail pylons modified, and the ever-expanding war frustrated the plans. Helicopters would be assigned to the reserve units, only to be withdrawn and shipped back to the active forces. By 1968 only 38 were available.[37] Not until 1970 could the expanded authorization of 105 UH-34s be diverted from the active forces and assigned to the reserves.[38]

The reserves were not the only source of UH-34s to meet the needs of the helicopter program. In the fall of 1965 when it was obvious that the war in Vietnam would make it necessary to find more helicopters for the Marines, the Navy proposed that the ancient CH-19 be brought out of storage in Arizona and substituted for the UH-34s utilized in the training command at Pensacola. It was quickly pointed out that it would cost over $3 million to restore 53 of the CH-19s to flyable condition. In addition, there were few mechanics and pilots left who knew how to fly and maintain the CH-19, and new ones would have to be retrained. Such an effort would delay the progress of students completing the syllabus in a training program that was already beginning to show signs of strain at the increased pace caused by the war. Most of all, the CH-19 was "not configured for instrument flight." If the CH-19 were used instead of the UH-34, "The Navy, Marine Corps and Coast Guard would receive helicopter pilots with no helicopter instrument time."[39] It had been a lengthy struggle to procure aircraft which were capable of flying on instruments for the training command, and any step backward now would be disastrous. When the potential results of the plan were presented, it—fortunately—was dropped. Had it been adopted, a whole new generation of Marine Corps helicopter pilots would have become personally acquainted with the "can't let go to scratch my nose" technique which had so bedeviled Colonel Dyer 15 years earlier.

A similar proposal was made the following spring and it was "tentatively planned to replace UH-34 helos at 24 specific sites with CH-19E types. This shift will create a source of UH-34s needed to replace losses in Southeast Asia."[40] Most of the UH-34s to be replaced were assigned to Navy and Marine Corps air stations for search and rescue duties. Once again, it was pointed out that the CH-19 had neither the stability systems nor the instruments to provide for flight in clouds or at night except in dire emergencies. This program was also abandoned. Even then, the Marine Corps continued to operate three CH–19s at MCAS El Toro until the fall of 1967.

The UH–34s in the training command remained until 1969 when their replacement began. The new advanced trainer was the TH–1L, basically a standard UH–1E painted bright red and white for improved visibility in the crowded air at Pensacola. Initially, UH–1Ds had to be borrowed from the Army until production of the Navy models could begin in the fall, when 45 TH–1L trainers were procured from Bell.[41]

In the meantime, the UH–34 continued to serve around the world. Its days, however, were seemingly soon to come to an end, and preparations began to insure its rightful place in history.

### Last Flights of the "Huss"

In early 1968, the Marine Corps began a search for the oldest UH–34 still on active duty. The helicopter was to be displayed in the Marine Corps Aviation Museum in Quantico, Virginia. The search led to Vietnam, and the proper aircraft was located. Being a UH–34, the "Huss" was little impressed by the distinction and impending place of honor. It kept on flying missions in support of the combat Marines, and in May "before the oldest of the choppers could be brought in, she was downed by enemy mortar fire near the Demilitarized Zone and destroyed."[42]

A renewed check of the records indicated that the oldest UH–34 now remaining was also in Vietnam and was assigned to H&MS–36 at Phu Bai. On August 17, with Lieutenant Colonel Duwayne W. Hoffert at the controls, First Lieutenant Peter A. Cacciola as co-pilot, Gunnery Sergeant Leland R. Lindley as crew chief, and Staff Sergeant Richard J. Purtell as gunner, the aircraft, Bureau Number 143971, was flown to Da Nang for shipment back to the United States.[43] The trip to Da Nang was not the last flight of "971" for there had been a change of plans and the aircraft eventually was assigned to the Marine Corps reserve unit at NAS Glenview, Illinois. There, like all UH–34s, it continued to be a work horse. Three years later, in August 1972, "971" once again made headlines as the aircraft "now the last one, has been retired from active duty in the Marine Corps."[44]

The UH–34's last combat flight in Vietnam occurred, appropriately, in HMM–362, the first Marine helicopter squadron to enter the country (with UH–34s) in April 1962 at Soc Trang. Over seven years later, the squadron was still flying UH–34s in the war. On 18 August 1969, at Phu Bai, ceremonies were held marking the end of the combat role of the UH–34s. Two days later, the squadron, now under the command of Lieutenant Colonel Jack E. Schlarp, flew the final six aircraft to Da Nang for shipment back to the United States.[45] The squadron's title was transferred to New River where a new HMH–362 was formed equipped with CH–53s.

At the time of last combat flight, General Leonard F. Chapman, Jr., who had been appointed Commandant on 1 January 1968, sent a message to the Sikorsky plant in Connecticut. In it he said:

> As the last UH–34 is phased out of Marine Corps forces in Vietnam, it is appropriate to express our appreciation for the outstanding record compiled by this aircraft. Over 500 of these helicopters have flown one and a half million flight hours in 15 years. They have proven their dependability in an amazing variety of roles. They have accomplished every task from space capsule recovery to disaster relief in peacetime, and

USMC Photo A422466

*Marines of HMM–326 salute after folding the blades of a squadron UH–34D at the squadron's decommissioning ceremony on 18 August 1969 at Phu Bai. With the decommissioning of this squadron, the UH–34 at last retired from combat service.*

assault troop lifts to medical evacuations in war. In the rigorous combat environment in Vietnam, they have proven the Marine Corps concept of helicopter assault. Many hundred of Marines owe their lives to this aircraft. As we look to the future with more modern aircraft, the UH-34 takes its place in our memories along with such aircraft as the F-4F, SBD, and F4U as one of the giants of Marine Aviation.* [46]

By the end of September 1969 there were no more Marine UH-34s operating in Vietnam. Even though these aircraft were no longer engaged in combat, they were not yet quite ready to disappear from the scene.

Of the two temporary transport squadrons authorized for the duration of the war, one had never been formed for lack of aircraft and personnel available for assignment. The other unit, HMM-561, remained at Santa Ana with a complement of 12 UH-34s. On 14 October 1969, all 12 aircraft flew in formation over the airfield.[47] The occasion was in honor of the decommissioning of the last UH-34 squadron left in the active Marine Corps. On 27 October, Lieutenant Colonel William C. Anderson, in the presence of Major General Robert G. Owens, Commanding General, 3d Marine Aircraft Wing, carried out his orders and the squadron was disbanded. Now the Marine Corps was down to the original 15 medium transport squadrons authorized in the permanent force.

The next "last flight" did not occur for almost another two years. In March of 1972, it was announced that "The last active Marine Corps UH-34D helicopter flew its final mission on March 22 when it arrived at Marine Corps Air Station, Quantico."[48] The aircraft, Bureau Number 147161, was piloted by Lieutenant Colonel Daniel P. Prudhomme, commanding officer of the Headquarters Squadron of FMFLant at Norfolk. It was to be put on display at the Marine Corps Aviation Museum, instead of the originally selected "971."

The report of the final flight gained widespread publicity in professional journals and newspapers. The response from the readers was a shock. Not so, wrote Captain James E. Henshaw, to the *Naval Aviation News* which had reprinted the story. While "161" had indeed gone to the museum, the aircraft at FMFLant had been replaced by another UH-34, Bureau Number 147191. This aircraft, he wrote, "served previously with the Headquarters Squadron, FMFPacific, and now doubtless holds the distinction of being the only UH-34 still on active duty." He continued that he wanted "to take this opportunity to clarify the status of an old and honored aircraft and to let you know that there's still at least one alive and kicking."[49]

---

* The F-4F, SBD, and F4U were all famous World War II aircraft.

Captain Henshaw, as did many other Marines, underestimated the durability of these old helicopters. Even more indignant over the announcement was Colonel Kenneth M. Scott, commanding officer of the Marine Corps Air Reserve Training Detachment at Glenview, Illinois. In another letter to the hapless editors of the magazine, he wrote that HMM-776 still had UH-34s. "Not only is the squadron still flying the UH-34, but continues to use it in a tactical environment."[50] Though the unit was making the transition to UH-1Es, as Colonel Scott was writing in late June, it still had six UH-34s assigned. Just to make sure there was no doubt, he included a copy of the 17 June flight schedule in which the UH-34s had flown a total of 18.9 hours in the one day. By the end of July, however, UH-1Es had replaced all the UH-34s in the squadron and no additional flights were made.

As the "last flight" claims were being disputed, three more UH-34s took to the air. On 21 May 1972, Bureau Numbers 149317, 145787, and 145729 arrived at Davis-Monthan Air Force Base in Tucson, Arizona to be put in storage. For as dependable an aircraft as the "Huss", the 1000-mile trip from Dallas was routine. They are the last recorded arrivals at the vast desert aircraft preservation facility.[51]

A few more flights were made during the late summer of 1972, all by aircraft belonging to headquarters units, but one by one each aircraft had a "last" flight. It now seemed certain that the UH-34 had finally left the Marine Corps service.

Nevertheless, the morning of 3 October 1973, the Marines at New River were jolted to hear a strange sound in the air. Unmistakably it was the distinctive noise of a UH-34. Bureau Number 147191 had remained at Norfolk after "161" had been transferred to the museum at Quantico. Colonel Grover C. Doster, commanding officer of the air station at New River, knew of "191" and at the first opportunity requested that it be delivered to New River to be installed as a permanent memorial display at the front gate. Approval was granted. The only remaining problem was how to transport the aircraft to its new home. Once again, the Marines who knew the UH-34 were confident that the easiest way was the same as the UH-34 had always arrived—flying. So Colonel Doster went to Norfolk, climbed in the aircraft and casually flew the ancient veteran to New River. His co-pilot, ironically enough, was Lieutenant Colonel Prudhomme who had flown "161" the year before on the previous "final flight" to Quantico. When Colonel Doster arrived at New River, Bureau Number 147191 was stricken from the records of active UH-34s in the Marine Corps. It was the last "last one" left.[52]

Public Affairs Office, MCAS(H) New River, N.C., Photo 1079

*In honored retirement, UH-34 Number 147191 stands at the main gate of MCAS(H) New River in November 1977.*

It is difficult to determine accurately the position of the UH-34 in the development of helicopters in the Marine Corps. It was, after all, only a very slight modification from the Navy anti-submarine aircraft. In addition, it was initially procured as a temporary measure and was never intended to become the backbone of the vertical assault capability—much less for the length of time its position was preeminent. It was one of the first helicopters in the Marine Corps which could be flown with some degree of confidence on instruments. It was the first armored helicopter; the first armed one; and, in spite of the unimpressive performance of the TK-1 kit, the first gunship which belonged to the Marine Corps. For five years it had made up the bulk of the lift capability in Vietnam. Many Marines learned to fly it in the training command, flew it in war, and then flew it in the reserves when they left the active forces. It also was the last piston-engined helicopter in the Marine Corps.

Probably one of the better evaluations of its service was given by an experienced helicopter pilot who had flown the "Deuces," the UH-34, and the CH-53. Major Dwight L. ("Ike") Bledsoe summed up his feelings as: "Well, if we ever get into a scrape where we need lots of helicopters in a hurry, I won't be surprised a bit to see someone find some UH-34s and have me flying them again."[53] It is unlikely that Major Bledsoes's fears will ever come to pass. At the same time, no one who knew the helicopter will ever say conclusively that the last Marine UH-34 has had its final "last flight."

# CHAPTER ELEVEN

# A GENERAL AND HIS PILOTS

## Conscience and Will Power

> I particularly pride myself in the fact that I can carefully and meticulously plan and organize my work in a most efficient manner; and not only to plan the work, but to execute it with rapidity and accuracy.
>
> The ability to do these things lies in my will-power and conscience. Anything I have been made responsible for, or anything I have undertaken, I have always endeavored to complete.
>
> It also seems that my capacity increases with the pressure, that is, the more work there is for me to do, the more efficiently I perform it.
>
> Keith B. McCutcheon
> 26 February 1937 [1]

In these words, written as a young man applying for a job with an insurance company, General McCutcheon expressed the quiet determination and self-confidence which, with experience and expertise in his field, made him one of the most effective promoters and defenders of Marine Corps aviation. During 1967, these inner resources helped sustain General McCutcheon in a long, complicated struggle with the Office of the Secretary of Defense. At issue was the perennial problem of Marine aviation—a shortage of pilots.

## "There Is No Shortage"

> My next topic has held the number one spot in DC/S (Air) this spring—pilots. Surely everyone knows that there is no pilot shortage; it is merely that requirements exceed resources.
>
> Major General Keith B. McCutcheon
> Speech to General Officers'
> Symposium.
> July 1967 [2]

The first days of 1967 brought no lessening of the war in Vietnam. Marines were fighting major battles against the Viet Cong and the North Vietnamese Army. In Washington, a serious battle of a different kind was shaping up—one which would test the capabilities of General Greene, General McCutcheon, and most of the rest of the staff at HQMC. It also was one of the most vivid examples of why a Marine is proud of his Corps.

The root cause of the disagreement was the fact that the military services of the United States were involved in a major war in Southeast Asia without the backing of an all-out mobilization of the nation's men and material. The problem affected all the services, but none so seriously as the Marine Corps which had almost half of its Fleet Marine Forces engaged in combat. Within the Marine Corps, there were few areas which were not affected, but no difficulty was more serious, or eluded solution longer, than the provision of trained pilots for the war. The situation was particularly critical for helicopter pilots.*

From 1957 to 1964 total pilot requirements for the Marine Corps had remained at approximately 4,000. Slightly over half were assigned to tactical squadrons. The rest were divided about equally among staff positions requiring aviation experience, students and instructors at schools, and an assortment of other miscellaneous duties. Included in the latter portion were those pilots who were in transit from one duty station to another, a status usually referred to as the "pipeline."

In five of those years, the Marine Corps actually had a surplus of pilots, though the number was extremely small. The only significant shortage occurred in 1963, when 226 retired, leaving an identical number of unfilled billets. The rest of the pilot attrition that year was made up of 191 reserves who chose not to remain in the Marine Corps beyond their initial obligation, and 22 who were killed. Only three pilots resigned. To compensate for these losses, 490 new pilots graduated from the training command. The Marine Corps ended FY–63 in June, with 3,927 pilots against an authorized strength of 4,201. The next year there was again a small surplus of 11 aviators.

While the total numbers were encouraging, the imbalance between fixed wing and helicopters continued.

---

* Unless otherwise noted, all information on pilots is for lieutenant colonels and below.

129

The forced transition program had been quite successful and the shift in training goals at Pensacola was beginning to show results. Still, the number of helicopter crews never quite caught up to the demand for them.

Even after the Marines made the inital landings at Da Nang and Chu Lai, it seemed possible that the formation of the three new helicopter transport squadrons instituted by General Shoup, and the transition into turbine helicopters, could be completed smoothly. After more than a year in combat, the Marine Corps was short only 45 pilots out of an authorized total of 4,284.[3]

Many Marines, however, harbored no illusions as to what the future held. Marines had, historically, been stationed in the Orient and knew well that Occidental solutions do not apply to Asian problems. The Marines in Vietnam were engaged in a brutal "nose to nose, toes to toes" war with a determined enemy who sought the conquest of South Vietnam as his only goal. General Greene was particularly aware of what was happening. A plan for prosecuting the war to a swift and successful conclusion had been developed by the Marine Corps in 1965 and had served as a basis for much of the initial effort. Unfortunately, only parts of it were adopted, and without all of

USMC Photo A422093

*How many Marine helicopters arrived in Vietnam. These CH–53s, cocooned in canvas for protection, are being towed from the docks at Da Nang to Marble Mountain in 1968.*

them, the plan was doomed to failure. The plan was termed "Echo," not for any secrecy, but simply an alphabetical listing of the alternatives. Plan "Echo" included an increase of 441 pilots. Brigadier General Alan J. Armstrong, DC/S (Air) in 1966, could report that by "12 October 1965—the increased pilot training rate associated with Plan "E" (Echo) was absorbed by the Naval Air Training Command." [4] A further development was needed.

In July 1966, Lieutenant General Leonard F. Chapman, Chief of Staff of the Marine Corps, told the generals assembled at the annual symposium: "Many of you will remember that at last year's symposium we at Headquarters were heavily engaged in preparing Plans A, B, C, D, and E." [5] It was the last of these which was adopted, "giving us an increase of 30,000" Marines. "Then, in October," he continued, "the Headquarters Staff produced in 4½ days, from a standing start, including 8 hours of printing time, Plans 1A, 1B, 2A, and 2B. 1A provided another 55,000 Marines." [6]

Plan 1A was submitted to the Secretary of the Navy on 21 October 1965 and approved by him on 1 December the same year. Simultaneously, General Armstrong was developing a program for 447 additional pilots to carry out the provisions of the plan. When the Navy was preparing the requirements for the new effort, "Plan 1A had not [yet] been approved by OSD, and consequently [the Navy] did not deem it appropriate to include a pilot requirement in the" proposals.[7] The day after CMC submitted Plan 1A, on 22 October, General Armstrong requested an increase in the training rates at Pensacola from the FY 65 goal of 450. He estimated that a total of 502 new aviators would be necessary in FY 66; 588, in FY 67; 683 in FY 69. "The . . . training rates were tailored to provide an orderly build-up which could be realistically absorbed by the Training Command," and, he wrote, "at the same time satisfy the activation and augmentation schedules required by Plans E and 1A."

The lack of the requirements for additional aviators being stated when the Navy sent its plans to OSD was to come back and haunt the Marine Corps. For when the plans were approved, "the Marine pilot training rate for FY 67 [was only] 525." [8] When the news of the low training levels was received DC/S (Air) submitted a letter to the CNO pointing out that the 525 new pilots a year "did not provide an adequate pilot training rate for the Marine Corps and it was in conflict [with the decision] which has approved 1A increases." The letter "also reiterated requirements and recommended that CNO initiate action to insure that OSD documents reflect the Marine Corps requirement."

The Marine Corps was in for a shock, for on 21 December, it was informed that "no further action could be taken until the completion of the study of pilot production and aviator inventory problems, required . . . to be submitted to OSD by 1 April 1966." As a basis for the study, the Marine Corps was directed to make all its plans on the assumption that the war would end at midnight 30 June 1968—the end of the fiscal year for the U.S. Government. It was an order which, with a change in the year, would be repeated more than once in the years that followed.

General Armstrong and his staff rolled up their sleeves and went to work. On 23 March, the approved plan was sent to the Secretary of the Navy, via the CNO. Although the plan recognized that fewer pilots would be needed after 1968, it called for even higher training goals than had been requested the previous October.

Required Training Rates

FY–67: 572; FY–68: 838; FY–69: 629; FY–70: 681; FY–71: 471; FY–72: 647.

There could be no delay in increasing the number of Marines reporting to Pensacola for flight training because "predicated on a fifteen month training cycle, the student input to the Training Command commencing April 1966 will [not] be reflected [until] the FY–68 output." [9] The report concluded "that slippage of input increases beyond April 1966 will directly affect augmentation and activation schedules connected with Southeast Asia commitments." During this brief time between July 1965 and July 1966 the Marine Corps pilot requirement had climbed from 4,307 to 5,292. [10] Most of the increase was related to more helicopter units needed for Vietnam. The two "add-on" transport squadrons had been authorized. Two new VMOs were to be commissioned.

Equally important, all aviation units in the combat area had been operating under a "peacetime" manning level and the tempo of war was beginning to have serious effects on the thinly stretched pilots and crews. The squadrons were to be brought up to full wartime strength. Additionally, and this was often misunderstood at the time, with the increase of pilots and crews traveling across the Pacific back and forth from the war, and with the casualties being suffered —particularly in helicopters—additional pilots would be necessary to compensate for the larger "pipeline." A final new need was to staff with flight instructors combat training squadrons, both for helicopters and for fixed wing. These units would complete the training of pilots just graduated from the Training Command.

The prospects were summarized at the July 1966 General Officers' Symposium by Major General Richard G. Weede, Director of Personnel. General Weede was intimately familiar with the war in Vietnam, for from February 1962 until May 1964 he had served in Saigon as the Chief of Staff of the newly-created U.S. Military Assistance Command, Vietnam (USMACV). He reported "Our Marine aviators face accelerated assignments to unaccompanied overseas tours." He continued:

> Helicopter pilots present a special problem. Over one-half of the WestPac aviator requirements are for helicopter pilots and losses in this skill are unusually heavy. . . . We can anticipate a shortage of helicopter pilots.[11]

The late summer and early fall of 1966 was a frustrating time for the Marine Corps. After a series of conferences, letters, messages, memos, and meetings, in August the Navy settled on a pilot training rate (PTR) which was a compromise among all the services which had their pilots trained at NATC. The share for the Marine Corps was 725 a year. At that rate, the Marine Corps would not catch up with its approved needs for some years into the future. On 26 September it reiterated that a higher rate was required for "as long as SEA commitments continue, and assuming we receive the 725 pilot training rate by FY 69, the pilot shortage will continue until FY 74." A month later, on 19 October, the Secretary of the Navy went ahead and approved the original plan and forwarded it to OSD. It called for the Navy to produce 1,700 pilots each year; the Coast Guard and foreign military services were to get another 100, but the Marine Corps remained at 725.

Once again the Marine Corps received a jolt. Even after having compromised on its requirements, "OSD Systems Analysis recomputed both the Navy and Marine Corps attrition factors as submitted . . . to arrive at a revised Navy/Marine Corps distribution of the 2,525" total graduates.[12] According to OSD the proper balance for the Navy was 1,902 pilots and the Marine Corps only 523.

All during the month of December 1966, there were intense negotiations between General McCutcheon, who had returned in June as DC/S (Air), and his staff and their counterparts in the Navy "in an effort to resolve the problem . . . to arrive at a fair distribution." Finally, on 17 December, "the Navy concluded that an 1800/625 compromise was in order and it was recommended." Five days later "The joint Navy/Marine Corps memorandum to SecNav requested an 1800 Navy and 625 Marine Corps PTR for FY 69 and stated that additional actions have been taken and others are to be initiated to increase the pilot resources." This time, to avoid any doubt, the "memorandum was signed jointly, the Marine Corps on 22 December 1966 and the Navy on 27 December 1966."

It was a significant document—but not in the usual sense of the word. In the intense negotiations to achieve the compromise, the request had concentrated on only one aspect of the problem and had neglected to cover other important factors. As General McCutcheon informed the Commandant, the memorandum "was deficient in that it did not state what the Marine Corps originally requested (725) and it did not address specific training rates for FY 67 and 68." He added, "to preclude restaffing the joint . . . letter, a CMC memorandum was initiated to CNO to reiterate CMC stipulations in connection with the 625 compromise."[13] Thus the Marine Corps found itself in a position where it needed up to 838 new pilots in a single year, had worked out a compromise with the Navy of 725, which had been rejected by OSD who ordered it to receive no more than 525, and now was jointly, with the Navy, requesting a further compromise of 625.

The situation was becoming grave. It was further aggravated by the fact that many pilots, faced with repeated tours in Vietnam, and deployments away from their home bases during the short time they were back in the United States, were finding Marine Corps careers less attractive. Though the final results would not be known until 30 June, FY 67 was rapidly shaping up as a near disaster for retention of pilots. By the end of the year 288 of the reserve pilots had been released from the service, and another 107 had asked for retirement. More ominous, 125 pilots had been killed or taken prisoner and 257 voluntarily resigned their commissions. The Marine Corps in the end gained slightly more than its allotted 525, a total of 573; but it lost 777 pilots.[14] It ended the year with a shortage of 706; and the situation promised to get worse.

General Greene and General McCutcheon found the Marine Corps in a three-way squeeze. They needed more pilots to fill the new units authorized by plans Echo and 1-A; they could not obtain approval for an increased training rate which, even though the results would not have much effect for nearly 18 months after the additional students reported to Pensacola, was one of the best long-range solutions; and now they were having difficulty keeping the pilots they already had.

As the magnitude of the expected shortage became apparent in the last months of 1966, all of the Marine Corps knew that the question of additional pilots—

particularly those for helicopters—was becoming extremely critical. Starting in July 1967, pilots who had been back in the United States 22 months were scheduled to start returning for a second year in combat. By the end of 1968, it was estimated, almost 300 who had left since 1 March 1965, would have to be ordered back to Vietnam. The situation for fixed-wing pilots was only a little better.[15] At the same time the Marine Corps was becoming alarmed at the continued drain on its pilots, the situation became a matter of concern to the Congress.

## Congress Investigates

Senator John Stennis (D.-Mississippi) was a respected and powerful figure. On 19 January 1967, as Chairman of the Preparedness Investigating Subcommittee of the Senate Committee on Armed Services, he announced that "the Subcommittee will hold formal hearings in the near future on the aircraft pilot programs of the Army, Navy, Air Force, and Marine Corps." Senator Stennis said "that the Subcommittee has had a continuing interest in this matter for several months and the hearings will follow staff investigations and inquiries which commenced last fall." The subcommittee, he continued, would:

> ... address themselves to all aspects of the programs, and all problems which they present with particular attention being given to the adequacy of the present and proposed pilot production programs to meet existing and anticipated demands.[16]

Simultaneously, in the House of Representatives, the Chairman of the Committee on Armed Services, L. Mendel Rivers (D.-South Carolina) wrote to Secretary of Defense Robert S. McNamara. Congressman Rivers said that "I am very much concerned about a serious situation which exists in the Department of Defense. I am referring to the fact that we have been losing pilots at a faster rate than we are replacing them."[17] He continued that "This problem seems to have received little attention in the Department of Defense, insofar as the expansion of pilot training is concerned, until recently. I am sure the situation could have been anticipated some time ago." Never noted as a fond admirer of Secretary McNamara's style of management of the Department of Defense, he kept pointing out in the letter that some action had to be taken!

> Pilots who have completed their obligated service and wish to retire or resign are not permitted to do so.\*
> This, of course, cannot help but have an adverse effect upon our ability to attract young men into our pilot training program.
> Perhaps the Defense Department has expressed no concern about the shortage of pilots . . .
> We have got to come up with an answer.
> But it seems to me that we need more pilots now, and the faster the better. Half measures will not be sufficient. A gradual buildup will not solve the problem.

He concluded that "I intend to go into this matter fully at the first opportunity," and that "this situation needs immediate attention."[18]

In the hearings that followed in February and March, General Greene was among those called to testify before Senator Stennis' and Representative Rivers' committees. In each case the Commandant reviewed the needs of the Marine Corps, the number of new pilots being produced by the Training Command, and the losses being experienced. He also explained that "management actions" had reduced the number of pilots required to 5,002; but even with that, there remained a shortage of 851 aviators, 416 of them for helicopters. He estimated that by July 1968, the shortage would increase to 1,021.

The Congress was not the only place where General Greene was describing the situation. On 15 February, he spoke briefly to the Marine Officers' Wives Club. He explained some of the impact of the shortage. "Now about rotation policy. If your husband comes back from South Vietnam, how long are we going to let him stay here before he has to go out again?"[19] The answer was not reassuring:

> Well, our policy is two years. That's our optimum time, but I'm finding that in certain specialties and helicopter pilots . . . I don't have enough . . . to let the individual remain at home for two years. . . . and that's the kind of sacrifice you ladies are going to make, and you're going to have to look forward to. . . . And I'm asking you to do it.

Though less a matter of debate at the time, the shortage was not confined just to helicopter pilots. The crew chiefs, mechanics, and their wives faced nearly the same conditions. To most people concerned with the problem, the existence of a serious shortage was evident, but a few key men in DOD were not convinced.

The crux of the controversy lay in the statements General Greene had made before committees in both houses of Congress. The Commandant repeatedly had told the legislators that the Marine Corps was experiencing a severe shortage of pilots and the situation would get worse if steps were not taken immediately to cure it. With full-scale hearings on military pilot training, requirements, and inventories scheduled in April before Senator Stennis' Preparedness Investigating Subcommittee, OSD became concerned about the testimony which might be given by the witnesses.

---

\* One of the "management actions" taken to maintain pilots, though it was applied on a selective, almost case-by-case basis by the four services.

Dr. Alain C. Enthoven, Assistant Secretary of Defense (Systems Analysis), initially challenged the Marines' need for additional pilots, but after thorough review of the problem partially agreed with the Marines.

On 21 March, General McCutcheon was called to the Pentagon to meet with Mr. Russell Murray from the office of Dr. Alain C. Enthoven, Assistant Secretary of Defense (Systems Analysis). "Mr. Murray stated that Mr. McNamara simply could not have programs where resources and requirements were out of balance," General McCutcheon reported.[20] The general responded by recounting the reasons for the increased requirement, including all the steps the Marine Corps had taken to make more pilots available, but concluded that the only long-term solution was an increase in the pilot training rate. "Mr. Murray then showed us a chart which depicted a new projection of resources vs. requirements." After going over the new OSD calculations, General McCutcheon told him:

I would be glad to take the chart and study it and come up with some suggested dialogue to reconcile the Department of Defense view of 'no shortage' vs. the Marine Corps statement, which is now a matter of record in the Congress, that we will be short 851 on 30 June 1967.

The next day, in response to a telephone call from Dr. Enthoven to General Greene, General Chapman (Chief of Staff) and General McCutcheon returned to the Pentagon for another meeting. There, General Chapman explained to Dr. Enthoven that he thought the Department of Defense "was taking a rather narrow definition of 'requirement'." Dr. Enthoven, for instance, had suggested that if the Marine Corps would just restrict pilots' leave to 20, rather than the more customary 30 days, prior to leaving for Vietnam and on returning from combat, additional aviators would be available at any one time. While General Chapman agreed that such a program might be necessary, instituting it did not eliminate the need for sufficient pilots so that the pipeline could accommodate 30 days' leave. He repeated that "The Marine Corps had not complained about not having assets equal to total requirements. . . . What we [do] not have [is] an adequate approved pilot training rate to get us well." The meeting broke up with Dr. Enthoven "stating he was in hopes we could draft a paper that would show a balanced program and thus come to a meeting of the minds."[21] Neither of the two generals had much doubt what was meant by a "meeting of the minds."

On 29 March, the chief of staff approved a memorandum for the Secretary of the Navy in which he stated: The Secretary of Defense "intends to have all programs in balance, i.e., resources to match requirements. He proposes to accomplish this by reducing requirements in FY 1968 and 1969."[22] Apparently OSD had underestimated the courage and determination of the generals, for, as General Chapman stated in the memo, "The Marine Corps has refused to acquiesce in this method of eliminating the 'shortages'." The increases required by plans Echo and 1-A were valid; the statements by General Greene as to the shortage were valid; and regardless of what actions the Marine Corps took to temporarily relieve the problem, a long-term solution had to be found. As it was, the memo pointed out, "The situation as seen by the pilots is one of repetitive tours to WestPac, two years or less in [the United States] between tours," and "reduced chances for professional schooling, reduced leave to and from WestPac, family separation even in [the United States] due to other deployments, exercises," and squadrons on the east and west coast woefully undermanned.

The "effect on the pilots," he wrote "runs counter to those [actions] taken to increase pilot retention. The situation looks better on the outside and the pay is higher." Worst of all, "The Marine Corps prediction of wartime pilot retention has proved to be too optimistic, thereby contributing to the 'shortage.' The pilot retention rate can get worse." Under the circumstances, he continued, the Marine Corps could only consider that, "the present pilot situation is tolerable only for a short, interim period. There must be a 'get well' program we can publish" to our aviators and reassure them that the sacrifices they are making are not to become a continuing way of life. "To summarize the essence of the matter," he concluded, "The Marine Corps refuses to agree to exorcize the 'shortage' because no 'cure' *we can rely on*" had been approved and started by OSD.[23]

On 30 March, there was another meeting between Mr. Murray, Dr. Enthoven, and General McCutcheon. It was quickly apparent that little progress had been made toward a "meeting of the minds," for "the primary concern of [OSD] was the forthcoming testimony before the Stennis Committee."[24] Dr. Enthoven "objected to the Marine Corps showing what it considered to be its full requirements." One of his ideas was that since deliveries of some aircraft were slightly behind schedule, "the requirement [for pilots for them] was not valid for that year, but should be shown in some future year." A particularly deep point of disagreement concerned the squadrons in combat. OSD had previously agreed that they should have a full wartime complement of pilots instead of the peacetime level with which they were fighting the war. Dr. Enthoven stated that OSD "would issue a paper negating" the decision, and the units would remain at a peacetime allocation of pilots. General McCutcheon said, "that we carried this as a requirement since we had received it in writing and if he wanted to cancel the requirement, he would have to do so in writing."

"The end result of the conversation . . . was that [Dr. Enthoven] was still adamant that our true requirements should not be shown and that he questioned the validity of many of them." As the meeting broke up, Dr. Enthoven stated "he regretted that we couldn't get together and agree, and that it might be necessary to 'air our dirty linen' in public before Congress." He also warned that OSD "found it necessary to attack and that they would have to point out that the Marine Corps requirements were fictitious and that they had resources necessary to carry out their assigned missions." General McCutcheon was not cowed, for "I told Dr. Enthoven I understood his position but we would be happy to accept the challenge."[25]

That night, Dr. Enthoven's secretary called General McCutcheon's home and left word with his son to get in touch. It was past midnight when the general arrived from work, but early the next morning he returned the call. Dr. Enthoven told the general "that he was taking personal charge of the Marine Corps pilot requirement problem," and that he wanted to meet with General McCutcheon "and go over all [the] requirements line by line.'[26] A few hours later, he arrived at HQMC and they went to work immediately.

It is not often that a single room contains two more intelligent, analytical—and determined—men as when the experienced, perceptive Marine general sat down at the same table as the brilliant economist. It is also seldom that each and every Marine aviator and his billet receive as careful scrutiny from such high ranking officials. At the end of the first day, General McCutcheon could report that as a result of their efforts, "He certainly will know a whale of a lot more about Marine Corps aviation, and I will have a fuller appreciation of his systems analysis procedures."[27]

After another full day of effort, the Marine general and the systems analyst had finished their review and come close to agreement. McCutcheon had started out with the initial need for 5,002 aviators, had pressed for 5,222 but "wherever my new figure was above the previous . . . requirements, I told him I would drop to the lower number."[28] Dr. Enthoven had accepted 4,705. The difference was the manning at wartime levels of the squadrons engaged in combat. General McCutcheon held out for a full strength of pilots; Dr. Enthoven remained convinced that they could operate at peacetime levels. At the conclusion of the line-by-line justification, the general reported, "we then turned to a discussion of ways and means to improve our situation. He took notes . . . and I'm sure we will get some action."

After it was all over, General McCutcheon concluded that "it was a most interesting and worthwhile session. Dr. Enthoven learned a great deal about the Marine Corps and I believe we have established a good harmonious, close rapport with him." He concluded "I believe that anytime we have a good hard case to present that he will hear us out and decide the issue fairly and squarely."[29]

On 3 April, in a telephone conversation with General Greene, Enthoven further clarified both the areas of agreement and the remaining issues between himself and the Marine Corps. Enthoven declared that after his working session with McCutcheon, he was "satisfied that you definitely need more pilots than you've got" and that he was "quite sure that we are going to be able to figure out one way or another . . . to improve your training rate."

At the same time, Enthoven again tried to persuade Greene not to use the word "shortage" in relation to the pilot problem. The OSD analyst urged the Marine Commandant to concentrate in all public statements on three points: First, that "We do have enough pilots to fly our planes today;" second, that DOD, the Navy Department, and the Marine Corps all agreed that over the long run more aviators were needed; and, third, that all agencies and services concerned were examining ways to "increase our pilot inventory." Enthoven made it clear that he was concerned about the effect on public opinion of any official statement that the Marines (or anyone else) did not have enough pilots. Such statements, he said, would be used by antiwar elements in the U.S. and by enemies abroad to claim that the nation no longer could carry on the war, thereby undermining the overall political effort of the Johnson administration to defend its Vietnam policy. Greene acknowledged the importance of the political problem but made no commitments on what Marines would tell the Congress.[30]

In spite of these lingering differences, it appeared that enough agreement had been reached that steps could be taken to begin a program to produce sufficient pilots for plans Echo and 1–A. The Marine Corps, however, had not taken into account fully the fears of OSD over the rapidly approaching Stennis committee hearings. The results were spelled out in a memorandum written by General McCutcheon:

> General Chapman received a call from Dr. Enthoven late Wednesday afternoon, 19 April and agreed to meet with the Doctor in his office at 0830 the following day. We prepared a modification of the current tables [of pilot requirements] which had been under discussion. . . .
>
> Lieutenant General Chapman, Colonel [Mervin B.] Porter [who had commanded HMM-261 in Vietnam and now was an assistant to General McCutcheon] and I arrived at Dr. Enthoven's office at 0830, Thursday, 20 April.
>
> The session lasted until about 1315. Several times it got rather heated and I thought that we would conclude the meeting with no agreement between us.
>
> The main point at issue remained the one that has been prominent since the beginning, i.e., "shortage." The Department of Defense cannot accept the fact that requirements can in fact be in excess of capabilities without the corresponding shortfall being publicized as a shortage. Dr. Enthoven made it clear that if we did not accept his chart and cooperate in front of the Stennis Committee by saying that we are not short that he would have no alternative but to analyze Marine Corps aviation in depth and he assured us that he would cut us apart. He emphasized that he had lots of experience in this line of work, i.e., [the Air Force's hoped-for new bomber] the B-70, and that he had the organization to do it. He said he did not want to but if we didn't cooperate he would have to. I got the impression that he was on the defensive and that they were afraid of what we might say in front of Stennis and more important what the aftermath might be.
>
> In spite of this blackmail threat we continued to negotiate and General Chapman was very successful in extracting nearly everything we asked for.
>
> Several hours after we had left Dr. Enthoven's office Mr. Sullivan [an assistant of Dr. Enthoven] called Colonel Porter and requested a lot of data on our pilots going back to 1961. He wanted the information by 1000 the following morning. I tried to get in touch with Sullivan but could not; but I did call Dr. Enthoven and told him we could not provide it in that short of notice but would get it as soon as possible. Most of it was provided late the following day.[31]

If the Marine Corps had miscalculated the sensitivity of OSD to the Stennis committee hearings, then OSD miscalculated the integrity and determination of the Marines who were called to testify. Friday, 5 May 1967, General McCutcheon was the witness. Within minutes of the afternoon session's beginning, James T. Kendall, chief counsel for the committee, asked, "General McCutcheon . . . I trust that you will not be offended if I am so bold as to use the word 'shortage' in my questioning. Is that word in your vocabulary, sir?"

The general shot back a brisk "Yes sir; it is."[32]

Three and a half hours later, there was no doubt in the minds of the Senators. The Marine Corps had a serious shortage of pilots.

## CHAPTER TWELVE

## MORE PILOTS FOR THE WAR

### Busy Helicopter Crews

The Stennis Committee hearings established as common knowledge that the Marine Corps had a shortage of pilots. Recognition of the problem, however, was not equivalent to a solution. Even if the pilot training rate could be increased immediately—and it could not—there would be no noticeable effect for almost two years. In the meantime the situation continued to worsen. Among fixed-wing pilots it was serious. Among helicopter pilots it was critical.

No Marine will ever detract from the heroic efforts of the fixed-wing crews. Flying under seemingly impossible weather conditions, the jets performed miracles to protect the helicopters as well as the combat riflemen on the ground. They encountered a thicket of surface-to-air missiles while attacking targets in North Vietnam. They operated from expeditionary airfields and aircraft carriers. Always they fought with the highest degree of skill and dedication and, whenever possible, as a member of the Marine air-ground team.

If the speed and altitude of a jet made the war a slightly impersonal experience to the pilots, the same was not true of the helicopter crews. Theirs was a very personal war. They were seldom out of range of enemy fire from the moment of takeoff until the final landing. With rocket and mortar attacks against forward bases, even when they completed a flight, they were subjected to continuing enemy fire.

The continued combat at close quarters between the helicopter crews and enemy gunners brought a new dimension into the pilot shortage. Attrition, either as a direct or an indirect result of this new factor, was climbing beyond all previous estimates. Prior to the Stennis Committee hearings, General McCutcheon had prepared an analysis of the conditions.

Since Archie's Angels had first landed at Soc Trang—and they had never suffered a combat casualty—up to 23 April 1967, 719 pilots and crew members had become casualties in Vietnam. After the landings in 1965 both fixed-wing and helicopter crews were exposed to enemy fire in approximately equal numbers. The results were revealing. Of the total casualties, 638 had been in helicopters. Among pilots, 37 helicopter and 21 fixed-wing had been killed. For crew members, the ratio was 52 against 16. Most indicative, 311 helicopter crew members and 229 pilots had been wounded or injured. The equivalent numbers for fixed-wing were 19 and 10.[1]

Two months earlier, a similar study on a different facet of the problem had been completed. It was a part of General Chapman's and General McCutcheon's strenuous efforts to have sufficient pilots approved by OSD to bring the squadrons in combat up to wartime allowance of pilots. The report had made a detailed and comprehensive analysis of the duties of pilots in Vietnam. The conclusion was that as a *routine average*, fixed-wing pilots were on duty 86 hours per week.[2] For the helicopter crews, the *normal* was 14 hours a day, the equivalent of 100 hours a week. The study added that;

> ... not portrayed in the above data are the following considerations: irregular hours and interrupted sleep, heat and humidity preventing recuperative daytime rest, continuous seven-day week duty period up to six months with little respite, and almost continual exposure to enemy fire on the part of helicopter pilots and frequent periods of being downed in the midst of a fire fight as evidenced by two CH–46 crews who were recently downed and joined in with other friendly troops in repelling an attacking force."[3]

If a large assault operation was underway, the hours for fixed-wing per day increased from 12.3 to 12.5. For helicopters, every single pilot assigned would have to average "15.5 hours crew time . . . per day," and "these increased rates continue for periods of 5 to 10 days."[4] General McCutcheon also calculated that a helicopter pilot on a 13-month tour in combat would complete more than 1,100 individual sorties. Jet pilots averaged about 250, though those flying the Grumman-built, all-weather A–6 attack aircraft would spend half of them flying into North Vietnam, rather than supporting the Marines in the south.[5]

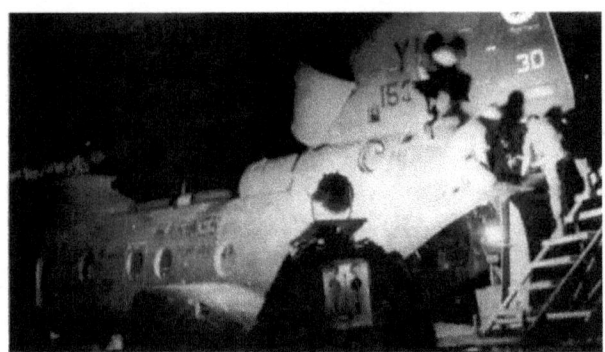

USMC Photo A421989

*Under portable lights, Marines of HMM-364 work through the night at Marble Mountain readying a CH-46D for an early morning mission in 1967. Such efforts were routine for helicopter crews in Vietnam.*

Though no equivalent studies were made for crew chiefs, they worked even harder, flying in their aircraft on missions and manning the guns, maintaining the helicopters, and trying to catch a few moments of rest before again taking off on another mission. Their exploits provide one of the proudest moments in the history of the Marine Corps. More than anyone else, the flying mechanics and crew chiefs of the helicopter units made the prosecution of vertical assault warfare possible.

Even when the crews returned to the United States, there was little let-up in the pace. General Greene had hoped that no Marine would be sent back to Vietnam without at least two years between tours. This meant that for every pilot in the Western Pacific area, at least two were needed elsewhere to provide a "rotation base requirement." General Chapman calculated that by the summer of 1967, 881 helicopter pilots would be needed for the overseas units if they were to be brought up to full wartime strength. This meant that there should be 2,643 elsewhere. There were only 1,966, almost 700 individuals and 25 percent short of the number needed. In jets and transports, there was a tiny surplus of 80 pilots.[6]

At the General Officers' Symposium in July 1967, there were few bright spots in the outlook. General McCutcheon could report that the change from the UH-34s to the CH-46s was progressing and that the last squadron was due to make the transition to the new helicopter by the end of 1970. "More than one half of our medium helicopter squadrons are deployed," he said. "Rotation of the CH-46s to WestPac to replace the UH-34s has nearly doubled the Marines' lift capability without"—and it was a vital point—"increasing the demand for helicopter pilots." The impending difficulty with the tail pylon still was unknown at the time.

He continued that "of the (medium) squadrons deployed, two are assigned to the Special Landing Forces; the other seven are with MAG-16 in Vietnam." Remaining in the United States, "we have six squadrons of the permanent force structure plus two temporary add-on squadrons of MAG-56 which have been activated in a cadre status on the West Coast." The shortage of pilots and crew members, however, "has prevented our manning MAG-56 as an active group." For the "heavy" transports, production of the CH-53 was beginning to catch up with the schedule, and "all three squadrons will be fully outfitted this fiscal year." HMH-463 had arrived in Vietnam two months previously and had joined the four-plane detachment which had retrieved so many downed aircraft. In observation units, "at present, three of our five VMO squadrons, with 70 percent of our UH-1s, are in" Vietnam.

He concluded his presentation by reviewing the pilot situation. "Retention of aviators on active duty fell far below our earlier projections," and "the attrition is forecast to stay higher than in the past. This includes losses due to death, disability, retirement, resignation . . . and all other causes." Not for another two years could any improvement be foreseen. In the meantime, a series of steps had been "taken and [are] to be taken to ease the pressure on our pilots."[7]

## Management Actions

Even as General McCutcheon was talking, the results of the FY 67 pilot program were being added up. The news, while not quite as bad as expected, was grim. New pilots numbered 573. Attrition from all causes was 777. Now the Marine Corps was short 706 from a requirement of 4,705.[8] Although the steps taken to remedy the shortage were, at the time, called "management actions," there was really only one meaning to them: scrape up every available pilot in the Marine Corps for assignment to the operating units, until sufficient new ones could be recruited and trained.

Some of these efforts had begun in the fall of 1965 when it first became readily apparent that Vietnam could expand into a major conflict. Unless there was a personal hardship involved, all regular officers who had requested retirement or resignation beyond 31 August 1965, were to be retained in the Marine Corps for an expected additional 12 months. For the regular enlisted Marines, much the same program went into effect and, in addition, there were some involuntary extensions of enlistment for up to four months. The message announcing the freeze on Marines getting out went on to say:

> Reserve officers and enlisted personnel are not affected by involuntary extensions, not because their numbers are not needed, but because of legal considerations. The large number of reserve officers and enlisted personnel whose terms of active service . . . expire each month represent a tremendously important source of skill and experience which is vitally needed for the leadership of our Corps during this time of expansion.[9]

When the restrictions on leaving the Marine Corps were lifted the next year, a surge of resignations and retirements contributed to the ever-widening gap between requirements and resources. Once again, involuntary extensions were ordered. In a message to all Marines, the Commandant explained the necessity of such a move:

> During the past year, every effort has been made to obtain sufficient officers with necessary qualifications to meet all requirements. Despite these efforts, some deficiencies exist. Therefore, in order to provide the needed officer strength to maintain an adequate rotation policy, the Secretary of the Navy has approved the reinstitution of a program of selective deferrals of acceptance of resignations and requests for retirement or termination of temporary appointments.
>
> The Commandant is fully aware of the many inconveniences, personal hardships, and sacrifices caused by similar action in 1965, and therefore takes this present action with the greatest reluctance. However, there is no alternative if the Marine Corps is to continue to meet its expanding contribution to our nation's defense effort. Assurance is given that case-by-case attention will be given each request to ensure full consideration of personal problems resulting from this policy.
>
> Acceptance of resignations, requests for retirement, or termination of temporary appointments of regular officers of the grades Lieutenant Colonel or below will be selectively deferred [and] will be based on critical needs for officers with particular skills . . . including naval aviators.[10]

The deferrals would "remain in effect indefinitely," the message concluded.

Even though there was no way to retain reservists without Congressional legislation, at least the regular pilots would remain in the Marine Corps. The policy was effective, and resignations and retirement of aviators dropped off sharply during FY 68.

There was another source for more pilots. Borrowing the systems analyst's technique of carefully scrutinizing each billet requiring an aviator might be a way to reduce the number of pilots needed. The biggest savings was also the most difficult for the Marine Corps. Reluctantly, Generals Greene, Chapman, and McCutcheon agreed that there was no way possible to fill the units in combat at a full wartime complement of pilots without jeopardizing any semblance of a rotation policy back to the United States.[11] They ordered the squadrons to remain at peacetime levels. This reduced the needs of the WestPac squadrons by a total of 166 pilots. It meant that the deployed Marines were going to continue to be fully committed, but it also meant that they could have a somewhat longer period back home before returning to Vietnam.

Another bitter pill was the loss of MAG-56, the long-fought-for and finally approved "add-on" helicopter group formed at Santa Ana after MAG-36 departed for Chu Lai. It was left in a cadre status and staffed with ground officers who carried aviation specialties designations, thus eliminating the need for another 124 helicopter pilots. The Marine Corps finally had to accept OSD's proposal for only 20-day leaves for pilots when departing to or returning from Vietnam, an action which produced the equivalent of 102 more pilots. Aviator students at the Amphibious Warfare School at Quantico, normally considered a vital part of the training of a Marine officer, were cut by 50. Bit by bit, the Marine Corps whittled away at any place where a pilot could be spared. Nothing was overlooked. Two were replaced by civilians at air stations, and even one was subtracted from the staff at FMFPac. When it was all over, 709 billets had been identified as being able to be reduced.

One more approach was substituting ground officers for pilots. Though not as productive as eliminating billets, the effort still netted 245 more pilots. Generals no longer could have aviators as aides, and squadron staffs were carefully screened from top to bottom for billets which could be filled by a ground officer. HQMC gave up 20, including 10 from DC/S (Air).

Finally, the Marine Corps had to curtail commitments in areas other than Southeast Asia. Nowhere was there a greater impact than on the helicopter pilots of MAG-26 at New River. Lieutenant General Richard G. Weede had been promoted and assigned as the Commanding General, Fleet Marine Force, Atlantic after his tour as Director of Personnel at HQMC. He also spoke at the 1967 symposium.

Up to June 1965, he pointed out, the Marine landing force of the Sixth Fleet in the Mediterranean Sea had included a small detachment of eight UH-34s. A lack of LPHs, which were then still being built, had prevented the assignment of any larger vertical assault capability. Since then, General Weede continued, "we have been forced to withhold even this [limited UH-34] support due to our critical shortage of helo pilots."[12] He went on that "We consider it essential to provide full helicopter support for this unit—by that I mean an LPH embarked squadron." In the Caribbean the helicopter unit of the ready force, which

*CH–46s and a CH–53 lift off from a logistics support area with supplies for 3d Marine Division firebases and units in the field in September 1969. The demand for helicopters in the war for both logistical and tactical missions never slackened.*

normally was a full squadron of transports reinforced with two UH–1s, was down to "six UH–34s and two 'Hueys' due to nonavailability of LPHs." We were actually a bit thankful for this," he continued, "since it gave us a breather and temporarily alleviated our pilot shortage somewhat." [13]

Even with the units in Vietnam being held to peacetime pilot strengths, with the elimination and substitution of billets, involuntary extensions of active duty, and cutbacks of Atlantic fleet commitments, there were still not enough helicopter pilots to go around. General Weede displayed two charts. One showed that the 2d Marine Aircraft Wing, which made up the aviation member of the FMFLant air-ground team, had only enough pilots to satisfy 71 percent of the wartime, and 88 percent of the peacetime requirements. Discussing the shortage, he said, "I won't harp on this. We are all aware of it." [14] Then he displayed where the bulk of the shortages lay. MAG–26 had 58 percent of the pilots it would need in wartime. "Many of our problems or situations we can work with, on, and around," the general concluded, "But only a long lead time pilot can fill that cockpit seat and 42 percent of MAG–26's helo seats are empty, with no significant relief in sight." [15]

Not only was no relief in sight, the shortage continued to get worse. In 1966, the obligated service of pilots graduating from the training command had been increased from three to three and a half years after earning their wings.[16] In 1968, approval was gained for another increase to four and a half years starting with those officers beginning flight training after 1 January 1970.[17] A new program of warrant officer pilots was suggested, but not approved.[18] The disadvantages of pilots who were restricted in their assignment still remained a major issue. In addition, it would take just as long to train a warrant officer as a commissioned officer, and the plan offered no real benefit.

Fixed-wing pilots again were ordered to transition into helicopters. On completion of training, they were sent to Vietnam. The reaction of most was similar to that expressed by the Marines in the forced transition program in the early 1960s. One of the first to be sent to helicopter training was Major Jerry D. Boulton. He wrote HQMC pointing out his long experience in jets and requesting that he be assigned to a fixed-wing squadron in Vietnam. The answer was not reassuring, for DC/S (Air) said that while "taking fixed wing pilots, transitioning them into helicopters and sending them to SEA was undesirable...the bottom of helicopter assets had been reached." [19] Each case would be reviewed individually, but the Marine Corps desperately had to find some way to obtain more helicopter pilots. By 1 July 1968 it needed almost 1,000 more aviators than it had. The worse shortage remained with helicopters. For a total requirement of 5,010, there were only 4,045 available.[20]

The "management actions" had not solved the problem, only softened its blows. The only cure for the shortage was more pilots from the Training Command.

## A New Source of Helicopter Pilots

Any increase in the pilot training rate did not automatically produce more pilots. If additional students were to be taught how to fly, more aircraft, classrooms, and instructors were required. Like everything in aviation, a major change could not be produced overnight. In the spring of 1967, plans were being made for a total production of 2,525 pilots in FY 69. Vice Admiral Alexander S. Heyward, Jr., Commander, Naval Air Training Command stated "That in view of the expected phase in of assets which lag real requirements, a 2,525 pilot production capability in FY 69 is in some doubt." Such an objective, he added, "in any event represents the absolute maximum attainable goal short of mobilization or similar measures." If aircraft, instructors and maintenance personnel, and construction programs were all provided on schedule—and he had misgivings that they would be—the Naval Air Training Command might be able to reach a rate of 2,700 students per year by FY 70 and to sustain it through "over utilization of assets." [21]

When representatives from CNO discussed the matter with the admiral they reported that "It is not a simple matter to address a specific phase without analyzing the overall effect." At Ellyson Field, where helicopter training was given, the problem was serious. "Increasing the number of helicopters would enable us to increase that phase of the program providing the instructors were available," but "the whole training syllabus is a series of interacting phases, the effects on other phases would have to be analyzed to see if a total increase could be achieved, just by adding to the helo phase." Such an action as adding more aircraft and instructors to Ellyson, "could create bottlenecks in other areas and students would be delayed." The admiral pointed out that "it is impossible to project an increase in production merely by addressing one specific part of the overall syllabus. The entire program must be examined." [22]

At the time, a syllabus for a Marine Corps helicopter pilot consisted of 11 weeks of preflight academic training, two weeks of learning how to survive if forced to land in uninhabited areas, and other scholastic instruction. Flight in aircraft was normally eight weeks and 26 hours in a very light Cessna-built, fixed-wing T-34, followed by 21 weeks and 100 flight hours in the T-28—the same aircraft utilized to evaluate the LARA concept. This stage was followed by three weeks of intensive practice, and finally, landings on board an aircraft carrier.

At the conclusion of carrier qualification, the student was assigned to advanced training, and if ordered to helicopters, reported to Ellyson. There he received an additional 11 weeks of instruction, divided between classroom work, 20 hours of flight in the H-13 (HTLs), followed by 50 hours in an H-34. [23]

In 1967 the helicopter pilot syllabus was shortened and the carrier qualifications phase and some of the basic flight training were eliminated. This allowed 48 more pilots to be trained per year, still nowhere near the number needed by the Marine Corps. Ellyson could produce no more, at least for the immediate future. Another source for training had to be found.

The idea of one military service conducting aviation training for another was not new. In World War I there had been the "training of 23 seaplane pilots for the Army by the Navy." In return, the Army had trained "61 naval pilots in the operation of aeroplanes for use on board ship." [24] Though it was often difficult to explain to anyone unknowledgeable in military matters, the arrangement existing for many years at Pensacola was not that of one service training the pilots of another. Both the Navy and Marine Corps were—and are—members of the same naval service, tied closely together by history, custom, and missions. The Training Command was staffed jointly by both Marines and Navy personnel. But the training of pilots by the Army or the Air Force definitely involved another service.

In April of 1967 a peculiar set of circumstances set the stage for a change. The U.S. Air Force had been training many of the fixed-wing pilots of the Federal Republic of (West) Germany, and it also was attempting to increase its own pilot training rate for the buildup of the war in Vietnam. To do this Air Force pilot training had been "programmed to maximum capacity." Training bases had a policy "to fly every day that the weather permits, including weekends and holidays to maintain student schedules." Then the German government announced to the Air Force that "beginning in FY 68, they [would] be unable to fill their contracted agreement" up to the full allotment of students. As a result, Germany "proffered 108 of these spaces for Air Force students." Originally the Air Force planned "to utilize these spaces to relieve the somewhat saturated conditions on other" bases. [25]

The Marine Corps learned of these events and quickly requested that the spaces left unfilled by Germany be utilized to train Marines, since any fixed-wing aviator who received his instruction from the Air Force would free a space for a helicopter pilot to be trained at Pensacola. The proposal was agreed to by OSD, and the first of a total of 507 pilots over the next four years began flight training with the Air Force in the summer of 1967.

The speedy acceptance of this program opened up new avenues to General McCutcheon. Though there was no way to prevent the 1,000-pilot shortage forecast for 30 June 1968, if a program similar to that with the Air Force for fixed-wing pilots could be worked out with the Army for helicopter pilots, the training rate could be increased above that which was possible just at Pensacola.

Army aviation consisted almost exclusively of helicopters, with only a few light fixed-wing aircraft assigned, and during the years since its commitment to combat in Vietnam, the Army had established a large complex for the training of its helicopter pilots. In November, Secretary McNamara had approved a pilot training rate of "7,320 Army pilots plus 180 foreign" students for the fiscal year beginning 1 July 1968. The Army, however, estimated that it could train up to 8,100 pilots in FY 69. The Marine Corps jumped at the chance and on 9 November 1967, Secretary McNamara directed the Army to "please develop plans for training Marine pilots with the Secretary of the Navy and provide my Systems Analysis office [Dr. Enthoven] with a schedule as soon as possible." [26] The goal was 150 graduates in FY 69. The first nine were to report in July 1968.

Within three weeks of Secretary McNamara's approval, General McCutcheon was exploring ways to expand even further the training of Marine helicopter pilots by the Army. On 30 November, he wrote the Army, requesting that it not wait until the start of the new fiscal year, but begin accepting Marine students as soon as possible.[27] The Army tentatively agreed to add 67 more between February and 30 June. The Deputy Secretary of Defense Paul H. Nitze, who previously had been the Secretary of the Navy, wrote on 2 February, "I would like the Army to start training helicopter pilots for the Marine Corps as soon as possible." He added, that though the original program was not to begin until July "I understand your staff has proposed entering the first Marines into training in February 1968. That schedule appears satisfactory providing the build up is fast enough to produce 150 Marine pilots during FY 69." [28] The approval of the accelerated schedule should have brought some relief to the hard-pressed Marine Corps. The increase, while small compared to the overall requirements, was at least a step in the right direction. As so many other times in the development of helicopters, however, what seemed like a solution to a problem still required refinement.

Colonel Edwin L. Powell, Jr., Director of Army Aviation, wrote on 29 January, "that the FY 68 training of USMC pilots was contingent on training being conducted on a reimbursable basis, and also requested action to reimburse the Department of the Army with $179,719 to cover the cost of the FY 68 training." [29] In addition, as there were no suitable government quarters available at the Army training bases, the Marine Corps would have to provide each of the students an extra allowance of pay. The entire cost for the FY 68 classes, Major General William K. Jones, Deputy Director of Personnel at HQMC, wrote, amounted to "approximately $241,000, none of which . . . is available." [30] A search by the Fiscal Director of the Marine Corps, Mr. Joseph F. Wright, indicated that "this office does not know of any slippage elsewhere that can fund this deficiency." [31] A plea to the Navy brought no relief. The Army responded on 29 January that "since no indication has been received that FY 68 funds will be provided, the training previously discussed for FY 68 cannot be accomplished." [32] The first classes were scheduled to begin in two weeks, and sufficient funds had been found for only five Marine students. The level of frustration within DC/S (Air) was definitely on the rise as January ended. Deputy Secretary Nitze was briefed on the problem, and on 2 February, directed that the "FY 68 costs should be financed within the funds available in the Army's FY 68 budget." [33] It had been a close call, but the Marine Corps was back in the accelerated program and students began reporting to the Army for training as helicopter pilots.

## Army Helicopter Training

There were some differences between the flight training a Marine would get at Pensacola and what he would receive under the Army system. Most were minor. There was, however, one great difference. Under Army training, all flights would be in helicopters. There would be no fixed-wing time as there was at Pensacola.

The first students reported to Fort Wolters at Mineral Wells, Texas, where the Marines joined a class of "120 officers from the Army, the National Guard, and various Allied nations." There were two main phases to the training. The first one consisted of 18 weeks of primary training at Fort Wolters. Instructor pilots were civilians under contract by Southern Airways. The fledgling aviator received a total of 50 hours of flight, 20 of which were solo, along with extensive classroom work. One of the small trainer helicopters used was the OH–23D "Raven," a much-improved version of the HTL which had proved so underpowered in the early days of Ellyson. After successfully completing this part of the syllabus, and still at Fort Wolters, the Marine flew an additional 60 hours "performing a countless number of confined and pinnacle operations. These involve a high and low reconnaissance of each area, planning an approach into the area, and selecting the type of takeoff."

Lieutenant Colonel Warren G. Cretney, a former commanding officer of HML–367 in Vietnam and Marine liaison to the Army Aviation Center in 1971, described the results. "Since the terrain in Texas offers an infinite number of confined areas and pinnacles, and the wind conditions vary from day to day, the officer student is constantly presented with new problems to tax his planning ability and judgment." At the completion of the training at Fort Wolters, the Marines were transferred to either Fort Rucker in Alabama, Hunter Army Airfield at Savannah, Georgia or Fort Stewart, South Carolina, for advanced maneuvers.

A total of 50 hours of instruction on flight under instrument conditions followed. The aircraft was the TH–13, essentially the same aircraft being flown at Ellyson. Since this was the only phase of the entire syllabus which was flown in that particular aircraft, to save time, the Army did not teach the student how to start it or take off and land in it. The instructor accomplished all of those maneuvers, and the student flew the aircraft only during the required exercise. This practice, while unusual, is not uncommon.

In a final phase of the training, the student learned to fly and conduct operations in the familiar UH–1 series. As Lieutenant Colonel Cretney recounted, during the last two weeks "of the Army Flight Program, the entire unit (made up of several classes) actually lives and functions in the field, under simulated Vietnam conditions." While there, "students have the opportunity to plan and execute complete operations involving live troop lifts at Eglin (Florida) Air Force Base, and Fort Benning, Georgia." [34]

The first six Army-trained Marines graduated in September 1968 at Hunter Army Airfield. All were second lieutenants: Robert L. Barnes, George W. Haufler, Jr., Jeffery D. Monaghan, Stanley W. Taylor, Edward L. Watson, and Joseph E. Sturtevant, Jr. The Deputy Director of Army Aviation, Colonel Jack W. Hemingway, was the speaker at the graduation ceremonies.[35] Also on hand was General McCutcheon. The first Marine to complete the course was Second Lieutenant Watson.[36]

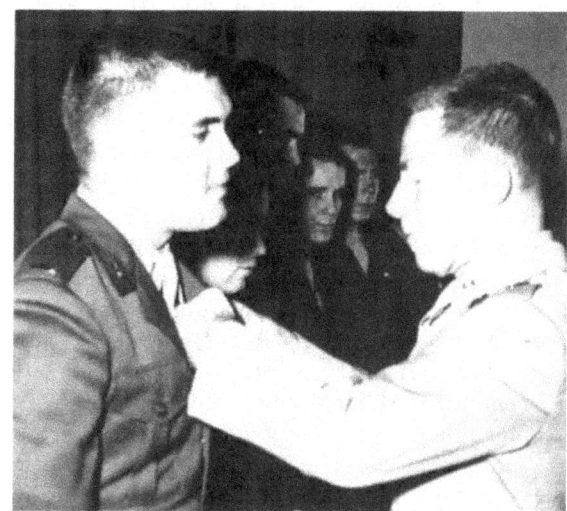

USMC Photo 532038

*Major General McCutcheon DC/S (Air), presents Army wings to the first Marine helicopter pilots to complete training with the Army at Hunter Army Airfield in September 1968.*

By the end of FY 69, 142 Marines had graduated from Army helicopter training. As a result of this program and the similar one with the Air Force, for the first time since July 1965, the shortage of Marine Corps pilots decreased. The situation continued to improve. Pensacola had gained additional facilities, and both the Marine Corps and the Navy became anxious to have all pilot training returned to the Naval Air Training Command. The Army was requested on 22 February 1971 that "the remaining Marine quotas for FY 71 be cancelled and that no quotas be allocated for Marine Corps use in FY 72 and FY 73." [37] The Air Force program also was dropped.

Five months later, the last of the Army-trained helicopter pilots graduated. The Commandant, General Chapman, wrote a personal letter to the Chief of Staff of the Army, General William C. Westmoreland. The letter stated that "the training was accomplished in a timely and professional manner and contributed greatly to the accomplishment of the Marine Corps mission during an extremely turbulent and trying period." General Chapman concluded, "please accept my sincere thanks for a job well done." [38]

There were several attempts to continue the association of the Army and Marine helicopter pilots. In June 1970 the Army made a proposal "to allow Marine and Navy company grade helicopter pilots to volunteer to serve for one year with Army aviation units in Vietnam."[39] While the shortage of helicopter pilots had eased somewhat, it certainly had not eased that much! Lieutenant General Louis B. Robertshaw, Deputy Chief of Staff for Personnel at HQMC, answered the request, in an almost classic understatement, "The Marine Corps has enjoyed sufficient commitment in Southeast Asia to provide combat experiences for all Marine helicopter pilots." In addition, "our commitment during the fiscal year 1971 will still provide adequate opportunity for combat service of all new pilots. Accordingly," he added dryly, "the Marine Corps does not anticipate a requirement for additional combat opportunity for its helicopter pilots."[40]

A few months later, a more serious proposal was made. For some time Congress had been looking into the reason for separate helicopter training programs. In early 1971, OSD agreed that it might be possible to have the Army take over the training of all service helicopter pilots, including those of the Navy, Air Force, Coast Guard, and Marine Corps. The Army was happy to oblige. The Air Force, which had few helicopters other than for Search and Rescue missions, was indifferent. The Navy and Marine Corps were violently opposed. They objected on a number of grounds.[41] One minor, but often mentioned fact was that the Army-trained helicopter pilots had most of their instruments instruction based on what was termed, "tactical instrument flight." Prior to being certified to fly on the FAA-controlled airways in the United States, additional training had to be given. This normally was accomplished in a short syllabus which consisted of classroom work and about 12 hours of flight.

OSD calculated that the Army could train the pilots at less expense than the Training Command. The costs were subjected to repeated analyses. In the end, the difference, if there was one at all, was based more on accounting procedures than any real savings. The Marine Corps was particularly concerned about the fact that Army-trained helicopter pilots would lack fixed-wing qualifications. The problem was the same as with the warrant officer programs. Marine Corps aviation was too small to have any segment of its pilots restricted to a single type of aircraft. In an emergency, as had been proven repeatedly, the Marine Corps could order pilots to make the transition from fixed-wing aircraft to helicopters with a minimum amount of time needed. The opposite also was true. A helicopter pilot who had fixed-wing experience would take less time to train in jets than one who had flown nothing but helicopters. It was an important point.

Most of all, however, any attempt to have the Army train all Marine helicopter pilots ignored the fact that learning how to fly is just a part of a much larger education. The young officer student also must learn the ways of the naval service in general, and of the Marine Corps in particular. He must become familiar with the organization, mission, customs, and procedures of the amphibious assault force. Much of this knowledge comes from informal association with Marine and Navy instructors, and by living and working in a naval organization. During the first formative year in the service, it was particularly critical that the students operate in such an environment. It was difficult to put a price tag on this type of training, but after a year of study, even more analysis, and effort, Congress and OSD relented and the Marine Corps and the Navy were permitted to train their own helicopter pilots at Pensacola. The issue, while not dead, at least remains temporarily dormant.*

## Post Graduate Flight Training

Regardless of who trains the Marine pilot, the Air Force, the Army, or the Naval Air Training Command, on graduation he is not ready to fly in combat. First, with a few exceptions, the aircraft in which he trains will not be the aircraft in which he goes to war. Equally important, all the training is aimed at producing a competent pilot, and not necessarily a competent combat pilot. There is quite a difference between the two. Another problem, for which there is no instant solution, is that experience in flight operations is closely tied with capability in flight operations. The newly designated pilot has been trained in the shortest time possible. He needs additional experience before he flies in an attack on the enemy. Thus all the instruction given prior to graduation is, accurately, termed undergraduate flight training. Prior to being ready for combat, the pilot needs postgraduate flight training.

From the late 1950s until shortly after the build-up began in Vietnam, the most common method for providing this instruction was to use a stabilized squadron which completed phase training together. A unit would be formed and almost its entire complement of Marines ordered in from other organizations. At this point, most of the men would be "stabilized" in the squadron and would remain with it for the next few years. The crews and pilots, clerks and technicians simultaneously would begin the first of three phases of training. The initial period was devoted to basics on how to main-

---

* The idea of a single service—in this case the Army—training all helicopter pilots was raised again in Congress in 1976 but later dropped.

tain, repair, and fly the aircraft. Next the squadron would enter a phase which concentrated on combat maneuvers, tactics, and techniques. At the conclusion of these two, which could last as much as two years, the unit was deemed ready for combat. If scheduled for deployment overseas, the squadron went together as a unit. A year later, when the Marines returned to the United States, they were reassigned, new men ordered in, and the entire process repeated.

It was an excellent peacetime system. In the normal three-year cycle, commanders had ample time to make their policies known and followed. Pilots and crews who had flown together for almost two years before deploying had been honed into a smooth-running and efficient combat team. Shortly after it was initiated, the system brought an enthusiastic response from Major General John C. Munn, Director of Aviation. He said, "two complete cycles of rotations with units of the 1st Marine Aircraft Wing have proved the significant benefits provided by this program." He went on to add that "never before has the Marine Corps had a more capable, more ready Marine Aircraft Wing deployed than the one now stationed in Japan." [42]

Unit rotation had three drawbacks, however. The system required a larger pipeline than if Marines were sent overseas on an individual basis. It made no provision for casualties. It also meant that at any one time, one third of the squadrons were not ready for combat as they learned the basics, another third were only partially ready as they learned tactics, and only those in phase three could be considered fully capable of going to war. By the fall of 1965, with the demands of the war in Vietnam being felt by all Marines, the pipeline had to be shortened. As General McCutcheon was to write, the Marine Corps "was forced to go to a system of replacement by individuals rather than units," and "had no time to devote to team or unit training except for those units which were reforming with new aircraft." To prevent all of a unit which was committed to combat from being replaced at one time:

> ... the 1st Marine Aircraft Wing went through a reassignment program ... in an effort to smooth out the rotation dates of men's tours. All like squadrons, for example all HMMs, had their men interchanged to take advantage of different squadron arrival times in WestPac so that their losses through rotation would be spread over several months rather than one.

General McCutcheon, who commanded the 1st MAW at the time, had to admit that the program" was a difficult one to administer, but it accomplished the objective." [43] Appropriately enough, it was called Operation Mixmaster.

Though units could not train and deploy together, the need for post-graduate flight training of new pilots remained. Initially, the task fell to the squadrons remaining in the United States. MAG-36 had deployed from Santa Ana and MAG-56 was still in a cadre status, so much of the burden fell on MAG-26 at New River.

## "We View Our Present Posture With Concern"

In July 1965, Lieutenant General Alpha A. Bowser became Commanding General, FMFLant. Already a veteran of more than 33 years service in the Marine Corps, he had spent much of his career up to the end of World War II in artillery units. A year after assuming command of FMFLant, in July 1966, he arrived in Washington to speak to the general officers' symposium. The war in Vietnam was being felt acutely in his units. He began his presentation with a photograph flashed on a large viewing screen. It portrayed a possum stranded in a very precarious position. "At FMFLant," he said, "like the possum, we view our present posture with concern." He continued:

> Our challenge was not one of combat in the literal sense, but rather combating the dual problem of supporting operations in WestPac, and at the same time, meeting our own deployments, contingencies, and [other] war responsibilities.

In many ways, his units had been converted into a giant training command to meet the needs of the war in Vietnam, yet at the same time they had to be prepared to respond to any emergencies which might occur in the Atlantic theater of operations. "One thing became readily apparent early in the year," he added, "FMFLant could no longer enjoy the luxury of concentrating its efforts in only one direction. We are not two-faced in FMFLant but we have been facing in two directions." [44]

While the problem existed throughout FMFLant, it was again most critical in MAG-26. The squadrons there already were stretched thin by the transfer of experienced pilots and crews to Vietnam, the shipment of UH-34s and UH-1Es to replace the losses at Marble Mountain, and the demands of converting to the CH-46 and CH-53. To compound the problem, helicopters and crews from New River were required to train the increasing number of new Marines arriving at the near-by Camp Lejeune complex in the art of vertical amphibious assault. The final element of the dilemma was that new pilots arriving from Pensacola had to receive their post-graduate flight training prior to being ready for combat. The heavily committed operating squadrons were the only places where such training was available.

In the initial phases of post-graduate training, the new aviator co-pilot was prohibited from landing and taking off with passengers on board. This, and other restrictions, effectively limited any meaningful training for him while flying on an operational commitment, including the training at Lejeune. The pilots and crews of helicopters in the United States were almost fully committed to operational flights, and training suffered accordingly.

Thus, while units in General Bowser's command might have but slightly more than one half of the pilots required for wartime, many of these were still undergoing post-graduate training and would not be ready for combat, if it occurred in the Atlantic area. General Bowser had to admit reluctantly that though "we have shuffled, strained, and trained in order to accomplish the second half of our mission—that of fulfilling our Atlantic Command requirements—the overriding demands to the Pacific" had lowered the combat readiness to the point where "we cannot field a formidable, fighting, expeditionary force." By an all-out effort, only a small unit could be deployed "for any time of sustained combat operations." He had ample reason to "view our present posture with concern." [45]

The key to solving the problem was to relieve the operating squadrons from the post-graduate training requirements, and provide them only with pilots who were completely combat capable. In this way, the tactical units—even if they were short of Marines—at least would have all their personnel ready for war. Even more important, if the post-graduate flight training could be conducted in specialized units specifically designed and staffed for the purpose, the quality of the training—which had suffered under the demands of operational commitment in the tactical squadrons—could be greatly improved. The idea, like many in the development of helicopters in the Marine Corps, was not a new one.

## The Training Groups

Until 1958, the Marine Corps had been authorized post-graduate flight training groups with squadrons for fighters (VMFT), attack aircraft (VMAT), and specialized instrument instruction (VMIT). With cutbacks in the Marine Corps, the groups had to be disbanded and by 1965 the individual squadrons had been whittled down until just two remained, one on each coast. In 1966, General McCutcheon reported that "for some years now, we have been trying to reinstate the training groups." "For the last two years," he continued, "our objective consisted of utilizing the two existing VMTs to form a fighter and an attack training squadron within the authorized force levels." Any progress in getting OSD to agree to an increase in squadrons in the Marine Corps was obviously going to be slow and often doomed to disappointment. Suddenly, in November of 1965, "The Secretary of Defense recognized the requirement for the Marine Corps to have a permanent training capability comparable to those of the Navy and Air Force." Two groups were to be formed for fixed-wing aircraft. Entitled, Marine Combat Crew Readiness Training Groups (MCCRTGs), "the east coast" unit, he said, "is scheduled to activate this [1966] December. The west coast group forms in January 1969," at MCAS Yuma, Arizona.[46]

Not only did OSD agree to the fixed-wing organizations, but General McCutcheon convinced Secretary McNamara to accept two helicopter post-graduate flight training groups though, "in contrast to the fixed wing, they are only approved on a temporary basis and their number is not adequate." He continued to press for "authority and means to expand, modernize, and retain permanently two helicopter training groups." The purpose of these units, he explained, "is to accomplish all transition and familiarization training and provide aircrew qualifications in the primary weapon system of the assigned aircraft." By doing this, "replacement inputs to the tactical squadrons will be combat-capable aircrews." With the shortage of experienced pilots for the United States-based squadrons, and the flow of new aviators from the Training Command, General McCutcheon pointed out, "Presently, the typical squadron has only about 25 percent of its pilots Phase III combat capable at any one time." He predicted that "after the readiness training groups are operating, the squadrons will be filled with combat-capable pilots, will be relieved of much of the training load, and will be combat deployable at all times." [47]

At Santa Ana, on 20 January 1966, the first of the Marine helicopter training groups (MHTG–30) was commissioned. Colonel Russell R. Riley, the fifth Marine to be designated a helicopter pilot, was commanding officer. The same day, H&MS–30 was activated and Captain Peter N. Samaras began to assemble the team of Marines who not only would support the training squadrons, but also assist in training the technicians who were destined to maintain the aircraft in the tactical squadrons. The dual ceremony, though a major landmark in the development of helicopters in the Marine Corps, went almost unnoticed, for at the time of commissioning, the total personnel of the group consisted of six officers and four enlisted men. Initially, the buildup was slow, but by 1 April, the group was ready to inaugurate post-graduate flight training, and Marine Medium Helicopter Training (HMMT) Squadron 301 was commissioned under the command of Lieutenant Colonel William R. Duncan. It had been hoped that the unit could be equipped with CH–46s, but the buildup in Vietnam had priority and there were no aircraft available.

Once again the ever faithful H-34 series came to the rescue. The demands put on this versatile aircraft by the Marine Corps, however, were so heavy that sufficient UH-34s could not be spared to fully equip the squadron. Over half of the helicopters were a Navy anti-submarine warfare version, the SH-34J. They had been transferred to the Marines earlier to help alleviate the shortage created by combat losses and the expansion of units. The training syllabus for the helicopter pilot newly graduated from Ellyson provided for about 75 hours of flight time. This included initial familiarization, formation flying—which was not taught at Pensacola—flight with the aircraft at or near maximum weight, and additional instrument training. The post-graduate instruction required a minimum of 90 days.[48] The first of the students began on 13 April, and by the end of June, 12 had completed the course and were rated as combat-capable co-pilots.

During the same period, on 11 May, a subunit of H&MS-30 which conducted post-graduate flight training in the UH-IE at Camp Pendleton, was added to the group. A second training squadron, HMMT-302, was activated on 1 November under the command of Lieutenant Colonel Elvyn E. ("Happy") Hagedorn. Sufficient CH-46s were made available to equip this unit.

A month and a half later, on 15 December, the H&MS-30 subunit at Camp Pendleton was redesignated VMO-5 and became a full-fledged training squadron as part of MHTG-30. By the end of 1966, the training group could offer post-graduate flight training in the UH-34 series, the CH-46, and the UH-1E. Equally vital, it offered courses of instruction to mechanics, crew chiefs, and technicians in the maintenance and repair of all three different models of helicopters. It appeared that the Marine Corps had regained a major device to improve combat readiness.

As so often before, what had been planned and hoped for, was not what happened. The "requirements exceed resources—there is no shortage" disagreement was in full bloom and in July 1967, General McCutcheon had to state, "because of aircraft and pilot shortages, we were able to form only two helicopter training squadrons and slipped the activation of the four [two helicopter, two fixed wing] Marine combat crew readiness training groups to Fiscal 1968."[49] Even that projection proved optimistic.

It was not until 30 June 1969, the last day of FY 69, that MHTG-40 was commissioned at New River under the command of Lieutenant Colonel Morris G. Robbins, who served in that billet until 23 July the next year when he was succeeded by Colonel Robert B. ("Big E") Engesser. At the same time, all three of its squadrons were also activated. H&MS-40 was commanded by Major James T. Gordon and HMMT-402 was under Lieutenant Colonel Donald R. Carpenter. The "heavy" squadron, HMHT-401, was commissioned, but neither aircraft nor Marines were available to be assigned so it was held at "zero" strength until 12 January 1970. The first commanding officer later was Major Chester L. Whipple. The number of mechanics and technicians to be trained created the need for another organization. Officially a subunit of H&MS-40, and initially under the direction of Captain John W. Shoaff, the subunit controlled and monitored all of the training of the crew members.

Unlike its sister training group at Santa Ana, which had been located in old buildings, MHTG-40 moved into a brand new, $10 million complex, specifically designed for post-graduate training. There was a classroom building, new hangars, and administrative spaces, warehouses, and shops. The group even had its own barracks and dining hall. Flight operations began 21 August with the arrival of a CH-46D which was assigned to HMMT-402.[50] This aircraft was followed on 29 January 1970, with the acceptance of a CH-53 by HMHT-401.[51] By the end of June, 20 CH-46D, and four CH-53s were on hand. At the same time, HMMT-301 at Santa Ana, was redesignated as a "heavy" training squadron and replaced its UH-34s with CH-53s.

In addition to the post-graduate flight and maintenance training, the groups conducted several specialized schools. Courses of instruction on instrument flight were offered. Jet pilots who had been ordered into helicopters completed the transition in the training groups. Likewise, helicopter pilots who had not recently—or who had never—flown the UH-1E, CH-46, or CH-53 received refresher training.

Another school trained crew chiefs and mechanics on the operation of the machine guns firing from the aircraft. If the gunner was not careful, it was possible to shoot the helicopter's own rotor blades. Thus the initial airborne live firing could be dangerous. The pilots in the operating squadrons, being no different than Marine aviators of any time or type, felt that all officers on the group headquarters staffs were the bane of their lives and had nothing better to do than shuffle papers and interfere with the "real" work in the units. Thus, a custom quickly grew up in which squadron aviators seldom flew the gunners on their first firing flight. That exciting task was always reserved for pilots on the headquarters staff. Any loss would just reduce the number of reports that had to be submitted, so went the logic.

HMMT-402 conducted one school which was unique. The AV-8 "Harrier" jet attack aircraft procured by the Marine Corps was fully capable of taking off and landing vertically, and actually hovering in flight. Jet pilots assigned to the unusual aircraft seldom were familiar with the techniques of such maneuvers. With a slight adjustment of the stability system in the CH-46, the helicopter could be made to handle very similarly on takeoff and landing to the AV-8. Thus, prior to flying the new attack aircraft, the jet pilots were given a special course of instruction in the helicopter to develop the coordination and techniques for VTOL flight. The mutual understanding generated between the helicopter and AV-8 pilots, though not as widespread as that which resulted from the forced transition program in the early 1960s, was a definite and additional benefit to the Marine Corps.

From the time MHTG-30 was first commissioned in 1966, for the next six years, these two training groups repeatedly would validate General McCutcheon's hopes for them. In 1967 he had spelled out what was to be their service to the Marine Corps.

> Even in a stable peacetime situation at least 25 percent of the squadrons are not combat-ready because of aircrew training requirements. In war time there is the difficult choice of holding back a Wing as a training base or of deploying everything and shutting off the rotations. Now [July 1967], for example, we are 50 percent deployed and have been heavily committed for two years, and we cannot muster one combat ready squadron in the United States. The main reason for this condition is the crew training requirement.
>
> With the readiness training groups doing the Phase I and II training, the fleet squadrons can be staffed with Phase III crews and be combat deployable all the time.[52]

The officers and men of MHTG-30 and -40 provided the combat capable Marines, just as had been expected of them.

# CHAPTER THIRTEEN

## TWINS AND MIXES

### Continue the March

On the first day of January 1968 at exactly one minute after midnight, Washington time, a message from HQMC was flashed to all the Marines in the world. It read:

    FROM: CMC
    TO: ALL MARINES
    1. I HAVE THIS DATE ASSUMED DUTIES AS COMMANDANT OF THE MARINE CORPS.
    2. MY PREDECESSOR HAS SET THE DIRECTION AND THE PACE.
    3. CONTINUE THE MARCH.
    CHAPMAN SENDS.[1]

General Greene, after serving four years as Commandant and guiding the Marine Corps through one of its most turbulent periods, retired. He chose a small estate in a Virginia suburb of Washington, D.C. In over 37 years of duty, it was the first time he and his wife ever owned a home of their own. He still keeps an active interest in Marine Corps matters, but now has time for other pursuits. His impact on the development of helicopters in the Marine Corps is difficult to measure, not because his influence was in any way nebulous, but because he had such a direct role in so many facets. Seldom before had a Commandant played such an intimate part in the development of vertical amphibious assault.

His successor, General Leonard F. Chapman, Jr., was born on 3 November 1913 in Key West, Florida.[2] A graduate of the University of Florida at Gainesville, Chapman, like McCutcheon, had been a member of the Army ROTC and in 1935 was commissioned a second lieutenant in the Field Artillery Reserve. The Marine Corps at that time offered a certain number of commissions annually to honor ROTC graduates at each university. Chapman applied for the one opening given to the University of Florida and of all the applicants was determined to be the best qualified. He resigned from the Army and was commissioned in the Marine Corps on 8 July 1935. Basic School at Philadelphia, duty at Quantico, and Field Artillery School at Fort Sill, Oklahoma, followed.

Chapman participated in the early action in the Pacific in World War II as commanding officer of the Marine detachment on the heavy cruiser USS *Astoria*. He served in this ship in the battles of Coral Sea and Midway but left her for another assignment in June 1942, just two months before she was sunk by the Japanese in the Battle of Savo Island. After a tour as an artillery instructor in the United States, Chapman returned to the Pacific in June 1944. In command of an artillery battalion, he took part in the assaults on Peleliu and Okinawa. Korea saw him held in a series of assignments in the United States, but in 1953 he went to Japan to command the 12th Marines, another artillery unit. Then came tours as commander of the Marine Barracks, Washington, D. C., and of Force Troops, Atlantic, at Camp Lejeune.

In September 1961, Chapman reported to HQMC as Assistant Chief of Staff (G–4), and three years later, as General Greene assumed the post of Commandant, Chapman, promoted to lieutenant general, became chief of staff. On 1 July 1967, he was designated as the Assistant Commandant. Six months later, he was

USMC Photo A190309

*General Leonard F. Chapman Jr., 24th Commandant of the Marine Corps, greets South Korean Marine officers at Chu Lai during a tour of Vietnam in January 1968. Chapman presided over the redeployment of Marines from Vietnam.*

listening to his first New Year's Day concert as Commandant of the Marine Corps.

In the development of helicopters in the Marine Corps, the last two years of General Shoup's commandancy could be characterized as being a period of struggle to define new missions, develop new aircraft, and overcome the chronic shortage of funds. General Greene had been faced with the explosive growth of Marine helicopter forces, the actual introduction into combat of the new designs, and the difficulties of conducting a major war for a nation that remained essentially on a peacetime basis.

For General Chapman, the years 1968 to 1972 would bring a period of retrenchment in the military, a further refinement of the helicopters already in operation, and the laying of the groundwork for yet another generation of vertical amphibious assault aircraft and techniques. As he assumed the duties of Commandant, the CH-46 had been modified and was back in the battle. The CH-53s were deployed in strength. The UH-1E had proved itself invaluable in a variety of missions. The role of the armed helicopter, if not unanimously agreed on, at least was no longer a burning issue.

## Further Improvements of the CH-46

On 24 July 1968, still another version of the CH-46 was accepted at the Vertol plant in Morton. Bureau number 154845 looked exactly like the "D" on the outside.[3] Even on the inside, most observers could see little difference. The new aircraft had the same performance and could lift the same amount as the "D" and for all practical purposes, was in fact the same—with one major exception.

The CH-46F, as it was designated, had provisions for the installation of the long-awaited Integrated Helicopter Avionics System (IHAS) which held promise of giving helicopters a true all-weather, low-level, formation flight capability. To an experienced CH-46 crew member, the most obvious difference in the new model was that the avionics compartments had space provided for the electronic components of the IHAS. In the cockpit, the radio control console between the pilots had been rearranged to leave room for the IHAS display.

Once the contract for the instrument system had been awarded to Teledyne and the initial designs completed, a schedule was prepared in 1966 which called for the "navigation system of IHAS" to be installed "in the 360th aircraft delivered from the production line." It was anticipated that the first aircraft to be equipped should be ready in December 1967. Bureau number 154845 was that helicopter. Once the "F" models were coming off the production line, NavAirSysCom confirmed to the Marine Corps that "earliest retrofit is planned to get this navigation capability in all aircraft."[4] Before the first CH-46F could be delivered, however, the IHAS program was in trouble and Teledyne was recommending that only the Self Contained Navigation System (SCNS) portion of the system be installed. Continued delays in production of the electronics and constant increase in the cost of even the SCNS made the future of the CH-46F navigation system doubtful. The end came when the SCNS blanked out all radio transmission from the helicopter. Five months of testing at Vertol in the first half of 1969 could not solve the problem. The CH-46F never went into operation with the IHAS or SCNS that were the sole reason for its new designation.

In spite of the disappointing results of the IHAS, Vertol engineers continued trying to improve the CH-46 series. In late 1966 and early 1967, they conducted a series of experiments with an H-46 which had been converted into a compound helicopter similar to that which had created so much interest prior to the design of the CH-53. Short "stub wings" were mounted directly behind the cockpit and also on the rear tail pylon as part of the company's "effort to improve speed and payload." The concept, as in all compound helicopters, was that in forward flight the wings would provide some of the lift necessary, allowing the rotor blades to move faster and give the aircraft a higher speed. Also "The aircraft's rear rotor pylon has been moved aft and the forward one streamlined," the company announced.[5] Provisions were made for fuel tanks carried on the outside of the aircraft, and the entire fuel system was adaptable for inflight refueling. The helicopter was also used as a "flying guinea pig... to try out new ideas."[6] After a number of successful flights, the aircraft crashed and was destroyed, but Vertol continued to experiment with ways to improve the CH-46 series.

On 2 July 1969, the CH-46 passed a milestone. At ceremonies at the plant in Morton, Pennsylvania, the 500th such helicopter was delivered. Accepting the aircraft for the Marine Corps was Brigadier General Homer S. (Dan) Hill, General McCutcheon's assistant and eventual successor. It was appropriate that General Hill was on hand for the event for he was an experienced helicopter pilot. He had been first commissioned in June 1942 and had flown combat missions throughout World War II. In Korea he had commanded VMF-314. He reported to Ellyson in 1957 to complete the transition to helicopters, and had served as air officer on the *Princeton* after her conversion to an LPH.

At the time General Hill traveled to Vertol to accept the 500th aircraft, the CH-46 in Vietnam had already flown more than 625,000 sorties while carrying 1,330,000 passengers. In addition it had lifted nearly 100,000 tons of cargo, and most important, had evacuated "more than 120,000 wounded or injured personnel to safety."[7]

Almost two years later, General Hill, who was now the DC/S (Air), as General McCutcheon had returned to Vietnam, visited the Vertol plant again. At 1100, 2 February 1971, the final production model of the CH-46F rolled out of the plant.[8] Since 30 April 1962 when the first CH-46 had made its debut, a total of 624 A, D, and F models had been delivered.[9] The CH-46 had become, and remains, a versatile, hard working member of the vertical amphibious assault team.

### The "Huey" Changes Its Skin

The determination of the U.S. Army to develop an airborne attack capability was understandable and natural. In the aftermath of the bitter fights following World War II over the unification of the armed forces, each had been allowed—and restricted—to very specific missions. Fixed-wing attack was the domain of the Air Force. There was no question that it was extremely competent in providing close air support for the Army; but the many demands on the aircraft and pilots, conflicting priorities, and lack of mutual training often could lead to misunderstandings. The coordination required, no matter how good, just was no substitute for direct control. It was only in the Marine Corps that the air and ground elements were cemented together by a common uniform, a common training, a common doctrine— and most important—a common commander.

The Army had tried to expand its air capability and had built up a modest fleet of small- and medium-sized fixed-wing transports, but shortly after the war in Vietnam began, it had to relinquish most of this to the Air Force. Thus, if the Army was going to have any aircraft of its own, particularly those for attack missions, they would have to be helicopters. The manufacturers capable of developing such an aircraft, specifically designed for the Army's needs, were aware of the requirement and a number of them proposed attack helicopters.

Most of these manufacturers proposed entirely new helicopter models. The design, testing, and production of these, particularly of the critical drive system— engines, transmissions, connecting shafts, and rotors— would take much time. Thus, even under an accelerated schedule, any new aircraft proposed could not be ready for the operating units for several years, too late to meet the Army's requirements.

One company, Bell helicopters, had an easy solution to the Army's problem. A proven drive system from the long-since-tested and -operated UH-1 series could serve as the basis of a helicopter specifically designed for the airborne attack role. A different fuselage would be needed, but compared to designing or building an entirely new aircraft, the problem was minor, and such an aircraft could be put into production in a relatively short time. Bell decided to gamble, though not without some assurance of success, and built an attack aircraft without any firm orders for it. The first model was unveiled in September 1965. It was officially designated the UH-1H, but was more commonly called the Huey Cobra, or just simply "The Cobra."

On 11 March 1966, Bell announced that "after its development as a company project [The Cobra] has since been flown extensively by both company and military pilots in rigorous test and evaluation programs," and that "The U.S. Army . . . would order the high speed Bell UH-1H Huey Cobra, the world's first helicopter developed as an aerial weapons platform." The aircraft, "featuring functional streamlining, record-breaking speed and tremendous fire-power capabilities, was developed by Bell as a modified version of the Army's UH-1B Iroquois, which is now being used extensively throughout Vietnam," the company added. The new machine had demonstrated sustained speeds of 200 miles per hour in level flight during company tests. "The speed attainments have been hailed by Bell engineers as a performance breakthrough for aircraft of pure helicopter design and are considerably better than the world's speed record for helicopters of the Huey-Cobra's weight class," Bell boasted. The speed record at the time for light helicopters was 180.1 miles per hour set by the UH-1D in 1964.

Bell's Vice President for Military Contracts, Hans Weichsel, said that the Cobra "is not a new product, but a modified version of the UH-1B, which can be readily deployed directly from production to field units now equipped with the UH-1 series helicopters."[10] Not only could testing be shortened, but "transition for pilots and mechanics will be simplified due to the similarity of dynamic systems and flying characteristics between the UH-1H and UH-1B." The new aircraft "retains the UH-1B dynamic components, including the Lycoming T-53-L-13 gas turbine engine. Utilizing proven components currently in the supply system," it was stated, "results in a highly reliable machine that can be easily maintained with maximum use of on-site parts."[11]

USMC Photo A419219

*This Marine AH–1G Cobra, parked at Hunter Army Airfield in 1969, has automatic grenade launchers in its chin turret and rocket pods mounted on its stub wings. The first five Cobras received by the Marine Corps were loaned to the Army for use in training Marine pilots.*

It was difficult for an observer to believe that what they saw as a Cobra had anything but the most distant relationship to the UH–1 series.[12] The new attack aircraft was a streamlined, extremely thin helicopter. Viewed from the front, the fuselage was only three feet-six inches wide as compared to over eight feet on the standard UH–1. The narrow profile, however, was effective in presenting any enemy with an exceedingly small target. To accommodate the crew in such an aircraft, the cockpit was arranged so that the pilot sat directly behind and slightly above the front seat. From there, he could have sufficient visibility to maneuver the aircraft in almost any situation. The front seat, which had a slightly better view of the ground immediately to the front of the aircraft, was occupied by the gunner. He had a few of the control mechanisms available to the pilot, but was not a co-pilot in any conventional respect.

A careful observer would find similarities between the Cobra and its ancestors. At extreme length, the Cobra was less than one half inch shorter than the UH–1. There was also the familiar 44-foot diameter main rotor, and a tail rotor which was but one inch larger than that of the previous models. Typical of the design, the new aircraft had no wheels and used skids instead.

Even though the fuselage was much smaller than the UH–1 series, the Cobra weighed more when empty —5,517 pounds as compared to 4,734. Likewise, the maximum weight was also more—8,620 to 8,500. The difference was mostly due to the armament, and there was no doubt that the Cobra was armed as an attack helicopter. Two short wings, slightly less than two feet long, protruded from the aircraft. On each of them there were two positions for installing gun and rocket pods and other armament. In addition, the aircraft could be fitted with several models of remote controlled turrets mounted in the "chin" of the fuselage. Depending on the particular model of turret, they could fire 7.62mm machine guns, 40mm grenades, or a combination of both. The pilot, gunner, and the vital parts of the aircraft were protected by armor.

The Army was delighted with the aircraft, and ordered it into full-scale production. On 29 August 1967, the first Cobras arrived in Vietnam. One week later the aircraft logged its first combat kill—an enemy sampan and crew. Within a year, Bell had delivered more than 350 Cobras to the Army.[13]

Since the Cobra and the "Huey" were designed for such different roles, and—at least externally—appeared to be different aircraft, the designation UH-1H was confusing. It was subsequently changed to AH-1G (Attack Helicopter-1G)

The Marine Corps watched the development of the Cobra with interest. It requested that sufficient attack helicopters be procured to provide a squadron of 24 in each of the three active wings. In 1967, Brigadier General Earl E. Anderson reported on the results. At the time he was the Deputy Chief of Staff for Research and Development. General Anderson had flown helicopters in Korea with VMO-6 and had been the commanding officer of MAG-36 at Santa Ana during the Cuban missile crisis. He was the youngest active duty Marine ever promoted to general and, later, became the first Marine aviator to hold the rank of full general while on active duty when he was assigned as Assistant Commandant 1 April 1972.*

In July 1967, he said "funding and production of the AH-1G for the Marine Corps have been approved by the Secretary of the Navy. We are now awaiting approval from OSD."[14] General Anderson was destined to be disappointed for only 38 aircraft were approved for FY 69. They were "designed to support 24 operating in South East Asia in FY 70 (2 VMOs with 12 AH-1 each)." This program," a report concluded, "is not in keeping with the 'Force in Readiness' concept."[15]

Two weeks after General Chapman had become Commandant, on 15 January 1968, General McCutcheon submitted the latest information on the Cobra program:

> Experience in Vietnam has clearly shown that armed helicopters are an essential member of the fire support team. Due to continued circumstances of weather and terrain the armed helicopter has proven to be an absolute necessity in the delivery of close-in fire suppression support during vertical assault operations.
> Existing UH-1Es were modified to fulfill this requirement. However, in so doing, the availability of the UH-1E for performing the missions for which the aircraft was procured was degraded. While the modified UH-1Es are now doing a creditable job, the AH-1 will provide greater speed and firepower and more flexibility in the performance of the armed helo mission. The AH-1 will also free the UH-1s for light helicopter utility mission, many of which are now neglected.[16]

He concluded by assuring the Commandant that efforts would continue to have sufficient AH-1s approved, but for the present, the number of AH-1Gs remained at just 38. In February 1969, the first ones were delivered to the Marines at the Bell plant in Fort Worth, Texas.[17] Since the total number of Cobras was so small, no postgraduate flight training program was established. Instead, the first five aircraft were loaned to the Army "as training vehicles for instructing Marine pilots."[18] Three months later, the first Marine Cobra pilots graduated from Hunter Army Airfield. They were Majors Jimmie A. Creech, James W. Rider, Ronald J. Thrasher, and John L. "Jack" Pipa. Out of a class of 39 pilots, the four Marines graduated in class standing as one, two, three, and four respectively.[19]

By the end of June, 17 AH-1Gs had been received. In addition to the five on loan to the Army, two had been sent into a research and development program to study further the potential of such an attack helicopter. The rest had been sent directly to Vietnam,[20] the first shipment of four aircraft arriving 10 April. They were assigned to Lieutenant Colonel Clark S. Morris's VMO-2. At the time, the squadron had a complement of 8 UH-1Es and 23 OV-10s, in addition to the new Cobras. After a week of test and orientation flights, "the first Marine Corps AH-1G in Vietnam went operational 18 April 1969" by flying escort for a medical evacuation flight.[21] The pilot was Major Donald E. P. Miller with First Lieutenant Tommy L. James as the gunner in the front seat.

In the next few months the Cobras brought some surprises to the enemy who were more acquainted with the UH-1E gunship or the machine guns of the CH-46 and CH-53. One incident was related by Colonel Kenneth S. Foley. He wrote:

> With [Cobras] covering, a Marine rifle company was moving out cautiously. Shots came from around the bend and the [Cobras] covered the area with fire. When the Marines got there, five Viet Cong were horizontal; four dead and one wounded. The wounded VC was shouting

---

* General McCutcheon was placed on the retired list the same day as his promotion.

and banging his fists into the dust. One company commander asked the interpreter what all the shouting was about.

"He's apparently the squad leader," the interpreter replied. "He's yelling, 'If I told them once I told them a thousand times—*don't shoot at that kind of helicopter!*" [22]

On 11 July a report was submitted evaluating the AH–1G in its first months of combat. The conclusions were very favorable. When compared with the armed UH–1E the new attack aircraft was called "a far superior weapons platform precluding the need to fly rocket and gun runs below 1000 feet for the required accuracy." The aircraft "has a much improved armament system that provides greater firepower and flexibility . . . and permits steeper dive angles . . . providing greater accuracy." The cruise speed was such that it was "compatible with that of transport helicopters, allowing the AH–1G the capacity to lead troop transport helos into the objective area and be able to loiter overhead for an entire lift." [23] The biggest problem was that most of the spare parts that were not the same as those for the UH–1E had to be ordered from the Army, and delays had been encountered.

By December, VMO–2, now commanded by Lieutenant Colonel Stanley A. Challgren, had its full authorization of 24 Cobras. Then, on 16 December, in a reorganization which affected all units in Vietnam equipped with the AH–1G, UH–1E, and OV–10As, the aircraft were transferred to HML–367. The commanding officer was Lieutenant Colonel Warren G. Cretney who later would serve as liaison officer with the Army during the time it was training Marine Corps helicopter pilots. [24]

### The "Sea Cobra"

Slow delivery of parts, however, was not the only difficulty with the AH–1G. It was an aircraft designed for the Army. Like the UH–1B/D which had led to the Marine UH–1E, the Cobra had no rotor brake and thus was only marginally suitable for use on board ships. It also had Army avionics which, though satisfactory, created additional supply problems. The Marine Corps preferred a different chin turret. It wanted one which had heavier 20 millimeter guns rather than the 7.62mm installed in the Army version. Most important, the Marine Corps felt that the helicopter should have two engines. From the very start of the program it had been pushing for such a twin-engined Cobra. General Anderson had said that such a version "which the Marine Corps desires, offers a substantial increase in relative combat power and reliability over the present [AH–1G]. Its gun platform, stability, cruise, dive, and maximum allowable speeds are marked improvements. Moreover," he continued, "it can deliver twice the ammunition and operate in the objective area twice as long." [25]

Colonel, later Lieutenant General, Thomas H. Miller was the Head, Air Weapons Systems Branch, DC/S (Air) during the time the Marine Corps was attempting to win approval for the "twin" Cobra. A highly decorated combat pilot, he had won 18 medals in World War II and Korea, and four Distinguished Flying Crosses, one of which was for setting the world's speed record of 1,216.78 miles per hour in an F4B "Phantom" on 5 September 1959. He summed up the arguments. "Justification for the twin-engine power plant is based on four major factors: improved crew safety, increased reliability in mission performance, increased payload, and growth potential." He went on to point out the "Records of the Naval Aviation Safety Center indicate that during 1956–1967, 17 USN/USMC UH–1 [type] helicopters were lost or damaged in combat or operational mishaps directly attributed to the failure or malfunction of its single engine." The result, he emphasized, was *eight fatalities* and *four major* and *20 minor injuries.*" [26]

Another factor, which the Army did not have to face, was that the Marine Corps mission was based on amphibious landings. At sea, in an aircraft with only one engine, a malfunction almost invariably led to the loss of the helicopter and often some of the crew. Recent experience with the twin-powered CH–53 and CH–46 had proved that with two engines, if one malfunctioned, not only could the crew be saved, but often the aircraft, too. Even the mighty "Deuce" had made safe landings on board a ship with one engine not operating, though the event was usually the highlight of excitement for any amphibious force. Over land, it was pointed out, "while it is true that a single engine helicopter can auto-rotate a power-off, controlled descent to a landing in the event of power failure, aircraft losses still occur when the terrain is unfavorable to a landing." Not only that, "in some cases missions can and have been completed on the remaining engine when a single power loss has occurred." [27]

There were other reasons, but they all added up to the fact that the Marine Corps required Cobras with two engines and not the Army single-engined version. The Marine Corps model was to be designated the AH–1J. Approval turned out to be more lengthy and difficult than anyone had anticipated. The Marine Corps found itself having to thread its way through a thicket of opposition to the "twin" Cobra. By early 1968 it was apparent that, even if approval could be gained, the additional engineering, design, and testing of the improved model would delay its introduction into combat. Thus General McCutcheon agreed to accept the single-engine Army version and gained OSD approval "but only until the end of the war." He added, that "simultaneously with our fight to get Cobras, we have been fighting to get them with two engines. . . . This has been quite a battle in itself both with SecNav, OSD, and the Congress." Part of the problem, he continued, was that OSD "requested that we offer both equal effectiveness as well as equal cost trade offs of fixed-wing aircraft in order to retain the armed helos." The staff of OSD remained unconvinced that, in the Marine Corps, armed helicopters and fixed-wing attack aircraft complemented, not competed with each other. General McCutcheon concluded that "We are challenging the validity of the equal effectiveness concept, but we are examining ways to get an equal cost trade off."[28] The old dictum that for every additional helicopter, a fixed-wing aircraft had to be deleted, was still very much in effect.

The FY 69 Defense Budget proposed the procurement of 38 AH-1Js. These aircraft were not exactly what the Marine Corps had hoped for. They did have the rotor brake, Navy avionics, and the desired chin turret, but they did not have two engines. Though such a "power pack" was available, the cost of buying enough for such a limited number of aircraft proved to be too high. The AH-1Js requested would still be equipped with a single Lycoming T-53 engine.

In the early spring of 1968, the Marine Corps received a boost in its efforts to obtain twin Cobras from an unexpected—though not necessarily appreciated—source: the North Vietnamese Army. During the annual holidays of "Tet," it launched an all-out attack on the allied forces. In the resulting battles, the UH-1E armed helicopters played a large role in defeating the enemy and inflicting heavy casualties on him. The aircraft had ample opportunity to demonstrate their effectiveness. It was not without cost, however. A number had been hit by enemy fire and either severely damaged or destroyed.

The Marine Corps was quick to point out the need not only for replacements of the aircraft lost, but for more Cobras to be readied for the war. It also emphasized that as long as additional aircraft were required, they should be twin engined. Such a "power pack" was now available at a suitable cost from Pratt and Whitney of Canada.

The Secretary of Defense, in April, asked Congress for permission to take funds from less urgent programs and divert them to the "Twin" Cobra, which was now also known as the Sea Cobra. Not only was the Marine Corps finally to have its Cobra with two engines, the Secretary of Defense increased the number to 49.

During hearings on the new program before the Senate and House Armed Services and Appropriations Committees, a new controversy broke out. It centered around the use of the Canadian-built, twin-engine pack. On 9 April 1968, the Chairman of the House Armed Services Committee, L. Mendel Rivers, wrote Secretary McNamara voicing his concern over not buying an American-built engine. Congressman Rivers was assured that there would be a competition prior to selecting the engines for the AH-1J. The Naval Air Systems Command sent out requests for proposals on 3 July to all eligible manufacturers, including those in Canada. A month later, at the deadline, only two had answered. They were United Aircraft of Canada, which was the parent company of Pratt and Whitney who had made the original offer, and Continental Aviation and Engineering Corporation, an American concern. Both engines were suitable, but United Aircraft's entry already was in production and had been thoroughly tested. The Continental engine would not be available until sometime in the future. The United Aircraft "power pack" was selected and the contract awarded.

On 14 October 1969, Bell Helicopter unveiled the first AH-1J twin-engined Sea Cobra. The ceremony, and a conference on details of delivery and design, was attended by a group of Marine officers including Brigadier General Victor A. Armstrong. He had been designated a helicopter pilot 25 August 1949 and was the 28th Marine to be officially qualified in rotary wing aircraft. He had commanded HMR-161 in Korea and had participated in some of the earliest helicopter combat operations. He had also served as commanding officer of HMX—1 in 1960 and MAG-36 in Vietnam in 1966. In World War II, Korea, and Vietnam he had been awarded a Silver Star, seven Distinguished Flying Crosses, and 12 Air Medals, among numerous other decorations. At the Bell plant, General Armstrong was accompanied by Colonel Edwin H. Finlayson, Head, Weapons Group, at HQMC, and Colonel Henry ("Hank") Hart, program manager for assault helicopters at Naval Air Systems Command.

The helicopter they saw was almost exactly the one the Marine Corps had wanted. The chin turret was an XM-197 model equipped with a three-barrel 20 millimeter gun firing up to 750 rounds per minute. Also available for mounting on the stub wings were an XM-18 self-contained 7.62 millimeter "minigun" pod and seven-tube XM-157 and 19-tube XM-159 aerial rocket pods. The aircraft had a rotor brake for shipboard operations, standard Navy avionics, and most important, twin engines.[29]

USMC Photo A419089

*The first AH-1J "Sea Cobra" to be delivered to the Marine Corps stands ready for inspection at the Bell plant in Forth Worth, Texas in November 1969. These aircraft had increased firepower and greater reliability with their two engines.*

When the Marine Corps had purchased the Army version of the Cobra, no testing had been required prior to introducing the aircraft into combat. The modifications necessary to create the AH-1J, however, were sufficiently extensive that the first four aircraft were delivered to Patuxent River for Board of Inspection and Survey (BIS) trials in July 1970. The next seven arrived in September at New River "to start crew and maintenance training." [30] The aircraft were assigned to Lieutenant Colonel Robert D. Myer's VMO-1. There had not been time to install all the parts of the new armament system in the first 11 aircraft, so eventually all were returned to Bell for further modifications.

As soon as pilots and crews could be trained, and all the required changes installed on aircraft at the plant, four Sea Cobras were to be shipped to Vietnam for an evaluation in combat. This test was to be conducted under the supervision of Colonel Paul W. ("Tiny") Niesen. On 12 February 1971 he, eight other officers, and 23 enlisted Marines departed the United States for Marble Mountain. The same day, the four AH-1Js left in Air Force turboprop C-133 cargo aircraft.[31] The crews arrived 16 February and the aircraft two days later. The evaluation unit was assigned to Lieutenant Colonel Clifford E. Reese's HML-367. The first combat test of the new twin-engined Cobra came four days after the aircraft had been unloaded. Colonel Niesen and Lieutenant Colonel Reese joined the Army-version aircraft while supporting transport helicopters around a hostile landing zone.[32]

For the next two months, the small detachment kept its four aircraft busy. By 28 April, when the evaluation was completed and the aircraft shipped from Vietnam, they had flown a total of 614 hours, shot 14,950 rounds of 7.62mm ammunition, 72,945 of 20mm, and 2,842 rockets in addition to several other items of ordnance. The Commandant received a report which summarized that "the combat evaluation determined that the AH-1J provides a significantly greater effectiveness in firepower over the AH-1G." [33]

There were two basic ways to load the AH-1J, depending on the type of targets which could be expected and the amount of fuel required for the mission. A "light" load of 1,475 pounds consisted of a full amount of 20 millimeter ammunition, 14 2.75-inch rockets, and either forward firing gun pods or other light ordnance. For the "heavy" version, 2,400 pounds of armament were included. A total of 76 rockets and 300 rounds of of 20 millimeter ammunition shells for the chin turret made up this load.[34] The Sea Cobra was capable of speeds up to 155 knots in level flight and could dive at 190 knots. Even with one engine malfunctioning at the maximum weight of the aircraft, it could maintain flight at 2,000 feet.

Coincidentally, on the same day that Colonel Niesen and Lieutenant Colonel Reese began combat operations with the Sea Cobra in Vietnam, at New River the first helicopter attack squadron (HMA) began to form. An "activation cadre" with Lieutenant Colonel Lloyd W. Smith, Jr., as officer-in-charge became a part of MAG-26. Initially, while waiting for its aircraft, the unit was assigned UH-1Es. On 7 April, five AH-1Js arrived from the Bell factory. By the end of June the "cadre" had received 23 more Cobras.[35]

At ceremonies on 1 July, the "cadre" was disbanded and HMA-269 became the first of three helicopter attack squadrons in the active forces and one in the reserves. Armed helicopters had come a long way since the first efforts to give weapons to the crew members of the SHUFLY squadrons in early 1962.

## The Twin "Huey"

Simultaneously and in conjunction with the efforts to have approved a twin-engined Cobra, the Marine Corps set out to procure a twin-engined version of the UH-1E. The reason was identical to that for the attack helicopter: safety during amphibious operations and improved performance particularly in high altitude or heat. If the Marine Corps had encountered difficulty in obtaining the twin-engine "power pack" built in Canada for the Cobra, it was nothing compared to the difficulties in procuring one for the UH-1E. In February 1968, the Canadian Department of Industry had sent representatives to Washington to sound out the military services on the possibilities of using a twin engine on the UH-1 series. It was reported that the Canadian armed services were planning to purchase "about 100 twin UH-1s" and the "U.S. Air Force has a buy of 125 UH-1Ds scheduled during FY 70 and they may buy the twin pack also in lieu of the Lycoming T-53."[36]

At the same time, the Army had "completed a series of studies into the cost and technical aspects of installing a twin engine power plant in the UH-1D helicopter." The conclusions reached were "that the benefits to be gained do not justify the expense of increased development, production and operations." Thus, the Army did "not intend to further pursue the development of a twin engine power plant for the UH-1 Helicopter."[37] Part of the reason for the reluctance of the Army to join in the program was that, at the time, it was heavily committed to several new helicopters including a large, super-sophisticated armed one, the Lockheed-built AH-56A "Cheyenne." Any major program with the UH-1 series might affect the new aircraft.

The Marine Corps, Navy, and Air Force remained enthusiastic about the possibility of a twin-engined UH-1.[38] It was to be designated the UH-1N. By shifting funds from other projects in FY 68, the Air Force was able to gain approval for five of the aircraft, and with FY 69 money, 74 more. For the following year, the Navy requested 40 UH-1Ns and the Marine Corps, 22. They were all to be equipped with the United Aircraft of Canada PT-6T (T400-CP-400) twin "power pack." OSD agreed that the program was a good one and forwarded the request to Congress but during testimony of 15 July 1969, the Chairman of the House Armed Services Committee, L. Mendel Rivers, unexpectedly and strongly opposed the Navy and Marine Corps' request.

Several factors influenced the committee's stand. There was always the question of "gold flow" which occurred when purchases were made from foreign nations. Also, at the time, the government of Canada was publicly expressing its displeasure over the United States commitment to Vietnam—no small item to the Congressmen. A further complicating feature was that Lycoming Corporation, which built the engines for the single-engined UH-1 series, had just developed a new model, which was almost as powerful as the "twin power pack" offered by the Canadian company. Lycoming recently had built a new plant near Charleston, South Carolina, to produce these engines.

Almost simultaneously, the Army's AH-56 "Cheyenne" armed helicopter had become bogged down in cost and development problems. Other than a few helicopters for test purposes, the program was canceled. Now the Army was faced with having no armed helicopter other than the single-engined UH-1B/D and AH-1G series. It immediately began to show interest in the Marine Corps Sea Cobra and the UH-1N twin-engined model. If the Army, which needed many more helicopters than the rest of the services combined, joined in the program, the resulting contract for engines would be a very large one. The economic and political impact of buying the engine in Canada would be greatly increased.

On 7 August 1969, Colonel Miller and General Lewis W. Walt, Assistant Commandant, met with Chairman

Rivers. "General Walt outlined the Marine Corps' critical UH-1N requirements, and emphasized the points in justification for the twin engine configuration," Colonel Miller reported. "He further stressed the importance of these aircraft in support of our forces in South East Asia. After approximately 55 minutes the Chairman indicated that he would support this year's limited procurement of the twin engine UH-1N." While the argument as to the increased safety of a twin-engine helicopter had saved the FY 70 program, Congressman Rivers "clearly indicated that his committee would not stand for any follow-on procurement of this engine unless the engine could be built in the United States."[39] United Aircraft chairman of the board, W. P. Gwinn, lost no time in reassuring both the military and the congressmen that the company "is prepared to establish a U.S. source for this powerplant and we have now set in motion the necessary planning."[40] The Navy, which was responsible for procuring the engines for all services, quickly agreed to cooperate and informed the congressmen of the impending developments. The UH-1N program was back on track.

On 7 April 1971, the first of the twin "Hueys" was delivered to the Marine Corps at New River. It had been flown there from the plant at Fort Worth, Texas, by Colonel Glenn R. Hunter, commanding officer of MAG-26. Accompanying him on the same flight was Lieutenant Colonel Smith, officer-in-charge of the HMA-269 "activation cadre." He and other crews simultaneously delivered the first four twin Cobras.

As there were neither sufficient aircraft nor trained crews to operate two squadrons at the time, both the UH-1N and AH-1Js were assigned to Lieutenant Colonel Smith's unit.[41] The similarities between the two aircraft, particularly in the propulsion train, aided both training and maintenance.

Four months later, on 10 June, HML-167 was officially transferred from Vietnam to New River. Some members had arrived earlier and it would be a few more weeks before the commanding officer, Lieutenant Colonel Richard J. Blanc, would have his whole unit reassembled. By 28 June, however, enough had checked in that he could begin accepting the UH-1Ns that had been kept in HMA-269. Three days later, Lieutenant Colonel Blanc turned over command of the squadron to Lieutenant Colonel Horace S. ("Hoss") Lowrey, Jr. HML-167 was the first of the planned "light" helicopter squadrons to be equipped with the new "twin Huey."

The Marine Corps now had at least one unit operating with a new and improved version of all the original turbine-powered helicopters. There was the CH-46F, the CH-53D, the AH-1J, and now the UH-1N. Though the older models continued to serve, the acceptance of aircraft by HML-167 marked the beginning of a new era in helicopter development in the Marine Corps.

## Change in the Mix

The difficulty in winning approval for the improved models of helicopters was just one of the problems

USMC Photo A331874

*The twin-engine UH-1N offered greater safety in amphibious operations and had more power than the UH-1E, yet required no more fuel to operate than did the single-engine Huey.*

facing the Marine Corps. How many of each type were required, and how they would be organized was a serious issue.

Given a specific and reasonable mission to be performed, any designer can produce an aircraft which will be suitable. Such an approach, however, often results in an aircraft which can perform well only the mission for which it was built. There is no way to predict accurately just what missions will be necessary in a war, and equally important, how much of the total effort will be needed for the specific task. As an example, the UH-34, designed as a utility helicopter, proved to be a poor observation aircraft simply due to the cockpit and cabin arrangements. Likewise, on emergency medical evacuation flights, it was vulnerable to enemy fire because of the height of the cockpit and transmission. Attempts to use the UH-34 as an armed gunship also were unsuccessful. If specialized missions, like observation and helicopter escort, were to be performed, aircraft had to be designed specifically for these tasks. Once that was accomplished, the next problem was how many observation or armed helicopters were needed within the Marine Corps limit on total aircraft. It was not an easy job. Nowhere did the relative mix of types of aircraft receive more deep and constant attention than in the assault transports.

The Marine Corps Operations Analysis Group (MCOAG), a part of the Center for Naval Analyses, was created to study such problems as the relative mix of different types of aircraft. In 1966 MCOAG was directed by the Headquarters Marine Corps Transport Helicopter Study Advisory Committee "to examine the possibility of including the smaller and less expensive UH-1D aircraft in the over-all mix," and requested "an analysis of the cost and effectiveness of the [CH-53, CH-46, and UH-1D] aircraft in a search for the mix that would provide the Marine Corps with the most effective initial assault lift capability." [42]

The basic assumption was that the Marine Corps had to have a vertical assault capability of "11,000 troops, 850 tons of equipment and supplies . . . to landing zones up to 50 miles from the launching area within 60 to 90 minutes." The study was detailed and comprehensive. Factors such as the cost of training the crews, their pay, and the necessary bases were included as well as the actual cost of the aircraft and the fuel and parts to operate them. Various combinations were tried, including the inclusion of what was then the promising IHAS instrument navigation system. Assaults from the different types of LPHs were scrutinized. It was quickly apparent that the Army version UH-1D, even though it was single engined and had no safety margin for amphibious operations, was by far the least expensive to buy, maintain, and operate per aircraft. Next was the CH-46. The CH-53, which was just coming into production, was estimated at both a "high" and "low" cost depending on how many aircraft were eventually procured.

Average Costs per Operating Aircraft
(millions of dollars)

| Aircraft | 5 year cost | 10 year cost |
|---|---|---|
| CH-46 | $2.2 | $3.0 |
| CH-53 Low | 3.7 | 4.8 |
| CH-53 High | 4.0 | 5.1 |
| UH-1D | 1.1 | 1.6 |

When each of the aircraft was compared as to its lift capability, and its operation from an LPH, the results were reversed. The study concluded:

> The least-cost alternative for meeting the Marine Corps' initial vertical assault requirement is procurement of the CH-53 helicopters only, from now on. This conclusion [which remains valid with] changes in assumed aircraft [procurement amounts] and operating variations, is supported by considerations of ship utilization and command and control, and is not contradicted by analyses of the vulnerability of the aircraft.[43]

The report went on that though "helicopter requirements for post assault operations have not been examined in this study . . . some general comments on the subject come out of the analysis of the ship to shore assault phase." Once the Marines had landed, "resupply and replenishment of assault forces require essentially the same capability as the initial assault: delivery of a given payload in a certain time." It could be assumed that "if the CH-53 is the least-cost way to provide the initial assault, then it is probably the best way of providing resupply." In addition, "the same reasoning for expecting the CH-53 to be the best resupply alternative also holds for the general ship offloading, if there is a need to do this as quickly as possible." The CH-53 "Superbird" could not do everything, however, and the study said that "medical evacuation and utility missions, such as rescue and liaison requirements are another important category." In these missions, "there may be a need to have flexibility, in terms of numbers of aircraft rather than tons of payload, because of the possible numbers and diversity of tasks to be taken care of simultaneously." [44] Thus, in addition to the CH-53, a number of small, relatively inexpensive aircraft would be needed to make up the vertical assault force.

MCOAG was not the only organization studying the problem of the proper mix of helicopters. Even before the report was released, Boeing Vertol had completed one which, naturally enough, concluded that the

CH-46 could perform almost all of the missions required. In the Vertol study "The CH-53 and CH-46 were considered as equally suitable aircraft for retrieval, Air Search and Rescue, helicopter control, and a pathfinder transport on a 1 for 1 basis."[45] Such an assumption, it was later pointed out, "overlooks the payload and speed advantage of the CH-53, which might enable it to perform these missions with a smaller force than the CH-46." The conflicting analyses prompted further investigations. In September 1966, MCOAG released a new report which traced the development of the mix and summarized the progress and problems in resolving the question.

In first establishing a helicopter force which could conduct the required initial assault, the Marine Corps had determined that 360 CH-46s and 72 CH-53s would be needed in the operating forces. Subsequent to this decision, the cost of the CH-46 had risen considerably. The increase in price upset the "cost/effectiveness" calculations and "was cause for a reevaluation of the helicopter program mix."[46] It was this study which had resulted in the recommendation to buy only CH-53s. "Because a force with more CH-53s and fewer CH-46s would have a smaller total number of helicopters, there was some concern about flexibility to perform follow-on missions," MCOAG stated. Therefore:

> ... the War Games Division of the Marine Corps Landing Force Development Center [at Quantico] was asked to examine the overall helicopter mission, assault and follow-on, to determine whether mixes capable of transporting assault elements were also capable of supporting subsequent operations.

There was one major difficulty with a study of this type. As MCOAG had to admit, "First of all, there is no established doctrine to be satisfied in providing helicopter support of post-assault operations." Up until the war in Vietnam, the Marine Corps had concentrated the development of its doctrine, tactics, equipment, and even organization almost exclusively on the initial vertical amphibious landings. Little attention was given to any operations after the beachhead had been secured. At first glance, this appears to be an oversight. It was not.

In 1973, Major General Henry R. Paige recalled the events 20 years earlier that led up to the neglect of a post-assault doctrine. General Paige had served as the first president of the Tactics and Techniques Board at the Marine Corps Development Center from September 1950 until July 1953. He was also the officer who had made such a strong case for enlisted Marines as helicopter pilots. He wrote:

> To understand this, you must go back to the 1945-1950 era when the Marine Corps was literally fighting for its life. The roles and missions of the various services were finally spelled out and the Marine Corps ended up with a task of "Developing Tactics, Techniques and Equipment for *Landing Force* Operations."
>
> This led to the organization of the Marine Corps *Landing Force* Development Center in the fall of 1950. The Navy was assigned "Amphibious Operations" so you can see the Marine Corps was limited to only the *Landing Force* phase. The Army had the responsibility for land operations, and we were guided by their manuals.
>
> So to avoid conflict, we devoted our efforts principally on how to get Marines and equipment and supplies ashore. The roles and missions were put to a test in Korea. You may recall that the Army controlled land operations, and the Air Force air operations, while the Navy looked after the sea (and amphibious operations in conjunction with the Marine Corps). That, in essence, is why . . . we did not pursue postlanding operations at that time.[47]

It was difficult to determine the proper mix of transport helicopters for a type of war for which there was no Marine doctrine. By the summer of 1966 it was becoming increasingly apparent that the majority of the Marine combat operations which had been ordered in Vietnam would not require amphibious landings, but would be post-assault warfare.

The Marine Corps intensified its efforts to develop an appropriate doctrine. In the meantime, MCOAG could conclude only that "requirements for helicopter lift in post-assault operations may well be a function of the tactical situation, the terrain, and the number of helicopters available."[48] Thus, "rather than a requirement for a minimum number of helicopters, whatever helicopters are available might be used. Their effectiveness may not be determined easily." As this study was being written, the shortage of helicopter pilots was beginning to be felt acutely and the crews in Vietnam were on duty up to 15 hours a day for months on end. There was no question in their minds that "whatever helicopters were available" were being used.

The attempt to establish a proper mix, not only for the amphibious landings but in post-assault combat, continued. The war game analysis conducted by MCLFDC at Quantico in 1966, "originally used a 5:1 (CH-46:CH-53) helicopter mix." MCOAG pointed out that "to use the follow-on missions generated in this case as a basis for comparing various mixes assumes that these are the only such missions which could be performed, and which are of any value." The fact was that, "other mixes might perform other kinds of missions, with more or less tactical value." Not only that, it was pointed out: "The use of Vietnam experience, based on UH-34 operations, can also bias the results. The UH-34 missions were naturally geared to the payload, speed, and number of these helicopters available. To assume that the same kind of missions may be performed if other helicopters are available," could make a small helicopter more efficient and effective than it, in fact, was, the report concluded. The only recommendation MCOAG could give was:

> The implications of the assumptions made in the Vertol and MCLFDC studies clearly point out the need for a much broader study of Marine Corps missions and transportation. An analysis of the trade offs between forms of transportation, surface, and air, in support of overall tactical and strategic goals, is necessary before any long-run program decisions can be made.[49]

The Marine Corps was not the only one wrestling with the problem. OSD was also taking a hard look at the cost/effectiveness of the transport helicopter mix. In July 1968, General McCutcheon reported that OSD "proposed that the mix of medium to heavy helicopter squadrons in our wings be changed from 5:1 to 4:2 and that the number of helicopters in each medium squadron be reduced from 24 to 21." Reluctantly, the Marine Corps had to accept the decision. At the same time SecDef "indicates his belief that we do not need the number of medium and heavy helos in each wing that we requested and which he had previously authorized. It is now proposed," General McCutcheon continued, "that ¼ of the currently authorized total active helo assets be placed" in the reserve squadrons. If such a plan was forced on the Marine Corps, it "would end up with two 18-plane heavy and three 21-plane medium squadrons in each of the four wings." The Marine Corps was "fighting this plan, of course, but it is too early to know how successful we are going to be."

The new 2:1 mix was agreed to by the Marine Corps "on the condition that our light helicopter structure would be increased," for, he said, "Vietnam has proven that we do not have enough small helicopters for all the tasks that Marine ingenuity can devise."[50]

During the next year, the switch to the new mix got underway. There were to be 12 squadrons equipped with 252 CH–46s and six with 144 CH–53s. It was not the only change in the organization of helicopters taking place. As planning started for the FY 68 program, "the Marine Corps stated a requirement for armed and light helicopters in the base line [permanent peacetime] force."[51] The need for these squadrons had been amply demonstrated in Vietnam. "This requirement was recognized by OSD, but only if the Marine Corps would identify an equal cost force trade." It was the same old problem: any increase in the number of helicopter units had to be compensated by a reduction in fixed-wing aircraft. By October 1970 the Marine Corps was ready to recommend where the cuts would be made. One F–4 Phantom jet fighter/attack squadron was to be deactivated. In addition, one fixed-wing group headquarters with all the associated elements was to be abolished. Since the flow of students from the training command was beginning to taper off, the need for postgraduate flight training would be reduced in the future and additional deactivations were planned.

## Marine Helicopters around the World

The first Marines began their withdrawal from South Vietnam in August 1969. In the next year and a half, one by one, the helicopter squadrons departed and were reassigned to other bases. On 26 May 1971, the last unit, HML–167, ceased combat operations and redeployed to New River where it was to receive the new twin-engined UH–1N. Two UH–1Es remained behind "for last minute administrative support."[52] Three weeks later, on 15 June, the two aircraft flew on board ship for transfer to Okinawa. They were the last Marine helicopters stationed in Vietnam. It seemed that the Marine commitment was over. It was not.

With the Americans gone, the North Vietnamese sensed that, finally, they had an opportunity to conquer the south. On 30 March 1972 they launched a massive invasion. The northern areas were quickly overrun. The two special landing forces sailed back to Vietnam and arrived off the coast the first week of April. On board the USS *Tripoli* (LPH 10) was Lieutenant Colonel Paul L. Moreau's HMM–165 and on board the USS *Okinawa* was HMM–164 under the command of Lieutenant Colonel Edward C. Hertberg. In addition to their normal complement of CH–46s, the squadrons were reinforced with detachments of CH–53s, UH–1Es, and Cobras. Meanwhile, Marine fixed-wing units returned to combat. Eventually the aircraft were stationed at Nam Phong in Thailand. A detachment of CH–46s from H&MS–36 under the leadership of Major John G. McCabe supported the jet operations. The squadrons were not withdrawn until 21 September when they returned to their home bases.

Off the coast of Vietnam the two SLFs assisted in recapturing the territory conquered by the enemy. U.S. ground forces were not used, but the helicopters made repeated assaults with the Vietnamese Marine Corps. It was some of the most bitter fighting of the war. By the end of the year, the invasion had been repulsed. Though the Marine helicopters would continue to patrol in the area—and later were used to clear mines from the waters of North Vietnam—they were not actively engaged in combat.

December 1972 found Marine helicopters, once again, around the world. Many of the places were

*These Marine CH-46s of HMM-161, partially dismantled and rigged for shipment, have been loaded onto an amphibious ship at Da Nang for redeployment out of Vietnam in August 1970.*

familiar, Futema, Kaneohe, Santa Ana, Camp Pendleton, Quantico, New River, and the LPHs in the Caribbean, Mediterranean, and Pacific. It seemed just like 1962. But there was a difference. All aircraft now had turbine engines, and it would not be long until all had two engines. The observation squadrons, while still a part of the helicopter groups, had no helicopters assigned. All aircraft were the fixed-wing OV-10s. There were now light HML squadrons, in addition to the HMMs and HMHs. There were attack helicopter units equipped with Cobras. There were other changes. The much sought for postgraduate training groups had been reduced to a single composite squadron on each coast offering instruction in the CH-46 and CH-53. The biggest difference, however, was in the pilots and crews. Many of those from 1962 were gone. Some permanently. For those who remained, there was no question of them being second-class citizens. The events of the decade had proved beyond any doubt that they were among the finest in all of the Marine Corps.

## The "Father of Helicopters" Leaves the Ranks

Missing from the ranks of Marine aviators in December 1972 was the man who had contributed as much as any other individual to the development of helicopters in the Marine Corps—General McCutcheon. On 5 February 1970, McCutcheon's nomination for promotion to lieutenant general had been approved by President Nixon. The Senate confirmed it less than three weeks later, and soon after General McCutcheon left the post of DCS (Air) for a new assignment.

*CH—53Ds of HMM—463 make their last flight over Marble Mountain Air Facility before redeployment on 18 May 1971. With its wooden huts and protective arches for aircraft, Marble Mountain in 1971 contrasts sharply with the improvised facility established almost six years before.*

*Marine helicopters return to war. Aircraft of HMM—164 land near Hue to embark South Vietnamese Marines for a counterattack against invading North Vietnamese forces in June 1972.*

He returned to Vietnam as Commanding General, III Marine Amphibious Force (III MAF). In this post he helped to direct the redeployment of III MAF from Vietnam. Eight months after going to Vietnam, he was selected for promotion to the rank of full general and in January 1971 returned to Washington and an assignment as the Assistant Commandant of the Marine Corps. This time, however, he could not keep to the dictum he had laid down for himself 34 years before, that "anything I have been made responsible for, or anything I have undertaken, I have always endeavored to complete." [53]

McCutcheon was seriously ill and was not responding to medical treatments. Sadly he had to notify the Commandant that he would be unable to assume his new position for reasons of ill health. His failing strength forced him prematurely into retirement, but in recognition of his 34 years of distinguished service, Congress passed special legislation placing McCutcheon on the retired list in the grade of general effective 1 July 1971.[54] Just 13 days later, the general died of cancer at the National Naval Medical Center, Bethesda, Maryland. He was only 55.

A year later at a dual ceremony, the airfield at New River was named in honor of him, and the chapel renamed "Memorial Chapel" for all those who had served with the Marine Corps' first active duty four-star aviator. [55] *

At the dedication, the Assistant Commandant, an aviator, General Earl E. Anderson reflected:

> He was one of the finest and most distinguished Marine Officers [whose career] reads like a history of Marine aviation. He was a pioneer whose great determination, aggressive, innovative spirit produced so many long lasting programs.[56]

General Anderson went on to add: "All the Marine Corps shares with great pride in this recognition of the unparalleled accomplishments," of General Mc-

---

* The first to be promoted while on active duty, though he was placed on the retired list the same day.

MCAS(H) New River Photo 0978 5 72
*Mrs. McCutcheon attends the ceremony at New River naming airfield in honor of the late General McCutcheon in 1972. Pointing out the ceremony site to Mrs. McCutcheon is General Earl E. Anderson, Assistant Commandant of the Marine Corps.*

Cutcheon. Undersecretary of the Navy Frank P. Sanders said:

> America was built on the lives of those who have gone before. Faith, in God, in country, in desire has made this great country what it is today. General McCutcheon, throughout his career and his long illness, displayed this faith. He was a great Marine, a great American.[57]

General McCutcheon is often best remembered in connection with Marine Corps helicopters. But he had an equally significant impact on close air support command and control techniques, guided missile weapons systems, combat air operations doctrine, and the introduction of the true VTOL attack aircraft—the AV-8 "Harrier."

McCutcheon has been called "The Father of Helicopters," a title which ignores both his other aviation achievements and the contributions of many other Marines to helicopter development. If Marine Corps helicopters had a father, however, it undoubtedly would have been General Keith Barr McCutcheon.

# CHAPTER FOURTEEN

# LOOKING TO THE FUTURE

## The LHA

As 1972 came to a close, there were two major developments under way. Neither one would be completed until some years later. One was at Pascagoula, Mississippi, where a new type of ship was taking form.[1] Termed a Landing Helicopter Assault ship (LHA), it bore little resemblance to the original LPH, the "Teddybear," USS *Thetis Bay*.

At the time the true LPHs of the *Iwo Jima* class were being designed, the Marine Corps still had hopes of being able to conduct an "all helicopter" amphibious assault. Helicopter manufacturers continued to be optimistic that they could design and build a helicopter which could lift all the equipment needed for the attack. If this were to be the case, there would be no need for conventional landing craft and amphibious vehicles. Helicopters would carry everything. Thus the LPHs were designed with no provision for any landing boats, and the Landing Ship Dock (LSD), Landing Platform Dock (LPD), and Landing Ship Tank (LST) were built for surface attack.

The LSD and LPD were constructed with a "well deck." This ingenious arrangement allowed the ships to carry smaller landing craft inside them. When such a vessel reached its objective area, a large gate at its stern would be opened and, by taking on ballast, the ship would partially submerge, allowing the well deck to flood. The landing craft then could swim out and conduct the assault. On their return they could reenter the ship, the gate would be closed, ballast pumped out, and the well deck would once again be dry. It was an excellent system for surface assaults.

In the mid and late 1950s, the concept of an all-helicopter landing began to be questioned. The difficulties in producing the "Deuce" were a clear indication of the problems which would be encountered in any large helicopter. Attempts to reduce the weight of combat equipment to fit current aircraft were not all successful. There just seemed to be no lightweight substitute for some items, particularly tanks and heavy artillery. Thus the "all-helicopter" amphibious assault was set aside in favor of a balanced air and surface landing, which if not ideal, was obtainable. By now, the LPHs had been built and the lack of any facilities for landing craft was a matter of serious concern. In large-scale attacks, assault Marines often had to be transferred from the LPHs to the LSDs and LPDs to board landing craft. This posed constant problems for commanders and reduced the inherent flexibility of a balanced amphibious attack.

These problems and the testing of solutions to them pointed to a need for a ship which had facilities for both helicopters and landing craft. The answer was the LHA.

On 28 May 1968, the Secretary of Defense announced the award of a contract to build the new ships to the Ingalls Shipbuilding Division of Litton Industries. They would combine a helicopter flight deck and hangar space with a well deck for landing craft. They were to be very different from the first conversion into an LPH. Where the "Teddybear" at a full load displaced 10,000 tons, the new models are four times as large, displacing 39,000 tons. The LHAs are larger even than the *Boxer*-class conversions. The flight decks are 820 feet long. Their beam of only 106 feet permits passage through the Panama Canal with a scant three feet to spare. Their tallest masts reach 221 feet above the keel, and are designed to fold so that the ships can pass under the Brooklyn Bridge, if it ever were necessary to do so.

If the "keel-up" LPHs were three ships stacked on top of each other, the LHA is at least five different ones. Large holds are included to handle essential cargo. There are living facilities for a total of 262 officers and 2,542 enlisted personnel, including 1,672 combat marines. The well deck can accommodate an assortment of landing craft and amphibian tractors. And, of course, there are spaces for the helicopters and the necessary spare parts and machinery.

Originally, the Marine Corps requested nine of these ships. Tentative approval had been given, but on 20 January 1971 the number was reduced to five. It was a blow to the Marine Corps, but at least produc-

165

USMC Photo A702362
*General Robert E. Cushman, Jr., 25th Commandant of the Marine Corps, presided over the christening of the Navy's first LHA, USS* Tarawa, *in December 1973.*

tion began on the ones approved. Litton Industries had long been a manufacturer of aerospace equipment and had only recently entered the field of shipbuilding. It had constructed a new shipyard at Pascagoula and attempted to apply the techniques of the aerospace business to the new venture. There were, understandably, problems. By the end of 1971, most had been corrected and the first LHA was back almost on schedule.

The date of 1 December 1973 was to be an important one for the Marine Corps. On that day, the Commandant, General Robert E. Cushman, Jr., arrived in Pascagoula. He had succeeded General Chapman as CMC on 1 January 1972. General Cushman, winner of the Navy Cross for heroism in the recapture of Guam in 1944, had come to Mississippi to attend the launching of the first LHA. It was to be named the USS *Tarawa* (LHA 1).

In his speech at the launching he said he felt a sense of exhilaration "at the impending arrival of a versatile amphibious assault ship designed from the keel up with the requirements of its landing forces in mind. In the current vernacular, this one really 'gets it all together.' "[2] He went on to predict that "The LHA will be the backbone of our amphibious forces for the rest of this century." At the conclusion of the speech he turned and said: "It is with great personal pride that I present to you the sponsor of *Tarawa* ... my own personal wife."[3] A few minutes later she broke the traditional bottle of champagne on the bow of the *Tarawa*—a major development had arrived.

## The CH-53E

On the opposite end of the nation from Pascagoula, in Stratford, Connecticut, the other major development at the end of 1972 was underway. Sikorsky was building a true "flying crane" for the Marine Corps. The idea that a helicopter could have a lift capability greater than its own weight always had been tantalizing, but the design and construction of such a machine

USN Photo 1166266
*The USS* Tarawa *(LHA 1) here steaming in the Gulf of Mexico during her sea trials in 1976, is the first of a new class of amphibious assault ships which can accommodate both helicopters and landing craft.*

had eluded all manufacturers. In spite of the tremendously impressive record of the CH-53 "Superbirds" as retrievers in Vietnam, if one of them was forced to land in enemy territory, the aircraft still had to be dismantled partially before another CH-53 could pick up the various components and take them back to the home airfield. In addition, there remained items of equipment which the assault Marines needed in any amphibious landing which still were beyond the lift capability of the CH-53D. The idea of attaching several helicopters to a single piece of equipment no longer was seriously considered. What was needed was a helicopter which, in an emergency, could lift another one just like it, as well as the heavy equipment of an amphibious landing.

On 24 October 1967, a specific operational requirement (SOR-14-20) was approved by the CNO. It called for a helicopter with an 18-ton lift capability to be used by both the Navy and the Marine Corps.[4] The document specified that the new helicopter had to be able to be operated, not only from the LHA, but also from the older *Iwo Jima* class LPHs. As this proposal was being studied, the Army, recognizing a similar need, requested a much larger and more powerful helicopter for its shore-based operations. OSD directed that the three services continue to study the problem to see if a single model could not be acceptable. What followed was, by now, a familiar story.

Even though the last of the CH-53Ds would not be delivered to the Marine Corps until January 1972, Sikorsky had begun efforts to improve the lift capability of the CH-53 much earlier. By 1968 it had determined that it was feasible to install a third engine in the aircraft. Such a development promised a significant increase in power with relatively little increase in the empty weight of the helicopter. Even more attractive, it would not require extensive redesign of the aircraft with usual delays and expenses.

On 8 November 1968, General McCutcheon met with representatives from the Navy "to determine the direction the Navy should take in satisfying the well recognized heavy lift helo requirement."[5] At stake was the necessary funds for Sikorsky to build a test bed to evaluate the idea. This test bed would consist of nothing but the propulsion train, and could be used to confirm the engineering and design of the third engine installation. At the meeting it was concluded that the three-engined CH-53 "was an acceptable method to satisfy the Crane heavy lift requirement for the Navy and Marine Corps."[6] Approval was recommended, and limited funding approved.

OSD, believing that the requirements of the Army and the Marine Corps were similar, directed that both proposals be reviewed. Early in 1970 it became apparent that the needs were different and two aircraft should be developed. Secretary of Defense Melvin R. Laird disagreed. On 21 September he announced that he favored the Army version and designated it to pro-

Photo courtesy of Sikorsky Aircraft Division, United Aircraft Corporation
*Two CH–53Es, one with Navy and the other with Marine markings, fly in formation. The three-engine CH–53E can lift its own weight.*

ceed with the development of a single heavy-lift helicopter for all services. The Navy and the Marine Corps protested vigorously. OSD partially relented and decided that, though the Army would continue the joint development, the Navy could support the Sikorsky testbed program—if it could find the money from funds already budgeted for other items. In December, the Navy had scraped up $1.97 million, and OSD approved the continuing effort.[7]

Meanwhile, the Army went ahead and asked manufacturers to submit their proposals. They were received on 11 February 1971, and turned over to a Source Selection Advisory Council for evaluation. This council was made up of senior officers from the Army, Navy and Marine Corps. Five companies submitted proposed designs: Sikorsky, Boeing/Vertol, Hughes, Gyrodyne, and Kamman. After studying the designs, the members of the council unanimously agreed on 2 April 1971 that all the proposals "leave no doubt that" any aircraft meeting the Army's requirements "will be minimally suitable for LHA use, and not suitable at all for" the *Iwo Jima* class LPHs.

There were two problems. First, the Army wanted an aircraft which could lift 22.5 tons, while the Marine Corps would now be satisfied with 16. This meant that if the Army type was adopted, it would be an aircraft which empty would probably weigh as much as 60,000 pounds, and fully loaded "in excess of 108,000 pounds."[8] The elevators and flight decks of the *Iwo Jima* class LPHs simply could not handle aircraft of that weight, and if they were ever to be used on such ships, major—and very expensive—modifications would have to be made. The second problem revolved around the blade fold capability. The Army did not need it; the Marine Corps had to have it. Just as in the conversion of the YH-1C into the CH-46, the addition of blade folding calls for major changes in the entire aircraft and greatly complicates the design and production. Finally, though not a factor in the council's decision, the Navy and Marine Corps were wary of a brand-new design which called for a helicopter so much larger than those flying. The memory of the "Deuce" lingered on. Also, the Army had just recovered from the cancellation of its AH-56A "Cheyenne" super-sophisticated attack helicopter, and the Marine Corps was anxious to avoid being tied to any program that could end the same way.

This time OSD agreed that no one aircraft could meet both sets of requirements. In May, it authorized the Army to continue to work on its helicopter, and the Navy to proceed with the development of a three-engined CH-53. On 1 November, OSD approved the program and a month later Congress gave its blessing. Only two aircraft were to be built until the design was proven acceptable and reliable. Then additional production could be begun. The aircraft would be the CH-53E, "Super Stallion."

The third engine was mounted to the rear and slightly above the one on the left side of the aircraft. To accept the power developed by these three General Electric T-64-415 engines, a new transmission, capable of accepting up to 11,340 horsepower, was installed. Likewise, the main lifting rotor was enlarged to 79 feet in diameter and to seven blades. The tail rotor was also

USMC Photo A355822

*An AH-1G Cobra of HMA-169 sits on the pad at an auxiliary Marine landing field near Camp Pendleton in January 1972. Attack squadrons (HMAs) equipped with Cobras now were part of the permanent Marine helicopter force.*

Photo courtesy of LtCol William R. Fails, USMC (Ret.)
*On board the USS* Iwo Jima *(LPH 2), the helicopters currently in the Marine inventory are ready for an amphibious assault. CH–46Ds are spotted along the starboard side, CH–53Ds at bow and stern, AH–1Js near the elevators, and UH–1Ns beside the island.*

made larger, and in an unusual design, canted to the left. In this position, in addition to providing antitorque control, the rotor produced some lift and allowed greater flexibility in loading cargo near the center of gravity of the aircraft. Earlier, specialized versions of the CH–53 had provisions for inflight refueling and for carrying additional fuel on the outside of the aircraft. These were adapted to the "Super Stallion."

Like all the CH–53 series, the new one could trace its ancestry directly to the "Deuce." When the first CH–53E made its maiden flight on 1 March 1974, it proved that it was a worthy descendant of the helicopter which had taken the first step toward fulfilling the dreams of the early Marine Corps planners of developing the capability for true vertical amphibious assaults.

## The First Concert

New Year's Day 1973 dawned cloudy in Washington, D.C., with a light drizzle falling. Shortly after daybreak, the sky cleared and the temperature would soar to 63 degrees. As most of the residents of the Nation's Capital slept away the revelry of the night before, in the same full block of staid but substantial brick buildings located in the southeast section of the city, there was a flurry of activity.

Drum Major Dennis Carroll and Master Gunnery Sergeant Charles P. Erwin were readying the United States Marine Band for yet another New Year's Day concert. All were in position in front of the Commandant's house at 1020. Lieutenant Colonel Dale L. Harpham, director of the band, who had been a Marine since July 1935, took his post. As the band began to play for the well-rehearsed "impromptu" concert, General Robert E. Cushman, Jr., Commandant of the Marine Corps, appeared at the door of his house "looking suitably surprised."

The contrast between spring-like weather and bitterly cold snow-laden skies was not the only difference between the New Year's Day concert of 1973 and the one 11 years before. Great changes had occurred throughout the Marine Corps between the two holidays, and nowhere had the changes been greater than in Marine helicopters. In 1962, as General Shoup had listened to the band, Marine helicopters consisted of a few rapidly aging "Deuces"—the remnant of the original dream of massive vertical amphibious assaults—the ubiquitous but interim UH–34s, and a collection of the unusual OH–43s with their excellent visibility but notorious low speed. Helicopter carriers, then, were all makeshift conversions including the tiny *Thetis Bay*. The entire concept of a helicopter-supported air/ground team remained untested except in small-scale maneuvers and exercises. Combat experience in helicopters was confined to a handful of Korean War veterans. Helicopter pilots and crews were firmly entrenched at the bottom of the heirarchy of aviation prestige, regarded as second-class citizens by their high-flying fixed-wing brethren.

As General Cushman listened to the concert, he knew that all Marine helicopters were jet powered and shortly would be joined by the 16-ton lift capability of the CH–53E. Helicopter carriers were all keel-up LPHs, and the vastly improved LHA soon would be in service. Amphibious vertical assault doctrine and tactics had been tested and proven repeatedly in fullscale maneuvers, international crises, and shooting war. The Marine Corps had a wealth of pilots and crews hardened by combat experience in Vietnam, where the "second-class syndrome" had been exploded once and for all.

For all Marines, and indeed for all Americans, there was a final and even more important difference between the two days: This was the first New Year's Day Concert since 1962 when Marines, including helicopters and their crews, were not actively fighting a war. For Marines and their helicopters, it had been a long 11 years.

# NOTES

Note: Unless otherwise indicated, all material is located in the Support Branch, History and Museums Division, Headquarters, USMC, Washington, D.C.

## CHAPTER I

### The Last Concert

#### New Year's Day 1962

1. USMC Band Log, dtd 1Jan62 (HistFile, USMC Band. Washington, D. C.).
2. *Ibid.*

#### Marine Helicopters around the World

3. CMC, ltr to Dist List, dtd 18Jun62, Subj: Marine Aviation Status Board Photograph as of 31Dec61, encl (1); Ser 08B1762, hereafter cited as *Aviation Status Board Photograph*, dtd......
4. *Naval Aviation News*, Aug65, p. 7.
5. LtCol Eugene W. Rawlins, *Marines and Helicopters, 1946–1962* (Washington: History and Museums Division, Headquarters, U.S. Marine Corps, 1977), hereafter cited as Rawlins, *Marines and Helicopters.*
6. Department of Defense Directive 4505.6 dtd 6Jul 62, Subj: Designation, Redesignation and Naming of Military Aircraft.

#### Helicopters are Different

7. Transcript provided and permission to reprint granted by "ABC Evening News with Howard K. Smith and Harry Reasoner."
8. LtCol Alvah J. Kettering, Intvw by HistBr, HQMC, dtd 12Dec74 (Oral Hist Coll, Hist&MusDiv, HQMC).
9. BGen Jay W. Hubbard, ltr to HistBr, HQMC, dtd 16Jan73.
10. LtCol David A. Spurlock, Intvw by HistBr, HQMC, dtd 24Jan64 (Oral HistColl, Hist&MusDiv, HQMC).
11. MajGen Marion E. Carl, Intvw by HistBr, HQMC, dtd 1May73, (Oral HistColl, Hist&MusDiv, HQMC).
12. Chronological List of Qualified Helicopter Pilots, p. 1.
13. BuAir memo to CNO, dtd 3Sep52, Subj: Model HRS–1 Helicopter JATO Installation, Investigation of; Recommendations Concerning. (Ser 016983).
14. Subject accident report at Naval Safety Center, Norfolk, Va.
15. Chief, BuAir ltr to CNO, dtd 26Aug52, Subj: Model HRS–1 Helicopter, JATP installation, Investigation of; Recommendations Concerning, 1st Endor. (No serial).
16. BuAir, memo to CNO, dtd 3Sep52, *op. cit.*

#### The "Huss"

17. *Aviation Status Board Photograph*, dtd 31Dec61.
18. Sikorsky Aircraft, *Helicopter History: U. S. Marine Corps. . . Sikorsky Aircraft, 1967.* (Sikorsky Aircraft, Stratford, Connecticut), p. 3, hereafter cited as *Sikorsky History, 1967.*
19. CMC ltr to CNO, dtd 1Apr55, Subj: Marine Corps requirements for utility aircraft. (S&C, MCDEC, Quantico, Va.).
20. Rawlins, *Marines and Helicopters*, p. 79.
21. Commander, Naval Air Systems Command, Standard Aircraft Characteristics, Navy Model, UH–34D Aircraft, dtd 1 July 67 (Ser NAVAIR 00–110AH34–1), hereafter *Standard Aircraft Characteristics, UH–34D*; *Aviation Status Board Photograph*, dtd 28Feb62.
22. Rawlins, *Marines and Helicopters*, pp. 70–72.
23. *Standard Aircraft Characteristics, UH–34D*, p. 6.
24. *Sikorsky History, 1967*, p. 3.
25. *Standard Aircraft Characteristics, UH–34D*, p. 4.
26. *Sikorsky History, 1967.*
27. *Standard Aircraft Characteristics, UH–34D.*
28. *Naval Aviation News*, Apr61, p. 53.
29. Major Herbert A. Nelson, "Bigger Payloads for the HUS," *Naval Aviation News*, Apr61, p. 52.
30. CNO ltr to Chief, BUWEPS, dtd 28Aug62, Subj: Reimbursement for HUS–1 Helicopters delivered for the Military Assistance Program in Laos, p. 1.
31. *Aviation Status Board Photographs*, dtd 30Jun62, 21Jul62, and 31Aug62.
32. *Marine Corps Gazette*, Vol 41, No. 9 (Sep57), p. 15.
33. DirAvn ltr to FDMC, dtd 1Sep59, Subj: Projected expenditure rates for HUS program, FY 60 and 61. (Ser 008C24359).

#### The HOK

34. Chares H. Kaman, "Design Considerations in the Kaman Servo-controlled intermeshing-rotor helicopter" (Address delivered before the New England Region, the American Helicopter Society, Windsor Locks, Conn. 9Feb53), p. 2, hereafter Kaman, "Design Considerations."
35. BuAir, Standard Aircraft Characteristics, HOK–1, 1Mar52, hereafter cited as *Standard Aircraft Characteristics, HOK–1.*
36. NavAirSysCom, Standard Aircraft Characteristics, Navy Model CH46A Aircraft, dtd 1Jul67. (Ser NAVAIR 00–110AH46–1).
37. LtCol David A. Spurlock USMC, Intvw by HistBr, HQMC, dtd 14Jan74 (Oral HistColl, Hist&MusDiv, HQMC).
38. Mr. E. J. Polaski, Assistant Supervisor, Kaman Service Engineering Section. "Intermeshing Rotor System—What it is—How it works," *Kaman Performance*, Nov/Dec 61, p. 7.

39. Board of Inspection and Survey rpt to SecNav, dtd 30Jun58, Subj: Contracts No's 51-645 and 54-317 Service Acceptance Trials of Model HOK-1 Aircraft, final report of (Ser 011P45).
40. *Ibid*, p. 4.
41. *Standard Aircraft Characteristics, HOK-1.*
42. DirAvn memo to AC/S (G-2, G-3, and G-4), dtd 27Mar59, Subj: Future Programming of Reconnaissance Aircraft. (Ser 08B8259)
43. *Ibid.* p. 2.
44. *Marine Corps Gazette*, Vol. 41, No. 1, (Jan57), p. 7; and Vol. 43, No. 8 (Aug58), p. 2.
45. *Aviation Status Board Photograph*, dtd 31Dec61.
46. *Aviation Status Board Photographs*, dtd 30Apr, 31May, and 30June65.

### The Deuce

47. BGen Edward C. Dyer, USMC (Ret.) Transcript of Interview by Oral History Unit, HQMC, dtd 19Aug68 (Oral HistColl, Hist&MusDiv, HQMC), p. 198, hereafter *Dyer Transcript.*
48. *Ibid.*
49. CMC ltr to DCNO (Ops), dtd 24Mar47, Subj: Employment of helicopters in amphibious warfare (Ser 003C7347 S&C MCDEC, Quantico, Va.).
50. Igor Sikorsky, "Military Future of the Helicopter," *Marine Corps Gazette*, Vol. 33. No. 8 (Aug49), p. 10, hereafter, Sikorsky, "Military Future of the Helicopter."
51. Carol Demand and Heiner Emde, *Conquerors of the Air: The Evolution of Aircraft 1903-1945* (Lausanna Edita S. A., 1963), p. 124-127.
52. CNO ltr to Commander Amphibious Forces, US Pacific Fleet, dtd 9Apr52, Subj: Amphibious Material New Development Program Guide, as cited in Rawlins, *Marines and Helicopters*, p. 46.
53. *Army, Navy, Air Force Journal*, 23Jan54, p. 11.
54. Rawlins, *Marines and Helicopters*, pp. 66-68.
55. Bureau of Aeronautics, Standard Aircraft Characteristics: HR2S-1, dtd 30Aug58.
56. *Army, Navy, Air Force Journal*, 23Jan54, p. 11.
57. Rawlins, *Marines and Helicopters*, pp. 70-72.
58. 1st Lt Roy L. Anderson, "The Marine Corps and the Helicopter," *Marine Corps Gazette*, Vol. 33, No. 8 (Aug49), p. 13.
59. *Marine Corps Gazette*, vol 41, no. 6, (Jun57), p. 16.
60. Rawlins, *Marines and Helicopters*, p. 79.
61. *Sikorsky History, 1967*, p. 3; *Marine Corps Gazette*, Vol. 41, No. 1 (Jan57), p. 28 and Vol. 44, No. 10 (Oct60), p. 25.
62. *Aviation Status Board Photograph*, dtd 31Dec61.
63. Rawlins, *Marines and Helicopters*, p. 79.

### Last of a Breed

64. *Sikorsky History, 1967*, p. 2; Bureau of Aeronautics, Standard Aircraft Characteristics: HRS-3, dtd 1Jun54.
65. LtCol David A. Spurlock, USMC, Interview by HistBr, HQMC, dtd 22Jan74, (Oral HistColl, Hist&MusDiv, HQMC), hereafter *Spurlock Interview.*
66. *Dyer Transcript*, p. 220.
67. Charles H. Kaman, "Design Considerations," p. 5.
68. *Aviation Status Board Photograph*, dtd 31Dec61.

### The White Tops

69. *Marine Corps Gazette*, Vol. 52, No. 1 (Jan68), p. 28.
70. CMC ltr to CO HMX-1, dtd 29Nov57, cited in CO, HMX-1 ltr to CMC, dtd 16Dec60, Subj: Presidential Mission (Ser 01A35160).
71. Administrative Aide to SecNav memo to Chief, BuWeps, dtd 31Jul61, Subj: Programs for providing increased safety in Presidential Mission Helicopters, 1st Endorsement of BuWeps, ltr to SecNav, dtd 27Jun61.

### An Extended Range

72. As cited in Rawlins, *Marines and Helicopters*, p. 59.
73. Igor Sikorsky, "Military Future of the Helicopter."
74. *Marine Corps Gazette*, Vol. 40, No. 5 (May56), p. 23.
75. All American Engineering Co. ltr to Marine Corps Development Center, dtd Apr59; Subj: Automatic pick-up systems (J. C. Breckinridge Library, MCS, Quantico, Va.).
76. MGen Norman J. Anderson, USMC (Ret) ltr to Director, Hist&MusDiv, dtd 26Jul76, in Marines and Helicopters, Pt. II, Comment File, hereafter cited as *Anderson Comments.*

### The Conversion

77. USN photo No. 694642 dtd 24Sep56 (ADCNO (AW) Code Op 05d, Washington, D.C.).
78. CMC memo to CNO, dtd 16Jun58, Subj: Use of CVE Aircraft Carriers as interim LPHs to support the Vertical Amphibious Assault (Ser 04D16458m MCDEC, Quantico, Va.).
79. *Ibid.*
80. *Dictionary of American Naval Fighting Ships.*

### Soldier Mechanics of the Sea

81. As cited in *A Chronology of the United States Marine Corps* (Washington: Historical Division, HQMC, 1971) III, p. 39.
82. *U.S. Naval Institute Proceedings*, Vol. 90, No. 6 (Jun64), p. 153.
83. CO, USS *Boxer* ltr to CNO (no date), Subj: Aviation Historical Summary, OPNAV Form 5720-2 for period 1Oct58 through 31Dec58; and same form for period 1Jan60 through 31Mar60 (ADCNO (AW) Code OP 05D, Washington, D.C.).
84. DirAvn memo to AC/S (G-1), dtd 29Jul60, Subj: Additional permanent personnel for the USS *Boxer*, LPH-4 (Ser 08B20160, S&C files, HQMC, Washington, D.C.).
85. *Marine Corps Gazette*, Vol. 44, No. 2 (Feb60), p 1.
86. Policy Analysis Division ltr to Dist. List, dtd 28Jun60, Subj: Periodic Information (Ser 007A17560).
87. *Marine Corps Gazette*, Vol 44, No. 2 (Feb60).

### Keel-Up LPH

88. *Marine Corps Gazette*, Vol 44, No. 8 (Aug 60), p. 24.
89. Unless otherwise noted, all information on the *Iwo Jima* is taken from CO, USS *Iwo Jima* ltr to CNO, dtd 1Jan62, Subj: Historical Report, 26Aug61 through 31Dec61; and Cdr L. W. Garrison, USN, "USS *Iwo Jima*. LPH-2," *US Naval Institute Proceedings*, Vol. 89, No. 11 (Nov63), p. 162.
90. Garrison, *op cit*, p. 101.

# NOTES

## CHAPTER 2

### Maneuvers and Deployments

#### Possible Deployment

1. Gen Wallace M. Greene, Jr., USMC (Ret) ltr to History & Museums Div, HQMC, dtd 5Dec73.
2. SSgt Charles Kester, "The Twenty Third Commandant", *Leatherneck*, Vol. 47, No. 1(Jan 62), pp. 24, 27.
3. *Ibid.* p. 27.
4. *Ibid.* p. 28.
5. *Ibid.* p. 29.
6. Gen Wallace M. Greene, Jr., USMC (Ret) ltr to History&Museums Div, HQMC, dtd 5 Dec 73.
7. *Ibid.*

#### SHUFLY

8. MCCC Items of Significant Interest, dtd 3Feb62.
9. *Spurlock Interview.*
10. Capt. Robert H. Whitlow, *U.S. Marines in Vietnam, 1954-1964: The Advisory and Combat Assistance Era* (Washington: Hist&MusDiv, HQMC, 1977), hereafter cited as Whitlow, *Advisory Era.*
11. MCCC Items of Significant Interest, dtd 28Feb62.
12. *Ibid.*, dtd 14Mar62.
13. *Ibid.*, dtd 9Mar62.
14. *Ibid.*, dtd 19Mar62.
15. MGen John P. Condon, Transcript of Interview by Hist Br, HQMC, dtd 3Dec70 (Oral HistColl, Hist&MusDiv, HQMC), p. 126.
16. BGen Ormond R. Simpson, "Expeditionary Medal: 1962 Thailand," *Marine Corps Gazette*, Vol. 49, No. 11 (Nov 65), p. 89.
17. MCCC Items of Significant Interest, dtd 4Apr62.
18. LtCol Archie J. Clapp, "Launch the Runways," *Marine Corps Gazette*, Vol. 42, No. 4 (Apr 58), p. 20.
19. LtCol James P. Kizer Intvw by Hist&MusDiv, HQMC dtd 20Feb74 (Oral HistColl, Hist&MusDiv, HQMC), hereafter *Kizer Interview.*
20. Unless otherwise noted, information on the establishment of Operation SHUFLY is taken from: LtCol Archie J. Clapp, "Shu-Fly Diary," *U.S. Naval Institute Proceedings*, Vol. 89, No. 10 (Oct63), p. 42, hereafter Clapp, "Shu-Fly Diary," HMM-362 Cruise Book for WestPac tour 1 Aug 62-1 Aug 63, provided through the courtesy of Maj William C. Cowperthwait; and *Kizer Interview.*
21. *Kizer Interview.*
22. *Ibid.*
23. *Ibid.*
24. USMC Service Information Release, No. REA 63-63, dtd 26Mar63.
25. MCCC Items of Significant Interest, dtd 29 and 30Mar62.
26. USMC FMFM 3-3, *Helicopter Operations*, p. 45.
27. Clapp, "Shu-Fly Diary," p. 44.
28. *Ibid.*, p. 45.
29. *Ibid.*, p. 52.
30. *Ibid.*
31. *Ibid.*
32. *Ibid.*, p. 53.
33. DirAvn memo to DCS (Plans), dtd 1Mar62, Subj: Aviation Program Document (Ser 08A5962).
34. Whitlow, *Advisory Era*, pp. 58-59.
35. CMC msg to CGFMFPac and CGAirFMFPac, dtd 7May-62.
36. MCCC Items of Significant Interest, dtd 3Jun62.

#### The 1962 Missile Crisis

37. II MEF Command Diary 1Oct-15Dec62, p. 1-3-B-2.
38. MCCC Items of Significant Interest, dtd 8Oct62.
39. *Marine Corps Gazette*, Vol. 49, No. 10 (Oct62), p. 3.
40. CTF 144 and ComPhibLant OpO 502-62, dtd 21Sept62.
41. *Dictionary of American Fighting Ships.*
42. *New York Times*, 23Oct62, p. 20.
43. MCCC Items of Significant Interest, dtd 23, 25, 26, 27 and 28Oct62.
44. HMM-361, Unit Subject File.
45. *Dictionary of American Fighting Ships.*
46. MCCC Items of Significant Interest, dtd Nov62.
47. *Ibid.*, dtd 2Dec62.
48. *Ibid.*, dtd 1Dec62.
49. *Ibid.*, dtd 13Dec62.
50. Marine Corps General Officers' Symposium, dtd 26Jul 63, Tab L, p. 5. (Ser 007A20763).

#### STEEL PIKE I

51. LtGen James P. Berkeley, USMC (Ret), Transcript of Intvw by HistBr, HQMC, dtd 1Dec62 (Oral HistColl, Hist&MusDiv, HQMC), p. 459.
52. *Ibid.*, p. 460.
53. Text of Post-exercise briefing by FMFLant Staff to SecNav and others, dtd 8Dec64 (Subj file, Reference Section, Hist&MusDiv, HQMC), p. 1.
54. *Ibid.*, p. 4.
55. *Ibid.*, p. 7 and MCCC items of Significant Interest, dtd 20 and 24Jul64.
56. LtCol James B. Soper, USMC (Special Observer for the Commandant), "Observations: STEEL PIKE and SILVER LANCE," *U.S. Naval Institute Proceedings*, Vol. 91, No. 11 (Nov 65), p. 45, hereafter Soper, "Observations."
57. AC/S (G-3) memo to CMC, dtd 4Nov64, Subj: Trip Report.
58. FMFLant briefing, dtd 8Dec64, in *Ibid.*
59. MCCC Items of Significant Interest, dtd 27Oct64.
60. CTF 187 msg to CincLant, dtd 28Oct64.
61. MCCC Items of Significant Interest, dtd 28Nov64.
62. DC/SA memo to AC/S (G-3), dtd 30Oct64, Subj: Aviation Activities—STEEL PIKE.
63. Soper, "Observations," p. 56.

#### Dominican Republic

64. Unless otherwise noted, material on the Dominican Republic crisis of 1965 is taken from: Maj Jack K. Ringler, and Henry I. Shaw Jr., "U.S. Marine Corps Operations in the Dominican Republic, April-June 1965" (HistDiv, HQMC, 1970).
65. Col Frederick M. Klepsattel, Intvw by HistDiv, HQMC, dtd 6Mar74 (Oral HistColl, Hist&MusDiv, HQMC).
66. GySgt Paul A. Berger, "Peace Force on the Line," *Leatherneck*, Vol. 49, No. 7 (Aug65), p. 18.
67. Maj Thomas P. McBrien, Intvw by HistDiv, HQMC, dtd 7Mar74 (Oral HistColl, Hist&MusDiv, HQMC).

## CHAPTER 3

## Introduction of the Turbines

### More Lift Per Aircraft

1. General Officer Symposium, 1963, Tab A, p. 24.

### The Turbine Engines

2. ComNavAirSysCom, Standard Aircraft Characteristics, Navy Model, CH-53A Aircraft, dtd 1Jul67.
3. Capt David A. Spurlock (USMC), Naval Air Test Command, "The Practical Problems of Gas Turbine Operation in Helicopters," Transcript, dtd 5May61, hereafter Spurlock, "Practical Problems."
4. David Richardson, "What Has the Free Turbine Done for the Helicopter," Transcript, dtd 5May61.
5. *Ibid.*
6. Spurlock, "Practical Problems."

### The "Huey"

7. DivAvn ltr to Dist. List, dtd 18Jan62. Subj: Newsletter (Ser. 008A1862/A).
8. CMC ltr to CMCLFDC, dtd 23Aug60, Subj: Assault Support Helicopter program, policy concerning (Ser. 08A18360).
9. CMC ltr to CMCLFDA, MCS, dtd 4Feb61, Subj: Assault Support Helicopter; background concerning (Ser. 08A-35460 MCDEC, S&C files, Quantico, Va.).
10. CNO ltr to CBuWeps, dtd 5Sep, 1961, Subj: Assault Support Helicopter (ASH) Program, PAMN funds; request for (Ser. 06123P50).
11. *Ibid.*
12. *Ibid.*
13. *Ibid.*
14. *Ibid.*
15. *Ibid.*
16. *Ibid.*
17. Chronology of Key Dates for Development of UH-1E (Subject file ADCNO-AW, OP 05-D).
18. CNO ltr to Chief, BuAir, dtd 26Oct50, Subj: Provisions for canvas litters in helicopters (Ser 212P551).
19. DC/S (Air) memo to CFS, dtd 26Dec63, Subj: OH5A Information.
20. All data from NASC, Standard Aircraft Characteristics, Navy Model UH-1E Aircraft, dtd 1Jul67.
21. *Spurlock Interview.*
22. *Ibid.*
23. (Ser. 008B29862).
24. BuWeps ltr to Dist. List, dtd 15Oct62, Subj: Program Evaluation Meeting of 9Oct62 (NavAirSysCom Hist).
25. Bell Helicopter News Release, dtd 30Jan63.
26. BuWeps ltr to Dist. List, dtd 12Jul63, Subj: Program Evaluation Meeting of 9Jul63 (NavAirSysCom Hist).
27. BuWeps ltr to Dist. List, dtd 17Dec63, Subj: Plans and Programs Brief for the week ending 17Dec63, (NavAirSysCom Hist).
28. Bell Helicopter News Release, dtd 21Feb64.
29. BuWeps ltr to Dist. List, dtd 25Feb64, Subj: Plans and Programs Brief for week ending 25Feb64, p. 3 (NavAirSysCom Hist).
30. Bell Helicopter News Release, dtd 21Feb64.

### Replacement for the HUS

31. CMC ltr to CNO, dtd 9Jan58, Subj: Future procurement of a transport version of the HSS-2 (Ser. 008A32657).
32. *Ibid.*
33. Asst Chief for Program Management, BuWeps, ltr to Dist. List, dtd 8Feb62, Subj: CH-46A Program Summary, Encl (1), p. B-1, hereafter cited as *CH-46 Program Summary.*
34. HSS-2 Subject File, Contract No. 58-208C of 24Dec58, w/periodic updates.
35. *CH-46 Program Summary.*
36. *Ibid.*
37. DirMCLFDC ltr to CMC, dtd 4Aug59, Subj: HR3S Program (Ser 04158, MCDEC S&C, Quantico, Va.).
38. *Ibid.*, p. 2.
39. *CH-46 Program Summary*, p. B-2.
40. *Ibid.*
41. DirAvn memo to C/S, dtd 14Dec59, Subj: Objectives for 1960 (Ser. 08A34259).
42. DirAvn memo to Dist. List, dtd 29Dec59, Subj: Information Concerning the HR3S-1 (Ser. 08A35659).
43. *Ibid.*, p. 2.
44. CNO, ltr to Dist. List, dtd 7Mar60, Subj: Development Characteristic No. AO 1750-2, VTOL Assault Transport Helicopter, promulgation of, Encl (1), pp. II, 1, 2, and 3, (Ser. 04P70).
45. ComNavAirSysCom, Standard Aircraft Characteristics, Navy Model SH-3A Aircraft, dtd 1Jul67.
46. Rawlins, *Marines and Helicopters*, p. 82. See also: BuWeps ltr to CNO (undated *circa* Aug60), Subj: Model HR3S-1/107 M Programs, status report.
47. DirAvn memo to Dist List, dtd 9Jul59, Subj: Vertol Model 107A presentation.
48. DirMCLFDC ltr to CMC, dtd 8Apr60, Subj: Procurement of the YHC-1A helicopters for evaluation; recommendations for.
49. LtCol Victor A. Armstrong ltr to CO MCAS Quantico, dtd 31Mar60, Subj: YHC-1A, comments on.
50. Maj Frederick M. Klepsattel memo, dtd Mar60, Subj: Comments concerning evaluation flight in Vertol YHC-1A helicopter.
51. DirMCLFDC ltr, dtd 8Apr60.
52. *Ibid.*, p. 2.
53. *Ibid.*, First Endorsement, dtd 18Apr60.
54. *CH-46 Program Summary*, p. B-2.
55. *Ibid.*
56. DirMCLFDC ltr to CMC, dtd 1Jul60, Subj: Comparison of the Vertol 107-M with HR3S (Ser. 046158-60, MCDEC S&C, Quantico, Va.).
57. *CH-46 Program Summary.*
58. *Ibid.*
59. Ch BuWeps ltr to CMC, *circa* Aug60, *op. cit.*
60. CMC ltr to CMCLFDA, dtd 11Oct60, Subj: Review of proposed helicopter development characteristic, AO 17501-3, Assault Transport Helicopter (Medium) (S&C, HQMC).
61. VAdm Paul D. Stroop, USN (Ret.) ltr to Director, Hist and MusDiv, dtd 25Jun76, in Marines and Helicopters, Pt. II, Comment File hereafter cited as *Stroop Comments.*

# NOTES

62. ChBuWeps ltr to SecNav, dtd 17Feb61, Subj: Acceleration of Procurement of FY62 Lot of HRX (L), Request for (Ser 0817); ASecNavMat memo for SecNav, dtd 17Feb61, Subj: Helicopters for the Marine Corps (HRX).
63. Memo for Files, dtd 20Feb61, signed by VAdm Paul D. Stroop, Subj: HRX Competition, notification of results of.
64. ASecNavMat memo for SecNav dtd 17Feb61, Subj: Helicopters for the Marine Corps (HRX).
65. *Stroop Comments.*
66. ChBuWeps ltr to SecNav, dtd 17Feb61, Subj: Acceleration of Procurement of FY 62 Lot of HRX (L), Request for (Ser 0817).
67. White House ltr of 2Feb61, as cited in *Ibid.*
68. *Stroop Comments.*

## The CH-46

69. All data from the CH-46A Standard Characteristics.
70. *CH-46 Program Summary*, p. C2.
71. Vertol Division Public Relations Release, dtd 16Oct62, no. VN-200 (NavAirSysCom Hist).
72. CNO notice to Dist. List, dtd Mar62 OpNavNotice 03110 (Ser 02503P50) (ADCNO-AW, OP-05D). Washington, D.C.).
73. LtCol Perry P. McRoberts memo for the record, dtd Feb63, file AAP-3.
74. *Ibid.*
75. *Ibid.*
76. DirAvn memo to DCS (Plans), dtd 1Mar62, Subj: Aviation Program Document (Ser. 08A5962).
77. *CH-46 Program Summary*, p. F-1.
78. OpNavNotice, dtd Mar62.
79. BuWeps ltr to Dist. List, dtd 14Jan63, No subject (NavAirSysCom Hist).
80. *Ch-46 Program Summary*, p. A 3.
81. BuWeps ltr to Dist List, 20Jan64, Subj: Program Evaluation Meetings of 14Jan64 (NavAirSysCom Hist, Washington, D.C.).
82. *Ibid.*
83. BuWeps ltr to Dist. List, dtd 1Sep64, Subj: Plans and Program Brief for Week Ending 1Sep64 (NavAirSysCom Hist.).
84. Fact Sheet for CMC's visit to the Boeing Company, Seattle, Washington, dtd 7May65. (Unprocessed "General McCutcheon's CH-46 Historical Data File").
85. *Marine Corps Gazette*, Vol. 47, No. 6, (Jun63), p. 2.

## The VH-3A and CH-3

86. Admin Aide to SecNav memo to Chief of BuWeps, dtd 31Jul62, Subj: Program for Providing Increased Safety in Presidential Mission Helicopters (NavAirSysCom Hist).
87. BuWeps ltr to DistList of 11Dec62, Subj: Plans and Programs Brief for Week ending 11Dec62 (NavAirSysCom Hist).

## The VTOLs

88. LtCdr James R. Williford, "The Slumbering V/STOL Program," *U.S. Naval Institute Proceedings*, Vol. 90, No. 3 (Mar64), pp. 76–79.
89. C/S USMC ltr to VCNO, dtd 14Aug62, Subj: Marine Heavy Helicopter Program (HHX), comments concerning (Ser. 08B22562), Encl (1).
90. DivAvn memo to Dist. List, dtd 25Nov59, Subj: VTOL Assault Transport Program, review of (Ser. 0832859).
91. *Ibid.*
92. *Ibid.*
93. *Ibid.*, p. 2.
94. C/S ltr to VCNO, dtd 14Aug62, p. 2, Encl (1).
95. "VTOL Transitions," *Naval Aviation News*, Mar65, p. 24.
96. "Bell Rolls out the X-22A V/STOL Aircraft," *Naval Aviation News*, Jun65, p. 29.
97. *Ibid.*
98. C/S ltr to VCNO, dtd 14Aug62.
99. BuWeps memo for Files, dtd 16Nov62, Subj: HH (X) Assault Transport Helicopter Competition, Evaluation and Recommendation, Encl. (2), p. 2, hereafter cited as *CH-53A Program History.*

## The CH-53

100. DirAvn ltr to Dist. List, dtd 18Jan62, Subj: News Letter (Ser. 008A1862/A).
101. *CH-53 Program History.*
102. CMC ltr to CNO, dtd 3Jul51, Subj: Flying Crane Helicopter, Marine Corps Requirement for (Ser. 007D18051).
103. Sikorsky Aircraft, Subject File No. SP 138 (ADCNO-AW, OP-05D).
104. DirMCLFDC ltr to CMC, dtd 8Jun59, Subj: Heavy Lift Helicopter, requirements for (Ser. 046126-59).
105. Background material for funding difficulties was by: Maj William C. Cowperthwait (USMC); "The Impact of New Contract Policy Changes, and Certain External Factors on Aircraft Procurement in the Department of the Navy." (Washington, D.C.: Unpublished thesis submitted to the School of Government and Business Administration of the George Washington University, May71).
106. BuWeps memo, dtd 10Oct62, Subj: CH-53A Program with Sikorsky Aircraft, incremental funding, comments on, Encl (1), p. 3 (Code CW-5 to CW).
107. *Ibid.*
108. CS ltr to VCNO, dtd 14Apr62.
109. *Ibid.*, p. 8.
110. DOD News Release No. 1565-62, dtd 26Sep62.
111. DC/S (Air) ltr to FisDirMC, dtd 19Sep62, Subj: NavCompt mark up of FY64 Budget (Ser. 08A26262).
112. *Ibid.*
113. BuWeps memo, dtd 10Oct62.
114. All data from: NavAirSysCom, Standard Aircraft Characteristics, Navy Model CH-53A Aircraft, dtd 1Jul67.
115. DC/S (Air) memo to CS dtd 25Jul63, Subj: Heavy Helicopters (Ser. 008A206613), Encl. (1).
116. BuWeps memos to Dist. List, dtd 30Aug63 and 10Sep63, Subj: Program Evaluation Meeting of 27Aug and 10Sep, (NavAirSysCom Hist).
117. Weapons System Development Master Plan (WSDMP) for CH-53A, Second Revision, for period 1Jul63–31Dec63, Preface, p. 1.
118. Unless otherwise cited, all material from: "CH-53A Program History, Sikorsky Aircraft" provided through the

courtesy of Mr. Gary Rast and Mr. Kenneth J. Kelly of Sikorsky Aircraft.
119. Memo for the record, dtd Mar62, subject file, CH-53A.
120. *Naval Aviation News*, April66, p. 9.
121. Briefing information folder for Admiral Townsend, dtd 24Feb67, Subj: CH-53A.
122. OpNavNotice 03110, dtd 29Sep64, Subj: CH-53A Weapons System, statement of planned introduction (Ser. 02542P50).
123. NavAirSysCom ltr to Dist. List, dtd 14Sep66, Plans, Programs and Comptroller Group "Howgozit" report of week ending 14Sep.

## CHAPTER 4

## The Men Who Flew Helicopters

### Who Wants to Fly Helicopters?

1. "Message Center," *Marine Corps Gazette*, Vol. 39, No. 10 (Oct55), p. 2.
2. *Dyer Transcript*, p. 209.
3. *Ibid.*, p. 210.
4. CMC ltr to Dist. List, dtd 9Jun52, Subj: Helicopters conference, report of (Ser. 08B13552).
5. Summary of the General Officers' Conference at HQMC, 11–13Jul55, dtd 12Jul55 (Ser. 0007D19355).
6. *Ibid.*, p. 10.

### Sources of Marine Aviators

7. Col H. M. Hart memo, dtd 16Jun74, Subj: Aviation Officer Procurement.
8. *Ibid.*
9. ChNaAiAdTrnCom, PAO release #37-68, dtd 21Mar68, Subj: History of Naval and Marine Aviation Cadet Programs.
10. CNO ltr to CMC, dtd 26Dec57, Subj: Marine Corps Procurement of MarCads (Ser 3346P50); also see file VE. N121729, RefSec, Hist&MusDiv, HQMC.
11. *Ibid.*
12. *Ibid.*
13. NAAS Chase Field, Texas, *Beehive*, Vol. VII, No. 28 (26 Apr 61), p. 1.
14. MCAS Cherry Point *Windsock*, 10Feb61, p. 3.
15. DivAir memo, dtd 20May58, Subj: Establishment of Marine Aviation Program.
16. DirAvn memo to Dist. List, dtd 7Nov60, Subj: Mid Range Aviators, procurement of.
17. *Ibid.*
18. General Officers' Symposium, FY 63.
19. *Ibid.*
20. *Ibid.*
21. CMC ltr to CMS, dtd 3Jul63, Encl (1).
22. General Officers' Symposium, FY63.
23. CNAATC PAO release, dtd 21Mar68.

### Selection of Helicopter Pilots in Training

24. Maj W. H. Rodenberger, "Pilot Who's Behind the Aircraft Flies Beyond his Capabilities," *Marine Corps Gazette*, Vol. 49, No. 10 (Oct62), p. 60.
25. *Ibid.*
26. *Ibid.*
27. *Ibid.*
28. *Ibid.*
29. MajGen Paige personal ltr to Gen Pate, dtd 24Jan56 (MCDEC S&C, Quantico, Va.).
30. *Ibid.*
31. *Ibid.*, p. 2.
32. DirAvn ltr to Dist. List, dtd 18Jan62, Subj: News Letter (Ser. 008A1862), p. 2.
33. *Ibid.*
34. DCSA ltr to Dist. List, dtd 29Oct62, Subj: News Letter (Ser 008B29862).
35. Unless otherwise noted, all material on warrant officer program taken from: DCSA Point Paper: Warrant Officer Program for Helicopters, dtd 13Dec68 (HQMC Code AAZ), hereafter *DCSA Point Paper*.
36. BGen Paige ltr to Gen Pate, dtd 24Jan56 (MCDEC S&C, Quantico, Va.).
37. DivAvn Study #2-60, as cited in *DCSA Point Paper*.
38. DCSA ltr to Dist. List, dtd 18Jan62, p. 5.
39. *Ibid.*
40. MCAS Cherry Point *Windsock*, 6Oct61, p. 3.
41. DCSA ltr to Dist. List, dtd 18Jan62.
42. *Ibid.*
43. *DCSA Point Paper*.
44. *Naval Aviation News*, June 64, p. 2.
45. *Ibid.*
46. *Ibid.*
47. *Ibid.*
48. BGen Samuel R. Shaw, Transcript of Intrvw by Oral Hist Unit, Hist&MusDiv, dtd 21Jan70 (Oral Hist Coll, Hist&MusDiv, HQMC), p. 345.
49. *Ibid.*
50. CMC memo to SecNav, dtd 8Jul66, Subj: Warrant Officer Helo Pilot Program, as cited in *DCSA Point Paper*, p. 2.
51. *Ibid.*

### Transitions

52. *Marine Corps Gazette*, Vol. 49, No. 10 (Oct62), p. 3.
53. *Ibid.*
54. *Ibid.*
55. *Ibid.*
56. DCSA ltr to Dist. List, dtd 29Oct62, Subj: Newsletter (Ser 008B29862), p. 3.
57. *Ibid.*
58. *Ibid.*
59. *Ibid.*
60. DCSA ltr to DirPolAnaDiv, dtd 26Sep62, Subj: News-Letter (Ser. 008A26862).
61. *Ibid.*

### Training

62. Transcript of 16May62 (Personal papers of LtCol D. A. Spurlock, Washington, D.C.).
63. *Dyer Transcript*, p. 214.
64. *Ibid.*
65. Chronological Listing of Helicopter Pilots.
66. *Dyer Transcript*, p. 215.
67. CNO Avn Cir Ltr to All Ships, Stations and Units concerned with Naval Aircraft, dtd 11Jun48.
68. *Ibid.*
69. *Dyer Transcript*.
70. *Ibid.*
71. *Ibid.*, p. 2.
72. *Ibid.*
73. Chronological Listing of Helicopter Pilots.
74. HMX-1 ltr to CMC, dtd 27Sep52, Subj: Helicopter Flight Training, discontinuance of, request for (Ser. 011-52).

# NOTES

75. CMC ltr to HMX–1, dtd 15Nov52, Subj: Helicopter Pilot training at HMX–1 (Ser. 08B29552).
76. Unless otherwise noted, early history of HTU–1 is from "Historical Sketch of Helicopter Training Unit One, 1950–52," dtd 17Oct55 (AvHistU, DCNO A, Op 05D, Washington, D.C.).
77. *Naval Aviation News*, Feb51, p. 10.
78. All data from BuAir Standard Aircraft Characteristics, Model HTE–2, dtd 1Jun53.
79. All data from BuAir Standard Aircraft Characteristics, HTL–2, dtd 1Nov51,; HTL–7, dtd 15Sep59 and NavAirSysCom, Standard Aircraft Characteristics Navy Model TH–13N, dtd 1Jul67.
80. NAAS Ellyson News Release, dtd 20Feb69, No. 001169.
81. *Spurlock Interview*.
82. *Ibid*.
83. CNO ltr to CNATAC, dtd 25Sep63, Subj: NaTraCom Student Pipeline Distribution Proposal, approval of.
84. Marine Corps General Officers' Symposium, 1964, dtd 6Jul64 (Ser. 007F18864), p. 18 DCSA.
85. *Ibid*.

### Crew Training

86. CNO ltr to CMC, dtd 1 Nov 66, Subj: Talking Paper, forwarded by ends. to CMC 30Jan67 (Ser. 0040P34).
87. *Dyer Transcript*, p. 213.
88. *Ibid*.
89. "Fledging Whirlybirds," *Naval Aviation News*, Feb52, p. 1.
90. "Helicopter Mechanics School Graduates First Student," NAS Memphis *Bluejacket*, 25Apr58, p. 3.
91. *Ibid*.
92. Memo for the Record, dtd 1Dec65, Subj: Availability of Reciprocating Helicopter Mechanics (HQMC Code AAZ, Cameron 1965 file).
93. This description of crew chiefs and their work is based on: MSgt Jerome P. Sullivan, intvw by HistDiv. HQMC, dtd 9May74 (Oral HisColl, His&MusDiv, HQMC); quotations are from this interview.
94. HMM-263 Cruise Book, "Okinawa-Vietnam, 1965–1966," p. 36.

### Flight on Instruments

95. HU–2 ltr to CNO, dtd 17Apr50, Subj: Helicopter Instrument Flight Project, (Ser 297).
96. *Ibid*. End (2) notes, from BuAir, Op 05, dtd 8Jan51.
97. LtCol Archie J. Clapp, "Missing Link: All Weather Terminal Guidance for Helicopters," *Marine Corps Gazette*, Vol. 45, No. 12 (Dec61), pp. 3–34.
98. *Ibid*. p. 13.
99. *Ibid*. p. 32.
100. *Ibid*.
101. *Ibid*., p. 3.
102. CMCLFDA, ltr to CMC, dtd 6Oct61, Subj: Proposed Development Characteristic, Self-Contained Navigation System for Helicopters (Ser. 046327961, MCDEC S&C, Quantico, Va.).
103. Op–52 memo to Op 05, dtd 4Dec61, Subj: Proposed Development Characteristic AO 12501–2 (ser. 058P52).
104. *Ibid*., p. 2.
105. *Ibid*., Encl (1), p. 2.
106. *Ibid*., p. 3.
107. *Ibid*.
108. No. ltr to CNavMat, dtd 17Mar64, Subj: Specific Operational Requirement No. W 14–09, Assault Helicopter/VTOL All Weather Navigation System (Ser. 016P0).
109. NavAirSysCom memo from AIR 1042 to Air 01, dtd 8-Jun70, Subj: Review and Audit of IHAS, SNCS and MTAR programs (HQMC, Code AAW files).
110. *Ibid*. Hist. Encl., p. 1.

## CHAPTER 5

## Helicopters Shoot Back

### SHUFLY Ends

1. Senior Advisor, III Corps ltr to General Paul D. Harkins, dtd 30Jul62, as cited in Marine Corps General Officers' Symposium, 1963.
2. LtGen Keith B. McCutcheon, "Marine Aviation in Vietnam 1962–1970," *U.S. Naval Institute Proceedings*, Vol. 97, No. 819 (May71), p. 125, hereafter McCutcheon, "Marine Aviation in Vietnam."
3. Whitlow, *Advisory Era*, p. 83.
4. MCCC Items of Significant Interest, dtd 22Jul63.
5. *Ibid*., dtd 7Sep63, 20Sep63, 10ct63, 6Nov63, 22Jan64.
6. J. C. Sessler, "Marine Helicopter Operations at Da Nang, Republic of Vietnam," MCOAG, Center for Naval Analyses, Franklin Institute, Washington, D.C., p. A–9.
7. MCCC Items of Significant Interest, dtd 6Mar64, 24-Apr64, 9May64.
8. *Ibid*., dtd 10Jun64, 15Aug64.

### Land the Landing Force

9. MCCC items of Significant Interest, dtd 8Mar65.
10. *Ibid*., dtd 4May65.

### Armoring

11. CGMFPac msg to CMC, dtd 3Dec66.
12. CO, VMO–6 ltr to CMC, dtd 30Nov50, Subj: Battle damage received by helicopters, report of (Ser. 0478).
13. *Ibid*.
14. *Marine Corps Gazette*, Vol. 47, No. 1 (Jan63), p. 3.
15. DirMCLFDC ltr to Cord MCLFDA, dtd 26Jan60, Subj: Troop Test of Project 30–58–01 (Ser. 004624–60, MCDEC S&C, Quantico, Va.).
16. DirAvn memo to Dist Lts, dtd 7Nov60, Subj: Mid Range Program Objectives Relative to Armoring Helicopters (Ser. 08B29860).
17. *Ibid*.
18. MCOAG Study No. 1, "Characteristics of U.S. Marine Corps Helicopter Operation in the Mekong Delta," dtd 12Mar62, p. 20 (Ser 046A7163), hereafter *MCOAG Study No. 1*.
19. *Ibid*., p. 18.
20. *Ibid*.
21. *Marine Corps Gazette*, Vol. 54, No. 11 (Nov70), p. 61.
22. *Ibid*.
23. DCSA ltr to Dist List, dtd 29Oct62, Subj: Newsletter (Ser. 008B29862), p. 7.
24. *Ibid*.
25. CMC ltr to Dist. List, dtd 4Nov65, Subj: Provision of Armor for Helicopter Protection (Scr. 08C25365).
26. Advanced Research Projects Agency, R&D Field Unit ltr dtd 27Jan64, Subj: Trip Report to DaNang, Vietnam, by LtCol William R. Quinn, Encl (1), p. 7.
27. USMC ISO Release, MCS, Quantico, dtd 237–64, Subj: Assault Airlift.
28. CMC ltr, dtd 4Nov65, p. 2.
29. FMFPac msg, dtd 3Dec66.

### Helicopter Escorts

30. FMFM 3-3, *Helicopter Operations, op. cit.*, 12Jun63, p. 16.
31. *MCOAG Study No. 1*, p. 15.
32. *Ibid.*

### Early Studies of the LARA

33. CMC ltr to CNO, dtd 25Jul62, Subj: Assignment of T-28 Aircraft to Marine Observation Squadron Six (VMO-6) (Ser. 08B20562).
34. MCCC Items of Significant Interest, dtd 29Mar63.
35. CGFMFPac msg to CincPacFlt, dtd Apr63.
36. MCCC Items of Significant Interest, dtd 2May63.
37. *Ibid.*, dtd 5May63, 1Jun63.

### Arming the Transports

38. *Marine Corps Gazette*, Vol. 37, No. 7 (Jul53), p. 30.
39. Clapp, "Shu-Fly Diary," p. 52.
40. *MCOAG Study No. 1*, p. 16.
41. MCOAG Research Contribution, dtd 9May66, "Aspects of U.S. Marine Corps Helicopter Operations in South Vietnam—Late 1963," R. W. Randall, Jr (Center for Naval Analyses, the Franklin Institute, Washington, D.C.), p. 15.
42. Advanced Research Projects Agency report, dtd 27Jan64, p. 3.
43. MCCC Items of Significant Interest, dtd 16Feb63, 23Feb63.
44. *Ibid.*, dtd 16Mar63.
45. *Ibid.*, dtd 15May64.
46. Advanced Research Projects Agency report, dtd 27Jan64, p. 4.
47. MCCC Items of Significant Interest, dtd 20May64.

### Armed Helicopters

48. CMC ltr to selected CGs, dtd 29Apr49, Subj: Material for Special Lecturers during Organized Marine Corps Reserve—Ground—unit training, transmission of; Encl (1) p. 3 (Ser. 03C11249, MCDEC S&C, Quantico, Va.).
49. LtCol V. J. Croizat and Maj D. Riley ltr to CMC, dtd Jul57, Subj: Report on Temporary Duty performed as U.S. Marine Corps Observers with French Military Helicopter Units in Algeria during the period 29May to 27Jun, 1957, p. 70.
50. DivAvn ltr to Dist. List, dtd 11Mar59, Subj: Evaluation of Helicopter Armament Systems, Encl (1), p. 1 (Ser. 08B6859).
51. CNO (Air) memo to CNO, dtd 31Mar61, Subj: Status of Helicopter arming (Ser 0604P50).
52. DivAvn ltr to Dist. List, dtd 11Mar59, Subj: Evaluation of Helicopter Armament Systems, Encl (1), p. 1 (Ser. 08-B6859).
53. *Marine Corps Gazette*, Vol. 42, No. 4 (Apr58), p. 30.
54. Capt E. C. Riley (USA), "Air-propelled Artillery, a New Challenge," *Artillery Trends* (U.S. Army Artillery and Missile School, Instructional Aid No. 29, Feb64).

### Gunships for the Marines

55. Gen Greene ltr to Hist&MusDiv, dtd 5Dec73, Encl. (1), p. 2.
56. *Anderson Comments.*
57. Col Noah C. New, "Helicopter or Fixed Wing? Both!" *Marine Corps Gazette*, Vol. 55., No. 5 (May71), pp. 25-27.
58. Gen Greene, Marine Corps Position Regarding Armed Helicopters, dtd 6Feb64.
59. CMC ltr to All General Officers, dtd 10Mar64, Subj: Marine Corps Position re Armed Helicopters (Green Letter 4-64).

### Armed UH-34s

60. Advanced Research Project Agency report, dtd 27Jan64.
61. CMC "Talking Paper," circa Oct64, CMC File #11.
62. MCCC Items of Significant Interest, dtd 28Aug64.
63. CMC "Talking Paper" Oct64, CMC File #11, p. 2.
64. LtGen Victor H. Krulak ltr to Director, Hist&MusDiv, dtd 14Jun76, Marines and Helicopters, Pt. II Comment File, hereafter *Krulak comments.*
65. MCCC Items of Significant Interest, dtd 16Oct64, 17Nov64, 20Dec64.
66. *Ibid.*

### The Armed UH-1E

67. Briefing Memo, dtd 5Nov63, Subj: Ground Fire Suppression Kit for UH-1E (ASH) Helicopter (HQMC, Code AAW).
68. CNO ltr to ChBuWeps, dtd 19Sep64, Subj: Helicopter Ground Fire Suppression Armament Kits, requirement for (Ser. 06121P50, HQMC, Code AAW).
69. *Ibid.*, p. 2.
70. MCLFDC report, dtd 3May65, Project No. 54-64-08, "UH-1E Armament Final Report" (Ser. 08400).
71. *Ibid.*, p. 2.
72. *Ibid.*, p. 4.
73. MCCC Items of Significant Interest, dtd 31Mar and 12Apr65.
74. CMC ltr to Dist. List, dtd 13Jan65, Subj: UH-1E Defensive Fire Suppression Armament Program (Ser. 08-A36464).
75. MCCC Items of Significant Interest, dtd 7Sep64.
76. *Aviation Daily*, Vol. 151, No. 20 (27Mar64), p. 166.
77. Transcript of remarks by Gen Greene at National Press Club, 26Mar64.

## CHAPTER 6

## More Helicopters for an Expanding War

### The Buildup

1. Symposium Book, 1967 General Officers' Symposium, dtd 14Jul67, Tab F, pp. 26 and 29 (Ser 007F19367).
2. Aircraft Status Board Photo, dtd 1Mar65.
3. MCCC Items of Significant Interest, dtd 11Aug65, 27Aug65.
4. MCCC Status of FMF Book, Dec66, p. 18-2.
5. McCutcheon, "Marine Aviation in Vietnam," p. 130.
6. *Ibid.*
7. MCCC Items of Significant Interest, dtd 26Aug65, 4Sep65.
8. McCutcheon, "Marine Aviation in Vietnam."
9. MAG-36 ComdC, Sep-Dec65, p. 4; McCutcheon, "Marine Aviation in Vietnam."
10. MAG-36 ComdC, Sep-Dec65, pp. 5-6.
11. Symposium Book, 1967 General Officers' Symposium, dtd 14Jul67, TabF, p. 37 (Ser 007F19367).
12. McCutcheon, "Marine Aviation in Vietnam."
13. MCCC Items of Significant Interest, dtd 15Aug65, 30Aug65, 8Oct65, 22Oct65.
14. BuWeps msg to CMC, dtd 16Sep65.

# NOTES

### The Viet Cong Worsen the Helicopter Shortage
15. MAG–36 ComdC, Oct65, p. 11.
16. III MAF *Sea Tiger*, 10Nov65, p. 3.
17. CG III MAF ltr to CGFMFPac, dtd 29Nov65, Subj: Viet Cong Attack of Marble Mountain Air Facility and Chu Lai Airfield of 28October1965; report of (Ser. 0042865), hereafter cited as *III MAF report of 29Nov65*.
18. *Sea Tiger*, 10Nov65.
19. *III MAF report of 29Nov65*, p. 5.
20. MAG–16 ComdC, Oct65, p. 11.
21. *III MAF report of 29Nov65*, Tab. 1 to Encl. 1.
22. MAG–16 ComC, Oct65, p. 30.
23. MCCC Items of Significant Interest, dtd 28Oct65.
24. Aviation Status Board Photograph dtd 1Oct65.
25. AdminOFMFPac msg to CMC, dtd 29Oct65.
26. MCCC Items of Significant Interest, dtd 29Oct65, 2Nov65, 15Nov65, 1Dec65.
27. CGFMFPac msg to ComNavAirPac, dtd 1Dec65.

### The "Deuce" Finds a Mission
28. Maj Richard L. Hawley intvw with author, Apr71.
29. MAG–26 ComdC, Jul64–Jan65, p. 10.
30. CGFMFPac msg to CMC, dtd 12Sep65.
31. Unless otherwise noted, all material on the retrieval incident is taken from MAG–16 ComdC, Oct65, p. 13.
32. *Ibid*.
33. FMFPac ComdC, Jan-Jun66, pp. 9, 29.

## CHAPTER 7
## The CH-46 on Active Service

### The CH–46 Enters Combat
1. NavAirSysCom ltr to Dist. List, dtd 16Jun66, Subj: Project Management Review of 14 June 1966 (NavAirSysCom Hist).
2. MCCC Items of Significant Interest, dtd 4Mar66.
3. LtCol Alvah J. Kettering, Intvw by HistDiv, HQMC, dtd 17May74 (Oral HistColl, Hist&MusDiv, HQMC).
4. FMFPac msg dtd 14Apr66, FMFPac ComdC, Jul-Dec66, pp. 1–2.

### Problems and Improvements
5. DC/S (Air) memo for record, dtd 8Aug66, Subj: Introduction of the CH–46A aircraft into HMM squadrons, pp. 2–3, hereafter DC/S (Air), *CH–46A Introduction, dtd 8Aug66*.
6. *Ibid*.
7. NavAirSysCom memo, Op520c to Op53, dtd 3Nov65, Subj: Answers to questions for use by SecNav/CNO in preparations for FY67 Congressional Hearings (Ser 043-P52).
8. BuWeps Monitor, Weekly Howgozit, for Fleet Readiness and Training Group for the week ending 21Jan66, dtd 21Jan66, p. 2.
9. DC/S (Air), *CH–46A Introduction, dtd 8Aug66*, p. 2.
10. MAG–26 ComdC, 1Jan–30Jun66, p. 3.
11. NavAirSysCom, Howgozit for the Logistics/Fleet Support Group (Air-04), dtd 29Jul66 (NavAirSysCom Hist).
12. CGFMFPac msg to CMC, dtd 14Apr66, p. 2.
13. CGMFPac msg to CMC, dtd 3Dec66, p. 2.
14. *Ibid.*, p. 3.
15. FMFPac ComdC, Jul–Dec66, p. 18.
16. NavAirSysCom, Howgozit, dtd 29Apr66, for the Logistics/Fleet Support Group (NavAirSysCom Hist, Washington, D.C.).
17. FMFPac msg to CMC, dtd 14Apr66.
18. NavAirSysCom, Howgozit, dtd 29Apr66, for the Logistics/Fleet Support Group (NavAirSysCom Hist).
19. NavAirSysCom, Howgozit, dtd 11May66, for Plans, Programs and Comptroller Group (NavAirSysCom Hist).
20. NavAirSysCom, Howgozit, dtd 8Jun66, Plans, Programs and Comptroller Group, p. 3.
21. NavAirSysCom, Howgozit, dtd 1Jul66, Plans, Programs and Comptroller Group, p. 5.
22. NavAirSysCom, Howgozit, dtd 8Jun66, Plans, Programs, and Comptroller Group.
23. NavAirSysCom, Howgozit, dtd 11May66, Plans, Programs, and Comptroller Group, p. 4.
24. MAG–16 ComC, Jul66, pp. 3–4.
25. NavAirSysCom, Howgozit, dtd 27Jul66, Plans, Programs Comptroller Group, p. 2.
26. NavAirSysCom, Howgozit, dtd 31Aug66, Plans, Programs and Comptroller Group, p. 4.
27. FMFPac, U.S. Marine Forces in Vietnam, March 1965–September 1967, I, 6–34.

### A New Version
28. Roy L. Wilson, Intvw by HistDiv, HQMC, dtd 20May74 (Oral HistColl, Hist&MusDiv, HQMC).
29. Vertol Public Relations release, dtd 22Sep65, p. 1.
30. Unless otherwise noted, all material on the design of the CH–46D is taken from: President, BIS ltr to SecNav, dtd 22May67, Subj: Service Acceptance trials of Model UH/CH–46D Aircraft, BIS 21265, final report of. Hereafter cited as *BIS ltr of 22May67*.
31. *Ibid.*, p. 5.
32. *Ibid*.
33. *Ibid.*, p. 2, and NavAirSysCom ltr to Dist. List, dtd 16Jun66, Subj: Project Management Review of 14Jun66.
34. *BIS ltr of 22May67*, p. 2.
35. *Ibid*.
36. *Ibid.*, and INSURV, PaxRiv msg to CNO, dtd 7Oct66.

### General McCutcheon Takes Charge
Unless otherwise noted, all material on the life of General McCutcheon is taken from: Keith B. McCutcheon Manuscripts, Collections Unit, History and Museums Division, HQMC, hereafter cited as *McCutcheon Papers*; Keith B. McCutcheon Subject File, Reference Section, History and Museums Division, HQMC, hereafter *McCutcheon Subj File*; and Keith B. McCutcheon Biographical File, Reference Section, History and Museums Division, HQMC.

37. Keith B. McCutcheon, ltr to MGen Commandant, USMC, dtd 8Jun37, Item 14, Box 4, *McCutcheon Papers*.
38. For correspondence on McCutcheon's withdrawal from the Army flight school and Engineer reserve commissioning, see Item 14, Box 4, *Ibid*.
39. McCutcheon's correspondence related to his physical examination and commissioning in the Marine Corps is in *Ibid*.
40. 2dLt Keith B. McCutcheon ltr to MGenCommandant, dtd 22Sep38, MGen Commandant, ltr to McCutcheon, dtd 3Feb39, Subj: request for assignment to flight training, both in *ibid*.
41. DivAvn, HQMC ltr to McCutcheon, dtd 13Jun39 (Ser AA-251), copy in *Ibid*.

42. Quoted in George W. Garand and Truman R. Strobridge, *Western Pacific Operations: History of U.S. Marine Corps Operations in World War II*, Vol. IV (Washington, D.C.: Historical Division, HQMC, 1971), p. 304.
43. *Ibid.*, p. 306.
44. ComSeventhFlt Citation, *McCutcheon Subj File*.
45. CG, XCorps, Citation, dtd 26Jun46, General Orders No. 69, *Ibid.*
46. Capt Daniel B. McDyre, "History of Marine Corps Squadron One," dtd 15Jul69, p. 1.

## CHAPTER 8

## Two Separate Roles for the UH-1E

### Expansion and Shortages

1. Symposium Book, 1965 General Officers' Symposium, Tab V-B, p. 6.
2. *Ibid.*
3. MCCC Items of Significant Interest, dtd 6Oct65.
4. Symposium Book, 1966 General Officers' Symposium, Agenda Item III C., p. 1.
5. *Ibid.*, Agenda Item III E, p. 2.
6. DC/S (Air) memo to CMC, dtd 17Mar66, Subj: Marine Corps Light Helicopters Shortage (Ser 008D6266, S&C files, HQMC).
7. DC/S (Air) memo to DC/S (R&D), dtd 22Jun66, Subj: Marine Corps Position on Armed UH-1E helicopters (Ser. 008B17266, S&C files, HQMC).
8. NavAirSysCom, Howgozit, dtd 26Aug66, Logistics/Fleet Support Group, p. 4 (NavAirSysComHist).
9. DC/S (Air) memo for CMC Ref. Notebook, dtd 30Jun67, p. 1 (Code AAP—2D).
10. Symposium Book, 1966 General Officers' Symposium, Agenda Item III E, p. 23.
11. NavAirSysCom, Howgozit, dtd 4May66, Plan, Programs and Comptroller Group, p. 2.

### Guns or Eyes

12. MCCC, Status of FMF Book, dtd 29Jun67, p. 10-1.
13. Extracted from Symposium Book, 1967 General Officers' Symposium, Tab F., p. 26.
14. *Ibid.*
15. *Ibid.*, pp 26 and 27.
16. *Ibid.*, p. 27.
17. *Ibid.*, Tab I, pp. 6-7.
18. NavAirSysCom, Howgozit, dtd 16Dec66, Logistics/Fleet Support Group, p. 3.
19. Symposium Book, 1967 General Officers' Symposium, p. 6.

### Reorganization

20. Symposium Book, 1967 General Officers' Symposium, Tab I, p. 11.
21. Symposium Book, 1968 General Officers' Symposium, Tab G, p. 7.
22. *Ibid.*, Tab I, p. 8.
23. Symposium Book, 1967 General Officers' Symposium.
24. *Ibid.*
25. *Ibid.*
26. Symposium Book, 1968 General Officers' Symposium, Tab G, p. 9.

## CHAPTER 9

## The CH-53 Enters the War

### A New Role for the "Sea Stallion"

1. Igor Sikorsky, "Military Future of the Helicopter."
2. Vertol Feasibility Study: Multi-Helicopter Heavy Lift System, undtd *circa* Mar58, pp. 1, 4.
3. *Ibid.*, p. 1.
4. Lynn Montross, *Cavalry of the Sky* (New York: Harper and Brothers, 1954), p. 172; Capt Joseph H. Strain, "Sky Hook," *Marine Corps Gazette*, Vol. 37, No. 11 (Nov53), pp. 56-57; *Naval Aviation News*, Dec51, p. 8.

### A Helicopter Retriever

5. CMC ltr to CNO, dtd 7Jan66, Subj: Downed Aircraft Recovery Capability, requirements for (Ser. 08E36265), pp. 1-4.
6. Unless otherwise noted, data on the introduction of the CH-53 as a retriever aircraft is taken from progress reports on Chief of Staff Project No. 53-66 of the date indicated, hereafter cited as *C/S Proj 53-66*.
7. *C/S Proj 53-66*, dtd 30Jun66, p. 1.
8. *Ibid*, dtd 5Aug66, p. 1.
9. DC/S (Air) memo to DirPer, dtd 21Mar66, Subj: Personnel Actions in support of WestPac deployments (Ser. 0008A066, S&C files, HQMC).
10. *C/S Proj 53-66*, dtd 21Oct66, p. 1.
11. *Ibid.*, dtd 5Aug66, p. 1.
12. *Ibid.*, dtd 14Nov66, p. 1.
13. *Ibid.*, dtd 12Dec66, p. 1.
14. *Ibid.*, dtd 22Dec66, p. 1.
15. *Ibid.*, dtd 12Dec66.
16. *Ibid.*, dtd 22Dec66.
17. NavAirSysCom, Op 520C memo to Op52, dtd 3Nov66,
18. CGFMPac, msg to CMC, dtd 3Dec66, pp. 2-3.
19. NavAirSysCom Howgozit, dtd 10Aug66, Plan, Programs and Comptroller Group, p. 3.
20. *Marine Corps Gazette*, Vol. 52, No. 10 (Oct68), p. 11.
21. NavAirSysCom, Howgozit, dtd 10Aug66.
22. *C/S Proj 53-65*, dtd 23Sep66, p. 1.
23. "Veri-Frite," Sikorsky Aircraft, Oct66, p. 10.
24. NavAirSysCom, Howgozit, dtd 23Nov66, Plans, Programs and Comptroller Group (NavAirSysCom Hist), p. 2. p. 2.
25. NavAirSysCom, Howgozit, dtd 7Dec66, Plans, Programs and Comptroller Group (NavAirSysCom Hist). p. 2.
26. NavAirSysCom Howgozit, dtd 14Dec66, Plans, Programs and Comptroller Group, p. 4.

### Retrievers to Viet Nam

27. *C/S Proj 53-66*, dtd 23Sep66.
28. *Ibid.*, dtd 21Oct66, p. 2.
29. Det "A", HMH-463, ComdC, Jan67, pp. 4, 19.
30. NavAirSysCom, Howgozit, dtd 8Feb67, Plans, Programs and Comptroller Group, p. 4.
31. *C/S Proj 53-66*, dtd 7Jul67, p. 1.
32. *Ibid.*, dtd 7Jul67, p. 1, 11Aug66, p. 1, 23Sep66, p. 1.
33. *Aviation Status Board Photograph*, dtd 1Dec66.
34. *C/S Proj 53-66*, dtd 22Jan68, p. 1.

### Requiem for a Heavyweight

35. H&MS-16 Sub-Unit No. 1, ComdC, May67, Encl., p. 3.
36. MAG-16 ComdC, May67, p. 1-II.

37. *Sikorsky News*, Jul67, p. 7.
38. Joseph S. Black, Property Disposal, NavAirSysCom, Washington, D.C., Intvw by HistDiv, HQMC, dtd 15May74 (Oral HistColl, Hist&MusDiv, HQMC).

# CHAPTER 10

## Medium Transport Crisis

### The CH-46 in Trouble

1. Unit location data from the *Aviation Status Board Photograph*, dtd 1Jul67, and MCCC Status of Fleet Marine Forces, dtd 29Jun67.
2. Point Paper, dtd 30Jun67, Subj: CH–46 Seaknight (Ser. VB3d-2, AAP-2D).
3. Symposium Book, 1967 General Officers' Symposium, Tab I, p. 7.
4. CGFMFPac msg to ComNavAirPac, dtd 22Jul67, p. 2.
5. DC/S (Air) Point Paper, dtd 4Oct67, Subj: CH–46 Status (Ser. Code AAW-4A).
6. *Ibid.*, p. 2.
7. FMFPac, Operations of U.S. Marine Forces, Vietnam, 1967, May67, p. 53, Jun67, p. 79, hereafter FMFPac, *Vietnam Ops 67*.
8. NavAirSysCom msg dtd 13May67, as cited in Howgozit, dtd 17May67, Plan, Programs and Comptroller Group.
9. Point Paper, dtd 4Oct67, p. 3.
10. FMFPac, *Vietnam Ops 67*, Jun67, p. 80.
11. Point Paper, dtd 4Oct67, p. 4.
12. NavAirSysCom, Howgozit, dtd 12Jul67, Plans, Programs and Comptroller Group (NavAirSysCom Hist).
13. Point Paper, dtd 4Oct67.
14. FMFPac msg, dtd 22Jul67.
15. *Ibid.*
16. Point Paper, dtd 4Oct67, pp. 5–6.
17. NavAirSysCom Howgozit, dtd 4Aug67, Logistics/Fleet Support Group (NavAirSysCom Hist).
18. Point Paper, dtd 4Oct67.
19. *Ibid.* pp. 4–5.
20. 1st MAW ComdC, Sep67, p. 2-2.
21. *Ibid.*, p. 1-5.
22. FMFPac *Vietnam Ops 67*, Sept67, p. 59.
23. Point Paper, dtd 4Oct67, p. 6.
24. FMFPac *Vietnam Ops 67*, Sep67, p. 59.
25. Point Paper, dtd 4Oct67, p. 7.
26. FMFPac, *Vietnam Ops 67*, Oct67, p. 68.
27. *Ibid.*, Dec67, p. 107.
28. DC/S (Air) memo, dtd 8Aug66, p. 1.
29. FMFPac, *Vietnam Ops 67*, Dec67, p. 107.

### The CH-46D Arrives in Vietnam

30. HMM–364 ComdC, Jul-Dec67, p. 5.
31. *Aviation Status Board Photograph*, dtd 1Dec67.
32. Symposium Book, 1968 General Officers' Symposium, Tab F, p. 35.

### A Premature Funeral for the UH-34

33. Sikorsky Aircraft Information Release, dtd 27Jul64.
34. *Ibid.*, dtd 8Jan64, p. 1.
35. ACNO (Marine Aviation) memo to DCNO (Air), dtd 14Apr64, Subj: Marine Aviation Program Objectives (Ser. 018P52).
36. Symposium Book, 1967 General Officers' Symposium, Tab I, p. 9.
37. Symposium Book, 1968 General Officers' Symposium, Tab II–E, p. 1.
38. Symposium Book, 1970 General Officers' Symposium, Tab N, p. 13.
39. OP–502 (Capt E.J. Winger) memo to USMC aide (LtCol M. Spark) to UnSecNav, dtd 17Aug65, Subj: H–19 Helicopter for the Training Command (Ser 02047P50).
40. BuWeps, Howgozit, dtd 1Apr66, Fleet Readiness and Training Group (NavAirSysCom Hist), p. 3.
41. Bell Helicopter Information Release, dtd 21Mar69, No. 037.

### Last Flights of the "HUSS"

42. III MAF Press Release, dtd 27Aug68, Subj: War Horse Retires. No. 2603.
43. *Ibid.*
44. *Marine Corps Gazette,* Vol. 56, No. 9 (Sep72), p. 8.
45. HMM–362 ComdC, Aug69, p. 5.
46. CMC msg to NavPro, Stratford, Conn, dtd 18Aug69, Subj: UH–34 Aircraft.
47. HMM–561 ComdC, Oct69, p. 4.
48. MCAS Cherry Point *Windsock*, 24Mar72, p. 3.
49. Capt J. E. Hensaw ltr to *Naval Aviation News*, dtd 21Jun72, Subj: Erroneous Obituary.
50. CO, MARTD Glenview ltr to *Naval Aviation News*, dtd 28Jun72, Subj: UH–34D, Active Flying.
51. William Baka, Disposal Records, Davis-Monthan Air Force Base, telecon to HistDiv, 4Jun74.
52. Joseph S. Black, Property Disposal, NavAirSysCom, Intvw, HistDiv, HQMC, dtd 6Jun74 (Oral HistColl, Hist&MusDiv, HQMC).
53. Maj Dwight L. Bledsoe, Intvw, HistDiv, HQMC, dtd 6 Jun 74 (Oral HistColl, Hist&MusDiv, HQMC).

# CHAPTER 11

## A General and His Pilots

### Conscience and Will Power

1. Keith B. McCutcheon ltr to The Group Division, Aetna Life Insurance Company, dtd 26Feb37, Item 20, Box 4, *McCutcheon Papers*.

### "There Is No Shortage"

2. Symposium Book, 1967 General Officers' Symposium, Tab 1, pp. 12–13.
3. "Historical Information—Naval Aviator Inventory, LtCol and below, Fy57–74" prepared by Major Robert M. Rose, DC/S (Air), Code AAZ–23, hereafter cited as *Historical Summary*. In addition, Maj Rose provided verbal and written briefing for background for the entire section.
4. DC/S (Air) memo to CMC, dtd 31Mar66, Subj: Pilot Training (Ser. 08F8866, S&C files, HQMC).
5. Symposium Book, 1966 General Officers' Symposium, Tab 1-B, p. 3.
6. DC/S (Air) memo, dtd 31Mar66.
7. General McCutcheon, folder entitled "Senate Subcommittee on Preparedness Investigation Concerning Marine Corps Pilots Situation, 1967," Tab G, p. 1, hereafter cited as *Stennis Committee Hearings*.
8. *Ibid.*, p. 2.
9. *Ibid.*, p. 3.
10. Symposium Book, FY–66 General Officers' Symposium, Tab III–E, p. 11.
11. *Ibid.*, Tab III–B, p. 3.

12. *Ibid.*, p. J-4.
13. *Ibid.*
14. *Historical Summary.*
15. Comprehensive Study of Pilot Shortage, II, Tab A-h, p. 1.

### Congress Investigates

16. News Release by Sen Stennis, dtd 19Jan67.
17. Hon L. Mendel Rivers ltr to SecDef Robert S. McNamara, dtd 12Jan67.
18. *Ibid.*, p. 2.
19. Comprehensive Study of Pilot Shortage, Tab L.
20. DC/S (Air) memo for the record, dtd 23Mar67, Subj: Meetings with OSD (SA) regarding USMC pilot situation, p. 1.
21. *Ibid.*, p. 2.
22. C/S memo to SecNav, dtd 29Mar67, Subj: Key Issues Relative to Marine Corps Pilot Requirements and Inventory (Ser. 008A8867)
23. *Ibid.*, p. 3.
24. DC/S (Air) memo for the record, dtd 31Mar67, Subj: Marine Corps Pilot Requirements.
25. *Ibid.*, p. 2.
26. DC/S (Air) memo for the record, dtd 31Mar67, Subj: Review of USMC Pilot Requirements.
27. *Ibid.*
28. DC/S (Air) memo for the record, dtd 3Apr67, Subj: Review of USMC Pilot Requirements.
29. *Ibid.*, p. 2
30. Gen Wallace M. Greene, Transcript of Telecon with Dr Alain Enthoven, dtd 3Apr67 (Wallace M. Greene Papers, Collections Section, Hist&MusDiv, HQMC).
31. DC/S (Air) memo for the record, dtd 24Apr67, Subj: Meetings with Dr. Enthoven on Thursday, 20Apr67, pp. 1-2.
32. U.S. Congress, Senate, *Hearings before the Preparedness Investigating Subcommittee of the Committee on Armed Services* United States Senate, 90th Congress, First Session, April 24, May 5 and 11, 1967 (Washington, D.C.: U.S. Government Printing Office, 1967), p. 154.

## CHAPTER 12

### More Pilots for the War

#### Busy Helicopter Crews

1. "General McCutcheon's Statements to the Senate Subcommittee on Preparedness Investigation Concerning Marine Corps Pilot Situation," folder, *McCutcheon Papers*, hereafter cited as *McCutcheon Statements*, Tab F, p. 1.
2. Comprehensive Study of Pilots, *McCutcheon Statements*, Tab E., p. 3.
3. *Ibid.*, p. 4.
4. *Ibid.*, p. 6.
5. *McCutcheon Statements*, Tab G, p. 1.
6. CMC memo for UnSecNav, dtd 15Oct66, Subj: Pilot Training (Ser. 08C2866, S&C Files, HQMC), Encl. 1.
7. Symposium Book, 1967 General Officers' Symposium, Tab I, pp. 6, 13-14.

#### Management Actions

8. *Historical Summary.*
9. CMC msg to ALMar, dtd 13Aug65, pp. 1-2.
10. CMC msg to AlMar, dtd 17Oct66.
11. Unless otherwise noted, all information on the reduction and substitution in aviator billets is taken from Comprehensive Study of Pilot Shortages, *McCutcheon Statements*, Tab C and D.
12. Symposium Book, 1967 General Officers' Symposium, Tab D, p. 4.
13. *Ibid.*
14. *Ibid.*, p. 10.
15. *Ibid.*, p. 11.
16. DirPer memo to AC/S (G-1), dtd 24Mar66, Subj: Obligated Active Duty for Assignment to Flight Training.
17. MCBul 1120 of 30Apr68.
18. DC/S (Air) Point Paper, Subj: Warrant Officer Helicopter Pilots, p. 3.
19. DC/S (Air) memo to DepDirPer, dtd 4Nov69, Subj: Helicopter Transition Training, case of Major Jerry D. Boulton (Ser. 15000, DC/S [Air] Code AAZ files, HQMC).
20. *Historical Summary.*

#### A New Source of Helicopter Pilots

21. DirAvnPlns and Requirements Div, CNO memo to SecNav, dtd 30Mar67 (Ser. 071-50), p. 1.
22. *Ibid.*
23. Syllabus data extracted from: Memo for AScCDef (Manpower), dtd 16Jan67, Subj: Proposed visit by Mr. Morris, ASecDef (Mpr) to Ellyson Field (Ser 52P56, DC/S [Air] Code AAZ Files, HQMC).
24. Transcript of Naval Appropriation Bill Hearings, Naval Aviation, 66th Congress, 2nd Session, dtd 5Feb20, pp. 1492-1493.
25. SecUSAF memo for DepSecDef, dtd 17Apr67, Subj: Pilot Training.
26. OSD memo to SecUSA, dtd 9Nov67, Subj: FY69 Pilot Training Rate.
27. DirArmyAvn, OACSFOR memo to DC/S (Air), dtd 29Jan68, Subj: Army Training U.S. Marine Helicopter Pilots.
28. DepSecDef memo to SecUSA, dtd 2Feb68, Subj: Training U.S. Marine Corps Pilots.
29. DirArmyAvn memo, dtd 29Jan68.
30. DC/S (Air) memo to A/CS (G-1), dtd 29Jan68, Subj: Army Training of Marine Pilots, Encl. 3.
31. *Ibid.*, Encl. 2.
32. DirArmyAvn memo, dtd 29Jan68.
33. DepSecDef memo, dtd 2Feb68.

#### Army Helicopter Training

34. All information on the Army helicopter is extracted from LtCol W. G. Cretney and Lt R. J. Dooling, "Above the Best," *Marine Corps Gazette*, Vol. 55, No. 6 (Jun71), pp. 32-35.
35. MCLiaO ltr to Col S. F. Martin, dtd 26Sep68, Subj: Graduation of First Marine Helicopter Students, Hunter AAF (DC/S [Air] Code AAZ files, HQMC).
36. MGen McCutcheon ltr to 2d Lt Watson, dtd 30Dec68.
37. CMC ltr to DC/S for personnel, USA, dtd 22Feb71, Subj: Army Training of Marine Helicopter Pilots, termination of.
38. *Historical information.*
39. Gen Chapman ltr to Gen W. C. Westmoreland, dtd 4Aug71.
40. CMC ltr to CNO, dtd 15Jun70, Subj: USMC/Navy Helicopter Pilots in Vietnam (DC/S [Air], Code AAZ, files, HQMC).

# NOTES

41. Information extracted from 1500/15 files and numerous misc. documents (DC/S [Air] Code AAZ files, HQMC).

### Post-Graduate Flight Training

42. DirAvn memo to Dir. Policy Analysis Div, dtd 3Jun59 (Ser. 08A15359), p. 1.
43. McCutcheon, "Marine Aviation in Vietnam," p. 133.

### "We View our Present Posture with Concern"

44. Symposium Book, 1966 General Officers' Symposium, Tab II B, p. 1.
45. *Ibid.*

### The Training Groups

46. *Ibid.*, Tab III–E, pp. 2-3.
47. *Ibid.*
48. 3d MAW ComdC, Jan-Jun66, p. 21.
49. Symposium Book, 1967 General Officers' Symposium, Tab I, p. 7.
50. MHTG–40 ComdC, Jul-Dec69, p. 2.
51. HMMT–401 ComdC, Jan-Jun70, p. 2.
52. Symposium Book, 1967 General Officers' Symposium, Tab I, p. 8.

## CHAPTER 13

## Twins and Mixes

### Continue the March

1. CMC msg to AlMar, dtd 1Jan68.
2. Unless otherwise noted, biographical information on General Chapman is extracted from official subject files.

### Further Improvements of the CH-46

3. Command History, Naval Plant Representative, Morton, Pa., dtd 23Jul68 (NavAirSysComHist).
4. NavAirSysCom ltr to Dist. List, dtd 16Jun66, Subj: Project Management Review of June 66, p. 15.
5. *Naval Institute Proceedings*, Vol. 92, No. 10 (Oct66), p. 173.
6. *Naval Institute Proceedings*, Vol. 93, No. 10 (Oct67), p. 13.
7. *Marine Corps Gazette*, Vol. 53, No. 8 (Aug68), p. 5.
8. DC/S (Air) C/S Conference Item, dtd 5Feb71, Subj: Acceptance of final production CH–46.
9. *Marine Corps Gazette*, Vol. 55, No. 3 (Mar71), p. 4.

### The "Huey" Changes Its Skin

10. Bell Helicopter news release, dtd 11Mar66, as cited in *Naval Institute Proceedings*, Vol. 92, No. 5 (May66), p. 163.
11. *Ibid.*
12. Unless otherwise noted, specifications are taken from: Bell Helicopter Company Technical Data, Model AH–1G, dtd 15Nov67.
13. *Marine Corps Gazette*, Vol. 52, No. 9 (Sep68), p. 2.
14. Symposium Book, 1967 General Officers' Symposium, Tab M, p. 28.
15. CMC Reference Notebook, 1968, V, p. v-c-4-e.
16. *Ibid.*
17. *Marine Corps Gazette*, Vol. 53, No. 3 (Mar69), p. 5.
18. Symposium Book, 1969 General Officers' Symposium, Tab I., p. 4.
19. *Marine Corps Gazette*, Vol. 53, No. 6.
20. Symposium Book, 1969 General Officers' Symposium.
21. VMO–2 ComdC, Apr69, pp. 6–9.
22. *Marine Corps Gazette*, Vol. 55, No. 10 (Oct71), p. 27.
23. CG 1st MAW msg to CMC, dtd 11Jul69.
24. HML–167 ComdC, Dec69, p. 4.

### The "Sea Cobra"

25. Symposium Book, 1967 General Officers' Symposium, Tab M., p. 28.
26. Point Paper, dtd 2Aug69, Subj: Status of Navy/Marine FY–70 UH–1N Procurement (DC/S [Air] Code AAW files, HQMC, Wash., D.C.).
27. "Background Briefing," dtd 16Jul69, Subj: AH–1J/UH–1N Multi Engine Requirements (DC/S [Air] Code AAW files, HQMC).
28. Symposium Book, 1968 General Officers' Symposium, Tab G, p. 7.
29. Bell Helicopter News Release, dtd 14Oct69, No. 133/10. 1369 (DCNOHist Subject file: H–1).
30. Notes for briefing for SecNav, CMC, and C/S, undtd, circa mid-1972, Subj: AH–1J., p. 4 (DC/S [Air] Code AAW subject files, HQMC), hereafter *SecNav Briefing*.
31. DC/S (Air), C/S Conference Item, dtd 19Feb71, Subj: AH–1J Program (DC/S [Air] Code AAW subject files, HQMC).
32. DC/S (Air), C/S Conference Item, dtd 3Mar71, Subj: AH–1J Combat Evaluation (DC/S [Air] Code AAW subject files, HQMC, Washington, D.C.).
33. *SecNav Briefing*.
34. *Ibid.*, p. 3.
35. HMA–269 ComdC, 22Feb-30Jun71, p. 4.

### The Twin "Huey"

36. DC/S (Air) memo AAW–4 to AA–1, dtd 6Feb68, Subj: Information from Mr. Beam for your background prior to meeting with General Smith, USA (DC/S [Air] Code AAW subject files, Wash., D.C.).
37. DeptArmy msg to CMC, dtd 3Feb68, Subj: Multi-Engine Power Plant for Helicopters.
38. Unless otherwise noted, all information is extracted from: DC/S (Air) Code AAW subject files HQMC, containing varied background documents.
39. Memo for the record, dtd 7Aug69, Subj: ACMC Meeting with Chairman, House Armed Services Committee Concerning FY–70 UH–1N Procurement (DC/S [Air] Code AAW, HQMC, Wash. D.C.).
40. United Aircraft ltr to ComNavAirSysCom, dtd 25Aug69.
41. HMA–269 ComdC, 22Feb-Jun71, p. 3.

### Change in the Mix

42. Unless otherwise noted, all information on the intial recommendations to change the mix of the transport helicopters is from: MCAG Study No. 3, "Cost-Effectiveness Analysis of Marine Corps Assault Transport Helicopters," dtd 20Jun66. Authors listed are T. E. Anger and J. C. Sessler. Contract No. NONR 3732 (OO), entire study hereafter cited as *MCOAG Study No. 3*.
43. *Ibid.*, p. 3.
44. *Ibid.*, p. 26.
45. Boeing Vertol Division, "USMC Medium and Heavy Helicopters is from: MCOAG Study No. 3, "Cost-Effectiveness in MCOAG Research Contribution No. 7, dtd 30Sep66. Listed author T. E. Anger. Contract No. NONR–3732 (OO)., p. 3, hereafter cited as *MCOAG Study No. 7*.

46. *Ibid.*, p. 1.
47. General Paige ltr to HistDiv, dtd 4Nov73.
48. *MCOAG Study No. 7.*
49. *Ibid.*
50. Symposium Book, 1968 General Officers' Symposium, Tab II-E, pp. 6-7.
51. "Major Accomplishments Book," 1Jul69-30Jun70, Vol. I, Tab 2, p. 1.

### Marine Helicopters around the World

52. FMFPac, Operations of U.S. Marine Forces, Vietnam, May-June 1971, p. 16.

### The "Father of Helicopters" Leaves the Ranks

53. Keith B. McCutcheon ltr to The Group Division, Aetna Life Insurance Company, dtd 26Feb37, *McCutcheon Papers*, Item 20, Box 4.
54. HQMC News Release No. CAB-215-71, dtd 1Jul71.
55. JPAO, MCAS New River, Release No. 06-028-72, dtd 8Jun72.
56. *Ibid.*
57. *Ibid.*, p. 2.

## CHAPTER 14

## Looking to the Future

### The LHA

1. Unless otherwise noted, information on the LHA is from: James D. Hessman and Bernadine M. Kopec, "The Navy, the Marines and the Nation Take a Giant Step," *Seapower*, Vol. 16, No. 11 (Nov73), p. 27.
2. ASecDef (PA) News Release, dtd 1Dec73, Subj: Remarks by General Robert E. Cushman Jr., USS *Tarawa* launching.
3. *Ibid.*

### The CH-53E

4. Much of the information, unless otherwise noted, on the CH-53E program is from: Colonel Frederick M. Kleppsattel, "CH-53E Super Stallion," *Marine Corps Gazette*, Vol. 56, No. 5, (May72), p. 43.
5. NavAirSysCom memo, dtd 13Nov68, Subj: Heavy Lift Helicopter.
6. *Ibid.*
7. DC/S (Air) C/S Conference Item, dtd 18Dec70, Sub: Status of Funding for Sikorsky Propulsion System Test Program.
8. *Ibid.*, dtd 26Feb71.

# CHRONOLOGY

## 1962

| | |
|---|---|
| 17 Jan | CG FMFPac, LtGen Alan Shapley, recommended to CMC that, instead of sending Marine pilots to augment Army helicopter squadrons in Vietnam, as suggested by the U.S. Military Assistance Advisory Group, Vietnam, an entire Marine Corps helicopter squadron be sent to the area. |
| 5 Feb | Capt L. Kenneth Keck, USMC, set a new world's speed record for helicopters of 210.6 mph while flying a HSS-2. |
| 1 Mar | The Secretary of the Navy approved adoption of the Bell Helicopter Company's UH-1B (Marine designation UH-1E) as the new Marine light reconnaissance and utility helicopter. |
| 19 Mar | The Joint Chiefs of Staff approved dispatch of a Marine Corps helicopter squadron to Vietnam in place of an additional Army helicopter company, to be in position in Vietnam on or about 15 April 1962. |
| 22 Mar | 1st Marine Aircraft Wing was ordered to prepare to deploy a squadron to Vietnam. Planning began for what would become Operation SHUFLY. |
| 15 Apr | The first SHUFLY helicopter squadron, HMM-362, under LtCol Archie J. Clapp, began operations from Soc Trang airfield, Republic of Vietnam. |
| 23 Apr | The first SHUFLY helicopter received combat damage in Vietnam but was able to land safely. |
| 30 Apr | The first Boeing/Vertol CH-46 was accepted by the Navy for testing. |
| 25 Jul | Gen David M. Shoup, CMC, asked the Chief of Naval Operations to furnish the Marine Corps six T-28 aircraft for use in target-marking, escort and protection of helicopters, and limited close air support in lightly defended areas. |
| 26 Jul | The Navy Bureau of Weapons (BuWeps) announced its selection of the Sikorsky S-64 (CH-53) as the new heavy helicopter for the Marine Corps. |
| 30 Aug | CNO, at recommendation of HQMC, issued order that about 500 Marine fixed-wing aviators were to be transferred into helicopters in order to relieve a severe helicopter pilot shortage in the Marine Corps. |
| 16 Sep | The SHUFLY squadron began movement from Soc Trang in the Mekong Delta to Da Nang. |
| 18 Sep | The Navy revised its directive establishing pilot criteria so that single-engine helicopters could be flown under certain conditions by only one pilot instead of the previously required two. |
| 24 Sep | The Department of Defense announced that Sikorsky, with its S-64, had won the competition to design the HHX, the new heavy Marine Corps helicopter transport, which now would be known as the CH-53A. |
| Oct–Nov | HMMs–261, -263, -264, and -361 participated in operations in the Caribbean during the Cuban Missile Crisis and quarantine. |

## 1963

| | |
|---|---|
| 16 Feb | The Joint Chiefs of Staff temporarily permitted helicopter crews in Vietnam to "engage clearly defined VC elements considered to be a threat to the safety of the helicopters and their passengers" without waiting for the VC to shoot first. |
| 23 Feb | The Joint Chiefs of Staff again restricted helicopter crews in Vietnam to returning enemy fire "for defensive purposes only." |
| 13 Mar | The SHUFLY squadron announced that three armed UH-34s for the first time had provided close air support from helicopters. |
| 29 Mar | Gen Shoup, CMC, proposed that armed T-28s be sent to Vietnam to provide escort for the SHUFLY squadron. |
| 13 Apr | Six Army UH-1B gunships from the Utility Tactical Company based at Da Nang began escorting the Marine UH-34s of the SHUFLY squadron on all troop-carrying missions and missions into Viet Cong-infested areas. |

## 1964

| | |
|---|---|
| 1 Jan | Gen Wallace M. Greene, Jr. became 23d Commandant of the Marine Corps. |
| 15 Jan | The last Marine crew members, "Soldier-Mechanics of the Sea," were removed from the U.S.S. *Boxer* (LPH-4). |
| 22 Jan | The Joint Chiefs of Staff approved extension of the SHUFLY operation in Vietnam until 30 June 1964. |
| 31 Jan | The last Marine crew members, "Soldier-Mechanics of the Sea," were removed from the U.S.S. *Princeton* (LPH-5). |
| 21 Feb | At Fort Worth, Texas, Bell Helicopter Company delivered the first UH-1E to a Marine tactical squadron, VMO-1. |
| 17 Mar | CNO published Specific Operational Requirements No. W-14-09 for an all-weather navigation system for helicopters called the integrated helicopter avionics system (IHAS). |
| 20 May | The Joint Chiefs of Staff announced that helicopters were to use their on-board weapons only for protection of the aircraft passengers and that armed helicopters were not to be used as "substitutes for Close Air Support." |

|  |  |
|---|---|
| 28 May | The first CH-53A to roll off the production line was accepted by the Sikorsky Flight Test Division. |
| 10 Jun | The Joint Chiefs of Staff ordered that Operation SHUFLY continue indefinitely. |
| 30 Jun | The first three CH-46As were delivered to LtCol Eldon C. Stanton's HMM-265 at New River, the first squadron to receive the turbine-powered medium helicopter. |
| 1 Jul | The second CH-46 squadron in the Marine Corps, HMM-164 under LtCol Herbert J. Blaha, was commissioned at MCAS Santa Ana but did not receive its aircraft until 21 Dec 64. |
| 4 Aug | North Vietnamese patrol boats attacked two U.S. destroyers on patrol in the Gulf of Tonkin, and the U.S. launched retaliatory air strikes at targets in North Vietnam. |
| 17 Aug | Gen Greene, CMC, directed MCLFDC and HMX-1 to begin work on an armament kit for the UH-34. |
| 13 Oct | CMC directed HMX-1 at Quantico to begin a high-priority project to "develop, evaluate, and service test a readily installable weapons kit for the UH-1E helicopter to provide armed helicopter support for transport helicopters." |
| 14 Oct | The first test flight of a CH-53A was made by the Sikorsky Aircraft Company. |
| 26-31 Oct | Marine Aircraft Group 26, under Col Stanley V. Titterud, with six helicopter squadrons and 105 aircraft, participated in Operation STEEL PIKE I, on the Mediterranean coast of Spain, the largest amphibious assault ever made using helicopters. |
| 16-23 Nov | HMM-162 joined the SHUFLY squadron, HMM-365, in rescuing thousands of Vietnamese in the Da Nang area who were endangered by floods caused by Typhoon Kate. |
| mid-December | TK-1 machine gun and rocket pod kits were installed on UH-34s of HMM-365, the SHUFLY squadron. |

## 1965

|  |  |
|---|---|
| 15 Jan | The first TK-2 armament kits were shipped to Camp Pendleton for installation in UH-1Es of VMO-6. |
| 6-7 Mar | The Joint Chiefs of Staff ordered the landing of the 9th MEB at Da Nang. |
| 8 Mar | The headquarters of MAG-16 moved from Futema to Da Nang, and Col John H. King, Jr., commander of SHUFLY at the time, assumed command of the helicopter group. |
| 9 Mar | HMMs -365 and -162 switched equipment and aircraft at Da Nang, HMM-365 delivering its aircraft to Da Nang, where officers and men from HMM-162 flew from Futema to take them over. The personnel from HMM-365 then embarked on the U.S.S. Princeton and sailed to Futema to take over the helicopters of HMM-162. |
| 25 Apr | In response to reports of rioting and an attempted coup in the Dominican Republic, U.S. naval forces, including the U.S.S. Boxer (LPH-4) with HMM-264 embarked, were ordered into Dominican waters. |
| 27 Apr | HMM-264, under Lt Col Frederick M. Kleppsattel, evacuated 558 civilians from the civil war-torn Dominican Republic. |
| 27 Apr-31 May | HMMs-263 and -264 and elements of VMO-1 and HMH-461 participated in Marine peacekeeping operations in the Dominican Republic, lifting troops, evacuees, and supplies, and performing reconnaissance missions. |
| 3 May | Six armed UH-1Es of LtCol George Bauman's VMO-2 arrived at Da Nang, the Marines' first gunship helicopter escorts in Vietnam. |
| 6 May | Capt Thomas P. McBrien, flying a UH-1E attached to HMM-263 over Santo Domingo City during peacekeeping operations there, was wounded by ground fire but safely landed his aircraft, becoming one of the few Marine aviators to become a combat casualty in the Western Hemisphere. |
| 8 Jun | HMM-361 arrived at Futema from Santa Ana, under LtCol Lloyd F. Childers, bringing to five the number of Marine transport helicopter squadrons in the western Pacific. |
| 12 Jun | HMM-161 (LtCol Gene W. Morrison) arrived at Phu Bai, South Vietnam, from Kaneohe. |
| 21 Jun | HMM-261, under LtCol Mervin B. Porter, arrived at Da Nang from New River as part of the Marine helicopter buildup in Vietnam. |
| 1 Jul | Aircraft, Fleet Marine Force, Pacific (Air-FMFPac) was consolidated into Fleet Marine Force, Pacific (FMFPac), under LtGen Victor H. Krulak, with aviation MGen Avery R. Kier becoming Deputy Commander, FMFPac. |
| 28 Jul | President Lyndon B. Johnson announced that U.S. forces in Vietnam would be increased to 125,000 men and that additional reinforcements would be sent if required. |
| 11-30 Aug | MAG-36 under Col William G. Johnson deployed from Santa Ana to Vietnam with three UH-34 squadrons, one squadron of UH-1Es, and a detachment of six HR2Ss. |
| 26 Aug | MAG-16 moved from Da Nang Airbase to Marble Mountain Air Facility. |
| 2 Sep | MAG-36 began construction of a helicopter facility on the Ky Ha Peninsula near Chu Lai. |
| 12 Sep | A HR2S of MAG-16 performed what was called "the first helo lift of a downed aircraft under tactical considerations" by retrieving a downed helicopter in Vietnam about 15 miles from Chu Lai and carrying it externally back to the airfield. |
| 15 Sep | HMH-461 (Maj Richard L. Hawley) deployed as the aviation component of the Caribbean Ready Force with 12 HR2Ss, the only squadron-size force of these helicopters ever operationally deployed. |
| 22 Sep | The Department of Defense notified Vertol to accelerate production of the CH-46 by 100 percent over the previously planned production rate, to meet the need for more helicopters in Vietnam. |
| 27 Oct | Viet Cong sappers attacked Marble Mountain Air Facility, destroying 19 helicopters of MAG-16 and heavily damaging 11 more. |

# CHRONOLOGY

## 1966

| | |
|---|---|
| 20 Jan | Marine Helicopter Training Group (MHTG) 30 was commissioned at Santa Ana. This was the first of two temporary helicopter post-graduate flight training groups authorized by Secretary of Defense McNamara to meet Vietnam war pilot requirements. |
| 8 Mar | The first CH-46 squadron to enter the Vietnam war, HMM-164 under LtCol Warren C. Watson, arrived at Marble Mountain with 27 of the new jet-powered medium transports. |
| 15 Jun | MGen Keith B. McCutcheon, long associated with aviation and helicopter development, became Deputy Chief of Staff (Air) at HQMC. |
| 9 Sep | MGen Keith B. McCutcheon, DC/S (Air), accepted delivery of the first operational CH-53A for the Marine Corps. |
| 20 Sep | The first CH-53A was delivered to an operational Marine squadron, HMH-463 at Santa Ana. |
| 19 Dec | HMM-161 received the first "D" model CH-46s at New River MCAS. |

## 1967

| | |
|---|---|
| 8 Jan | The first four CH-53As of HMH-463 arrived at Marble Mountain Air Facility, where a detachment of the squadron was waiting to put them into operation as helicopter retrievers. |
| 25 Jan | A CH-53A from LtCol William R. Beeler's HMH-463 performed the first helicopter retrieval accomplished in Vietnam by this aircraft, lifting a disabled UH-34 off the landing platform of a Navy hospital ship. |
| 14 May | A HR2S made the last operational flight of a HR2S in Vietnam, carrying 20 troops and 3,000 pounds of cargo. |
| 22 May | The main body of HMH-463, with 22 CH-53s, arrived at Marble Mountain, completing the deployment of the new heavy helicopters to Vietnam. |
| Jul | The Secretary of the Navy approved funding and production of the Bell AH-1G Huey Cobra gunship for the Marine Corps. |
| 30 Jul | Naval Air Systems Command directed that all stored HR2Ss be stricken from the records and disposed of at the least expense to the government. This action marked the end of the association of this first true heavy-lift helicopter with the Marine Corps. |
| 31 Aug | MGen Norman J. Anderson, CG, 1st MAW, ordered all CH-46s grounded, except for missions to meet "emergency combat requirements which could not be met by other aircraft," after a series of fatal crashes caused by disintegration of the CH-46s' tail pylons. |
| 24 Oct | The Chief of Naval Operations approved Operational Requirement SOR-14-20, which called for a helicopter with an 18-ton lift capability, to be used by both the Navy and Marine Corps, operable from both *Iwo Jima* class LPHs and the new LHAs. |
| 9 Nov | Secretary of Defense Robert S. McNamara directed the U.S. Army to prepare plans for training helicopter pilots for the Marine Corps at Army facilities. This measure was intended to help remedy the Marines' wartime shortage of helicopter pilots. |
| 29 Nov | The first 32 "D" model CH-46s arrived at Phu Bai, to equip LtCol Louis A. Gulling's HMM-364. Personnel of the squadron had deployed to Vietnam earlier and had flown UH-34s to help relieve the lift shortage caused by the grounding of the CH-46. |
| 20 Dec | The CH-46 structural modification program at Futema, Okinawa, instituted to correct the problems which had caused the crashes and grounding of the CH-46 during the summer, was officially completed. During it, 80 CH-46s had been completed and returned to operation in Vietnam. |

## 1968

| | |
|---|---|
| 1 Jan | Gen Leonard F. Chapman, Jr., became the 24th Commandant of the Marine Corps. |
| 22 Mar | 2d Lt Larry D. Mullins was commissioned on this date and was the last Marine aviator to be commissioned from the MarCad program, which now came to an end. |
| 28 May | The Secretary of Defense announced the award of a contract to build a new type of amphibious assault ship for the Navy. This was the LHA (Landing Helicopter Assault Ship). |
| 24 Jul | The first CH-46F was accepted by the Marine Corps at the Vertol Plant in Morton, Pennsylvania. This model was designed to carry the long-awaited integrated helicopter avionics system (IHAS), which, however, quickly proved a failure in tests and was never installed. |
| 8 Nov | MGen McCutcheon, DC/S (Air), and Navy representatives recommended funding of tests of Sikorsky's proposed three-engine CH-53E as a heavy lift helicopter for the Navy and Marines. |

## 1969

| | |
|---|---|
| 18 Apr | The first Marine AH-1G Huey Cobra gunship flew its first operational mission in Vietnam, assigned to VMO-2. |
| 30 Jun | Marine Helicopter Training Group (MHTG)-40 was commissioned at New River, with the mission of providing post-graduate helicopter flight training to Marine pilots. |
| 2 Jul | The 500th CH-46 was delivered to the Marine Corps in a ceremony at the Vertol factory at Morton, Pennsylvania. Accepting the aircraft for the Marine Corps was BGen Homer S. "Dan" Hill, General McCutcheon's assistant and eventual successor as DC/S (Air). |
| 18 Aug | Ceremonies were held by HMM-362 at Phu Bai to mark the end of combat operations in Vietnam for the UH-34. The last six of these aircraft were flown to Da Nang for shipment to the U.S. two days later. |

| | |
|---|---|
| 14 Oct | The first Bell AH-1J twin-engine Sea Cobra was unveiled at the Bell factory before a board of Marine officers headed by BGen Victor A. Armstrong. |
| 27 Oct | The last Marine squadron equipped with UH-34s, HMM-561 at Santa Ana, a temporary wartime augmentation squadron, was decommissioned. |
| 16 Dec | All AH-1G Cobra gunships in Vietnam were transferred to HML-367, under LtCol Warren G. Cretney. |

### 1970

| | |
|---|---|
| 29 Jan | HMHT-401, the heavy helicopter training squadron of MHTG-40 at New River, accepted its first CH-53. |
| 9 Mar | Lieutenant General McCutcheon, who had just left the post of DC/S (Air), took command of the III Marine Amphibious Force in Vietnam. |
| July | The first four AH-1J Sea Cobra gunships were delivered to the Naval Air Test Center at Patuxent River for Board of Inspection and Survey trials. |

### 1971

| | |
|---|---|
| 20 Jan | The number of LHAs to be built was reduced from nine to five. |
| 2 Feb | BGen Homer S. "Dan" Hill, DC/S(Air), accepted the final production model of the CH-46F for the Marine Corps at the Vertol plant in Morton, Pennsylvania. This was the last of 624 A, D, and F models of the CH-46 to be delivered to the Marine Corps. |
| 18 Feb | Four AH-1J Sea Cobras arrived in Vietnam for combat evaluation and were assigned to HML-367. |
| 7 Apr | The first Bell UH-1N twin-engine Huey was delivered to HMA-269 at New River MCAS. |
| 28 Apr | Combat evaluation of the AH-1J in Vietnam was completed, with the twin-engine gunship having proved its ability to deliver "significantly greater effectiveness in firepower" than the AH-1G. |
| 26 May | The last Marine helicopter unit in Vietnam to cease combat operations, HML-167, stood down for redeployment to New River, leaving two UH-1Es behind for last-minute administrative support of the 3d Marine Amphibious Brigade. |
| 15 June | The last two UH-1Es of HML-167 flew on board ship for transfer to Okinawa. These were the only Marine helicopters then remaining in Vietnam. |
| 21-28 Jun | HML-167, just returned from Vietnam, was re-equipped at New River with the twin-engine Bell UH-1N Huey, becoming the first Marine light helicopter squadron to be so equipped. |
| 1 Jul | HMA-269, the first of three helicopter attack squadrons in the active Marine forces, was formally commissioned at New River MCAS. |
| 1 Nov | OSD approved continued development by the Navy of a three-engine CH-53 and separate development by the Army of a flying crane helicopter. |

### 1972

| | |
|---|---|
| 1 Jan | Gen Robert E. Cushman, Jr., became 25th Commandant of the Marine Corps. |
| Apr | The two special landing forces of the Seventh Fleet returned to the coast of South Vietnam to support Allied forces against the 30 March North Vietnamese invasion. The SLFs included HMM-164 and HMM-165. |

### 1973

| | |
|---|---|
| 1 Dec | Gen Cushman, CMC, attended the launching of the U.S.S. *Tarawa* (LHA-1) at Pascagoula, Mississippi. |

### 1974

| | |
|---|---|
| 1 Mar | The first three-engine CH-53E made its initial flight. |

# STANDARD AIRCRAFT CHARACTERISTICS

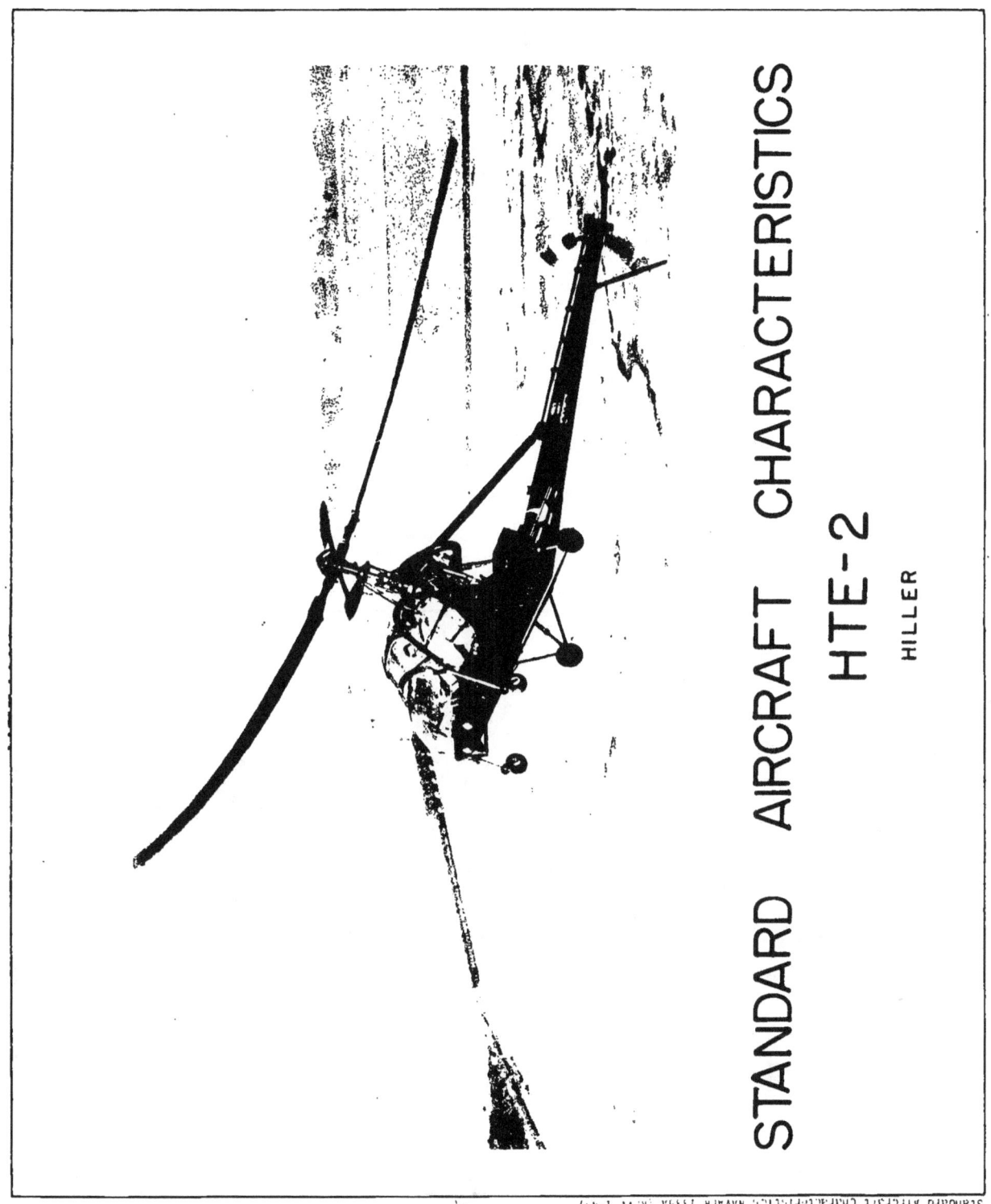

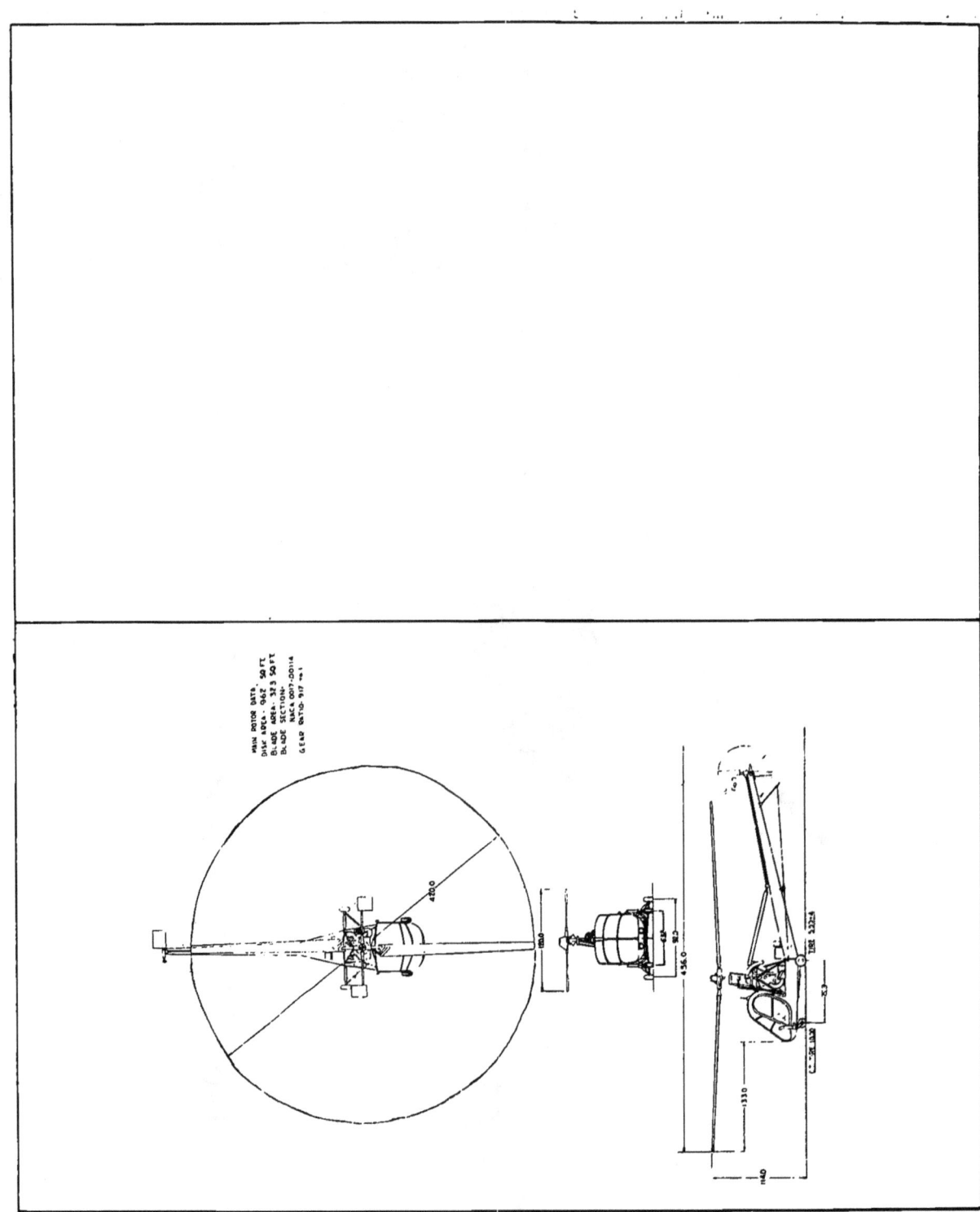

# STANDARD AIRCRAFT CHARACTERISTICS

## WEIGHTS

| Loadings | Lbs. | L.F. |
|---|---|---|
| EMPTY | 1,762 | |
| BASIC | 1,769 | |
| DESIGN | 2,500 | 2.84 |
| MAX.T.O. | 2,400 * | |
| MAX.LAND. | 2,400 | |

* Limited by performance

All weights are actual

## FUEL AND OIL

| Gals. | No. Tanks | Location |
|---|---|---|
| 28 | 1 | Fuselage |

FUEL GRADE......91/96
FUEL SPEC......MIL-F-5572

### OIL

CAPACITY (Gals.)......2.5
GRADE......1100
SPEC......MIL-O-6082

## ELECTRONICS

Receiver......R-19
Transmitter......T-11A
Transmitter......T-13
Receiver......R-11A

## MISSION AND DESCRIPTION

The HTE-2 helicopter is procured primarily for use as a trainer. It is similar in general configuration and rotor dimensions to the HTE-1 helicopter but has a 200 HP engine in place of the 178 HP engine and quadricycle instead of tricycle landing gear. These changes result in an increase in gross weight.

The model HTE-2 helicopter is a three-place (side-by-side) aircraft equipped with dual controls operated from the left and center seat positions. The aircraft has a two-bladed, teetering main rotor, a two-bladed, anti-torque tail rotor, and is equipped with an aerodynamic servo control rotor, whereby cyclic control is obtained through the aerodynamic action of two small airfoils mounted to the rotor hub at right angles to the main rotor blades.

## DEVELOPMENT

Service use............January 1951

## DIMENSIONS

DISC AREA......962.0 sq.ft.
BLADE AREA......32.3
BLADE DIA......35'
SPAN *......10'
LENGTH......40' -5"
HEIGHT......9' -6"
TREAD......7' -8"
CONTROL ROTOR
BLADE AREA...3.55 sq.ft.
STABILIZER AREA..2.49 sq.ft.

*Rotor stationed fore and aft.

## POWER PLANT

NO. & MODEL.....(1) O-335-6
MFR......Franklin
ROTOR GEAR RATIO......0.109
TAIL ROTOR RATIO......0.629

### RATINGS

| | Bhp. @ Rpm | @ Alt. |
|---|---|---|
| T.O. | 200 3100 | S.L. |
| NORMAL | 200 3100 | S.L. |

SPEC. NO. 19261A

## ACCOMMODATIONS

CREW......2
PASSENGER......1
LITTERS......2

## PERFORMANCE SUMMARY

| TAKE-OFF LOADING CONDITION | | (1) TRAINER<br>1 Pilot<br>1 Student | (2) UTILITY<br>1 Pilot<br>1 Passenger |
|---|---|---|---|
| TAKE-OFF WEIGHT | lb. | 2,338 | 2,400 |
| Fuel | lb. | 168 | 168 |
| Payload | lb. | 190 | 252 |
| Disc loading | lb./sq.ft. | 2.4 | 2.5 |
| Vertical rate of climb at S.L. (A/B) fpm. | | 0 | -- |
| Absolute hovering ceiling (A/B) ft. | | 0 | -- |
| Max. rate of climb at S.L. (A) fpm. | | 780 | 740 |
| Service ceiling (100 fpm) (A) ft. | | 7,400 | 7,000 |
| Speed at S.L. (A) kn. | | 73 | 72 |
| Max. speed/altitude (A) kn./ft. | | 73/S.L. | 72/S.L. |
| Combat range | n.mi. | 110 | 105 |
| Average cruising speed | kn. | 67 | 67 |
| Cruising altitude | ft. | 1,500 | 1,500 |
| Max. Endurance | hrs. | 2.0 | 2.0 |
| Average cruising speed | kn. | 40 | 41 |
| Cruising altitude | ft. | 1,500 | 1,500 |

### NOTES

(A) Normal power
(B) Take-off power

Performance is based on NATESTCEN flight test of the HTE-2

Combat range and maximum endurance are based on engine specification fuel consumption data increased by 5% and allowing fuel for warm-up and take-off (5 minutes at NRP) and a 10% fuel reserve. 3100 RPM is used at all speeds.

All performance is out of ground effect.

# STANDARD AIRCRAFT CHARACTERISTICS

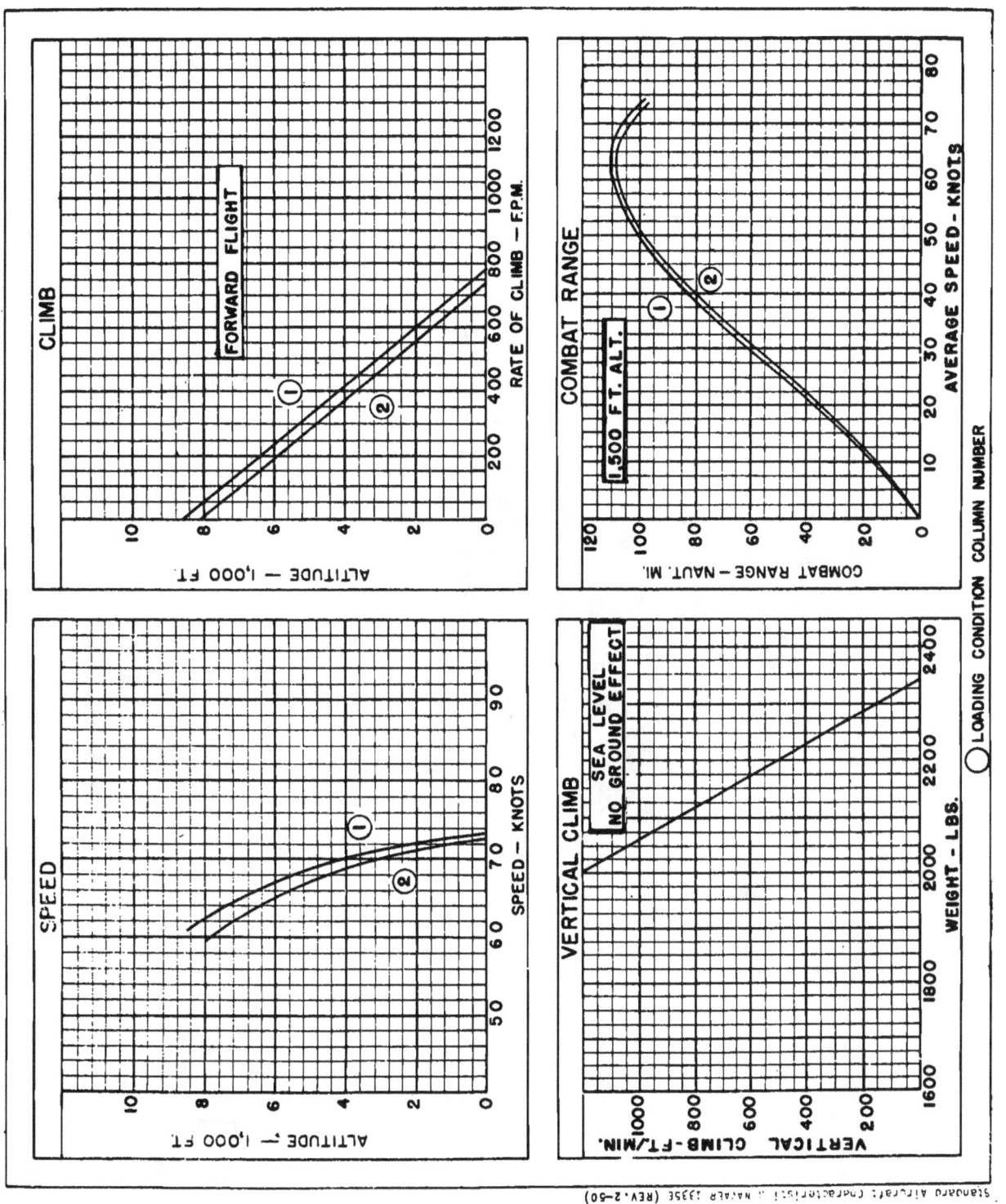

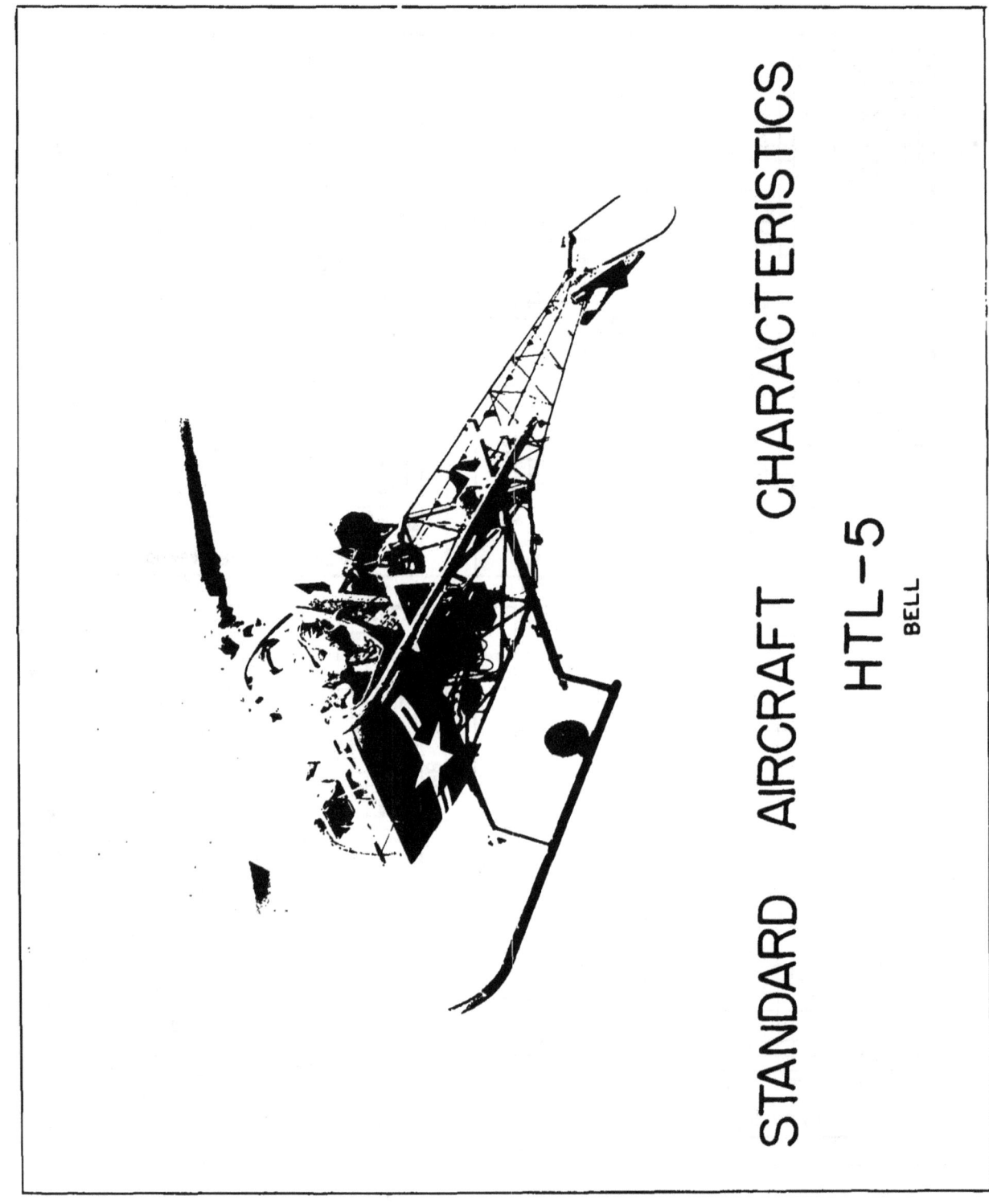

# STANDARD AIRCRAFT CHARACTERISTICS

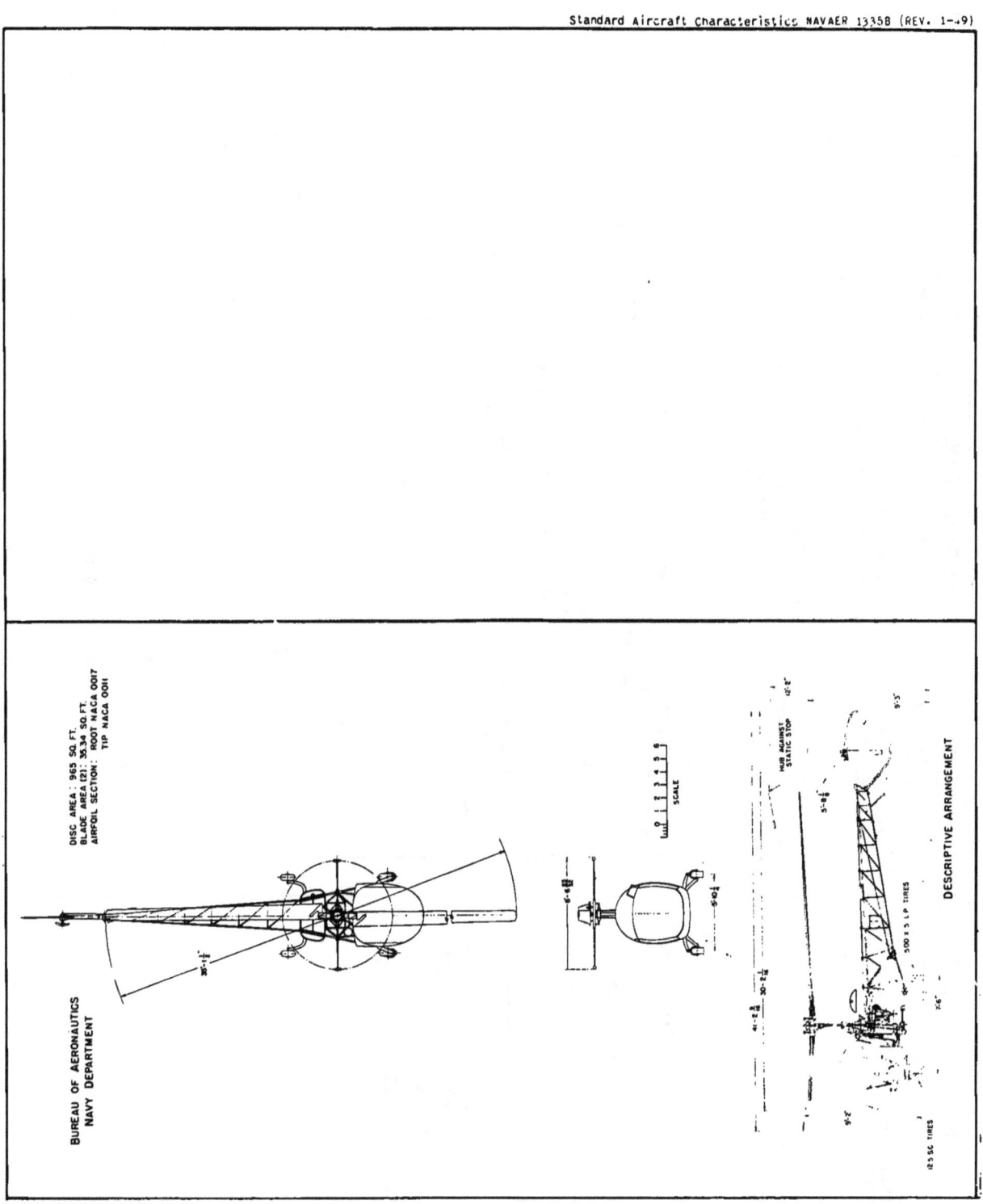

## WEIGHTS

| Loadings | Lbs. | L.F. |
|---|---|---|
| EMPTY | 1,561 | |
| BASIC | 1,570 | |
| DESIGN | 2,350 | 2.5 |
| MAX.T.O. | 2,350 | 2.5 |
| MAX.LAND | 2,350* | 2.5 |

All weights are calculated.

* Limited by performance

## FUEL AND OIL

| Gals. | No. Tanks | Location |
|---|---|---|
| 29 | 1 | Fuselage |

FUEL GRADE...91/98
FUEL SPEC...AN-F-48

### OIL

CAPACITY (Gals.)......2
GRADE................1100
SPEC..............AN-O-8

## ELECTRONICS

VHF TRANSMITTER.......T-11A
VHF TRANSMITTER.......T-13
VHF REC.(118-148 mcs).R-19
RANGE REC.(190-550 kcs).R-11A

## MISSION AND DESCRIPTION

The primary mission of the HTL-5 is training. It will also be used in combat areas for the evacuation of wounded, mine spotting, liaison, carrying limited amounts of critical supplies, and general utility.

It is similar in general configuration and rotor dimensions to the HTL-4, but an improved transmission and a rotor brake have been installed with a 15 pound increase in empty weight.

Some of these helicopters are being delivered with skid type gear and some with wheel type gear. Kits containing the other type of gear are being supplied with each helicopter.

The HTL-5 is a three-place, single engine helicopter equipped with a two-bladed main rotor with a gyroscopic action stabilizer bar. The main rotor is of the see-saw type, the blade being rigidly interconnected by means of the hub except that each blade is separately journaled to the hub for pitch change.

In service use -- November 1951

## DIMENSIONS

DISC AREA.........969 sq. ft.
BLADE DIA.........35' - 2"
LENGTH............41' - 5"
HEIGHT*...........11' - 3"
TREAD.............5' - 11"
BLADE AREA........35 sq. ft.

* Blades in stowed position.

## POWER PLANT

NO. & MODEL......(1) O-335-5
MFR........Aircooled Motors
ROTOR GEAR RATIO.......0.111
TAIL ROTOR RATIO........0.60

### RATINGS

| | Bhp @ Rpm @ Alt. |
|---|---|
| NORMAL | 200  3,100  S. L. |

SPEC. NO. 19178

## ACCOMMODATIONS

CREW AND PASSENGERS ON
SEAT....................3
EXTERNAL LITTERS........2

## PERFORMANCE SUMMARY

| LOADING CONDITION | | (1) TRAINER 1 Pilot 1 Student | (2) TRAINER 1 Pilot Cargo/Passen. |
|---|---|---|---|
| TAKE-OFF WEIGHT | lbs. | 2,141 | 2,350 |
| Fuel | lbs. | 174 | 174 |
| Pay Load | lbs. | 190 | 400 |
| Engine Power | bhp/rpm | 200/3,100 | 200/3,100 |
| Disc Loading | lbs./sq.ft. | 2.2 | 2.4 |
| Power Loading (A) | lbs./bhp. | 10.7 | 11.7 |
| Maximum Speed—S.L. (B) | kn. | 80 | 80 |
| Maximum Speed/Alt. (B) | kn./ft. | 82/1,900 | 80/S.L. |
| Rate of Climb—S.L. (B) | ft./min. | 985 | 850 |
| Speed for Rate of Climb—S.L. (B) | kn. | 45 | 45 |
| Time-to-Climb 5,000 ft. (B) | min. | 6.3 | 7.5 |
| Time-to-Climb 10,000 ft. (B) | min. | 18.0 | 25.0 |
| Service Ceiling (B) | ft. | 12,500 | 10,600 |
| Vertical Rate of Climb—S.L. (B/C) | ft./min. | 300 | -- |
| Abs. Hover Ceil. No Grd. Effect (B/C) | ft. | 1,400 | -- |
| Abs. Hover Ceil. In Grd. Effect (B/C) | ft. | -- | -- |
| Combat Range/Vav 1,500 ft. | n.mi./kn. | 105/65 | 95/65 |
| Max. Endur./Vav 1,500 ft. | hr./kn. | 1.9/45 | 1.7/45 |

### NOTES

(A) BHP at Maximum Critical Altitude
(B) Normal BHP
(C) Take-Off Power

Performance is based on NATC flight test of the HTL-3 helicopter.

Combat range and maximum endurance are based on flight test fuel consumption data increased by 5% and allowing fuel for warm-up and take-off (5 minutes at NHP) and a 10% fuel reserve.

All performance is based on 3,100 RPM and is out of ground effect.

Maximum speed is restricted to 80 knots IAS by BUAER Technical Order No. 40-51 of 1 June 1951.

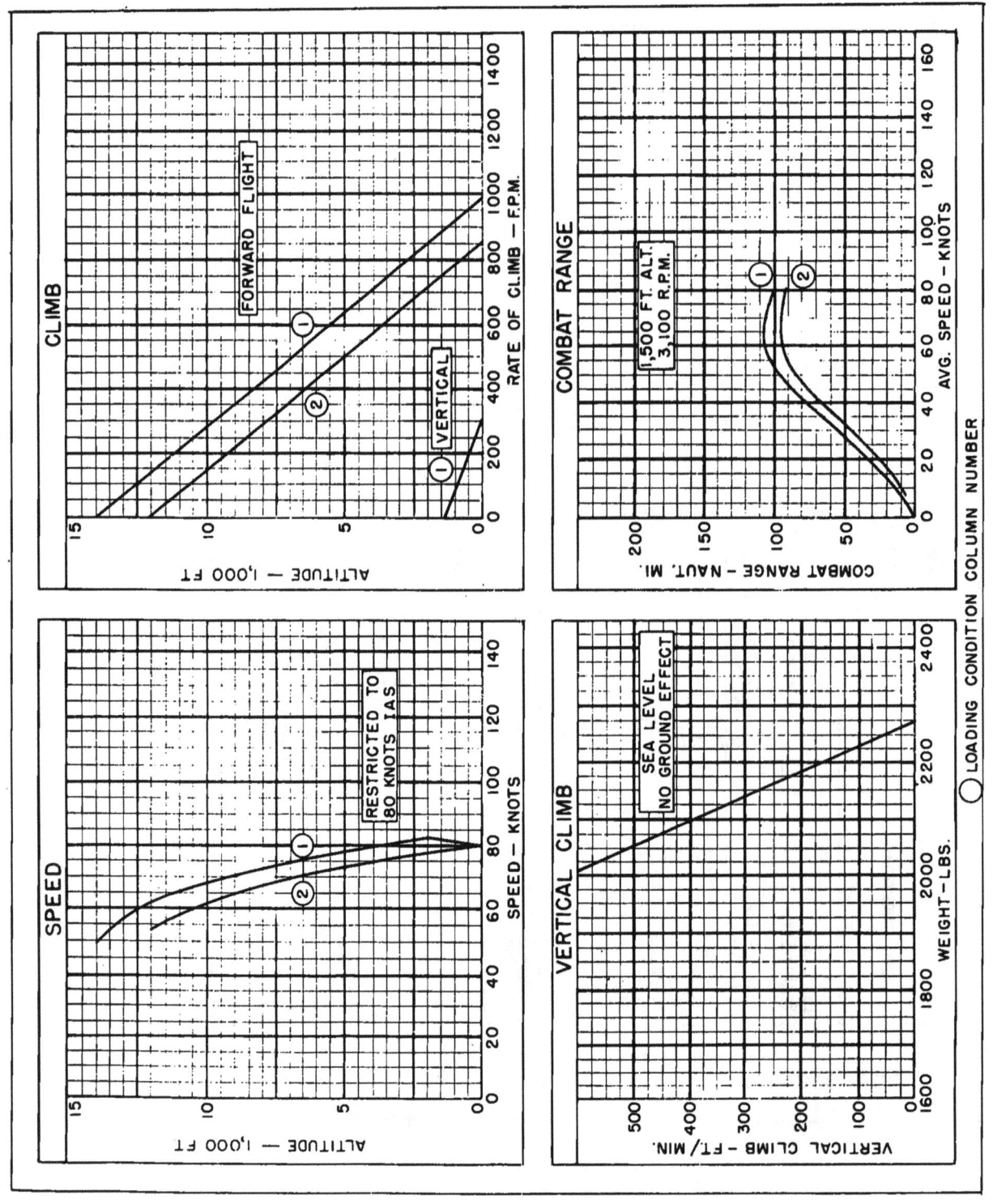

# STANDARD AIRCRAFT CHARACTERISTICS

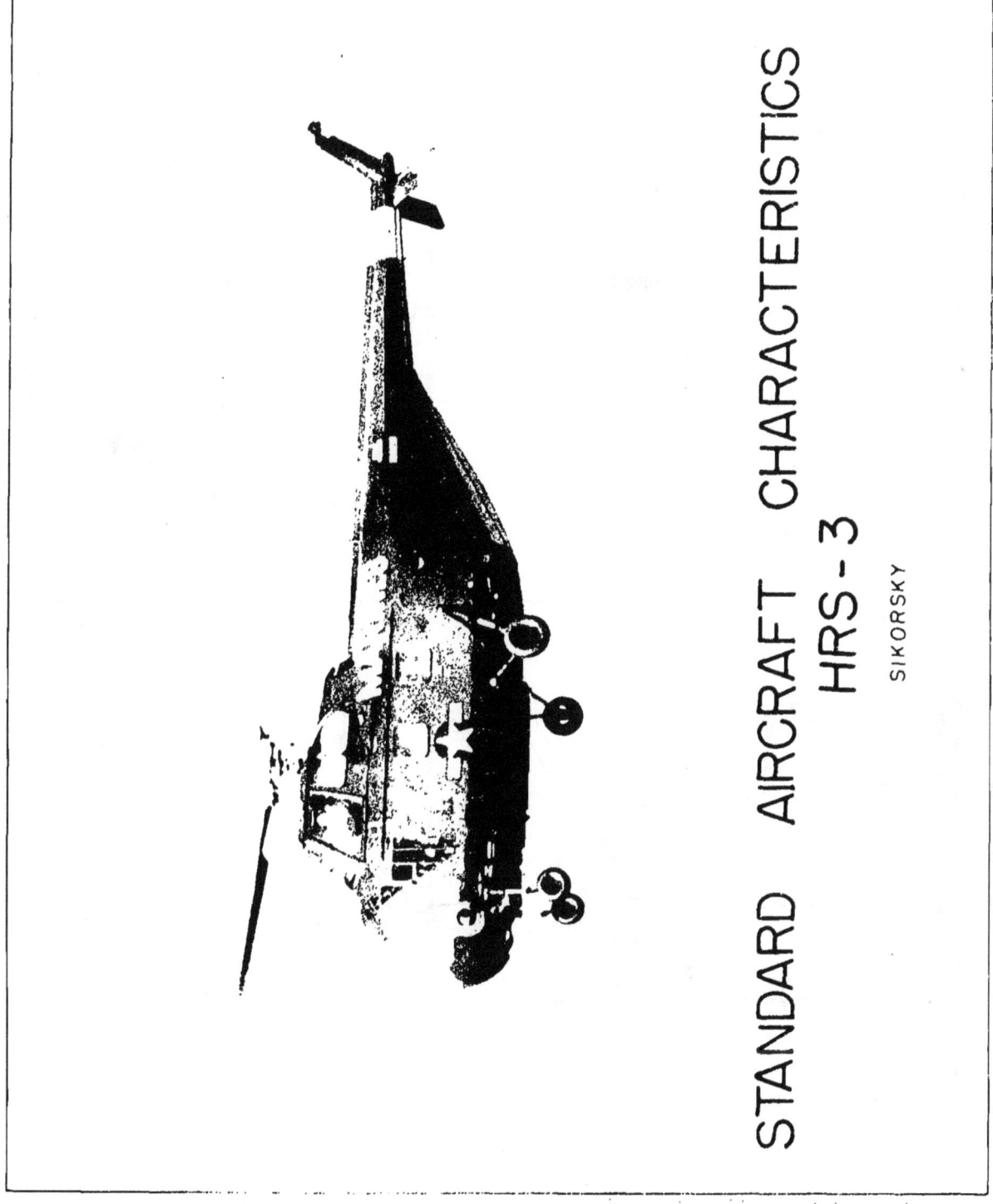

# STANDARD AIRCRAFT CHARACTERISTICS
## HRS - 3
SIKORSKY

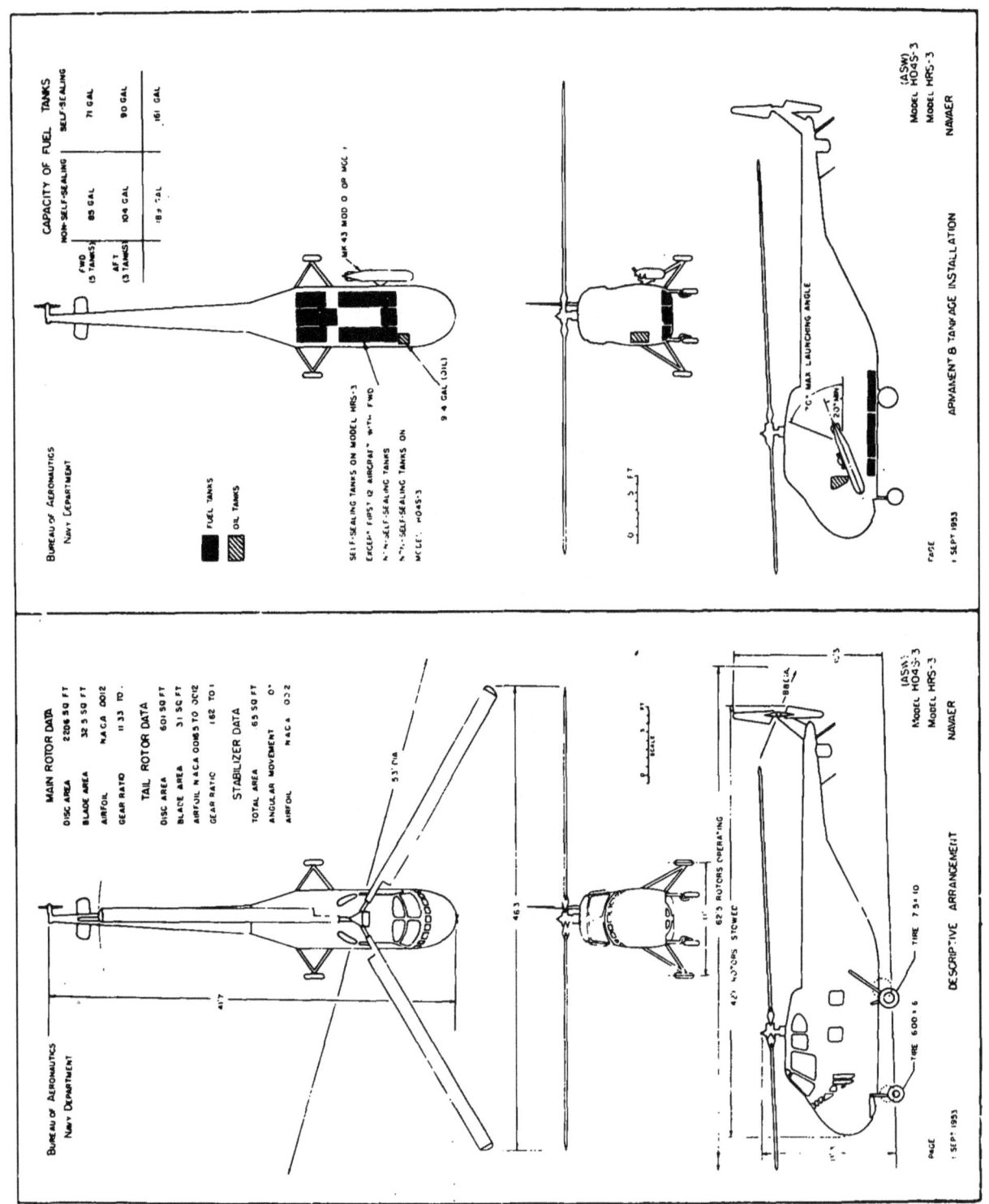

# STANDARD AIRCRAFT CHARACTERISTICS

## POWER PLANT

NO. & MODEL......(1)R-1300-3
MFR.............................Wright
SUPERCH.........................1 Speed
ROTOR GEAR RATIO..........0.0582
TAIL ROTOR RATIO...........0.617

### RATINGS

|       | BHP | RPM  | ALT  |
|-------|-----|------|------|
| T.O.  | 800 | 2600 | S.L. |
| NORMAL| 700 | 2400 | 5,700|

See not on performance summary page

SPEC. NO. W.A.D. AC-9322:

## ACCOMMODATIONS

Pilot............................1
Dual-Pilot......................1
Combat Troops..................10
Litters..........................3
Door size...............48" X 48"

## MISSION AND DESCRIPTION

The HRS-3 is a transport helicopter. The primary mission of this helicopter is to transport assault troops and equipment from ships or land bases to the objective area and the evacuation of wounded. It may also be used for ship-to-ship liaison and general utility.

The most significant change incorporated in this model was the installation of a more powerful engine. The engine is mounted facing rearward in the nose of the aircraft with the shaft inclined 35° from the horizontal. Access is provided through clam-shell type nose doors and through a removable panel in the firewall.

Design features include an external cargo sling, provisions for a hydraulic hoist for airborne loading or rescue, equipment for night contact flying, hydraulically operated servo controls, a hydraulic clutch to accelerate the transmission to engine speed, and cockpit and cabin ventilation.

Accommodations for ten passengers are provided in the cabin of the HRS-3. Alternate arrangements for three litters and an attendant can be carried.

### DEVELOPMENT

Development of the HRS-2 Service Use.........February 1953

## WEIGHTS

| LOADINGS | LBS | L.F. |
|----------|-----|------|
| EMPTY    | 5,193 | |
| BASIC    | 5,261 | |
| DESIGN   | 7,100 | 2.67 |
| MAX.T.O.*| 7,761 | 2.44 |
| MAX.LAND.| 7,761 | 2.44 |

* Maximum anticipated loading

## FUEL AND OIL

| NO.TANKS | TOT.GALS | LOCATION |
|----------|----------|----------|
| 2        | 161      | Fuselage |

FUEL GRADE.........91/96
FUEL SPEC......MIL-F-5572

### OIL

CAPACITY(Gals)..........9.4
GRADE.....................1100
SPEC................MIL-O-6082

## ELECTRONICS

R-19 A.R.C. Type Receiver
R-26/ARC-5 MHF Receiver
T-19/ARC-5 MHF Transmitter
T-23/ARC-5 VHF Transmitter
R-11A A.R.C. Type Receiver

## DIMENSIONS

DISC AREA..........2206 sq.ft.
BLADE AREA.........97.5 sq.ft.
STABILIZER AREA....6.5 sq.ft.
BLADE DIA...........53' -0"
LENGTH..............42' -1"
OVERALL LENGTH**....62' -6"
HEIGHT..............13' -4"
TREAD...............11' -0"

* Blades Folded
** Rotors operating

## PERFORMANCE SUMMARY

| TAKEOFF LOADING CONDITION | | (1) Troop Transp. Crew (1) Passengers (8) | (2) Rescue Crew (1) Litter Patients (3) | (3) Cargo Transp. Crew (1) |
|---|---|---|---|---|
| TAKEOFF WEIGHT | lb. | 7,761 | 7,065 | 7,725 |
| Fuel | lb. | 455 | 966 | 210 |
| Payload | lb. | 1,800 | 510 | 2,000 |
| Disc loading | lb./sq.ft. | 3.5 | 3.2 | 3.5 |
| Vertical rate of climb at S.L. (A/B) fpm. | | 145/— | 745/— | 180/— |
| Absolute hovering ceiling (A/B) ft. | | 2,000/— | 7,100/— | 2,550/— |
| Max. rate of climb at S.L. (A) fpm. | | 1,095 | 1,345 | 1,110 |
| Service ceiling (100 fpm) (A) ft. | | 12,800 | 14,700 | 12,900 |
| Speed at S.L. (A) kn. | | 103 | 105 | 103 |
| Max. speed/altitude (A) kn./ft. | | 105/5,000 | 108/5,700 | 105/5,000 |
| Combat range | n.mi. | 110 | 280 | 40 |
| Average cruising speed | kn. | 77 | 79 | 76 |
| Cruising altitude | ft. | 1,500 | 1,500 | 1,500 |
| Combat radius | n.mi. | 45 | 108 | 10 |
| Average cruising speed | kn. | 77 | 78 | 77 |
| Cruising altitude | | 1,500 | 1,500 | 1,500 |
| Max. endurance | | 1.7 | 4.4 | 0.6 |
| Average speed | | 54 | 49 | 54 |
| Altitude | | 1,500 | 1,500 | 1,500 |
| %BHP req'd to hover at S.L., no wind | | 97 | 86 | 96 |

### NOTES

(A) Normal power
(B) Take-off power

Performance basis: NATESTCEN flight test of the HRS-3 helicopter and Air Force flight test of the H-19B helicopter.

All performance is out of ground effect and in standard atmosphere (59°F).

Range, radius, and endurance are based on NATESTCEN fuel consumption test data increased by 5% and allowing fuel for warm-up and take-off (5 minutes at NRP) and a 10% fuel reserve. 2,400 rpm is used at all speeds.

Power is limited to a maximum value of 700 BHP by helicopter transmission capacity. Engine is limited to 2400 rpm.

# STANDARD AIRCRAFT CHARACTERISTICS

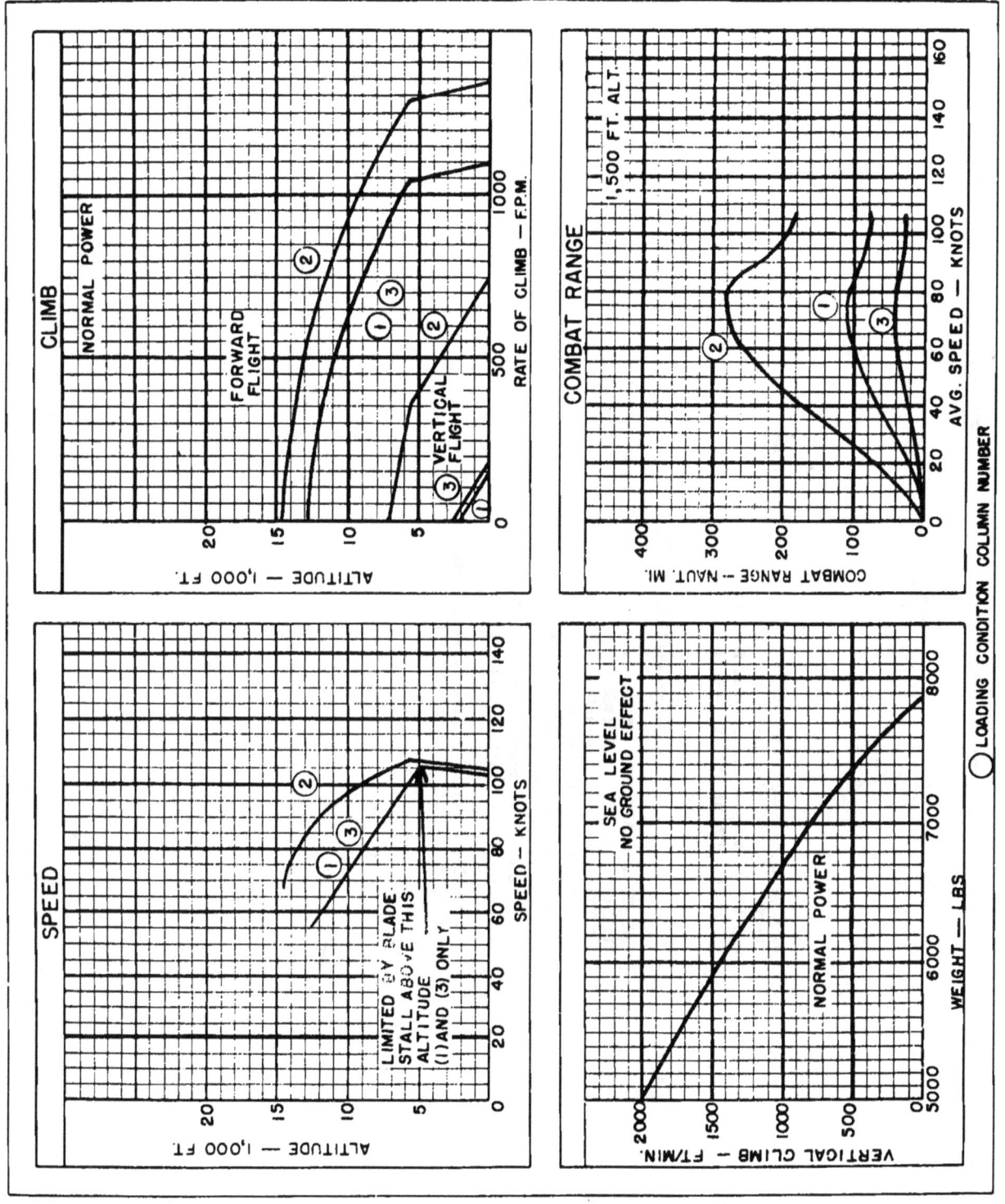

# NOTES

## ENDURANCE PROBLEM

WARM-UP AND TAKE-OFF: 5 minutes at normal rated power
CLIMB: To 1500 ft. altitude
CRUISE: At speed for minimum fuel flow
RESERVE: 10% of initial fuel load

## COMBAT RADIUS PROBLEM

WARM-UP AND TAKE-OFF: 5 minutes at normal rated power
CLIMB: To 1500 ft. altitude
CRUISE: At speed for maximum range
LAND AT REMOTE SEA LEVEL BASE
RESTART, WARM-UP AND TAKE-OFF: 5 minutes at normal rated power
CLIMB: To 1500 ft. altitude
CRUISE-BACK: At speed for maximum range
RESERVE: 10% of initial fuel load

NOTE: Weight of cargo carried both ways.

# STANDARD AIRCRAFT CHARACTERISTICS
## TH-13N

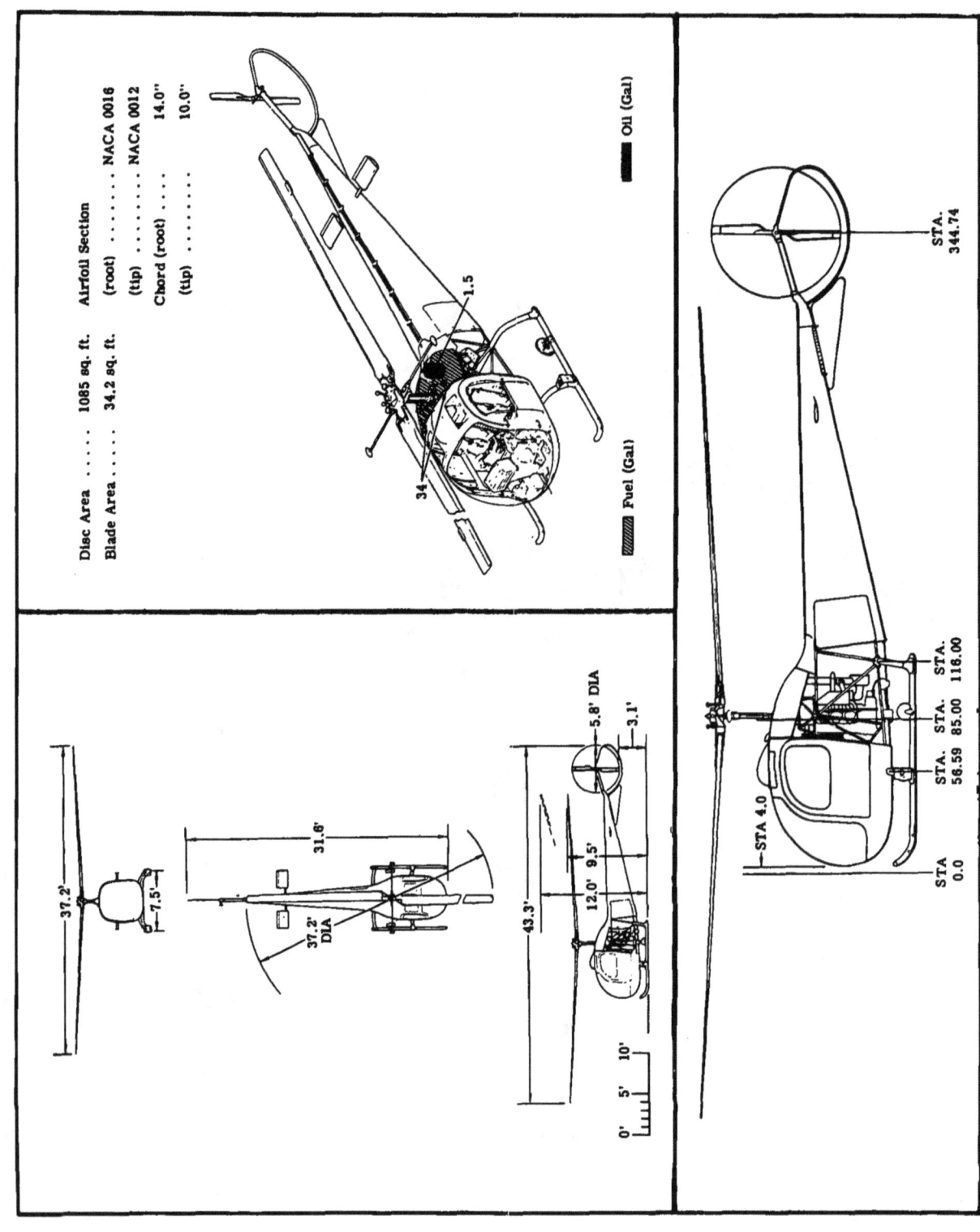

# STANDARD AIRCRAFT CHARACTERISTICS

## POWER PLANT

No. and Model..............(1) VO-435-6
Manufacturer.....................Lycoming
Main Rotor Gear Ratio.............0.111
Tail Rotor Gear Ratio.............0.600

### RATINGS

|  | BHP @ RPM @ ALT |
|---|---|
| Take-off (5 Min) | 240  3200  1300 |
| Normal | 220  3200  3800 |

Spec. No. 2207-B

## MISSION AND DESCRIPTION

The basic mission of the HTL-7 is to train pilots for both primary and instrument flight.

The HTL-7 has a two-blade semi-rigid rotor with a stabilizer bar, and a two-blade semi-rigid tail rotor mounted on a delta hinge. The rotor, transmission and engine are suspended as a unit on rubber mounts in the fuselage. Mechanically the HTL-7 is nearly identical to the HUL-1. The fuselage is semi-monocoque except for the engine compartment, or center frame, which is of steel tube construction.

The control system has conventional dual controls, with full hydraulic motivation on the cyclic stick, and direct mechanical linkage to the rotor. The cabin has a military standard arrangement in all respects with side by side seating. Blind flying is possible using the A.C. powered gyro horizon and gyro stabilized compass. The stand-by blind flying instruments include a D.C. turn and slip indicator, a barometric rate of climb indicator, and a magnetic compass. A radio system is provided to permit communication and radio navigation. The landing gear is of the skid type with small handling wheels.

## WEIGHTS

| Loading | Weight |
|---|---|
| Empty | 1892 |
| Basic | 1916 |
| Design | 2565 |
| Maximum T.O. | 2565 |

All weights are actual

## FUEL AND OIL

| No. of Tanks | Gals. | Location |
|---|---|---|
| 2 | 35 | Fuselage |

Grade.................91/96
Specification.........MIL-F-5572

### OIL

Capacity (Gals)........1065/1100
Grade..................3
Specification..........MIL-L-6082

## DEVELOPMENT

First Flight...............December 1957
Service Use................February 1958

## DIMENSIONS

Disc Area...............1085 sq. ft.
Rotor Dia...............37'.2 sq. ft.
Blade Area..............34'.2 sq. ft.
Length (Fuselage).......31'.6 sq. ft.
Height..................9' 6"
Tread...................7' 6"

## ACCOMMODATIONS

Pilot.....................1
Passenger.................1

or

Instructor................1
Student...................1

## ELECTRONICS

UHF......................ARC-TYPE 12
UHF RECEIVER.............R-fy
UHF TRANSVERTER..........TV-10
UHF RELAY OSCILLATOR UNIT....K-13
AIF RADIO................AN/ARN-41A

## PERFORMANCE SUMMARY

| TAKE-OFF LOADING CONDITION | | (1) TRAINER<br>1 pilot<br>1 student | (2) TRAINER<br>1 pilot<br>1 passenger+cargo |
|---|---|---|---|
| TAKE-OFF WEIGHT | lb. | 2450 | 2565 |
| Fuel | lb. | 210 | 210 |
| Payload | lb. | 170 | 285 |
| Disc loading | lb./sq.ft. | 2.26 | 2.36 |
| Vertical rate of climb at S.L. (A)/(B) | fpm. | 700/220 | 525/25 |
| Absolute hovering ceiling (B) | ft. | (C) 4400/7725 (C) | 200/6400 (D) |
| Max. rate of climb at S.L. (B) | fpm. | 835 | 680 |
| Service ceiling (100 fpm) (B) | ft. | 15,750 | 13,800 |
| Speed at S.L. (B) | kn. | 82 | 81 |
| Max. speed/altitude (B) | kn./ft. | 83/3500 | 82/3500 |
| Max. range (B) | n.mi. | 130 | 125 |
| Average cruising speed | kn. | 72 | 72 |
| Cruising altitude | ft. | S.L. | S.L. |
| Max. endurance | hrs. | 2.2 | |
| Average cruising speed | kn. | 40 | |
| Cruising altitude | | S.L. | |

## NOTES

(A) MILITARY POWER (5 min. limit)
(B) NORMAL POWER
(C) IN GROUND EFFECT
(D) OUT OF GROUND EFFECT

Performance is based on NATESTCEN evaluation of the Model HTL-7 Helicopter
Range and Endurance are based on NATESTCEN fuel consumption test of the Model HTL-7 Helicopter
All performance data presented is for the skid gear configuration

### Maximum Range Mission

Warm-up and take-off: 5 minutes at Normal Rated Power
Cruise out: At speed for maximum range at sea level
Reserve: 10% of initial fuel load

### Maximum Endurance Mission

Warm-up and Take-off: 5 minutes at Normal Rated Power
Cruise out: At speed for maximum endurance at sea level
Reserve: 10% of initial fuel load

# STANDARD AIRCRAFT CHARACTERISTICS

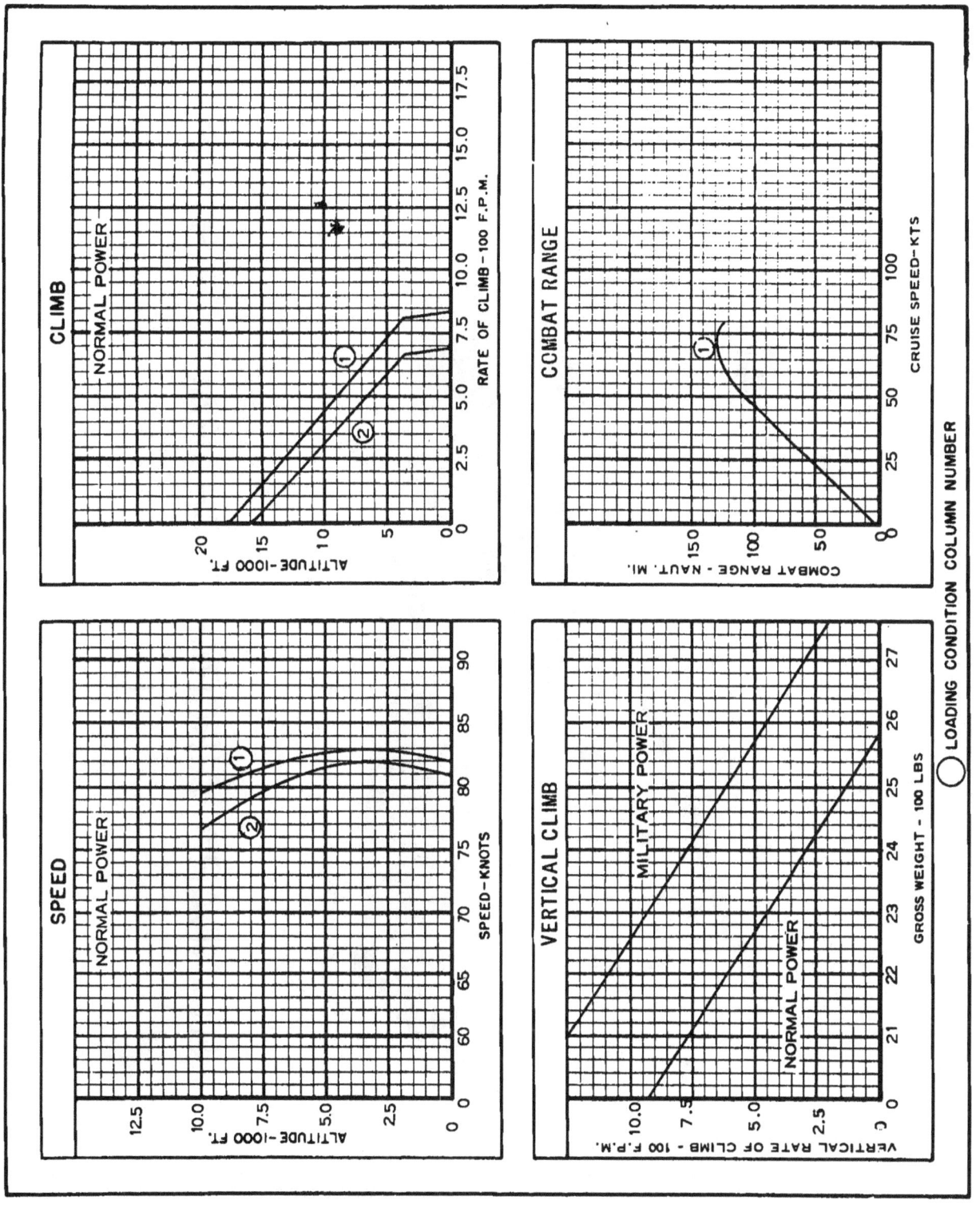

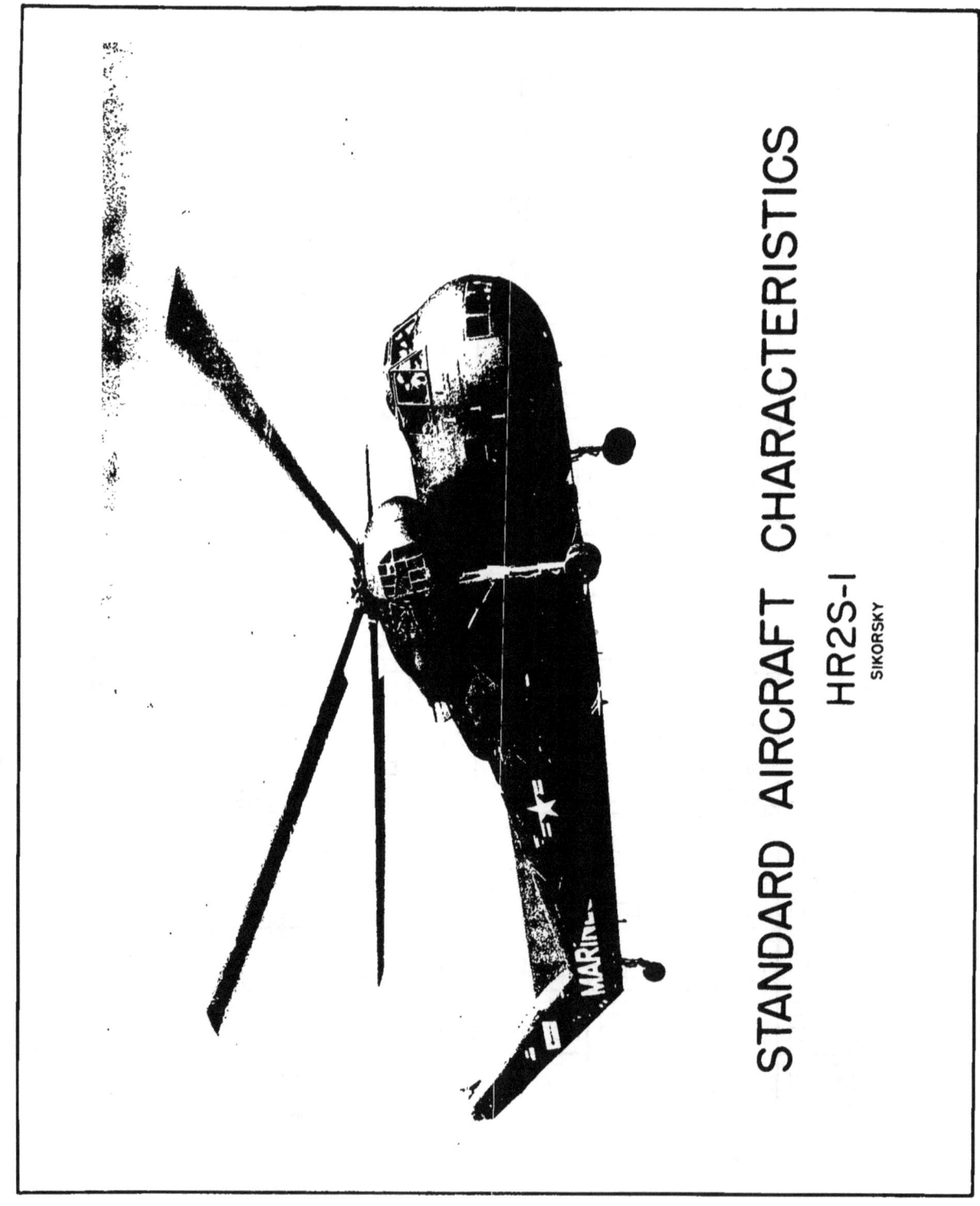

# STANDARD AIRCRAFT CHARACTERISTICS

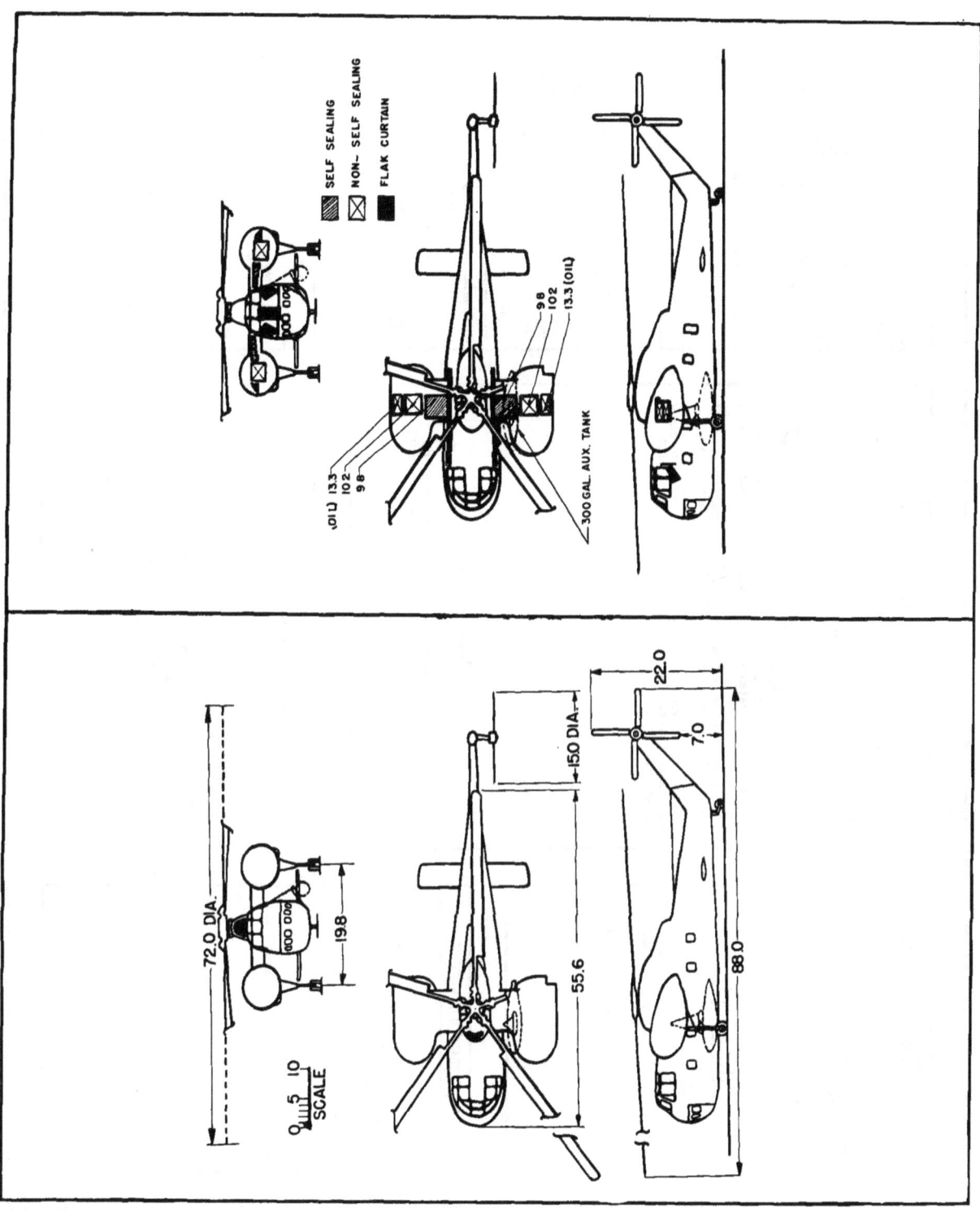

## POWER PLANT

| | |
|---|---|
| NO. & MODEL | (2) R-2800-54 |
| MFR | Pratt & Whitney |
| SUPERCHARGER | 1 Stage, 1 Speed |
| ROTOR GEAR RATIO | 14.01 to 1 |
| TAIL ROTOR RATIO | 2.9 to 1 |

### RATINGS

| | BHP @ | RPM @ | ALT |
|---|---|---|---|
| T.O. | 2100 | 2700 | 5000 |
| NORM. | 1900 | 2600 | 7000 |

Spec. No. M-8143B

## MISSION AND DESCRIPTION

The primary mission of the model HR2S-1 helicopter is to transport assault troops and equipment from ships or land bases to a target and return. It is suitable for operation from aircraft carriers (except for CVE and CVL class) and from land bases.

The HR2S-1 has a twin engine, single main rotor with an automatic torque compensation tail rotor and a controlled stabilizer. It incorporates a dual control system. The mechanical flight controls are augmented by a primary and secondary servo system with an automatic stabilization device.

A blade flapping restrainer and a rotor brake are provided for starting and stopping the rotor in winds up to 60 knots.

There are provisions for an auxiliary fuel system to allow installation of two-300 gallon external tanks or two-150 gallon tanks.

## WEIGHTS

| LOADING: | LBS | L.F. |
|---|---|---|
| EMPTY | 21,502 | |
| BASIC | 21,502 | |
| DESIGN | 31,000 | 2.5 |
| COMBAT (Basic) | 28,706 | 2.7 |
| T.O. (Normal) | 31,000 | 2.5 |
| T.O. (Overload) | 31,000 | 2.5 |
| MAX. LANDING | 31,000 | 2.5 |

All weights are actual

## ACCOMMODATIONS

| | |
|---|---|
| PILOT | 1 |
| CO-PILOT | 1 |
| COMBAT TROOPS | 20 |
| or | |
| LITTERS | 16 |

MAXIMUM CARGO CAPACITY ... 10,000 lbs.

## DEVELOPMENT

| | |
|---|---|
| First Flight | December 1953 |
| Service Use | June 1956 |

## DIMENSIONS

| | |
|---|---|
| DISC AREA | 4017.5 sq. ft. |
| BLADE AREA | 261.5 sq. ft. |
| NO. OF BLADES(MAIN) | 5 |
| ROTOR DIA. | 72' - 0" |
| LENGTH | 58' - 5" |
| HEIGHT | 16' - 8" |
| (tail rotor folded and tail rotor positioned) | |
| TREAD | 19' - 9" |
| STABILIZER AREA | 111.7 sq. ft. |

## FUEL AND OIL

| GALS. | NO. TANKS | LOCATION |
|---|---|---|
| 196 | 2 | Nacelles |
| 204 | 2 | Wing * |
| 600 | 2 | Fuse. Sides (ext.) |

* Self Sealing

| | |
|---|---|
| FUEL GRADE | 115/145 |
| FUEL SPEC (applicable) | MIL-F-5572 |

### OIL

| | |
|---|---|
| CAPACITY (Gals.) | 26.6 |
| GRADE | 1100 |
| SPEC (applicable) | MIL-O-6082 |

## ELECTRONICS

| | |
|---|---|
| CODER GROUP | AN/APA-89 |
| UHF TRANS/RECOR | AN/ARC-27A or AN/ARC-55 |
| MHF TRANS/RECOR | AN/ARC-2A |
| ICS | AN/AIC-4A |
| DIR. FINDER GROUP | AN/ARA-25 |
| RADAR ALTIMETER | AN/APN-22 |
| TRANS/RECOR | AN/APX-6B |
| RADIO SET (TACAN) | AN/ARN-21 |
| RADIO RECEIVER | AN/ARN-41A |
| FM COMMUNICATIONS SET | AN/ARC-44 |

## STANDARD AIRCRAFT CHARACTERISTICS

### PERFORMANCE SUMMARY

| TAKE-OFF LOADING CONDITION | | (1) ASSAULT TRANSPORT (Normal) 1 Ext. Fuel Tank | (2) CARGO (Overload) | (3) FERRY Maximum Fuel 2 Ext. Fuel Tanks |
|---|---|---|---|---|
| TAKE-OFF WEIGHT | lb. | 31,000 | 31,000 | 28,533 |
| Fuel internal/external | lb. | 2400/1527 | 2400/0 | 2400/3600 |
| Payload | lb. | 4500 | 6673 | 0 |
| Disc loading | lb./sq.ft. | 7.61 | 7.61 | 7.00 |
| Vertical rate of climb at S.L. (A) | fpm | 0 | 0 | 950 |
| Absolute hovering ceiling (A) | ft. | 0 | 0 | 5400 |
| Max. rate of climb at S.L. (B) | fpm | 1280 | 1280 | 1580 |
| Service ceiling (100 fpm) (B) | ft. | 11,500 | 11,500 | 13,800 |
| Speed at S.L. (B) | kn. | 115 | 119 | 121 |
| Max. speed/altitude | kn./ft. | 115/S.L. | 119/S.L. | 121/S.L. |
| Combat range | n.mi. | -- | -- | 335 |
| Average cruising speed | kn. | -- | -- | 100 |
| Cruising altitude | ft. | -- | -- | 0 |
| Combat radius | n.mi. | 100 | 71 | -- |
| Average cruising speed | kn. | 100 | 100 | -- |

### NOTES

(A) TAKE-OFF RATED POWER
(B) NORMAL RATED POWER

PERFORMANCE BASIS: NATESTCEN flight test data.

COMBAT RANGE and RADIUS are based on NATESTCEN fuel consumption data.

All performance is out of ground effect.

Maximum airspeed limited by blade tip stall and Mach Number effects on rotor blades.

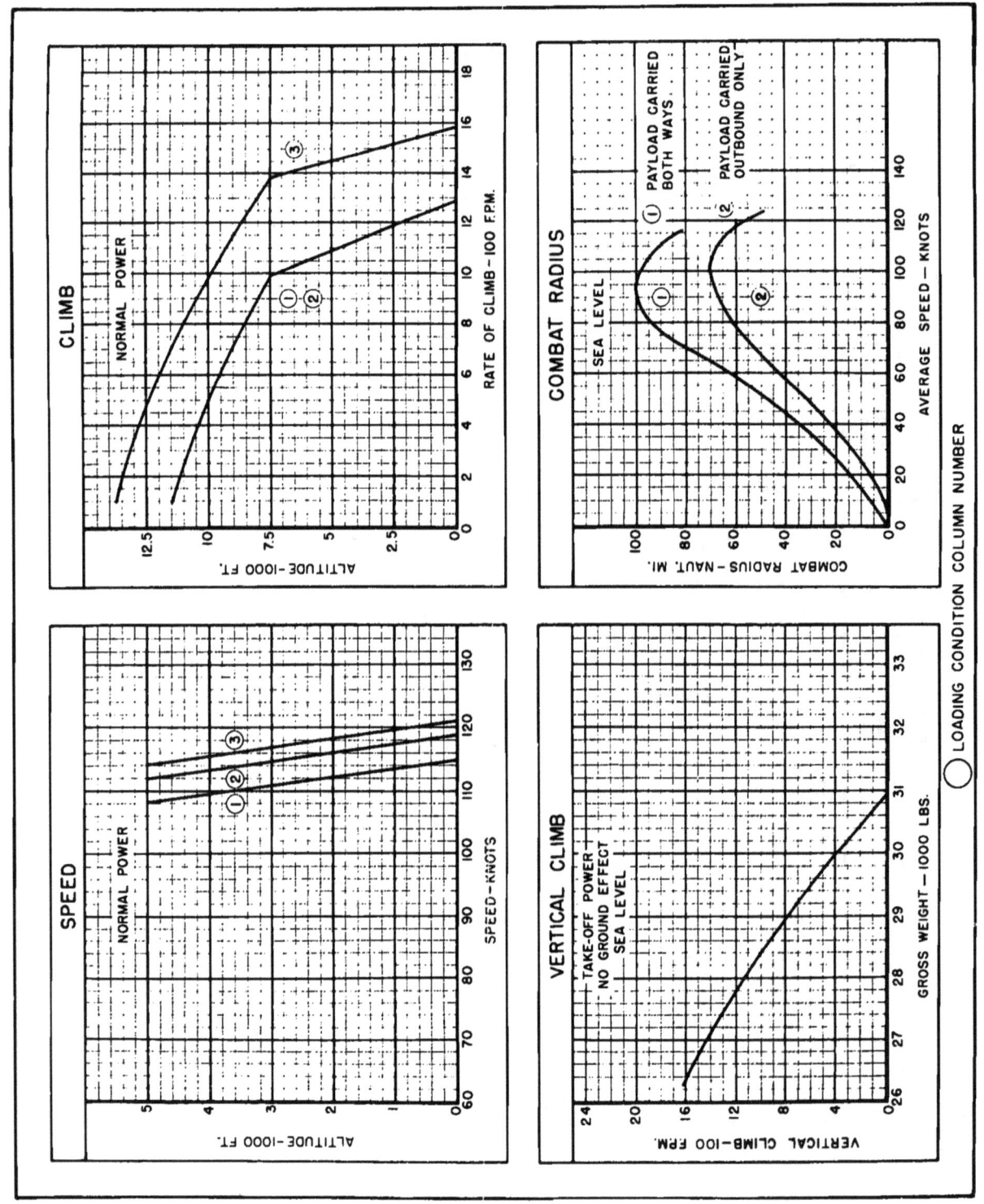

# NOTES

## ASSAULT COMBAT RADIUS MISSION

WARM-UP, TAKE-OFF, RENDEZVOUS: 10 minutes fuel allowance at normal rated power.
CRUISE-OUT: At sea level at 80% normal rated power.
LAND AT TARGET AND TAKE-OFF: No change in payload; fuel allowance of 5 minutes at normal rated power.
CRUISE-BACK: At sea level at 80% normal rated power.
RESERVE: 10% of initial fuel load.

## CARGO MISSION

Same as Assault Combat Radius Mission except in lieu of 20 assault troops, 6673 lbs. of cargo is carried out and unloaded at target.

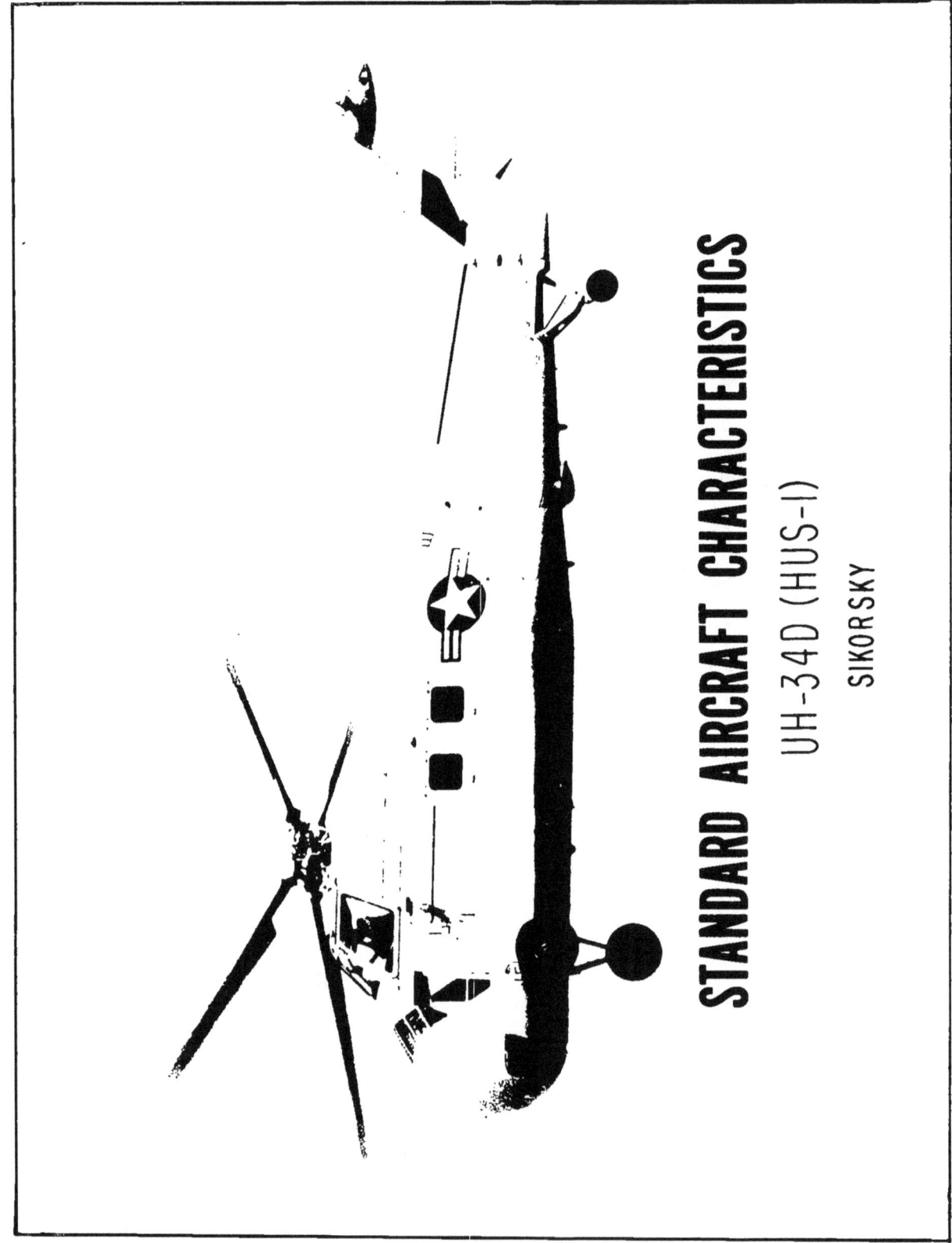

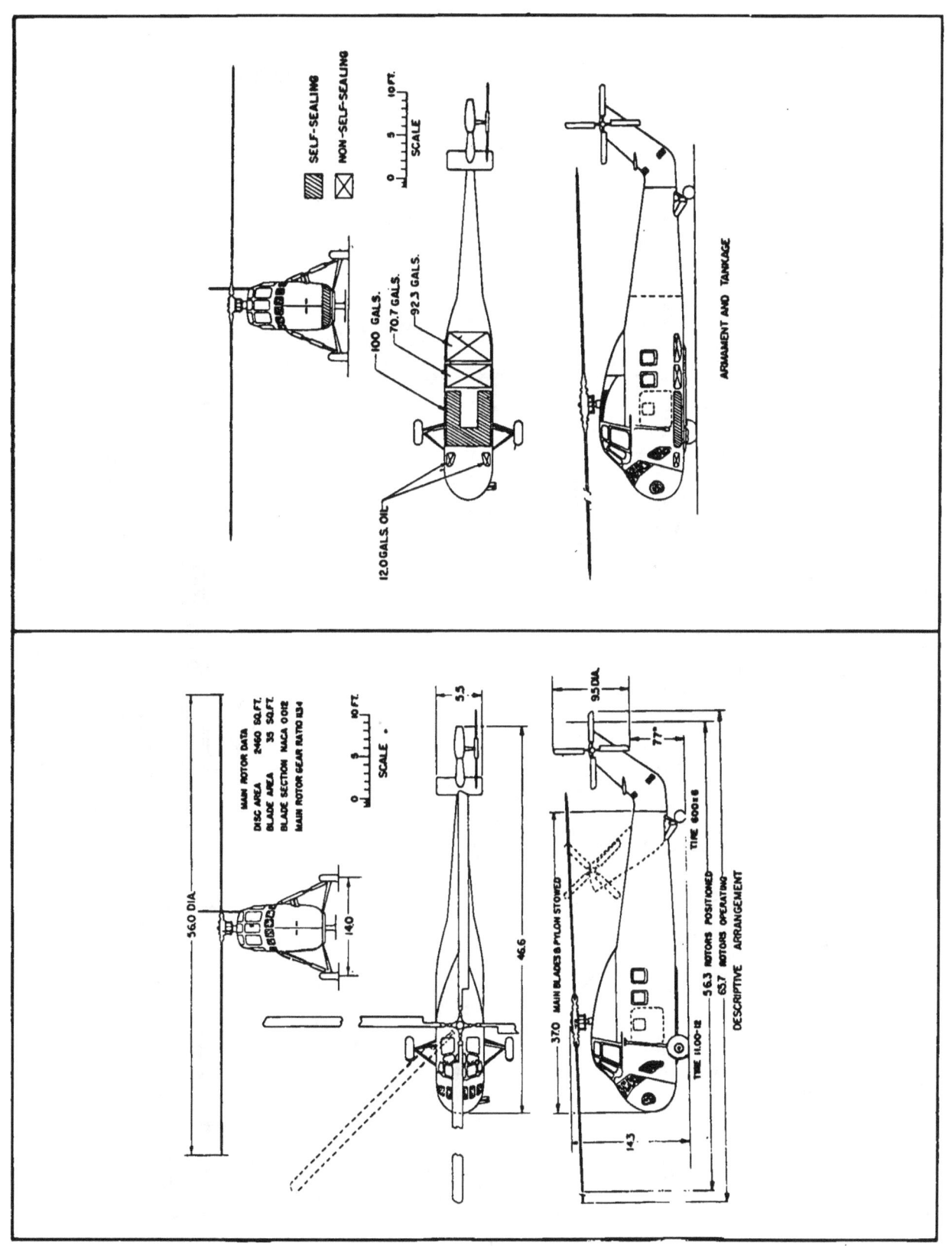

## POWER PLANT

| | |
|---|---|
| NO. & MODEL | (1)R-1820-84 |
| MFR | WRIGHT |
| SUPERCH | 1 STAGE, 1 SPEED |
| ROTOR GEAR RATIO | 11.3 to 1 |
| TAIL ROTOR RATIO | 1.9 to 1 |

### RATINGS

| | BHP | RPM | ALT | TIME |
|---|---|---|---|---|
| T.O. | 1525 | 2800 | 700' | 5 Min. |
| MIL. | 1425 | 2700 | 2400' | 30 Min. |
| NORM. | 1275 | 2500 | 3500' | Cont. |

ENGINE SPEC. N-895 of 26 Nov 1952

## ACCOMODATIONS

| | |
|---|---|
| Crew (Pilot & Co-Pilot) | 2 |
| Troops | 12 |
| or | |
| Litters | 8 |

## CARGO

| | |
|---|---|
| Internal/Capacity | 4000 lbs. |
| External Capacity (on sling) | 5000 lbs. |

Cargo Compartment:
- Length ... 13' 7"
- Width ... 4' 11"
- Height ... 6' 0"

## MISSION AND DESCRIPTION

The principal mission of this helicopter is to transport general cargo and large aircraft maintenance spare components.

The HUS-1 is a four bladed all metal main rotor type helicopter with a four bladed all metal automatic torque compensating tail rotor. The engine is mounted in the nose facing rearward inclined 35° from the horizontal. This helicopter incorporates a dual control system of the conventional stick and rudder pedal type, supplemented by a collective pitch control lever synchronized with the throttle to provide constant rotor speed. Automatic stabilization equipment is provided capable of maneuvering and maintaining heading, altitude, and attitude established by the pilot under stick and pedal free conditions. The tail pylon and main rotor blades flod without disconnecting transmission or controls, thus permitting stowage on the smallest carrier or cruiser deck elevator. The fixed type landing gear consists of a main two wheel alighting gear and a tail wheel.

Hoist Capacity          400#

## DEVELOPMENT

| | |
|---|---|
| First Flight | January 1957 |
| Service Use | January 1957 |

## DIMENSIONS

| | |
|---|---|
| ROTOR DIA | 56' 0" |
| DISC AREA | 2460 sq. ft. |
| *LENGTH | 37' 0" |
| HEIGHT (MAX) | 15' 8" |
| TREAD | 12' 0" |
| STABILIZER AREA | 12.4 sq. ft. |

*ROTOR AND TAIL PYLON FOLDED.

## WEIGHTS

| LOADING | LBS | L.F. |
|---|---|---|
| EMPTY | 8090 | |
| BASIC | 8598 | |
| DESIGN | 11305 | 2.68 |
| MAX T.O. | 13300 | 2.29 |
| MAX LANDING | 13300 | 2.29 |

All weights are actual

## FUEL AND OIL

| NO. Tanks | Gals. | Location |
|---|---|---|
| 3 | 263 | Fuselage |

| | |
|---|---|
| FUEL GRADE | 115/145 |
| FUEL SPEC | F-5572-1 |

### OIL

| | |
|---|---|
| Capacity (Gals) | 12.4 |
| Grade | 1065/1100 |
| Spec | MIL-L-6082A |

## ELECTRONICS

| | |
|---|---|
| UHF RADIO SET | AN/ARC-55 |
| MHF | AN/ARC-39 |
| ICS | AN/AIC-4A |
| RADAR ALTIMETER | AN/APN-117 |
| FINDER GROUP | AN/ARA-25 |
| RADAR ID SET | AN/APX-6 |
| CODER GROUP | AN/APA-89 |
| ADF | AN/ARN-59 |
| TACAN | AN/ARN-21 |
| FM RADIO SET | AN/ARC-44 |
| COURSE INDICATOR | ID-250/ARN |
| VIDEO CODER | KY-81/APA-89 |

## PERFORMANCE SUMMARY

| TAKE-OFF LOADING CONDITION | | (1) Cargo Transport | (2) Troop Transport | (3) Combat Evacuation | (4) Cargo Transport (Overload) | (5) Ferry Range |
|---|---|---|---|---|---|---|
| TAKE-OFF WEIGHT | LB. | 11297 | 12936 | 11837 | 13300 | 10284 |
| FUEL | LB. | 1240 | 1446 | 1562 | 504 | 1562 |
| PAYLOAD | LB. | 1335 | 2700 | 1520 | 4110.9 | --- |
| DISC LOADING | LB./SQ.FT. | 4.59 | 5.26 | 4.82 | 5.41 | 4.18 |
| VERTICAL RATE OF CLIMB AT S.L. (B) | FPM. | 1350 | 500 | 1060 | 320 | 1910 |
| ABSOLUTE HOVERING CEILING (B) | FT. | 7900 | 3875 | 6480 | 3000 | 10700 |
| MAX. RATE OF CLIMB AT S.L. (B) | FPM | 2020 | 1570 | 1860 | 1475 | 2350 |
| SERVICE CEILING (100 FPM.) (A) | FT. | 14300 | 10800 | 13100 | 10000 | 16550 |
| SPEED AT S.L. (A) | KN. | 132 | 123 | 129 | 121 | 135 |
| MAX. SPEED/ALTITUDE (A) | KN./FT. | 132/S.L. | 123/S.L. | 139/S.L. | 121/S.L. | 135/S.L. |
| COMBAT RANGE (A) | N.MI. | 210 | 218 | 263 | 58 | 298 |
| AVERAGE CRUISING SPEED | KN. | 94 | 98 | 94 | 99 | 93 |
| CRUISING ALTITUDE | FT. | 1500 | 1500 | 1500 | 1500 | 1500 |
| COMBAT RADIUS (A) | N.MI. | 100 | 110 | 128 | 24 | --- |
| AVERAGE CRUISING SPEED (C)(D) | KN. | 94/93 | 98/93 | 94/93 | 99/93 | --- |
| Cruising Altitude | ft. | 1500 | 1500 | 1500 | 1500 | --- |

NOTES:

(A) NORMAL RATED POWER
(B) TAKE-OFF POWER
(C) AVERAGE CRUISE SPEED OUTGOING
(D) AVERAGE CRUISE SPEED RETURNING

PERFORMANCE BASIS: NATESTCEN Evaluation of HSS-1 and HUS-1 helicopters.

RANGE AND RADIUS Are based upon NATESTCEN fuel consumption data.

All performance is out of ground effect and for standard atmospheric conditions.

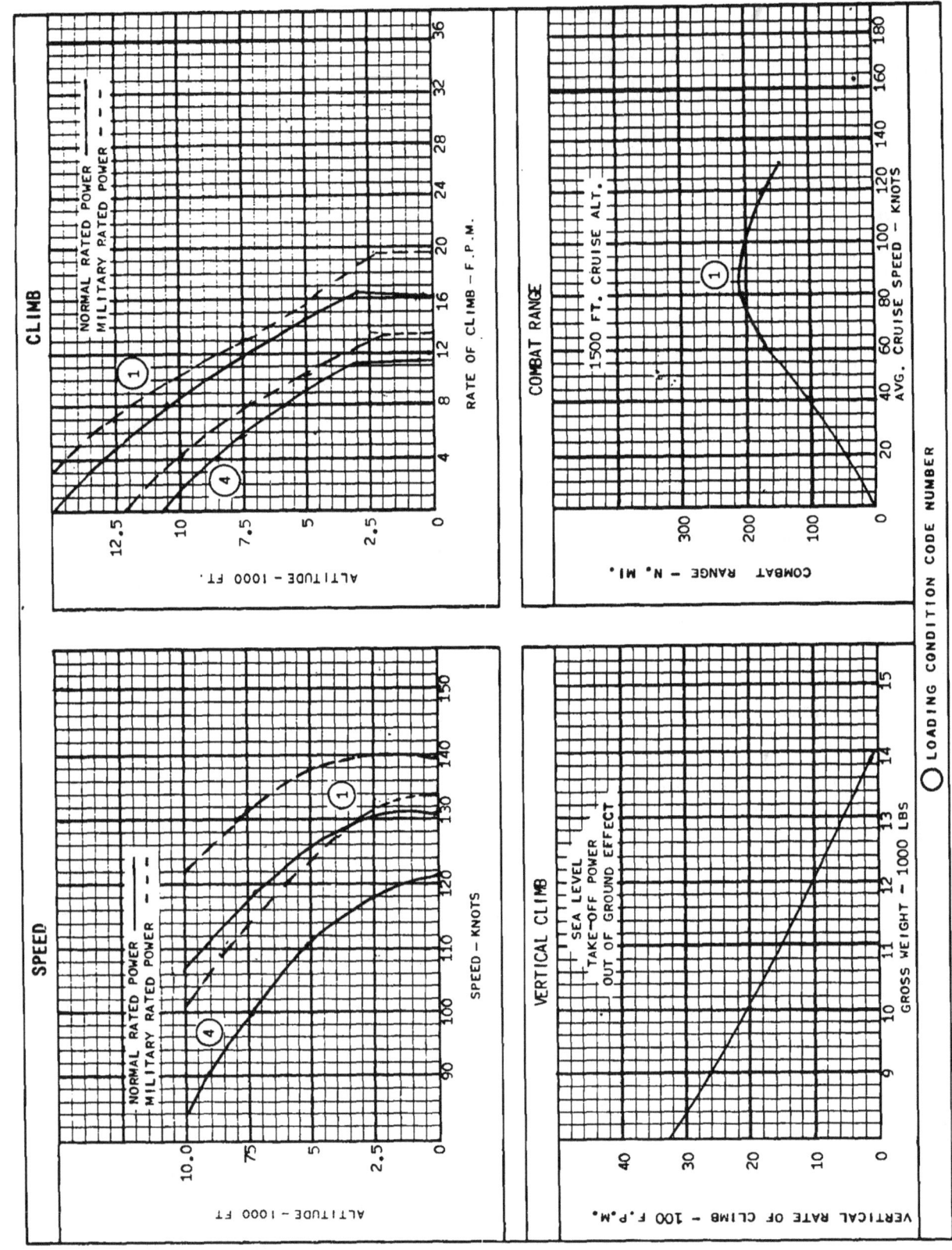

## NOTES

### COMBAT RADIUS MISSION:

Warm-up and Take-off: 10 Minutes at Normal Rated Power
Climb: To 1500 feet at Normal Rated Power
Cruise: At long range speed to advanced area
Land: Deposit Cargo or Discharge Troops
Climb: To 1500 feet at Normal Rated Power
Cruise: Back to base at speed for best range
Reserve: 10% of initial fuel load

### EVACUATION MISSION:

Warm-up and Take-off: 10 Minutes at Normal Rated Power
Climb: To 1500 feet at Normal Rated Power
Cruise: At long range speed to advanced area
Land: Pick up evacuees (8)
Climb: To 1500 feet at Normal Rated Power
Cruise: Back to base at speed for best range
Reserve: 10% of initial fuel load

### COMBAT RANGE MISSION:

Warm-up and Take-off: 5 minute at Normal Rated Power
Climb: To 1500 feet at Normal Rated Power
Cruise: At speed for best range
Reserve: 10% of initial fuel load

○ LOADING CONDITION COLUMN NUMBER

# STANDARD AIRCRAFT CHARACTERISTICS

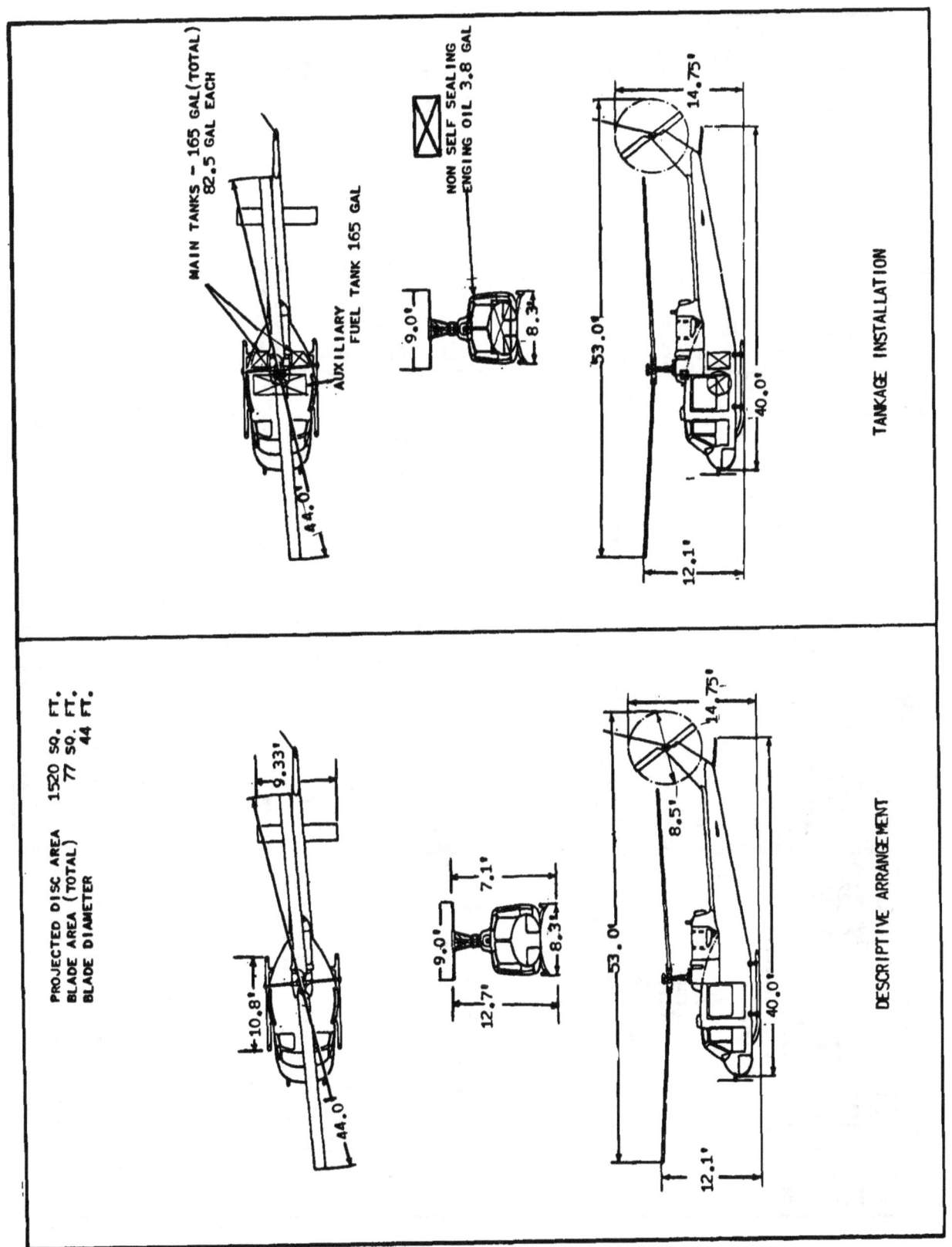

## POWER PLANT

| | |
|---|---|
| No. and Model | (1)T53-L-9 |
| Mfg. | Lycoming |
| Engine Spec. No. | 104.22-B |
| Type | Free Power Turbine |
| Red. Gear Ratio | 0.3119 |
| Tail Pipe | Fixed Area |
| Augmentation | None |

### RATINGS

| | ESHP | SHP | Net Jet Thrust (lb) | RPM | MIN |
|---|---|---|---|---|---|
| Sea Level Std. | | | | | |
| T.O. | 1150 | 1100 | 124 | 6610 | 5 |
| MIL. | 1046 | 1000 | 115 | 6610 | 30 |
| Nor. | 943 | 900 | 107 | 6610 | Cont. |

## ACCOMMODATIONS

Basic Mission
- Crew .......... 1
- Observer .......... 1

Transport (Personnel) Mission
- Normal
  - Crew .......... 1
  - Passengers .......... 4
- Alternate
  - Crew .......... 1
  - Passengers .......... 7

Litter Evacuation
- Crew (Pilot & Medical Attend.) .......... 2
- Litters .......... 3

Ferry Mission
- Crew (Pilot) .......... 1

Hoist Capacity .......... 600 lb.

## MISSION AND DESCRIPTION

The basic missions of the UH-1E are visual observation and target acquisition, reconnaissance and command control. The UH-1E is capable of flight from established airfields, carriers of the LPH and CVS class, advanced bases, areas or ships with individual landing platforms or limited landing facilities, and from unprepared fields. It may be handled on carrier elevators without any folding of components.

In addition, the UH-1E may be used for medical evacuation, to transport personnel, special teams or crews, equipment and supplies. These missions may be performed under instrument operations including light icing and day or night flight. By the attachment of appropriate weapons it is possible to deliver point target and area fire.

The gas turbine powered UH-1E is of compact design having a low silhouette. The two-bladed main and tail rotors are of all metal construction. The fuselage is of semi-monocoque construction.

The cabin has large sliding doors allowing straight-through loading. Litters may be loaded from either side or from both sides simultaneously. The cargo floor is knee high for easy loading. The copilot's controls are easily removed; thus providing accomodations for a passenger in the copilot seat or when the copilot seat is removed, an additional 8.75 square feet of cargo area for a total of 47.2 square feet.

## DEVELOPMENT

Three (3) production articles being procured for the Department of the Navy.
First Flight (Est) .......... Feburary 1963
First Deliver (Est) .......... March 1963

## DIMENSIONS

| | |
|---|---|
| Rotor Diameter | 44.0' |
| Disc Area | 1520.0 – Blade Area..77.0' |
| Length – Rotors Operation | 53.0' |
| Fuselage | 39.5' |
| Span (Max. Lateral) | 9.3' |
| Height | 14.7' |
| Tread | 8.4' |
| Rotor Ground Clearance (Static, Against Stops) | 7.4' |

## WEIGHTS

| LOADING | LB. | L.F. |
|---|---|---|
| Empty | 4734(A) | |
| Basic | 5145 | |
| Design | 6600 | 3.0 |
| Combat | 6171 | 3.0 |
| Max T.O. | 8500 | 2.3 |
| Max Land | 8500 | |

(A) Actual

## FUEL AND OIL

| LOCATION | NO. TANKS | GALS |
|---|---|---|
| Fuselage | 2 | 165.0 |
| Fuselage, Ferry | 1 | 165.0 |
| External, Ferry | 2 | 200.0 |
| | Total | 530.0 |

Grade .......... JP-4
Specification .......... MIL-J-5624D

### OIL

Fuselage .......... 3.8
Specification .......... MIL-L-7808D

## ELECTRONICS

| | |
|---|---|
| UHF Transceiver | AN/ARC-52 |
| LF Automatic Direction Finder | AN/ARN-59 |
| HF-AM/SSB Transceiver | AN/SRC-94 |
| Intercom System | AN/AIC-14 |
| UHF-DF Homing Group | AN/ARA-25A |
| Gyro Compass System | MA-1 |
| IFF Radar Identification Set | AN/APX-6B |
| Coder Group | AN/APA-89 |
| Radar Altimeter | AN/APN-141 |
| FM Radio Set | AN-ARC-44 |
| TACAN Radio Set | AN/ARN-52(V) |

## PERFORMANCE SUMMARY

| TAKE-OFF LOADING CONDITION | | (1) PRIMARY OBSERVATION | (2) TRANSPORT | (3) OVERLOAD TRANSPORT | (4) LITTER EVACUATION | (5) FERRY |
|---|---|---|---|---|---|---|
| TAKE-OFF WEIGHT | LB. | 6600 | 6868 | 7500 | 6701 | 8500 |
| FUEL INTERNAL/EXTERNAL | LB. | 1072/- | 1072/- | 1072/- | 1072/- | 1072/2056 (4) |
| PAYLOAD | LB. | 332 | 800 | 1432 | 400 (5) | 0 |
| DISC LOADING | LB./SQ.FT. | 4.34 | 4.52 | 4.93 | 4.15 | 5.59 |
| VERTICAL RATE OF CLIMB AT S.L. (1) | FPM. | 2300 | 2050 | 1470 | 2210 | 560 |
| ABSOLUTE HOVERING CEILING (1) | FT. | 11900 | 10500 | 6800 | 11300 | 1700 |
| MAX. RATE OF CLIMB AT S.L. (2) | FPM. | 1985 | 1840 | 1565 | 1932 | 1200 |
| SERVICE CEILING (100 FPM.) (2) | FT. | 19700 | 18450 | 15700 | 19200 | 11600 |
| SPEED AT S.L. (3) | KN. | 120 | 116 | 108 | 120 | 95 |
| MAX. SPEED/ALTITUDE (3) | KN./FT. | 120/S.L. | 116/S.L. | 108/S.L. | 120/S.L. | 95/S.L. |
| COMBAT RANGE | N.MI. | 243 | 230 | 214 | 214 | 548 |
| AVERAGE CRUISING SPEED | KN. | 98 | 104 | 100 | 107 | 90 |
| CRUISING ALTITUDE | FT. | 10000 | 10000 | 10000 | 10000/50000 | 10000 |
| COMBAT RADIUS /MISSION TIME | N.MI. | 105/2.27 | 112/2.21 | 109/2.24 | 104.9/2.12 | 219/- |
| AVERAGE CRUISING SPEED | KN. | 107 | 105 | 102 | 106 | 90 |
| MAXIMUM ENDURANCE @ S.L. | HRS. | 2.40 | 2.30 | 2.25 | 2.37 | 5.20 |
| MISSION TIME - FERRY RANGE | N.MI. | | | | | 6.11 |

NOTES:
(1) Take-Off Power
(2) Normal Rated Power
(3) Vne Limit
(4) Additional fuel in two 100-gallon external tanks (External Tank System under Development By Navy - Not Presently Available) and one 165-gallon Internal Tank

PERFORMANCE BASIS: YHU-1B Category II (Air Force) Flight Test
Range and Radius are based on engine specification fuel consumption increased by 5%

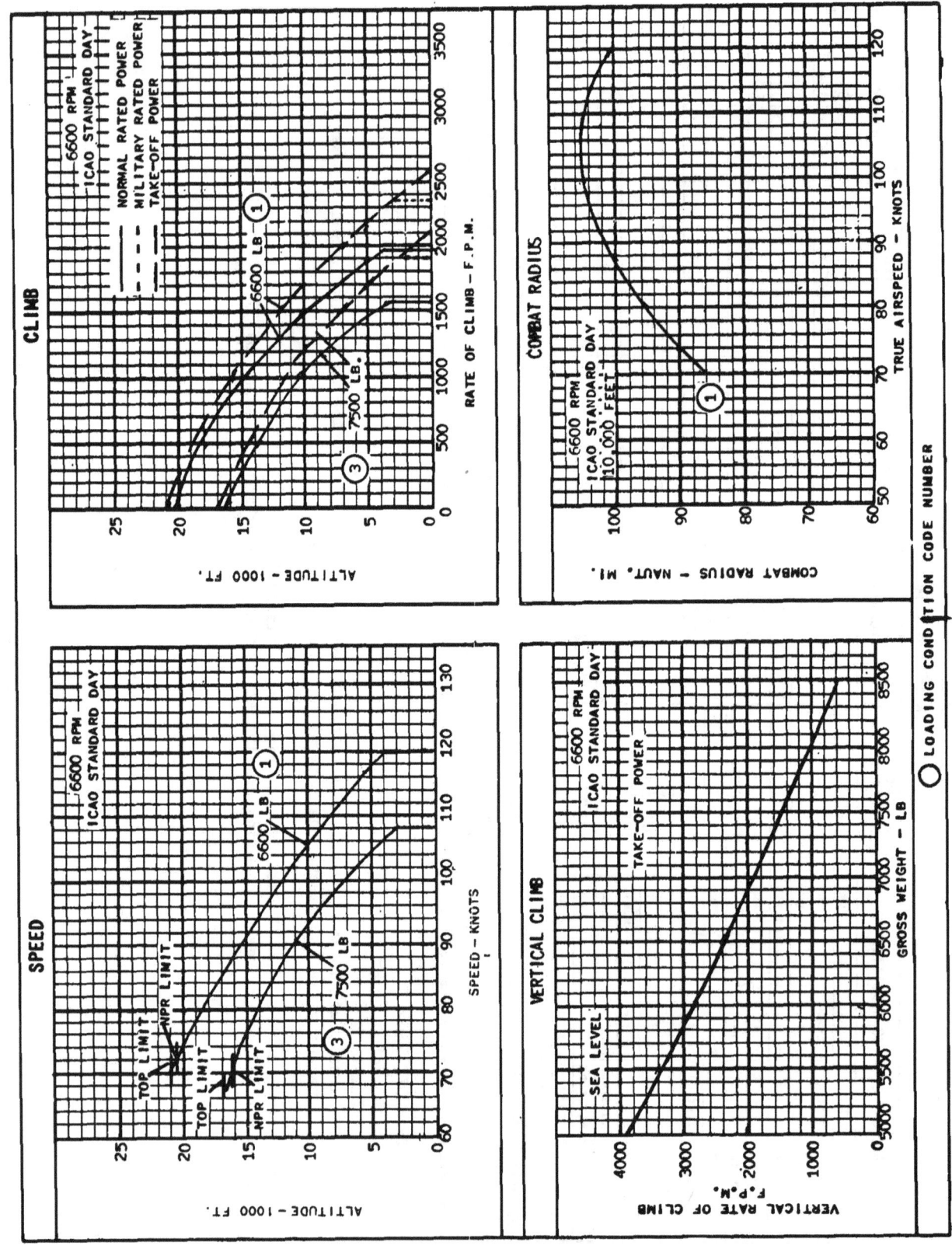

## NOTES

### Observation and Reconnaissance (1)

1. Warm-Up and Take-Off: 2 minutes at Normal Rated Power at Sea Level
2. Climb: On course to 10,000 feet
3. Cruise Out: At speeds for best range at 10,000 feet
4. Descent: To sea level loiter for 10 minutes at speeds for maximum endurance
5. Climb: On course to 10,000 feet
6. Cruise Back: At speeds for best range at 10,000 feet
7. Reserve: 10% of initial fuel load

### Transport (2), (3), (5)

1. Warm-Up and Take-Off: 2 minutes at Normal Rated Power at Sea Level
2. Climb: On course to 10,000 feet
3. Cruise: At speeds for best range at 10,000 feet
4. Reserve: 10% of initial fuel

### Litter Evacuation (4)

1. Warm-Up and Take-Off: 2 minutes at Normal Rated Power at Sea Level
2. Climb: On course to 10,000 feet
3. Cruise out at speeds for best range at 10,000 feet
4. Land: At remote base and discharge 2 passengers, pick up two litter patients
5. Warm-up and Take-off: 2 minutes at normal rated power at sea level
6. Climb: On course to 5000 feet
7. Cruise Back: At speeds for best range at 5000 feet
8. Reserve: 10% of initial fuel load

Mission Time: Excludes Warm-Up, Take-Off and Reserve Loiter Time
Cycle Time: Excludes Warm-Up and Take-Off Time

O LOADING CONDITION COLUMN NUMBER

STANDARD AIRCRAFT CHARACTERISTICS
CH-46A (HRB-1) "SEA KNIGHT"
BOEING-VERTOL

# STANDARD AIRCRAFT CHARACTERISTICS

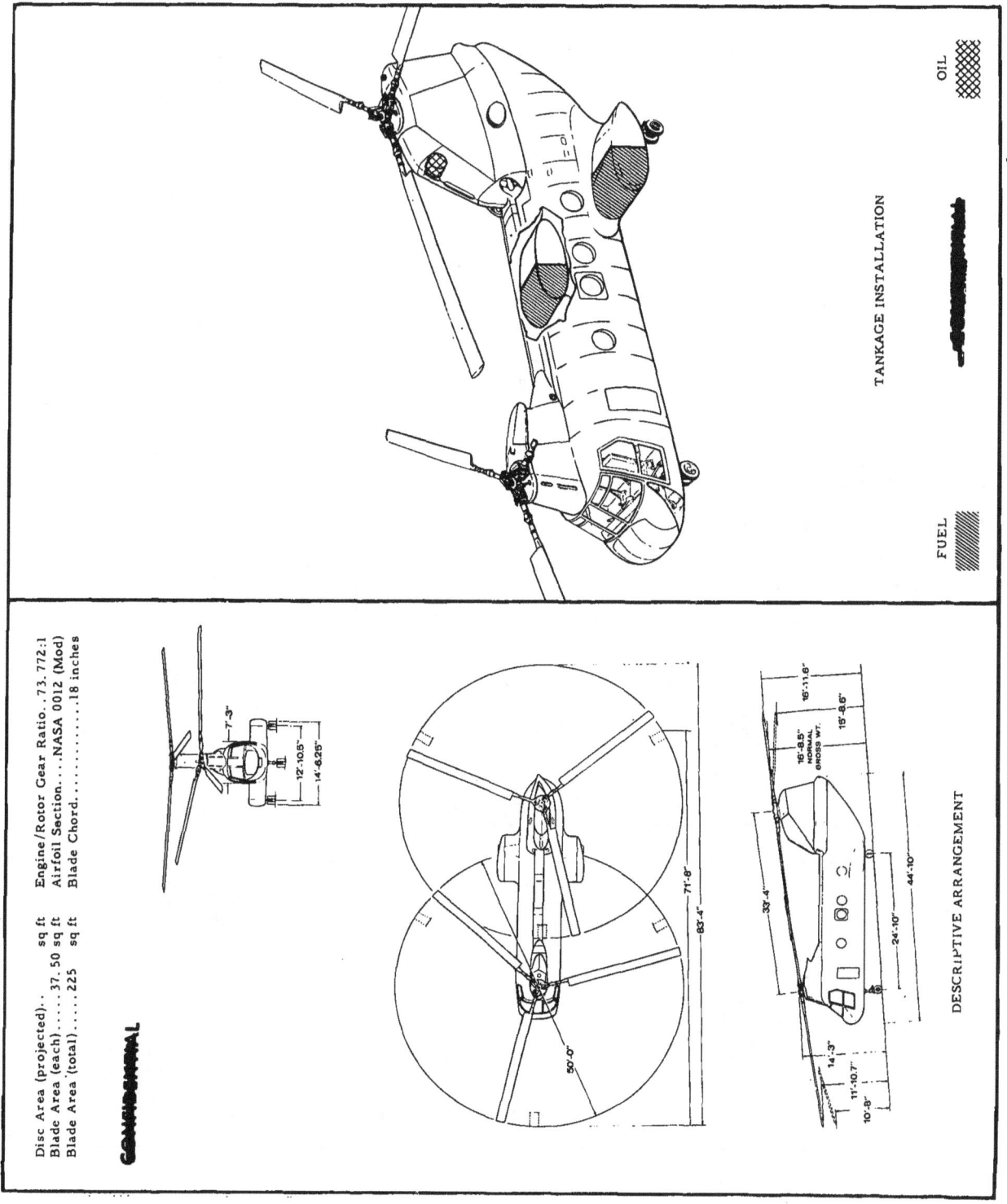

Disc Area (projected).. sq ft  
Blade Area (each).....37.50 sq ft  
Blade Area (total)....225 sq ft  
Engine/Rotor Gear Ratio..73.772:1  
Airfoil Section...NASA 0012 (Mod)  
Blade Chord..........18 inches

TANKAGE INSTALLATION

FUEL  OIL

DESCRIPTIVE ARRANGEMENT

## POWER PLANT

No. & Model (2)T58-GE-8B
Manufacturer General Electric Co.
Rotor Gear Ratio 73.772:1

**RATINGS**

|  | SHP/RPM/ALT |
|---|---|
| Military | 1250/19500/SSL |
| Normal | 1050/19500/SSL |

Engine Spec. No. E-1025B
15 Sept. 1961

## MISSION AND DESCRIPTION

The primary mission of this aircraft is to rapidly disperse combat troops, support equipment and supplies from amphibious assault landing ships and established airfields to advanced bases in undeveloped areas with limited maintainance and logistic support under all-weather conditions, day or night.

The Sea Knight is a twin turbine, tandem-rotor helicopter with an all-metal fuselage of semi-monocoque stressed skin construction. The engines drive two three-bladed fully articulated partially overlapping rotors, which are synchronized by positive gearing and an interconnecting drive shaft. The all-metal steel-spar rotor blades are interchangeable and have provisions for electrically heated deicing boots. Automatic blade folding within 60 seconds under 45/knot wind conditions is another feature included in the rotor system design.

By sealing the fuselage during assembly, inherent flotation capability is achieved in the normal configuration for emergency water landings and take-offs. A rear loading ramp provides access to the unobstructed payload space for rapid straight-in loading and unloading of personnel, supplies, equipment and vehicles. The ramp is capable of being operated both on the ground and in flight.

For instrument flight capabilities, a dual Stability Augmentation System (SAS) is included as standard equipment. It is a normal and integral part of the control system, and provides positive dynamic stability about the yaw, pitch, and roll axes throughout the entire speed range from hover to maximum forward speed.

**DEVELOPMENT**

FIRST FLIGHT ............................................. Aug. 1962
SERVICE USE ............................................. Sept. 1963

## WEIGHTS

|  | Lbs. | L.F. |
|---|---|---|
| Empty: | 11,708 |  |
| Basic: | 11,729 |  |
| Design: | 18,700 | 2.67 |
| Max. T.O.: | 21,400 | 2.3 |
| Max. Landing: | 21,400 | 2.3 |

Weights are 39% actual, 3% estimated. and 58% calculated

## FUEL AND OIL

| Tanks | Gals | Location |
|---|---|---|
| 2 | 190 | Left and Right Stub Wings |

Fuel Grade JP-4
Fuel Spec Mil-F-5624C

**OIL**

| Capacity (Gals) | |
|---|---|
| Engine | 4.2 |
| Transmission | 14.4 |
| Oil Grade | 1065 |
| Oil Spec | Mil-L-7808C |

## DIMENSIONS

Disc Area: 3495 sq ft (projected)
No. of Blades: 6 (2 rotors)
Total Blade Area: 225 sq ft
Rotor Diameter: 50 ft
Length (Blades Folded) 44' 10"
 "   ( "    Turning) 83' 4"
Height (Blades Folded) 16' 8.5"
 "   ( "    Turning) 16' 11.6"
Width (Blades Folded) 14' 11.6"

## ELECTRONICS

| | |
|---|---|
| Radio Set (UHF) | AN/ARC-52 |
| Radar Ident. Set | AN/APX-6B |
| ICS | AN/AIC-14 |
| ADF | AN/ARN-59 |
| TACAN | AN/ARN-52 |
| Radio Finder Group | AN/ARN-25A |
| Radar Altimeter | AN/APN-117 |
| Coder | AN/APA-89 |
| FM Liaison | AN/ARC-44 |
| Compass | MA-1 |

## CARGO

Cargo Compartment 1023 cu ft
 (including Ramp Area)
Dimensions 6' x 6' x 24' 2"
External Cargo Hook Capacity
 10,000 lbs
Floor Area 180 sq ft
 (incl. Ramp)
Floor Limit Loads
 Roller Beams for 3000 lb
 Pallet 40" x 48"
 Wheel Tread 1000 lb Dead Weight
 Wheel Load @33 psi Tire Pressure
 Remaining Floor Area 300 lb/sq ft

## ACCOMMODATIONS

| | |
|---|---|
| Crew | 3 |
| Troops (Combat Equipped) | 17 |
| or | |
| Litters | 15 |
| Attendants | 2 |

# STANDARD AIRCRAFT CHARACTERISTICS

## PERFORMANCE SUMMARY

| TAKEOFF LOADING CONDITION | | ① ASSAULT TRANSPORT | ② CARGO | ③ CARGO OVERLOAD | ④ FERRY |
|---|---|---|---|---|---|
| TAKEOFF WEIGHT | lb. | 18708 | 18708 | 21400 | 21400 |
| Fuel | lb. | 2387 | 2364 | 2470 | 8609 |
| Payload | lb. | 4000 | 4023 | 6611 | 0 |
| Disc Loading | lb./sq.ft. | 4.77 | 4.77 | 5.45 | 5.45 |
| Vertical rate of climb at S L (A) | fpm. | 1290 | 1290 | 220 | 220 |
| Absolute hovering ceiling (A) | ft. | 7300 | 7300 | 2050 | 2050 |
| Max. rate of climb at S.L. (B) | fpm. | 1540 | 1540 | 1060 | 1060 |
| Service ceiling (100 fpm) (B) | ft. | 12800 | 12800 | 8300 | 8300 |
| Speed at S.L. (B) | kn. | 131 | 131 | 124 | 124 |
| Max. speed/altitude (A) | kn./ft. | 139/SL | 139/SL | 134/SL | 134/SL |
| Range | n.mi. | 211 | 209 | 204 | 843 |
| Average cruising speed | kn. | 120 | 120 | 119 | 116 |
| Cruising altitude | ft. | SL | SL | SL | 5000 |
| Radius | n.mi. | 100 | 100 | 98 | --- |
| Average cruising speed | kn. | 130 | 130 | 127(C) | --- |
| Cruising altitude | | SL | SL | SL | --- |

## NOTES

(A) MILITARY POWER.
(B) NORMAL RATED POWER.
(C) CRUISE AT NORMAL RATED POWER.
ALL PERFORMANCE IS OUT OF GROUND EFFECT.
PERFORMANCE BASIS: CALCULATED DATA BASED ON CONTRACTOR'S FLIGHT TESTS OF BOEING-VERTOL 107-II HELICOPTER.
RANGE AND RADIUS ARE BASED ON ENGINE SPECIFIC FUEL CONSUMPTION INCREASED 5% PER MIL-C-5011A.

CH-46A (HRB-1)

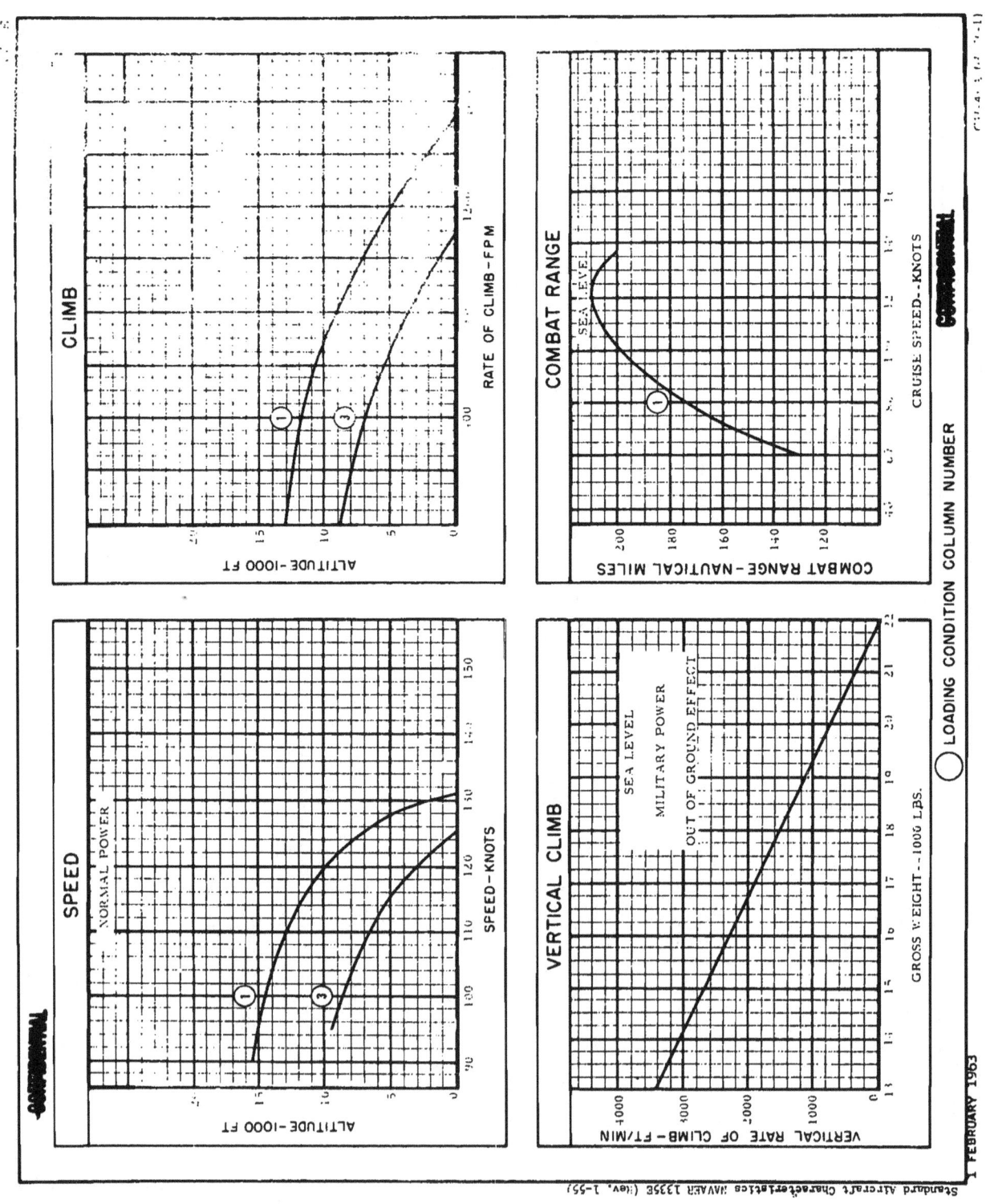

# NOTES

## COMBAT RANGE MISSION:

W.U. and T.O.: 2 min. at Normal Power
CRUISE: at speed for best range at sea level
RESERVE: 10% of initial fuel load

## RADIUS MISSION (ASSAULT TRANSPORT):

W.U. and T.O.: 7 min. at Normal Power
 (includes allowance for warm-
 up and take-off at remote base)
CRUISE OUT: at 130 knots at sea level
LAND: at remote base and unload troops
CRUISE BACK: at 130 knots at sea level
RESERVE: 10% of initial fuel load

## FERRY RANGE MISSION:

W.U. and T.O.: 2 min. at Normal Power
CLIMB: on course to 5000 ft.
CRUISE: at speed for best range at 5000 ft.
DESCEND: to sea level (no fuel consumed, no distance gained)
RESERVE: 10% of initial fuel load

## RADIUS MISSION (CARGO):

W.U. and T.O.: 2 min. at Normal Power
CRUISE OUT: at 130 knots at sea level
LAND: at remote base, do not unload cargo
W.U. and T.O.: 2 min. at Normal Power
CRUISE BACK: at 130 knots at sea level
RESERVE: 10% of initial fuel load

MISSION TIME: INCLUDES ALL ITEMS OF THE MISSION
EXCEPT TIME AND FUEL FOR WARMUP, TAKE-OFF AND RESERVE.

CYCLE TIME: INCLUDES ALL ITEMS OF THE MISSION EXCEPT
TIME AND FUEL TO WARM-UP AND TAKE-OFF

◯ LOADING CONDITION COLUMN NUMBER

# STANDARD AIRCRAFT CHARACTERISTICS

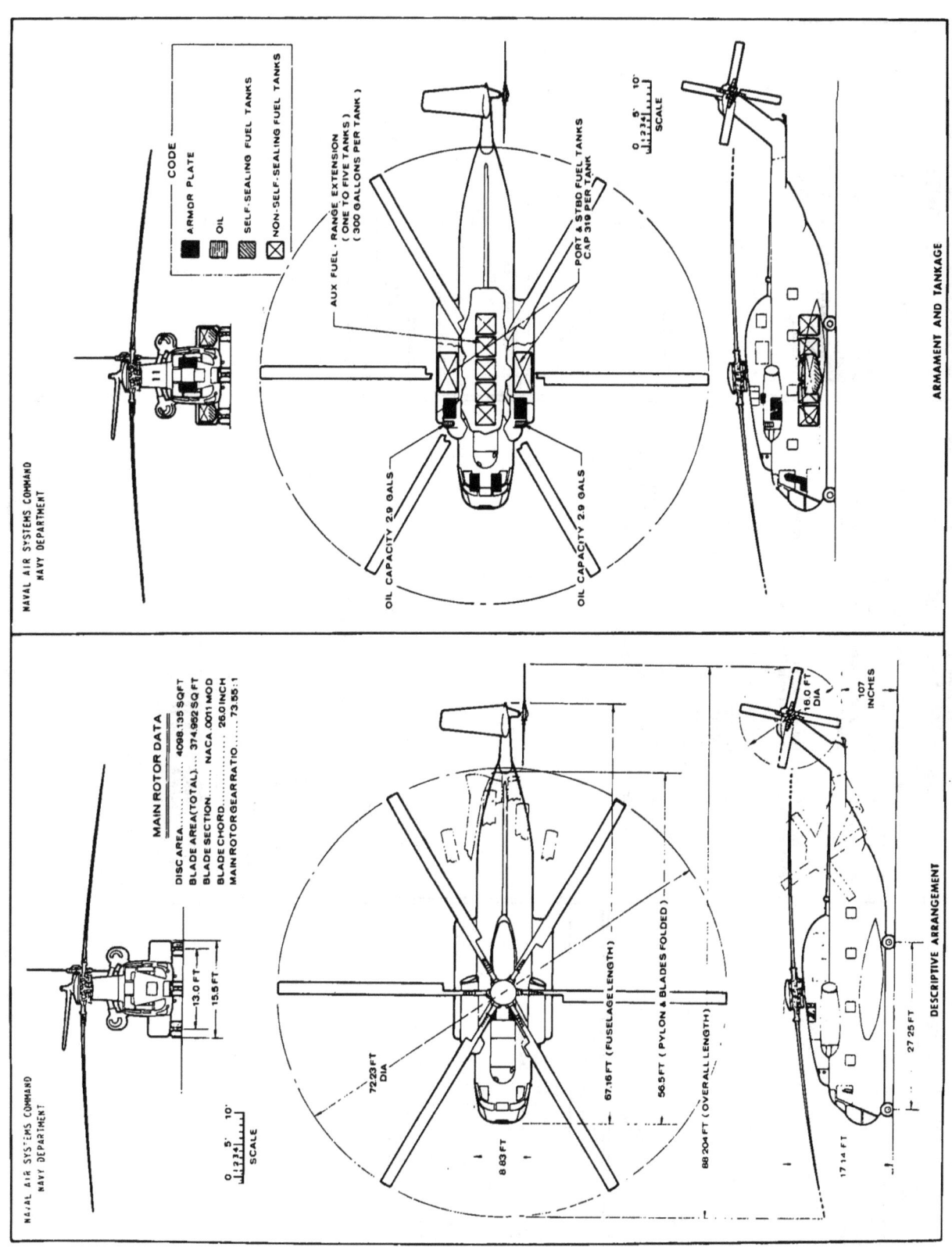

## POWER PLANT

No. and Model: (2)T64-GE-413  
Manufacturer: General Electric  
Engine Spec. No.: E1159(19 March 1969)  
Type: Axial  
Length: 78.8 inches  
Diameter: 23.8 inches  
Gear Ratio (Eng/Rotor) 73.55 to 1  

### RATINGS

| S. L. STATIC | SHP | RPM | MIN. |
|---|---|---|---|
| Max. | *3925 | 13600 | 10 |
| Military | 3695 | 13600 | 30 |
| Normal | 3230 | 13600 | Cont. |

* See Note Performance Summary page for transmission ratings.

## ELECTRONICS

AN/ARC-51A Radio Set (UHF)  
AN/ARN-52 Tacan Navigation Set  
AN/APX-64 IFF Transponder Set  
AN/ARC-94 Radio Set  
AN/ARN-59 ADF  
AN/ARC-54 or 131 Radio Set (VHF)  
AN/AIC-14 Interphone System  
AN/APN-154 Radar Beacon Set  
AN/APN-171 Radar Altimeter  
ID-351 or 387/ARN Course Indicator  
ID-663A/U or B/U or C/U Bearing Distance Heading Indicator  

## MISSION AND DESCRIPTION

Primarily designed as an assault transport, the helicopter is employed in the movement of cargo and equipment and in the transportation of troops. When appropriately equipped, it may be used in the recovery of downed aircraft and personnel, performing mine countermeasure missions, and towing of vehicles and ships.

The twin turbine engine helicopter uses a single main rotor and a single anti-torque tail rotor. The blades are all metal construction. Main rotor blades are equipped with Sikorsky BIM® to eliminate mandatory blade retirement. Conventional helicopter controls are provided for both pilot and copilot. The mechanical controls are augmented by two parallel and independent hydraulic servo systems. An automatic flight control system (AFCS) is also provided. Landing gear is retractable. Main rotor blades and tail pylon fold for stowage aboard an aircraft carrier. To facilitate cargo loading, the aircraft is equipped with a hydraulically operated rear ramp, two cargo winches, roller conveyors, and tie-down facilities.

## DEVELOPMENT

First Flight: 27 January 1969  
First Service Use: 7 March 1969  
Production Status: In Production  

## DIMENSIONS

Main Rotor Dia. 72'-2.8"  
Length (blades & pylon folded) 56'-6"  
Height (blades & pylon folded) 17'-1.7"  
No. of Blades, main 6  
Blade Area (each) 62.5 sq. ft.  
Disc Area 4098.1 sq. ft.  
Main Wheel Tread 13'-0"  
Max. Width (Main Blades and Pylon Folded) 15'-6"  

## WEIGHTS

| LOADING | POUNDS | L.F. |
|---|---|---|
| Empty (A) | 23628 | |
| Basic | 23634 | |
| Design | 33500 | 3.0 |
| **Design Alternate | 42000 | 2.39 |
| *Combat | 34958 | |
| *Take-off | 36693 | |

(A) Actual  
\* For Basic Mission  
\*\* ECP 6144 Part II

## FUEL AND OIL

| LOCATION | NO. TANKS | GAL. |
|---|---|---|
| L. Sponson* | 1 | 319 |
| R. Sponson* | 1 | 319 |
| Cabin** | 5 | 1500 |
| | TOTAL | 2138 |

Grade ——————————————— JP-4, JP-5  
Specification ———————————— MIL-J-5624D  
\*Bottom third self-sealing  
\*\*Aux. tanks for range extension  

### OIL

Nacelles — 2 (tot. 5.8)  
Specification — MIL-L-23699  

## ACCOMMODATIONS

Crew (Normal) 3  
Cargo (basic mission) 8000 lb.  
or  
Cargo (overload mission) 12742 lb.  
or  
Troops 38  
or  
Litters 24  
Cabin Size Clearance:  
  Length 30'-0"  
  Height 6'-6"  
  Width 7'-6"

# STANDARD AIRCRAFT CHARACTERISTICS

## PERFORMANCE SUMMARY

| TAKE-OFF LOADING CONDITION | | BASIC ASSAULT MISSION I | OVERLOAD ASSAULT MISSION II | COMBAT RANGE MISSION III | FERRY RANGE MISSION IV | RETRIEVAL (TROPICAL DAY)* MISSION V |
|---|---|---|---|---|---|---|
| TAKE-OFF WEIGHT | LB. | 36693 | 41435 | 36693 | 41513 | 28693 |
| FUEL | LB. | 4338 | 4338 | 4338 | 14538 | 4338 |
| PAYLOAD | LB. | 8000/4000 | 12742/4000 | 8000/0 | 0/0 | 0/9289** |
| DISC LOADING | LB./SQ.FT. | 8.95 | 10.11 | 8.95 | 10.13 | 7.00 |
| VERTICAL RATE OF CLIMB AT S.L. (B/C) | FPM | 1590/1740 | 580/840 | 1590/1740 | 560/820 | 2110/2325 |
| ABSOLUTE HOVERING CEILING (B/C) | FT. | 6250/7200 | 1700/2900 | 6250/7200 | 1650/2850 | 7900/8900 |
| MAX. RATE OF CLIMB AT S.L. (A/B) | FPM | 2180/2460 | 1845/2160 | 2180/2460 | 1855/2150 | 2320/2710 |
| SERVICE CEILING (100 FPM.) (A) | FT. | 16750 | 13350 | 16750 | 13300 | 17500 |
| SPEED AT S.L. (A) | KN. | 166 | 158 | 166 | 157 | 172 |
| MAX. SPEED/ALTITUDE (A) | KN./FT. | 166/S.L. | 158/S.L. | 166/S.L. | 127/8000 | 169/3000 |
| COMBAT RANGE | N.MI. | --- | --- | 228 | 886 | --- |
| AVERAGE CRUISING SPEED | KN. | --- | --- | 140 | 135 | --- |
| CRUISING ALTITUDE | FT. | --- | --- | 0 | 8000 | --- |
| COMBAT RADIUS | N.MI. | 100 | 95 | --- | --- | 106 |
| AVERAGE CRUISING SPEED | KN. | 150 | 150 | --- | --- | 138 |
| Cruising altitude | FT. | 0 | 0 | --- | --- | 3000 |
| Total-mission time | HRS. | 1.48 | 1.40 | 1.63 | 6.62 | 1.55 |

NOTES:
(A) Normal power
(B) Military power
(C) Maximum power
* Tropical Day: 91.5°F. at 3000 ft. cruise altitude.
** Inbound payload is carried externally ($\Delta f = 35$ sq. ft.)

Performance Basis:
(1) ICAO Standard conditions (except Mission V), no wind, no ground effect.
(2) Calculated data based on Navy flight tests on CH-53A helicopter.
(3) Range and radius based on General Electric specification fuel consumption data using fuel grade JP-5.
(4) Fuel consumption data are increased 5% above engine specification values.
(5) Transmission ratings are 7560 HP dual engine and 3780 HP single engine operation.
(6) Aircraft red line airspeed is 170 knots IAS.
(7) Weight data based on "Actual Weight and Balance Report", SER-65575 dated 10 March 1970.
(8) Performance reference: Sikorsky Report, SER-65583, "Substantiating Data for Standard Aircraft Characteristics and Performance Charts for CH-53D Helicopter."

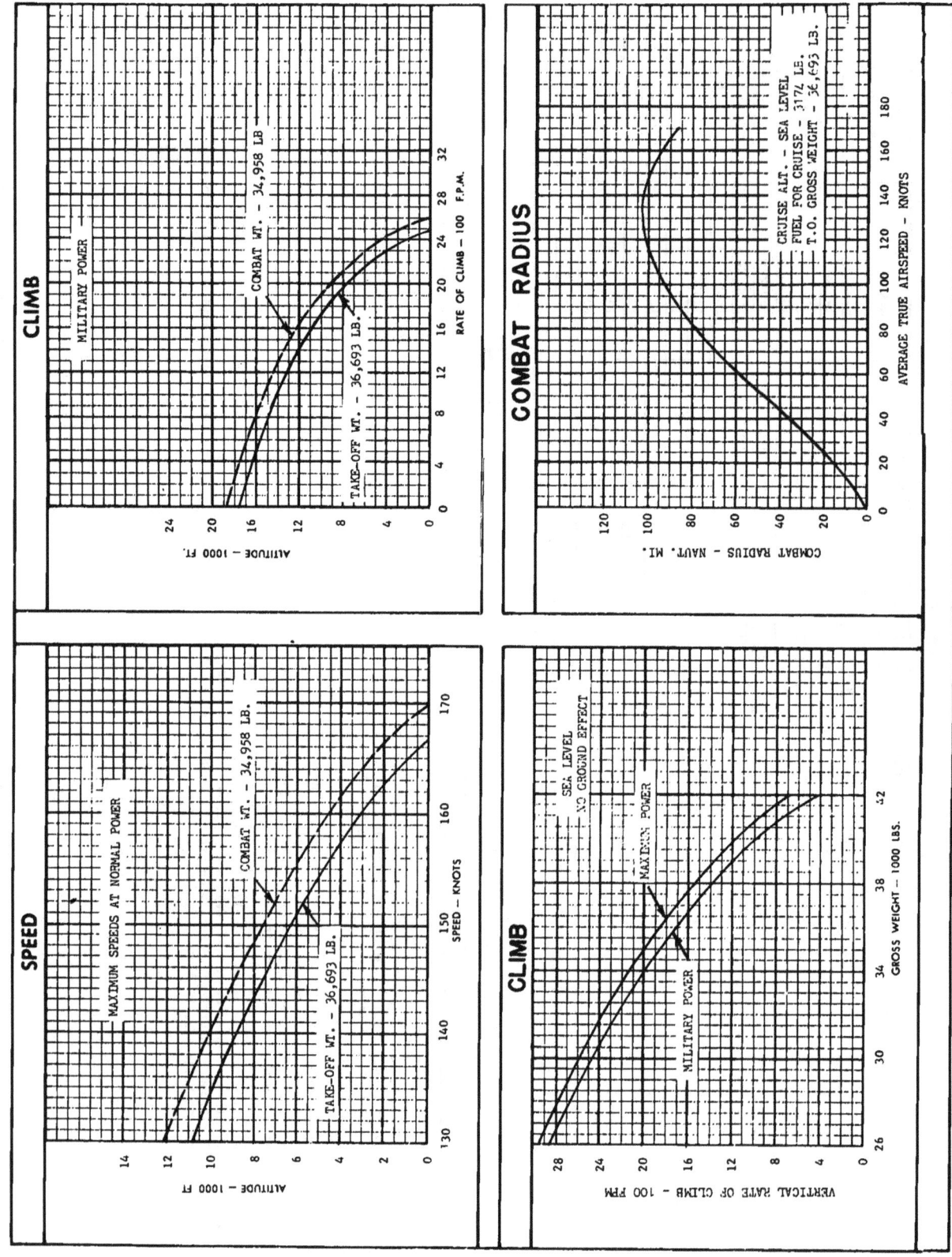

# STANDARD AIRCRAFT CHARACTERISTICS

## NOTES

### BASIC ASSAULT

Warm-Up & Take-Off: 2 min. at S.L., NRP
Cruise Out: At 150 kts. air-speed at S.L. to remote base
Hover Over Remote Base: At S.L. out of ground effect, for 10 min.
Land At Remote Base: Discharge 8000 lbs. and accept 4000 lbs. for return
Warm-Up & Take-Off: 2 min. at S.L., NRP
Cruise Back: At 150 kts. air-speed at S.L.
Reserve: 10% of initial fuel load

### OVERLOAD ASSAULT

Warm-Up & Take-Off: 2 min. at S.L., NRP
Cruise Out: At 150 kts. air-speed at S.L. to remote base
Hover Over Remote Base: At S.L. out of ground effect, for 10 min.
Land At Remote Base: Discharge 12,742 lbs. and accept 4000 lbs. for return
Warm-Up & Take-Off: 2 min. at S.L., NRP
Cruise Back: At 150 kts. air-speed at S.L.
Reserve: 10% of initial fuel load

### DUD RETRIEVAL (TROPICAL DAY)

Warm-Up & Take-Off: 5 min. at S.L., 90°F, NRP
Climb: On course to 3000 ft. 91.5°F with Mil power
Cruise Out: At best range speeds to remote base
Hover Over Base: Out of ground effect, at 3000 ft., 91.5°F for 10 min. Pick up external maximum payload (O.G.E. hover, $\Delta f = 35$ ft$^2$)
Cruise Back: At best range speeds 3000 ft., 91.5°F
Descend: To S.L. (no fuel used, no distance gained)
Reserve: 10% of initial fuel load

### COMBAT RANGE

Warm-Up & Take-Off: 5 min. at S.L., NRP
Cruise Out: At S.L. at best range speeds until reserve fuel remains
Reserve: 10% of initial fuel load

### FERRY RANGE

Warm-Up & Take-Off: 5 min. at S.L., NRP
Climb: On course to 8000 ft. with Mil power
Cruise Out: At best range speeds until reserve fuel remains
Descend: To S.L. (no fuel used, no distance gained)
Reserve: 10% of initial fuel load

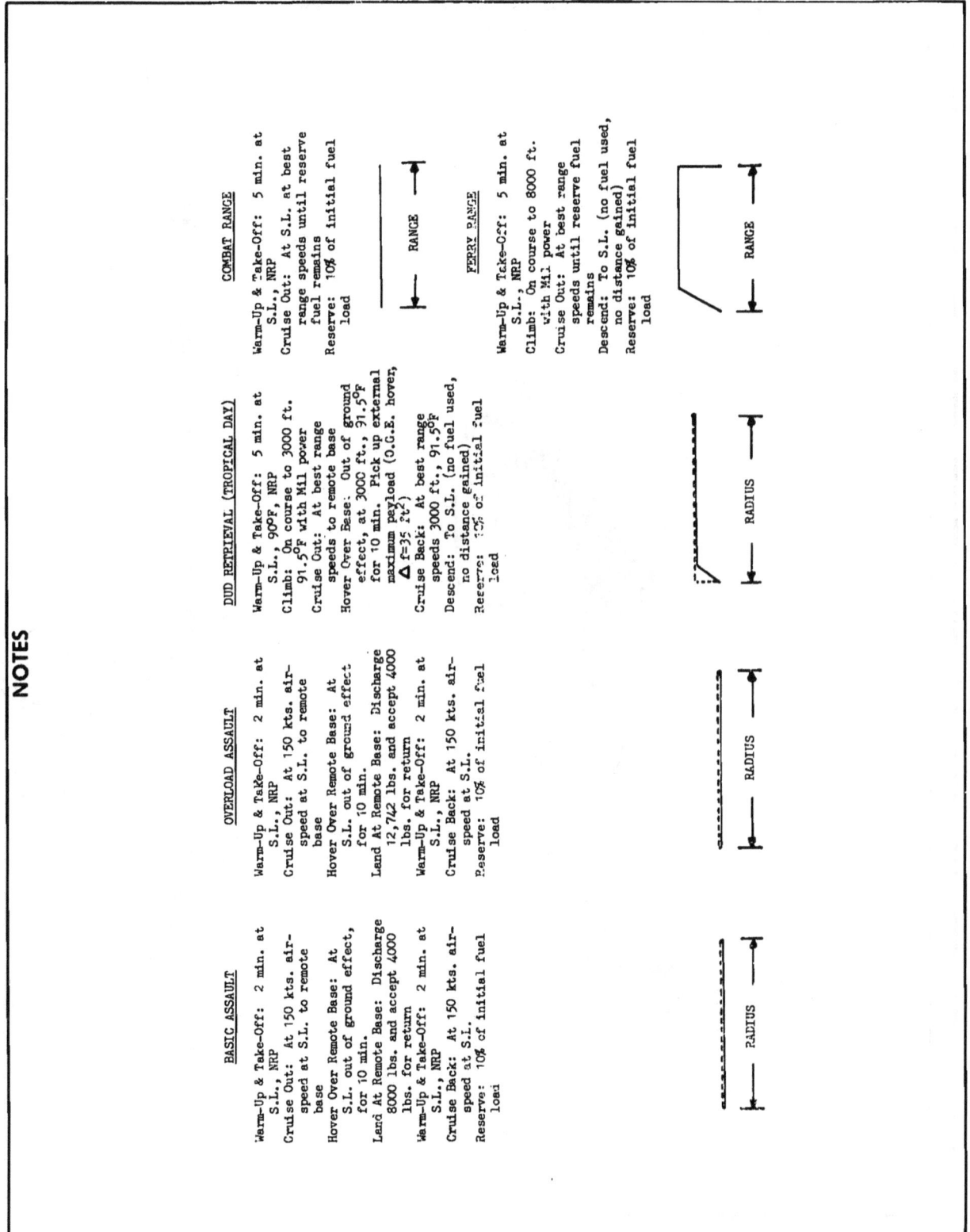

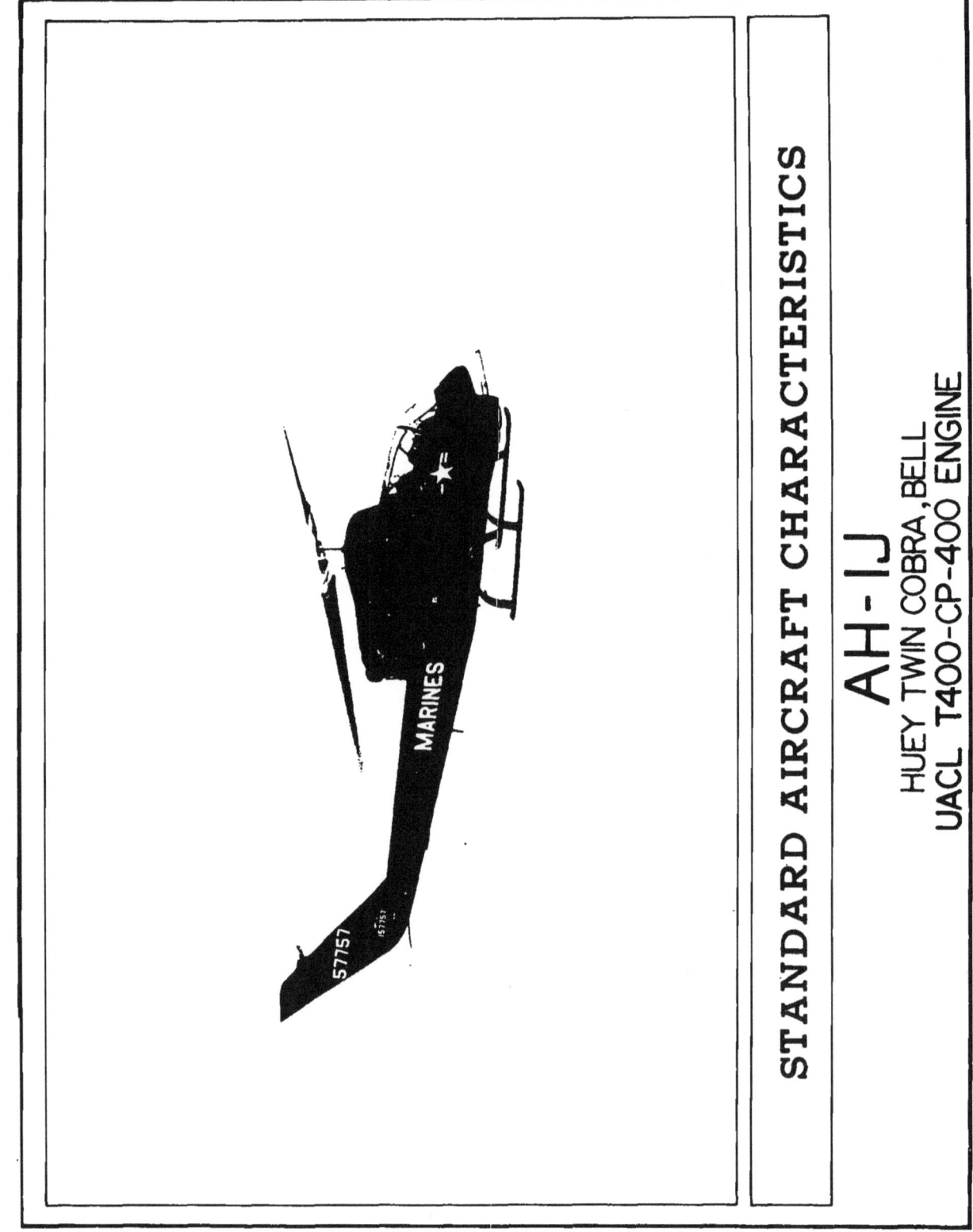

STANDARD AIRCRAFT CHARACTERISTICS

AH-1J
HUEY TWIN COBRA, BELL
UACL T400-CP-400 ENGINE

# STANDARD AIRCRAFT CHARACTERISTICS

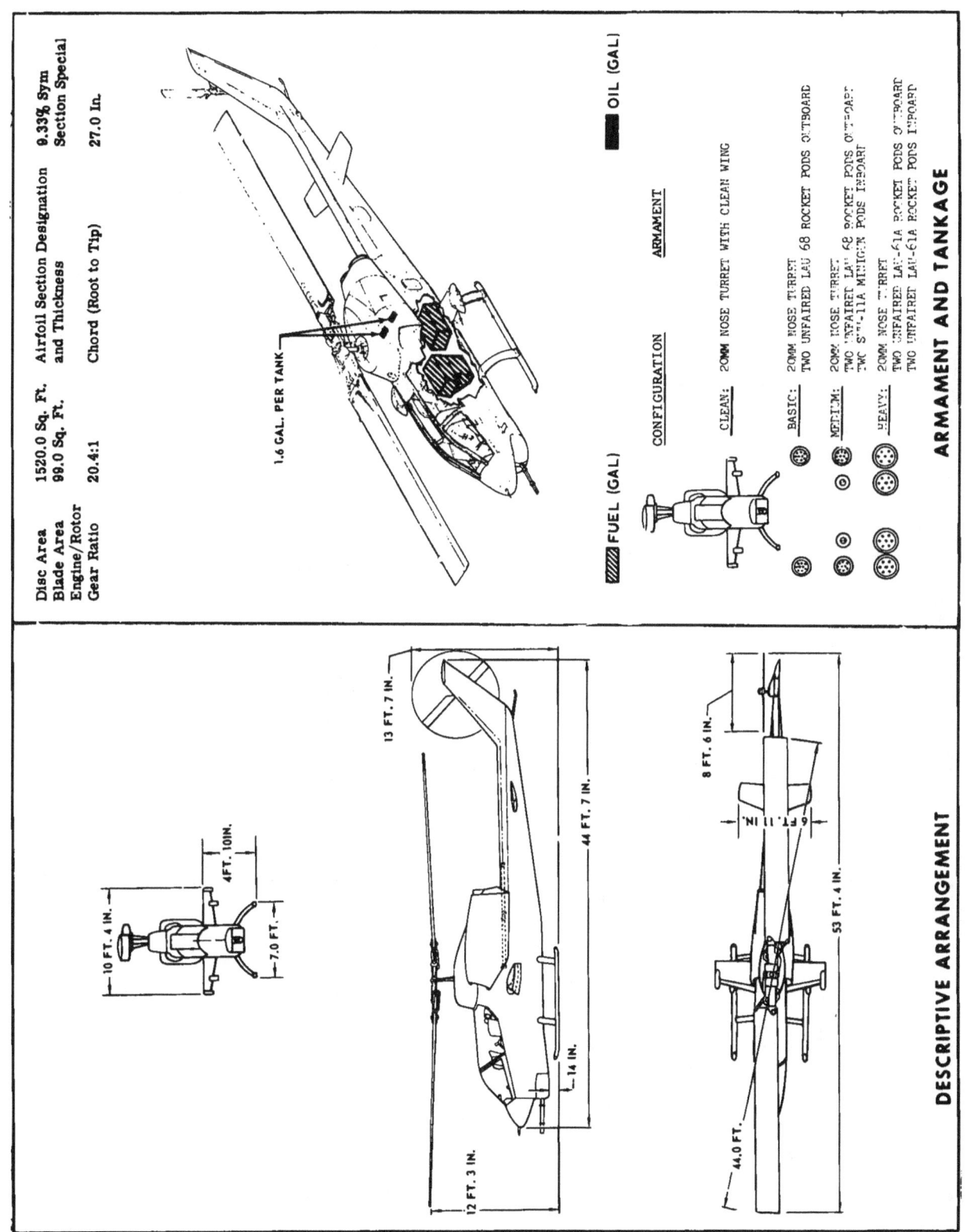

## ARMAMENT AND TANKAGE

## DESCRIPTIVE ARRANGEMENT

241

## POWER PLANT

No. & Model .....(1) T400-CP-400
Manufacturer.....United Aircraft of Canada
(Pratt and Whitney)
Engine Spec. No........7120
Type..............Twin Section Free Power
Turbine with Reduction
Gearbox

Gear Reduction Ratios
Main Rotor.....20.383:1
Tail Rotor.....3.974:1

### RATINGS

|  | SHP | RPM | ALT |
|---|---|---|---|
| Intermediate | 1800* | 6600 | SL |
| Maximum Continuous | 1530** | 6600 | SL |
| Intermediate Single Power Section | 900 | 6600 | SL |
| Maximum Continuous | 765 | 6600 | SL |

Transmission Limits
*1290 SHP
**1134 SHP

## ELECTRONICS

UHF Command Set............AN/ARC-51AX
FM Tactical Set............AN/ARC-131
Intercom...................AN/AIC-18
TACAN Nav Sys..............AF/ARN-52(v)
UHF Direction Finder.......AN/ARA-50
Gyrosyn Compass............AN/ASN-75
Direction Finder Set.......AN/ARN-83
Radar Altimeter............AN/APN-171(v)
IFF Transponder Set........AN/APX-72
Radar Beacon...............AN/APN-154(v)
Two Juliet 28 Controls.....C-8057
Two Mounts.................Barry Controls 21078-1

PROVISIONS FOR

Two Voice Security Units...Juliet 28
Transponder Test Set.......TS-1843( )/APX
Mounting...................MT-3513/APX
Computer, MX XII...........KIT-1A/TSEC
Mounting...................MT-( )/C

## MISSION AND DESCRIPTION

The primary mission of this aircraft is that of an armed tactical helicopter capable of delivering weapons fire, low-altitude high-speed flight, multiple weapons fire support, and troop helicopter support. The aircraft is capable of performing this mission from prepared or unprepared areas and operation from ships at sea.

The gas turbine powered Huey Twin Cobra is of compact design, featuring tandem seating to give both pilot and gunner nearly unlimited visibility. Both crew stations have flight control and fire control systems permitting flexibility in division of functions under all normal and emergency situations.

The twin engine installation improves both hot day and altitude performance and enhances overall reliability. A mission designed fuselage coupled with 540 "door hinge" rotor system gives a low vibration level plus increased maneuverability and speed. Four wing stores stations and integral chin turret provide a high degree of armament versatility with the capability of quickly changing a wide combination of weapons to match the desired mission. Many UH-1 parts which have been combat proven assure reliability and maintainability.

## DEVELOPMENT

Contract Placement        May 20, 1965
First Flight AH-1J        November 1969
BIS                       November 1970
First Delivery            January 1971
Final Delivery            In Production

## DIMENSIONS

Rotor diameter....................44.0 ft
Length
  Rotors operating................53.3 ft
  Rotors static...................53.3 ft
Fuselage..........................44.6 ft
Span (max lateral)................10.3 ft
Height............................13.6 ft
Tread.............................7.0 ft
Rotor ground clearance
  (static against stops)..........7.9 ft

## WEIGHTS

| Loading | Lb | LF |
|---|---|---|
| Empty | 6503 |  |
| Basic | 6702 |  |
| Design | 6600 | 3.5 |
| Combat |  |  |
|   Clean | 8202 | 2.8 |
|   Basic | 9272 | 2.5 |
|   Medium | 9534 | 2.4 |
|   Heavy | 9821 | 2.4 |
| Maximum Takeoff | 10000 | 2.3 |
| Maximum Landing | 10000 |  |

## FUEL AND OIL

### FUEL

| Location | No. Tanks | Gals. |
|---|---|---|
| Fuselage | 2 | 270 |
| Grade |  | JP-4 JP-5 |
| Specification |  | MIL-J-5624 |

### OIL

| | | |
|---|---|---|
| Engine | 2 | 3.2 |
| Specification | | MIL-L-7808 |

## ORDNANCE

20MM CHIN TURRET
WING STORES PYLONS (FOUR)
Any combination of the following
(1) LAU-68 rocket launcher (or equivalent)
(2) LAU-61A rocket launcher (or equivalent)
Outboard wing station only:
(3) Smoke grenade dispenser
Inboard wing station only:
(4) SUU-11A minigun pod
Maximum ammunition capacity for the 20 mm chin turret is 750 rounds.

## ACCOMMODATIONS

Basic, Medium, or Heavy combat
  Pilot.............1
  Gunner............1
Clean Mission
  Pilot.............1
  Copilot...........1

## PERFORMANCE SUMMARY

| TAKE-OFF LOADING CONDITION | | ① CLEAN | ② BASIC COMBAT | ③ MEDIUM COMBAT | ④ HEAVY COMBAT |
|---|---|---|---|---|---|
| **TAKE-OFF WEIGHT** | lb. | 8976 | 10000 | 10000 | 10000 |
| Fuel internal (JP-5) | lb. | 1836 | 1819 | 1164 | 446 |
| Payload (A) | lb. | 0 | 1041 | 1696 | 2414 |
| Disc loading | lb./sq.ft. | 5.90 | 6.58 | 6.58 | 6.58 |
| Vertical rate of climb at S.L. (B) | fpm. | 1160 | 285 | 285 | 285 |
| Absolute Hover Ceiling | ft. | 10,000 (D) | 4200 | 4200 | 4200 |
| Max. rate of climb at S.L. (B) | fpm. | 2230 | 1820 | 1814 | 1776 |
| Service Ceiling | ft. | 10000 (D) | 10000 (D) | 10000 (D) | 10000 (D) |
| Speed at S.L. (C) | kn. | 151 | 141 | 139 | 131 |
| Max. speed/altitude (C)kn./ft. | | 153/3000 | 142/2000 | 140/2000 | 133/2000 |
| O.E.I. Service ceiling | ft. | 10000 (D) | 10000 (D) | 10000 (D) | 10000 (D) |
| Min. Speed (O.E.I.) | kn. | 30 | 35 | 35 | 35 |
| Max. Speed (O.E.I.) | kn. | 128 | 116 | 115 | 108 |
| Combat radius | n.mi. | - | 134 | 72 | 7 |
| Mission time (E) | hrs. | - | 1.87 | 1.08 | 1° |
| Average cruising speed | kn. | - | 150 | 142 | 132 |
| Cruising altitude | ft. | - | SL | SL | SL |
| Range | n.mi. | 288 | 257 | 134 | 2 |
| Average cruising speed | kn. | 134 | 132 | 131 | 120 |
| Cruising altitude | ft. | SL | SL | SL | SL |
| Max. endurance | hrs. | 2.8 | 2.55 | 1.32 | .02 |
| Endurance speed | kn. | 71 | 71 | 70 | 69 |
| Endurance altitude | ft. | SL | SL | SL | SL |

## NOTES

(A) Includes Ammo
(B) Take-off Transmission rating of 1290 HP
(C) Maximum Continuous Transmission rating of 1134 HP
(D) Limited by oxygen requirement
(E) Mission Time - Time in air (excludes time before start of enroute climb and reserve, unless otherwise specified and noted.)

Performance Basis:
(1) All performance at standard day conditions.
(2) Aerodynamic flight test data.
(3) Engine specification fuel consumption increased 5%.
(4) 20 MM nose turret on all configurations.

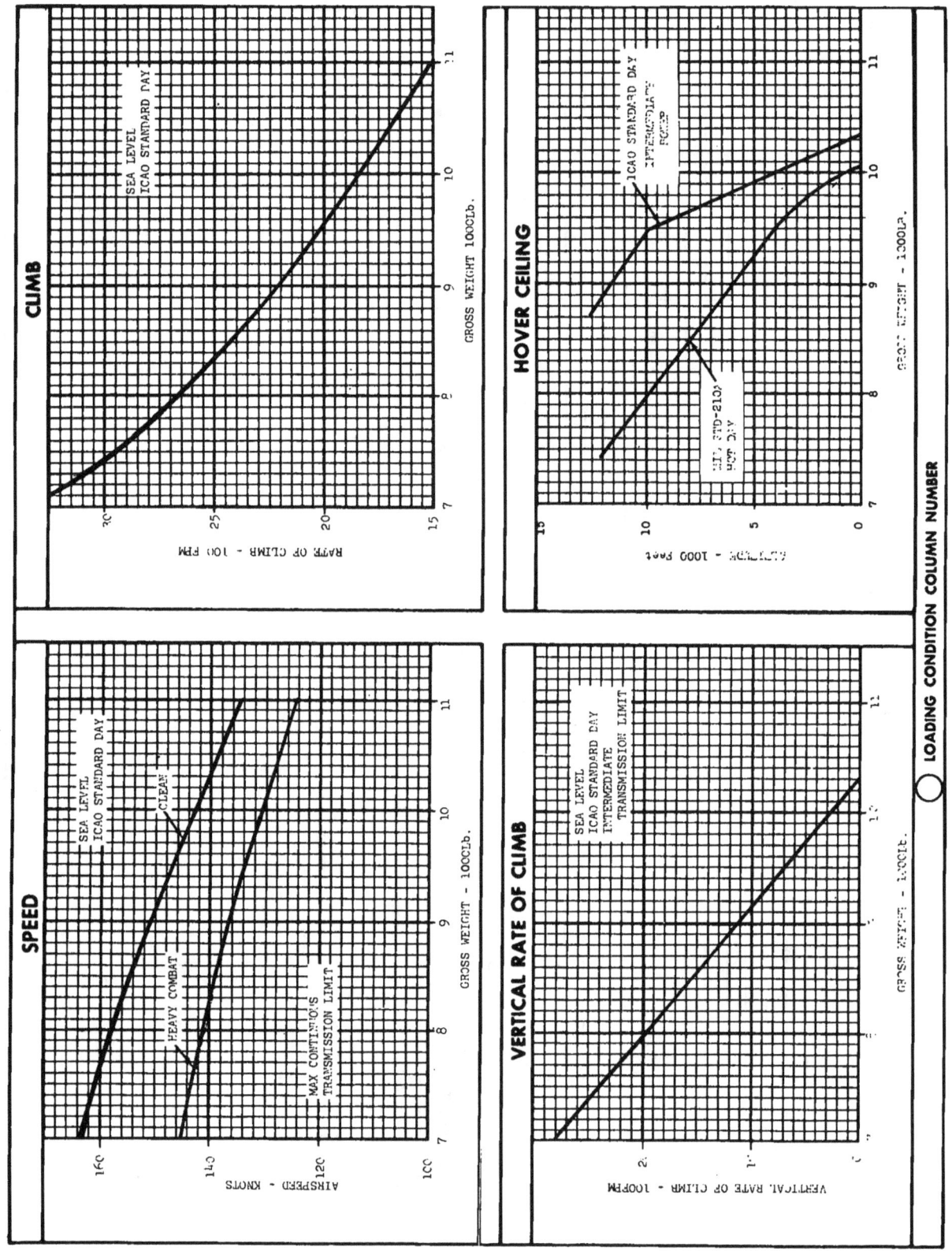

# STANDARD AIRCRAFT CHARACTERISTICS

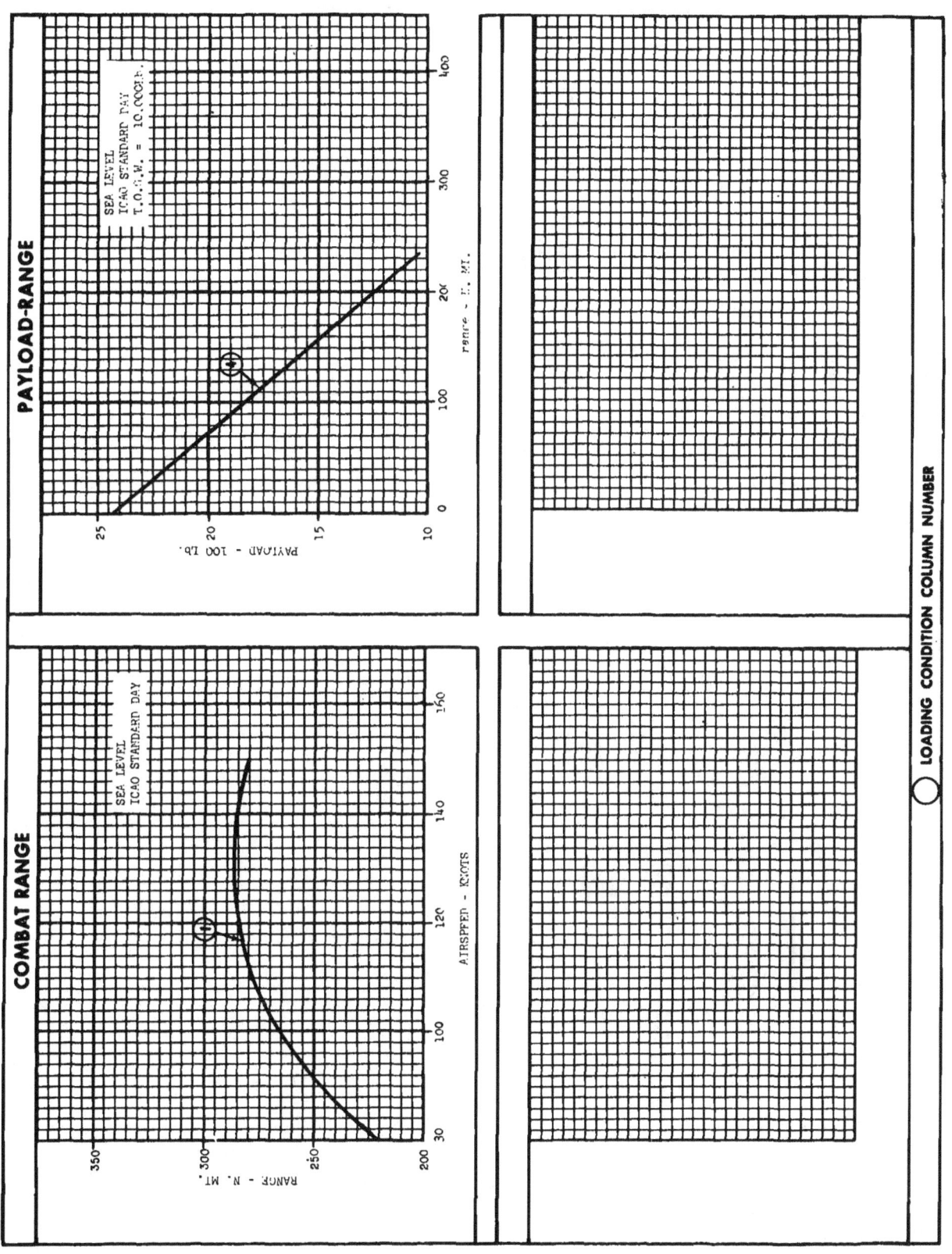

## NOTES

**RANGE MISSION**

1. Warm-up and take-off: Fuel allowance of 5 minutes at maximum continuous power at sea level.
2. Cruise out: To remote base at speed for maximum range at sea level.
3. Landing reserve: Fuel for 30 minutes at speed for maximum range at sea level.

**ATTACK MISSION**

1. Warm-up and take-off: Fuel allowance of 5 minutes at maximum continuous power at sea level.
2. Dash out: To target at maximum continuous power at sea level.
3. Combat: 5 minutes at intermediate power at sea level at $V_{max}$.
4. Expended all ordnance.
5. Dash back: To home base at maximum continuous power at sea level.
6. Landing reserve: Fuel for 20 minutes at speed for maximum range at sea level.

○ LOADING CONDITION COLUMN NUMBER

## STANDARD AIRCRAFT CHARACTERISTICS

# UH-1N
### BELL
### T400-CP-400 ENGINE

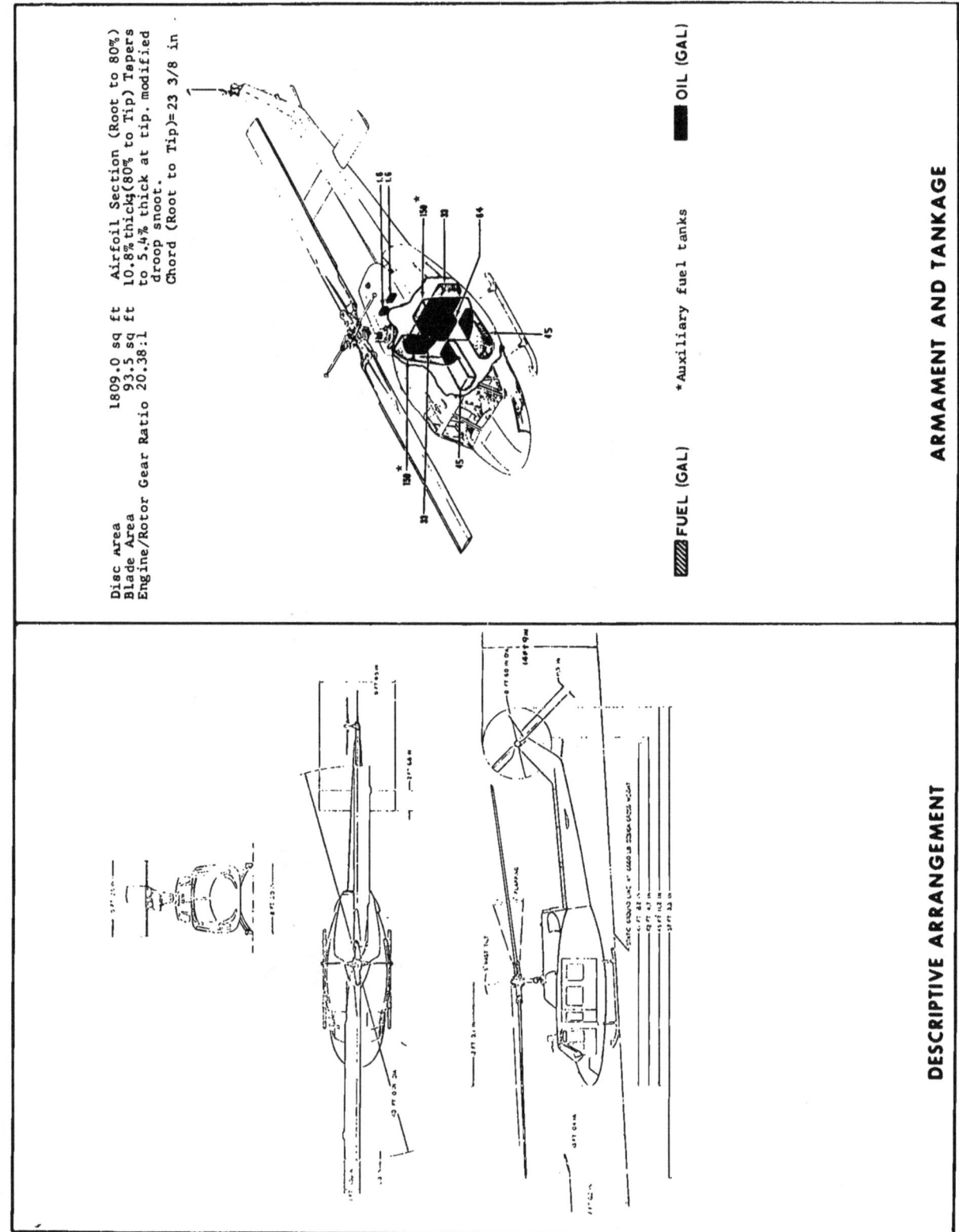

# STANDARD AIRCRAFT CHARACTERISTICS

## POWER PLANT

No. & Model.....(1) T400-CP-400
Manufacturer....United Aircraft of Canada
(Pratt and Whitney)
Engine Spec. No......712 C
Type...............Twin Section Free Power
Turbine with Reduction
Gearbox

Gear Reduction Ratios
Main Rotor.....20.383:1
Tail Rotor......3.974:1

### RATINGS

|  | SHP | RPM | ALT |
|---|---|---|---|
| Intermediate | 1800* | 6600 | SL |
| Maximum Continuous | 1530** | 6600 | SL |
| Single Power Section | | | |
| Intermediate | 900 | 6600 | SL |
| Maximum Continuous | 765 | 6600 | SL |

Transmission Limits
*1290 SHP
**1134 SHP

## ELECTRONICS

| | |
|---|---|
| VHF-FM Radio Set | AN/ARC-114 |
| Altimeter Encoder | AAU-21/A |
| UHF-AM Radio Set | AN/ARC-116 |
| Communication Sys | C-6533/ARC |
| Gyromag Compass Set | AN/ASN-43( ) |
| UHF Dir Find Sys | AN/ARA-50 |
| TACAN Navigation Set | AN/ARN-105 |
| Transponder Set | AN/APX-72 |
| HF Radio Set | AN/ARC-102 |
| Auto Direc Finder | AN/ARN-89 |
| Radar Altimeter | AN/APN-171(V) |
| Transponder Test Set | TS-1843A/APX |

### PROVISIONS FOR

| | |
|---|---|
| Loudspeaker System Kit | TSEC/KY-28 |
| Commun Security Set | AN/ARC-115 |
| VHF-AM Radio Set | KIT-1A/TSEC |
| Mark XII Computer | |

## MISSION AND DESCRIPTION

The basic missions of the UH-1N are visual observation and target acquisition, reconnaissance and command control. The UH-1N is capable of flight from established airfields, carriers of the LPH and CVS class, advanced based, areas or ships with individual landing platforms or limited landing facilities, and from unprepared fields. It may be handled on carrier elevators without any folding of components.

In addition, the UH-1N may be used for medical evacuation, to transport personnel, special teams or crews, equipment and supplies. These missions may be performed under instrument operations including light icing and day or night flight.

The twin power section installation improves both hot day and altitude performance.

The semi-monocoque fuselage is of all metal construction as are the tail rotor blades and the two main rotor blades. The large sliding door along each side allows rapid entry and exit and simplified straight-through loading from either side or both sides simultaneously. The knee-high cargo floor also contributes to loading ease.

## DEVELOPMENT

| | |
|---|---|
| Contract Placement | September 1969 |
| First Flight (Comm. 212) | April 1969 |
| (USAF UH-1N) | March 1970 |
| (USN UH-1N) | January 1971 |
| First Delivery | March 1971 |
| Final Delivery | In Production |

## DIMENSIONS

| | |
|---|---|
| Rotor Diameter | 48.0' |
| Length | |
| Rotors Operating | 57.3' |
| Rotors Static | 57.3' |
| Fuselage | 42.4' |
| Span (Max Lateral) | 5.2' |
| Height | 14.9' |
| Tread | 8.5' |
| Ground Clearance | 7.0' |
| (Static, Against Stops) | |

## WEIGHTS

| Loading | Weight | L.F. |
|---|---|---|
| *Empty | 6032 | |
| Basic | 6277 | |
| Operating | 7101 | |
| Design | 6600 | 3.0 |
| Combat | 7968 | 2.5 |
| Overload | 10,500 | 1.9 |
| Maximum Takeoff | 10,500 | 1.9 |
| Maximum Landing | 10,500 | 1.9 |

*UH-1N (Navy) is 91 lbs. Heavier

## FUEL AND OIL

### FUEL

| Gal. | No. of Tanks | Locations |
|---|---|---|
| 220.0* | 5 | Fuselage |
| 300.0 | 2 | Fuselage |

Fuel Grade......JP-4/JP-5
Fuel Spec.......MIL-J-5624
*Estimated with Foam

### OIL

Engine (Gal.)........3.2
Spec.............MIL-L-7808

## ORDNANCE

## ACCOMMODATIONS

| | |
|---|---|
| Crew (Observation) | 4 |
| Cabin Size Clearance: | |
| Length (Overall) | 7'8" |
| Width (Maximum) | 7'7" |
| Height (Maximum) | 4.1' |
| Usable Volume | |
| Cargo Area 220 Cu-ft | |
| Copilot Area 20 Cu-ft | |
| Provision for Troop Seats | 8 |
| Provision for Litters | 6 |
| Cargo Hook Capacity | 5,000 lb |
| Limit Floor Loading | 100 lb/sq.ft. at 1.5/2.5 |

## PERFORMANCE SUMMARY

| TAKE-OFF LOADING CONDITION | | ① OBSERVATION | ② RESCUE | ③ MEDICAL EVACUATION | ④ TROOP TRANSPORT | ⑤ EXTERNAL TRANSPORT | ⑥ FERRY |
|---|---|---|---|---|---|---|---|
| **TAKE-OFF WEIGHT** | lb. | 8546 | 8704 | 8586 | 9946 | 10,500 | 10,000 |
| Fuel internal/external (JP-5) lb./lb. | | 1445/0 | 1445/0 | 1445/0 | 1445/0 | 799/0 | 3186/0 |
| Payload Outbound/Inbound | lb/ lb. | 0/0 | 200/0 | 0/1200 | 1800/0 | 3000/0 | 0/0 |
| Disc loading | lb./sq.ft. | 4.72 | 4.81 | 4.74 | 5.50 | 5.80 | 5.52 |
| Vertical rate of climb at S.L. (A) | fpm. | 2010 | 1880 | 1970 | 900 | 460 | 880 |
| Absolute hovering ceiling (OGE) | ft. | 13,000 (A) | 12,500 (A) | 12900 (A) | 7800 (A) | 4000 (A) | 7400 (A) |
| Max. rate of climb at S.L. (A) | fpm. | 2310 | 2260 | 2300 | 1830 | 1660 | 1810 |
| Service ceiling (C) | ft. | 21,600 | 21100 | 21400 | 17800 | 16500 | 17700 |
| Speed at S.L. (D) | kn. | 122 | 120 | 121 | 111 | 110 | 110 |
| Max. speed/altitude (D) | kn./ft. | 128/3000 | 126/3000 | 127/3000 | 115/3000 | 115/3000 | 115/3000 |
| O.E.I. Service ceiling (B) | ft. | 14450 | 14000 | 14400 | 10600 | 9100 | 10400 |
| Min. speed (O.E.I.) | kn. | 11 | 15 | 11 | 29 | 34 | 30 |
| Max. Speed (O.E.I.) | kn. | 120 (D) | 119 | 120 | 111 (D) | 110 (D) | 110 (D) |
| Combat radius | n.mi. | 96 | 87 | 105 | 97 | 31 | ---- |
| Mission time (E) | hrs. | 1.58 | 1.68 | 1.77 | 1.59 | .69 | ---- |
| Average cruising speed | kn. | 128 | 125 | 122 | 122 | 105 | ---- |
| Cruising altitude | ft. | SL | SL | 5000 | SL | SL | ---- |
| Range | n.mi. | 181 | -- | -- | -- | 46 | 565 |
| Average cruising speed | kn. | 128 | -- | -- | -- | 80 | 117 |
| Cruising altitude | ft. | SL | -- | -- | -- | SL | 8000 |
| Maximum endurance | hrs. | 2.02 | -- | -- | -- | -- | -- |
| Endurance speed | kn. | 67 | -- | -- | -- | -- | -- |
| Endurance altitude | ft. | SL | -- | -- | -- | -- | -- |

**NOTES**

(A) Take-off Transmission Rating of 1290 HP  
(B) Military Rated Power  
(C) Maximum Continuous Power  
(D) ---  
(E) Mission Time - Time in air (excludes time before start of enroute climb and reserve, unless otherwise specified and noted).

Performance Basis:
1. All performance at standard day conditions.
2. Aerodynamic flight test data.
3. Engine specification fuel consumption increased 5%

# STANDARD AIRCRAFT CHARACTERISTICS

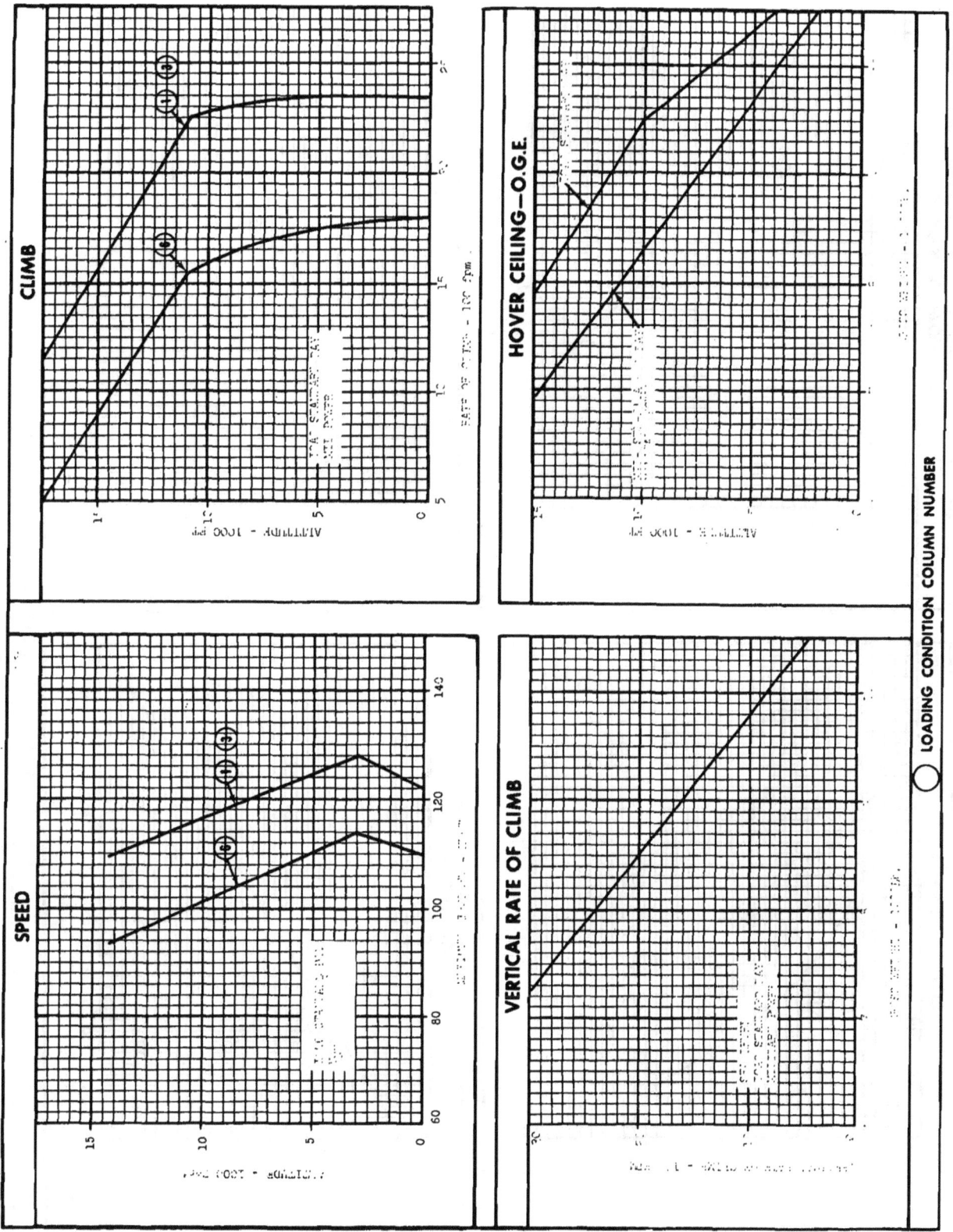

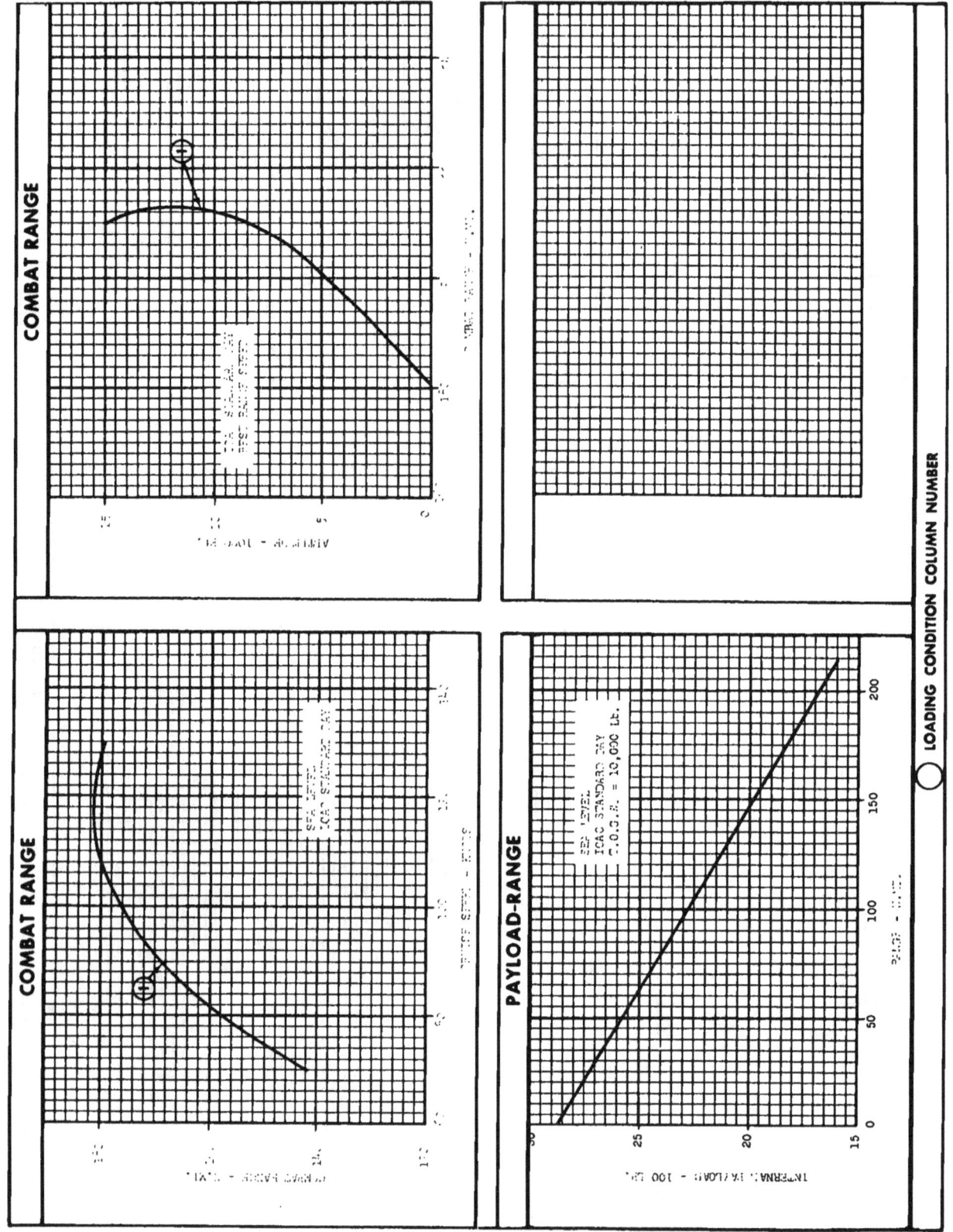

# STANDARD AIRCRAFT CHARACTERISTICS

## NOTES

| ① OBSERVATION | ② RESCUE | ③ MEDICAL EVACUATION | ④ TROOP TRANSPORT | ⑤ EXTERNAL TRANSPORT | ⑥ FERRY |
|---|---|---|---|---|---|
| RADIUS MISSION | RADIUS MISSION | RADIUS MISSION | RADIUS MISSION | RADIUS MISSION | RANGE MISSION |
| 1. Warm-up and take-off: Fuel allowance of 5 minutes at maximum continuous power at sea level.<br>2. Cruise out: At speed for best range at sea level.<br>3. Hover: 5 minutes out of ground effect at mid-mission.<br>4. Cruise back: To home base at speed for best range at sea level.<br>5. Landing Reserve: Fuel for 20 minutes at speed for maximum range at sea level.<br><br>RANGE MISSION<br><br>1. Warm-up and take-off: Fuel allowance of 5 minutes at maximum continuous power at sea level.<br>2. Cruise out: To remote base speed for maximum range at sea level.<br>3. Landing Reserve: Fuel for 30 minutes at speed for maximum range at sea level. | 1. Warm-up and take-off: Fuel allowance of 5 minutes at maximum continuous power at sea level.<br>2. Dash out: To target at maximum cruise speed for maximum continuous power at sea level.<br>3. Search: Over target at speed for best endurance for 15 minutes at sea level.<br>4. Pick up survivor; Hover out of ground effect 2 minutes at sea level.<br>5. Cruise back: To base at speed for maximum range at sea level.<br>6. Landing reserve: Fuel for 20 minutes at speed for maximum range at sea level. | 1. Warm-up and take-off: Fuel allowance 5 minutes at maximum continuous power.<br>2. Climb out: On course at speed for best climb at intermediate power to 5000 feet.<br>3. Cruise out: To remote base at 5000 feet at maximum continuous power.<br>4. Descend to sea level: No fuel used, no distance gained.<br>5. Land pick up six (6) litter patients; Mid-point fuel allowance of 2 minutes at maximum continuous power at sea level.<br>6. Climb back: On course at best climb speed at maximum continuous power to 5000 feet.<br>7. Cruise back: To home base at 5000 feet at maximum continuous power.<br>8. Descend to sea level: No fuel used, no distance gained.<br>9. Landing reserve: Fuel for 20 minutes at speed for maximum range at sea level. | 1. Warm-up and take-off: Fuel allowance of 5 minutes at maximum continuous power at sea level.<br>2. Cruise out: To remote base at maximum continuous power at sea level.<br>3. Land and unload troops: Mid-point fuel allowance of 2 minutes at maximum continuous power at sea level.<br>4. Cruise back: To home base at maximum continuous power at sea level.<br>5. Landing reserve: Fuel for 20 minutes at speed for maximum range at sea level. | 1. Warm-up and take-off: Fuel allowance of 5 minutes at maximum continuous power at sea level.<br>2. Cruise out: To remote base with payload at 80 knots at sea level.<br>3. Hover: 5 minutes out of ground effect at sea level with payload.<br>4. Release payload<br>5. Cruise back: To home base without payload at speed for best range at sea level.<br>6. Landing Reserve: Fuel for 20 minutes at speed for maximum range at sea level.<br><br>RANGE MISSION<br><br>1. Warm-up and take-off: Fuel allowance of 5 minutes at maximum continuous power at sea level.<br>2. Cruise out: To remote base with payload at 80 knots at sea level.<br>3. Landing Reserve: Fuel for 30 minutes at speed for maximum range at sea level. | 1. Warm-up and take-off: Fuel allowance of 5 minutes at maximum continuous power at sea level.<br>2. Climb out: On course at best climb speed at intermediate power to optimum cruise altitude not to exceed 10,000 feet (unless limited by cruise ceiling).<br>3. Cruise out: To remote base at speed for maximum range at optimum cruise altitude not to exceed 10,000 feet (unless limited by cruise ceiling).<br>4. Descend to sea level: No fuel used, no distance gained.<br>5. Landing reserve: Fuel for 30 minutes at speed for maximum range at sea level. |

○ LOADING CONDITION COLUMN NUMBER

# INDEX

Air America, 9
Air Force, 9–10, 13, 20, 55–57, 90–91, 97, 108–109, 111, 118, 133, 136, 141–144, 146, 151, 157, 160
Air Weapons Systems Branch, 154
Aircraft Types:
  A–4 (Skyhawk), 37, 109
  A–6, 137
  AH–1G (Huey Cobra), 151–154, 156–157, 161; illus., 152, 168
  AH–1J (Sea Cobra), 154–158; illus., 156, 169
  AH–56 (Cheyenne), 78
  AH–56A (Cheyenne), 157, 168
  AV–8 (Harrier), 56n, 63n, 148, 164
  B–26, 82
  C–47, 20
  C–117, 31, 79
  C–124, 97
  C–133, 156
  CH–19, 5, 17, 73, 84, 125–126
  CH–19E, 5, 13n, 17–19, 21, 125; illus., 18
  CH–37 (Mohave, "Deuce"), 12–17, 16n, 19–21, 34–35, 37–39, 41, 48–49, 56–58, 60, 63n, 64, 74–77, 81, 96–99, 114–116, 119–120, 125, 128, 154, 168–169; illus., 14, 36, 98, 118
  CH–37C, 12–15, 17, 24
  CH–46 (Sea Knight), 50, 52–55, 62, 73, 78, 82, 92, 99, 101–103, 114, 116, 118, 121–125, 137–138, 145–148, 150–151, 154, 159–162, 168; illus., 95, 102–103, 118, 140, 162
  CH–46A, 10, 99–100, 102–104, 115, 121, 123; illus., 53, 122
  CH–46D, 102–104, 121–125, 147; illus., 104, 124, 138, 169
  CH–46F, 4, 150–151, 158
  CH–47 (Chinook), 57n, 58, 60–61
  CH–53 (Sea Stallion), 58–59, 61–62, 75, 78, 82, 97–98, 114–119, 124–126, 128, 130, 138, 140, 145, 147, 150, 154, 159–162, 167–169
  CH–53A, 59, 60n, 62, 155–116
  CH–53D, 158, 167; illus., 62, 163, 169
  CH–53E, 166–169; illus., 167
  CH–54A, 117
  CH–54E, 167
  DC–3, 9, 20, 31
  F–4 (Phantom), 63, 161
  F4B, 154
  F–4F (Wildcat), 127, 127n
  F4U (Corsair), 127, 127n
  H–13, 141
  H–21, 28, 33, 79
  H–34, 5–6, 86, 141
  HH(X), 58
  HO3S, 2
  HO3S–1, 81
  HOK–1; see OH–43
  HR2S; see CH–37, CH–37C
  HR2S–1, 13n
  HR2S–1W, 16n
  HR3S, 48–50, 55, 59
  HR3S–1, 50
  HR–34, 6
  HRB, 54
  HRB–1, 52
  HRP–1, 107
  HRS, 11n, 20, 114
  HRS–1, 5, 73
  HRS–2, 73
  HRS–3; see CH–19E
  HS–3, 47
  HSS–1; see SH–34
  HSS–2, 47–50, 55, 59
  HTE–1, 71
  HTE–2; see OH–23
  HTL (Sioux), 72; illus., 72
  HTL–4, 72; illus., 72
  HTL–5, 72
  HTL–7, 72
  HUS–1; see UH–34
  KC–130, 31
  O–1, 35, 44, 46–47, 79, 83, 92, 112
  OE, 44
  OE–1 (Bird Dog), 11, 31–32
  OE–2 (Bird Dog), 11
  OH–23 (Raven), 71–72
  OH–23D (Raven), 142
  OH–43, 10–12, 34–35, 44–47, 56, 85, 92, 109, 169
  OH–43D, 10–12, 13n; illus., 10
  OV–10 (Bronco), 86n, 153, 162
  OV–10A, 109, 112–113, 154; illus., 113
  S–60 (Flying Crane), 58; illus., 59
  S–64, 58
  S–65, 12
  SBD (Dauntless), 127n
  SH–34, 5, 47
  SH–34J, 147
  SM–14, 90
  SS–11, 85
  T–28, 82–83, 86, 141
  T–28B, illus., 83
  T–34, 141
  TH–1L, 126
  TH–13, 73, 143
  UH–1 (Huey), 46, 110, 124, 138, 140, 143, 151–152, 157
  UH–1A, 46
  UH–1B (Iroquois), 45–46, 87–88, 90, 110, 112, 151, 154, 157
  UH–1D, 88, 126, 151, 157, 159
  UH–1E, 37–41, 44–47, 59, 62, 81–82, 88–92, 95–98, 109, 111–113, 115, 117n, 125–127, 145, 147, 150, 153–155, 157, 161; illus., 45, 89–90, 105, 110, 112
  UH–1H, 151, 153
  UH–1N, 157–158; illus., 158, 169
  UH–34 (Sea Horse), 5, 5n, 6–7, 9–11, 11n, 15–17, 19–20, 31, 33–39, 41–42, 47–48, 54–56, 62, 63n, 70, 73–76, 79, 80–85, 87–90, 92, 95, 97–99, 100–101, 104, 107n, 108, 112,

255

114-118, 117n, 121, 124-128, 138-140, 145, 147, 159-160, 169; illus., 6, 21-22, 36, 38-40, 84, 89, 98, 117, 128
UH-34D, 5-6, 8, 19, 83, 115, 127; illus., 126
Vertol 107M, 50, 52
VH-3, 20
HSS-2, 47-50, 55, 59
VH-3A, 55; illus., 56
VH-34, 19; illus., 19
VX-3, 71
"Wessex," 9
X-19A, 57
X-22A, 57
XC-142A, 57-58
XHR2S-A, 12
YH-1C, 168
YHC-1A, 49-50, 52, 114, 124
Alber, Major John W., 123
Aldworth, Lieutenant Colonel James, 92
Algeria, 85
All American Engineering Company, 20
Althoff, Major David L., 123
American Helicopter Society, 10, 43, 101
Amphibious assault ship (LPH), 6, 20-26, 28, 35, 58, 61, 63, 69, 80, 120, 139-140, 159, 162, 165, 167-169; illus., 25
Amphibious assault transport (APA), 24
Amphibious Warfare School Quantico, Virginia, 139
Anderson, General Earl E., 35, 153-154, 164; illus., 164
Anderson, Major General Norman J., 59-60, 65-66, 68-70, 73, 82, 86, 123-124, 123n
Anderson, Major Roy L., 16, 70
Anderson, Lieutenant Colonel William C., 127
Annamite Cordillera, 79
AR-15, 84
Armstrong, Brigadier General Alan J., 99-100, 110, 115, 119, 123, 131
Armstrong, Brigadier General Victor A., 49, 52, 155
Army, 13, 16n, 28-29, 33, 45-46, 49, 55, 57, 60-61, 67, 78-79, 82, 84-91, 96, 105-107, 109-110, 112, 117, 124, 126, 133, 141-144, 144n, 151, 153-154, 156, 159-160, 167-168
Army Air Corps, 106
Army Aviation Center, Fort Wolters, Texas, 143
Army Transportation Research and Engineering Command, 114
Assault-support helicopter (ASH), 44-45
Assistant Chief of Naval Operations (Air), 65
Assistant Chief of Staff, G-3, 109
Assistant DC/S (Air), 66, 99, 115, 119
Assistant Director of Aviation, 108
Attack cargo ship (AKA), 24
Attack transport ship (APA), 23
"The Attitude Song," 75
Automatic Stabilization Equipment, 75n
Aviation Officer Candidate Course (AOCC), 65

Baltos, Sgt Richard P., 75
Bancroft, First Lieutenant Arthur R., 81
Bare, Brigadier General Robert G., 13-14
Barnes, Robert L., 143
Basic School, Quantico, Virginia, 64-65, 106, 149
Batt, Staff Sergeant James A., illus., 75
Battle of Britain, 12
Bauman, Lieutenant Colonel George, 91, 96
Beal, Lieutenant Colonel Samuel G., 117-118
Beeler, Major William R., 62, 117-118
Belgian Congo, 87
Belieu, Assistant Secretary of the Navy Kenneth E., 50-51
Bell Helicopter Company, 45-47, 45n, 71-72, 88-89, 109-110, 126, 151, 153, 155, 157

Bennett, William Tapley, Jr., 38
Berkeley, Lieutenant General James P., 36-37
Berlin, Don, 50
Bianchi, Lieutenant Colonel Rocco D., 34
Binney, Major General Arthur F., 23, 48, 50, 81
"black box," 39
Blaha, Lieutenant Colonel Herbert J., 55
Blakeman, Major Wyman U., 123
Blanc, Lieutenant Colonel Richard J., 158
Bledsoe, Major Dwight L., 128
The Boeing Company, 50n
Boeing Airplane Company, 50n
Boeing-Vertol; (see Vertol Division, the Boeing Company)
Bougainville, 106
Boulton, Major Jerry D., 140
Bowser, Lieutenant General Alpha A., 145-146
Bremerton, Washington, 24
Brice, Lieutenant General William O., 64, 67
Bruce, Lieutenant Colonel Henry K., 35
Brule, Corporal Lawrence, 96
Brumley, Lieutenant Colonel Robert H., 70
"Bullpup" (ASM-N-7A), 85, 107n
Bureau of Aeronautics, (BuAir), 5, 13, 48, 107
Bureau of Naval Weapons (BuWeps), 20, 43-45, 47-48, 50, 54, 57-59, 62n, 89-91, 95-96

Cacciola, First Lieutenant Peter A., 126
Campo, Captain Guy R., 49n
Carey, Colonel John F., 29, 31, 80, 95; illus., 32
Caribbean, 96
Caribbean Ready Force, 37, 97
Carl, Major General Marion E., 5n, 45-46, 54, 70-71; illus., 51
Carnegie Institute of Technology, 105
Carpenter, Lieutenant Colonel Donald R., 147
Carroll, Drum Major Dennis, 169
Cassidy, Lieutenant Colonel Earl W., Sr., 34
Cates, General Clifton B., 20, 23
Cessna Aircraft Company, 45n, 112
Center for Naval Analyses, Washington, D.C., 159
Challgren, Lieutenant Colonel Stanley A., 154
Chapman, General Leonard F., Jr., 126, 131, 134, 136-139, 143, 149, 150, 153, 166; illus., 149
"Chickenhawk," 33
Chief of Naval Operations (CNO), 5, 22, 44-45, 47-50, 58-60, 66, 71, 77, 83, 89-90, 103-104, 115-116, 131-132, 141, 167
Childers, Lieutenant Colonel Lloyd F., 92, 96
Childress, 2d Lieutenant Clyde, 65
Chu Lai, Vietnam, 93, 97, 130, 139; illus., 22, 89; map, 94
Clapp, Colonel Archie J., 9, 29, 32-33, 76-77, 81, 84, 100; illus., 32
Clark, Lieutenant Colonel Truman, 37, 39, 96
Coast Guard, 71, 125, 132, 144
Cochran, Colonel Robert L., 34, 61
Colbert, Captain Bruce A., 125
Collins, General James F., 29
Collins, Major General William R., USA, 49-50, 109
Combat Information Center (CIC), 25
Commander, Amphibious Force, Atlantic (ComPhibLant), 36
Commander, Naval Air Forces, Pacific, (ComNavAirPac), 122
Commander Seventh Fleet, 80, 107
Commander, U.S. Military Assistance Command Vietnam, (ComUSMACV), 34, 79-80
Commander-in-Chief, Atlantic Fleet (CinCLantFlt), 36, 38
Commander-in-Chief, Pacific (CinCPac), 28, 34, 80, 83, 108
Commander-in-Chief, Pacific Fleet (CinCPacFlt), 80, 95
Commanding General, FMFPac, 28
Committee on Armed Services, 133

# INDEX

"compound" helicopter, 57
"compressor stall," 101
Condon, Major General John P., 29, 31; illus., 32
Congress, 133
Con Thien, Vietnam, illus., 117
Continental Aviation and Engineering Corporation, 155
Corliss, Lieutenant Colonel Gregory A., 99, 123
I Corps (Republic of Vietnam), 84; map, 94
Corps of Engineers Reserve, 106
Costa, 1st Lieutenant Anthony D., 98, 114
"crachin," 79
Crafton, Lieutenant Robert W., USN, 63n
Creech, Major Jimmie A., 153
Cretney, Lieutenant Colonel Warren G., 143, 154
Crew chiefs, 8, 73–75, 138, 147
Croizat, Lieutenant Colonel Victor J., 85
Cuba, 28, 35
Cuban Missile Crisis, 34–35, 153
Curtis, Lieutenant Colonel Oliver W., 80
Cushman, General Robert E., Jr., 124, 166, 169; illus., 166

Da Nang, Vietnam, 79–84, 87, 91–93, 93n, 97, 109, 124, 126, 130; illus., 130, 162; map, 30, 94
Da Nang River, Vietnam, 93n
Davis-Monthan Air Force Base, Arizona, 127
Dawson, Fred, 70
DeLalio, Major Armond H., 5, 70–71
Department of the Army, 142
Department of Defense, 3, 12, 23, 42, 57, 59, 77–78, 102–103, 112, 133–134, 136
Deputy Chief of Naval Operations (Air), 44
Deputy Chief of Naval Operations (Air Warfare) (DCNO-AW), 9n
Deputy Chief of Naval Operations (DCNO(OPS)), 12
Deputy Chief of Staff (Air), 37, 59, 59n, 62, 68–70, 73, 82, 104, 108–110, 115, 118, 122–123, 131–132, 139–140, 142, 151, 162
Deputy Chief of Staff for Research and Development, 46
Derning, Colonel Edmund G., Jr., illus., 105
Director of Aviation, 23, 45, 48, 54, 57, 59, 64, 67, 81, 145
Director of Policy Analysis, 68
Division of Aviation, 68, 85
Doman, 45n
Dominican Intervention (1965), 37–40
Dominican Republic, 36–38, 41, 46n, 49, 77, 95; illus., 39
Doster, Colonel Grover C., 127
Doyle, Lieutenant Colonel Griffith B., 16
Doyle, Sergeant Thomas, 41
Duncan, Lieutenant Colonel William R., 146
Dyer, Colonel Edward C., 2, 5, 12, 17, 63–64, 70–71, 73, 125

East Liverpool, Ohio, 105, 107
Eglin Air Force Base, Florida, 143
Eisenhower, President Dwight D., 19
Eldridge, Lieutenant Colonel William W., 29, 31
Engelhardt, Lloyd J., 49n
Engesser, Colonel Robert B., 147
Enthoven, Dr. Alain C., 134–136, 142; illus., 134
Erwin, Master Gunnery Sergeant Charles P., 169

Fairbourn, Brigadier General William T., 35
Fairey Rotodyne, 58
Federal Aviation Agency (FAA), 76
Federal Republic of (West) Germany, 141
*Federation Aeronautique International*, 16
Felt, Admiral Harry D., 28, 83
Ferris, Major James W., 49n

Field, Captain Steven E., 119
Finlayson, Colonel Edwin H., 155
Finn, Lieutenant Colonel Edward V., 71
Finn, Major Robert C., 113
Fire Support Coordination Center (FSCC), 25
Fisher, Master Sergeant Arnold G., 71
Fleet Introduction Program (FIP), 11, 54, 62
Fleet Marine Force, 2, 11, 90, 109
Floyd Bennett Field, New York, 70
"Flying cranes," 16n, 58, 114, 166
Flynn, Lieutenant Colonel Richard J., Jr., 5
Foley, Colonel Kenneth S., 153
Forced transition program, 69–70
Foreign object damage (FOD), 43
Fort Belvoir, Virginia, 46
Fort Benning, Georgia, 67, 143
Ford Ord, California, 29
Fort Rucker, Alabama, 85, 143
Fort Sill, Oklahoma, 149
Fort Stewart, South Carolina, 143
Fort Wolters, Texas, 142–143
Forward air controller (FAC), 111
Foss, Lieutenant Colonel Donald H., 31
Foster, 2d Lieutenant James R., 65
Freitas, Joseph L., Jr., 49n
French Army, 85
Fulton, Captain Samuel J., 85
Futema, Okinawa, 9, 12, 34, 62, 81, 88, 92, 162

Garber, Charles D., 70
General Electric Corporation, 101
Glenn, Lieutenant Colonel John H., 63
Glenview, Illinois, 126
Goebel, Lieutenant Colonel Jerome L., 96
Gordon, Major James T., 147
Greene, General Wallace M., Jr., 27, 37, 57–59, 61, 69, 86–87, 91, 109, 115, 129–130, 132–136, 138–139, 149–150; illus., 27
Ground effect, 4–5, 8
Guantanamo Bay, Cuba, 38, 106
Gulling, Lieutenant Colonel Louis A., 124
Gwinn, W.P., 158
Gyrodyne, 45n, 168

Hagedorn, Lieutenant Colonel Elvyn E., 147
Haina, Dominican Republic, 38
Haiti, 36, 87
Hai Van Peninsula, Vietnam, 79
Han River, Vietnam, 93
Harkins, General Paul D., USA, 28, 79–80, 83
Harpham, Lieutenant Colonel Dale L., 169
Harris, Captain Thomas D., USN, 26
Hart, Colonel Henry, 155
Hart, Captain Herbert M., 64–65
Haufler, George W., Jr., 143
Hawley, Major Richard L., 97–98, 119
Headquarters Marine Corps, 5, 23, 49, 59, 64, 69, 73, 109, 129, 135, 139–140, 142, 144, 149, 155
Headquarters Marine Corps Transport Helicopter Study Advisory Committee, 159
Helicopter Aircraft Commander, 75n
Helicopter Development Squadron Three (VX-3), USN, 70
Helicopter Direction Center (HDC), 25–26
Helicopter Squadron 2, USN, 107
Helicopter Training Unit One (HTU-1), USN, 71
Hemingway, Colonel Jack W., 143
Henshaw, Captain James E., 127
Hertberg, Lieutenant Colonel Edward C., 161

Heyward, Vice Admiral Alexander S., Jr., 141
Hill, Brigadier General Homer S., 23n, 150–151
Hiller Aircraft Corporation, 45, 45n
Hochmuth, Brigadier General Bruno A., 46
Hoffert, Lieutenant Colonel DuWayne W., 126
Hollowell, Colonel George L., 46, 59, 61
Hubbard, Brigadier General Jay W., 4
Hughes Aircraft Company, 45, 58, 168
House Appropriations Committee, 155
House Armed Services Committee, 155, 157
House of Representatives, 133
Hue, Vietnam, 92; map, 94
Huelva, Spain, 37
Hunter Army Airfield, Georgia, 143, 153
Hunter, Colonel Glenn R., 113, 158

Ingalls Shipbuilding Division, 165
Integrated Helicopter Avionics System (IHAS), 77–78, 150, 159
Ireland, Colonel Julius W., 80
Iwakuni, Japan, 19, 29, 31

Jacksonville, Florida, 100
Jamaica, 36
James, 1st Lieutenant Tommy L., 153
Jerome, Major General Clayton C., 13
Jet-assisted takeoffs (JATO), 5
Johnson, Lee, 50
Johnson, President Lyndon B., 92
Johnson, Admiral Roy L., 80
Johnson, Brigadier General William G., 66, 92–93, 95
Johnston, Colonel Paul T., 65
Joint Chiefs of Staff (JCS), 28–29, 36, 80–81, 84–85, 92
Joint Coordination Committee on Piloted Aircraft, 57
Jones, Major General William K., 142

Kaiser, 21
Kaman Aircraft Corporation, 11, 45n, 58, 168
Kaman, Charles H., 10
Kaneohe, 2, 19, 62, 74, 92, 162
Keck, Captain L. Kenneth, 55, 63
Kendall James T., 136
Kennedy, Major Jack A., 93
Kennedy, President John F., 28, 35, 52
Kettering, Captain Alvah J., 99
Kew, Lieutenant Colonel George D., 92
Kier, Major General Avery R., 2
King, Colonel John H., Jr., 92
Kinkaid, Admiral Thomas C., 107
Kirby, Lieutenant Colonel Edward K., 36–37
Kivette, Rear Admiral Frederick N., 65
Kizer, Captain James P., 31
Kleppsattel, Lieutenant Colonel Frederick M., 36, 38–39, 49, 77
Knapp, Commander William G., 5n
Koler, Lieutenant Colonel Joseph, 80–81
Korea, 107
Korean War, 17, 28–29, 114
Korth, Secretary of the Navy Fred, 50–52
Krulak, Lieutenant General Victor H., 2, 13, 80, 82, 88, 90, 92, 95–96, 98–102, 109, 111–112, 116–117, 121–122, 123n
Ky Ha, Vietnam, 93–96; map, 94

LaHue, Lieutenant Colonel Foster, 13
Laird, Secretary of Defense Melvin R., 167
Lakehurst, New Jersey, 70–71, 73, 107
Lamarr, Master Sergeant C. A., 62
Larry, Lieutenant Colonel John H., 80
Landing Helicopter Assault Ship (LHA), 165–169; illus, 166
Landing Platform Dock (LPD), 165
Landing Ship Dock (LSD), 165
Landing Ship Tank (LST), 23, 165
Laos, 9, 87, 95
Laterite, 31, 95
Lee, Lieutenant Colonel Reinhardt, 29
Lejeune, Camp, North Carolina, 2, 145–146, 149
Leu, Lieutenant Colonel Reinhardt, 34
Light Armed Reconnaissance Aircraft (LARA), 83, 86, 141
Light observation helicopter (LOH), 45
Limited duty officers (LDOs), 68
Lindley, Gunnery Sergeant Leland R., 126
Litton Industries, 165–166
Lockheed Aircraft Corporation, 45n, 105
Lowrey, Lieutenant Colonel Horace S., Jr., 158
Lucas, Lieutenant Colonel William R., 92
Luckey, Lieutenant General Robert B., 35–36
Luzon, Philippines, 107
Lycoming Corporation, 157

M-60 machine gun, 84–85, 87, 89–90, 100–101, 116; illus., 84
MacQuarrie, Colonel Warren L., 36
Malabang Airfield, Philippines, 107
Mangrum, Lieutenant General Richard C., 13, 87, 93
Mansfield, Lance Corporal James I., 81
Marble Mountain Air Facility (MMAF), Vietnam, 93, 95–101, 110, 113, 117–1.9, 121, 145, 156; illus., 124, 130, 138, 63; map, 94
Marine Air Reserve Training Command, 4
Marine Barracks Philadelphia, Pennsylvania, 106
Marine Combat Crew Readiness Training Group (MCCRTG), 146
Marine Corps Air Facility (MCAF), Camp Pendleton, California, 2, 11
Marine Corps Air Facility (MCAF), Futema, Okinawa, 2, 11, 123
MCAF New River, North Carolina, 2
MCAS Cherry Point, North Carolina, 65, 100, 124
MCAS El Toro, California, illus., 56; 67, 92, 126
MCAS (H) New River, North Carolina, 11, 16, 19, 34–35, 37–39, 41, 55, 62, 65, 74, 92, 97, 99, 104, 108–110, 123, 126–127, 139, 145, 147, 156–158 161–162, 164; illus., 128
MCAS Quantico, Virginia, 2, 127
MCAS Santa Ana, California, 2, 9, 16, 34–35, 55, 62, 70, 76, 92, 96–97, 100, 104, 109, 115, 117–118, 121, 123–124, 127, 139, 145–147, 153, 162
MCAS Yuma, Arizona, 146
Marine Corps Association, 29
Marine Corps Auxiliary Air Field (MCAAF), Camp Pendleton, California, 83, 110–111
Marine Corps Aviation Cadet (MarCad), 65–66, 68
Marine Corps Aviation Museum, Quantico, Virginia, 126–127
Marine Corps Development Center, Quantico, Virginia, 13, 84, 160
Marine Corps Equipment Board, 107
*Marine Corps Gazette*, 12, 16, 63, 67, 76
Marine Corps General Staff, 13
Marine Corps Landing Force Development Center, (MCLFDC), Quantico, Virginia, 8, 48–49, 77, 87, 90, 160–161
Marine Corps Operational Analysis Group (MCOAG), 81, 159–161
Marine Corps Schools, 13, 44, 64, 66, 107

# INDEX

Marine Corps Units:
  Fleet Marine Force, Atlantic (FMFLant), 2, 13, 36, 110, 127, 139–140, 145
  Fleet Marine Force, Pacific (FMFPac), 80, 83, 90, 96, 98, 127, 139
  Aircraft, Fleet Marine Force, Atlantic (AirFMFLant), 13
  Aircraft, Fleet Marine Force, Pacific (AirFMFPac), 2, 28
  Force Troops, Atlantic, 149
  II Marine Expeditionary Force, 35–36
  III Marine Amphibious Force, 108, 124, 164
  1st Marine Aircraft Wing, 29, 31, 90, 93, 108, 112, 117–118, 123n, 123–124, 145
  2d Marine Aircraft Wing, 140
  3d Marine Aircraft Wing, 127
  4th Marine Aircraft Wing, 4
  1st Marine Division, 35
  2d Marine Division, 35
  3d Marine Division, 79; illus., 140
  1st Marine Brigade, 2, 108
  5th Marine Expeditionary Brigade, 35
  Marine Aircraft Group (MAG) 13, 2
  MAG–16, 2, 16, 29, 34, 80, 88, 92–93, 95, 101, 119, 124, 138; illus., 98
  MAG–24, 106
  MAG–26, 2, 34, 36, 38, 47, 61–62, 65, 97, 101, 108, 139–140, 145, 157–158
  MAG–36, 2, 35, 62, 92–93, 95–96, 99, 124, 139, 145, 153, 155; illus., 22, 90
  MAG–56, 120–121, 138–139, 145
  Marine Helicopter Training Group (MHTG) 30, 146–148
  MHTG–40, 147–148
  Marine Wing Service Group (MWSG) 17, 19
  MWSG–37, 92, 99
  7th Marines, illus., 105
  12th Marines, illus., 119
  Headquarters and Maintenance Squadron (H&MS) 16, 2, 9, 95–96
  H&MS–26, 104
  H&MS–30, 146–147
  H&MS–36, 126, 161
  H&MS–40, 147
  Marine Attack Helicopter Squadron (HMA) 169, illus., 168
  HMA–269, 157–158
  Marine Heavy Helicopter Squadron (HMH) 461, 34, 37, 39, 62, 92, 97, 120
  HMH–462, 92
  HMH–463, 62, 115, 117–119, 138; illus., 62, 75, 118
  Marine Heavy Helicopter Training Squadron (HMHT) 401, 147
  Marine Light Helicopter Squadron (HML), 167, 113, 158
  HML–267, 113
  HML–367, 113, 143, 154, 156
  Marine Medium Helicopter Squadron (HMM) 161, 74, 92, 104; illus., 102, 162
  HMM–162, 29, 80–81, 83
  HMM–163, 34, 79
  HMM–164, 55, 92, 99–102, 161; illus., 163
  HMM–165, 161
  HMM–261, 29, 31–32, 34–36, 92, 95, 136
  HMM–262, 34, 36–38, 70, 123; illus., 122
  HMM–263, 35–36, 39–41, 95–97; illus., 89, 124
  HMM–264, 34–36, 38–39, 41, 49, 77; illus., 39–40
  HMM–265, 37, 92, 99–101
  HMM–361, 35, 80, 92, 96
  HMM–362, 2, 9, 29, 31–34, 70, 79–81, 92, 126, 137; illus., 126
  HMM–363, 92
  HMM–364, 80, 92, 122, 124; illus., 138
  HMM–365, 80–81, 88
  HMM–462, 111
  HMM–463, illus., 163
  HMM–561, 121, 127
  HMM–776, 127
  Marine Medium Helicopter Training Squadron (HMMT) 301, 146–147
  HMMT–302, 147
  HMMT–402, 147–148
  Marine Transport Helicopter Squadron (HMR) 161, 107, 155
  Marine Light Helicopter Transport Squadron (HMRL) 161, 2, 19
  HMRL–162, 2, 9
  HMRL–163, 2, 9
  HMRL–261, 2, 5, 9
  HMRL–262, 2, 65
  HMRL–263, 2, 19
  HMRL–264, 2
  HMRL–361, 2
  HMRL–362, 2
  HMRL–363, 2, 6
  Marine Medium Helicopter Transport Squadron (HMRM) 461, 2, 16
  HMRM–462, 2
  Marine Helicopter Squadron (HMX) 1, 2, 6, 11, 16, 19–20, 29, 55, 64, 70–71, 73, 75, 85, 87, 89–90, 92, 95–96, 107, 125, 155; illus., 18–19, 56
  Marine Air Base Squadron (MABS) 16, 2, 29, 96
  MABS–36, 93
  Marine Observation Squadron (VMO) 1, 2, 11, 34, 37, 39, 47, 156
  VMO–2, 2, 11–12, 31, 81, 91–92, 96–97, 111, 153–154
  VMO–3, 111, 113
  VMO–5, 111, 113, 147
  VMO–6, 2, 11, 35, 38, 83, 86, 90, 92, 111, 153; illus., 89
  VMO 151, 106n
  Battalion Landing Team (BLT) 1/2, 34, 39, 41
  BLT–3/8, 37
  2d Raider Battalion, 4
  Marine Corps Air Reserve Training Detachment, Glenview, Illinois, 127
Marine Officers' Wives Club, 133
"Marine One," illus., 56
Marston matting, 93
Martin, Colonel Samuel F., 119
Massachusetts Institute of Technology, Cambridge, Massachusetts, 106
Masud, Staff Sergeant Leo A., 84
Maughan, Master Sergeant John P., 73
McBrien, Captain Thomas P., 40–41
McCabe, Major John G., 161
McCain, Vice Admiral John S., Jr., 36
McCauley, Lieutenant Colonel Betram W., 82
McCutcheon, General Keith B., ii, 44, 47, 55, 58, 62, 67–68, 77, 79, 93, 104–110, 112–113, 115–116, 118, 121–123, 129, 132, 134–139, 142–143, 145–148, 151, 153, 153n, 155, 161–162, 164, 167; illus., 105, 143
McCutcheon, Mrs. Marion P. Thompson, 107; illus., 164
McDonnell Aircraft Corporation, 13
McNamara, Secretary of Defense Robert S., 133–134, 142, 146, 155
McRoberts, Lieutenant Colonel Perry P., 54
Mediterranean Ready Amphibious Squadron, 36
Megee, General Vernon E., 6, 107
Mekong Delta, Vietnam, 28–29, 81, 83
Mekong River, Vietnam, 32

Mendenhall, Lieutenant Colonel Herbert E., 99, 101
Meredith, James H., 34
Military Sea Transport Service, 36
Miller, Major Donald E.P., 153
Miller, Lieutenant General Thomas H., 63, 63n, 154, 157–158
Mindanao, Philippines, 107
Mitchell, Lieutenant Colonel William F., 6
Mittelstadt, 1st Lieutenant Richard C., 41
Monaghan, Jeffrey D., 143
Monsoon, 79
Moore, Commander Ben, Jr., 71
Moorer, Admiral Thomas H., 80
Moreau, Lieutenant Colonel Paul L., 161
Morris, Lieutenant Colonel Clark I., 153
Morrison, Lieutenant Colonel Gene W., 92
Mortimer, Corporal Eugene, 96
Morton, Pennsylvania, 122, 150
Mounts, Master Sergeant Leonard J., 71, 73n
Mullins, 2d Lieutenant Larry D., 66
Munn, Major General John C., 11, 48, 57, 85, 145
Murray, Major Francis R., 111
Murray, Russell, 134–135
Myer, Lieutenant Colonel Robert D., 156

Nam Phong, Thailand, 161
National Guard, 142
National Press Club, 91
National War College, Washington, D.C., 108
NAS Cubi Point, Philippines, 31
NAS Memphis, Tennessee, 34
NAS, Patuxent River, Maryland, 90
NAS, Quonset Point, Rhode Island, 19, 61
Naval Air Station, Pensacola, Florida, 68
NAS, Pensacola, Florida, 68
  101–102, 115–116, 118–123, 150, 155
Naval Air Technical Training Command, Memphis Tennessee, 73
Naval Air Test Center (NATC), Patuxent River, Maryland, 5, 45–47, 49, 54, 66, 104, 115–116, 123, 156
Naval Air Training Command, 131–133, 140–141, 143–144, 146
Naval Auxiliary Air Station (NAAS) Ellyson, Florida, 71–73, 141, 143, 147, 150
Naval Aviation Cadets (NavCads), 65–66
Naval Aviation Pilots (NAPs), 68n
Naval Aviation Safety Center, Norfolk, Virginia, 121, 123, 154
Navorska, Major Donald R., 37
Navy, 13, 16n, 22–23, 25, 46–47, 50–51, 57–59, 65, 71, 75, 77–78, 96, 100, 102, 104, 108–109, 112, 121, 125, 128, 132–133, 141–142, 144, 146, 155, 157–158, 160, 167–168
Navy Department, 107, 136
Nelson, Major Herbert A., 8
Nelson, Lieutenant Colonel Joseph A., 47
Nelson, Major Wilbur O., 34, 70
New, Colonel Noah C., 86
Nghiem, Major General Le Van, 79
Nicaragua, 36
Niesen, Colonel Paul W., 156–157
Nitze, Paul H., 142
Nixon, President Richard M., 162
Norfolk, Virginia, 124, 127
Norman, Corporal Thomas F., illus., 105
North American Aviation, Inc., 83
North Island, San Diego, California, 100
North Korea, 87
North Vietnam, 137, 161
North Vietnamese, 98

North Vietnamese Army, 129, 155
Nortronics, 77

O'Connor, Colonel Thomas J., 92, 96
Office of the Secretary of Defense (OSD), 57, 61, 86, 113, 129, 132, 134–137, 139, 142, 144, 146, 153, 157, 161, 167–168
Okinawa, 9, 29, 31, 34, 41, 79–80, 88, 92, 123, 161
Olson, Major Virgil D., 19
Onslow Beach, North Carolina, 41
Operation DEWEY CANYON, illus., 110
Operation MIXMASTER, 145
Operation NANKING-SCOTLAND II, illus., 90
Operation PLACE KICK, 38
Operation PRAIRIE, 111
Operation SHUFLY, 28–29, 31, 33–34, 41, 70, 79–84, 86–89, 92, 95, 100, 109, 112, 157; illus., 32
Operation SILVER LANCE, 37, 41; illus., 38
Operation STEEL PIKE I, 36–37, 41; illus., 36
Operation TULUNGAN, 29, 31
Organization of American States, 41
Overhaul and Repair Activity, North Island, San Diego, California, 100, 117
Overhaul and Repair Activity, Jacksonville, Florida, 89
Owens, Major General Robert G., 127
Oxford, Mississippi, 34

Paige, Major General Henry R., 36, 67–68, 87, 160
Pascagoula, Mississippi, 165–166
Pate, General Randolph McCaul, 22, 47–48, 55, 65, 67, 69; illus., 47
Payne, Colonel Frederick R., 21
Pendleton, Camp, 86, 90–91, 112–113, 147, 162
Pennel, Captain Guss H., Jr., 96
Pensacola, Florida, 64–65, 71, 83, 106, 125–126, 130–132, 141–145, 147
PHIBEX 1–62, illus., 21
PHIBRIGLEX–62, 34–35
Philadelphia Navy Yard, Philadelphia, Pennsylvania, 106
Philippine Islands, 29, 92, 106–107
Phu Bai, Vietnam, 92, 96, 113, 124, 126; illus., 126; map, 94
Piasecki Aircraft Corporation, 13, 45n, 49n, 58
Piasecki, Frank, 12, 52
Pipa, John L., 153
Pirie, Vice Admiral Robert B., 44–45
Plan "Echo", 131–132, 134, 136
Platoon Leader's Class (PLC), 64–65
Plummer, Captain James R., 31
Policy Analysis Division, 23
Pope, Lieutenant Colonel Eugene J., 16–17, 34
Porter, Colonel Daniel B., Jr., USA, 79
Porter, Colonel Mervin B., 36, 92, 136
Powell, Colonel Edwin L., Jr., 142
Pratt and Whitney, 10, 14
Pratt and Whitney of Canada, 155
Preparedness Investigating Subcommittee, 133
"Presidential Mission", 2
"Project Tough", 100
Prudhomme, Lieutenant Colonel Daniel P., 127
Puerto Rico, 36, 38
Puget Sound Naval Shipyard, Bremerton, Washington, 24, 26
Purtell, Staff Sergeant Richard J., 126

Quang Ngai (Province), Vietnam, 80
Quantico, Virginia, 13n, 49, 62, 67, 89, 96, 100, 106–107, 127, 139, 162; illus., 10–12, 18
QUICK KICK VII, 38
Quinn, Lieutenant Colonel William R., 84

# INDEX

Randolph Field, Texas, 106
Rathbun, Lieutenant Colonel Robert L., 34, 79
Raymond, Morrison, Knudson-Brown, Root, and Jones (RMK-BRJ), 93
Republic Aviation Corporation, 45n
Republic of Korea Marines, illus., 89
Republic of Vietnam Air Force, 33, 80, 82–83, 85, 87
Republic of Vietnam Marine Corps, 161
Reese, Lieutenant Colonel Clifford E., 156–157
Reid, Master Sergeant J. A., 62
Reusser, Colonel Kenneth L., 47, 109
Richardson, David, 43, 101
Rider, James W., 153
Riley, Major David, 85
Riley, Colonel Russell R., 70, 146
Rivers, Representative L. Mendel, 133, 155, 157–158
Robbins, Lieutenant Colonel Morris G., 147
Roberts, Major General Carson A., 28, 34, 65
Robertshaw, Lieutenant General Louis B., 37, 73, 82, 87, 109–110, 115, 118–119, 123n, 125, 144
ROR (Rocket on Rotor), illus., 18
Ross, Lieutenant Colonel Thomas J., 35
Rota, Spain, 36
Royal Air Force, 12

Sabattus, Staff Sergeant Donald, 125
Sadowski, Lieutenant Colonel Joseph L., 61
Saigon, Vietnam, 31, 83
Samaras, Captain Peter N., 146
Sanders, Undersecretary of the Navy Frank P., 164
San Diego, California, 96, 120
San Francisco Naval Shipyard, San Francisco, California, 21
San Juan, Puerto Rico, 38, 106
Santo Domingo City, Dominican Republic, 38–39, 41; illus., 40
Schlarp, Lieutenant Colonel Jack E., 126
Schoech, Vice Admiral William A., USN, 32
Schoepper, Lieutenant Colonel Albert F., 1–2, 16
Schrider, Colonel Peter P., 64
Schriefer, First Sergeant Robert A., 31
Scott, Colonel Kenneth M., 127
Seabees, 93
Secretary of the Army, 110
Secretary of Defense, 60, 109–110, 113, 134, 146, 155, 161, 165
Secretary of the Navy, 45, 55, 60, 69, 111, 131–132, 134, 139, 142, 153, 155
Self-Contained Navigation System (SCNS), 77–78, 150
Senate Appropriations Committee, 155
Senate Committee on Armed Services, 133, 155
Shapley, Lieutenant General Alan, 28, 34
Sharp, Admiral Ulysses S. G., 80
Shaw, Brigadier General Samuel R., 12, 68–69
Shelton, Major James L., 117
Shepherd, General Lemuel C., Jr., 5–6, 12–13, 64, 71, 125
Sherman, Admiral Forrest, 12
Shinn, Vice Admiral Allen M., 115, 122
Ships, U. S. Navy:
  USS *Block Island* (LPH 1), 21–22, 24n
  USS *Boxer* (LPH 4), 22–23, 24n, 35–38, 41, 99; illus., 39
  USS *Croatan* (TAKV 43), 117
  USS *Donner* (LSD 20), 37
  USS *Guadalcanal* (LPH 7), 36–38, 46n, 47, 97; illus., 25, 36, 122
  USS *Hancock* (CVA 19), 32
  USS *Iwo Jima* (LPH 2), 24–26, 35, 92, 165; illus., 169
  USS *Lake Champlain* (CVS 39), 23, 61
  USS *Okinawa* (LPH 3), 34–36, 39, 41, 99, 161
  USS *Princeton* (LPH 5), 2, 22–23, 23n, 24, 24n, 29, 31–32, 35, 80–81, 92–93, 96, 99–100, 119, 150; illus., 22
  USS *Raleigh* (LPD 1), 38
  USS *Shadwell* (LSD 25) 34
  USS *Tarawa* (LHA 1), 166; illus., 166
  USS *Thetis Bay* (VHA 1) (LPH 6), 9, 21–24, 24n, 35, 165, 169; illus., 21
  USS *Tripoli* (LPH 10), 118, 161; illus., 6
  USS *Valley Forge* (LPH 8), 22–23, 24n, 35, 99, 124; illus., 38
  USS *Yorktown* (CV 5), 106
Shoaff, Captain John W., 147
Shook, Lieutenant Colonel Frank A., Jr., 34
Shoup, General David M., 1–2, 9, 16, 33–34, 44, 50, 54, 69, 83–84, 92, 109, 121, 130, 150, 169; illus., 1
Sienko, Lieutenant Colonel Walter, 125
Sikorsky Aircraft Division, United Aircraft Corporation, 5–7, 9, 12, 14–16, 16n, 17, 20, 45n, 47, 49–51, 55, 58–59, 61–62, 70, 73, 80 103, 116–117, 125-126, 166–168
Sikorsky, Igor, 3, 7n, 12–13, 20, 114
Sikorsky Flight Test Division, 61
Sixth Fleet, 139
Slaton Lieutenant Colonel Clyde H., Jr., 35
Smith, Lieutenant Colonel Lloyd W., Jr., 157–158
Smith, Lieutenant General Oliver P., 13–14
Snedeker, Lieutenant General Edward W., 44, 50, 109
Soc Trang, Vietnam, 31–34, 79, 81, 84, 126, 137; illus., 31–32; map, 30
"Soldier Mechanics of the Sea," 22–23
Somerville, Major Daniel A., 16–17
Soper, First Lieutenant Donald W., 37
South, Colonel Hamilton D., 21n
South, Captain Thomas W., II, USN, 21, 21n
South Vietnam, 28, 70; map, 30, 94
Southeast Asia Treaty Organization (SEATO), 29
Spain, 36
Special Landing Force (SLF), 29, 32, 34–35, 80, 92, 121, 123–124, 138, 161
"Spray-Lat," illus., 124
Spurlock, Captain David A., 46
Spurr, Major Thomas L., 39
Stanton, Lieutenant Colonel Eldon C., 37, 55
State Department, 32
Station Operations and Engineering Squadron (SOES), 88
Steele, Lieutenant Colonel Fred A., 9, 29, 34
Stennis, Senator John, 133, 135–137
Stolz, Gunnery Sergeant Donald D., 120
Stoner 63, 90
Stout, Rear Admiral Richard F., 11
Strieby, Robert A., 70
Stroop, Rear Admiral Paul D., 20, 44–45, 50–52, 55, 58
Sturtevant, Joseph E., Jr., 143
Subic Bay, Philippines, 92, 99
Sullivan, Master Sergeant Jerome P., 74

Tactical Air Controller (Airborne) (TACA), 113
Tactics and Techniques Board, 160
TAT-101 turret, 90; illus., 90
Taylor, General Maxwell D., USA, 28
Taylor, Stanley W., 143
Teledyne System Company, 77–78, 150
Texas Instruments, 77
Thailand, 29, 34
Tharrington, Robert W., 123
Thrasher, Ronald J., 153
Timmes, Major General Charles J., USA, 28
Titterud, Colonel Stanley V., 36–37

TK-1 (Temporary Kit-1), 87–90, 128; illus., 88
TK-2, 89–90, 97; illus., 89
Tooker, Lieutenant Colonel Donald K., 111
Tompkins, Brigadier General Rathvon McC., 35
Tourane River, Vietnam, 93n
Townsend, Major Kyle W., 111
Townsend, Rear Admiral Robert L., 62, 115
33d Transportation Light Helicopter Company, USA, 28–29
93d Transportation Light Helicopter Company, USA, 29
Translational lift, 4–5, 98
Trinidad, 36
"the twenty-one knot thump," 26
Twining, Colonel Merrill B., 12
Typhoon "Kate", 80, 88

Udorn, 29
United Aircraft, 158
United Aircraft of Canada, 155, 157
U.S. Army, Pacific, 29
United States European Command, 107
United States Marine Band, 1, 169
U.S. Military Assistance Advisory Group, Vietnam (MAAGV), 28
U.S. Military Assistance Command, Vietnam (USMACV), 132
U.S. Naval Academy, Annapolis, Maryland, 106
Upschulte, Lieutenant Colonel Phillip P., 113

Valente, Sergeant Martin F., 75
Vernon, Lieutenant Colonel Thomas E., 96
Vertical takeoff and landing (VTOL) aircraft, 56, 58
Vertol Division, the Boeing Company, 43, 49–52, 49n, 50n, 54–55, 59, 78, 103, 114, 121–124, 123n, 150–151, 159, 161, 168; illus., 51, 103

Vieques Island, Puerto Rico, 35–36, 38
Viet Cong, 81, 84–88, 95–98, 114, 117
Vietnam, 29, 31–34, 56, 79–82, 84–88, 91–93, 95–104, 107–119, 121–134, 136–140, 143–145, 147, 151, 153–158, 160–161, 167
Viner, Dimitry D., 70

Walt, General Lewis W., 157–158
Walters, 1st Lieutenant Francis M., Jr., 32
Warrant Officer, Helicopter Only (WOHELIO), 68–69
Watson, Edward L., 143
Watson, Major Royce W., 39
Watson, Lieutenant Colonel Warren C., 99–202, 121
Wede, Major General Richard G., 132, 139–140
Weichsel, Hans, 151
Westmoreland, General William C., USA, 143
Whelan, B. L., 13
Whipple, Major Chester L., 147
"White Tops", 19; illus., 19
Williford, Lieutenant Commander James R., USN, 56
Wilson, Roy L., 102
Wooley, Master Sergeant Samuel R., 71
Wright, Joseph F., 142
Wright R-1820-84, 7

XM-18 "minigun," 155
XM-157, 155
XM-159, 155
XM-197, 155

Yeager, Technical Sergeant Robert V., 73

Zitnik, Lieutenant Colonel Robert J., 92
ZUNI, 85

*The device reproduced on the back cover is the oldest military insignia in continuous use in the United States. It first appeared, as shown here, on Marine Corps buttons adopted in 1804. With the stars changed to five points, this device has continued on Marine Corps buttons to the present day.*